Public Speaking

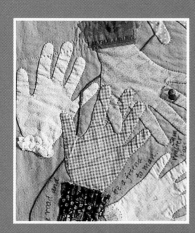

Public Speaking

FIFTH EDITION

Michael Osborn
University of Memphis

Suzanne Osborn
University of Memphis

Houghton Mifflin   *Boston   New York*

Senior Sponsoring Editor: George Hoffman
Assistant Editor: Jennifer Wall
Project Editor: Rachel D'Angelo Wimberly
Senior Production/Design Coordinator: Jennifer Waddell
Senior Manufacturing Coordinator: Priscilla Bailey
Senior Marketing Manager: Pamela J. Laskey

Cover Design: MINKO T. DIMOV, MINKOIMAGES
Cover Image: Threads of Friendship, 1990. Made by members of the Cocheco quilt guild, Dover, N.H. Courtesy of the New England Quilt Museum.

Printed in the U.S.A.

Library of Congress Catalog Card Number: 99-71957
Student Edition ISBN: 0-395-96008-8
Instructor's Annotated Edition ISBN: 0-395-96046-0

3 4 5 6 7 8 9 – DOC – 03 02 01 00

We dedicate this edition of Public Speaking *to the students in section 07, CMST 100 (Fundamentals of Public Speaking), Vanderbilt University, who studied public speaking with us during the spring semester of 1998. Their creativity, commitment, and suggestions have enriched the pages that follow.*

Contents

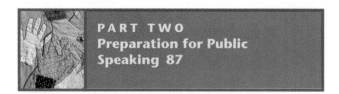

PART TWO
Preparation for Public
Speaking 87

PART FOUR
Types of Public Speaking 331

12 Informative Speaking 332

13 Persuasive Speaking 360

Preface

By the end of the fifth edition of *Public Speaking,* over one million college and university students will have used the book in public speaking classes. It is gratifying to speculate how the book may have touched so many lives! On the other hand, this realization also placed a large burden of responsibility on us as we approached the challenge of revision.

Fortunately, we had a lot of help. The process of revising has carried us from the coastline of California to the hills of Tennessee and to many points in between. We would especially like to thank colleagues and/or students at the Hope College Institute for Faculty Development, Indiana–South Bend University, Luzerne County Community College, Northwest Mississippi Community College, the Two-Year College Association of NCTE, and the Universities of Kutztown, Memphis, New Mexico, Northern Illinois, Pennsylvania State, Pepperdine, Pittsburgh, and Vanderbilt. At these various places we conducted workshops, advised teaching assistants and/or taught undergraduates. With all these colleagues and students we also explored and tested ideas that made their way into this new edition.

The overall result is perhaps the best edition yet of our book. This is a text complete with new discoveries, updated research, fresh examples, new sample speeches, and streamlined writing. Hopefully, those who have come to think of *Public Speaking* as an innovative textbook will not be disappointed by this revision.

Major Changes in the Fifth Edition

The revision themes for *Public Speaking,* Fifth Edition, are *enrichment* and *refinement.*

Enrichment

We enriched this new edition of *Public Speaking* in at least five substantial ways.

1. We improved our discussion of listening in two important ways. First, we introduced the concept of listener apprehension, which is presently receiving considerable attention in listening research. This new concept identifies an important challenge that both speakers and listeners must overcome to achieve authentic communication. Second, we created the idea of the *ladder of listening* as a graphic device to help students understand the various kinds of listening and the relationships among them. These changes should augment our approach to listening as a constructive and critical process.

2. We changed our approach to motivation in Chapter 4. Previously, like many other texts, we offered generic discussions of motivation drawn from various psychological theories. To make the discussion more useful, we examined the actual use of motive appeals in more than a hundred student speeches. The resulting change in our treatment of motivation has a practical, empirical grounding that students should find useful.

3. We added a new section in Chapter 5 that offers guidelines for the evaluation of Internet research to help students assess the quality of what they encounter. In addition, we included a research plan in which the Internet might play a substantial role. We also provided a list of web sites for Internet research. These were carefully selected with the speaker's needs in mind. In addition, we expanded our discussion in Chapter 9 of how computer technology can assist in developing effective presentation aids.

4. We underscored our emphasis on ethics by adding a new section on the challenges of ethical persuasion. In addition, recognizing that students often have problems differentiating between persuasive and informative speaking, we expanded our discussion of the characteristics of persuasion in Chapter 13.

5. We added five new student speeches at the ends of Chapter 2, 12, and 15, illustrating exceptional use of the principles discussed in these chapters. Throughout the book, new student and professional speaker examples enliven the fifth edition.

Refinement

The fifth edition of *Public Speaking* offers at least three major refinements.

1. The students we taught reminded us that they are under constant pressure to complete reading assignments in many courses in a limited amount of time. In response to this reality, we made a renewed effort to write more simply and economically in this edition. We also tried to present clearer definitions of major terms. For example, we redefined argument in Chapter 14 to bring that concept into sharper focus and to make our discussion of the interaction of evidence, proof, and argument more effective. We reduced the use of technical terms in Chapter 10's discussion of language, simplified the writing, and provided better examples for many of its concepts. While some repetition of ideas may be necessary and even desirable across chapters, we tried to reduce redundancy whenever possible.

2. We restructured several chapters to make the material more useful for a variety of teaching approaches. Chapter 2 continues to offer advice on how to present a successful first speech; but we also recognized that some teachers developed their own unique approaches to the first assignment. To accommodate such differences, we moved the discussion of the self-introductory speech to the end of the chapter, where it may be assigned at the teacher's discretion. We believe this change also improves the cohesiveness of the chapter. In Chapter 11, we moved the material on making video presentations to the end of the chapter as well, treating it as an enrichment application. We think this change improves the logical development of the chapter.

3. We made other specific refinements. In Chapter 9, we gave less emphasis to the "single big poster" approach to presentation aids and stressed instead the more flexible use of multiple, smaller aids and computer-generated materials that are more easily integrated into a speech. These revisions continue the transformation announced in our previous edition when we changed the traditional "Visual Aids" to "Presentation Aids." Finally, in Chapter 15 we updated and revised our section on presenting toasts, and streamlined our section on introducing speakers.

Continuing Themes in Public Speaking

Some themes have not changed in the new edition because they represent enduring values in the public speaking course. One such theme is the role of public speaking in a diverse society. The ancient writiers on rhetoric never had to contend with the reality of such an audience. Growing cultural diversity in society increases the importance of public speaking as a force that can counter division. For this reason, the theme of cultural diversity remains embedded throughout the book. We have also renewed our emphasis on ethics: A diverse society heightens the importance of values that can join people of different backgrounds.

We continue to believe that a major ethical obligation of textbooks about public speaking is to make students sensitive to the potential impact of public speaking on the lives of others. Because of the pervasive importance of values and ethics, we applied ethical considerations throughout the book rather than confining the discussion to a single chapter. For example, we direct the attention of students to ethical concerns as we consider listening, audience analysis and adaptation, cultural variations, topic selection, research, ways of structuring speeches, presentation aids, use of language, and the consequences of informing and persuading others.

We continue to honor a study that ancient educators thought belonged at the center of liberal education. What other discipline, they argued, requires that students think clearly, organize their thoughts, select and combine words artfully and judiciously, and express themselves with power and conviction, all while under the direct scrutiny of listeners? The study of public speaking should empower students in social, economic, and political situations that require open discussion. Not only personal success but also the fate of communities may depend upon such discussions.

For these reasons we believe that a college or university course in public speaking should offer both practical advice and an understanding of why such advice works. We emphasize both the *how* and the *why* of public speaking—*how* so that beginners can achieve success as quickly as possible, and *why* so that they can manage their new skills wisely. Consistent with this philosophy, we based our practical advice on underlying principles of human communication. As we offer advice on structuring speeches, we show how various speech designs connect with basic concepts of "good form," explaining why some speeches succeed and others fail. We grounded our advice on informative speaking in the principles of learning theory, and our suggestions on persuasive speaking on research from social psychology and the communication discipline. We illustrate how evidence, proof, and argument function together as an integrated system that makes persuasion work. As we consider ceremonial speaking, we show how two basic principles, identification and magnification, are essential for successful communication. We draw from the past and present from the social sciences and the humanities to help students understand and manage their public speaking experiences.

The Roman educator, Quintilian, held forth the ideal of "the good person speaking well" as a goal of education, and we join with him in stressing the value of speech training in the development of the whole person. We also emphasize that successful public speaking is excellent training for leadership. In addition, understanding the basics of public communication can make students more resistant to unethical speakers and more critical of the mass-mediated communication to which they are exposed. The class should help students become better producers and consumers of public communication.

We have continued and sharpened the focus on public speaking as a way to climb the barriers that separate speakers and their listeners. In the previous edition, we introduced the concept of "Interference Mountain" to dramatize these barriers and to demonstrate the power of public speaking to reduce them. In this edition we have continued to develop the metaphorical themes of the student as climber, builder, and weaver to show the important dimensions of personal growth and development that the public speaking class makes possible. The student learns to climb barriers of personal and cultural interference and grows in the process. The student also learns how to build ideas by mastering the arts of practical logic and organization, and determining how to utilize various forms of supporting materials. Finally, the student learns how to weave words into a clear, colorful fabric of communication and how to fashion a tapestry of argument using evidence and proof. Mastering these central metaphors is the key not only to effective communication, but also to successful living.

Plan of the Book

Overview of the Book

Public Speaking is designed to help students build knowledge and skills step by step. Positive initial speaking experiences are especially important. For this reason, Chapter 2 offers a basic overview to help students design and present successful first speeches. We included a detailed formula for developing speeches in which students introduce themselves or others. In our experience, these speeches can break the ice, build a sense of classroom community, and help students develop credibility for later speeches.

In the chapters that follow, students learn how to listen critically and constructively, analyze their audiences, select, refine, and research speech topics, develop supporting materials, arrange these materials in appropriate structures, outline their thinking, and create effective presentation aids. They also learn how to manage words and present their messages. Students become acquainted with the nature of information and how to present it, the process of persuasion and how to engage it, and the importance of ceremonial speaking in its various forms. Appendix A, "Communicating in Small Groups," provides concise practical advice on how to participate effectively in small groups. Teachers may adapt the sequence of chapters to any course plan, because each chapter covers a topic thoroughly and completely.

Detailed Plan of the Book

Part One, "The Foundations of Public Speaking," provides basic information that students need for their first speaking and listening experiences. Chapter 1 highlights the personal, social, and cultural benefits of being able to speak effectively in public, introduces public speaking as communication, and emphasizes the ethical responsibilities of speakers. Chapter 2 offers students procedures for inventing, organizing, practicing, and presenting their first speeches. The chapter also helps students handle communication apprehension. Chapter 3 identifies common listening problems and ways to overcome them, helps students sharpen critical thinking skills, and presents criteria for the constructive evaluation of speeches.

Part Two, "Preparation for Public Speaking," covers the basic skills needed to develop effective speeches—audience analysis, topic selection, research, development of supporting materials, and structuring and outlining procedures. Chapter 4 emphasizes the importance of the audience as it considers how to adapt a message and how to adjust to factors in the speaking situation. Chapter 5 provides a systematic way to select, refine, and research speech topics. We emphasize the ethical and practical importance of having *responsible knowledge* based upon personal experience, library and computerized resources, and interviewing. Chapter 6 covers the major types of supporting materials including facts and statistics, examples, testimony, and narratives. This chapter shows students how to select the most appropriate supporting materials and bring them to life through comparison, contrast, and analogy. Chapter 7 shows students how to develop simple, balanced, and orderly speech designs, how to select and shape their main points, how to use transitions, and how to prepare effective introductions and conclusions. Chapter 8 explains how to develop working outlines, refine them into formal outlines, and derive a key-word outline to use during presentation. An extended example in Chapters 6, 7, and 8 illustrates how a speech on an environmental topic might develop from its initial conception through to its final presentation. Chapter 8 ends with the annotated text of this speech.

Part Three, "Developing Presentation Skills," brings the speaker to the point of presentation. Chapter 9 explains the development of presentation aids including a discussion of how to use computers to produce aids and make multimedia presentations. Chapter 10 provides an understanding of the role of language in communication and offers practical suggestions for using words effectively. Chapter 11 offers exercises for the improvement of voice and body language and helps students develop an extemporaneous style that is adaptable to most speaking situations.

Part Four, "Types of Public Speaking," discusses informative, persuasive, and ceremonial speaking. Chapter 12 covers speeches designed to share information and increase understanding. The chapter discusses the different types of informative speeches, and presents the major designs that can be used. Chapter 13 describes the persuasive process, focusing on how to meet the many challenges of persuasion. The chapter also discusses designs that are appropriate for persuasive speeches. In Chapter 14 we explain the use of evidence, proof, and argument to help students develop strong, reasoned cases. The chapter also identifies the major forms of fallacies so students can avoid them in their speeches and detect them in the messages of others. Chapter 15 discusses the techniques of identification and magnification as it considers various forms of ceremonial speaking, emphasizing especially speeches of tribute and inspiration. The chapter features interesting annotated speech excerpts by and about Olympic track-and-field legends Jesse Owens and Wilma Rudolph, and concludes with two new, striking student speeches.

Appendix A, "Communicating in Small Groups," introduces students to the problem-solving process and the responsibilities of group participants. This appendix also provides guidelines for managing informal and formal meetings, and explains the basic concepts of parliamentary procedure. Appendix B contains additional sample speeches by professional and student speakers for classroom analysis and discussion.

Learning Tools

To help students master the material, we developed a number of special learning tools.

- We open each chapter with learning objectives that cue students to the content and prepare them for productive reading.
- The epigrams and vignettes that start each chapter help point out the topic's significance and motivate readers. The epigrams especially remain a signature of our book.
- We use contemporary art work and photographs to illustrate ideas, engage student interest, and add to the visual appeal of the book.
- Examples illustrate and apply the content in a clear, lively, and often entertaining way.
- We provide Speaker's Notes to help students remember the essentials. This innovation offers internal summaries as the chapters develop to reinforce the learning process.
- We end each chapter with In Summary and Terms to Know sections that further reinforce learning.
- Sample classroom speeches illustrate important concepts. The book contains many annotated speech texts so that students can see how the concepts apply in actual speeches. These speeches are found at the ends of chapters. Appendix B contains additional speeches for analysis. These speeches cover an interesting array of topics, contexts, and speakers. They illustrate the major functions of self-introductory, informative, persuasive, and ceremonial speeches.
- A glossary at the end of the book defines Terms to Know in an accessible format.

Supplementary Materials

The following materials are available to adopters of *Public Speaking:*

For Instructors

- An *Instructor's Annotated Edition* that includes general and ESL teaching tips for every chapter.
- The *Instructor's Resource Manual* written by Suzanne Osborn and Randall Parrish Osborn. Part I of the manual includes sections on the purpose and philosophy of the course, preparing a syllabus, various sample syllabi, an assortment of speech assignment options, a discussion of evaluating and grading speeches, a troubleshooting guide with teaching strategies for new instructors, and an extensive bibliography of resource readings. Part II offers a chapter-by-chapter guide to teaching *Public Speaking* including learning objectives, suggestions for teaching, lecture/discussion outlines, classroom activities, transparency/handout masters, and a bibliography of readings for enrichment. This comprehensive manual can be used as a text for training teaching assistants.
- A **Printed Test Bank** separate from the IRM to provide test security.
- A **Computerized Test Bank** including all the test items from the printed test bank. Available in PC and Mac formats.
- **Student Speeches Videos and Guides** including a compilation of student speeches accompanied by a guide that contains the text of each speech, an evaluation of the presentation, discussion items, and commentary.
- **Contemporary Great Speeches Videos**
- The **Using Presentation Aids Video** illustrating class lectures on presentation aids.
- **Speech Assessment Video and Guide** with training in speech evaluation.
- An **ESL Teaching Guide** available online.
- A *PowerPoint* **Presentation Program** on the Houghton Mifflin web site (http://www.hmco.com/college).
- A **companion web site** including links, research sites, exercises, and other ancillary material for both instructor and student use.

For Students

- The *Speech Designer* computer software program that offers students a self-directed, step-by-step electronic process for outlining speeches and includes formats for each major speech design discussed in the text.
- The *Speech Preparation Workbook* that contains materials for activities mentioned in the text and skeleton outline formats for the major speech designs.
- *Multicultural Activities Workbook for the Public Speaking Classroom*

- The ***Overcoming Your Fear of Public Speaking*** supplement written by Michael Motley that offers practical advice for controlling and making productive use of communication apprehension.

- The ***Classical Origins of Public Speaking*** supplement written by Michael Osborn that offers a concise overview of the ideas developed by early Greek theorists on the nature and importance of public speaking.

Acknowledgments

Many people helped improve *Public Speaking* as it passed through its revisions. For this edition, we especially wish to thank George Hoffman, our sponsoring editor. More than an editor, George has also been our friend and a constant source of encouragement. Pamela Laskey, marketing manager for our book, has inspired us with her enthusiasm and commitment, and has been a source of hugs when we needed them most. Jennifer Wall, assistant editor for communication at Houghton Mifflin, has been essential to the coordination of all the behind-the-scenes work that makes a revision possible, from the main text to the extensive ancillaries package that accompanies the book. Rachel D'Angelo Wimberly, our production editor, has prodded us through the final processes of the revision with a firm, patient, and friendly hand. The spirit of Karla Paschkis, our development editor through two previous editions, continues to animate this revision.

John Bakke, chair of the Department of Communication, and Dick Ranta, dean of the College of Communication and Fine Arts (both of the University of Memphis), have supported us in ways too numerous to mention, not the least of which has been their close friendship over many years. We would also like to record our admiration for Lane Rawlins, president of the University of Memphis. Lane continues to battle the odds to make the University a place where educational excellence can be pursued. His support of the University's Osborn Lecture Series in Communication and the Osborn Enrichment Fund for excellence in communication graduate education is greatly appreciated.

We thank our colleagues listed below, whose thoughtful and helpful critical readings guided our revisions for the fifth edition.

Ferald J. Bryan, Northern Illinois University; David Walker, Middle Tennessee State University; Marcia Litrenta, William Rainer Harper College; Glynis Holm Strause, Coastal Bend College; Alton Barbour, University of Denver; Elizabeth Threnhauser, Northeastern University; Janette Kenner Muir, George Mason University; Beth M. Waggenspack, Virginia Tech; Lynnda Upton, The Colorado Institute of Art; and Gretchen Weber, Midlands Technical College.

Special appreciation goes to the following: Phillip Anderson at Kansas State University, who brought Anna Aley's speech to our attention; Anna Aley, Bonnie Marshall, and Stephen Lee, who travelled to Memphis so that we could videotape their speeches; Valerie Banes, Tom Dean, Roxanne Gee, Kathryn Hendrix, David Liban, and Brooke Quigly, colleagues at the University of Memphis, who expertly prepared videotapes of student speeches; Pamela Palmer, Memphis State University librarian, who offered invaluable advice concerning resources of the reference room; and Hal Phillips, film writer and novelist from Corinth, Mississippi, who went out of his way to help us.

List of Speeches

Public Speaking

PART ONE

The Foundations of Public Speaking

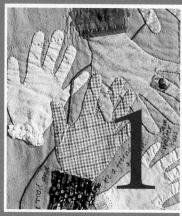

1

You as a Public Speaker

*S*peeches are
actions
among people,
and, indeed, most
effective ones.

— *Georg Wilhelm*
Friedrich Hegel

This chapter will help you

■ understand how a course in public speaking can help you
  personally
■ discover the social and cultural benefits of the course
■ grasp the nature of public speaking as communication
■ appreciate your responsibilities as an ethical speaker

Mary had worried about taking public speaking for some time. She didn't see herself as a public speaker and wasn't sure she could carry it off. But the time came when she simply couldn't put off taking the course any longer. At her first class, she saw about twenty other stone-faced students who looked as uncomfortable as she felt. Her teacher later confessed that he felt discouraged when he saw that sullen group. She thought about dropping the class, but realized that that was not an option. So she decided to try to stick it out.

Mary's first assignment was to present a speech of self-introduction. As she worked on this, it dawned on her why she found marine biology so fascinating. As she spoke, she forgot much of her nervousness in her excitement over the subject. While her speech was certainly not perfect, she did some things quite well. She helped others get to know her, and she built respect for later informative and persuasive speeches on the fate of the oceans. She was pleased when her classmates discussed the positive things she had done.

As she listened to her classmates, Mary found that she was beginning to enjoy the class. Some of the speeches were very interesting, and she joined in the discussion of how they worked well and how they might be improved. The "great stone faces" began to chip away and reveal the real human beings they had masked.

As Mary gave more speeches, she found that her classmates took her seriously. She began to care about her classmates and take joy in their successes. As she researched her speeches, she learned to keep her audience constantly in mind. She sought out facts, opinions, examples, and stories her listeners would find useful and interesting. Toward the end of the term it dawned on her: She was a public speaker! She also could now recognize the strategies, techniques, and even manipulations in the world of communication surrounding her. She knew she would be ready to accept the challenges of public speaking and careful listening whenever the need for these should arise in her life.

PERHAPS BY NOW you have guessed the point of our story. There is no one Mary, but there are many Marys. Mary represents all the successful students we have known in many years of teaching public speaking. To write your own success story, you need five essential ingredients. The first is *commitment*: You must want to succeed and be willing to work toward that goal. The second is *experience*: You must give speeches and learn from the constructive

3

suggestions of your classmates and your instructor. The third is an *instructor* who encourages your growth as a speaker. The fourth is a *supportive audience* of classmates who will encourage you and whom you can help in return. The fifth is this *textbook* to guide and enrich your learning process by pointing out the "hows" and "whys" of public speaking.

Perhaps the most important of these ingredients is your commitment. You must *decide* that you want to learn the art of public speaking, that you will select worthy topics, that you will treat listeners ethically and responsibly, and that you will listen constructively to others. In this chapter, we explain why this class deserves your commitment, help you understand the art you will be learning, and prepare you to meet the major ethical challenges of public speaking.

How a Public Speaking Course Can Help You

A course in public speaking offers personal, social, and cultural benefits that will enrich your life.

Personal Benefits

You should benefit personally from this class in two ways. First, you can grow to be a more sensitive and skilled communicator. Second, you should be able to enjoy the practical advantages of improved communication skills.

Growth as a Public Speaker.   The most basic benefits of this class, those that make all the rest possible, are the sensitivity and creativity you develop as you learn to be an effective speaker. Public speaking encourages you to look inside yourself and explore what really matters to you so that you can share these convictions and concerns with others. The class also helps you consider your listeners. What issues concern them? What *ought* to concern them? How might they react when you speak on these issues? What experiences will make your points come alive? How can you build a base of knowledge that will let you speak responsibly?

One important sensitivity you will acquire is an appreciation for the power of speech. The biggest lie we ever learn is "Sticks and stones can break my bones, but words can never harm me." Sometimes words hurt more than sticks or stones. But words can also create, build, and transform. There is a magic to the art of speaking that has been acknowledged since civilization began. From the time of Homer nearly three thousand years ago, poets have marveled over the forces that move speakers to eloquence. The Oglala Sioux, for example, think that speaking must have divine origins. They believe that "the ability to make a good speech is a great gift to the people from their Maker, Owner of all things."[1] This mystery may be hard to penetrate, but it involves the joint creation of meaning, as speaker and listener work together to make sense of the uncertainty that surrounds them.

There are other important skills that you will acquire as you grow to be a successful speaker. You will learn how to focus on a topic, how to use research to strengthen your message, how to structure and organize a presentation, how to use language that stamps your thoughts on the minds of listeners, and how to present a speech that commands attention. These are not only arts of speaking but arts of living as well. They can make you more effective not just as a speaker, but as a person.

You will also learn to be a more effective listener. Listening is a part of communication that is often neglected, even though we listen far more than we speak. Education in public speaking can help you critically evaluate what you hear. The daily barrage of media messages directed at us makes the ability to sort out honest from dishonest public communication a basic survival skill. You will also learn how to become a constructive listener who plays an essential role in the creation of meaning. We examine listening in more detail in Chapter 3.

A final personal bonus of your public speaking class is that it makes you an active participant in the learning process. You don't just sit in a class, absorbing lectures. You put communication to work. The speeches you give illustrate the strategies, the possibilities, and the problems of human communication. As you join in the discussions that follow these speeches, you learn to identify elements that can promote or block communication. In short, you become a vital member of a learning community. It is no accident that the words *communication* and *community* have a close relationship: They are both derived from the Latin word for *common,* meaning "belonging to many" or "shared equally."

Practical Benefits.   The personal growth you experience in a public speaking class also makes possible a number of practical benefits. The skills you build in this class can help you in other classes, in campus activities, and in whatever career you undertake.

How important are oral communication skills to getting a good job? Each year the National Association of Colleges and Employers surveys hundreds of corporate recruiting specialists. Based on a 1996 survey of 294 employers in various fields, NACE isolated eleven fundamental skills that recruiters seek in job candidates. *The most important of these skills—at the top of the list—was oral communication!* NACE concluded: "Learn to speak clearly, confidently, and concisely."[2] In a similar study, 250 companies surveyed by the Center for Public Resources rated speaking and listening as among the most critical areas in need of improvement for people entering the work force. Jerome Solomon, director at Pannell Kerr Forster in Boston, commented: "Courses in those areas are a must."[3] Echoed Martin Ives, vice chair of the Governmental Accounting Standards Board, "The difference between an average career and a 'special' career is the ability to communicate orally and in writing."[4] Finally, an American Council on Education report, *Employment Prospects for College Graduates,* advises readers that "good oral and written skills can be your most prized asset" in getting and holding a desirable position.[5]

The abilities you develop in this class also can help you in life outside the workplace. Picture the following scenarios:

The local school board has announced that it plans to remove *A Catcher in the Rye, Huckleberry Finn, Of Mice and Men,* and *To Kill a Mockingbird* from the high school library. It will hold a public hearing

on this issue at its next regular meeting. Because you feel strongly about this issue, you decide to speak out for your principles and your children.

A real estate developer is planning to build a shopping center on fifteen acres of undeveloped land near your home. You believe that this will not only devalue your property but also destroy the beauty and serenity of your neighborhood. The Land Use Control Board has scheduled a public hearing next week. To protect your pocketbook as well as your lifestyle, you need to speak at that hearing.

Clearly, the study of public speaking offers important personal benefits. Many students experience an incredible sense of personal growth in a public speaking class. What they learn and what they become prepares them for the opportunities and challenges they will encounter in life beyond the classroom.

Social Benefits

From the beginning of time we have lived in societies. It is in our nature to belong to groups and to seek out the company of others. We draw much of our personal identity from the groups we belong to, and our status and effectiveness within these groups depends largely on our communication skills.

Anna Aley, a student at Kansas State University, was living in substandard off-campus housing. She brought that problem to the attention of her classmates in a persuasive speech. Her persuasive speech (see Chapter 13) was selected by her classmates for presentation in a public forum on campus. During that presentation, she made such an impression that the local newspaper printed the text of her speech and launched an investigation of the off-campus housing problem. The paper then followed up with a strong editorial, and the mayor established a rental inspection program in the community. Anna's experience is a dramatic example of how speeches, even those given in a classroom, can benefit society.

Although not all the speeches we give and hear are so momentous, our words create ripples of meaning that can spread far beyond the time and place in which we speak. We can never know how the speeches we give may ultimately affect the lives of others. Even now, we recall brave classroom speeches given by students thirty years ago supporting civil and human rights in our nation. Their words continue to resonate in our memories and in our lives.

Clearly, the personal benefits of public speaking are tied to the social benefits. It is part of our nature to care about the groups we value. When we can help them, we also feel deeply confirmed as human beings. The social significance of speaking was captured very well by Isocrates, an educator of ancient Greece, when he said: "Because there has been implanted in us the power to persuade each other . . . , not only have we escaped the life of the wild beasts but we have come together and founded cities and made laws and invented arts." Those who are confident in their public speaking skills are ready to take active roles whenever social problems or opportunities arise.

The effectiveness of a democracy depends on our ability to deliberate and make wise judgments on public policy. At the very least, we must be able to listen critically to those who represent us in government, advise them concerning our positions, and evaluate their performance come election time. We should be able to take part in public discussions in which we learn from others, develop responsible convictions on important issues, and speak our minds for the benefit of others. Our entire system of governance is built on open public communication. Those who originally designed the United States of America realized the importance of freedom of speech when they wrote the First Amendment to the Constitution:

> **Congress shall make no law respecting an establishment of religion, or prohibiting the free exercise thereof; or abridging the freedom of speech, or of the press; or the right of the people peaceably to assemble, and to petition the government for a redress of grievances.**

Such freedom is not without its risks, as noted by Supreme Court Justice William Brennan:

> **Rulers always have and always will find it dangerous to their security to permit people to think, believe, talk, write, assemble and particularly to criticize the government as they please. But the language of the First Amendment indicates that the founders weighed the risks involved in such freedoms and deliberately chose to stake this Government's security and life upon preserving the liberty to discuss public affairs intact and untouchable by the government.**[6]

Public speaking is vital to the maintenance of a free society. The right to assemble and speak on public issues is guaranteed by the Bill of Rights.

To be able to speak without fear and to hear all sides of an issue are rights basic to our social system. Acquiring the presentation and evaluation skills you need to keep this freedom alive is a profound social benefit of this course.

Cultural Benefits

Several generations ago, if you listened to the radio (in those days before television) or read magazines, you would find one striking assumption: America was the best of all possible worlds. This attitude typified **ethnocentrism**, the tendency of any nation, race, or religion to believe that its way of seeing and doing things is right and proper, and that other perspectives and behaviors are incorrect. Ethnocentrism can touch everything from the clothes we wear and the food we eat to the values we affirm and the God we worship. Clearly, ethnocentrism is a human, not an American, trait as we shall see more clearly in Chapter 4. But we Americans certainly have our share of it. Forty years ago, Richard M. Weaver, a noted conservative critic of communication, suggested:

> **The Western World has long stood as a symbol for the future; and accordingly there has been a very wide tendency in this country, and also I believe among many people in Europe, to identify that which is American with that which is destined to be. . . . [To them] America is the goal toward which all creation moves. . . . [They] judge a country's civilization by its resemblance to the American model.**[7]

In the first half of this century, the "melting pot" was a popular metaphor that expressed this attitude about American culture. This theory suggested that as various ethnic and national groups came to this country, they would be blended and melted down in some vast cultural cauldron into a superior alloy called "the American Character." The idea assumed that all who came to our shores would be forged into a powerful new unity. In addition, the "melting pot" metaphor reinforced ethnocentrism and cultural arrogance—to be American was to be better.

Another problem with the "melting pot" metaphor was that it created a **stereotype**, a generalized picture of a race, gender, or nationality that *supposedly* represents the essential character of the group. We may have stereotypes of Latinos, or of athletes, or of "rednecks." If we look inside ourselves and confront ourselves honestly, we may discover many such stereotypes. They stick in our minds and become habits of thinking. We may use them because they simplify human interactions or because they are endorsed by a group important to us. Unfortunately, stereotypes can be quite damaging. They may entail harsh prejudgments about others, and they may keep us from seeing the real value of a unique person who just happens to be Latino, or an athlete, or from the rural South. They may impede our ability to communicate with others in a genuine way.

The stereotype inherent in the "melting pot" theory seemed harmless on the surface: It offered an image of the ideal American citizen. However, that citizen always had a decidedly white, definitely male face. Asians, Middle Easterners, and African Americans—just to mention some of the "out" groups—did not mix very readily into a common pot. Moreover, often these people, joined by Native Americans and others, *did not wish* to lose their ethnic identities. Within the melting pot, women simply disappeared. It was hard to champion the economic and political rights of women when the ideal citizen was always a man. Elizabeth Lozano summarizes the shortcomings of the melting pot stereotype, and begins to explore an alternative view of American character:

> **The "melting pot" is not an adequate metaphor for a country which is comprised of a multiplicity of cultural backgrounds and traditions. . . . [W]e might better think of the United States in terms of a "cultural [stew]" in which all ingredients conserve their unique flavor, while also transforming and being transformed by the adjacent textures and scents.**[8]

A public speaking class is an ideal place to savor this rich broth of many cultures. As we hear others speak, we often discover the many flavors of the American experience. If you examine your own identity, you may discover that you yourself are "multicultural." One of your authors describes herself as "part Swedish, part Welsh, part German, and all hillbilly." The other is Scots, Irish, and English with a dollop of Creek Indian. Just imagine the complex cultural heritage of our children! Communication scholar Dolores V. Tanno describes her cultural background as an "unfolding ethnic identity" that includes, in order of her own realization, "I am Spanish," "I am Mexican American," "I am Latina," and "I am Chicana," and expresses her joy in discovering these various identities.[9]

As we strive to understand our own and others' unfolding identities, we must guard against the subtle intrusion of stereotypes into our thinking. Casey Man Kong Lum has pointed out that the main problem confronted by Chinese immigrants in New York City may not be relating to the American culture, but relating to other Chinese. As he notes, there are seven major Chinese dialect groups, each with its own subgroups.[10] To the extent that different languages imply different cultures, any conclusion that "The Chinese feel . . ." or "The Chinese perspective on this problem is . . ." must surely be a distortion, if not an outright fiction. We quickly discovered a similar problem when we taught in New Mexico. We could not simply lump together the Native American students in our classes. Were they Navajos, Apaches, or Pueblos? And if Pueblos, to which one of the more than twenty northern New Mexico Pueblos representing five different language groups did they belong?

Perhaps the best protection against such "creeping stereotyping" is to remember that we are, in the final analysis, talking to individuals. Navita Cummings James, a communication scholar at the University of South Florida, sums up the attitude we must preserve:

> **I am a child of the American baby boom. I am a person of color, and I am a woman. All of these factors have influenced the creation of the person I am today, just as the time and place of each of our births, our genders, races, and ethnicities influence the people we are today.**[11]

Professor James reminds us that each of us is a unique expression of many backgrounds.

In this section, we have introduced the "melting pot" and the "cultural stew" as ways of thinking about the American character. One of our favorite metaphors for the complex culture of the United States entered into public discourse at the conclusion of Abraham Lincoln's first inaugural address, as Lincoln sought to hold the nation together on the eve of the American Civil War:

> **The mystic chords of memory, stretching from every battlefield, and patriot grave, to every living heart and hearthstone, all over this broad land, will yet swell the chorus of the Union, when again touched, as surely they will be, by the better angels of our nature.**[12]

Lost in the immediate crisis of that war, Lincoln's image of America as a harmonious chorus implied that the individual voices of Americans can not only survive but, when heard together, create a music that is more rich and beautiful than that of any one alone.

Lincoln's vision may seem out of place beside the noisy contemporary American scene, but it holds forth a continuing dream of a society in which individualism and the common good can not only survive but enhance each other. In your class and within these pages you will hear many voices: Native Americans and new Americans, women and men, conservatives and liberals, Americans of all different colors and lifestyles. Sometimes these voices may seem bitter, alienated, or dispossessed, but all of them are a part of the vital chorus of our nation. The public speaking class gives you an opportunity to hear these voices and to add yours to them.

Public Speaking as Communication

Seeing yourself as a public speaker may be difficult, just as it was for Mary in our opening vignette. At first Mary thought of public speaking as a mysterious skill possessed only by the leaders of our society. However, she soon realized that she had been preparing for public speaking for a long time. As an infant, she had developed the most essential tool of communication—language. When her grandfather explained to her why flowers bloom and why she must stay away from fire, she had been introduced to two of the great functions of human communication, *informing* and *persuading*. Later, as she developed close friends, Mary had begun practicing interaction skills that are vital to communication: These skills included when and how to listen as well as speak, and what kind of behaviors either advance or impede the flow of ideas.

What happens when three people become six, when six become twelve, or when twelve become twenty-four? Public speaking is really only an enlargement of the conversational skills we have been practicing all our lives. On the other hand, there are some distinctive features that make public speaking a unique form of communication.

Public Speaking as Expanded Conversation

Public speaking retains three important characteristics of good conversation. First, it preserves the natural directness and spontaneity of informal talk. Second, it is colorful and compelling. And third, it is tuned to the reactions of listeners.

Public Speaking Preserves Conversational Directness and Spontaneity.   Even though a message has been carefully planned and prepared, it must come to life before the live audience. Consider the following opening to a self-introductory speech:

> **It may seem hot here today, but it's not near as hot as Plainview, Texas, where I was born and reared. I almost said "roasted." John has just told us about the joys of urban living. Now you're going to hear about what you might call a "country-fried" lifestyle.**

Compare that opening with:

> **My name is Sam Johnson, and I come from Plainview, Texas.**

The first version, because of its references to weather conditions and to an earlier speech, seems fresh and spontaneous. The "us" and "you," together with the casual humorous remarks, suggest that the speaker is reaching out to his audience. The second, unless presented with a great deal of oomph, will sound quite ordinary. The first opening invites listening; the second invites yawning.

Public Speaking Is Colorful and Compelling.   We enjoy listening to good conversationalists often because of their colorful speech. Consider the following development of the "heat" theme from the above example:

> **That place was so hot it would make hell seem air-conditioned! It was so hot it would make an armadillo sweat! It was so hot that rattlesnakes would rattle just to fan themselves!**

Compare those words with the following:

> **The average summer day in Plainview was often over a hundred degrees.**

The literal meaning of both statements is not that different, but the first contains the kind of colorful conversational qualities that listeners usually enjoy.

Public Speaking Is Tuned to Listeners.   Public speakers must be aware of the reactions of listeners, and make both on-the-spot and carefully planned adjustments. As you develop basic conversation skills, you learn how to monitor listeners' reactions. Smiles and frowns, nodding heads, looks of boredom or confusion can all be meaningful signals. The technical term for these reactions is **feedback**. Feedback is absolutely vital to a public speaker.

Smiles and nods of agreement can raise your confidence and let you know that you are getting through. On the other hand, frowns or signs of confusion or disagreement should prompt you to rephrase a point or present more evidence. Imagine that you were giving a speech about global warming, and some members of the audience looked skeptical or perplexed. You might add, as you monitor such signals:

> **I know it may be hard to believe that we are responsible for global warming. But Dr. Tom Wigley, a climatologist at the National Center for Atmospheric Research, recently said in an interview with the *New York Times*: "I think the scientific justification for the statement is there, unequivocally." And Dr. Michael Oppenheimer, an atmospheric scientist with the Environmental Defense Fund, added: "The scientific community has discovered the smoking gun."**
>
> **For our own sakes, the sake of our children, and the sake of the human future, we'd better start believing it and asking what we can do about it.**

A wise speaker always has additional facts, examples, and expert opinions in reserve for such moments. We cover responding to audience feedback in greater detail in Chapter 11.

In addition to such impromptu adjustments, your entire speech should be designed to answer the questions that audiences—knowingly or unknowingly—will ask:

- Why should I be interested in your topic?
- What do you mean?
- How do I know that is true?
- What can I do about it?

You must answer "Why should I be interested?" in the introduction of your speech or you will lose your audience before you ever get started. "What do you mean?" suggests that your purpose and language must be clear and understandable. For example, if you said, "A pattern of climatic response to human activities is identifiable in the climatological record," listeners might well respond with, "Huh?" "How do I know that is true?" conveys listeners' natural skepticism about startling information or conclusions. This question calls for evidence, like that offered above on global warming. "What can I do about it?" comes up most often in persuasive speeches. It challenges speakers to present a course of action that is both practical and promising. If you can successfully answer these questions, the response to your speech may be more than immediate feedback: The lives of your listeners may be enriched in some lasting way. You and your speech will have made a difference.

It seems clear that public speaking, far from being a mysterious skill, is a natural but expanded application of abilities and sensitivities we develop as we learn how to converse with one another. On the other hand, as we move from three to six, six to twelve, and twelve to twenty-four listeners, there are some striking changes in the patterns of communication that make public speaking distinctive.

Distinctive Features of Public Speaking

Conversations represent a free-flowing, spontaneous, fluid process of communication. The conversationalist is *both* a speaker and a listener in an ongoing interaction. The conversation itself is a series of fragments that may or may not fit together well. In contrast, public speaking defines the roles of speaker and listener more clearly. Speeches may seem fresh and spontaneous, but good speeches are the product of carefully considered research, audience analysis, design, wording, and practice. In public speaking, the medium of communication can affect the message, as in the case of speeches presented on radio or television. Finally, the environment in which communication occurs can change dramatically.

Speaker and Listener Roles Are Clearly Defined.   In conversation, it is often hard to tell who is the speaker and who is the listener. In public speaking, however, there is seldom doubt as to who the speaker is and who the listeners are. Moreover, public speaking spotlights the role of the speaker. Whether speakers can take advantage of this prominence depends on their ability to reward listeners with interesting and useful messages. As Aristotle pointed out more than two thousand years ago, our impressions of speakers themselves affect how we respond to what they say. We are far more inclined, he observed, to react favorably when we think speakers are competent in their subject matter and when we trust them. These ancient qualities of competence and integrity form the basis of the modern term *credibility*. Aristotle also noted that audiences respond more favorably when speakers seem likable—when they seem to be people of good will. Modern researchers have uncovered still another important speaker characteristic, forcefulness (or dynamism).[13] Some speakers strike us as vital, action-oriented people. When

The more comfortable you are when speaking to an audience, the more effective you will be.

important interests are at stake and action seems called for, we may turn to such people to lead the way. These qualities of likableness and forcefulness combine to form the basis for another modern term, *charisma*.[14] Taken together, credibility and charisma provide an updated account of what Aristotle called the **ethos** of the speaker.[15] We consider ethos at greater length in Chapter 2.

In public speaking, the role of the **listener** is also essential. As we will see in Chapter 3, ideal listeners are supportive, yet listen carefully and critically. Such listeners seek the value in all messages and listen actively and enthusiastically, rather than passively and apathetically. Finally, listeners help construct the meaning in messages. Because the fate of a message depends on how listeners respond to it, speakers must always keep their audiences in mind. Indeed, Chapter 4 shows that effective speech preparation begins with audience analysis. What needs or problems concern them? What subjects interest them? What biases could distort their reception of messages? Such questions are crucial to the selection of your topic and to the way you frame your message.

Successful Public Speaking Offers Carefully Planned Messages.   As we have indicated, conversations are fragmentary. They are often unpredictable explorations, taking many wrong turns and sometimes ending there. In contrast, successful public speaking offers a **message** that is carefully designed to be internally consistent and complete. The message is based on responsible research and considered reflection. It is designed to guide an audience to give sympathetic attention to the speaker's ideas. It has been carefully worded and rehearsed so that it achieves maximum impact. The message is the product of the speaker's **encoding** processes, the effort to convey through words, tones, and gestures how the speaker thinks and feels about the subject. Encoding is the invitation to meaning that a speaker offers an audience. Audience members respond to that invitation by **decoding** the message, deciding what the speaker intended and determining the value of the message for their lives.

Shaping a message is a basic public speaking skill. You begin by selecting a worthwhile topic and deciding what you want to accomplish. Then you search for supporting material—facts, examples, testimony, and stories—that will strengthen and develop your speech. We discuss finding and using such material in Chapter 5, "Selecting and Researching Your Topic," and Chapter 6, "Using Supporting Materials in Your Speech." Next, you build a message structure that will incorporate these materials effectively, so that each point seems to follow naturally and appropriately from the point before it until an idea is completed. We discuss the arts of building and refining speech structure in Chapter 7, "Structuring Your Speech," and Chapter 8, "Outlining Your Speech." To clarify your points and add variety, you may decide to use illustrative maps, models, or charts. We discuss how to develop such materials in Chapter 9, "Presentation Aids."

Words can make or break a message. In 1994 Republicans effectively used the phrase "Contract with America" to describe their legislative program. It caught the public's imagination in a favorable way. On the other hand, the wrong words can destroy a speaker's ethos. One senator, speaking in support of a balanced federal budget, did not help the cause when he declared: "We're finally going to wrassle to the ground this gigantic orgasm that is just out of control."[16] We discuss how to use words effectively in Chapter 10, "Using Language Effectively."

Finally, you convey your message by the way you use your voice, facial expressions, and gestures. We cover these topics in Chapter 11, "Presenting Your Speech." Becoming a master of the message is a complicated process, but it is a goal that you can achieve through practice and constructive advice from your teacher and classmates.

The Communication Environment Changes.   Conversation can occur in a variety of settings, and the setting can influence the communication that takes place there. One of the most profound discussions of the ethics of communication, Plato's *Phaedrus,* written in ancient Greece some twenty-four hundred years ago, takes place in a woodland setting that frames and colors its message appropriately. This setting is described by Socrates as

> **. . . a fair resting-place, full of summer sounds and scents. Here is this lofty and spreading plane-tree and the [flowering vines] high and clustering, in the fullest blossom and the greatest fragrance; and the stream which flows beneath the plane-tree is deliciously cold to the feet.[17]**

In this setting, Socrates envisions the loving nature of communication at its finest. Such communication, he argues, promotes spiritual growth for both listeners and speakers. Beyond the physical setting, the moods and immediate concerns of participants can also affect the fate of a message. Taken together, these physical and psychological factors make up the **communication environment**.

In public speaking, the communication environment is both simple and more complex. In public speaking classes your speeches will probably all be presented in one place—your classroom. This simplifies the problem of the physical setting: You can get used to speaking in one place. On the other hand, the move from three people to twenty-four complicates the psychological aspects of the communication environment. That many more people can bring to the classroom that many more personal distractions that may prevent them from listening fully to what you say. Moreover, you sometimes cannot control the immediate context of events that can affect the reception of your speech. For example, your carefully planned presentation attacking "oppressive campus security" could be jeopardized if a major crime occurs on campus shortly before your speech. But a campus incident demonstrating the overreaction of security forces could be a real bonanza. You must adapt to such events as you make your speech.

At times this adaptation can be difficult, if not impossible. One of your authors once ran for the U.S. Congress, and during that six-month experience spoke before many audiences. On one occasion, he was speaking at a meeting of mothers who were dependent on welfare benefits to support their families. He had a good message, and he was expecting a warm reception. But the speech fell flat. Later someone explained to him that the welfare checks were late. The women's concern over this delay was such a distraction that no one could have addressed them successfully that day. They simply were in no mood for a speech.

Audience expectations are another important part of the communication environment. If your listeners are anticipating an interesting self-introductory speech and instead hear a tirade against tax reform, the communication environment may become a bit chilly. At another time or in another place, your speech might perhaps work—but not in that particular circumstance.

The negative or challenging factors in the communication environment that can disrupt effectiveness are called **interference**. Interference, which we discuss further in Chapter 3, can range from physical noise that impedes the hearing of a speech, such as a plane flying over the building, to psychological "noise" within speakers and listeners that prevents them from connecting.

While conversationalists are often close acquaintances who feel comfortable with each other, public speakers and their audiences can seem like strangers to each other, especially during first encounters. At such times, they may raise psychological barriers to protect themselves from the risks of genuine communication. Speakers troubled by communication anxiety may see listeners as distant, unfriendly, or threatening. Even before they begin to speak, they raise a barrier between themselves and their audience. Listeners may fear hidden agendas. They may be suspicious of a speaker's motives, cautious about accepting messages, or concerned that what a speaker asks of them may be costly or risky. They too may fear the change—even the growth—that can result from genuine communication.[18] Such suspicions and fears may raise the barrier even higher.

Moreover, listeners may be indifferent to a message or distracted by other concerns. Worries over money or an upcoming test, or dreams about the weekend ahead, can further block communication. Stereotypes about race, gender, nationality, etc., that clutter our heads with prejudice may multiply interference and dramatically raise the barriers between speakers and listeners.

As these formidable barriers develop, the speaker may lose control over what the listeners hear. As most of us have learned from experience, what speakers intend and what listeners hear can be miles apart, and messages may have unintended, unexpected, and unfortunate meanings. *When one masters the art of public speaking, one learns how to minimize interference so that listeners understand the intended message.*

At the beginning of a public speaking course, the barriers of fear, suspicion, indifference, distraction, and prejudice may seem quite formidable. Figure 1.1 illustrates the frustration that speakers and listeners may feel as they first confront this "Interference Mountain." Figure 1.2 suggests that climbing this mountain can be the first challenge students confront in the public speaking class. This book contains detailed instructions on how to make it to the top, both as speaker and as listener. You will discover that as you grow more confident and knowledgeable about public speaking, your topic area, and your listeners, Interference Mountain will become smaller. In most cases your anxiety will become controllable, trust will replace suspicion, involvement will overcome indifference, and mutual respect will reduce prejudice. By the end of the course, as Figure 1.3 suggests, you will have reduced Interference Mountain to a quite manageable hill.

FIGURE 1.1

Blocked by Interference Mountain

FIGURE 1.2

Climbing Interference Mountain

FIGURE 1.3

At the Summit

Communication as Transformation

While communication can be challenging, successful communication offers so many rewards that it deserves our commitment to improve our public speaking skills. Such communication can go beyond personal achievement and the sharing of vital information, ideas, and advice.

At some basic level, successful communication also implies the creation and sharing of selves. In the introduction to *Bridges Not Walls,* John Stewart, an interpersonal communication scholar, notes: "Every time persons communicate, they are continually offering definitions of themselves and responding to definitions of the other(s)." Therefore, Stewart suggests, communication is an ongoing transaction "in which *who we are . . .* emerges out of the event itself."[19] We agree: *Public speaking is often a self-creative event in which we discover ourselves as we communicate with others.* We can grow and expand when we communicate ethically with others. On the other hand, deceitful and dishonest communication will thwart the process of growth.

This is no more than what Plato told us long ago in the *Phaedrus.* Indeed, Plato went beyond the idea of communication as transaction to communication as **transformation.** *Transformation is the dynamic effect of successful communication on the identities of speaker and listener, and on public knowledge as well.* Plato realized that ethical communication that respects the humanity of listeners and nourishes it with responsible knowledge encourages the spiritual growth of both speaker and listeners. As you develop in your public speaking class, you may notice the phenomenon of personal growth. Like Mary in our opening vignette, you may discover the public speaker in you! You may also see your classmates change in response to the good speeches you give throughout the term. The transformative effect of successful public speaking on listeners can be quite dramatic.

Finally, as rhetorical scholar Lloyd Bitzer has noted, successful communication builds public knowledge, what we as a community decide is worth knowing.[20] Public speaking expands and builds this knowledge base. It develops the scope and accuracy of our public awareness.

In these fundamental ways, then, for the speaker, the listener, and the state of public knowledge, public speaking can be transformative. This is why Figure 1.3 shows the speaker and the listener as having drawn closer together and grown larger during their climb to the top of Interference Mountain. They both can also see farther, and their horizons of knowledge have expanded.

You as an Ethical Speaker

When we speak of **ethics,** we mean the moral dimension of human conduct, how we treat others and wish to be treated in return. We can hardly open our mouths without our words affecting those around us. The topics you select, the supporting materials and arguments you use, the way you structure your thoughts, and the words you choose can all have ethical consequences.

We shall return to ethics time and again as this book develops. Here we will develop two central themes: *(1) Ethics in public speaking emphasizes respect for the integrity of ideas, and (2) ethics in public speaking requires concern for the impact of our communication on listeners.* Listeners also must be willing to assume an important ethical role in the speaking situation. We shall examine this role in Chapter 3.

Respect for the Integrity of Ideas

Respect for the integrity of ideas means meeting the demands of responsible knowledge, carefully using communication techniques, and avoiding plagiarism.

Acquiring Responsible Knowledge.   In another of his dialogues, the *Gorgias,* Plato charged that the speakers of his day, especially politicians, were ignorant of their subjects, but that they shamelessly paraded their ignorance before the public anyway. Plato also charged that speakers pandered to public tastes, making listeners feel satisfied with themselves when actually they should have felt the need for improvement.

The growing cynicism of Americans concerning public affairs and politicians suggests that things haven't improved all that much in the last two thousand years. During a recent presidential campaign a poll conducted by *Time* magazine and CNN revealed that 63 percent of voting Americans "have little or no confidence that government leaders talk straight."[21] It is not a time of great faith in the spoken word.

Fortunately, you do not have to be an expert on a topic to speak effectively and ethically about it. If you speak from **responsible knowledge**, your audience will listen to you with respect, especially if you are able to show listeners that they will benefit from your message.

What is responsible knowledge, and what does it require of speakers? As we describe it in more detail in Chapter 5, responsible knowledge of a topic includes

- Knowing the main points of concern
- Understanding what experts believe about them
- Being aware of the most recent events or discoveries concerning them
- Realizing how these points directly affect the lives of listeners

Responsible knowledge requires that you know more about a topic than your listeners, so that your speech has something to give them. *Responsible knowledge is adapted, useful knowledge that takes into account the needs and interests of your listeners.*

Let's consider how one of our students, Stephen Huff, gained responsible knowledge for an informative speech. Stephen knew little about earthquakes before his speech, but he did know that earthquakes were on the minds of his listeners after some recent disasters in California. He also knew that Memphis was sitting right on top of the New Madrid fault, and that this was not good news. Finally, he knew that a major earthquake research center was located at the University of Memphis.

Stephen telephoned the center and scheduled an interview with its director. During the interview, Stephen asked a series of strategic questions: Where was the New Madrid fault, and what was the history of its activity? What was the probability of a major quake in the near future in the Memphis area? How prepared was Memphis for a major quake? How extensive might the damage be in the event of such a catastrophe? What could his listeners do to prepare for it? What readings would the director recommend that might shed additional light on such questions?

Notice that Stephen avoided such general questions as "what are earthquakes?" and "what makes them happen?" Such questions might well have prompted long, rambling answers that would simply have exhausted the time available for the interview. Rather, all his questions were designed to gain knowledge that would be of particular interest and value to his listeners. Armed with knowledge from the interview, Stephen was prepared to visit the library and track down the readings suggested by the director. He was well on his way to giving the good speech that appears in Appendix B. Acquiring responsible knowledge requires time and effort, but you are well rewarded by being able to bring the gift of such knowledge to your listeners.

Carefully Using Communication Techniques.   Respect for the integrity of ideas also requires that you handle the techniques of oral communication very carefully. For example, one frequently used technique is to quote respected authorities in support of your position. Used ethically, this technique helps establish the credibility of ideas by demonstrating that they are not just the notions of the speaker—rather, they are verified by experts. You must be careful, however, to avoid abusing this technique by **quoting out of context**. This unethical use of a quotation distorts its meaning. In effect, it lies and deceives its audience.

Harper Barnes, movie critic for the *St. Louis Post-Dispatch*, describes an all-too-typical case of quoting out of context:

> Jay Boyar of the *Orlando Sentinal* recently reported a fairly egregious example. . . . An ad for the Richard Gere–Sharon Stone stinker "Intersection" attributed this line to Boyar: "Sizzling! Hot stars, steamy sex." He replied, "What I actually wrote was that the premise of 'Intersection' is 'considerably less sizzling' than those of other movies . . . and those sex scenes, which I called only 'ostensibly steamy,' are, I noted, 'presented in a deliberately unsexual way.' As for the ad's suggestion that I had characterized Richard Gere, Sharon Stone and Lolita Davidovich as 'hot stars,' that much is correct. But I would now add that they're not quite so hot after appearing in 'Intersection.'[22]

Quoting out of context can have far more serious consequences. A high point of Dr. Martin Luther King, Jr.'s famed "I Have a Dream" speech came when he said that he wanted his children to be judged "not by the color of their skin but by the content of their character." Tom Teepen of the *Minneapolis Star Tribune* argues that when you hear that quote "being piously invoked these days, you can be sure black folks are about to get nailed again."

Gov. Pete Wilson flew the quote like air cover over his political turnaround when he supported the referendum that killed affirmative action in California. A man whose lawsuit has all but cleared the University of Texas law school of black students crowed, "It's kind of finishing Dr. King's dream . . ." Colorado Attorney General Gale Norton cited King, too, in her effort to end scholarships to the state's colleges and universities targeted for black students. Mississippi Gov. Kirk Fordice used the quote to explain why he was appointing only white men to the board that runs the university system. Robert Brustein, theater critic and artistic director of the American Repertory Theater, cited King in condemning the formation of black theatrical companies. And on and on goes this political grave robbery.[23]

Teepen's point is that King's words were quoted not only out of the context of his speech, but out of the context of his life. Such citations subverted all that King had fought and died for as a civil rights activist. In your speeches, be sure to quote people carefully and reflect the true spirit of their meaning.

As we talk about the use of supporting materials in Chapter 6 and about developing evidence and proofs for persuasive speeches in Chapter 14, we shall be especially attentive to the problem of the ethical and unethical uses of communication techniques.

Avoiding Plagiarism.   Finally, respect for the integrity of ideas requires that a speech be the original work of the speaker and that it acknowledges major sources of information and ideas. *Presenting the ideas and words of others as though they were your own, without acknowledging their contribution, is called* **plagiarism.** It is depressing to discover the extent of such intellectual theft in contemporary journalism, literature, scholarship, and scientific research as well as public speaking.[24] As writer Paul Gray said in *Time:* "An author's worst dream is to be accused of plagiarism, of stealing ideas and language from someone else and parading them as original."[25]

Given the shame and ruin that come when plagiarism is discovered, why do writers and speakers do it? Perhaps it is because of the pressure of time and deadlines in modern life, or the terrible temptation to "cut a few corners" in order to win recognition—or improve a grade. Whatever the answer, you should avoid plagiarism—or even the appearance of it—at all costs. Beyond the immorality of the practice, which should be reason enough to avoid it, remember that colleges and universities consider plagiarism a major infraction of the student code and impose penalties ranging from grade reduction to suspension.

So how should you avoid any hint of plagiarism? The grossest form of such theft, simply presenting someone else's speech word for word as though it were your own, is easy enough to avoid. However, there are more subtle forms of intellectual looting, which you can escape by observing certain rules of conduct.

You should not summarize an article from a newspaper or magazine and present it as your speech. For starters, the speech probably will not be very good, because it will not have been designed for your particular audience. Because it does not bear the stamp of your own thinking and feeling, it will not seem authentic. And because the speech is not really a part of you, it will be hard for you to present it effectively. Do not cheat yourself and disappoint an audience this way. You should also be careful about relying too much on any single source of information. Instead, gather facts and ideas from a variety of sources, develop your own thinking about what they mean to you and your listeners, and present them in your own words.

You should credit the sources of the ideas in your speech. When you quote someone, directly or by paraphrase, let your listeners know. Also give credit to the sources of the ideas and information in your speech. Rather than simply saying:

> **The Dean of the College of Communication at Boston University resigned after he presented a commencement address that was plagiarized.**

say instead:

> **According to the *Boston Globe* of July 2, 1991, the Dean of the College of Communication at Boston University presented a plagiarized speech at the University's commencement ceremonies that year. Then on July 15, the *Washington Times* confirmed that the president of the University had accepted the dean's resignation, saying "It's the duty of all responsible scholars and writers to credit their sources."[26]**

To make matters even worse, a reporter for the *New York Times,* writing a story about the plagiarized speech, himself plagiarized from the *Globe* account and was placed on suspension.

It doesn't make sense not to credit the sources of your information and ideas. As the above example shows, citing your sources can strengthen your speech. It helps your ethos by demonstrating that you have carefully prepared. And it provides borrowed ethos by associating your thinking with that of respected others—experts, well-respected publications, or opinion leaders.

Concern for Listeners

Recognizing the power of communication leads ethical speakers to a genuine concern for how words affect the lives of their listeners. We conclude this chapter by introducing two related ideas: how the "other" orientation of public speaking requires us to be more ethically sensitive, and how applying universal values may help us overcome the problems of audience diversity.

Developing an "Other" Orientation.   In our opening story, Mary began her public speaking class with a great deal of concern about her own fate. During the class, however, as she grew more confident about her competence and as she came to know and like her classmates, she increasingly prepared her speeches with them in mind. In so doing, Mary developed an "other" orientation and grew away from **egocentrism,** the tendency to believe that our thoughts, dreams, interests, and desires are or should be shared by others. Jaksa and Pritchard, in *Communication Ethics: Methods of Analysis,* offer a pertinent example: "After offering a lengthy explanation of the importance of egocentricity in Kohlberg's theory of moral development, [one of the authors of this text] . . . was greeted with this response from a student. "I think I understand what egocentric thinking is. Here's an example. You're interested in Kohlberg. So you assume we are, too.'"[27]

How to Avoid Plagiarism

speaker's notes

1 Never summarize a single article for a speech. You should not simply parrot other people's language and ideas.
2 Get information and ideas from a variety of sources; then combine and interpret these to create an original approach to your topic.
3 Introduce your sources as lead-ins to direct quotations: "Studs Terkel has said that a book about work 'is, by its very nature, about violence—to the spirit as well as the body.'"
4 Identify your sources of information: "According to *The 1990 Information Please Almanac,* tin cans were first used as a means of preserving food in 1811" or "The latest issue of *Time* magazine notes that. . . ."
5 Credit the originators of ideas that you use: "John Sheets, director of secondary curriculum and instruction at Duke University, suggests that there are three criteria we should apply in evaluating our high school."

The discipline of the public speaking class encourages the desirable growth into an "other" orientation, and into the expansion of the self that this growth implies.

Applying Universal Values.   We have already noted that the public speaking class encourages us to counter ethnocentrism, which is the group parallel to egocentrism in that it holds up our own culture as the most desirable model. We learn to respect one another's backgrounds, and to look on the world through different cultural windows. But this also presents us with a problem. If the members of your class represent many cultures, each offering a different outlook, then how can you frame a speech that will communicate and will have appeal across these many audiences-within-an-audience?

One answer to this perplexing problem has been offered by Rushworth M. Kidder, former senior columnist for *The Christian Science Monitor* and president of the Institute for Global Ethics. In his book *Shared Values for a Troubled World,* Kidder reports interviews with leading moral representatives of many cultures that indicate the existence of a global code of ethical conduct, centering on the deeply and widely shared values of *love, truthfulness, fairness, freedom, unity, tolerance, responsibility,* and *respect for life.*[28] If Kidder is correct, appeals to these fundamental values should resonate in any culture, and should be well received by the diverse members of your public speaking class. We shall say more about how to effectively engage such values in Chapter 4.

In Summary

How a Course in Public Speaking Can Help You.   This class deserves your commitment because of the significant benefits it offers. Personally, you should benefit from the opportunity to grow as a sensitive, skilled communicator, and from the practical advantages such growth makes possible. You should also become a more effective member of society. Self-government cannot work without responsible and effective public communication, and public speaking is the basic form of such communication. The public speaking class can expose you to different cultures as you hear others express their lifestyles, values, and concerns. Such exposure can counter *ethnocentrism*, the tendency to feel that our way to live is the right way.

Public Speaking as Communication.   Public speaking builds upon the basic communication skills that we originally develop as we acquire language and learn how to converse with others. As expanded conversation, public speaking preserves the natural directness and spontaneity and the colorful and compelling qualities of good conversation. Like conversation, public speaking is tuned to the reactions of listeners and makes adjustments to this *feedback*. Speeches are also designed with the reactions of listeners in mind.

In contrast with conversation, public speaking defines the roles of speaker and *listener* more clearly. Public speaking gives prominence to the speaker. The *ethos* of the speaker, based upon audience perceptions of that speaker's competence and integrity, likableness and forcefulness, can be crucial to the success of a speech. A successful speech is carefully planned to be internally consistent and complete. The speaker *encodes* the *message*; the listener *decodes* its meaning. Misunderstandings arise when message and meaning are far apart. The *communication environment* can promote or impede understanding. To achieve effective communication, the speaker must overcome *interference* that can block or distort the message. Successful communication can result in the *transformation* of speaker, audience, and the knowledge they share.

You as an Ethical Speaker.   Ethical considerations in public speaking are inescapable. Ethical public speaking respects the integrity of ideas and focuses on the impact of communication on listeners. Respect for the integrity of ideas means meeting the demands of *responsible knowledge,* carefully using communication techniques, and avoiding such practices as *quoting out of context* and *plagiarism.* Responsible knowledge is useful knowledge. It requires having up-to-date information on the major points of a topic, what the most respected experts have to say about it, and how these points affect your immediate audience. Plagiarism is intellectual theft. Being convicted or even suspected of such a crime can damage your ethos beyond repair.

Concern for listeners comes as you develop an "other" orientation in your public speaking class to balance the *egocentrism*, or excessive preoccupation with the self, that you may bring to such a class. You can solve the problem of adapting to the many cultures that may be represented in your class if you base your appeals in a global code of ethics.

Terms to Know

ethnocentrism	listener
stereotype	message
feedback	encoding
ethos	decoding

communication environment   responsible knowledge

interference   quoting out of context

transformation   plagiarism

ethics   egocentrism

Application

The Speech Communication Association has adopted the following code of ethics concerning free expression:

Credo for Free and Responsible Communication in a Democratic Society

Recognizing the essential place of free and responsible communication in a democratic society, and recognizing the distinction between the freedoms our legal system should respect and the responsibilities our educational system should cultivate, we the members of the Speech Communication Association endorse the following statement of principles:

We believe that freedom of speech and assembly must hold a central position among American constitutional principles, and we express our determined support for the right of peaceful expression by any communicative means available.

We support the proposition that a free society can absorb with equanimity speech which exceeds the boundaries of generally accepted beliefs and mores; that much good and little harm can ensue if we err on the side of freedom, whereas much harm and little good may follow if we err on the side of suppression.

We criticize as misguided those who believe that the justice of their cause confers license to interfere physically and coercively with the speech of others, and we condemn intimidation, whether by powerful majorities or strident minorities, which attempts to restrict free expression.

We accept the responsibility of cultivating by precept and example, in our classrooms and in our communities, enlightened uses of communication; of developing in our students a respect for precision and accuracy in communication, and for reasoning based upon evidence and a judicious discrimination among values.

We encourage our students to accept the role of well-informed and articulate citizens, to defend the communication rights of those with whom they may disagree, and to expose abuses of the communication process.

We dedicate ourselves fully to these principles, confident in the belief that reason will ultimately prevail in a free marketplace of ideas.[29]

Working in small groups, discuss how you would adapt this credo into a code of ethics for use in your public speaking class. Each group should present the code it proposes to the class, and the class should determine a code of ethics to be used during the term.

Notes

1. "The Lakota Family," *Bulletin of Oglala Sioux Community College, 1980–81* (Pine Ridge, S. Dak.), p. 2.
2. "Be the Person Employers Want to Hire," Job Web and Job Choices Online, 5 July 1998, <http//www.jobweb.org/jconline/Tips/tips4.shtml>.
3. Sandy Hock, "Communication Skills Top List of Student Advice," *Accounting Today* vol. 8 no. 5 (1994): 27.
4. *Ibid.*
5. From "Statements Supporting Speech Communication," ed. Kathleen Peterson (Annandale, Va., Speech Communication Association, 1986).
6. William Brennan, "Commencement Address," Brandeis University, 1986; cited in *Time,* 9 June 1986, p. 63.
7. Richard M. Weaver, "Ultimate Terms in Contemporary Rhetoric," *Language Is Sermonic: Richard M. Weaver on the Nature of Rhetoric,* eds. Richard L. Johannesen, Rennard Strickland, and Ralph T. Eubanks (Baton Rouge: Louisiana State University Press, 1970), p. 95.
8. Elizabeth Lozano, "The Cultural Experience of Space and Body: A Reading of Latin American and Anglo American Comportment in Public," in *Our Voices: Essays in Culture, Ethnicity, and Communication,* ed. Alberto Gonzalez, Marsha Houston, and Victoria Chen (Los Angeles: Roxbury Publishing Company, 1994), p. 141.
9. Dolores V. Tanno, "Names, Narratives, and the Evolution of Ethnic Identity," in *Our Voices,* pp. 30–33.
10. Casey Man Kong Lum, "Regionalism and Communication: Exploring Chinese Immigrant Perspectives," in *Our Voices,* pp. 146–151.
11. Navita Cummings James, "When Miss America Was Always White," in *Our Voices,* p. 43.
12. T. Harry Williams, ed., *Abraham Lincoln: Selected Speeches, Messages, and Letters* (New York: Holt, Rinehart and Winston, 1964), p. 148.
13. See the discussion summarizing ethos-related research in James C. McCroskey, *An Introduction to Rhetorical Communication* (Englewood Cliffs, N.J.: Prentice-Hall, 1993), pp. 78–98, and a critique of such research in Gary Cronkhite and Jo Liska, "A Critique of Factor Analytic Approaches to the Study of Credibility," *Communication Monographs* 43 (1976): 91–107.
14. *Fortune* magazine offers an interesting discussion of the importance of charisma in American business: Patricia Sellers, Shaifali Puri, and David Kaufman, "What Exactly Is Charisma?" *Fortune,* 15 January 1996, p. 68+; 15 May 1998, <http://www.pathfinder.com/fortune/magazine/1996/960115/charisma.html>.
15. Book 2.1 of the *Rhetoric,* trans. Lane Cooper (New York: Appleton-Century-Crofts, 1932), p. 92.
16. Cited in *Newsweek,* 25 May 1992, p. 21.
17. *The Dialogues of Plato,* trans. Benjamin Jowett, in *Great Books of the Western World,* vol. 7 (Chicago: Encyclopaedia Britannica, Inc., 1952), p. 116. See the analysis by Richard M. Weaver, "The *Phaedrus* and the Nature of Rhetoric," *Language Is Sermonic,* pp. 57–83.
18. Such fear may be part of the "receiver apprehension" described in Joe Ayres, A. Kathleen Wilcox, and Debbie M. Ayres, "Receiver Apprehension: An Explanatory Model and Accompanying Research," *Communication Education* 44 (1995): 223–235.
19. John Stewart, ed., *Bridges Not Walls: A Book About Interpersonal Communication,* 5th ed. (New York: McGraw-Hill Publishing Company, 1990), p. 22.
20. Lloyd F. Bitzer, "Rhetoric and Public Knowledge," *Rhetoric, Philosophy, and Lit-*

erature: An Exploration, ed. Don M. Burks (West Lafayette, Ind.: Purdue University Press, 1978), pp. 67–93.

21. "Lies, Lies, Lies," *Time,* 5 October 1992, 32.

22. Harper Barnes, " 'Distorted!' 'Pretentious!' 'Arrogant!'," *St. Louis Post-Dispatch,* 28 July, 1994, p. 1G. Reprinted with permission of the *St. Louis Post-Dispatch,* copyright © 1994.

23. Tom Teepen, "Twisting King's Words to Give His Antagonists Comfort," *Minneapolis Star Tribune,* 14 July 1997, p. 9A.

24. See, for example, the disheartening array of plagiarism discussed in Trudy Lieberman, "Plagiarize, Plagiarize, Plagiarize . . . Only Be Sure to Call It Research," *Columbia Journalism Review* (July/August 1995), http://www.cjr.org/html/95-07-08-plagiarize.html.

25. "The Purloined Letters," *Time,* 26 April 1993, 59.

26. According to *Washington Times,* 15 July 1991, p. B 10, and "Recycling in the Newsroom," *Time,* 29 July 1991, p. 59.

27. James A. Jaksa and Michael S. Pritchard, *Communication Ethics: Methods of Analysis,* 2nd ed. (Belmont, Calif.: Wadsworth Publishing Company, 1994), p. 94.

28. Rushworth M. Kidder, *Shared Values for a Troubled World: Conversations with Men and Women of Conscience* (San Francisco: Jossey-Bass Publishers, Inc., 1994).

29. National Communication Association's "Credo for Free and Responsible Communication in a Democratic Society." Used by permission of the National Communication Association.

2

Your First Speech

*W*ithout speech there would be no community. . . . Language, taken as a whole, becomes the gateway to a new world.

—*Ernst Cassirer*

This chapter will help you

- manage the first impressions you make
- design your first speech
- develop effective presentation skills
- control communication apprehension
- introduce yourself or someone else

Jimmy Green worried about his self-introductory speech. How could he give a speech about himself when nothing exciting had ever happened to him? Jimmy opened his speech on growing up in rural Decatur County by referring to a popular song, "A Country Boy Can Survive." Then he captivated his urban audience with delightful descriptions of jug fishing for catfish and night-long barbecues where "more than the pig got sauced."

James Norton, who was attending the university on an athletic scholarship, introduced Rosamond Wolford, who was enrolled in the music department on an arts scholarship. James said that while he expressed himself most easily on the basketball court, Rosamond communicated through her violin. He played a taped excerpt of her playing a Mozart concerto, then commented that both he and Rosamond would now have to learn to express themselves more through words. He seemed surprised when listeners enjoyed his speech and said they were not aware of his nervousness.

MANY OF US do not appreciate our own experiences or think that others may find us interesting. We just can't see ourselves as "public speakers." We are amazed when listeners get so caught up with what we are saying that they don't notice our anxiety. Both the students just described gave excellent first speeches.

The first speeches in a class can help build a communication climate that nurtures effective speaking and listening. No matter what the exact nature of your assignment, your most basic challenge is to present yourself as a credible source of ideas for your first and later speeches. As we noted in Chapter 1, people are more likely to respond favorably to those whom they respect and like. In this chapter we show you how to get off on the right foot by managing the all-important first impressions you make as a speaker. We also discuss how to develop your first speech, how to rehearse it for presentation, and how to control nervousness. We conclude with special advice on how to develop a speech introducing yourself or another.

Before the opening round of speeches, you and your classmates are usually strangers. These speeches are often called "icebreakers," because they give members of the class a chance to know one another better. You will probably discover that your classmates are both diverse and interesting. What you learn about them will help you prepare later speeches by giving you insights into their knowledge, interests, attitudes, and motivations. Because it is easier to communicate with people you know, you should also feel more comfortable about speaking before the class.

Learning how to control the impressions you make will help you in later life. You deserve to make a good impression on others, just as people deserve to have their best cases presented in a court of law. The analogy is good, because others are constantly judging us on the basis of such impressions.

Managing the Impressions You Make

When you stand before others to offer information or advice, you are acting as a leader. You may never have thought of yourself that way, but as you develop your speaking ability, you will also grow in leadership potential.

Both leading and communicating begin with listeners forming favorable impressions of your ethos, based on perceptions of your competence, integrity, likableness, and forcefulness. In this section we explore ways in which you can promote these impressions.

Competence

Competent speakers seem informed, intelligent, and well prepared. You can build a perception of your **competence** by selecting topics that you already know something about and by doing the research necessary to qualify you as a responsible speaker. You can further enhance your competence by quoting experts and authoritative sources who support your position. For example, if you are speaking on the link between nutrition and heart disease, you might quote a prominent medical specialist or a publication of the American Heart Association: "Dr. Milas Peterson heads the Heart Institute at Harvard University. During his visit to our campus last week, I spoke with him about this point. He told me . . ." Note the competence-related elements here:

- The speaker cited the qualifications of the expert and his connection to a prestigious institution.
- The quotation contains the most recent information.
- The connection between the expert and the speaker is direct and personal, suggesting a favorable association.
- The speaker demonstrates that he or she has prepared carefully for the speech by interviewing a visiting expert.

When you cite authoritative sources in this way, you are "borrowing" their ethos to enhance your own as you strengthen the points you make in the speech. Remember, though, that borrowed ethos enhances but does not replace *your* ethos. Personal experience related as stories or examples can also help a speech seem authentic, bring it to life, and make you seem more competent. "Been there, done that" can be a very effective technique. Your competence will be further enhanced if your speech is well organized, if you use language ably and correctly, and if you make a polished presentation.

Integrity

A speaker with **integrity** seems ethical, honest, and dependable. Listeners are more receptive when speakers are straightforward and concerned about the consequences of their words. You can enhance your integrity by presenting all sides of an issue and then explaining why you have chosen your position. You should also demonstrate that you are willing to follow your own advice. In a speech that calls for commitment or action, it should be clear to listeners that you are not asking more of them than you would ask of yourself. The more you ask of the audience, the more important your integrity becomes.

Let us look at how integrity can be conveyed in a speech. Mona Goldberg was preparing a speech on welfare reform. The more she learned about the subject, the more convinced she became that budget cuts for welfare programs were unwise. In her speech, Mona showed that she took her assignment seriously by citing many authorities and statistics. She reviewed arguments both for and against cutting the budget and then showed her audience why she was against reducing aid to such programs. Finally, Mona revealed that her own family had had to live on unemployment benefits at one time. "I know the hurt, the loss of pride, the sense of growing frustration. I didn't have to see them on the evening news." Her openness showed that she was willing to trust her listeners to react fairly to this sensitive information. The audience responded in kind by trusting her and what she had to say. She had built an impression of herself as a person of integrity.

This example also shows how a "halo effect" can cause competence and integrity to be linked in judgments of credibility.[1] Speakers who rank high in one quality may get positive evaluations in the other.

Likableness

Speakers who rate high on **likableness** radiate goodness and goodwill, which inspire audience affection in return. Audiences are more willing to accept ideas and suggestions from speakers they like. A smile and direct eye contact

The character and personality of a speaker can influence how well a message is received. Likableness is an important component of speaker ethos.

can signal to listeners that you want to communicate. Likable speakers share their feelings as well as their thoughts. They enjoy laughter at appropriate moments, especially laughter at themselves. Being able to talk openly and engagingly about your mistakes can make you seem more human and appealing as well as more confident.

The more likable speakers seem, the more audiences want to identify with them.[2] **Identification** is the feeling of sharing or closeness that can develop between speakers and listeners despite different cultural backgrounds. When these backgrounds differ, speakers can invite identification by telling stories or by using examples that help listeners focus on the experiences, values, or beliefs they have in common. Speaking before a class that included students from all sections of the United States, Marie D'Aniello invited identification in her self-introductory speech by developing a theme everyone could share, family pride. At one point in her speech, Marie pointed out how she had drawn inspiration from her brother's athletic accomplishments:

> **When I think of glory, I have to think of my brother Chris. I'll never forget his championship basketball game. It's the typical buzzer beater story: five seconds to go, down by one, Chris gets the ball and he drives down the court, he shoots, he scores! . . . I'll never forget the headline, "D'Aniello saves the game!" D'Aniello, hey wait, that's me. I'm a D'Aniello. I could do this too. Maybe I can't play basketball like Chris, but I can do other things.**

After this speech, which appears at the end of this chapter, it was hard not to like Marie. This impression, combined with other favorable impressions of her competence, integrity, and confidence, created respect for her point of view.

Likableness can also be enhanced by appropriate touches of humor. Marcos White, a point guard for the University of New Mexico basketball team, endeared himself to listeners during his first speech. Marcos introduced himself as the son of an African American father and a Mexican mother: "I guess," he said, "that makes me a blaxican."

Audiences often identify with speakers who talk or dress the way they do. Audiences prefer speakers who use gestures, language, and facial expressions that are natural and unaffected. You should speak a little more formally than you do in everyday conversation, but not much more. Similarly, you should dress nicely for your speech, but not extravagantly. You do not want to create distance between yourself and your listeners by language or dress that seems either too formal or too casual.

Forcefulness

James Norton, who introduced Rosamond Wolford as an accomplished violinist, later confessed that he was frightened before he gave his speech. He was not sure how his speech would be received, and he worried that he might make a mistake. But when James walked in front of the room to speak, he seemed confident, decisive, and enthusiastic. In short, he conveyed the qualities of **forcefulness**. Whatever he might have secretly felt, his audience responded only to what they saw and gave him high marks for his sense of command.

FIGURE 2.1
Components of Ethos

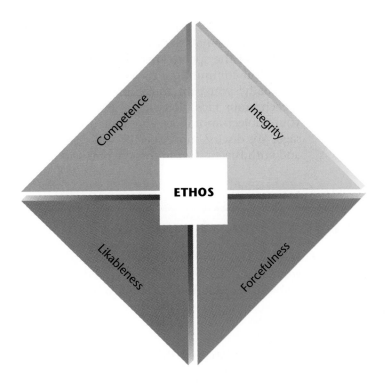

At first you may not feel confident about public speaking, but you should seem as though you are. If you appear self-assured, listeners will respond as though you are, and you may find yourself becoming what you seem to be. In other words, you can trick yourself into developing a very desirable trait! When you appear to be in control, you also put your listeners at ease. This feeling will come back to you as positive feedback and further reinforce your confidence. One of our students, John Scipio, was at first intimidated by the public speaking situation, but John was blessed with two natural virtues: He was a large, imposing person, and he had a powerful voice. And then he found a subject he truly believed in. When John presented his classroom tribute to the final speech of Dr. Martin Luther King, Jr., he radiated force, in addition to competence, likableness, and integrity:

> When I asked him during a telephone interview why he thought Dr. King was such an effective leader, Ralph Abernathy said, "He possessed a power never before seen in a man of color." What was this power that he spoke of? It was the power to persuade audiences and change opinions with his words. It was the power of speech. . . . In this speech, Dr. King had to give these people hope and motivate them to go on. . . . He spoke to all of us, but especially to those of us in the black community, when he said, "Only when it is dark enough can you see the stars." And when he talked of standing up to the firehoses in Birmingham, he said, "There's a certain kind of fire that no water can put out." And on the last night of his life, with less than twenty-four hours to live, he was still thinking—not of himself, but of our nation: "Let us move on," he said, "in these powerful days, these days of challenge, to make America what it ought to be."

To appear forceful, you must also be decisive. In persuasive speeches, you should consider all the important options available to your audience, but by the end of the speech there should be no doubt as to where you stand and why. Your commitment to your position must be strong.

Finally, you gain forcefulness from the enthusiasm you bring to your speech. Your face, voice, and gestures should indicate that you care about your subject and about the audience. Your enthusiasm endorses your message. We discuss more specific ways of developing confidence, decisiveness, and enthusiasm later in this chapter and in Chapter 11.

Building Your First Speech

So now you have your first speech assignment. Your teacher has explained what he or she would like you to do, but the creativity and excitement of working out the details are up to you. There is one thing you can count on: You will not have much time to speak. You will have to plan and rehearse carefully—*and time yourself as you practice*—to be sure you stay within the time limits.

As you plan, you should follow an orderly procedure to ensure that you will build a speech that represents you well. That includes

- Selecting a topic that is appropriate to you, your listeners, and the assignment
- Finding material that will add clarity and interest to your speech
- Designing your speech so that it fits together in a coherent pattern

Each of these considerations will be taken up in the chapters that follow. Here we simply want to introduce them and provide just enough information to help you build a successful first speech. How well you prepare will have a great deal to do with whether you succeed![3]

Selecting a Topic

The topic you select should be appropriate to you, your listeners, and the assignment. The best topic for your first speech is one that will not only win applause right away, but help you build desirable ethos for later speeches. The more you already know about a topic, the easier it will be to appear competent as you speak on it. Ask yourself, what am I most interested in? Can I make it interesting to my listeners as well? Might this speech help me give later, related speeches? As we have noted, Jimmy Green's first speech, "My Life as a River Rat," created favorable ethos for him and aroused interest for his later speeches on environmental policy. James Norton helped shape a receptive audience for Rosamond Wolford's later speeches on music as a form of communication and created an impression of himself as a person with interests that ranged beyond the basketball court.

Be sure to narrow and focus your topic so that you can accomplish your purpose within the limited time available. We shall have more to say as this chapter concludes about how to select topics for speeches introducing yourself and others.

Finding Material for Your Speech

Just as bridges and buildings require columns and beams to support them, a speech needs to have its main points reinforced. A well-developed speech will have the help of supporting materials such as facts and statistics, testimony, examples, and stories.

Facts and Statistics.   **Facts and statistics** are a major form of support for speeches. They lift your claims above mere assertions to the level of well-documented conclusions. For example, to support her statement that American business has a legal as well as a moral obligation to reach out to disabled persons, Karen Lovelace cited the Americans with Disabilities Act of 1990:

> **The ADA said that "privately owned businesses that serve the public such as restaurants, hotels, retail stores, taxi cabs, theaters, concert halls, and sports facilities are prohibited from discriminating against individuals with disabilities." The ADA went on to say that "companies have an ongoing responsibility to remove barriers to access for peoples with disabilities if it is readily achievable."**

Karen's factual knowledge of the law strengthened the foundations of her speech advocating reform.

Testimony.   **Testimony** in support of your ideas provided by experts or by respected persons can strengthen the authority of your speech. As she developed her speech, Karen cited Sandy Blondino, director of sales at Embassy Suites, who confirmed that the lodging industry is now more receptive to disabled travelers. She concluded with Ms. Blondino's exact words: "But that's just hospitality, right?" She followed up this *expert testimony* with *prestige testimony* by quoting President Clinton: "When I injured my knee and used a wheelchair for a short time, I understood even more deeply that the ADA isn't just a good law, it's the right thing to do." When you quote expert testimony, be sure to mention the expert's credentials, and state when and where she or he made the statement you are quoting.

Examples.   **Examples** illustrate points and make them seem authentic. An example says, in effect, this really happened. To illustrate her point that it is good business to serve the needs of disabled people, Karen Lovelace described a group called Opening Doors that encourages companies to improve travel for the disabled. "One hotel chain that has used this program is Embassy Suites. Their staff are taught by Opening Doors to problem-solve based on guests' needs. And you'd better believe that the word gets around to disabled travelers!" Her example made her claim seem realistic.

Stories.   **Stories** or narratives tell a tale to make a point more clear and convincing. Dramatic incidents told in a way that makes characters come to life can add great interest to your speech. To illustrate most of her points, Karen spoke of a day she had spent with a disabled person, describing all the barriers

Narratives based on personal experiences add interest and authenticity to speeches.

he had to overcome to achieve simple, everyday needs that most of us take for granted.

For the first speeches in a class, examples and narratives are often especially useful and appropriate. They help develop a feeling of closeness between the audience and the speaker that creates a positive learning community. They also enhance favorable ethos. They hold the interest of the audience while revealing some important truth about the speaker or the topic. Narratives should be short and to the point, moving in natural sequence from the beginning of the story to the end. The language of narration should be colorful, concrete, and active; the presentation, lively and interesting.

Taken as a whole, facts and statistics, testimony, examples, and stories provide the substance that can make us take a speech seriously. Karen's classmates at Vanderbilt felt that her speech was one of the most effective that they heard that semester.

Designing Your Speech

You must develop a design in which your points fit together to help you achieve your purpose. Your design provides the overall pattern into which you fit your supporting materials. Let us look at how a design might help structure a self-introductory speech.

If you wanted to explain how you were shaped by the neighborhood in which you grew up, you might select a *categorical* design. You could begin with the setting, a description of a street scene in which you capture sights, sounds, and smells: "I can always tell a Swedish neighborhood by the smell of *lutefisk* on Friday afternoons." Next you might describe the people, focusing on a certain neighbor who influenced you—perhaps the local grocer, who loved America with a passion, helped those in need, and always voted stubbornly for the Socialist party. Finally, you might talk about the street games you played as a child and what they taught you about people and yourself. This "setting–people–games" categorical design structures your speech in an orderly manner.

The example also suggests that the introduction, body, and conclusion of your speech must be closely related. Your **introduction**, in which you arouse interest and set the mood for what will follow, could be the opening street scene. In the **body** of the speech, where you develop your points using supporting materials, you could describe the people, using the grocer as an extended example. Then you could go on to describe the childhood games that reinforced the lessons of sharing. Your **conclusion** should make clear the point of the speech:

> **I hope you have enjoyed this "tour" of my neighborhood, this "tour" of my past. If you drove down this street tomorrow, you might think it was just another crowded, gray, urban neighborhood. But for me it is filled with memories of colorful people who cared for each other and who dreamed great dreams of a better tomorrow. That street runs right down the center of my life.**

Other topics and purposes might suggest other designs. If you select an experience that influenced you, such as "An Unforgettable Adventure," your speech might follow a *sequential* pattern as you tell the story of what happened. You would talk about events in the actual time sequence in which they occurred. Should you decide to tell about a condition that has had a great impact on you, a *causation* design might be most appropriate. Maria One Feather, a Native American student, used such a design in her speech "Growing Up Red—and Feeling Blue—in White America." In this instance she treated the condition as the cause and its impact on her as the effect. The various designs available to you are discussed in Chapters 12 and 13, and you may wish to refer to these chapters as you plan your first speech.

Just a bit more on introductions, bodies, and conclusions: In addition to arousing interest and preparing listeners for the rest of the speech, your introduction should also build a good relationship between yourself and your audience. That, of course, fits right in with the idea of building good ethos in the first speech. The best introductions are framed *after* the body of the speech has been planned—after all, it is difficult to draw a map if you don't yet know exactly where you are going. We provide other suggestions for preparing introductions in Chapter 7.

The body is where you develop your main points, the most important ideas in your message. For a three- to five-minute assignment, limit yourself to two or three main points so that you can develop them in depth. Determining and wording main points is covered in more detail in Chapter 7.

The conclusion often restates your main points and concludes with reflections on the meaning of the speech for the lives of your listeners. Good

Building Your First Speech

speaker's notes

1 Select a topic that fits you, your audience, and the assignment.

2 Choose a topic that will help you build ethos for later speeches.

3 Design your speech so that your thoughts develop in a coherent pattern.

4 Develop an introduction that arouses attention as it leads into your topic.

5 Limit yourself to two or three main points.

6 Use facts, statistics, and testimony to add authority to your speech.

7 Use examples and stories to add color and personal appeal, to clarify your meaning, and to bring your speech to life.

8 Prepare a conclusion that ties your speech together and reflects on your meaning.

9 Time yourself as you practice so that you stay within the time limits.

conclusions are easily remembered—even eloquent. Sometimes they quote well-known people who state the point very well. They may tie back to the introduction, completing a symbolic circle that the audience finds satisfying. They may try to end on a high note.

Outlining Your First Speech

To nail down your plan for your first speech and ensure that your thoughts all follow in sequence, prepare an outline using complete sentences. The outline should contain your introduction, the central point you are trying to make (the **thesis statement**), your main ideas and major supporting materials, and your conclusion. In addition, your outline should contain planned **transitions** to help you move from one point to another. Marie D'Aniello's first speech, "Family Gifts," which appears at the end of this chapter, illustrates especially skillful, subtle use of transitions.

You should also prepare a **key-word outline**, a shorter version of your full-sentence outline, to use as you practice and present your speech. As its name suggests, this outline contains only key words and phrases to prompt your memory. It can also contain presentation cues, such as "pause here" or "talk slowly and softly." Although the full outline may require several pages to complete, the key-word outline should fit on one or two index cards. We say more about outlining in Chapter 8.

In the following outline for a self-introductory speech, several critical parts of the speech—the introduction, thesis statement, and conclusion—are written out word for word. They stabilize the meaning you intend to convey and make your entrance into and exit from the speech both smooth and effective. Thus, it is important that they be planned exactly, even though you may vary your plan during the actual presentation to make adjustments to the immediate situation. Note, however, that the body of the speech is not written out, encouraging spontaneity in the actual presentation.

"Free at Last"

by Rodney Nishikawa

Introduction

Attention-arousing and orienting material: Three years ago I presented the valedictory speech at my high school graduation. As I concluded, I borrowed a line from Dr. Martin Luther King's "I Have a Dream" speech: "Free at last, free at last, thank God almighty we're free at last!" The words had a joyful, humorous place in that speech, but for me personally, they were a lie.

Thesis statement: I was not yet free, and would not be free until I had conquered an ancient enemy, both outside me and within me—that enemy was racial prejudice.

■ *Rodney's three main points are each supported with facts, examples, or narratives. The outline uses Roman numerals to indicate main points, capital letters to indicate the subpoints, and Arabic numbers to indicate sub-subpoints. These numbers and letters are indented to show the structure of the ideas in the speech.*

Body

I. When I was eight years old I was exposed to anti-Japanese prejudice.

    A. I was a "Jap" who didn't belong in America.

    B. The bully's words burned into my soul.

        1. I was ashamed of my heritage.

        2. I hated having to live in this country.

[Transition: "So I obviously needed some help."]

II. My parents helped me put this in perspective.

    A. They survived terrible prejudice in their youth during World War II.

    B. They taught me to accept the reality of prejudice.

    C. They taught me the meaning of *gaman:* how to bear the burden within and not show anger.

[Transition: "Now, how has gaman *helped me?"]*

III. Practicing *gaman* has helped me develop inner strength.

    A. I rarely experience fear or anger.

    B. I have learned to accept myself.

    C. I have learned to be proud of my heritage.

Conclusion

Summary Statement: Practicing *gaman*, a gift from my Japanese roots, has helped me conquer prejudice.

Concluding Remarks: Although my Japanese ancestors might not have spoken as boldly as I have today, I am basically an American, which makes me a little outspoken. Therefore, I can talk to you about racial prejudice and of what it has meant to my life. And because I can talk about it, and share it with you, I am finally, truly, "free at last."

Presenting Your First Speech

Once you have developed and outlined your first speech, you are ready to prepare for presentation. *An effective presentation spotlights the ideas, not the speaker, and is offered as though you were talking with the audience, not reading to them or reciting from memory.*

Spotlight the Ideas

The presentation of a speech is the climax of planning and preparation—the time to stand in the spotlight that you have earned. Though presentation is important, it should never overshadow the speech. Have you ever had this kind of exchange?

> **"She's a wonderful speaker—what a beautiful voice, what eloquent diction, what a smooth delivery!"**
> **"What did she say?"**
> **"I don't remember, but she sure sounded good!"**

Unfortunately, there are times when speakers use presentation skills to cover up a lack of substance or disguise unethical speaking. At such moments, the basic purpose of public speaking—communicating ideas—is lost.

As you practice speaking from your outline and when you present your speech, concentrate on the thoughts you have to offer. *You should have a vivid realization of these ideas during the moments of actual presentation.*[4] In other words, the thoughts should come alive as you speak, joining you and your listeners.

Sound Natural

An effective presentation, we noted in Chapter 1, preserves many of the best qualities of conversation. It sounds natural and spontaneous, yet it has a depth, coherence, and quality that are not normally found in social conversation. The best way to approach this ideal of improved conversation is to present your speech extemporaneously. An *extemporaneous presentation* is carefully prepared and practiced but not written out or memorized. If you write out your speech, you will be tempted either to memorize it word for word or to read it to your audience. Reading or memorizing usually results in a stilted presentation. DO NOT READ YOUR SPEECH! That defeats the purpose of public communication because it robs the audience of its chance to participate in the creation of ideas. *Audience contact is more important than exact wording.* The only parts of a speech that should be memorized are the introduction, the conclusion, and a few other critical phrases or sentences, such as the wording of main points or the punch lines of humorous stories.

Key-Word Outline

To sound conversational and spontaneous, use your key-word outline while you are speaking. *Do not make the mistake of using your full outline as you present your speech.* You may lapse into reading it and lose contact with your audience. (The following key-word outline is based on the outline presented earlier.)

"Free at Last"

Intro

■ *Rodney felt his notations would keep him on track during his presentation.*

"Free at last"—high school valedictory speech

Not free—enemy both outside and within was racial prejudice

I. Encounter with bully when I was 8
   A. "Jap," didn't belong here [Mime the bully]
   B. Words burned in soul
      1. Ashamed of heritage
      2. Hated living in America [Pause and smile]
II. Parents help
   A. Survived much worse
   B. Taught me to accept reality
   C. Taught me *GAMAN* [Pause and write on board]
III. *Gaman*—inner strength
   A. No fear or anger [Stress]
   B. Accepted self
   C. Proud of heritage [Pause]

Conclusion

Gaman from my Japanese roots conquers prejudice

But I am also American. Can talk about it: therefore, "free at last"

Practice Your Speech

Speech classrooms often have a speaker's lectern mounted on a table at the front of the room. Lecterns can seem very formal and can create a barrier between you and your listeners. Therefore, if you are attempting to build identification and good feelings, standing behind a lectern may be inappropriate. Moreover, short people can almost disappear behind a lectern. Because their gestures are hidden from view, their messages lose much of the reinforcing power of body language. For these reasons, when you practice, you may wish to experiment with speaking from the side of the lectern or in front of it.

If you plan to use the lectern, place your outline high on its surface so that you do not have to noticeably lower your head to look at it. That way, you reduce the loss of direct eye contact with your listeners. Print your key-word outline in large letters that you can read easily with a glance. If you are using note cards, don't try to hide them or look embarrassed if you need to refer to them. Most listeners probably won't even notice it when you use them. Remember, your audience is far more interested in what you have to say than in any awkwardness you may feel.

As you practice, imagine your audience in front of you. Begin practicing from your full outline, then move gradually to your key-word outline as the other becomes imprinted in your mind. Maintain eye contact with your

Practice speaking from your key-word outline until the main points of your speech are fully embedded in your mind.

imaginary listeners, just as you will during the actual presentation. Look around the room so that everyone feels included in your message. Try to be enthusiastic about what you are saying. Let your voice suggest that you are confident. Strive for variety and color in your vocal presentation; avoid speaking in a monotone, which never changes pace or pitch. Pause to let important ideas sink in. Let your face, body, and voice respond to your ideas as you utter them.

Controlling Communication Apprehension

Almost all speakers, veterans as well as rookies, have some degree of anxiety as they anticipate a communication situation. Barbra Streisand and Carly Simon—and countless other professional entertainers and communicators—have described their struggles to control this **communication apprehension**.[5] International students and students from marginalized cultural groups often have a great deal of it.[6] As you give your first speech, you may experience it as well. In fact, there might be something wrong if you didn't have feelings of anxiety. The absence of any nervousness could suggest that you do not care enough about the audience or your message. We once attended a banquet where an award was presented to the "Communicator of the Year." Before sitting down to eat, this recipient confessed privately to us, "I dread having to make this speech!" We were not surprised when this person, who is now governor of Tennessee, made an effective presentation.

There are many reasons why public speaking can be frightening. Speaking before large groups of people and being the center of attention are not every-

FIGURE 2.2
Public Speaking Fears

Type of Fear	Percent Reporting
Trembling or shaking	80
Mind going blank	74
Doing or saying something embarrassing	64
Being unable to continue talking	63
Not making sense	59
Sounding foolish	59

Source: Adapted from M. B. Stein, J. R. Walker, and D. R. Forde, "Public Speaking Fears in a Community Sample: Prevalence, Impact on Functioning, and Diagnostic Classification," *Archives of General Psychiatry* (February 1996), 169–174. *Thrive Online Health Library*, accessed July 1997, *http://www.thriveonline.com/ @14vdSwUA@G5s2ojN/thrive/health/Library/CAD/abstract25252.html.*

day occurrences for most of us. Moreover, these are often important moments: Much may depend on how well we speak. This element of risk, combined with the feeling of strangeness, can explain why many people dread public speaking. They are afraid they will make mistakes "and look bad to other people."[7] We have had students plunge into depression because they didn't say exactly what they planned and are certain that others were aware of the "mistake." Apparently, they think listeners are clairvoyant!

The truth is, listeners simply don't know what you've planned to say, and therefore have no way of knowing that you haven't said something exactly as you planned it. Furthermore, what you say on the spur of the moment may be *better* than the exact wording you had planned. That's why extemporaneous presentations are usually superior to memorized or read speeches. They are prompted by the moment, and by the interaction of speaker and listener. Finally, even if listeners are aware of a mistake, they really don't care that much about it. You will probably brood about an error much longer than your listeners will remember it.

So keep communication apprehension in perspective. Above all, do not be anxious about your anxiety. Accept it as natural, and be assured that the general effect of the public speaking class is to reduce it.[8] Even more significant, you can learn how to convert these feelings into positive energy. *One of the biggest myths about public speaking classes is that they can or should rid you of any natural fears.* Instead, you should learn how to harness the energy generated by anxiety so that your speaking is more dynamic. No anxiety often means a flat, dull presentation. Transformed anxiety can make your speech sparkle. The late Edward R. Murrow, a renowned radio and television commentator, once said: "The best speakers know enough to be scared. . . . The only difference between the pros and the novices is that the pros have trained the butterflies to fly in formation."

How can you train your butterflies to fly for you? If you find yourself building to an uncontrollable state of nervousness before a speech, don't stand around and discuss with your classmates how frightened you feel, especially with other speakers scheduled that day. You will only increase your own anxiety and make theirs worse as well.[9] Instead, go off by yourself and practice relaxation exercises. While breathing deeply and slowly, concentrate on tensing and then relaxing your muscles, starting with your neck and working down to your feet. These relaxation techniques will help you control the physical symptoms of anxiety.[10] While you are relaxed, identify any negative thoughts you may harbor about yourself as a speaker, such as "Everybody will think I'm stupid" or "Nobody wants to listen to me." Replace them with positive messages that focus on your ideas and your audience, such as "These ideas are important and useful" or "Listeners will really enjoy this story." This approach to controlling communication anxiety by deliberately replacing negative thoughts with positive, constructive statements is called **cognitive restructuring**.[11] Still another technique to help you control communication anxiety is **visualization**, in which you systematically picture yourself succeeding as a speaker, then practice with that image in mind. Athletes often employ visualization to improve their performance.[12] A memorable example occurred when Mark McGwire hit his sixty-second home run, breaking baseball's historic record. In the moments before McGwire came to bat, television caught him in the on-deck circle with his eyes closed. The announcer noted, "He's visualizing what will happen at the plate." Using this same technique, you picture a day of success, from the moment you get up to the moment you enjoy the congratulations of classmates and teacher on an excellent speech.[13] To make visualization work best, you will have to develop and enact the kind of script we suggest at the end of this chapter.[14] You must have a vivid sense of your successful day for visualization to be effective.[15]

There are other things you can do to control communication anxiety, which go under the general heading of **skills training**.[16] Actually, just about everything you learn in a speech class can help you harness your feelings of fear. First, select a topic that interests and excites you, so that you will get so involved with it that there is little room in your mind for worry about yourself. Second, choose a topic that you already know something about so that you will be more confident. Then build on that foundation of knowledge. Visit the library. Access the Internet. Interview local experts. The better prepared you are, the more confident you will be that you have something worthwhile to say. Third, consider whether you might use a presentation aid—a chart, graph, object, or model. Referring to a presentation aid during your speech encourages gesturing, and gesturing helps release excess energy in constructive ways. (For advice on preparing a presentation aid, see Chapter 9.) Fourth, practice, and then practice some more. The more you master your message, the more comfortable you will be, and the more successful you can expect to be.[17] Fifth, develop a positive attitude toward your listeners. Don't think of them as "the enemy." Expect them to be helpful and attentive.

Finally as we stated earlier, act confident, even if you don't feel that way. When it is your turn, walk briskly to the front of the room, look at your audience, and establish eye contact. If appropriate to your subject, smile before you begin your presentation. Whatever happens during your speech, remember that listeners cannot see and hear inside you. They know only what you show them. Show them a controlled speaker communicating well-researched and carefully prepared ideas. *Never place on your listeners the additional burden of sympathy for you as a speaker*—their job is to listen to what you are saying. Don't say anything like "Gee, am I scared!" Such behavior may make the audience uncomfortable. If your mind should go blank during a presentation, don't panic. Go back over what you have just said, as though you are giving your audience a reminder. They will appreciate the help, and you will give your mind a chance to get back on track. Above all, keep talking. You will find your way. If you put your listeners at ease with your confident appearance, they can relax and provide the positive feedback that will make you a more assured and better speaker.

When you reach your conclusion, pause, and then present your summary and concluding remarks with special emphasis. Maintain eye contact for a moment before you move confidently back to your seat. This final impression is very important. *You should keep the focus on your message, not on yourself.* Even though you may feel relieved that the speech is over, don't say "Whew!" or "I made it!" and never shake your head to show disappointment with your presentation. You probably did better than you thought, and at the very least, you don't want to encourage negative reactions to your message.

Do these techniques really work, and is such advice helpful? Research on communication apprehension has established the following conclusions: *(1) Such techniques do work, and (2) they work best in combination.*[18] Keep in mind that controlling anxiety takes time. As you become more experienced at giving speeches and at practicing the suggestions in the following Speaker's Notes, you will find your fears abating, and your ability to convert communication apprehension into positive, constructive energy should improve.[19]

Thus far, we have discussed controlling speech anxiety in terms of what the speaker can do, but the audience also can help speakers by creating a positive communication climate.[20] As an audience member, you should listen attentively and look for something in the speech that interests you. Even if you are not excited about the topic, you may pick up some techniques that will be useful when it is your time to speak. When you discuss or evaluate the speeches of others, be constructive and helpful. That's an attitude you will appreciate when others comment on your speech.

Ten Ways to Control Communication Apprehension

speaker's notes

1 To develop confidence, learn how to use speech skills.
2 To control tension, use relaxation exercises.
3 Replace negative, self-defeating statements with positive ones.
4 Visualize yourself being successful.
5 Select a topic that interests and excites you.
6 Narrow your topic to something you already know about and then learn more about it.
7 Use a presentation aid to release energy through movement.
8 Practice, practice, practice!
9 Expect your audience to be helpful and attentive.
10 Act confident, even if you don't feel quite that way.

Introducing Yourself and Others

A speech of introduction is sometimes the first assignment in a public speaking class because it helps warm the atmosphere, creates a sense of community, and provides an opportunity to develop credibility. Whatever the precise nature of your assignment, however, you can't avoid making first impressions—one way or another, you will be introducing yourself to your listeners. Of course there is no way to tell your entire life history or another person's history in a short speech. You have to be selective. What you should avoid is relating a few superficial facts, such as where you went to high school or what your major may be. Such information reveals very little about a person and is usually not very interesting.

One way to introduce yourself or others is to answer this question: *What is the one thing that best describes me or the person I am introducing as a unique person?* You should then develop a speech around the answer that will build positive ethos for later speeches.

To help stimulate your creativity, what the ancient, classical writers on public speaking called your "inventional processes," conduct a **self-awareness inventory** in which you consider the following possibilities:

1. *Is your cultural background the most important thing about you?* How has it shaped you? How might you explain this influence to others? In her self-introductory speech, Sandra Baltz described herself as a unique product of three cultures. She felt that this cultural background widened her horizons. Note how she focused on food to represent the convergence of these different ways of life:

   In all, I must say that being exposed to three very difficult cultures—Latin, Arabic, American—has been rewarding for me and has made a difference even in the music I enjoy and the food I eat. It is not unusual in my house to sit down to a meal made up of stuffed grape leaves and refried beans and all topped off with apple pie for dessert.

2. *Is the most important thing about you the environment in which you grew up?* How were you shaped by it? What stories or examples demonstrate this influence? How do you feel about its effect on your life? Are you pleased by it, or do you feel that it limited you? If the latter, what new horizons would you like to explore? In his self-introductory speech, "My Life as a River Rat," Jimmy Green concluded by saying:

   To share my world, come up to the Tennessee River some fall afternoon. We'll take a boat ride north to New Johnsonville, where Civil War gunboats still lie on the bottom of the river, and you will see how the sun makes the water sparkle. You will see the green hills sloping down to the river, and the rocky walls, and I will tell you some Indian legends about them. We'll "bump the bottom" fishing for catfish, drifting with the current. And if we're lucky, we might see a doe and her fawn along the shoreline, or perhaps some Canada geese or an eagle high overhead.

   Jimmy's descriptions of nature conveyed his feelings about his home without his having to tell us about them.

3. *Was there some particular person—a friend, relative, or childhood hero—who had a major impact on your life?* Why do you think this person had such influence? Often you will find that some particular person was a great inspiration to you. Here is a chance to share that inspiration, honor that person, and, in the process, tell us much about yourself. In her self-introductory speech, Marty Gaines explained how her two grandmothers had meant so much to her:

> Margaret Hasty was my "Memma." She was the kind of grandmother that everybody knows and loves. The kind that when you visit her house, she's waiting for you at the back door and you walk up the steps and she grabs you, and she gives you a big hug. And she's always got your favorite cookies hidden in the cabinet. . . .
>
> Martha Clark Akers . . . was my other grandmother. And that's what she was, my grandmother. Grandmother was very formal, very strict, very well educated. And when you went to visit Grandmother's house, she was at the door. But she didn't yank you up and give you a big hug. She held the door open so that you could walk in, file past, and give her a gentle kiss on the cheek. And then you'd go to the couch and sit down. And she would say, "Well, how are your grades?" or "What books have you read lately?"
>
> I didn't understand Grandmother for years. I finally realized that she loved me just as much as Memma, but in a different way. Where Memma loved me for who I was, Grandmother loved me for what she knew I could become and for what she wanted me to be. Both have given me a great blessing.
>
> Now, when I come home from work, there are some days that I'll just grab my children up, and give them a big hug, and tell them I love them. And I think to myself, "Thank you, Memma." And then there are other days when I come home and there may be a nasty note from the teacher, and I know I'm going to have to be strong and strict. And I say to myself, "Give me strength, Grandmother."

4. *Have you been marked by some unusual experience?* Why was it important? How did it affect you? What does this tell us about you as a person? Ashley Smith decided that the most definitive thing about her was what she had learned from her experiences as an exchange student in Costa Rica and Botswana. After she had told stories to illustrate how people's lives are controlled and limited in those countries, Ashley confided—in a speech that is reprinted at the end of this chapter—that her travel experiences had made her want to become an educator:

> I want to teach people to succeed on their merits despite the social and economic inequalities that they're faced with. And I want to learn from them as well. I want to teach the boy who never mastered welding that he could own the factory. And I want him to teach me how to use a rice cooker. I want to teach the girl who is exhausted each afternoon after walking to the

> river with a jar on her head to gather water that she could design an irrigation system. But I also want her to teach me how to weave a thatched roof. I want to travel and teach and learn.

Experiences need not be dramatic to be meaningful. Rodney Nishikawa related how an encounter with prejudice at an early age changed his life and helped him develop personal inner strength. His self-introductory speech, outlined earlier in this chapter, is reprinted in Appendix B.

5. *Are you best characterized by an activity that brings meaning to your life?* Remember, what is important is not the activity itself but how and why it affects you. The person being introduced must remain the focus of the speech. When you finish, the audience should have an interesting picture of you. As she reflected upon her identity, Julie Cunningham decided that the most meaningful thing in her life was her participation in a weekly off-campus ritual:

> Every Sunday morning before sunrise I arrive out at Shelby Forest State Park with a few friends of mine. My responsibilities are to gather wood and sweep the area for our sweat lodge. The sweat lodge is a Native American ceremony of spirituality and purification, and the lodge itself represents the womb of mother earth. You crawl in for the sweat ceremony, and when you crawl out you are reborn to this world. This is a time of respect and prayer, of singing and remembering our ancestors, of sharing our feelings. . . . It is a time for me to slow down and relax and remember things that are important to me in the past, present, and future. It's a time for me to exist as one part of a whole, to reflect on my ties to mother earth and to all of her children, to realize my kinship with my tree brothers, the four-leggeds, and the winged creatures as well as with my human brothers and sisters who sit with me in the sweat lodge. I listen to the wind and feel the warm sun on my face. And I feel so immune and so distant from the world outside, even though I know that I will return there.

6. *Is the work you do a major factor in making you who you are?* If you select this approach, focus on how your job has shaped you rather than simply describing what you do. What have you learned from your work that has changed you or made you feel differently about others? In introducing Mike Peterson, Carol Solomon told how his work as a bartender had influenced him. She explained that his job involved more than just mixing drinks—that it had made him an observer of people.

> He sees them in their times of happiness, when they are celebrating a promotion or a grandson or an anniversary. He sees the sadness of lonely people, trying to make a connection, and he sees the other people, the predators, who try to take advantage of them. He hears lots of good stories, and he thinks he may become a writer so that he can tell these stories. Maybe, if we're lucky, he'll tell us sometime about the land shark who got hooked by the hooker.

After her speech the audience saw both Mike and his work in a new light. Carol's introduction also communicated an impression of her as a thoughtful, enjoyable person.

7. *Are you best characterized by your goals or purpose in life?* A sense of commitment to a purpose will usually fascinate listeners. If you choose to describe some personal goal, be sure to emphasize why you have this goal and how it affects you. Tom McDonald had returned to school after dropping out for eleven years. In his self-introductory speech he described his goal of finishing college:

> **Finishing college means a lot to me now. The first time I enrolled, right out of high school, I "blew it." All I cared about was sports, girls, and partying. Even though I have a responsible job that pays well, I feel bad about not having a degree. My wife's diploma hangs on our den wall. All I have hanging there is a stuffed duck!**

As he spoke, many of the younger students began to identify with Tom; they saw a similarity between what caused him to drop out of school and their own feelings at times. Although he wasn't "preachy," Tom's description of the rigors of working forty hours a week and carrying nine hours a semester in night school carried its own clear message.

8. *Are you best described by some value that you hold dear?* How did it come to have such meaning for you? Why is it important to you? Values are abstract, so you must rely on concrete applications to make them meaningful to others. As she described her commitment to the value of justice, Valessa Johnson also established her goal—to become an attorney—and paid tribute to her personal role model:

> **If you go down to 201 Poplar at nine o'clock in the morning on any weekday, you will find yourself faced with hundreds of individuals and their quest for justice. Many of these will be convicted, and rightly so. Unfortunately, while they're incarcerated, the illiterate and unlearned will remain so, as will the unskilled and the uncrafted. Who's going to stand for these so that they have an alternative to standing in the revolving doors of the criminal justice complex? Or better yet, how about the ones that are truly innocent? Oh, yes, that's right, not everyone in the court system, not everyone institutionalized, is guilty. Who is going to stand for these? I will.**
>
> **You know, we were once blessed with a true advocate for justice, attorney Barbara Jordan. She fought a long, hard battle to ensure that we all abided by the constitutional creed, "All men are created equal" and "justice for all." Someone has to continue to beat the path of justice for all men. That includes black men, white men, yellow men, brown men, and *women*. Someone has got to continue to fight the good fight. And I submit to you that I am that someone.**

When Valessa concluded, no one questioned the sincerity of her commitment to justice, and all were impressed with the force of her ethos.

speaker's notes

Self-Awareness Inventory

1 Is your cultural background the most important thing about you?
2 Was your environment a major influence?
3 Did a person have an impact on you?
4 Were you shaped by an unusual experience?
5 Is there an activity that reflects your personality?
6 Can you be characterized by your work?
7 Do you have a special goal or purpose?
8 Does some value have great meaning for you?

As you explore your own background or that of a classmate, we suggest that you ask all the probe questions within the self-awareness inventory. Don't be satisfied with the first idea that comes to you. You should find this thorough examination of yourself and others to be quite rewarding. Just remember that you are not on a tabloid talk show. You don't want to embarrass listeners with personal disclosures that they would just as soon not hear. If you are uncertain about whether to include personal material, you should discuss it with your instructor. The general rule to follow is: *When in doubt, leave it out!*

In Summary

Many of us underrate our potential for public speaking. Starting with your first speech, you can work to build a positive communication environment for yourself and others. You can also develop your ethos as a speaker.

Understanding the Impressions You Make.   Listeners acquire positive impressions of you based on your ability to convey competence, integrity, likableness, and forcefulness. You can build your perceived *competence* by citing examples from your own experience, by quoting authorities, and by organizing and presenting your message effectively. You can earn an image of *integrity* by being accurate and complete in your presentation of information. You can promote *likableness* by being a warm and open person with whom your listeners can easily identify. *Forcefulness* arises from listeners' perceptions of you as a confident, enthusiastic, and decisive speaker.

Building Your First Speech.   Select a topic that is appropriate to you, your listeners, and the assignment and decide on what you want to accomplish. Seek *facts and statistics, testimony, examples,* and *stories* that will support your points and make them interesting and authoritative to listeners. Find a design for your speech that will let your ideas fit together in a cohesive pattern. Some basic designs include the use of categories, sequences of events, cause-effect relationships, and spatial patterns. Develop an *introduction, body,* and *conclusion* so that your speech forms a satisfying whole.

Outlining Your Introductory Speech. You can improve your chances of success with your speech by developing an outline. The outline should contain the central point you are trying to make (*thesis statement*) and *transitions* to help you move from one point to another. As you practice and present the speech, use a *key-word outline* to jog your memory.

Presenting Your Introductory Speech. When presenting your first speech, keep the spotlight on the message and strive for a conversational presentation. Never let presentation skills overshadow your ideas.

Controlling Your Communication Apprehension. Use your nervousness as a source of energy. Cope with communication apprehension by using relaxation exercises before your speak. Use *cognitive restructuring* to replace negative messages with positive ones. Use *visualization* techniques to build in your mind a vivid image of success as you address your audience. The skills training you receive in class will further increase your comfort and confidence. Select a topic that interests you and that you already know something about so that you can build on this foundation. Use presentation aids to give your nervous energy a constructive outlet. Practice until your outline is imprinted on your mind. During your actual presentation, you should appear confident and avoid expressions of personal discomfort.

Introducing Yourself and Others. The speech of introduction helps establish you or the person you introduce as a unique person. Prompted by your *self-awareness inventory*, it may focus on cultural background, environmental influences, a person who inspired you, an experience that affected you, an activity that reveals your character, the work you do, your purpose in life, or some value you cherish.

Terms to Know

competence	body
integrity	conclusion
likableness	thesis statement
identification	transitions
forcefulness	key-word outline
facts and statistics	communication apprehension
testimony	cognitive restructuring
examples	visualization
stories	skills training
introduction	self-awareness inventory

Application

To help in visualizing yourself succeeding as a speaker, write a script in which you describe specific details of an ideal experience of speaking. Start with getting up in the morning on the day of your speech, and continue to the moments after you have concluded. Once you have completed your script, relax, concentrate on it, and bring it to life in your mind. As a guide, follow the script and instructions for an informative speech developed by Professors Joe Ayres and Theodore S. Hopf:

Close your eyes and allow your body to get comfortable in the chair in which you are sitting. Move around until you feel that you are in a position that will continue to be relaxing for you for the next ten to fifteen minutes. Take a deep, comfortable breath and hold it . . . now slowly release it through your nose (if possible). That is right . . . now take another deep breath and make certain that you are breathing from the diaphragm (from your belly) . . . hold it . . . now slowly release it and note how you feel while doing this . . . feel the relaxation fluidly flow throughout your body. And now, one more REALLY deep breath . . . hold it . . . and now release it slowly . . . and begin your normal breathing pattern. Shift around, if you need to get comfortable again.

Now begin to visualize the beginning of a day in which you are going to give an informative speech. See yourself getting up in the morning, full of energy, full of confidence, looking forward to the day's challenges. You are putting on just the right clothes for the task at hand that day. Dressing well makes you look and feel good about yourself, so you have on JUST what you want to wear, which clearly expresses your sense of inner well-being. As you are driving, riding, or walking to the speech setting, note how clear and confident you feel, and how others around you—as you arrive—comment positively regarding your fine appearance and general demeanor. You feel thoroughly prepared for the task at hand. Your preparation has been exceptionally thorough, and you have really researched the target issue you will be presenting today. Now you see yourself standing or sitting in the room where you will present your speech, talking very comfortably and confidentially with others in the room. The people to whom you will be presenting your speech appear to be quite friendly, and are very cordial in their greetings and conversations prior to the presentation. You feel ABSOLUTELY sure of your material and of your ability to present the information in a forceful, convincing, positive manner. Now you see yourself approaching the area from which you will present. You are feeling very good about this presentation and see yourself move eagerly forward. All of your audiovisual materials are well organized, well planned, and clearly aid your presentation.

Now you see yourself presenting your talk. You are really quite brilliant and have all the finesse of a polished, professional speaker. You are also aware that your audience is giving head nods, smiles, and other positive responses, conveying the message that you are truly "on target." The introduction of the speech goes the way you have planned. In fact, it works better than you had expected. The transition from the introductory material to the body of the speech is extremely smooth. As you approach the body of the speech, you are aware of the first major point. It emerges as you expected. The evidence supporting the point is relevant and evokes an understanding response from the audience. In fact, all the main points flow in this fashion. As you wrap up your main points, your concluding remarks seem to be a natural outgrowth of everything you have done. All concluding remarks are on target. When your final utterance is concluded, you have the feeling that it could not have gone better. The introduction worked, the main points were to the point, your evidence was supportive, and your conclusion formed a fitting capstone. In addition, your vocal variety added interest value. Your pauses punctuated important ideas, and your gestures and body movements were purposeful. You now see yourself fielding audience questions with brilliance, confidence, and energy equal to what you exhibited in the presentation itself. You see yourself receiving the congratulations of your classmates. You see yourself as relaxed, pleased with your talk, and ready for the next task to be accomplished that day. You are filled with energy, purpose, and a sense of general well-being. Congratulate yourself on a job well done!

Now—I want you to begin to return to this time and place in which we are working today. Take a deep breath . . . hold it . . . and let it go. Do this several times and move slowly back into the room. Take as much time as you need to make the transition back.[21]

Notes

1. W. H. Cooper, "Ubiquitous Halo," *Psychological Bulletin* 90 (1981): 218-224.
2. Kenneth Burke, *A Rhetoric of Motives* (Berkeley and Los Angeles: University of California Press, 1969), pp. 20–23.
3. John A. Daly, Anita L. Vangelisti, and David J. Weber, "Speech Anxiety Affects How People Prepare Speeches: A Protocol Analysis of the Preparation Processes of Speakers," *Communication Monographs* 62 (1995): 383–397.
4. Donald C. Bryant and Karl R. Wallace, *Fundamentals of Public Speaking,* 4th ed. (New York: Appleton-Century-Crofts, 1969), p. 233.
5. Robert Hilburn, "Barbra on Tour: The Private Streisand," *Newsday,* 23 May 1994, p. BO3; and Edna Gundersen, "Carly Conquers Grand Central, Stage Fright," *USA Today,* 17 May 1995, p. 12d.
6. Marianne Martini, Ralph R. Behnke, and Paul E. King, "The Communication of Public Speaking Anxiety: Perceptions of Asian and American Speakers," *Communication Quarterly* 40 (1992): 280.
7. Laura J. Toler, "Scared of the Spotlight? You're Not Alone," Gannett News Service, 1995.
8. Heidi M. Rose, Andrew S. Rancer, and Kenneth C. Crannell, "The Impact of Basic Courses in Oral Interpretation and Public Speaking on Communication Apprehension," *Communication Reports* 6 (1993): 54–60. The physiological and neurological bases of communication apprehension are summarized in Terri Freeman, Chris R. Sawyer, and Ralph R. Behnke, "Behavioral Inhibition and the Attribution of Public Speaking State Anxiety," *Communication Education* 43 (1997): 175–187.
9. Ralph R. Behnke, Chris R. Sawyer, and Paul E. King, "Contagion Theory and the Communication of Public Speaking State Anxiety," *Communication Education* 43 (1994): 246–251.
10. Gustav Friedrich and Blaine Goss, "Systematic Desensitization," in *Avoiding Communication: Shyness, Reticence, and Communication Apprehension,* ed. John A. Daly and James C. McCroskey (Beverly Hills, Calif.: Sage, 1984), pp. 173–188.
11. William J. Fremouw and Michael D. Scott, "Cognitive Restructuring: An Alternative Method for the Treatment of Communication Apprehension," *Communication Education* 28 (1979): 129–133.

12. Joe Ayres and Theodore S. Hopf, "Visualization: Is It More Than Extra-Attention?" *Communication Education* 38 (1989): 1–5. Copyright by the Speech Communication Association. January 1989. Reproduced by permission of the publisher.

13. Tim Hopf and Joe Ayres, "Coping with Public Speaking Anxiety: An Examination of Various Combinations of Systematic Desensitization, Skills Training, and Visualization," *Journal of Applied Communication Research* 20 (1992): 183–198. Also see Joe Ayres and Brian L. Hewett, "The Relationship Between Visual Imagery and Public Speaking Apprehension," *Communication Reports* 10 (1997): 87–94.

14. The effectiveness of self-devised and enacted scripts has been demonstrated in Joe Ayres, "Comparing Self-constructed Visualization Scripts with Guided Visualization," *Communication Reports* 8 (1995): 193–199.

15. Joe Ayres, Tim Hopf, and Debbie M. Ayres, "An Examination of Whether Imaging Ability Enhances the Effectiveness of an Intervention Designed to Reduce Speech Anxiety," *Communication Education* 43 (1994): 252–258.

16. These techniques are summarized in Thomas E. Robinson II, "Communication Apprehension and the Basic Public Speaking Course: A National Survey of In-class Treatment Techniques," *Communication Education* 46 (1997): 179–197.

17. Kent E. Menzel and Lori J. Carrell, "The Relationship Between Preparation and Performance in Public Speaking," *Communication Education* 43 (1994): 17–26; and Joe Ayres, "Speech Preparation Processes and Speech Apprehension," *Communication Education* 45 (1996): 228–235.

18. Randolph H. Whitworth and Claudia Cochran, "Evaluation of Integrated Versus Unitary Treatments for Reducing Public Speaking Anxiety," *Communication Education* 45 (1996): 306–314.

19. Mike Allen, John E. Hunter, and William A. Donohue, "Meta-Analysis of Self-report Data on the Effectiveness of Public Speaking Anxiety Treatment Techniques," *Communication Education* 38 (1989): 54–76.

20. Peter D. MacIntyre, Kimly A. Thivierge, and J. Renee MacDonald, "The Effects of Audience Interest, Responsiveness, and Evaluation on Public Speaking Anxiety and Related Variables," *Communication Research Reports* 14 (1997): 157–168.

21. Joe Ayres and Theodore S. Hopf, "Visualization: Is It More Than Extra Attention?" *Communication Education,* 38 (1989): 2–3. Used by permission of the National Communication Association.

Sample Speeches of Self-Introduction

Three Photographs
Ashley Smith

■ *The three photographs are an ingenious way to structure this speech. Each photograph stands for a main point. Ashley's use of Spanish and her colorful language reinforce her competence. The contrast between the types of education in Costa Rica is dramatic and her on-the-scene report of life there makes her account both authentic and authoritative. In effect she provides her own expert testimony that is adequate for this brief speech. In an informative or persuasive speech, more supporting material would be needed.*

■ *Ashley uses examples as her major form of supporting material. Again stronger support would be needed for informative or persuasive speeches to support her assertion of European exploitation.*

■ *The scene she depicts of life in Jacksonville provides a vivid contrast with the other lifestyles she has sketched.*

Photographs often tell stories that only a few can hear. I would like to tell you the story told me by three snapshots that hang in my room in quiet, suburban Jacksonville, Florida. If you saw them, you might think them totally unrelated; together, they tell a powerful tale.

"Ashley, *levantete*!" I heard each morning for the month that I spent in Costa Rica as an exchange student. I would wake up at 5:30 to get ready for school and would stumble off to the one shower that the family of five shared. I had to wash myself in cold water because there was no warm water—that usually woke me up pretty fast! I then got dressed and breakfast would be waiting on the table. Predictably it would be fruit, coffee, and *gallo pinto*, a black bean and rice dish usually served at every meal. We would then walk to school and begin the day with an hour and a half of shop class. After shop we would have about 15- to 20-minute classes in what you and I might call "regular" academic subjects: math and Spanish, for example. Those classes had frequent interruptions and were not taken very seriously. The socialization process was quite clear: These children were being prepared for jobs in the labor force instead of for higher education. Each afternoon as we walked home we passed the elite school where students were still busy working and studying. The picture in my room of my Costa Rican classmates painting picnic tables in the schoolyard reminds me of their narrow opportunities.

The second photograph on my wall is of a little girl in Botswana who is not much younger than I. She's nearing the end of her education and has finished up to the equivalent of the sixth grade. She will now return to a rural setting because her family cannot afford to continue her schooling. To add to the problem, the family goat was eaten by a lion, so she had to return to help them over this crisis. But she didn't miss out on much—most likely, she would have gone on into the city and ended up in one of the shanty-towns, one more victim of the unemployment, poverty, even starvation endured by the people. Her lack of opportunity is due not so much to class inequalities as in Costa Rica, but more to the cultural tradition of several hundred years of European exploitation. Recently there has been extensive growth there, but the natives have been left far behind.

The third photograph in my room is of four high school students, taken where I went to school in Jacksonville, Florida. We're all sitting on the lawn outside school, overlooking the parking lot full of new cars that will take us home to warm dinners and comfortable beds and large homes and privileged lives. Many of us—including myself for most of my life—took this world for granted. But now, for me, no more. I may have gained a lot on my travels, but I lost my political innocence.

One thing I gained is an intense desire to become an educator. I want to teach people to succeed on their merits despite the social and economic inequalities that they're faced with. And I want to learn from them as well. I want to teach the boy who never mastered welding that he could own the factory. And I want him to teach me how to use a rice cooker. I want to teach the girl who is exhausted each afternoon after walking to the river with a jar on her head to gather water that she could design an irrigation system. But I also want her to teach me how to weave a thatched roof. I want to travel and teach and learn.

Three photographs, hanging on my wall. They are silent, mute, and the photographer was not very skilled. But together they tell a powerful story in my life.

Family Gifts
Marie D'Aniello

Lorraine, John, John Victor, Christopher, Michael, and Anthony. That's my family. My mom, my dad, and my four brothers—that's my life. Together these people have shaped me as an individual. Growing up in a small town with a large family teaches you a lot, especially if you grow up like I did, with a lot of love, a little money, and a whole lot of gifts. Not tangible gifts like clothes and jewelry (although those are nice, too), but gifts like strength, and glory, and pride, pride not only in myself, but also in them and in my family name. I am Marie D'Aniello . . . a D'Aniello. I belong to them like they belong to me. I'm a little bit like my Mom and a little bit like my Dad. I can work like my brother John and play like Chris. I can dream like Michael and love like Anthony. I'm Marie, exactly like no one but a little bit like everyone.

Every now and then I hear people say things like, "You know, my family just doesn't understand me." Well, yeah, I feel that way too at times. My family's not perfect. We have our hard times and disagreements. But I always walk away from these spats with a little more knowledge about myself. Maybe I learn that I'm stronger than I thought. That strength comes from my Mom.

It takes a strong woman to work a full-time job, hold together a family, and raise five children. But my mom does it all. I can remember when I was little, waking up at night and listening to the sound of the vacuum cleaner. My mom would stay up all night, cleaning the house and making sure everything was ready for the next day. She never complained about the hard work. She just did it because she loved us.

I never realized the influence my mother had on me until I went away. Now that I'm here, a thousand miles away from her, I sometimes see her smiling and working the night away. And when I get a grade and I don't think it reflects my effort, I can hear my Mom saying, "You're worth more than this, Marie. You'll get it next time." My mom's strength has given me my own strength and my own perseverance. I know these qualities are the keys to glory.

When I think of glory, I have to think of my brother Chris. I'll never forget his championship basketball game. It's the typical buzzer beater story: five seconds to go, down by one, Chris gets the ball and he drives down the court, he shoots, he scores! We all rush the floor, everyone. But Chris doesn't care about anyone else. All he looks for is us, his family. He wanted to share his glory with us. I'll never forget the headline, "D'Aniello saves the game!" D'Aniello, hey, wait, that's me. I'm a D'Aniello. I could do this too. Maybe I can't play basketball like Chris, but I can do other things.

So I started trying harder in school, "applying myself," as they say. And I had my own taste of glory. I became a valedictorian, won a scholarship, and now I'm here at Vanderbilt. Unbelievable. After I watched Chris drive toward the hoop to score the winning basket, I wanted to "drive" toward my future. And you know what? I just might make it!

And even if I don't make it, at least I'll try and I'll have my pride. At least, that's what my dad always says. He knows about pride. He knows what it's like to be scorned because you don't make as much money as other people or because you don't have an impressive job. My dad is a small-town mechanic. He couldn't go to school, so he taught himself everything he knows. And he knows a whole lot, not just about cars, but about honor. I hear my dad all the time, saying, "Marie, whatever you do, just try to put your whole heart into it. Make it count. Take pride in it." Not a day goes by that I don't hear those words. Because of him, I take pride in my work and I take pride in myself.

I practiced my speech in front of one of my friends, and she said, "Marie, are you sure you're really talking about yourself?" Yeah, I am. When I talk about my family, I'm talking about the main sources of myself. They've given me a world, but it's not like I'm trapped in it. I can go anywhere and do anything because of the gifts they've given me. Strength, glory, pride— thank you, John, Chris, Michael, Anthony, Mom, and Dad. You've made me an individual, Marie D'Aniello, a little bit different from each one of you, and a little bit like all of you.

Marie's praise of her father's pride and sense of honor was presented to an audience of students from mainly affluent families. The story reminded listeners that the most valuable gifts may not be material, and that you can't always measure the worth of a person by wealth or formal education.

In her conclusion Marie counters an impression that her identity relies too much on her family. She affirms that because of their influence she can be the individual that she is.

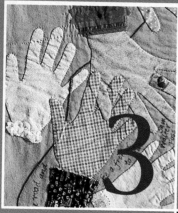

3 Becoming a Better Listener

*E*asy listening
exists only
on the radio.
    —David Barkan

This chapter will help you

- appreciate the importance of effective listening
- overcome the barriers to effective listening
- improve your critical thinking skills
- evaluate messages constructively
- become aware of the ethical responsibilities of listeners

You walk to the front of the room, ready to make your first presentation. You pause and make eye contact with your audience. This is what you see:

In a far corner of the room, a student is frantically trying to finish her accounting homework. A ledger is open on her desk, and a textbook is open on her lap. Her eyes move from the book to the ledger. She never stops writing, and she never looks up.

In the other far corner, a student is sleeping off last night's party. His eyes are closed most of the time. Occasionally his chin drops down onto his chest, and he jerks himself up and tries to look alert, but alas, within twenty seconds he has wandered off again.

Finally, you spot a friendly face—someone who actually looks as though he's ready to listen. His desk is empty except for a notebook. He is sitting alert, a pencil poised in his hand. His eyes are on you. He looks interested in what you have to say.

LEGEND HAS IT that President Franklin Delano Roosevelt was bemused by the poor listening behavior of people who attended social functions at the White House. To test his contention that people didn't really listen, he once greeted guests in a receiving line by murmuring, "I murdered my grandmother this morning." Typical responses ran along the lines of, "Thank you," "How good of you," or other platitudes of polite approval. Finally he met someone who actually listened and responded, "I'm sure she had it coming to her."[1]

Poor listening exacts a large price. As the eminent psychologist Carl Rogers once observed, "Man's inability to communicate is a result of his failure to listen effectively, skillfully, and with understanding to another person." The consequences can be enormous, both globally and personally. Nations may misunderstand each other's motives, and go to war over the misunderstanding. When people in a group don't listen well, they may make poor decisions. When juries don't attend to the evidence presented, they cannot render a just verdict. If you don't listen well to another person, you may lose his or her respect and affection. If you are not listening effectively in a classroom lecture or at new employee orientation at work, you may miss important information. At the very least, poor listening skills can create negative impressions of your competence that can hurt your ethos when you decide to speak.

The most encouraging thing is that better listening is a teachable and learnable skill.[2] You can improve as a listener if you work at it. In this chapter we consider the nature of effective listening and its benefits to both listener and speaker. We also discuss the external and internal sources of interference that impede effective listening and suggest ways to cope with these problems. Next, we relate effective listening to the analysis and evaluation of speeches. Finally, we consider what it means to be an ethical listener.

The Nature and Importance of Effective Listening

Although we spend the greatest amount of our communication time listening, we receive less formal training in listening than we do in speaking, writing, or reading.[3] Why is this so? Perhaps educators assume that we know by nature how to listen well, despite a great deal of evidence to the contrary. They may undervalue listening because they associate it with following, whereas they associate speaking with leading. In the dominant American culture, leadership is admired more than "followership," even though being a judicious follower is one definition of a good citizen. As S. I. Hayakawa once commented, "Living in a competitive culture, most of us are . . . chiefly concerned with getting our own view across, and we . . . find other people's speeches a tedious interruption of our own ideas." Perhaps this is why we frequently emphasize speaking while neglecting the obvious fact that listening is essential to any communication transaction. Finally, in a society that admires being "on the move," we may think of speaking as an active and listening as a passive behavior. This ignores the fact that effective listening is a dynamic activity that

- Seeks out the meaning intended in messages
- Considers apparent and not-so-apparent motivations
- Evaluates the soundness of the reasoning and the reliability of supporting materials
- Calculates the value and risk of accepting recommendations
- Integrates them creatively into the world of the listener

Other cultures place a higher premium on good listening behaviors. Some Native American tribes, for example, have a far better appreciation of their importance. The council system of the Ojai Foundation has three main rules for conducting business derived from tribal custom: "Speak honestly, be brief, and listen from the heart."[4] The Lakota also recognize the value of listening. In their culture:

Conversation was never begun at once, nor in a hurried manner. No one was quick with a question, no matter how important, and no one was pressed for an answer. A pause giving time for thought was the truly courteous way of beginning and conducting a conversation. Silence was meaningful with the Lakota, and his granting a space of silence to the speech-maker and his own moment of silence before

talking was done in the practice of true politeness and regard for the rule that, "thought comes before speech."[5]

We shall apply these lessons from the Ojai and Lakota people and regard listening as vital to successful communication.

The Ladder of Listening

The Chinese symbol for the verb "to listen" has four basic elements: undivided attention, ears, eyes, and heart.[6] This symbol suggests some of the basic differences between simply hearing and actually listening. *Hearing* is an automatic process in which sound waves stimulate nerve impulses to the brain. We may call it the **discriminative phase**, in which we detect the vital sounds of spoken communication. While it is a necessary condition to the listening experience, it is only the first step up the ladder that rises over communication barriers. *Listening* is a voluntary activity that goes beyond the mere physical reaction to sounds. At the very least, listening involves focusing, understanding, and interpreting:

- You must focus on the message and block out factors that compete for your attention.
- You must understand the speaker's verbal and nonverbal language.
- You must interpret what you hear in light of your own knowledge and experiences.

These elements make up the **comprehensive phase**, the next rung of the ladder. Beyond these basic processes is the **empathic phase**, which emphasizes the heart in the Chinese symbol. When we are empathic, we encourage speakers by suspending judgment and allowing them to be heard.[7] We try to see things from their point of view, even though we may not agree with them. Our next step up the ladder of listening is to the **appreciative phase**, in which we respond to beauty in the message. For example, we may enjoy the simplicity, balance, and proportion of a speech structure, or the eloquence of a speaker's words.

Critical listening represents another step up the ladder. Critical listeners analyze and evaluate the content of a message. They factor into the analysis their assessment of the speaker's motives and feelings. This step adds the element "mind" to the Chinese symbol for listening. Critical listeners also provide appropriate feedback to the speaker. As you evaluate, you may offer visual cues such as smiles or frowns, puzzled looks, or nods of agreement that let a speaker know how you are responding.

The final rung on the ladder of listening is **constructive listening.** Constructive listening involves seeking in messages their value for our lives. We often think of listeners as merely the "unpackers" of meaning in messages. Constructive listeners *add* to a message, finding in it special applications to their lives. As they listen to a speech on the importance of air bags in automobiles, they may question whether there are differences in the quality of air bags from one automobile to another. They may wonder if there are any drawbacks to air bags and, if so, how they might avoid them. If they don't hear the answers they seek in the speech itself, these listeners may question

FIGURE 3.1

The Ladder of Listening

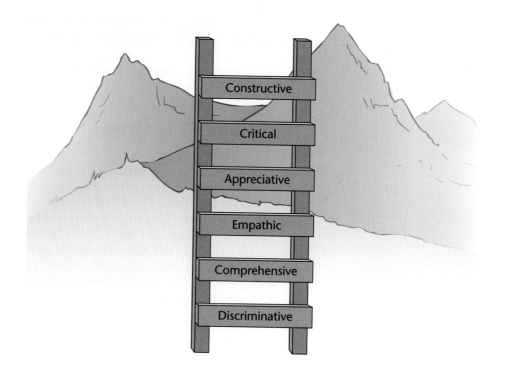

the speaker afterwards, creating a dialogue that *extends the meaning of the speech*. Such dialogues often produce discoveries, better realizations of values, and better answers to public questions.

Climbing the ladder of listening allows an audience to join with the speaker in creating meaning.[8] As speakers offer messages and listeners respond, their worlds interact to produce the transformative effect (described in Chapter 1) in which speaker, listener, and the state of public knowledge are enhanced as they are elevated by the communication experience.

Benefits of Effective Listening

Effective listening benefits both listeners and speakers.

Benefits to the Listener.   Charlatans often try to cover up a lack of substance or reasoning with a glib presentation or with irrelevant appeals.[9] How many times have you seen attractive, scantily clad young men and women appearing in ads to sell everything from soft drinks to automatic transmission repair services? Or consider ads that rely on celebrity endorsements. What are the ads really selling?[10] Ads may also ask you to buy what "doctors" recommend without explaining the credentials of these "doctors"—Ph.D.s in history may know very little about vitamins! Finally, political hucksters may hope that you won't notice their substitution of assertion for evidence, their appeals to prejudice in the place of good reasons. Effective listening skills may help ward off such deception.

Listening skills also have broad application to your academic and professional life. Students who listen effectively earn better grades and achieve beyond expectation.[11] The reasons would seem obvious: Effective listeners learn to concentrate on what is being said and to identify what is important. They

The ability to listen effectively can help you in your other classes.

motivate themselves to learn by exploring the value of information for their lives. The most effective student listeners read assignments ahead of time to familiarize themselves with the language and to provide a foundation for understanding. By listening well to the speeches presented in your class, you can discover the kinds of subjects that interest your classmates. You can also learn from their experience what techniques work best and the mistakes you should avoid. By observing how they structure, support, and deliver their speeches, you can tell why one presentation works better than another.

At work, improved listening skills can mean the difference between success and failure—both for individuals and for companies. A Department of Labor report emphasized the value of learning how to listen effectively.[12] A survey of over 400 top-level personnel directors suggested that the two most important factors in helping graduates find jobs are speaking and listening ability.[13] Another survey of major American corporations reported that poor listening is "one of [the companies'] most important problems" and that "ineffective listening leads to ineffective performance."[14] If you listen effectively on the job, you will improve your chances for advancement.[15] This is especially true in organizations that provide services rather than goods. Companies that encourage people at every level to develop effective listening skills enjoy many dividends. Employees are more innovative when they sense that management will listen to new ideas. Morale improves, and the work environment becomes more pleasant and productive. For these reasons, many *Fortune* 500 corporations provide listening training programs for their employees.[16]

Benefits to the Speaker. Speakers obviously benefit from an audience of good listeners. When audiences don't listen well, they can't provide useful feedback. Moreover, a good audience can help alleviate communication apprehension by creating a supportive classroom environment.[17] Speakers need to realize that their listeners want them to succeed. You can convey your support by being a pleasant and responsive listener rather than dour and inattentive.[18] Give speakers your undivided attention. Take an occasional note at appropriate moments—this suggests to them that you think their ideas are important.[19] Nod occasionally in response to what they say. Show respect for them as people, even when you disagree with their ideas. Look for value in what they say.

An audience of effective listeners also can boost a speaker's self-esteem and make speaking an exhilarating experience. How many times have you had people *really listen* to you? How often have you had an opportunity to educate others? How frequently have your ideas and recommendations been taken seriously? If your answer is "seldom" or "never," you may be in for a pleasant surprise when you make your presentations. You will soon discover that there are few things quite as rewarding as having people really listen to you and respect what you say. As Henry David Thoreau once commented, "The greatest compliment that was ever paid me was when one asked me what I thought, and attended to my answer." Negative evidence of the importance of this factor is provided by the difficulty many women executives have in American business.[20] Often they hold an organizational title, but are not regarded as company "insiders." Consequently, they are sometimes not taken seriously when they speak. They suffer, and the company suffers from the loss of their ideas.

Overcoming Barriers to Effective Listening

Some barriers to good listening arise from external sources of interference, such as a noisy room. But the most formidable barriers to effective listening are internal, rooted in the listener's own attitudes. At best, these barriers present a challenge; at worst, they may completely block communication.

Once we understand what our listening problems are, we can begin to correct them. Figure 3.2 should help you identify areas you will need to work on. Look through the list and place a check next to items that describe your listening attitudes and behaviors.

External Sources of Interference

External sources of interference may arise from the environment, from the message, or from the presentation. Most of the time, these sources of interference are relatively minor contributors to poor listening, and often they are better addressed by speakers than by listeners. For example, if a helicopter passes overhead, the speaker may need to talk louder in order to be heard. We cover how speakers can make such adjustments during their presentations in Chapter 11. Keep in mind, however, that communication is a joint enterprise. As a listener, you should provide feedback to let the speaker know that there is a problem. If you can't hear, give the speaker a signal, or move to a seat closer to the front of the room.

Environmental Problems. The most obvious source of environmental interference is noise. If the general noise level is high, you need to sit close enough to the speaker to hear comfortably. If the noise is intermittent or

FIGURE 3.2

Listening Problems Checklist

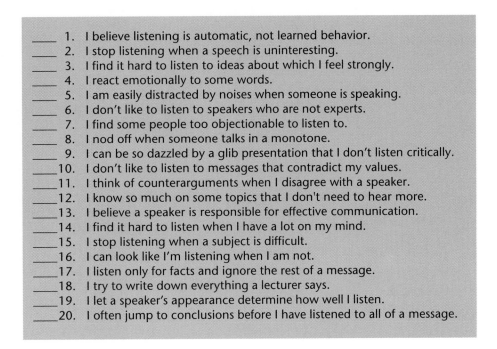

_____ 1. I believe listening is automatic, not learned behavior.
_____ 2. I stop listening when a speech is uninteresting.
_____ 3. I find it hard to listen to ideas about which I feel strongly.
_____ 4. I react emotionally to some words.
_____ 5. I am easily distracted by noises when someone is speaking.
_____ 6. I don't like to listen to speakers who are not experts.
_____ 7. I find some people too objectionable to listen to.
_____ 8. I nod off when someone talks in a monotone.
_____ 9. I can be so dazzled by a glib presentation that I don't listen critically.
_____10. I don't like to listen to messages that contradict my values.
_____11. I think of counterarguments when I disagree with a speaker.
_____12. I know so much on some topics that I don't need to hear more.
_____13. I believe a speaker is responsible for effective communication.
_____14. I find it hard to listen when I have a lot on my mind.
_____15. I stop listening when a subject is difficult.
_____16. I can look like I'm listening when I am not.
_____17. I listen only for facts and ignore the rest of a message.
_____18. I try to write down everything a lecturer says.
_____19. I let a speaker's appearance determine how well I listen.
_____20. I often jump to conclusions before I have listened to all of a message.

comes from outside the room, you may need to close a window or a door. Obviously it is best to do this before speakers start their presentations. If you must do so while someone is speaking, be as unobtrusive as possible.

Message Problems. Messages that are full of jargon or unfamiliar words, or that are poorly organized, make it difficult for people to listen effectively. We provide suggestions to speakers on using language effectively in Chapter 10, and on how to organize a message clearly in Chapters 7 and 8. As a listener, you have to put forth some effort to help overcome these problems. If you know that there may be unfamiliar words in a presentation, try to acquaint yourself with that vocabulary ahead of time. If a message is poorly organized, taking notes can help. Often you can find a pattern in the speaker's thoughts that will make them easier to remember and evaluate. Try to identify the main points or claims the speaker makes. Differentiate these from supporting materials such as examples or narratives. Figure 3.3 provides some helpful suggestions for taking notes.[21]

Presentation Problems. Speakers who talk too fast may be difficult to follow. On the other hand, speakers who talk too slowly or too softly may lull you to sleep. Speakers may also have habits that are distracting. They may sway to and fro or fiddle with their hair while they are talking. Occasionally, you may even encounter speakers whose dress or hairstyle is so unusual that you find yourself concentrating more on them than on what they are saying. We advise speakers on how to minimize such distractions in Chapter 11. As a listener, sometimes just being aware that you are responding to such cues may be enough to help you listen more attentively. If you find yourself drifting away because of such problems, remind yourself that what speakers say is the most important part of their message.

FIGURE 3.3

Guidelines for Taking Notes

1. Study background material ahead of time and have a notebook and a pen or pencil.
2. Leave a large margin on the left and take notes in outline form. Align the main points with the left-hand margin and indent supporting material. Leave spaces between main points.
3. Don't try to write down everything you hear. Omit nonessential words.
4. Be alert for signal words such as:
   A. *for example* or *case in point,* which suggest that supporting material will follow
   B. *the three causes* or *the four steps,* which suggest a list that you should number
   C. *before* or *after,* which suggest that the order is important
   D. *therefore* or *consequently,* which suggest a causal relationship
   E. *similarly* or *on the other hand,* which suggest that a comparison or contrast will follow
   F. *above all* or *keep in mind,* which mean this is an important idea
5. Review your notes and paraphrase, summarize, or indicate questions in the large left-hand margin.

Internal Sources of Interference

Internal listening problems may be caused by reactions to words, personal concerns, attitudes, cultural differences, bad listening habits, and listener apprehension. Fortunately, some of these problems can be anticipated by the speaker, and most are under the listener's control. Figure 3.4 shows how good and poor listeners respond differently to such problems.

One of the most common barriers to effective listening is simply not paying attention. How many times have you found yourself daydreaming, even when you know you should be listening to what is said? One reason for this problem is that our minds can process information far faster than people usually speak. Most people speak at about 125 words per minute in public, but can process information at about 500 words per minute.[22] This time lapse provides an opportunity for listeners to drift away to more delightful or difficult personal concerns. All too often daydreamers smile and nod encouragingly even though they haven't heard a word the speaker has said. This deceptive feedback is a major cause of failed communication. Both personal reactions to words and distractions can set off such reactions.

Reactions to Words.   As you listen to a message, you react to more than just the objective meanings of words. You respond to their emotional meanings as well. Some **trigger words** may set off such powerful emotional reactions that they dominate the meaning of the discourse. While some words deserve condemnation whenever they are used, people should control words and not the other way around. We should not let trigger words prevent us from hearing and evaluating the entire message within its overall context.

Let's consider a hypothetical case. Assume that you find the use of the word "girls" to refer to adult females demeaning and disrespectful. Now suppose a recruiter visiting your campus is describing opportunities for advancement in his company. He tells about "one of the girls from the office" who

FIGURE 3.4

Differences Between Good/Poor Listeners

Good Listeners	Poor Listeners
1. focus attention on the message.	1. allow their minds to wander.
2. control reactions to trigger words.	2. respond emotionally to trigger words.
3. set aside personal problems when listening.	3. let personal problems interfere with listening.
4. work to overcome distractions.	4. succumb easily to distractions.
5. don't let their biases interfere with listening.	5. let their biases interfere with listening.
6. don't let speaker mannerisms interfere with listening.	6. allow speaker mannerisms to interfere with listening.
7. listen for things they can use.	7. tune out dry topics.
8. recognize the role of the listener in communication.	8. hold the speaker responsible for communication.
9. listen actively.	9. listen passively.
10. reserve judgment until a speaker is finished.	10. jump to conclusions before a speaker is finished.
11. provide honest feedback to speakers.	11. feign attention, giving false feedback.
12. become familiar with difficult material ahead of time.	12. avoid listening to difficult material.
13. listen for main ideas.	13. listen only for facts.
14. don't demand that all messages be entertaining.	14. want all messages to be entertaining.

was recently promoted to a management position. His use of "girls" makes you think this may be a sexist organization. As you sit there stewing over his word choice, you miss his later statement that two-thirds of all recent promotions into management have gone to women and that an aggressive program aimed at promoting more females and minority employees is in effect.

How can you demystify such language and lessen its power over your reactions? Train yourself to look at the total message and analyze the particular case. For example, would it make any difference if the recruiter were a woman rather than a man? Ask yourself: Why is this person using such language? Is he personally insensitive, or is he testing me? Is this an attitude that is widespread in the company? By concentrating on such questions, you can reduce the power of trigger words and distance yourself somewhat from your own emotions. You can then decide whether you wish to confront the recruiter in order to clarify these questions. For example, you might tactfully say, "I'm impressed by what you have told me. But I'm troubled by your use of the term 'girls.' As a woman, would I really be respected in your company?" There is an obvious risk in this strategy: You might offend the recruiter and not get a highly desirable position. But there is also a risk in committing to a job situation that might not be good for you.

Trigger words can be positive as well as negative. Positive trigger words can blind us to flawed or dangerous messages. How many times have people been deceived by the use of such trigger words as "freedom," "democracy," or "progress" to justify courses of action?[23] Such techniques are related to *mythos*, a form of persuasion that appeals to people on the basis of traditions they hold dear. We discuss this more fully in Chapter 14. To gain control over your trigger words, Professor Richard Halley of Weber State University suggests that you observe your own behavior over a period of time and make a list of words that cause you to react emotionally.[24] You might then ask yourself the following questions:

- Did these words shape my responses to the messages?
- Were others trying to manipulate me?
- Should I have reacted differently?
- How can I gain more control over my reactions to words?

Chance associations with words can also derail your attention. For example, a speaker mentions the word "desk"—which reminds you that you need a better place to study in your room—which reminds you that you have to buy a new lamp—which starts you thinking about going shopping—which gets you thinking about the fried mushrooms at the restaurant in the mall—which reminds you that you didn't eat breakfast and you're hungry. By the time your attention drifts back to the speaker, you have lost the gist of what is being said. To prevent this kind of woolgathering, remind yourself of what is at stake in listening and commit yourself to do your part to make communication work.

Personal Concerns.   If you are tired, hungry, angry, worried, or pressed for time, you may find it difficult to concentrate. Your personal problems may take precedence over listening to a speaker. However, you can control inattention caused by internal distractions. Come to your classes well rested and well fed. Remind yourself that you can't really do your homework for another class when someone is talking. Decide to do your worrying later. Clear your mind and your desk of everything except paper on which to take notes. Sit erect, establish eye contact with the speaker, and commit to listen!

Attitudes.   You may have strong positive or negative attitudes toward the speaker or the topic that can diminish your listening ability. All of us have biases of one kind or another. Listening problems arise when our biases prevent us from receiving messages accurately. Some of the ways in which bias can distort messages are through filtering, assimilation, and contrast effects.[25]

Filtering means that you simply don't process all incoming information. You hear what you want to hear. You unconsciously screen the speaker's words so that only some of them reach your brain. Listeners who filter will hear only one side of "good news, bad news" speeches—the side that confirms their preconceived notions. **Assimilation** means that you see positions similar to your own as being closer to it than they actually are. Assimilation most often occurs when listeners have a strong positive attitude toward a speaker or topic. For example, if you believe that a speaker can do no wrong, you may be tempted to assimilate everything he or she says so that it seems consistent with all your beliefs. A **contrast effect** occurs when you see positions that differ from yours as being more distant than they actually are. For example, if you are a staunch Democrat, you may think anything Republicans say will be different from what you believe, even if that is not true. Biases can make you put words in a speaker's mouth, take them away, or distort them.

The attitudes that cause most listening problems are those related to the speaker or the topic. If you know a speaker or have heard something about him or her, you may have developed attitudes that cause listening problems. The more competent, interesting, and attractive you expect a speaker to be, the more attentive you will be and the more likely you are to accept what that speaker has to say. If your positive feelings are extremely strong, you may accept anything you hear from the speaker without considering the merits of the message. But if you anticipate an incompetent, uninteresting, or unattractive speaker, you may be less attentive and less likely to respect his or her ideas. You may dislike speakers because of positions they have previously defended or groups with which they are associated. Such biases may impair your listening ability.

Your attitudes toward certain topics also can affect how well you listen. If you believe that a topic is relevant to your life, you may listen more carefully than if you are indifferent. Speeches about retirement planning may fall on deaf ears with younger audiences. You may listen more attentively, although less critically, to speeches that support positions you already hold. If you feel strongly about a subject and oppose the speaker's position, you may find yourself rehashing counterarguments instead of listening. For example, if you have strong feelings against gun control, you may find yourself silently reciting the Second Amendment to the U.S. Constitution instead of listening to a speaker's arguments in favor of gun control. When you engage in such behaviors, you may miss much of what the speaker actually has to say. Finally, you may think that you already know enough about a topic. In such cases, you are not likely to listen effectively and may miss out on new, potentially useful information.

Attitudes are not easy to control. The first step in overcoming biases is to admit you have them. Next, decide that you will listen as objectively as you can, and that you will delay judgment until you have heard the entire message. Being objective does not mean that you must agree with a message—it only means that you believe a speech deserves to be heard on its own terms. What you hear may help you see clearly the faults or the virtues of an opposing position. As a result, you may feel confirmed in what you already believe, or you may decide to reevaluate your position. Finally, determine that you will find value in listening. Even if you are not interested in a topic, look for something in the speech that will benefit you personally. Even poor speeches can provide examples of what not to do when you are presenting your own speech.

Habits. Many listening problems are simply the result of bad habits. You may have watched so much television that you expect all messages to be fast-moving and entertaining. You may have learned how to pretend you are listening to avoid dull or difficult materials. Your experiences as a student may have conditioned you to listen just for facts. You may jump to conclusions before hearing a complete message. Such habits can interfere with effective listening.

William F. Buckley, Jr., has commented that "the television audience . . . is not trained to listen . . . to 15 uninterrupted minutes."[26] Our television-watching experiences may also lead us into the "entertainment syndrome," in which we demand that speakers be lively, interesting, funny, and charismatic to hold our attention.[27] Unfortunately, not all subjects lend themselves to such treatment.

Although honest feedback is important to speech effectiveness, we all have learned how to pretend to pay attention. We sit erect, gaze at the speaker, nod or smile from time to time (although not always at the most appropriate times), and do not listen to one word that is being said! You are most likely to feign attention when a message is difficult. If the speaker asks, "Do you understand?" you may nod brightly, sending false feedback just to be polite or to avoid seeming dimwitted.

Our fear of failure may cause us to avoid listening to difficult material. If we are asked questions later, we can always say "I wasn't really listening" instead of "I didn't understand." Additionally, our desire to have things simplified so that we can understand them without much effort makes us susceptible to oversimplified remedies for everything from fallen arches to failing government policies.

Your experiences as a student may contribute to another bad habit: listening only for facts. If you do this, you may miss the forest because you are so busy counting the leaves. Placing too much emphasis on facts can keep you from attending to the nonverbal aspects of a message. Effective listening includes integrating what you hear and what you see. Gestures, facial expressions, and tone of voice communicate nuances that are vital to understanding a message.

Overcoming bad habits requires effort. When you find yourself feigning attention, remember that honest feedback helps speakers, but that inappropriate feedback deceives them. Don't try to remember everything or write down all that you hear. Instead, listen to the main ideas and identify supporting materials. Paraphrase what you hear so that it makes sense to you. Try to build an overall picture of the meaning in your mind. Attend to the nonverbal cues as well. Does the speaker's tone of voice change the meaning of the words? Are the gestures and facial expressions consistent with the words? If not, what does this tell you?

Listening Apprehension.   Listening apprehension is the counterpart to the communication apprehension experienced by speakers that we discussed in Chapter 2. At first, this may surprise you: Do listeners really suffer from anxiety? The answer is, they can, and like speaker apprehension, this can be positive as well as negative.

Listener fear, which goes by the technical name **receiver apprehension**, is a relatively new research area in communication. As defined initially by Wheeless, it is "the fear of misinterpreting, inadequately processing and/or not being able to adjust psychologically to messages sent by others."[28] A later research team has connected it with motivation, evaluation, and message complexity.[29] To put the matter simply, we are apt to experience listener apprehension when we perceive that a message will be vital to our lives, when we expect to be judged on how well we respond to it, and when it challenges our ability to comprehend.

Assume for the moment that the first speaker of the day announces that her speech will contend that government student loan programs are unnecessary. You are attending school with the help of such a program, so you feel threatened by her message. The fear and resentment you initially feel cause you to listen to the message with some apprehension.

Now let's take this hypothetical situation a step further. Your teacher announces that he wants to designate a respondent for each speech to demonstrate the importance of constructive listening. In an impromptu critique after the speech, the respondent must demonstrate a grasp of the meaning of the speech, appreciation of its qualities, and sensitivity to the speaker's aims. The respondent also must be able to discuss possible shortcomings of content and presentation, and suggest a constructive application for the speech. Congratulations! You have just been designated the respondent for the speech on government loan programs. How can you meet the challenge of listening constructively on a subject on which you have strong initial bias? As you contemplate this challenge, you may experience an acute case of listener apprehension.

Take the case one more step. As you listen to the speech, it is presented with an incredible array of examples and statistics. The message is highly complex. As you attempt to follow the meaning of the speech, you feel your anxiety growing.

We hope we have made our point. Listener apprehension can be an important factor in communication. Thus far scientists have not discovered a great deal about it, nor can they yet tell us what to do about it. Until they can, we may assume the following: First, listener apprehension can be positive if it makes us *want* to listen to messages; nothing is worse than a bored audience.[30] But this same anxiety can distract us and even cause us to distort what we hear. If our discomfort is obvious, we may give speakers negative feedback and trigger communication anxiety in them! To control your listener apprehension and put it to work for you, we suggest that you experiment with procedures already demonstrated to work for speaker anxiety. That is, practice deep muscle relaxation, rewrite negative messages you may be giving yourself about the listening experience, and visualize successful outcomes.[31] Instead of telling yourself "I don't understand this at all," say "I can grasp the overall meaning here." Picture yourself giving a response that helps both the speaker and other listeners see the virtues as well as the problems in the message. Then, just as an anxious speaker can create confidence by acting confident, act as though you are interested and motivated by the speaker's message. After a time, you may discover that you actually *are* interested! Such techniques may help you put a positive spin on your experience as listener.

The Speaker's Notes, "Improving Your Listening Skills," summarize how you might listen more effectively to messages.

Improving Your Listening Skills

1 Identify your listening problems and work to correct them.
2 Motivate yourself to get everything you can out of messages.
3 Put problems and biases aside so that you listen more effectively.
4 Control your reactions to trigger words and other distractions.
5 Postpone judgments until you have heard all a speaker has to say.
6 Don't try to write down everything a speaker says.
7 Listen for the main ideas.

speaker's notes

Developing Critical Thinking and Listening Skills

Developing your critical thinking and listening skills will further increase your effectiveness as a listener. *Critical thinking and listening* is an integrated process of examining information, ideas, and proposals. It involves

- Questioning and exploring what you hear, accepting nothing at face value
- Developing your own position on issues by examining competing ideas
- Being receptive to new thoughts and new perspectives on old subjects
- Evaluating evidence and reasoning
- Discussing with others the meanings of events[32]

Throughout this course, the skills and knowledge you acquire as you learn to prepare speeches will also be useful in analyzing and evaluating the messages you receive. You will learn how to use and evaluate supporting materials and language resources in speeches. As you learn to prepare responsible arguments, you will also be learning how to evaluate the arguments of others. Although these topics will be covered in more depth in later chapters, here we will preview some questions that are important to critical listening.

Does the speaker support ideas or claims with facts and figures, testimony, and examples or narratives? Whenever speakers claim, "This statement is beyond dispute!" it is a good time to start a dispute. Listen for what is *not* said, as well as what is said. *No supporting material equals no proof. No proof should equal no acceptance.* Don't hesitate to ask such speakers challenging questions.

The ability to listen effectively is valued in the workplace.

Does the speaker use supporting materials that are relevant, representative, recent, and reliable? Supporting materials should relate directly to the issue in question. They should be representative of the situation as it exists rather than exceptions to the rule. The speaker who shouts, "Television is destroying family values!" and then offers statistics that demonstrate a rising national divorce rate has not demonstrated a causal relationship between television and family values. Facts and figures should be the most recent ones available. This is particularly important when knowledge about a topic is changing rapidly. Supporting materials should come from sources that are trustworthy and competent in the subject area. Controversial material, especially, should be supported by more than one source, and the sources should represent different perspectives on the issue.

Does the speaker cite credible sources? Ethical speakers specify the credentials of their sources. When the credentials are left out or described in vague terms, the testimony may be questionable. We recently found an advertisement for a health food product that contained "statements by doctors." A quick check of the current directory of the American Medical Association revealed that only one of the six "doctors" cited was a member of the AMA and that his credentials were misrepresented. Always ask yourself, "Where does this information come from?" and "Are these sources qualified to speak on the topic?" This was a major problem during the recent investigation of President Bill Clinton: Many media outlets during that time quoted unnamed or anonymous sources for the "facts" they were reporting. This created a formidable barrier to critical thinking by making it hard to judge the reports intelligently. We cover the use of supporting materials in greater detail in Chapters 6 and 14.

Does the speaker clearly distinguish among facts, inferences, and opinions? Facts are verifiable units of information that can be confirmed by independent observations. Inferences are projections based on facts. Opinions add personal judgments to inferences: They tell us what someone thinks about a subject. For example, "Mary was late for class today" is a fact. "Mary will probably be late for class again tomorrow" is an inference. "Mary is an irresponsible student" is an opinion. It may sound easy to make these distinctions among facts, inferences, and opinions, but you must be constantly alert to detect confusions of them in the messages you hear.

At the height of the media frenzy during the investigation of President Clinton, White House Press Secretary Mike McCurry charged that "in our political culture now, opinion often is pronounced as judgment before there are facts to support opinion." Walter Isaacson, managing editor of *Time* magazine, and Kathleen Hall Jamieson, dean of the Annenberg School of Communication, supported his charge by pointing out a kind of "echo-chamber" effect in modern journalism. The echo chamber works this way: An unconfirmed rumor is initially published by one news source, and then is repeated by others as though it had been substantiated. Of one such rumor, Isaacson said: "Within one day, it had spun around the city of Washington as if it were fact, and it had gotten embellished."[33]

Facts, inferences, and opinions all have a legitimate place in public discourse, but they also can be misused. Evaluating supporting material is covered in more detail in Chapter 6. Inferences are discussed as part of the reasoning process in Chapter 14.

Does the speaker use language that is concrete and understandable or purposely vague?   When speakers have something to hide, they often use incomprehensible or vague language. Introducing people who are not physicians as "doctors" to enhance their testimony on health subjects is one form of such vagueness. Another trick is to use pseudoscientific jargon such as "This supplement contains a gonadotropic hormone similar to pituitary extract in terms of its complex B vitamin–methionine ratio." If it sounds impressive but you don't know what it means, be careful. We cover other problems relating to language use in Chapter 10.

Does the speaker ask you to ignore reason?   Vivid examples and stories often express the speaker's deep passion for a subject and invite the listener to share this feeling. An ethical speaker will also include sound information and good reasons to justify such a feeling. In politics, those who try to inflame feelings in order to promote their own agendas, without regard to the accuracy or adequacy of their claims, are called **demagogues**. We should always ask, *what are these speakers asking us to ignore?* Republican leaders recently charged that their Democratic opponents were asking voters to ignore the fact that without significant change, the entire Medicare program would collapse. Democratic leaders countered that the Republicans were asking voters to ignore the fate of the poor and elderly who would be affected by their reforms. In the face of such conflicting claims, the critical thinker will investigate carefully before coming to a conclusion.

Does the speaker rely too much on facts and figures?   Although we have just cautioned you to be wary of speakers who rely solely on emotional appeals, you also should be wary of speakers who exclude emotional appeals. You can never fully understand an issue unless you understand how it affects others, how it makes them feel, how it colors the way they view the world. Suppose you were listening to a speech on environmental pollution that contained the following information: "The United States has 5 percent of the world's population but produces 22 percent of the world's carbon dioxide emissions, releases 26 percent of the world's nitrogen oxides, and disposes of 290 million tons of toxic waste."[34] Although these numbers are impressive, what do they really tell you about the human problem of pollution? Consider how much more meaningful this material might be if it were accompanied by the story of Colette Chuda, a five-year-old California girl who died recently from cancer that some feel resulted from direct exposure to a polluted environment.[35]

Does the speaker use plausible reasoning?   When reasoning is plausible, conclusions appear to follow from the points and supporting materials that precede them. In other words, they make good sense. The basic assumptions that support arguments should be those on which most rational people agree. Whenever reasoning doesn't seem plausible, ask yourself why, and then question the speaker or consult with independent authorities before you commit yourself. We cover the use of appeals and reasoning in more detail in Chapter 14.

Does the message promise too much?   If an offer sounds too good to be true, it probably is. The health-food advertisement previously described contained the following claims: "The healing, rejuvenating and disease-fighting effects of this total nutrient are hard to believe, yet are fully documented. Aging, digestive upsets, prostrate [sic] diseases, sore throats, acne, fatigue, sexual

Guides for Critical Thinking and Listening

speaker's notes

1 Require all claims to be supported with facts and figures, testimony, examples, or narratives.
2 Evaluate supporting materials in terms of relevance, representativeness, recency, and reliability.
3 Assess the sources' competence and trustworthiness.
4 Distinguish among facts, inferences, and opinions.
5 Be wary of language that is vague or incomprehensible.
6 Look for a balance between rational and emotional appeals.
7 Be on guard against claims that promise too much.
8 Check what you hear against what you know.
9 Consider alternative perspectives.
10 Ask questions whenever you have problems understanding or accepting a message.

problems, allergies, and a host of other problems have been successfully treated. . . . [It] is the only super perfect food on this earth. This statement has been proven so many times in the laboratories around the world by a chemical analyst that it is not subject to debate nor [sic] challenge." Maybe the product is also useful as a paint remover and gasoline additive.

Does this message fit with what I already know?   Although we have stressed the importance of being open to new knowledge, inconsistent information should set off an alarm in your mind. You should always evaluate information that is inconsistent with your beliefs very carefully before you accept it. Yet keep in mind that what you think you know might not necessarily be so. Ask the speaker tough questions suggested by the considerations summarized in the Speaker's Notes "Guides to Critical Thinking." Use the library to further verify information.

What other perspectives might there be on this issue?   How would people from a different cultural background perceive the problem? How would someone older see it? How might someone of the other gender see it? Why might these people see it differently from you? Would their solutions or suggestions be different? Whenever a message addresses a serious topic, try to examine the issue from several points of view. New and better ideas often emerge when we look at the world from a different angle.

These questions provide a framework for critical thinking. When we add these skills to the improved listening behavior that comes when we confront our listening problems, we are on the way to becoming effective listeners.

Evaluating Speeches

Your overall improvement as a listener should enhance the quality of the feedback you offer to speakers. Up to now, we have been emphasizing immediate feedback, your body language as a listener. Alert attention and cues such

Effective listeners provide valuable feedback to speakers. A puzzled expression may suggest a lack of understanding.

as nods of agreement or puzzled looks can be important *during* a speech. But you may also have an opportunity to give oral feedback *after* speakers have made their presentations. You may ask questions, comment on effective techniques, or offer suggestions for improvement.

To participate in this oral feedback, you must understand one important distinction: There is a difference between criticizing a speaker and giving a **critique**, or evaluation, of a speech. Criticism suggests emphasizing what someone did wrong. It can create a negative communication environment. In contrast, when you give a critique, your manner should be helpful and supportive. Point out strengths as well as weaknesses. Whenever you point out a problem, do so tactfully and try to suggest remedies or solutions. This type of interaction stresses the willingness of students to help one another.

To provide a constructive oral feedback, you need a set of standards to help you answer the question *What is a good speech?* These standards can vary in importance according to the assignment; for example, the critique of an informative speech might focus on the adequacy of information and examples, and that of a persuasive speech might emphasize evidence and reasoning. Nevertheless, there are four general categories of guidelines you can use to evaluate all speeches: overall considerations, substance, structure, and presentation.

Overall Considerations

Considerations about commitment, adaptation, purpose, freshness, and ethics apply to the speech as a whole.

Commitment.   Commitment means caring. You must feel that the speaker cares deeply about the subject and also about your welfare as a listener. Committed speakers will have invested the time and effort needed to gain responsible knowledge of their subject. Commitment also shows up in how well a speech is structured. A good speech cannot be prepared at ten-thirty the night before a presentation. It takes time to analyze an audience, select a topic and research it adequately, organize a message, and practice its presentation. Finally, commitment shows up in the energy, enthusiasm, and sincerity the speaker projects. Commitment is the spark in the speaker that can touch off fire in the audience.

Karen Lovelace became a model of commitment in her class at Vanderbilt University by developing a series of informative, persuasive, and ceremonial speeches on the fate of disabled people in our society. By the end of her class, no one doubted the passion of Karen's commitment, and many of us were ready to join her crusade for reform of laws and customs.

Adaptation.   For a speech to be effective, it must meet the particular requirements of the assignment and be adapted to the listeners' needs. An assignment will typically specify the **general purpose** of the speech: an **informative speech** that aims at extending your understanding of a topic, a **persuasive speech** that attempts to influence your attitudes or actions, or a **ceremonial speech** that celebrates shared values. The assignment may also specify time limits, the number of references required, and the manner of presentation (such as a required presentation aid or extemporaneous mode of speech).

Effective speakers are listener-centered. This means that as speakers plan and prepare their messages, they should weigh each technique and each piece of supporting material in terms of its appropriateness for the particular audience. Will this example interest listeners? Is this information important for them to know? How can the speaker best involve the audience with the topic? The close involvement of subject, speaker, and listener, called **identification**, is vital for effective speaking. One way in which speakers can invite identification is to ask involving questions at the beginning of a speech: "Have you ever thought about what it would mean not to have electricity?" Also, the pronoun *we* used artfully throughout a speech may draw audience, speaker, and subject closer together.

Purpose.   Beyond a general purpose, a speech should also have a specific purpose. For example, an informative speech may have the specific purpose of increasing listeners' knowledge of the causes of global warming. The specific purpose of a speech will typically be evident by the time the speaker finishes the introduction, and must be unmistakably clear by the time the speaker begins the conclusion.

A speech that lacks a clear sense of purpose will seem to drift and wander as though it were a boat without a rudder, blown this way and that by whatever thought occurs to the speaker. Developing a clear purpose begins with the speaker considering audience needs. Speakers must determine precisely what they want to accomplish: what they want listeners to learn, think, or do as a result of their speeches.

Freshness.   Any speech worth listening to will bring something new to you. The topic should be fresh and interesting. If the topic has been overused, then the speech must be innovative to sustain attention. One frequently overused topic for persuasive speeches is drinking and driving. When speakers choose such a topic, they can't simply reiterate the common advice "if you drink, don't drive" and expect to be effective. The audience will have heard that message hundreds of times. To get through to listeners on such a subject, speakers have to find a fresh way to present the material. One student of ours gave a speech on "responsible drinking and driving" that stressed the importance of understanding the effects of alcohol and of knowing your own tolerance limits. Her fresh approach and important information gave us a new perspective on an old problem.

Ethics.   Perhaps the most important measure of a speech is whether it is good or bad for you. *An ethical speech demonstrates respect for the audience, responsible knowledge, and concern for the consequences of exposure to the message.*

Respect for the audience means that speakers are sensitive to the cultural composition of their audience and are aware that well-meaning people often hold varying positions on an issue. Ethical speakers try not to offend others unnecessarily even as they dispute their arguments or question their information. We discuss additional audience considerations in Chapter 4.

Ethical speakers base their messages on responsible knowledge of their subject. They assess the accuracy and objectivity of their sources of information, and watch for potential bias. They are sensitive to their own prejudices and try to be accurate and objective in their presentation of information. Ethical speakers try not to pass off opinions and inferences as facts. An ethical speaker will report the sources of factual data and ideas, especially if this information runs counter to what is generally believed. Finally, ethical speakers do not fabricate data or present the ideas or words of others without acknowledging their contributions.

Ethical speakers are aware that words have consequences. Inflammatory language can arouse strong feelings in audience members that sometimes block constructive deliberation. Ethical speakers think through the possible ramifications of their messages before they present them. The greater the possible consequences, the more carefully speakers must assess the potential effects of their messages, support what they say with credible evidence, and temper their conclusions with regard for listener sensitivities.

Evaluating Substance

A speech has **substance** when it has a worthwhile message that is supported by facts and figures, testimony, examples, and/or narratives. The starting point for a substantive presentation is a well-chosen topic that interests both speaker and listeners, once they are shown how it affects their lives. Generally, speakers should already know something about the topics they select. This knowledge serves as the foundation for further research that enables them to speak responsibly and authoritatively. While personal experiences are a valuable source of information, speakers should always validate, update, and broaden such experience with research or interviews with knowledgeable people. We discuss selecting and researching topics in more detail in Chapter 5.

Speakers add substance by weaving reliable information into the fabric of their speeches. *Facts and figures* give precise focus to a speaker's points. *Testimony* adds the authority and prestige of others to the speaker's claims. Such testimony from knowledgeable or respected others can include expert opinions or eloquent quotations. At other times, speakers may rely on lay testimony from ordinary people with whom listeners might identify. For example, the opinions of other students might be meaningful on issues that pertain to campus life. *Examples* can help you understand better what speakers are talking about. *Narratives* can engage the audience by telling some colorful story that illustrates the speaker's message.

Skillful speakers often combine different types of supporting material to make their points more accessible to listeners. Combining statistical data with an example can make ideas more clear and compelling. For instance, a speaker might say, "The base of the Great Pyramid at Giza measures 756 feet on each side." While precise, this may be difficult for you to visualize. But what if the speaker adds, "More than eleven football fields could fit in its base." Aha! This example gives you a concrete point of reference by comparing the unfamiliar or hard to understand with something you can relate to. We discuss the use of supporting materials in greater detail in Chapter 6.

Evaluating Structure

A good speech is carefully planned so that it carries you through an orderly progression of ideas, making it easy for you to follow. Without a good design, a speech may seem to consist of random ideas that have been thrown together willy-nilly. A worthwhile message can get lost in the confusion. There are three main parts to every message: an introduction, the body of the speech, and a conclusion. The introduction should arouse interest in the topic and preview the message to follow. The body of the speech presents a speaker's main ideas and the supporting material needed to develop them. The conclusion should summarize the main points, reflect upon the meaning of the message, and provide a sense of closure.

The introduction may begin with an example, a quotation, or a question that draws you into the topic, such as "So you think there's no need to worry about global warming?" Once speakers gain their listeners' attention, they will usually prepare the listeners for what is to come by focusing on their purpose and previewing the main points. More suggestions for developing introductions can be found in Chapter 7.

The organization of the body of the speech will vary according to the subject and purpose. If a speech tells you how to do something—for instance, how to plan a budget—its main points should follow the order of the process that it describes. If the subject breaks naturally into parts, such as the three major causes of global warming, speakers can use a categorical design to present them. Chapters 12 and 13 discuss these and other designs for speeches.

A variety of concluding techniques can be used to end a speech. If speakers have covered several main points in the body, they should summarize them and then make a final statement that will help the audience remember the essence of the message. Chapter 7 provides additional information on developing conclusions.

Effective speeches also contain transitions that link together the various parts of the speech. Transitions bridge ideas and aid understanding. They signal that something different is coming and help the speech flow better. Transitions should be used between the introduction and body of a speech, between the body and the conclusion, and between the main points within the body. You will learn more about transitions in Chapter 7.

Evaluating Presentation Skills

No speech can be effective unless it is presented well. Both the actual words speakers use and the way they convey these words are important factors in presentation.

The oral language of speeches must be instantly intelligible. This means that speakers' sentences should be simple and direct. They should avoid complex chains of dependent clauses. Compare the following examples:

> **Working for a temporary employment service is a good way to put yourself through school because there are always jobs to be found and the places you get to work are interesting—besides, the people you work for treat you well, and you don't have to do the same thing day after day—plus, you can tailor the hours to fit your free time.**

> **Working for a temporary employment service is a good way to put yourself through school. Jobs are readily available. You can schedule your work to fit in with your classes. You don't stay at any one place long enough to get bored. And you meet a lot of interesting people who are glad to have your services.**

Which is easier to follow? The first example rambles on; the information is presented in no particular order, and the speaker pauses only to catch a breath. In the second example, the sentences are short, inviting the effective use of pauses to separate ideas. As a result, the meaning is more clear.

Concrete words are generally preferable to abstract ones because they create vivid pictures for you and enhance the speaker's meaning. Consider the following levels of abstraction:

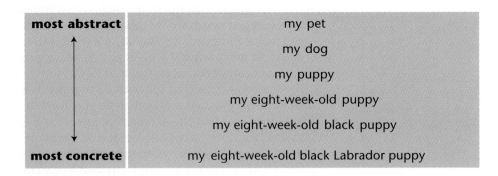

most abstract	my pet
	my dog
	my puppy
	my eight-week-old puppy
	my eight-week-old black puppy
most concrete	my eight-week-old black Labrador puppy

As the language becomes more concrete, you can better visualize what is being talked about, and there is less chance of misunderstanding. We discuss other language factors that help improve communication in Chapter 10.

An effective presentation sounds natural and enthusiastic. Speakers draw attention to their ideas rather than themselves and avoid distracting mannerisms. To achieve these qualities, most class assignments call for an **extemporaneous presentation**. In this style of speaking, the speech is carefully prepared and practiced but *not* written out or memorized. Extemporaneous speaking allows speakers to adapt to the audience during a presentation. If listeners look confused, speakers can rephrase what they have said or provide another example. This kind of speaking does require practice, however. Extemporaneous does *not* mean "off the top of the speaker's head."

Practice may not make perfect, but it certainly improves a speaker's chances of doing a good job. While rehearsing, a speaker may discover that a technique that looked good on paper sounds stilted or silly when spoken. It often helps if speakers can tape-record their speeches, leave them overnight, then play them back the next day. Supportive roommates or friends can listen to the speech before presentation and offer suggestions for further improving it. They should be able to identify the purpose and the main points of the speech. Speakers should imagine their audiences before them as they practice. If possible, they should find a time when the classroom is not being used so that they can try out the speech where it actually will be presented. The more they can practice under these conditions, the better the speech should flow when the class actually hears it. As we saw in Chapter 2, practice can also help speakers reduce communication anxiety.

During actual presentations, speakers should talk loud enough to be heard easily in the back of the room. Body language is also an important part of effective presentation. The speaker's posture should be relaxed. Movements should seem natural and spontaneous. Speakers who point to their heads every time they say "think" or who spread their arms out wide every time they say "big" will seem artificial and contrived. Gestures should complement what a speaker has to say, not compete with it for attention. Additional suggestions for effective presentation can be found in Chapter 11.

Keep these points in mind as you prepare to offer constructive feedback. Figure 3.5 summarizes these categories of guidelines. You may use it as a checklist for critiquing the speeches that you hear in class and in everyday life.

Ethical Responsibilities of a Listener

Listeners as well as speakers have ethical responsibilities. Ethical listeners do not prejudge a speech, but keep an open mind. John Milton, a great English poet and intellectual of the seventeenth century, observed in *Areopagitica,* his treatise on freedom of communication, that listening to our opponents can be beneficial. We may learn something from them and gain a new and better perspective on an issue. Or, as we question and argue with them, we may discover *why* we believe as we do. When we protect ourselves from opposing ideas, we deprive ourselves of the chance to engage, apply, and strengthen our own convictions.

Just as we should be open to ideas, we should also remain open to people of different lifestyles and cultural backgrounds. We should not deprive ourselves of the chance to explore other worlds. In comparing and contrasting our lifeways with those of others, we learn more about ourselves.

While ethical listeners should remain open to ideas that may at first seem strange or even hostile, we do not suggest that you lower your guard entirely. Some ideas, after fair consideration, prove to be faulty, risky, or even evil. Not every speaker has our good at heart. Perhaps our best advice to you is to be an open but cautious listener, combining the best traits of ethical and critical listening.

FIGURE 3.5

Guidelines for Evaluating Speeches

Overall Considerations
____ Was the speaker committed to the topic?
____ Did the speech meet the requirements of the assignment?
____ Was the speech adapted to the audience?
____ Did the speech promote identification among topic, audience, and speaker?
____ Was the purpose of the speech clear?
____ Was the topic handled with imagination and freshness?
____ Did the speech meet high ethical standards?

Substance
____ Was the topic worthwhile?
____ Had the speaker done sufficient research?
____ Were the main ideas supported with information?
____ Was testimony used appropriately?
____ Were the sources documented adequately?
____ Were examples or narratives used effectively?
____ Was the reasoning clear and correct?

Structure
____ Did the introduction arouse interest?
____ Did the introduction preview the message?
____ Was the speech easy to follow?
____ Were the main points of the speech evident?
____ Were transitions used to tie the speech together?
____ Did the conclusion summarize the message?
____ Did the conclusion help you remember the speech?

Presentation
____ Was the language clear, simple, and direct?
____ Was the language colorful?
____ Were grammar and pronunciations correct?
____ Was the speech presented extemporaneously?
____ Were notes used unobtrusively?
____ Was the speaker appropriately enthusiastic?
____ Did the speaker maintain good eye contact?
____ Did body language complement ideas?
____ Was the speaker expressive?
____ Were the rate and loudness appropriate?
____ Did the speaker use pauses?
____ Did presentation aids enhance the message?
____ Were presentation aids integrated into the speech?
____ Was the presentation free from distracting mannerisms?

Finally, keep in mind the impact of your listening on others. Good listeners help develop good speakers. Good listeners seek out the value in ideas, often finding unexpected worth in a speech. Good listeners are also concerned about the ethical impact of messages on others who may not be present. Good listeners do not only apply a version of the Golden Rule—"Listen to others as you would have them listen to you"—but extend it. They learn the communication values of other people so that they can apply what Bennett has called the Platinum Rule: "Listen to others as *they* would have you listen to them."[36] All sides benefit when speakers and listeners take their ethical roles seriously.

In Summary

Listening is as important to communication as speaking. Bad listening can devastate both nations and individuals. To climb the ladder of effective listening, we must first be able to hear a message, the *discriminative phase*. Thereafter, we must master the skills of focusing, understanding, and interpreting, the *comprehensive phase*. In the *empathic phase*, we share the speaker's point of view, and in the *appreciative phase,* we enjoy the speaker's ability to structure messages skillfully and to word ideas attractively. *Critical listening* requires us to have the ability to evaluate messages, and *constructive listening*, the final rung of the ladder, challenges us to find the value in messages for our lives.

Benefits of Effective Listening. Effective listening benefits both listeners and speakers. Listeners become less vulnerable to unethical advertising or to dishonest political communication. Improved listening skills can enhance both your academic performance and your chances for a successful career. Feedback from good listeners can help communication work better. Supportive listeners help relieve a speaker's communication apprehension and can boost the speaker's self-esteem.

Overcoming Listening Problems.   Some listening problems may arise from external sources, such as noisy surroundings. They may also result from a poorly organized message, unfamiliar language, or a speaker whose presentation is distracting. Most serious listening problems arise from factors internal to the listener, such as personal reactions to words, worries, attitudes, bad listening habits, or listener apprehension. Personal reactions to *trigger words* may set off strong emotions that block effective listening. Biased attitudes toward the speaker or the topic can interfere with listening. For example, *filtering* is a form of message distortion in which you hear only what you want to. *Assimilation* occurs when you interpret some favored person's views as identical with your own when there is actually a significant distance between the two positions. A *contrast effect* occurs when you see a position only slightly different from yours as quite different, because you have a negative bias towards the source.

Bad habits, such as pretending we are listening when we are not or listening only for facts, can also impair listening behavior. Fear of listening is a major form of *receiver apprehension*. We are often fearful listeners when we know that a message will be important for us personally, when we will be held responsible for it, and when it is difficult to understand.

Effective listening skills can be developed. The first step is to identify your listening problems. Concentrate on the main ideas and the overall pattern of meaning in the speech. Strive to be as objective as you can be, and withhold judgment until you are certain you understand the message.

Developing Critical Thinking Skills.　Critical thinking skills help you analyze and evaluate messages more effectively. Critical listeners question what they hear, require support for assertions and claims, and evaluate the credentials of sources. Critical listeners differentiate among facts, inferences, and opinions. They become wary when language seems overly vague or incomprehensible, when inflammatory speech takes the place of cool reason, or when a message promises too much. When what they hear does not fit with what they know, critical listeners start asking the tough questions.

Evaluating Speeches.　Speech evaluation in the classroom takes the form of a *critique*, a positive and constructive effort to help speakers improve. Criteria for speech evaluation include overall considerations, substance, structure, and presentation skills. Overall considerations encompass the speaker's commitment, adaptation to the audience and occasion, clarity of purpose, freshness of perspective, and ethical standards. Substance involves the value of the topic, the sufficiency of research, the adequacy of supporting material, and the speaker's ability to reason. Structural criteria include the presence of an effective introduction, a clearly organized body that includes the main points and supporting materials, and a conclusion that provides closure. Presentation questions touch upon how well speakers use words and their ability to convey their messages through voice and gesture.

Listeners have ethical responsibilities. Ethical listeners do not prejudge a speech, but are open to ideas and receptive to different perspectives. Ethical listeners test what they hear and are sensitive to the impact of ideas on others. They represent all who might be affected by the message.

Terms to Know

discriminative phase	receiver apprehension
comprehensive phase	demagogues
empathic phase	critique
appreciative phase	general purpose
critical listening	informative speech
constructive listening	persuasive speech
trigger words	ceremonial speech
filtering	identification
assimilation	substance
contrast effect	extemporaneous presentation

Notes

1. Cited in Clifton Fadiman, ed. *The Little, Brown Book of Anecdotes,* (Boston: Little, Brown, 1985), pp. 475–476.
2. Thomas L. Means and Gary S. Klein, "A Short Classroom Unit, but a Signficant Improvement, in Listening Ability," *Bulletin of the Association for Business Communication* 57 (1994): 13.

3. L. Barker et al., "An Investigation of Proportional Time Spent in Various Communication Activities by College Students," *Journal of Applied Communication Research* 8 (1980): 101–109; Larry L. Barker, *Listening Behavior* (Englewood Cliffs, N.J.: Prentice-Hall, 1971), pp. 3–9; and Walter Pauk, *How to Study in College,* 4th ed. (Boston: Houghton Mifflin, 1989), pp. 121–133.

4. Richard Bruce Hyde, "Council: Using a Talking Stick to Teach Listening," *The Speech Communication Teacher,* Vol. 7.2 (Winter 1993): 1–2.

5. Luther Standing Bear, Oglala Sioux chief, cited in *Native American Wisdom: Photographs by Edward S. Curtis* (Philadelphia: Running Press, 1993) pp. 58–59.

6. Ronald B. Adler and George Rodman, *Understanding Human Communication,* 5th ed. (Fort Worth, Tex.: Harcourt Brace, 1994), p. 130.

7. C. Glenn Pearce, "Learning How to Listen Empathically," *Supervisory Management* 36 (1991): 11.

8. We describe this concept further in Michael and Suzanne Osborn, *Alliance for a Better Public Voice: The Communication Discipline and the National Issues Forums* (Dayton, Ohio: National Issues Forums Institute, 1991).

9. Waldo Braden, "The Available Means of Persuasion: What Shall We Do About the Demand for Snake Oil?" in *The Rhetoric of Our Times*, ed. J. Jeffry Auer (New York: Appleton-Century-Crofts, 1969), pp. 178–184.

10. Jean Folkerts, "The Ethics of Questionable Advertising Campaigns," *The World & I,* Vol. 11, 1 September 1996, pp. 310ff, online, e-library (http://www.elibrary.com), accessed 8 September 1998; Bob Greene, "When Athletes Endorse, Why Does Anyone Listen?" *USA Today*, 8 April 1997, online, e-library (http://www.e-library.com), accessed 8 September 1998; "Michael Jordan's Magical Powers," *The Economist*, 1 June 1991, p. A28; and Jeffrey A. Trachtenberg, "Beyond the Hidden Persuaders: Psychological Aspects of Marketing, *Forbes,* 23 March 1987, pp. 134–137.

11. W. B. Legge, "Listening, Intelligence, and School Achievement," in *Listening: Readings*, ed. S. Duker (Metuchen, N.J.: Scarecrow Press, 1971), pp. 121–133.

12. U.S. Department of Labor, "What Work Requires of Schools" (Washington, D.C.: U.S. Government Printing Office, 1991).

13. Dan B. Curtis, Jerry L. Winsor, and Ronald D. Stephens, "National Preferences in Business and Communication Education," *Communication Education* 38 (1989): 7–14.

14. Gary T. Hunt and Louis P. Cusella, "A Field Study of Listening Needs in Organizations," *Communication Education* 32 (1983): 399.

15. B. D. Sypher, R. N. Bostrom, and J. H. Seibert, "Listening Communication Abilities and Success at Work," *Journal of Business Communication* (Fall 1989), 293–303.

16. Andrew D. Wolvin and Carolyn Gwynn Coakley, "A Survey of the Status of Listening Training in Some Fortune 500 Corporations," *Communication Education* 40 (1991): 152–164.

17. Lou Davidson Tillson, "Building Community and Reducing Communication Apprehension: A Case Study Approach," *The Speech Communication Teacher* (Summer 1995): 4–5.

18. Some material for this section was synthesized from William B. Gudykunst, Stella Ting-Toomey, Sandra Sudweeks, and Lea P. Stewart, *Building Bridges: Interpersonal Skills for a Changing World* (Boston: Houghton Mifflin, 1995), pp. 228–229.

19. Hank Trisler, "Now Hear This," *American Salesman* 39 (July 1994): 8.

20. Patricia O'Brien, "Why Men Don't Listen . . . and What It Costs Women at Work," *Workng Woman* 18 (1993): 56.

21. Adapted from Dave Ellis, *Becoming a Master Student,* 7th ed. (Boston: Houghton Mifflin, 1994), pp. 136–150; and Pauk, pp. 136–161.

22. Andrew D. Wolvin and Carolyn Gwynn Coakley, *Listening*, 2nd ed. (Dubuque, Iowa: William C. Brown, 1985), p. 177.

23. Richard M. Weaver, "Ultimate Terms in Contemporary Rhetoric," in *Language Is Sermonic: Richard M. Weaver on the Nature of Rhetoric*, ed. Richard L. Johannesen, Rennard Strickland, and Ralph T. Eubanks (Baton Rouge: Louisiana State University Press, 1970), p. 95.

24. He discussed this "Triggering Stimuli Assignment" on the web site of the International Listening Association, accessed 4 August 1998.

25. J. J. Makay and W. R. Brown, *The Rhetorical Dialogue: Contemporary Concepts and Cases* (Dubuque, Iowa: William C. Brown, 1972), pp. 125–145.

26. William F. Buckley, Jr., "Has TV Killed Off Great Oratory?" *TV Guide*, 12 February 1983, p. 38.

27. James J. Floyd, *Listening: A Practical Approach* (Glencoe, Ill.: Scott, Foresman, 1985), pp. 23–25.

28. L. R. Wheeless, "An Investigation of Receiver Apprehension and Social Context Dimensions of Communication Apprehension," *The Speech Teacher* 24 (1975): 263.

29. Joe Ayres, A. Kathleen Wilcox, and Debbie M. Ayres, "Receiver Apprehension: An Explanatory Model and Accompanying Research," *Communication Education* 44 (1995): 223–235. Also see Michael J. Beatty, "Receiver Apprehension as a Function of Cognitive Backlog," *Western Journal of Speech Communication* 45 (1981): 277–281; Michael J. Beatty and Steven K. Payne, "Receiver Apprehension and Cognitive Complexity," *Western Journal of Speech Communication* 45 (1981): 363–369; and Raymond W. Preiss, Lawrence R. Wheeless, and Mike Allen, "Potential Cognitive Processes and Consequences of Receiver Apprehension: A Meta-analytic Review," *Journal of Social Behavior and Personality* 5 (1990): 155–172.

30. C. V. Roberts, "A Validation of the Watson-Barker Listening Test," *Communication Research Reports* 3 (1986): 115–119.

31. Anthony J. Clark may have indicated indirectly the value of such exercises when he demonstrated a positive relationship between communication confidence and listening comprehension: "Communication Confidence and Listening Competence: An Investigation of the Relationships of Willingness to Communicate, Communication Apprehension, and Receiver Apprehension to Comprehension of Content and Emotional Meaning in Spoken Messages," *Communication Education* 38 (1989): 237–248.

32. John Chaffee, *Thinking Critically*, 2nd ed. (Boston: Houghton Mifflin, 1988), p. 59.

33. See their discussion in "Investigating the President: Media Madness?" transcript of a special report on CNN, 28 January 1998.

34. *Time*, 18 December 1989, cover.

35. Jim Motavalli, "In Memory of Colette," *E: The Environmental Magazine*, May/June 1994, pp. 30–31.

36. Milton J. Bennett, "Overcoming the Golden Rule: Sympathy and Empathy," in *Communication Yearbook 3*, ed. Dan Nimmo (New Brunswick, N.J.: Transaction Books, 1979), pp. 407–422.

PART TWO

Preparation for Public Speaking

4

Adapting to Your Audience and Situation

*O*rators have
to learn the
differences of
human souls.

—*Plato*

This chapter will help you

- understand audience dynamics
- adapt your message to your audience
- meet the challenges of audience diversity
- adjust your message to the speaking situation

*I*t's the beginning of the fall term, and the president of Students for Environmental Action (SEA) has a busy day ahead. In the morning she will welcome the students assembled in the field house. She wants to inform and inspire them about SEA's work and to recruit new members. Later in the day she will address the County Industrial Development Board to tell the board members about SEA's plans for the year. She wants to assure them that the group is sensitive to both business and environmental needs, and she wants to win their support.

 THE TOPIC OF the president's speeches will not change, but the two audiences and situations will require quite different approaches. Her listeners must be at the center of her thinking as she designs her speeches. Moreover, the setting for these speeches can make a big difference in how she presents them. Her manner of presentation, as well as the language she chooses, may vary from the field house to the boardroom.

This chapter begins with a basic assumption: *The more you know about your audience and speaking situation, the more effective your speech should be.* A good audience analysis will help you determine what your listeners may already know about your topic, what they need to know, and how they feel about it. Your audience analysis can also help you select the most effective supporting materials, decide on the design and structure of your speech, and choose the best techniques to help listeners understand and relate to your topic.

You may question the ethics of adapting a message to fit a particular audience. "Waffling," the taking of one position with one audience and a different position with another audience, is clearly unethical. But you can adapt to your audience without changing the essence of your message or surrendering your convictions. You can ethically adapt your message to a given audience in terms of the language you use, the examples you provide, the stories you tell, the authorities you cite, and your manner of presentation. Ask yourself, "How can I tailor my message so that I can reach my audience without compromising my principles?"

In this chapter, we open with *audience dynamics*, the motivations, attitudes, and values of listeners. Second, we consider *demographic factors* such as age, political and religious preferences, and gender. Next, we discuss some of the major challenges of *audience diversity* that make communication difficult. Finally, we focus on features of the *communication situation* that may call for adaptations.

Adapting to Audience Dynamics

Audience dynamics are the motivations, attitudes, beliefs, and values that influence listeners from deep within. An understanding of how these factors work is central to understanding your listeners. The more you understand what makes people tick, the better you can adapt your message so that it serves their interests and needs.

Motivation

Our needs and wants make up our **motivation**, the force that draws our attention to certain objects and makes us act in certain ways. Motivation helps explain *why* people behave as they do.[1] Therefore, motivation is important to both persuasive and informative speeches. *People will listen, learn, and remember a message only if it relates to their needs, wants, or wishes.* Understanding motivation can also help a speaker appeal to the common humanity in listeners that crosses cultural boundaries.

Motives can vary in importance according to the person, situation, and culture. *People are motivated by what they don't have that they need or want.* If you have recently moved to a new town, your need to make friends may attract you to places where you can meet others. Even when needs are satisfied, people respond to wants. Suppose you have just eaten a very filling meal. You're not hungry, but if someone enters the room with a plate of warm, freshly baked cookies, the sight and smell can make you want some.

The study of human motivation has had an interesting history within twentieth-century psychology. Social scientists first concentrated on identifying the different types of motivation. In a pioneering study published during the 1930s, Henry A. Murray and his associates at the Harvard Psychological Clinic identified more than twenty-five different human needs.[2] Later, another research pioneer, Abraham Maslow, arranged needs in a five-level hierarchy beginning with the most basic physiological needs and culminating in self-actualization needs.[3] Contemporary psychologists now argue that almost all motivations, even needs that seem purely social in nature, express a central preoccupation with the self.[4] Therefore, they contend that our most basic needs are to understand and control the world around us in order to protect and enhance our selfhood.[5] Beyond these general master needs, people may also have quite powerful, more specific physical, social, and personal needs. These needs often become motivational themes and appeals in speeches.

To get an idea of motivation as it actually surfaces in classroom speeches, we looked at more than a hundred speeches presented in recent years by students at the Universities of California-Davis, Indiana, Memphis, and Vanderbilt. We identified seven motives that were often used in those speeches: understanding, control, health and safety, nurturance and altruism, friends and family, self-actualization, and the desire for fairness.

Understanding.   The students in our sample confirmed the importance of the master need of understanding. Speakers attempted to help their listeners understand a wide range of subject matter, explaining such things as cloning, genetic testing, and the legal and moral issues involved in sexual harassment. Apparently, we all need to understand the world and the people around us, so we look for the causes of events and try to figure out why people act as they do. This curiosity may also explain the appeal of foreign travel and cross-cultural comparisons. One student talked about what she had learned in a cultural exchange visit to China. Another compared holiday customs in Mexico and the United States. This suggests that you can make almost any topic interesting to your audience if you can show them how understanding it might empower them. Speeches that emphasize the need for understanding are typically informative.

Control. Control goes along with understanding. We need to understand things, or at least think that we understand them, because this makes us feel less vulnerable. It gives us a sense of having some control over our lives—of being able to influence events and people—of shaping our own destiny. Our desire for control may place us in competition with others. Speeches that show listeners how they can gain control over their environment, over themselves, or over others typically hold the audience's attention. In the student speeches, however, the theme often was not so much exercising control as warning about controllers. Cloning and genetic testing, as well as other forms of technology, could have dire as well as favorable consequences for the human species. The powerful forces of advertising, in the hands of the tobacco, firearms, or insurance industry, can turn control against us. Thus the fear of control is often a powerful motivational appeal. Speeches that satisfy our need to gain, regain, or resist control over the forces around us are typically persuasive in nature.

Health and Safety. These two basic physical needs are often discussed together. All of us need to feel free from threats to both health and safety. Speeches describing the endangered ozone layer and the warning signs of deadly diseases obviously involve both. Our student speakers warned of the dangers of smoking and of the need for clean air and water, and expounded on the advantages of exercise and herbal medicines. They described rising crime rates, discussed the potential dangers of earthquakes, and urged classmates to be organ donors. Appeals to our safety needs often arouse fear in the audience. Fear appeals in a speech, if they are too obvious or frightening, can give listeners the impression that you are manipulating them. Therefore, use this technique with caution. If you develop fear appeals, be sure to show listeners how they can protect themselves from the dangers you describe.[6]

Nurturance and Altruism. While we may seem to be concerned primarily with ourselves, we also have strong needs to care for others. Protecting and comforting the helpless or those in need makes us feel good. We had moving student speeches describing the plight of the disabled and homeless, urging listeners to become volunteers in the community, and exhorting them to support programs and laws ensuring the rights of marginalized groups. Helping others is a basic tenet of most religious groups, reflected, for example, in the story of the good Samaritan.

Appeals to this motive can be especially strong when speakers discuss children who are deprived of nurturance. We had powerful speeches describing child abuse and the plight of "children at risk." Speakers engaged this need positively when they advocated educational reform, promoted arts education, or debated bilingual education. The central issue was always, "Would this program help children develop?"

Friends and Family.   People value friendship and family ties. Friends and family help define who we are, warm us with affection, and make the world a less lonely place. The importance of these needs is demonstrated by the intense feelings of homesickness many people develop when they move away from the support of family and friends. They may feel isolated, diminished, or uprooted, and may even develop physical illnesses.

In an era that advocates strengthening "family values," it is not surprising that we heard many speeches like Marie D'Aniello's tribute to her family, seen at the end of Chapter 2. Other speakers praised the importance of both traditional and nontraditional families. The importance of family can express itself in traditions and rituals. Our families can give us a sense of roots, of cultural and personal history. It can be comforting to know that some things don't change. In many families, Thanksgiving dinner is always turkey and dressing, cranberries, and pumpkin pie. Such holiday rituals convey the meaning of family.

The need for friendship may explain our desire to join with others and take pride in our group memberships. We like being with those who share similar backgrounds and values. Friendship is probably the most prevalent appeal in contemporary American advertising. How many ads have you seen that suggest that if you don't use the "right" deodorant, drink the "right" beverages, or drive the "right" car, you risk losing friends?

Self-Actualization.   One of the most powerful and persistent motive appeals in the student speeches we heard was the need for self-actualization. When we self-actualize, we realize our potential for growth and success, and we strive to become the better selves we can imagine. Perhaps it is not surprising to find that self-actualization has so high a priority among the needs of college students. As young adults, they stand on the threshold of self-actualization. As college students, they are part of a privileged population, the most able and promising. They are prime candidates for self-actualization.

For this reason, self-actualization seems to tie together a number of other personal needs, including the needs for self-esteem, independence, success, and recognition.

Self-Esteem.   Healthy self-esteem is a condition for self-actualization. Before we can hope to grow and develop, we must have some degree of confidence in our own abilities. Marie D'Aniello expressed her personal sense of self-esteem as she paid tribute to her father: "Because of him, I take pride in my work and I take pride in myself." As you achieve success in this class and begin to develop more confidence, you may notice an increase in your own self-esteem. This increased sense of self-esteem can become a key to greater self-actualization, both in the class and outside the classroom. This is why the public speaking class is valued by so many people. As Professor Rod Hart of the University of Texas has put it, "Communication is the ultimate people-making discipline."[7]

Independence.   While family and friends are vital to us, it is also important for us to learn that we can stand on our own two feet. The quest for independence allows young people to develop into fully functioning adults, making decisions on their own and taking responsibility for their own lives. For this reason, college audiences may be especially responsive to the need for freedom from arbitrary constraints on their ideas, actions, or lifestyles. One speech in our sample attacked censorship of books in the public schools precisely on the grounds that it places restrictions on self-actualization by young people, who must be free to explore ideas. Also, speeches that show listeners how to "do it yourself" often appeal to this need for independence.

Success.   The need for success or achievement is one of the most thoroughly studied human motives.[8] A sense of success provides assurance that self-actualization is going forward. There are numerous outstanding speeches in our sample on the theme of success. Ashlie McMillan inspired her Vanderbilt classmates by her tribute to her cousin Tina, who is a dwarf. Ashlie painted a picture of her cousin as a very short person with a very large personality. Tina, she said, is fiercely independent and has received undergraduate and graduate degrees from Texas Christian University. Now she is planning marriage and entrance into the University of Texas law school. And if Tina, against all odds, can self-actualize, so could members of Ashlie's audience. Ceremonial speeches often establish models for emulation as they praise achievers in public life. They challenge audiences to set high goals for themselves, to work hard to achieve them, and to enjoy success as well.

To learn more about the need for success, visit the Achievement Resource Center on the Internet (http:www.cyber-nation.com/victory/achievement/achievement_menu.html). Speeches that show how to be successful or how to master a difficult skill will have an attentive audience.

Recognition.   If we harbor any doubts about our quest for self-actualization, recognition from others can reassure us. The need for recognition may lead us to place great value on trophies or awards as tangible symbols of success. Speakers who recognize the accomplishments of listeners and the institutions or groups they represent may also satisfy this need. This can be especially helpful when speakers are not well known or are uncertain of acceptance.

Self-actualization is so complex that it touches other needs as well. There is, for example, an important "play instinct" in humans that may express itself in the needs for *enjoyment* and *variety*. All work and no play will make Jill about as dull as Jack, and will retard the full expression of our humanity. College students, inundated as they are with tests and papers and speeches to prepare, not to mention full- or part-time jobs, are not exempt from this need. If you can show listeners how to put some fun into their lives, you can be sure of their attention.

As for variety, too much of anything—even a good thing—can be dull. The need for variety can include a longing for adventure, a desire to do something different or exciting, or a yen to travel to exotic places. Offer listeners something different, a topic out of the ordinary, or a different point of view on a familiar subject, and you will be rewarded with their attention.

Fairness.   Fairness is one of the universal values (this is discussed in Chapter 1) that bridge the cultural differences among us. Fairness is also such a constant theme in student speeches that it may qualify as a motive. Our desire for fairness epitomizes the Golden Rule, "Do unto others as you would have them do unto you." It envisions a perfect moral balance in the world, in which we deserve what happens to us, both good and bad. For college audiences, especially those who are more idealistic, fairness is a compelling theme in speeches. Thus our students argued that homosexuals are treated unfairly in our society, that the disabled don't get a fair break, and that affirmative action assures (or denies) fairness. They expressed outrage over human rights abuses in China, over sexism in America, and over the past and present treatment of Native Americans. They pleaded for justice, the legal form of fairness, in our courts. The conclusion one draws from these speeches is that fairness is a dream that is sometimes denied, abused, and repudiated in our society. The students sought ways, especially in their persuasive speeches, to restore it. The quest for fairness might enter into your speeches as well.

Figure 4.1 contains capsule summaries of these seven motives that appear frequently in classroom speeches.

Attitude Systems

As you plan and prepare presentations, you should also consider the attitude systems of your listeners. A person's attitude system is composed of attitudes, beliefs, and values. **Attitudes** refer to our feelings—whether we like or dislike, approve or disapprove of people, events, or ideas—and how we are inclined to act towards them.[9] **Beliefs** are more conceptual, what we know or think we know about subjects. Our more important attitudes and beliefs are anchored by our **values**, how we think we should behave or what we regard as an ideal state of being.[10] Our values influence the attitudes we form and the beliefs we develop. If you can point out that listeners' attitudes and beliefs are *inconsistent* with their values, you may be able to lead them to change.

Information about your audience's attitudes, beliefs, and values is important in planning your speech. If your listeners' beliefs are based on faulty knowledge or incomplete information, you may be able to provide new infor-

FIGURE 4.1

Seven Motives Often Used in Classroom Speeches

Understanding:	satisfying your curiosity, understanding yourself, determining the causes of events, knowing why people act as they do, exploring the unusual.
Control:	having a hand in your own destiny, developing plans of action, fixing things, influencing others, resisting control and manipulation.
Health and Safety:	feeling secure in your surroundings, protected from crime, pollution, accidents, and natural disasters; doing things and avoiding dangers that promote or menace physical well-being.
Nurturance and Altruism:	caring for others, especially marginalized people and children, and promoting their well-being.
Friends and Family:	establishing warm relations with others, being a member of a group or organization, feeling secure and accepted within your family, having someone to love and be loved by.
Self-Actualization:	seeking to fulfill your potential for growth, satisfying your needs for self-esteem, independence, success, and recognition.
Fairness:	seeking to establish and restore moral balance in the world so that people receive the treatment they deserve.

mation or improve their understanding. Being aware of audience attitudes can suggest strategies that you might use to get a fair hearing. For example, suppose you are preparing a speech favoring capital punishment, and you know that most members of your audience strongly oppose this policy. An audience that disagrees with you may distort your message, discredit you, or even refuse to listen. Given these conditions, how can you reach your listeners? One way of dealing with a negative audience includes establishing identification between you and your audience, avoiding emotional appeals, limiting what you hope to accomplish, and acknowledging that others may disagree with you.[11] You should consider such strategies as you plan your presentation. These and other techniques for handling reluctant audiences are discussed in detail in Chapter 13.

How can you find out in advance about your audience's values, beliefs, and attitudes? In the classroom this is not difficult because people reveal this kind of information constantly as they take part in class discussions. Outside the classroom, you might question the person who invites you to speak about those aspects of the audience's attitude system that are related to your topic.

To understand more fully how your audience's attitude system may relate to your presentation, you could conduct a survey to explore what your listeners know about your topic, how they feel about it, and how they might respond to different sources of information. Classroom surveys can yield helpful results if you use the following guidelines to prepare your questionnaire:

- Use simple, concrete, clear language.
- Keep your questions short.
- Avoid words such as *all, always, none,* and *never.*
- Keep your own biases out of the questions.
- Provide room for comments.
- Keep the questionnaire short.

Figure 4.2 (on the following page) shows a sample survey questionnaire on the subject of capital punishment that may be used as a guide to developing a questionnaire on your subject.

Adjusting to Audience Demographics

Audience demographics include the age, gender, education, group affiliations, and sociocultural background of your listeners. If you are not familiar with the group you will be addressing, ask the person who invited you about these factors. Demographic analyses are often used in marketing and political campaigns to identify important attitudes, preferences, or concerns. In the classroom, demographic information can help you estimate interest in your topic and how much your listeners may already know about it. When you combine this information with an understanding of audience dynamics, you can better understand how they feel about your subject and how you can best motivate them.

The insights you can get from classroom demographics and from published public opinion surveys can help you tailor an effective message. The richest source of information on current public opinion is the Internet.

For each question, please circle the number that most clearly represents your position.

1. How interested are you in the topic of capital punishment?

Very Interested			Unconcerned			Not Interested
7	6	5	4	3	2	1

2. How important do you think the issue of capital punishment is?

Very Important			No Opinion			Very Unimportant
7	6	5	4	3	2	1

3. How much do you know about capital punishment?

Very Little			Average Amount			Very Much
7	6	5	4	3	2	1

4. How would you describe your attitude toward capital punishment?

Total Opposition			"On the Fence"			Total Support
7	6	5	4	3	2	1

5. Please place a check beside the sources of information on capital punishment that you would find the most acceptable.

_____ Attorney general's office

_____ FBI

_____ Local police department

_____ Criminal justice department of the university

_____ American Civil Liberties Union

_____ Local religious leaders

_____ Conference of Christians and Jews

_____ NAACP

_____ Other (please specify) _____

Comments:

Figure 4.3 contains a list of public opinion web sites that may be helpful as you plan your speeches. Most of these sites contain complete data from recent surveys on a wide variety of topics. Many of them include searchable archives of previous surveys, which are useful for tracing trends and drawing comparisons across time. Public opinion information is also available in many popular print periodicals: *Harper's* magazine regularly includes "Harper's Index," a compilation of unusual and interesting statistics; *USA*

Common values and inter-
ests can help bring groups
together despite differences
of age, gender, race, or ethnicity.

Today provides tidbits of poll results on a daily basis (these are also available on *USA Today*'s Web site, http://www.usatoday.com/). Each winter the American Council on Education releases the results of a national survey of the attitudes of college freshmen; this is available on the Internet (http://www.gseis.ucla.edu/heri/heri.html). At least once a week the network news shows mention poll results. With a little effort and ingenuity, you can usually find the complete text of the poll, either in hard copy or on the Internet.

FIGURE 4.3

Audience Analysis Web Sites

VALS:	http://future.sri.com/vals/survey.html
Equifax:	http://www.ends.com/low/lifequiz.html
Pew Political Ideology:	http://www.people-press.org/fit.htm
National Opinion Research Center:	http://www.icpsr.umich.edu/gss/about/gss/gssintro.htm
Gallup Organization:	http://www.gallup.com
Maritz Ameripoll:	http://www.maritz.com/
American Demographics:	http://www.demographics.com/
Cyberpages Polls:	http://www.cyberpages.com/poll
University of North Carolina IRSS:	http://www.unc.edu/deps/irss/
Princeton Survey Research Center:	http://www.princeton.edu/~abelson/index.html
Cornell Survey Research Center:	http://www.ciser.cornell.edu/Welcome.html#pubs
Roper Center for Public Opinion Research:	http://www.lib.uconn.edu/RoperCenter
The Polling Report:	http://www.pollingreport.com/

A word of caution is needed when it comes to interpreting demographic data. Most information on audience demographics—as well as on attitudes and values—is gathered through surveys that rely on self-reports. In such surveys people tend to give "socially appropriate" responses to questions. This doesn't necessarily mean that people are lying, just that they sometimes report what they "think they ought to say" or how they "think they ought to feel."

Finally, be aware that the relevance of specific demographic factors will vary from topic to topic. For example, if you were speaking on "Government Services—Get What Your Taxes Pay For," age might be an important consideration, but gender or religious affiliation might be less germane.

Age

Age has been used to predict audience reactions since the time of Aristotle, who suggested that young listeners are pleasure-loving, optimistic, impulsive, trusting, idealistic, and easily persuaded. Older people, he said, are more set in their ways, more skeptical, cynical, and concerned with maintaining a comfortable existence. Those in the prime of life, Aristotle argued, present a balance between youth and age, being confident yet cautious, judging cases by the facts, and taking all things in moderation.[12]

Contemporary communication research supports the relationship between age and persuasibility that Aristotle predicted. Susceptibility to persuasion is at a maximum during childhood and declines as people grow older. Most research also suggests that younger people are more flexible and open to new ideas, whereas older people tend to be more conservative and less receptive to change. Some recent research, however, suggests that older adults may be more willing to change than was previously thought.[13] You can change the minds of older adults, but you'll have to work harder to do it.

Age can be an important factor in the selection of speech topics. For example, an audience consisting mainly of eighteen- and nineteen-year-olds might be interested in a speech on campus social activities. To an older audience, this topic could seem trivial or uninteresting. Age can also be important in terms of the language you use and the people, places, things, or events you refer to in your speeches. For example, an older audience probably read *The Grapes of Wrath*, probably listened to "Strawberry Fields," and probably would ask "What is 'Smashing Pumpkins'?"

What do demographics tell us about the average classroom audience? Perhaps the most striking feature of today's college classrooms is their diversity. According to recent research, the demographics of people born between 1965 and 1985 are as follows: "69 percent Caucasian, 13 percent African American, 13 percent Hispanic, 3 percent Asian American, and 1 percent Native American."[14] If you live in New Mexico, California, Hawaii, New York, or the District of Columbia, there is a greater than 50 percent chance that any two individuals you encounter will differ ethnically or racially.[15]

The average college student is also older than you might expect. In 1994, 31 percent of college students were over thirty, with 21 percent over thirty-five. These figures are expected to hold steady within the foreseeable future.[16] If your classroom is typical, there will probably be more females than males in the class. Over 55 percent of students enrolled in colleges and universities are female, and this percentage is expected to grow in the near future.[17]

A 1998 survey of high school students suggests that over 85 percent of the females polled planned to continue their education beyond high school, compared with only 78 percent of the males.[18]

What else does contemporary research tell us about today's college students? In 1997, first-year students expressed less interest in political affairs than in any of the more than thirty years the Higher Education Research Institute at UCLA has conducted this research.[19] The survey of more than 250,000 students indicated that students also were less likely to participate in community action programs, environmental cleanup activities, or programs designed to help promote racial understanding. A large generational marketing survey conducted by the Yankelovich firm yields some interesting insights into the age group they call "Generation X."[20] To begin with, "X'ers" don't like being pigeonholed or labeled and are really put off by the stereotype of them in the mass media.[21] They resent being talked down to or having anyone try to put something over on them. They are skeptical, especially of politicians and the media.[22] A Nike ad targeted at this group announces, "Don't insult our intelligence. Tell us what it is, tell us what it does, and don't play the national anthem while you do it."[23] They believe there is a good side and bad side to almost everything and are accepting of alternative lifestyles.[24]

Such survey information is interesting, but keep in mind that these conclusions are based on national data. Your own observations can help you confirm or correct this portrait of the contemporary college student insofar as your listeners are concerned.

Gender

In our society, ideas about gender differences are changing rapidly. The changes are especially marked in the areas of "gender-appropriate" roles and interests. During the 1950s, when your authors were in undergraduate school, one of them could not be on the debate team because she was female and this activity was deemed more useful for males, who were more likely to become lawyers or politicians and thus would benefit more from the experience. During that same period, *Life* magazine interviewed five (male) psychiatrists who suggested that women's ambitions were the "root of mental illness in wives, emotional upset in husbands, and homosexuality in boys."[25] As late as 1981, this same publication introduced the first female Supreme Court justice, Sandra Day O'Connor, with the headline, "President Goes A-Courtin' ".[26]

Some of the greatest changes in gender differences have been in education and work. In 1950, only 24 percent of all college degrees went to women; in 1994, women earned 53 percent of all degrees awarded.[27] In 1962, 43 percent of females between the ages of twenty-five and fifty-four were in the labor force; by 1990, this was up to 75 percent. Between 1980 and 1990 the number of female professionals rose 100 percent and the number of female managers just about doubled. These changes in education and work are beginning to show up in changes in women's perceived leadership potential. A recent study reported that, for the first time, women were slightly more likely than men to emerge as leaders in mixed-sex groups.[28] Moreover, these female leaders do not simply take on "masculine" traits, such as dominance and control motives. They represent a blend of gender-related qualities: They are competitive and independent, yet sensitive and supportive. These trends are likely to continue.

As you consider gender, be careful not to fall into the trap of stereotypes. For example, many people still think of automobiles as a traditionally "male domain," yet in 1997 females influenced over 80 percent of car purchases.[29] Moreover, women tend to be more discriminating buyers. A *U.S. News/CNN* poll conducted in 1995 reported that women rated safety features, fuel economy, resale value, *Consumer Reports* ratings, and horsepower as more important factors in their purchasing decisions than did men. In fact, the only factor in the survey that men rated as more important was the color of the car.[30]

Given such rapid changes, is there any way you can use gender as a reliable factor in audience analysis? First, be sure that any differences reported *really make a difference.* Often the communication differences between genders, while statistically significant, can be so small that they have no practical importance.[31] Next, be certain that any assumptions you make are based on the most current data available because the differences are often a matter of "now you see them, now you don't." Differences that seem true even as we write may be outdated by the time you read this text. Finally, be careful to avoid sexism and gender stereotyping. These two topics are covered in detail later in this chapter.

Educational Level

You can better estimate your listeners' knowledge of and interest in a topic from their educational level than from their age or gender. The more educated your audience, the more you can assume they know about general topics and current affairs, and the broader their range of interests is apt to be. Research suggests that better-educated audiences are more interested in social, consumer, political, and environmental issues. They are more curious, and they enjoy learning about new ideas, new things, and new places. If your speech presents a fresh perspective on a problem, they should be avid listeners. Finally, better-educated audiences tend to be more open-minded. They are more accepting of social and technological changes and more supportive of women's rights and alternative lifestyles than less educated listeners.[32]

Educational differences can also affect the strategies you use in a speech. For example, if there are several positions on an issue, you should assume that a better-educated audience will be aware of them. Therefore, you should be especially careful to acknowledge alternative viewpoints and explain why you have selected your position.[33] Although you should always speak from responsible knowledge, knowing that your listeners are highly educated places even more pressure on you to be well prepared. A well-educated audience will require that you supply evidence and examples that can stand up under close scrutiny. If you are not well prepared, such listeners will question your credibility.

Group Affiliations

The groups people belong to reflect their interests, attitudes, and values. Knowing the occupations, political preferences, religious affiliations, and social group memberships of an audience can provide useful information. This knowledge can help you design a speech that better fits the interests and needs of your listeners. It can make your message more relevant and can help promote identification between listeners and your ideas.

Occupational Groups. Knowing your listeners' occupational affiliations, or in the case of your classmates their work aspirations, can provide insight into how much they know about a topic, what type of vocabulary you should use, and which aspects of the topic should be most interesting to them. For example, speeches on tax-saving techniques given to professional writers and to certified public accountants should not have the same focus or use the same language. With the writers you might stress record keeping and business deductions and avoid using technical jargon. With the CPAs you might concentrate on factors that invite audits by the IRS, and you would not have to be so concerned about translating technical terms into lay language. Knowledge of listeners' occupations also suggests the kinds of examples you may wish to provide and the authorities the listeners will find most credible. If many of your classmates are business majors, for instance, they may place more credence in information drawn from the *Wall Street Journal* than in information from *USA Today.* Use this knowledge to guide your selection of topics and choice of examples.

Political Groups. Members of organized political groups tend to be interested in problems of public life. Knowing how interested in politics your listeners are and their political party preferences can be useful in planning and preparing your speech.[34] People with strong political ties usually make their feelings known. Some of your classmates may be members of the Young Democrats or Young Republicans. Your college may conduct mock elections or take straw votes on issues of political interest, reporting the results in the campus newspaper. Be on the alert for such information.

Religious Groups. Knowing the religious affiliations of listeners can provide useful information because religious training often underlies many of our social and cultural attitudes and values. Members of fundamentalist religious groups are likely to have conservative social and political attitudes. Baptists tend to be more conservative than Episcopalians, who in turn are often more conservative than Unitarians. In addition, a denomination may advocate specific beliefs that many of its members accept as a part of their religious heritage.

A word of caution needs to be added here. You can't always assume that because an individual is a member of a particular religious group, he or she will embrace all the teachings of that group. One thing you can count on, however, is that audiences are usually quite sensitive concerning topics related to their religious convictions. As a speaker, you should be aware of this sensitivity and be attuned to the religious makeup of your anticipated audience. Appealing to "Christian" values before an audience that includes members of other religious groups may offend listeners and diminish the effectiveness of your message. The classroom audience of today is likely to be made up of students from different religious backgrounds. Since religious affiliation may be a strong indicator of values, it is wise not to ignore its potential importance.

Social Groups. Membership in social groups can be as important to people as any other kind of affiliation. Typically, we are born into a religious group, raised in a certain political environment, and end up in an occupation as much by chance as by design. But we choose our social groups on the basis of our interests. Photographers join the Film Club, businesspeople become involved with the Chamber of Commerce, environmentalists may be members of the Sierra Club, and feminists may join the National Organization for Women.

Knowing which social groups are represented in your audience and what they stand for is important for effective audience adaptation. The focus of a speech favoring pollution control measures might be different depending on whether the speech is presented to the Chamber of Commerce, or to the Audubon Society. With the Chamber of Commerce, you might stress the importance of a clean environment in inducing businesses to relocate in your community; with the Audubon Society, you might emphasize the effects of pollution on wildlife. People tend to make their important group memberships known to others around them. Be alert to such information from your classmates and consider it in planning and preparing your speeches.

Sociocultural Background

People often are grouped by sociocultural background, a broad category that can include everything from the section of the country in which they live to their racial or ethnic identity. There is a wealth of information available on such groups. The web sites listed at the end of this chapter provide access to a wide array of resources and information relevant to a variety of sociocultural groups. While such material may be fascinating, take the findings with a grain of salt. Remember, it is *your* audience for *your* speech that is important.

People from different sociocultural backgrounds often have different experiences, interests, and ways of looking at things. Consider, for example, the different perspectives that urban and rural audiences may have on gun control. Urban audiences may associate guns with crime and violence in the streets, and rural audiences may associate guns with hunting and recreation. A white, middle-class audience might have difficulty understanding what it means to grow up as a member of a minority. Midwesterners and southerners may have misconceptions about each other.

Since most college classes represent a variety of backgrounds, you must strive to reach the majority without ignoring or offending the minority. With diverse audiences, your appeals and examples should relate to those experiences, feelings, values, and motivations that people hold in common. It also may be helpful to envision smaller audiences within the larger group. You may even want to direct specific remarks to these smaller groups. You might say, for example, "Those of you majoring in the liberal arts will find computer skills just as important in your work as they are for business majors," or "Those of you majoring in business may discover that large corporations are looking for employees with the breadth of perspective that comes from a liberal arts education." Direct references to specific subgroups within the audience can keep your speech from seeming too general.

If your classmates gave introductory speeches or responded to one another in class, you should have a good idea of the diversity of their backgrounds and interests. This specific information will be much more valuable than anything you can learn from reading about college students in magazines or books. *They* are the listeners you will address. The more information you have about them, the better you should be able to adapt your message and the better it should be received.

Meeting the Challenges of Audience Diversity

Some thirty years ago Marshall McLuhan, an English professor at the University of Toronto, suggested that technological changes in the media of communication were turning the world into a "global village."[35] Today we live in the village that McLuhan envisioned.[36] Satellite transmissions bring news into our living rooms as it happens. The Internet provides access to information that was previously available only in the libraries of colleges and universities. Speeches that once were dusty relics in the pages of anthologies come to life on videotape. Computer conferencing makes it possible for executives in Singapore to "meet" with executives in New York without having to travel. National boundaries are dissolving as time and space no longer impede the flow of information and ideas.[37]

As we move into the twenty-first century, we must adapt to our diverse world. Although speaking to a diverse audience is a challenge, it is also an opportunity. Learning to communicate with diverse others can be one of the most rewarding experiences of your public speaking class. To find out more about your own sociocultural background, or about those of others, consult the relevant web sites listed at the end of this chapter. Again, keep in mind that the information you access relates to groups in general and not necessarily to your particular classmates. Try to integrate and reconcile such information with the information you derive about them firsthand.

To make the most of the opportunities of addressing varied audiences, you must be able to avoid some pitfalls. You must understand the power of stereotypes and bias and of the problematic "isms"—ethnocentrism, sexism, and racism. Finally, you should know how to find and build common ground with your listeners.

Stereotypes and Bias

We all use our past experiences to make sense of new information and to guide our interactions with others. To use our past experience efficiently, we react in terms of categories.[38] For example, having heard many stories about poisonous reptiles, we are leery of all snakes. Severe problems can arise, however, when we start categorizing people. The categories can harden into stereotypes. **Stereotypes** are rigid sets of beliefs and expectations about people in a certain group. They reflect our attitudes or biases toward the group.[39] When stereotypes dominate our thinking, we react more to them than to the people within those groups. Wilma Mankiller, who served as principal chief of the Cherokee nation, offers a good idea of the practical problems posed by stereotypes:

> **Sometimes in Oklahoma, it's really discouraging to sit down with a group of people from different backgrounds and cultures and try to work on a common problem, whether it's education or economic development or whatever the problem is, because everybody's sitting around this table, and they're all looking at each other with stereotypes, and they can't get past that. It's like everybody's sitting there and they have some kind of veil over their face, and they look at each other through this veil that makes them see each other through some stereotypical kind of viewpoint. If we're ever gonna collectively begin**

to grapple with the problems that we have collectively, we're gonna have to move back the veil and deal with each other on a more human level.[40]

People often form stereotypes based on easily visible characteristics such as gender, race, or age.[41] Stereotypes also may be related to ethnic identity, religion, occupation, or place of residence. We can form them from direct experiences with a few individuals who we assume are representative of a group. Most stereotypes, however, are learned indirectly from our families and friends, schools and churches, or media exposure. For example, our stereotype of Native Americans may fall into the "Tonto syndrome" often portrayed in Western movies, or our stereotype of southerners may be shaped by TV shows like "Designing Women."[42]

Whatever their origin, stereotypes can have a powerful influence on our thinking. We may judge people on the basis of stereotypes rather than on their merits as individuals. Stereotypes are also persistent: We are reluctant to give them up, especially when they agree with the stereotypes held by our friends and families. When we encounter people who do not fit our stereotypes, we may discount them as "exceptions to the rule." Beyond their obvious unfairness, stereotypes can also lead to disastrous behaviors. In their most extreme form they can justify the genocide that took place in Hitler's Germany or the more recent "ethnic cleansing" in places like Bosnia.

Ethnocentrism, Sexism, and Racism

Ethnocentrism, sexism, and racism represent the most common types of problems that impede effective communication with a diverse audience.

Ethnocentrism.   As we noted in Chapter 1, **ethnocentrism** is the belief that our way of life is the "right" and superior way. Actually, ethnocentrism is not always bad. In its milder form, ethnocentrism expresses itself in patriotism and national pride. It helps people unite and work toward common goals. It encourages immigrants to assimilate into a new national identity that provides common ground for living and getting along with one another.

But ethnocentrism has a darker side. Charles de Gaulle, who led the French people during the mid-twentieth century, once noted: "Patriotism is when love of your own people comes first; nationalism, when hate for people other than your own comes first."[43] When ethnocentrism goes beyond pride in one's own group and comes to include the rejection or derogation of others, it becomes a real problem in human relations and a barrier to cross-cultural communication.

The first step in controlling ethnocentrism is to recognize any tendencies you may have to undervalue other cultures.[44] *We must learn to respect the humanity in all people, and to recognize that this humanity transcends race and culture.* As part of this respect, you should avoid using offensive language that puts others down on the basis of their race or group affiliation.

Sexism.   **Sexism** occurs when we allow gender stereotypes to control our interactions with members of the opposite sex. **Gender stereotyping** involves making broad generalizations about men or women based on outmoded assumptions, such as "men don't know how to take care of children" or "women don't understand business." Such beliefs transcend national boundaries and have been reported in over thirty countries in North and South America, Europe, Africa, Asia, and Australia.[45] Gender stereotyping is especially problematic when it implies that the differences between men and women justify discrimination. As you plan and prepare your message, try to be aware of any gender stereotypes you might have that could interfere with effective communication. Be careful not to portray gender roles in ways suggesting superiority or inferiority. For instance, when you use examples or stories to illustrate a point, don't make all your authority figures male.

Gender stereotyping often reveals itself in the use of sexist language. As you plan your speeches, you must think about the language you use so that you can avoid such problems. **Sexist language** involves making gender references in situations where the gender is unknown or irrelevant. It may involve the generic use of masculine nouns or pronouns, such as referring to "man's advances in science" or using *he* when the intended reference is to both sexes. You can avoid this problem simply by saying "she or he" or by using the plural "they." Some people have criticized this practice, saying that it makes the wording of messages awkward. They scoff at the seriousness of the problem. In her book on gender and communication, Julia Wood demonstrated how important such language practices can be through the experience of a skeptical male student who suddenly found the situation reversed:

> **For a long time I thought all this stuff about generic *he* was a bunch of junk. I mean it seemed really clear to me that a word like *mankind* obviously includes women or that *chairman* can refer to a girl or a guy who chairs something. I thought it was pretty stupid to hassle about this. Then last semester, I had a woman teacher who taught the whole class using *she* or *her* or *woman* whenever she was referring to people as well as when she meant just women. I realized how confusing it is. I had to figure out each time whether she meant women only or women and men. And when she meant women to be general, I guess you'd say generic for all people, it still made me feel left out. A lot of the guys in the class got pretty hostile about what she was doing, but I kind of think it was a good way to make the point.[46]**

Racism.   Just as gender stereotyping and sexist language can block communication, so can racism. Although blatant racism and discrimination are no longer socially acceptable in most circles, a subtle form of such prejudice can still infect our thinking. While we may pay lip service to the principles of racial equality, we may still engage in **symbolic racism**, which is expressed subtly or covertly.[47] For example, if we say, "In our [white] neighborhood we believe in family values," the unspoken message may be, "You don't, and therefore we are superior." Or we might say, "We believe in hard work and earning our way," when we really mean, "Why don't you [blacks] get off welfare!" Thus we may excuse the vestiges of racial stereotypes by appeals to values like family stability or the Protestant work ethic. In such cases our underlying message may be, we honor such values and you don't.

It may be helpful to view the impact that symbolic racism can have from the perspective of someone on the receiving end. Television commentator Bryant Gumbel commented on how it feels:

> **It is very hard for any white person to appreciate the depth of what it means to be black in America. . . . Racism isn't only being called a nigger and spit on. It's being flipped the bird when you're driving, or walking into a store and being asked to check your bag, or being ignored at the checkout counter, or entering a fine restaurant and being stared at.**[48]

As you take the factor of race into consideration in your audience analysis, examine your thinking for biases and stereotypes that you may rationalize as value or lifestyle differences. Be sensitive about the language you use. When you are referring to a different racial or ethnic group, use the terms that *members of that group* prefer. Stay away from examples that cast members of a particular ethnic group in stereotypical roles that imply inferiority. And of course, avoid racist humor.

One language problem that relates to all three of these negative "isms" is **marking**, adding an irrelevant reference to gender, ethnicity, race, or sexual preference when none is needed. For example, if you refer to "Thompson, the African American engineer," you may be trivializing her contribution by drawing attention to her race when it is irrelevant. Some audience members may interpret your remarks as suggesting that "Thompson is a pretty good engineer *for a person of color,*" whether you intend that or not. The following excerpt from a speech by Martina Navratilova, who was the world's top-rated female tennis player for seven years, shows how marking affects people:

> **Labels, labels, labels—now, I don't know about you, but I hate labels. Martina Navratilova, the lesbian tennis player. They don't say Joe Montana, the heterosexual football player. One's sexuality should not be an issue. . . . I did not spend over 30 years of my life working my butt off trying to become the very best tennis player that I can be, to then be called Martina, the lesbian tennis player. Labels are for filing. Labels are for bookkeeping. Labels are for clothing. Labels are not for people.**[49]

Finding Common Ground

A recent study sponsored by the National Conference of Christians and Jews demonstrated that stereotypes and prejudice are present in all groups in our culture. The survey revealed that people of color see whites as "bigoted, bossy, and unwilling to share power."[50] Although each of the minority groups surveyed also demonstrated negative stereotypes of and feelings toward other people of color, they were united by a sense of being victims of discrimination. Some 80 percent of African Americans, 60 percent of Latino Americans, and 57 percent of Asian Americans are convinced that their opportunities in work, housing, and education are not equal to those enjoyed by whites. On the other hand, over 50 percent of all whites believe that people of color enjoy equal opportunities. The survey concluded that "most whites simply do not acknowledge the tangible effects that discrimination has on the daily lives of minorities."

Lest you think the situation is hopeless, we should also point out that there were some positive results in this research. More than 80 percent of all groups polled expressed admiration of Asian Americans for the value they

Avoiding Racist and Sexist Language

speaker's notes

1 Do not use slang terms to refer to racial, ethnic, religious, or gender groups.

2 Avoid using the generic *he* and gender-specific titles such as chair*man*.

3 Avoid "markers" that introduce irrelevant references to race, gender, or ethnicity.

4 Avoid stereotypic references that imply inferiority or superiority.

5 Do not use sexist, racist, ethnic, or religious humor.

presumably place on intellectual and professional achievement and for having strong family ties and respecting their elders. Similarly large majorities felt that Latino Americans take pride in their culture, work hard to attain a better life, and have deep religious and family ties. Equally sizable majorities agreed that African Americans work hard when given a chance, believe strongly in American ideals and the American Dream, are deeply religious, and have made valuable contributions to American society. Over 90 percent of all groups surveyed also agreed that learning to understand and appreciate the lifestyles, tastes, and contributions of other groups was either "very important" or "important." *The most heartening finding of the study was the indication that nine out of ten Americans from all groups would be willing to work with one another to try to solve the most pressing problems in their neighborhoods and communities.* They expressed a willingness to work together to help protect their children from gangs and violence, to help improve schools, including teaching understanding and respect for the cultural heritage of all groups, and to look for ways to ease racial, religious, and ethnic tensions.

In Chapter 1 we noted that the Institute for Global Ethics identified eight **universal human values** that transcend cultural differences: love, truthfulness, fairness, freedom, unity, tolerance, responsibility, and respect for life.[51] Contemporary social scientific research has also demonstrated the existence of transcendent social values. Shalom Schwartz and his associates at the Hebrew University of Jerusalem conducted a study of values in twenty different countries. They identified ten universal values: achievement, tradition, power, enjoyment, self-direction, security, universalism, benevolence, conformity, and stimulation.[52] Figure 4.4 (on the following page) lists these universal values and shows how they appear to come together.

If you can appeal to these common values in your speeches to a diverse audience, you can often unite your listeners behind your ideas or suggestions.

Adjusting to the Communication Situation

Finally, we come to the setting for your speech. You must consider the time, place, occasion, size of the audience, and overall context of your speech in making your final adaptations.

FIGURE 4.4
Universal Values

Power	Social power, authority, recognition from others, wealth
Achievement	Success, ambition, influence
Tradition	Acceptance of one's fate, devoutness, humility, respect for cultural heritage
Enjoyment	Pleasure
Self-Direction	Freedom, independence, choice of own goals, self-respect, curiosity, creativity
Security	National security, social order, family security, sense of belonging, personal health and cleanliness, reciprocity in personal relationships
Unity	Unity with nature, protecting the environment, inner harmony, social justice, equality, tolerance, a world at peace
Benevolence	Honesty, helpfulness, forgiveness, loyalty, responsibility, friendship, love, spiritual life, meaning in life
Conformity	Politeness, obedience, self-discipline, honoring parents and elders
Stimulation	Variety, excitement, daring

Time

The time of day, day of the week, time of the year, and amount of time allotted for speaking must be taken into account.[53] If you are speaking early in the morning, you may need to be more forceful to awaken your listeners. The vigor of your voice must assert the importance of your message. Since we tend to grow drowsy after we eat, after-dinner speeches (discussed in detail in Chapter 15) need lively examples and humor. Speeches given in the evening also present a problem. Most listeners will have completed a day's work and will have left the comforts of home to hear you. You must justify their attendance with good ideas that are well presented.

speaker's notes

Checklist for Analyzing the Communication Situation

____ 1 Will the time or timing of my speech present any challenges?

____ 2 Will room arrangements be adequate? Will I have the equipment I need for presentation aids?

____ 3 What does the audience expect on this occasion?

____ 4 Is there any late-breaking news on my topic?

____ 5 Will I possibly have to adjust to previous speakers?

____ 6 How large will the audience be?

If your speech is scheduled for a Monday, when people have not yet adjusted to the weekend's being over, or a Friday, when they are thinking of the weekend ahead, you need interesting material to hold their attention. Similarly, gloomy winter days or balmy spring weather can put people in different frames of mind, and their moods can color how they receive your speech.[54] Your materials and presentation style will have to be bright and engaging to overcome the blahs or forestall daydreaming.

The amount of time allotted for your presentation is also critical. *A short speech does not necessarily mean shorter preparation time.* Short speeches require you to focus your topic so that it can be handled in the time allotted. You must limit the number of main points and use supporting materials selectively. Choose the most relevant and impressive facts, statistics, and testimony, the most striking examples and stories. Plan your speech so that you begin with a burst and end with a bang.

Place

The place where you will be speaking should also be considered in your planning. When speaking outside, you may have to cope with unpredictable distractions. When speaking inside, you need information concerning the size and layout of the room and whether a lectern or electronic equipment you may need is available.

Even in the classroom, speakers must learn to cope with distractions—noises may filter in from outside or people in the hall may be raucous and loud. How can you handle such problems? If the noise is temporary, you should pause and wait until it stops, then repeat your last words and go on with your message. If the noise is constant, you may have to speak louder in

Elie Wiesel, recipient of the 1986 Nobel Peace Prize, had to overcome many distractions when speaking at this Holocaust memorial service. A compelling message and a forceful presentation can help speakers cope with problems of traffic noise and inclement weather.

order to be heard. You may even have to pause and close a window or door. The important thing is to take such problems in stride and not let them distract you or your audience from your message.

Occasion

As you plan your message, you need to take into account *why* people have gathered to listen. When an audience is required to attend a presentation, such as a mandatory employee meeting, you may have to work hard to arouse interest and sustain attention. When audience members voluntarily attend a presentation, they usually are more motivated to listen. But you need to know why they are there and what they expect from your speech. When a speaker does not offer the kind of message listeners expect, they may be annoyed. For example, if they are expecting an informative presentation on investment strategies and instead get a sales pitch for a mutual fund, they may feel exploited. This could result in more irritation than persuasion.

Size of Audience

The size of your audience can affect how you speak. A small audience provides feedback and an opportunity for interaction. Generally, a small audience invites a more casual presentation. You could easily overwhelm a small audience with a formal oratorical style, too loud a voice, or exaggerated gestures.

On the other hand, large audiences offer less feedback. Because you cannot make or sustain eye contact with everyone, you should choose representative listeners in various sections of the audience and change your visual focus from time to time. Establishing eye contact with listeners in all sections of the room helps more people feel included. With large audiences you also should speak more deliberately and distinctly. Your gestures should be more emphatic so that everyone can see them, and any visual aids used must be large enough for those in the back of the audience to see without strain.

Context

Anything that happens near the time of your presentation becomes part of the context of your speech. Both recent speeches and recent events can influence how the audience responds to you.

The Context of Recent Speeches.   Any speeches presented immediately before yours create an atmosphere in which you must work. This atmosphere has a **preliminary tuning effect** on listeners, preparing them to respond in certain ways to you and your message.[55] At political rallies, patriotic music and introductions prepare the audience for the appearance of the featured speaker. At concerts, warm-up groups put listeners in the mood for the star.

Preliminary tuning may also affect classroom presentations. Earlier speeches may affect the mood of the audience. If the speech right before yours aroused strong emotions, you may need to ease the tension in the introduction to your speech. You can do this by acknowledging the listeners' feelings and using them as a springboard into your own speech:

> **Obviously, many of us feel very strongly about the legalization of same-sex marriages. What I'm going to talk about is also very important—but it is something I think we can all agree on—the challenge of finding a way to stop children from killing other children in our community.**

Another technique might be to begin with a story that involves listeners and refocuses their attention. At times humor can help relieve tension, but people who are upset may be in no mood for laughter. Your decision on whether to use humor must be based on your reading of the situation: the mood of the listeners, the subject under discussion, and your own ability to use the technique effectively.

In addition to dealing with the mood created by earlier speeches, you may also have to adapt to their content. Suppose you have spent the past week preparing a speech on the *importance* of extending endangered species legislation. Then the speaker before you makes a convincing presentation on the *problems* of extending endangered species legislation. What can you do? Try to turn this to your advantage. Point out that the earlier speech established the importance of the topic but that—as good as that effort was—it did not give the total picture: "Now you will hear the *other* side of the story."

The Context of Recent Events. When listeners enter the room the day of your speech, they bring with them information about recent events. They will use this knowledge to evaluate what you say. If you are not up on the latest news on your topic, your credibility can suffer. A student in one of our classes once presented an interesting and well-documented speech comparing public housing in Germany with that in the United States. Unfortunately, she was unaware of a local scandal involving public housing. For three days before her presentation, the story had made the front page of the local paper and had been the lead story in area newscasts. Everyone expected her to mention it. Her failure to discuss this important local problem weakened her credibility.

At times the context of events to which you must adjust your speech may be totally unexpected. When that happens, you must make on-the-spot adjustments so that things work in your favor. During a graduation ceremony at Loyola Marymount University, the school's president fell off the platform immediately before the commencement address. While the only thing injured was his dignity, the fall certainly distracted the audience. The speaker, Peter Ueberroth, organizer of the 1984 Los Angeles summer Olympic Games, recaptured their attention and brought down the house by awarding the president a 4.5 in gymnastics.[56]

Figure 4.5 (on the following page) provides an Audience Analysis Worksheet that will help you consider all the factors we have discussed in this chapter as you plan for the audience and situation of your speech.

FIGURE 4.5

Audience Analysis Worksheet

	Factor Description	Adaptations Needed
	Topic: _____	
	Audience: _____	

Audience Dynamics

Factor Description	Adaptations Needed
Audience Attitude: _____	_____
Relevant Values: _____	_____
Motivational Appeals: _____	_____

Audience Demographics

Factor Description	Adaptations Needed
Age: _____	_____
Gender: _____	_____
Education: _____	_____
Group Affiliations: _____	_____
Sociocultural Background: _____	_____
Interest in Topic: _____	_____
Knowledge of Topic: _____	_____

Speaking Situation

Factor Description	Adaptations Needed
Time: _____	_____
Place: _____	_____
Occasion: _____	_____
Audience Size: _____	_____
Context: _____	_____

In Summary

Both the audience you anticipate and the setting of your speech are critical to your planning. Successful audience adaptation requires that you understand *audience dynamics*, have relevant information concerning audience demographics, be sensitive to the challenges of audience diversity, and be able to adjust to situational factors.

Adapting to Audience Dynamics. *Motivation* explains why people behave as they do. People will listen, learn, and retain your message only if you can relate it to their needs, wants, or wishes. Some motives you may call on include understanding, control, health and safety, nurturance and altruism, friends and family, self-actualization, and the desire for fairness. Your audience's *attitudes*, *beliefs*, and *values* will also affect the way they receive and interpret your message. If your listeners are initially negative toward your topic, you will have to adjust your presentation to receive a fair hearing.

Adjusting to Audience Demographics.   *Audience demographics* include information about more specific characteristics of your listeners, such as their age, gender, educational level, group membership, and sociocultural makeup (race, social class, etc.). The more you know about such factors, the better you can tailor your speech so that it serves your listeners' interests and needs.

Meeting the Challenges of Audience Diversity.   Today we live in a global village composed of many diverse groups. Learning to understand and adapt to diversity will help you prepare more effective messages. Examine your thinking to identify any *stereotypes* that might categorize people inflexibly and attribute positive or negative traits to them. Be on guard against *ethnocentrism*, *sexism*, and *racism* as you plan and prepare your presentations. When speaking to a diverse audience, search for common ground based on *universal human values*.

Adjusting to the Communication Situation.   You must be flexible enough to adjust to particular features of the speaking situation. The time at which you speak, the place of your speech, the constraints of the occasion, and the size of your audience can all pose challenges. In addition, you will be speaking in a context of other speeches and recent events, to which you must adjust as you make your presentation.

Terms to Know

audience dynamics
motivation
attitudes
beliefs
values
audience demographics
stereotypes
ethnocentrism

sexism
gender stereotyping
sexist language
symbolic racism
marking
universal human values
preliminary tuning effect

Notes

1. Barbara Engler, *Personality Theories: An Introduction,* 4th ed. (Boston: Houghton Mifflin, 1995), pp. 273–280, 340–363; and Thane S. Pittman, "Motivation," in *The Handbook of Social Psychology*, 4th ed., ed. Daniel T. Gilbert, Susan T. Fiske, and Gardener Lindzey (Boston: McGraw-Hill, 1998), vol. 1, pp. 549–590.

2. Henry A. Murray, *Explorations in Personality* (New York: Oxford University Press, 1938). Interest in Murray's research continues, and Radcliffe College maintains a Web site for the Murray Research Institute at http://www.radcliffe.edu/.

3. Abraham H. Maslow, *Motivation and Personality*, 2nd ed. (New York: Harper & Row, 1970).

4. S. Solomon, J. Greenberg, and T. Pyszczynski, "A Terror Management Theory of Social Behavior: The Psychological Functions of Self-esteem and Cultural World-views," in *Advances in Experimental Social Psychology*, vol. 24, ed. M. Zanna (New York: Academic Press, 1991).

5. Pittman, pp. 550–577.

6. Richard E. Petty and Duane T. Wegener, "Attitude Change: Multiple Roles for Persuasion Variables," in *Handbook of Social Psychology*, vol. 1, pp. 353–354.

7. Roderick P. Hart, "Why Communication? Why Education? Toward a Politics of Teaching," *Communication Education* 42 (1993): 101.

8. The study of achievement motivation began with the work of the Murray group, op. cit., and was extended by D. C. McClelland, *Human Motivation* (Glenview, Ill.: Scott, Foresman, 1985). Research in this area continues with the investigation of such elements as the influences of situational factors on achievement motivation and the various dimensions of this factor. Minette A. Bumpus, Sharon Olbeter, and Saundra H. Glover, "Influences of Situational Characteristics on Intrinsic Motivation," *Journal of Psychology,* July 1998, 451–453, online, e-library (www.elibrary.com), downloaded 7 August 1998; and Edward A. Ward, "Multidimensionality of Achievement Motivation Among Employed Adults," *Journal of Social Psychology,* August 1997, 542–544, online, e-library (www.elibrary.com) downloaded 7 August 1998.

9. Alice A. Eagly and Shelly Chaiken, "Attitude Structure and Function," in *Handbook of Social Psychology*, vol. 1, pp. 323–390; and James M. Olson and Mark P. Zanna, "Attitudes and Attitude Change," *Annual Review of Psychology* 44 (1993): 117–154.

10. Rushworth M. Kidder, *Shared Values for a Troubled World* (San Francisco: Jossey-Bass, 1994); Milton Rokeach, *Beliefs, Attitudes and Values: A Theory of Organization and Change* (San Francisco: Jossey-Bass, 1970) and *The Nature of Human Values* (New York: Free Press, 1973); Shalom H. Schwartz and Wolfgang Bilsky, "Toward a Theory of the Universal Content and Structure of Values: Extensions and Cross-Cultural Replications," *Journal of Personality and Social Psychology* 58 (1990): 878–891; and Shalom H. Schwartz, Sonia Roccas, and Lilach Sagiv, "Universals in the Content and Structure of Values: Theoretical Advances and Empirical Tests in Twenty Countries," *Advances in Experimental Social Psychology* 25 (1992): 1–65.

11. Herbert W. Simons, *Persuasion: Understanding, Practice, and Analysis,* 2nd ed. (Reading, Mass.: Addison-Wesley, 1986), pp. 121–139.

12. *The Rhetoric of Aristotle,* trans. George Kennedy (New York: Oxford University Press, 1992), pp. 163–169 (Book 2, Chs. 11-14).

13. S. J. Ceci and M. Bruck, "Suggestibility of the Child Witness: A Historical Review and Synthesis," *Psychological Bulletin* 113 (1993): 403–439; J. A. Krosnick and D. F. Alwin, "Aging and Susceptibility to Attitude Change," *Journal of Personality and Social Psychology* 57 (1989): 416–425; Petty and Wegener, "Attitude Change," p. 358; Milton Rokeach, *The Open and Closed Mind* (New York: Basic Books, 1960); and T. R. Tyler and R. A. Schuller, "Aging and Attitude Change," *Journal of Personality and Social Psychology* 61 (1991): 689–697.

14. J. Walker Smith and Ann Clurman, *Rocking the Ages: The Yankelovich Report on Generational Marketing* (New York: HarperCollins, 1997), p. 89.

15. "Measuring Diversity: How Does Your State Rate?" *National Education Association Today,* September 1992, p. 8.

16. "Total Fall Enrollment in Institutions of Higher Education, by Attendance Status, Sex, and Age: Fall 1970 to Fall 2006," *The Digest of Education Statistics 1996/Table 171,* http://nces.ed.gov/pubs/d96/D96T171.html, undated posting, downloaded 10 August 1998.
17. Ibid.
18. Horatio Alger Association, "State of Our Nation's Youth: 1998–1999," http://www.horatioalger.com/pubmat/glance.htm, undated posting, downloaded 11 August 1998.
19. "Academic and Political Engagement Among Nation's College Freshmen Is at All-time Low, UCLA Study Finds," 1997 CIRP Press Release, online, http://www.gseis.ucla.edu/heri/press97.html, posted January 1998, downloaded 4 February 1998.
20. Smith and Clurman.
21. Smith and Clurman, p. 90; and Susan Nix, "Students Say Gen-X Image Stereotypical," *Arkansas Traveler via U-Wire,* 17 February 1998, downloaded 18 July 1998 from e-library, http://www.elibrary.com.
22. Northwestern Mutual Life, "Generation 2001 Survey Results—Executive Summary," http://www.northwesternmutual.com/2001/summary-main.html, undated posting, downloaded 11 June 1998.
23. Smith and Clurman, p. 90.
24. Smith and Clurman, p. 88.
25. Cited in Allison Adato and Melissa G. Stanton, "If Women Ran America," *Life,* June 1992, p. 40.
26. James R. Gaines, "A Note from the Editor," *Life,* June 1992, p. 6.
27. "Total Fall Enrollment"; and Lisa DeMona and Constance Herndon, eds. *The 1995 Information Please Women's Sourcebook* (Boston: Houghton Mifflin, 1994).
28. Russell L. Kent and Sherry E. Moss, "Effects of Sex and Gender Role on Leader Emergence," *Academy of Management Journal,* October 1994, pp. 1335–1346.
29. Hester Lacy, "Girls Behaving Affluently . . ." *Independent on Sunday,* 23 March 1997, pp. 1, 2, online, e-library, http://www.elibrary.com, accessed 18 August 1998.
30. "New Wheels," *U.S. News & World Report,* 5 June 1995, p. 70.
31. Daniel J. Canary and Kimberley S. Hause, "Is There Any Reason to Research Sex Differences in Communication?" *Communication Quarterly* 41 (1993): 129–144.
32. James Atlas, "Beyond Demographics," *Atlantic Monthly,* October 1984, pp. 49–58; Arnold Mitchell, *The Nine American Lifestyles: Who We Are and Where We're Going* (New York: Macmillan, 1983); Rockeach, *Open and Closed Mind;* and P. Schonback, *Education and Intergroup Attitudes* (London: Academic Press, 1981).
33. William McGuire, "Attitudes and Attitude Change," in *Handbook of Social Psychology,* ed. Gardner Lindzey and Elliot Aronson (New York: Random House, 1985), vol. 2, pp. 271–272.
34. For a detailed analysis of this topic, see Donald R. Kinder and David O. Sears, "Public Opinion and Political Action," in *Handbook of Social Psychology*, vol. 2, pp. 659–741.
35. Marshall McLuhan, *Understanding Media: The Extensions of Man* (New York: McGraw-Hill, 1964).
36. Lewis Lapham, "Prime-Time McLuhan," *Saturday Night,* September 1994, pp. 51–54.
37. "Mass Communication: Mass Culture, Global Culture," *The New Grolier Multimedia Encyclopedia,* CD-ROM (Novato, Calif.: Software Toolworks, 1993).
38. Sharon S. Brehm and Saul M. Kassin, *Social Psychology,* 3rd ed. (Boston: Houghton Mifflin, 1996), pp. 120–161; Susan T. Fiske, "Stereotyping, Prejudice, and Discrimination," in *Handbook of Social Psychology*, vol. 2, pp.

357–414; and Annie Murphy Paul, "Where Bias Begins: The Truth About Stereotypes," *Psychology Today,* May/June 1998, pp. 52–55, 82.

39. R. C. Gardner, "Stereotypes as Consensual Beliefs," in Mark P. Zanna and James M. Olson, *The Psychology of Prejudice: The Ontario Symposium* (Hillsdale, N.J.: Erlbaum, 1994), vol. 7, pp. 1–32.

40. Wilma Mankiller, "Rebuilding the Cherokee Nation," presented at Sweet Briar College, 2 April 1993; retrieved 18 September 1998 from the World Wide Web: http://gos.sbc.edu/index.html. Reprinted by permission of the author.

41. Susan T. Fiske, "Social Cognition and Social Perception," *Annual Review of Psychology* 44 (1993): 155–194.

42. Leah Eskin, "The Tonto Syndrome," *Scholastic Update,* 26 May 1989, pp. 21–22.

43. Cited in *The Merriam-Webster Dictionary of Quotations* (Springfield, Mass.: Merriam-Webster Inc., 1992), p. 309.

44. It may also be helpful to take a look at the culture of the United States from an outsider's perspective. In a book entitled *USA Business,* available online through the e-library (www.elibrary.com), the others define the cultural norms while advising foreigners who plan to do business in the United States.

45. Brehm and Kassin, p. 164.

46. Julia T. Wood, *Gendered Lives: Communication, Gender, and Culture* (Belmont, Calif.: Wadsworth, 1994), p. 126.

47. Fiske.

48. G. Plaskin, "Bryant Gumbel," *Us,* 5 September 1988, pp. 29–35.

49. From a speech presented 4 April 1993, reprinted in DiMona and Herndon, pp. 344–345.

50. The data in this section come from The National Conference of Christians and Jews, "Taking America's Pulse: A Summary Report of the National Conference Survey on Inter-Group Relations," undated, available from The National Conference, 71 Fifth Avenue, New York, NY 10003.

51. Kidder, pp. 1–19.

52. Schwartz, Roccas, and Sagiv.

53. James W. Gibson and Michael S. Hanna, *Audience Analysis: A Programmed Approach to Receiver Behavior* (Englewood Cliffs, N.J.: Prentice-Hall, 1976), pp. 25–26.

54. N. Schwarz, H. Bless, and G. Bohner, "Mood and Persuasion: Affective States Influence the Processing of Persuasive Communications," *Advances in Experimental Social Psychology* 24 (1991): 161–199.

55. For more about preliminary tuning, see Theodore Clevenger, Jr., *Audience Analysis* (Indianapolis: Bobbs-Merrill, 1966), pp. 11–12.

56. Reported in *Time,* 17 June 1985, p. 68.

Diversity Resources on the Internet

General

Diversity University: http://www.du.org/places/du/

Diversity: http://www.execpc.com/~dboals/diversit.html or http://latino.sscnet.ucla.edu/diversity1.html

East Palo Alto Community Plugged In: http://www.pluggedin.org

In Motion (communities of color): http://www.cts.com/browse/publish

Atlantic Public Communications Network: http://www.cfn.cs.dal.ca/communications/Apcn/index.html

ITI's Multi-Cultural Network: http://www.fcg.com/iti/iti_cultnet.html

ESL Index: http://199.72.49.25/esl/index.html

Diversity Links: http://latino.sscnet.ucla.edu/diversity/html#AA

American Historical Images on File: http://www.csulb.edu.lgc/libarts/am-indian/nae

American Demographics (check current issue for password): http://www.demographics.com

Human Rights

Global Democracy Network: http://www.gdn.org/

Human Rights Web: http:// http://www.traveller.com/~hrweb/hrweb.hmtl

International Human Rights and Humanitarian Assistance: www.webcom.com/hrin/

U.S. House of Representatives Internet Law Library: Civil Liberties and Civil Rights: http://law.house.gov/93.htm

Religious Diversity

General

Finding God in Cyberspace: http://users.ox.ac.uk/~mikef/durham/gresham.html

Comparative Religion: http://weber.u.washington.edu/~madin

Facets of Religion: http://sunfly.ub.uni-freiburg.de/religion

Ontario Center for Religious Tolerance: http://www.kosone.com/people/ocrt/ocrt_hp.htm

APS Research Guide: http://www.utoronto.ca/stmikes/theobook.htm

Judaism

Anti-Defamation League: http://www.adl.org/

Jewish Family & Life: http://www.jewishfamily.com

B'nai B'rith: http://www. bnaibrith.org/ijm/

Jewish Communication Network: http://www.jcn18.com/index.htm

Shamash Home Page: http://shamash.nysernet.org

Buddhism

Mind Only Cafe: http://www2.uncwil.edu/p&r/wilson

Buddhist Studies WWW Library: http://coombs.anu.edu.au/
WWWVL-Buddhism.html

BuddhaNet: http://www2.hawkesbury.uws.edu.au/ BuddhaNet/budnet.htm

Shin Buddhist: http://www.well.com/users/shinshu/SBRG

Hinduism

Overview of Hinduism: http://www.geocities.com/RodeoDrive/1415/
indesd.html

Global Hindu Electronic Network: http://www.hindunet.org

Hindu Tantrik Home Page: http://www.hubcom.com/tantric

Hinduism Today: http://www.HinduismToday.kauai.hi/ashram/htoday.html

Islam

Caltech Muslim Students Association: http://www.cco.caltech.edu/~calmsa/
calmsa.html

Islam Homepage: http://web.syr.edu/~maalkadh or http://www.utexas.edu.
students/amso/indext.html

Holy Qur'an: http:chestnt.enmu.edu/~stjeanp/quran.index.html

CyberMuslim Information Collective: http://www.uoknor.edu/cybermusli

Christian (general)

Christian Coalition: http://www.cc.org

First Church of Cyberspace: http://www.goodweb.org/

Roman Catholic

Catholic.Net: http://www.catholic.net

Vatican: http://www.vatican.va

Latter Day Saints

LDS Info on the Internet: http://205.162.176.69/links/main.html

Episcopal/Anglican

Anglicans Online: http://infomatch.com/~hailbeck/anglican.html

Episcopal Church Home Page: http://www.ai.mit.edu/people/mib/anglican/
anglican.html

Lutheran

Project Wittenberg: http://www.iclnet.org/pub/resources/text/wittenberg/
wittenberg-home.html

Presbyterian

Presbyterian Church USA: http://www.pcusa.org

Methodist

United Methodist Information: http://www.umc.org

Society of Friends

The Religious Society of Friends Online Resources: http:www.misc.org/geeks/bnorum/quaker

Unitarians

Unitarian Universalist Association: http://www.uua.org

Racial/Ethnic Diversity Web Sites

African American

The Book: http://www.blackhistory.com

AfriNet: http://www.afrinet.net/main

NAACP: http://www.bin.com/assocorg/naacp/naacp.htm

Black Information Network: http://www.bin.com/homepage.htm

U. Penn African Studies WWW Links: http://www.sas.upenn.edu/African_Studies/Home_Page/WWW_Links.html

Afro-American Newspapers: http://www.afroam.org

Universal Black Pages: http://www.gatech.edu/bgsa/blackpages.html

National Civil Rights Museum: http://www.mecca.org/~crights/ncrm.html

Latino/Chicano/Hispanic

Electric Mercado: http://www.mercado.com

Azteca Web Page: http://www.directnet.com/~mario/aztec

Hispanic Heritage: http://www.clark.net/pub/jgbustam/heritage/heritage.html

Puerto Rican Home Page: http://www.iprnet.org./IPR

LatinoWeb: http://www.catalog.com/favision/latnoweb.htm

Mundo Latino: http://www.mundolatino.org./latingle.htm

Chicano-Latino Net: http://latino.sscnet.ucla.edu

LatinoLink: http://www.latinolink.com

LatinoWeb: Education and History: http://www.catalog.com/favision/history.html

Midwest Consortium for Latino Research: http://members.xoom.com/Indig_P_Lit3/mclr/

Native American

Native American Home Pages: http://www.pitt.edu/~lmitten/indians.html

Native American Information: http://www.freenet.ufl.edu/~native

Anasazi: http://www.sscf.uscb.edu/anth/projects/great.kiva

National Tribal Development Association: http://www.ntda.rockyboy.org/

Native American Resources: http://www.uark.edu/depts/comminfo/www/native/html

Index of Native American Resources on the Internet: http://hanksville.phast.umass.edu/misc/NAresources.html

New Mexican Pueblo Cultures: http://LAHS.LosAlamos.K12.nm.us/sunrise/work/piaseck/homepage.html

The Native American Adventure: http://www.indians.org

National Museum of the American Indian: http:www.si.edu/nmai

Asian-American

Asian American Network: http://www.aaa.net

Filipino Express Online: http://www.filipinoexpress.com

Asian Community Network: http://www.igc.apc.org/acon/

China Home Page: http://solar.rtd.utk.edu/~china/china/html

Japan Window: http://jw.nttam.com/HOME/index.html

A Magazine: http://www.amagazine.com

Asian-American Resources: http://www.mit.edu:8001/afs/athena.mit.edu/user/i/r/irie/www/aar.html

Italian-American

http://www-personal.engin.umich.edu/~danregjo/Dream/Italy

European

European Community Home Page: http://s700.uminho.pt/ec.ng.html

French

Les Carnet de Route de FranceWeb: http://francenet.fr/franceweb/FWCarnetRoute.html

Nordic

The Nordic Pages: http://algonet.se/~nikos/nordic.html

Russian

St. Petersburg Web: http://www.spb.su

Polish

Poland Home Page: http://info.fuw.edu.pl/pl/PolandHome.html

Greek

Hellas List Home Page: http://velox.stanford.edu/hellas

Canadian

The Heritage Project: http://heritage.excite.sfu.ca/hpost.html

Middle Eastern

Pakistan Students Association: http://www.rpi.edu/dept/union/paksa

Gender Issues

Women's Resources

The Web for Women (directory of sites for women): http://www.dogpatch.org/women.html

League of Women Voters: http://www.lwv.org/~lwvus/index.html

Women's Web: http://www.womweb.com/index.html

Women@work: http://www.nafe.com/

Women Online Worldwide: http://www.wowwomen.com/TOC.html

Advancing Women: http://www.advancingwomen.com

Women Leaders Online: http://www.wlo.org/

National Organization for Women: http://now.org/now/

Women's Studies Resources: http://www.inform.umd.edu/EdRes/Topic/WomensStudies/

Women Organizing for Change: http://www.wlo.org/woc/

Men's Issues

Women from Mars . . .: http://www.marsvenus.com

Menstuff: http://www.menstuff.org

Men's Issues Page: http://www.vix.com/men/index.html

Men's Action Network: http://www.vix.com/men/orgs/blurb/meanet.html

Men's Studies: http://www.libraries.wright.edu/libnet/subj/gen/men_index.html

MenWeb: http://www.vix.com/menmag/netresor.html

National Coalition for Men: http://www.ncfm.org

Backlash: http://www.backlash.com/master/dir.html

Promise Keepers: http://www.ccad.uiowa.edu/~timv/promise/general.html

Alternative Lifestyles

Alternative Sexuality/Sexual Politics Resource List: http:www.infoqueer.org/queer/qis/vl-queer.html

OUT.com: http://www.out.com

Q World: http://www.qworld.org

Above and Beyond Gender: http://www.abmall.com/cb/tg/res.html

Gay Lesbian and Bisexual Resources: http://www.yahoo.com/Society_and_Culture/Sex/Gay_Lesbian_and Bisexual_Resources/

Political Issues

General

U.S. Constitution: http://www.ecst.csuchico.edu/~rodmur/docs/USConstitution.html

Information Warfare (on terrorism, espionage, and privacy): http://www.infowar.com/

Politics Now: http://www.politicsnow.com

Congressional Quarterly: http://voter.cq.com/

Marketplace of Political Ideas: http://info.lib.uh.edu/politics/markind.html

American Political Network: http://www.apn.com/

Political Education for Everyday Life: http://english-www.cmu.edu/bs/

Republican

Senate Republican Policy Committee: http://www.senate.gov/~rpc/

Hill Source (House Republican Conference—Clinton bashing): http://hillsource.house.gov

Republican National Committee: http://www.rnc.org/

Democratic

Senate Democratic Policy Committee: http://www.senate.gov/~dpc/general/dpc.html

Democratic National Committee: http://www.democrats.org

Conservative

Right Side of the Web (conservative): http://www.clark.net/pub/jeffd/index.html

Media Research Center (conservative): http://www.mediaresearch.org

Christian Coalition: http://www.cc.org/

John Birch Society (conservative): http://www.jbs.org/

Liberal

Turn Left (liberal): http://www.cjnetworks.com

Feminist Majority: http://www.feminist.org/

Progressive Directory (peace/ecology/conflict/labor/women): http://www.igc.apc.org/

Other Political Groups

Libertarian Party: http://www.lp.org/lp/lp.html

Green Parties of North America: http://www.greens.org/

United We Stand America: http://www.uwsa.com:8972/uwsa//

Other

Age

Seniornet: http://www.seniornet.org
AARP: http://www.aarp.org
Seniors-Site: http://www.seniors-site.com
*Senior*Com:* http://www.senior.com

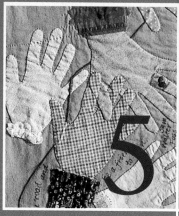

5 **Selecting and Researching Your Topic**

This chapter will help you

- select a topic for your speech
- focus your topic so that it is manageable
- determine your general and specific purposes
- develop a clear thesis statement
- obtain responsible knowledge on your topic

" I have to speak for five whole minutes? Why, I don't know that much about anything!" Your instructor has just given you your assignment. You are to prepare an informative speech on a subject of your choice. Your stomach starts to tighten as you worry. "Speech about what? How do I begin?"

PREPARING TO SPEAK before an audience can seem overwhelming, especially if you've never done it before. Simply getting started may be the most difficult part of speech preparation. If the task before you seems to be too much, take it in small steps, advises Robert J. Kriegel, a performance psychologist who has counseled many professional athletes. While working as a ski instructor, Kriegel found that beginners would look all the way to the bottom of a slope. The hill would seem too steep and the challenge too difficult, and the skiers would back away. However, if he told them to think only of making the first turn, this would change their focus to something they knew they could do.[1]

The "first turn" in speech preparation is deciding on a good topic that fits both you and your audience. Fortunately, there are some good ways to meet this challenge. Your "second turn" will be to develop a clear sense of purpose for your speech. Your "third turn" is to expand your knowledge so that you can make a responsible presentation. This chapter will help you negotiate these turns.

Selecting your topic, determining your purpose, and acquiring responsible knowledge form the first phase of the flow chart in Figure 5.1: "Major Steps in the Preparation of a Speech." As the chart indicates, you will work back and forth between these steps. In later chapters, we will deal with the second phase, structuring and outlining your speech, and with the third phase, preparing for presentation.

But for now, back to that first turn. What is a good topic? It is one that involves you, that allows you to express something that is important to you, and/or that explores something that fascinates you. It should also enrich the lives of your listeners by providing them with useful information or advice. Finally, a good topic is one that you can speak about responsibly, given the time allowed for your speech and the preparation time available.

A good topic involves you. Imagine yourself speaking successfully:

You're excited about what you're saying. Your face shows your interest in your topic. Your voice expresses your feelings. Your gestures

125

FIGURE 5.1

Major Steps in Speech
Preparation

Major Steps in Speech Preparation

```
┌──────────────────┐              ┌──────────────────┐
│ Analyze situation │◄──────────►│ Select and       │
│ and audience      │            │ focus your topic │
│ factors           │            │                  │
└──────────────────┘            └──────────────────┘
        ▲                               ▲
        │                               │
        ▼                               ▼
┌──────────────────┐            ┌──────────────────┐
│ Determine        │◄──────────►│ Research         │
│ your purpose     │            │ your topic       │
└──────────────────┘            └──────────────────┘
        │                               │
        │    ┌──────────────────┐       │
        └───►│ Develop your     │◄──────┘
             │ preliminary      │
             │ outline          │
             └──────────────────┘
                      │
             ┌──────────────────┐
        ┌───►│ Check the        │◄───┐
        ¦    │ adequacy of your │    ¦
        ¦    │ preparation      │    ¦
        ¦    └──────────────────┘    ¦
        ¦             │               ¦
        ¦    ┌──────────────────┐    ¦
        ¦    │ Prepare your     │    ¦
        ¦    │ formal outline   │    ¦
        ¦    └──────────────────┘    ¦
                      │
             ┌──────────────────┐
             │ Practice your    │
             │ presentation     │
             └──────────────────┘
```

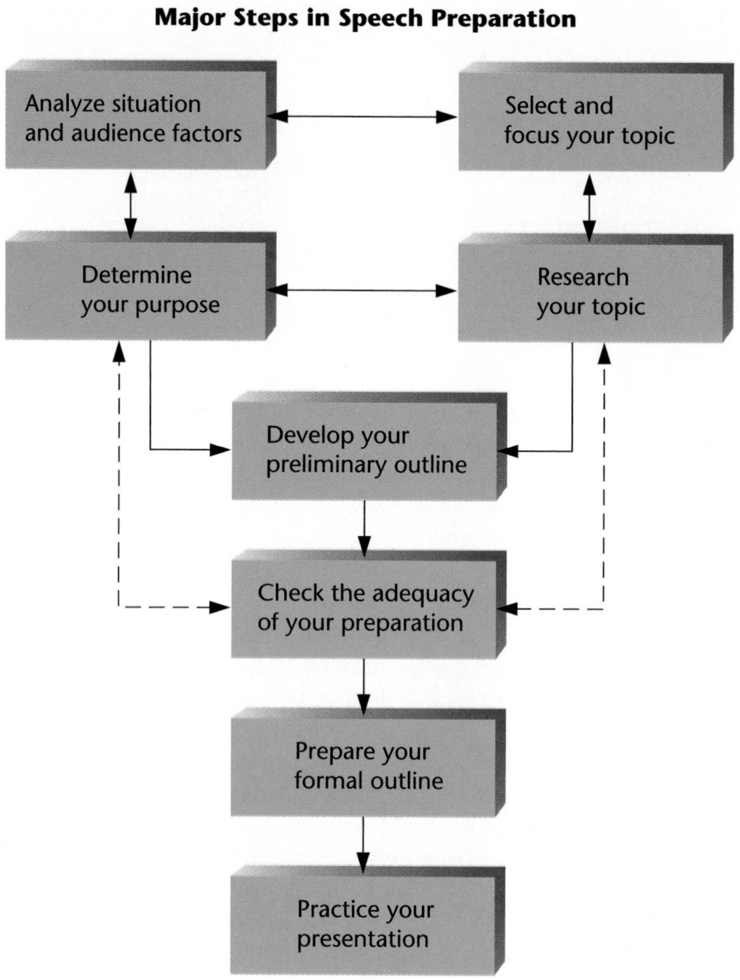

reinforce your meaning. Everything about you says, "This is important!" "You're going to love this!" or "This will make a real difference
in your lives!"

Now, let's work backwards from this image. What subject might make you
feel or act this way? That's the topic you want! If you don't care about your
topic, you will find it hard to put in the time and effort needed if you are to
speak responsibly and effectively. The enthusiasm you generate when you
speak on topics to which you are committed is contagious. It gets listeners involved as well.

A good topic involves your listeners. Now imagine an audience of ideal listeners:

Their faces are alive with interest. They lean forward in their seats, intent on hearing you. They nod or smile appropriately. You enjoy their
attention. At the end of your speech, they break out in applause. They
want to ask you questions about your ideas or to voice their own reactions. They really don't want you to sit down!

Questions to Ask on Your Speech Topic

speaker's notes

1   Have I selected a topic that has value for my listeners?
2   Do I really care about this topic?
3   Does the topic satisfy the assignment?
4   Have I narrowed the topic sufficiently?
5   Can I develop responsible knowledge on this topic?

What topic will help you reach this audience ideal? By now, you probably have heard the first speeches in your class, and you will have begun collecting audience analysis information. Ask yourself, "What are the interests of my listeners? What do they care about? What do they need to know about?"

Perhaps one of your classmates gave a speech honoring his family doctor. It sparked a lively classroom discussion and got you thinking about your less pleasant experiences with doctors. The lights come on in your mind. You could present an informative speech on the relationship between physician skills and malpractice complaints or a persuasive speech recommending training in interpersonal communication skills for doctors. Although these topics may seem intrinsically interesting, you still can't take audience involvement for granted. Your introduction must arouse their interest. You must show your audience how the topic affects *them* and what *they* stand to gain from hearing your message. For a topic to be really effective, it also must fit the time, place, and occasion for the speech, as we noted in Chapter 4. For example, a celebration in honor of a friend is not an occasion for a political tirade.

The final test of a good topic is whether you can acquire the knowledge you need in order to speak responsibly on it. The time you have for the preparation and presentation of your speech is limited. Consequently, you should select a topic area that you already know something about, then concentrate on developing a *manageable part* of that topic area for your presentation. Instead of trying to cover all the problems involved in the disposal of nuclear waste, it would be better to limit yourself to discussing your state's role in nuclear waste disposal or to focus on whether your community has an adequate plan to cope with the problem. The limited topic would be more manageable, could be better adapted to your audience, and should allow for responsible preparation.

Finding a Good Topic

One way to go about finding a good topic is to chart your personal interests and then those of your listeners so that you can analyze topic ideas in terms of their appropriateness and practicality.

Charting Interests

Begin your search for a good topic by listing your interests and those of your listeners to determine points of convergence. To develop these interests charts, use a system of prompt questions similar to the self-awareness inventory introduced in Chapter 2:

1. What *places* do you find interesting?
2. What *people* do you find fascinating?
3. What *activities* do you enjoy?
4. What *objects* do you find interesting?
5. What *events* are foremost in your mind?
6. What are your long- and short-range *goals*?
7. What *values* are important to you?
8. What *problems* concern you most?
9. What *campus concerns* do you have?

Write out brief responses to these questions. Try to come up with at least five alternatives for each question. Your interests chart might look like that in Figure 5.2.

Getting Ideas from the Media.   Sometimes it is hard to come up with a list of topics. If your mind goes blank, try using newspapers or magazines to generate ideas. Go through the Sunday paper, scan *Time, Newsweek,* or *People.* Study the headlines, titles, advertisements, and pictures. What catches your attention? Add these topics to your interests chart.

FIGURE 5.2
Your Interests Chart

Places	People	Activities
Chaco Canyon	Cesar Chavez	hiking
Freeport, Maine	Sammy Sosa	playing chess
San Francisco	Wilma Mankiller	watching baseball
Route 66	Charles Lindbergh	drying flowers
Manhattan	Sojourner Truth	traveling

Objects	Events	Goals
Kachinas	World Series	starting own business
movie posters	hurricanes	work in D.C.
antique fishing lures	canoeing the Colorado	visit Africa
political cartoons	Mardi Gras	live in Santa Fe
graffiti	Cody Rodeo	have a family

Values	Problems	Campus Concerns
close family ties	environmental pollution	race relations
tolerance	sensationalism in news	off-campus housing
physical fitness	substance abuse	date rape
respect	Internet censorship	campus security
world peace	prayer in schools	parking

One student developed an idea for a topic after seeing an advertisement for bank services. The ad stirred some unpleasant memories of having written a bad check. This suggested in turn an informative speech on keeping better personal financial records. His problem was getting listeners to see the importance of this topic to their lives. His solution was to develop an introduction that startled the audience into attention.

> **Last month I committed a crime! I wrote a check, and it bounced. The check was for $4.67 to a local grocery store where I bought the makings of a spaghetti supper. The bank charged me $25.00 for the overdraft, and the store charged me $10.00 to retrieve my bad check. That was the most expensive spaghetti I've ever eaten!**

Similarly, the headline "Travel Money Tips Offered" might inspire you to speak on "Champagne Travel on a Beer Budget." Or the personals section in the classified ads might prompt a speech on "The Dangers of Computer Dating Services."

Be careful not to misuse media sources. The media can suggest ideas for speeches, but you can't simply summarize an article and use it as a speech. The article should be only a starting point for your thinking. Search out more information about the topic. *Your* speech must be *your* message, designed to appeal to *your* specific audience. You should always bring something new to your topic—a fresh insight or a special application for your listeners.

Matching Your Interests to Your Audience.   Once you have completed your personal interests chart, make a similar chart of audience interests as revealed by class discussion and your audience analysis. What places, people, events, activities, objects, goals, values, problems, and campus concerns seem

Personal experiences, such as building houses for Habitat for Humanity, can be a useful source of examples or narratives for use in speeches.

to spark discussions in class? Study the two charts together, looking for shared interests in order to pinpoint your best topic possibilities. To do this systematically, make a three-column **topic area inventory chart**. In the first column (your interests), list the subjects you find most appealing. In the second column (audience interests), list the subjects that seem uppermost in the minds of your listeners. In the third column, match columns one and two to find the most promising areas of speech topics. Figure 5.3 shows a sample topic area inventory chart.

In this example, your interests in travel and hiking are matched with the audience's interest in unusual places and developed into a possible speech topic area: "Weekend Adventures Close to Campus." Similarly, your concern for physical fitness is paired with the audience's interest in deceptive advertising to generate another possible topic area: "Exercise Spa Rip-offs." Your interest in environmental pollution could combine with audience interests in leisure to lead to the topic area: "Should Cars Be Outlawed in Our National Parks?"

Analyzing Your Topic

The problem with these topic areas is that they are areas, not actual topics for speeches. They may be too broad for a short classroom speech. You must narrow them so that they are more specific and concrete. To do this, you need a system for analysis. You might ask the questions beginning reporters are taught to assure that they investigate a story thoroughly: what, why, when, how, where, and who. Apply these probes to your topic. Not all will apply to every topic area, but by working through the list systematically, you should be able to develop a number of possible topics. Let's take "Environmental Pollution" as a topic area and see where these questions can lead us:

What is environmental pollution? What are the major airborne pollutants? What are the major water pollutants? What causes environmental pollution? What are the effects of environmental pollution? What can we do to control environmental pollution? What can individuals do to reduce environmental pollution? What is the greatest pollution problem in our area?

Why do we have environmental pollution? Why are some companies reluctant to stop polluting? Why are some rural areas polluted? Why do some cities have more environmental pollution than others?

When did environmental pollution first become a problem? When did people first become concerned about environmental pollution? When was the first important book about environmental pollution published? When were the first laws protecting the environment passed?

How can air pollution be reduced? How can water pollution be reduced? How can companies be brought into compliance with pollution laws? How can individuals help reduce air pollution? How can individuals help reduce water pollution?

Where is air pollution the greatest problem? Where is water pollution the greatest problem? Where have cities or states done the most to control pollution?

FIGURE 5.3
Topic Area Inventory Chart

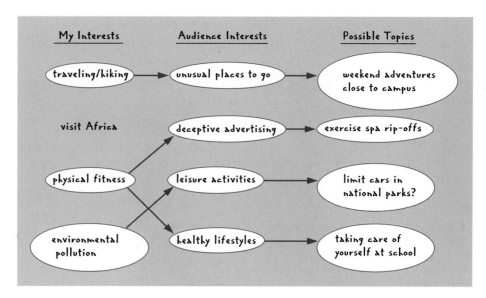

Who suffers most from air pollution? Who suffers most from water pollution? Who is responsible for enforcing pollution controls? Who brought the pollution problem to public awareness?

As you consider the six prompts, write down as many specific ideas about your topic area as you can. You may notice that certain clusters of ideas emerge: Some entries may center on air pollution, some on water pollution; some may relate to the history of environmental pollution, others to efforts to control pollution, and still others to the effects of pollution on wildlife or business interests. What would be the best topic for your speech on environmental pollution? That depends a great deal on your audience and locale. If you live in an area with a major pollution problem, a speech describing the pollution might offer little new information. However, your audience might be quite interested in the history of environmental legislation or in local efforts to solve the problems. On the other hand, if you live in an area where pollution is not an immediate or apparent problem, you may need to work hard to convince listeners that they should be concerned about the situation.

Your final choice of a topic should be made in light of your purpose: what you hope to accomplish in your speech for the benefit of your listeners. We shall discuss purpose in the next section, and defer discussion of the final selection process until then.

Our example of topic analysis has related to an informative speech topic. The same type of analysis can also be used to find topics for persuasive speeches. Because persuasion often addresses problems, you simply change the focus of the questions and add a few that are specific to persuasive situations:

Who is affected by this problem?

What are the most important issues?

Why did the problem arise?

Where is this problem happening?

When did the problem begin?

How is this problem like or unlike previous problems?

How extensive is the problem?

What options are available for dealing with the problem?

Selecting Your Topic

After you have completed the interests charts and analyzed the topic areas they suggest, two or three specific topics should emerge as important and appealing possibilities. Now you should ask of each:

Does this topic fit the assignment?

Could I give a speech on this topic in the time available?

Can I learn enough about this topic to give a responsible speech?

Why would I want to speak on this topic?

As you consider your options in light of these questions, a final choice should become clear.

Determining Your Purpose

"Why would I want to speak on this topic?" To answer this final question, you must know the general function of your speech, determine your specific purpose, and develop a clearly worded thesis statement and preview.

General Function

Invitations to speak outside class will usually indicate the **general function** for your speech. In class, the general function is often assigned. The general functions of speeches are to inform, to persuade, or to celebrate. The general function of a speech to inform is to share knowledge with listeners. If your general function is to persuade, you will advise listeners how to believe or act, and give them sound reasons to accept your advice. A speech of celebration emphasizes the importance of an occasion, event, or person. Speeches of celebration include toasts, tributes, eulogies, after-dinner speeches, and inspirational messages. Although it is easy to separate these functions on paper, they sometimes overlap in practice. For example, a speech celebrating the end of the twentieth century may also inform you of the major accomplishments of that century and urge you to strive for certain goals in the twenty-first century.

As we noted earlier, people who invite you to speak outside the classroom will usually suggest the general function for your speech. One of your authors was recently invited to speak to the county historical society on his work with the Tennessee Humanities Council. He knows that this audience will be most interested in the council's grants for local activities in the humanities. His speech will be largely informative, but he will also introduce himself and try to create good feelings toward the council. Were he to launch an attack on senators who want to reduce financial support for the arts and humanities, he would violate the audience's expectations by presenting a persuasive speech. That would be his last invitation to address the Decatur County Historical Society!

Specific Purpose

Your **specific purpose** helps focus your topic. It spells out what you want your listeners to understand, believe, feel, or do. Having a specific purpose clearly in mind helps direct your research toward relevant information so that you don't waste valuable time. You should be able to state your specific purpose clearly as a single idea. Let's look at how a specific purpose statement gives focus to your speech:

Topic:	**National parks**
General function:	**To inform**
Specific purpose:	**To inform my audience about hiking trails in Shenandoah National Park**

Topic:	**Global warming**
General function:	**To persuade**
Specific purpose:	**To persuade my audience that global warming poses a serious threat to our environment**

How can you tell if you have a good specific purpose? Your specific purpose should ensure that you provide listeners with new or useful information or advice. When you tell listeners something they already know, you simply bore them and waste their time. Your specific purpose also should be manageable in the time allotted to you. In a five-minute speech you have only about seven hundred words to get your message across. If you can't cover the material in the time allowed, then you must narrow your focus to something you can handle. Let's look at some examples of poor specific purpose statements and see how they might be improved:

Poor:	**To inform my audience about our national parks**
Improved:	**To inform my audience of the lesser-known attractions in Yellowstone Park**

Poor:	**To persuade my audience that driving while drinking is dangerous**
Improved:	**To persuade my audience to accept the idea of responsible drinking and driving**

In the first example, the specific purpose is too general. It does not narrow the topic sufficiently. With this *nonspecific* purpose, you could prepare a speech on the fate of grizzly bears in Yellowstone Park, on the differences between national parks and national forests, on national parks in urban areas, or on any of a multitude of other related subjects. The *improved* version limits the topic so that it can be handled within the time permitted. This helps you concentrate your research on those materials that are most useful to your speech. The second *poor* specific purpose is also too general, and it tells the audience nothing new. Who would argue that driving while drinking is not dangerous? Unless the speaker can offer a fresh perspective on the subject, holding the audience's attention or motivating the audience will be difficult. The *improved* version is more focused and offers a new perspective: the idea of *responsible* drinking and driving.

Thesis Statement and Preview

Most of the time your specific purpose will be reflected in the **thesis statement** for your speech. The thesis statement condenses your message into a single declarative sentence. It is usually offered as you introduce your speech so that your listeners will understand your intentions. Notice how the following speaker presents his thesis statement:

> **Today I want to discuss a moral blight on our campus—the problem of date rape—and what we can do about it.**

The thesis statement should be followed by a **preview.** The preview signals the main points that will be developed in the body of the speech. In effect, it presents an oral agenda for the speech:

> **I will define date rape, show its causes and consequences, and end with some advice on how to prevent it.**

In this example, listeners have been alerted to three main points in the speech:

    I. The nature of date rape

   II. Its causes and effects

  III. The prevention of date rape

Now the audience has a blueprint to help them follow the speech. In long or complicated speeches, the preview helps audience members listen effectively, thereby reducing misunderstandings.

In ethical speaking, the thesis statement will reveal the speaker's specific purpose. *But let the listener beware!* Not all speakers will be totally candid. While a speaker's specific purpose may be to sell the listeners an encyclopedia, the thesis statement may suggest a different intention:

> **I want to help you improve the quality of your lives by offering you—free of charge—this wonderful encyclopedia set [thesis statement]. Your only obligation is to help us demonstrate this encyclopedia in your neighborhood. We only ask that you keep your set up to date by purchasing at a special discount rate the annual supplements for the next ten years.**

Such disguises of a speaker's intention may be fairly trivial (unless you buy the set!), but if you substitute a political philosophy or a religious cause for an encyclopedia, you can see how serious the problem can be. The greater the distance between the hidden specific purpose and the thesis statement expressed in the speech, the larger the ethical problem.

At times ethical speakers may omit the thesis statement from their presentations, leaving it to be constructed by listeners from cues within the speech. Note how Cecile Larson left the thesis statement implicit in her speech, "The

'Monument' at Wounded Knee," which appears in Appendix B. Speakers may leave the thesis statement unstated in order to create a dramatic effect as listeners discover it for themselves. While it has some artistic merit, this technique also entails considerable risk. Listeners may miss the point! In most cases speakers should integrate the thesis statement into the introduction of their speeches.

Within a speech, the thesis statement should sharpen the focus of your specific purpose, and the preview should indicate the major points of your message

Specific purpose:	**To inform my audience about the less well-known attractions in Yellowstone Park**
Thesis statement:	**Many visitors leave Yellowstone Park without seeing some of its most interesting attractions**
Preview:	**Today I want to introduce you to three of the less well-known attractions in Yellowstone: the Fountain Paint Pots, the Grand Canyon of the Yellowstone, and the Firehole River.**
Specific purpose:	**To persuade my audience to accept the idea of responsible drinking and driving**
Thesis statement:	**Responsible drinking and driving can solve a serious social problem and might even save your life.**
Preview:	**You can practice responsible drinking and driving by knowing your tolerance for alcohol, having a designated driver, and not letting friends drive while intoxicated.**

Let us now look at the entire process of moving from general topic area to preview to see how these steps may evolve in speech preparation:

Topic area:	**Vacations in the United States**
Topic:	**Camping in the Rockies**
General function:	**To inform**
Specific purpose:	**To inform my audience that there are beautiful, uncrowded places to camp in the Rockies**
Thesis statement:	**You can get off the beaten path and find some wild and wonderful places to camp in the Rockies.**
Preview:	**Three beautiful yet uncrowded camping areas in the Rockies are Bridger-Teton National Forest in Wyoming, St. Charles Canyon in Idaho, and Dinosaur National Monument in Utah.**

A speech titled "Camping in the Rockies: Getting Off the Beaten Path" might then take the following form:

Introduction:	**Page 43 of the tour guide to Grand Teton National Park reveals this idyllic picture of camping [show enlarged photo]. As you can see, the area is beautiful**

and uncrowded. With this picture in mind, I went on my first camping trip to the Rockies two summers ago. Was I ever disappointed! After a long drive I arrived at Jenny Lake campground about two in the afternoon—early enough to set up camp, take a hike, and prepare a leisurely dinner. But, no! All the campsites had been taken since eight-thirty that morning. Not only were no sites available, but after driving through the campground, I realized I wouldn't have wanted to camp there anyway. Hundreds of tents were crowded on top of one another. It looked like a refugee relocation center after a disaster. And it wasn't only the crowding that was bad, but the noise! Radios and televisions blasted you with an unholy mixture of music and game shows and soap operas. I might just as well have been back in our freshman dorm.

Transition: Not every camping area in the Rockies is like this.

Thesis statement: You can get off the beaten path and find some wild and wonderful places to camp in the Rockies.

Preview: Three of the most interesting, beautiful, and uncrowded are Bridger-Teton National Forest in Wyoming, St. Charles Canyon in Idaho, and the Dinosaur National Monument in Utah.

Main points:
1. Bridger-Teton National Forest at Slide Lake has a magnificent view of the Tetons. [Show enlarged photo.]

2. St. Charles Canyon, on a white-water stream, offers the ultimate in seclusion. [Show enlarged photo.]

3. At Dinosaur National Monument you can watch the excavation of gigantic skeletons that are millions of years old. [Photo.]

Transition and conclusion: There are interesting, beautiful, and uncrowded places to camp if you know where to look. Try the National Forest Service campgrounds or national monuments rather than the overcrowded national parks. Last summer I enjoyed the peace and serenity of Slide Lake while reveling in its view of the Tetons. I caught native cutthroat trout in secluded St. Charles Canyon, and I saw the ancient petroglyphs at Dinosaur National Monument. I can't wait to get back!

Although the thesis statement appears in the foregoing example, you will note that the speaker *does not* begin with "My thesis statement is. . . ." Rather, it appears naturally in the introduction as a lead into the preview. Both thesis statement and preview suggest that this speech should give us interesting information, vivid examples, and engaging stories. The thesis statement indicates what kind of informative speech we will hear (descriptive), and the preview implies the overall design or pattern the speech will follow (categorical).

With a clear thesis statement in mind, speakers can focus their research to acquire responsible knowledge of the topic. In this case the speaker might use materials obtained at the sites, attendance figures from almanacs or newspaper articles, and materials available in the government documents section of the library or on the Internet.

Acquiring Responsible Knowledge

Although we have discussed selecting and focusing your topic before taking up research, your background reading for a speech often begins before you form your thesis statement. In order to determine your approach and the main points you will develop, you will probably have to find out more about your topic. Once you have your specific purpose in mind, you can begin a quest for responsible knowledge. **Responsible knowledge** is the most comprehensive understanding of your topic that you can acquire in the time available for preparation. It includes information on

- The main issues concerning your topic
- What respected authorities say about it
- The latest developments relevant to it
- Related local applications of interest to your audience

When you ask an audience for their time and attention, you must give them something of value in return. Having responsible knowledge earns you the right to speak to your audience.[2] In addition, whenever you speak, you put your mind and character on display. If you haven't made an effort to acquire responsible knowledge, you are saying in effect, "I haven't much to offer, and I don't really care." Having responsible knowledge of your topic should enhance your perceived ethos in terms of both competence and character.[3]

Although you cannot become an authority on most topics with ten hours or even ten days of research, you can learn enough to speak responsibly. Your research should result in your knowing more about your topic than the rest of the class does. The major sources of information available to you are your own knowledge and experience, Internet and library resources, and interviews. Each of these sources can supply facts, testimony, examples, or narratives to use as supporting materials in your speech.

As you pursue your quest for responsible knowledge, keep in mind the checklist offered in Figure 5.4 (see next page), "Quest for Responsible Knowledge". It offers an overview of possible resources. Not every source will be appropriate for every speech, and for any given speech, some sources will be more appropriate than others. By checking off the items one by one as they apply in your situation, you can be assured that you have conducted the research phase of your speech preparation thoroughly and systematically.

FIGURE 5.4

Quest for Responsible Knowledge

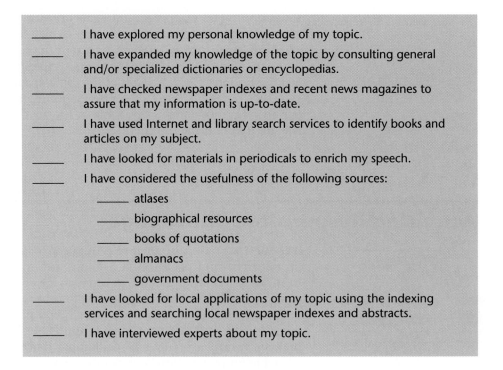

_____ I have explored my personal knowledge of my topic.

_____ I have expanded my knowledge of the topic by consulting general and/or specialized dictionaries or encyclopedias.

_____ I have checked newspaper indexes and recent news magazines to assure that my information is up-to-date.

_____ I have used Internet and library search services to identify books and articles on my subject.

_____ I have looked for materials in periodicals to enrich my speech.

_____ I have considered the usefulness of the following sources:

_____ atlases

_____ biographical resources

_____ books of quotations

_____ almanacs

_____ government documents

_____ I have looked for local applications of my topic using the indexing services and searching local newspaper indexes and abstracts.

_____ I have interviewed experts about my topic.

Because your preparation time will be limited, you should begin by developing a research strategy. Having a strategy will help you make more efficient use of your time and enable you to locate and evaluate the materials you need. You should start by assessing your personal knowledge and experience to determine what additional information you might need in order to make a responsible presentation. Next, you should develop a strategy for obtaining this information by accessing library resources, using the Internet, and/or interviewing for information and opinions. Finally, you should conduct your research and make note cards to use as you organize your speech.

Personal Knowledge and Experience

Personal knowledge and experience add credibility, authenticity, and interest to a speech. Being able to describe your feelings about a problem will gain and hold the audience's attention and may make them more receptive. You may not be an acknowledged authority on a subject, but personal stories suggest that you have a special kind of intimate knowledge of it. They make it easier for an audience to identify with you and the topic.[4]

If you lack direct experience with a topic, you can always try to arrange some. Suppose you are planning a speech on how local television stations prepare newscasts. You have gathered information from books and periodicals, but it seems rather dry and lifeless. Call a local television station and ask the news director if it would be possible for you to spend an afternoon in the newsroom of the station so that you can get a feel for what goes on during that hectic time right before a broadcast. Take in the noise, the action, and the excitement that occur before and during a show. All of this can help enrich your speech. You might also try to schedule an interview with the news director while you are at the station (see the section "Interviewing for Information" later in this chapter).

As valuable as it is, experience is rarely sufficient to provide all the information, facts and figures, and testimony that you will need for your speech. Your personal knowledge may be limited, the sources from which you learned may have been biased, or your experiences may not have been typical. Even people who are acknowledged authorities on a subject look to other experts to give credence to their messages. Use personal knowledge and experience as a starting point and expand it through research. Prepare a personal knowledge and experience summary similar to the one shown in Figure 5.5. Include on your summary sheet what you know (or think you know) about the topic, where or how you learned it, and what additional information you might need to find. Also jot down any examples or narratives based on your experience so that you can remember them as you put your speech together. Use your summary sheet to give direction to your research.

The Internet as a Research Tool

The Internet can be a very useful research tool in the preparation of speeches. It contains a wealth of information that is easily accessible through a personal computer. Most colleges and universities make Internet access available to their students, either through their own personal computers or through the library.

FIGURE 5.5
Personal Knowledge Summary

What I Know (or Think I Know)	Where/How I Learned It	What I Need to Find Out
Not many grizzly bears in park	Worked there 2 summers. Heard rangers talk about it. Only saw 1 and I was looking	Approximately how many bears are in the park
Go to back country to see the grizzlies	Same as above/personal experience	Where in park they are most likely to be seen; specify trails and areas
Grizzly attacks are rare	Same as above	When was first attack recorded? Last? # of attacks relative to # of tourists; relative to other types of injuries
Camping precautions	See above, brochure, personal experience	Information probably sufficient

Examples/Narratives I Might Use in Speech:

For the past two summers I've worked waiting tables at Mammoth Springs Lodge in Yellowstone Park. We got two days a week off, and I spent nearly all my free time hiking and camping in the back country, far away from the tourists and crowds in the park. I counted up the number of hours I spent that way and discovered that I had logged in more than 350 hours in these remote locations—in the grizzly bear habitat of the park—hoping to see one. Only once, in all those hours, did I see a grizzly bear, and that was from a distance of about half a mile. If I hadn't been sitting quietly with my binoculars focused on a watering area, I probably would have missed seeing that one!

Electronic access to information helps speed the research process. Most college libraries provide computerized databases for your convenience.

If you have never used the Internet before, the following books might be helpful:

John R. Levine and Carol Baroudi, *The Internet for Dummies,* IDG Books. (latest edition.)

Wayne Ause and Scott Arpajian, *How to Use the World Wide Web,* Ziff-Davis Press, 1996.

Joe Kraynak et al., *The Big Basics Book of the Internet,* Que Corp., 1996.

Mary Micco and Therese D. O'Neil, *Using the Internet,* Houghton Mifflin, 1996.

Gary Gach, *The Pocket Guide to the Internet,* Simon & Schuster, 1996.

Online, check out "Understanding and Using the Internet" (http://www.pbs.org/uti/) or "An Internet Tutorial" (http://www.msn.com/tutorial/default.html). These online guides may be even more useful than the books listed above because the Internet changes from day to day; therefore, anything written about it may be obsolete before the ink dries.

It has been said—and it certainly is true!—that anyone can put anything on the Internet. This being the case, how can you be sure that the information you find satisfies the requirements of responsible knowledge? One way to approach this problem is to apply the critical thinking skills discussed in Chapter 3. In addition to using these basic skills, you should consider the following guidelines that are applicable to Internet materials. Begin by evaluating the source of the material:

- Is the author of the document identified?
- Is a URL or email address provided?
- Is the source an authority on the subject?
- Are the credentials of the source specified?
- Does he or she list a professional affiliation? occupation? educational background?
- Can I verify the credentials of the source?
  - Check the home page of the web site (delete all information in the URL after the server name).
  - Run a search with the author's name in quotation marks.
  - Check organizations/associations via the Scholarly Societies Project (http://www.lib.uwaterloo.ca/society/overview.html).
  - Run a search with the name of the organization/association in quotation marks.

Evaluate the information provided:

- Is the source of statistical information identified?
- Are dates of information provided within the document? Is the information recent?
- When was the document last updated?
- Is information linked to other sources you can check?
- Is a bibliography provided?
- How does this compare with other information in the field?
- Are differing points of view presented?
- Is there more sizzle than substance in the document?
- Are the spelling and grammar correct?
- Is the writing clear or obscure?

If the material checks out well using these questions as a guide, it probably falls within the realm of responsible knowledge. You can find a list of useful web sites in the "Guide to Library and Internet Resources" following the endnotes of this chapter.

Using Library and Internet Resources

The major research resources available for speakers include (1) sources of background information, (2) sources of access to information, (3) sources of in-depth information, (4) sources of current information, and (5) sources of local information. You should use all of these resources to acquire responsible knowledge of your subject. In this section we explore the types of resources available and show you how to prepare a research strategy that will help you use your time efficiently.

Sources of Background Information.   Even if you feel you know almost everything you need to know about your topic, you should begin by reading an authoritative review of your subject. This allows you to check the comprehensiveness and accuracy of your personal information. You may find new information or discover areas of the topic you hadn't considered. The review also can help you focus your topic by pointing out the most important ideas. Review articles are found mainly in encyclopedias and specialized dictionaries, housed in the reference section of the library. On the Internet, go to The Page Site (http://www.thepagesite.com/encycl_p.htm) for links to most of the encyclopedias online. General encyclopedias, such as *Encyclopaedia Britannica* (http://www.eb.com/), contain background information, specify key words to use in your search for in-depth information, and often list references for additional research. The articles are brief and written in lay language. Specialized encyclopedias, such as the *International Encyclopedia of the Social Sciences,* cover specific topics in greater detail. Specialized dictionaries, available on diverse subjects ranging from American slang to zoology, provide more than definitions and pronunciations. For example, the *Oxford English Dictionary* presents the origin, meaning, and history of English words. A directory of dictionaries on the Internet is located at http://www.thepagesite.com/dict_p.htm.

Sources of Access to Information.   Since your preparation time for speeches is limited, you must know how to find information quickly. The major sources of access to information in the library are periodical indexes, newspaper indexes, and the card catalog. Some of the periodical indexes, such as the *Reader's Guide to Periodical Literature,* cover publications of general interest. Others, such as the *Business Periodicals Index,* are specific to a subject area. Many indexes are now available on computers, which should save you research time. To access information from an index, you must identify key terms related to your topic. As noted above, most encyclopedia entries list relevant key terms. The *Library of Congress Subject Headings* gives the key terms that are used in the library card catalog.

On the Internet, the major sources of access to information are the search engines. Your service provider will probably offer links to a variety of search engines. Many of these tools are described and rated in Magellan (http://www.mckinley.com/) and the Encyclopedia Britannica Internet Guide (http://www.ebig.com/). The following search engines may be useful in the preparation of your speeches.

Yahoo (http://www.yahoo.com/): contains subject guides

Excite (http://www.excite.com/): searches by concepts

Northern Light (http://www.nlsearch.com/): groups the results for better focus

The Mining Company (http://www.miningco.com/): has mini-sites designed by humans.

Inference Find (http://www.infind.inference.com/): a superfast search engine that clusters results.

Sources of In-depth Information.   Most of the facts and figures, testimony, examples, ideas for narratives, and material for presentation aids will come from in-depth sources of information such as periodicals and books. The "Guide to Library and Internet Resources" at the end of this chapter contains an annotated list of periodicals that may be useful in speech preparation. As you research your speech, try to use a variety of sources representing different perspectives on your topic. Keep in mind that periodicals have a reputation of their own. Some periodicals, such as the *Wall Street Journal,* will be perceived as highly credible and objective, whereas other periodicals may be less acceptable to your audience. Even highly credible sources may be tinged with bias on certain topics. For example, the American Cancer Society might be an excellent source of information about the relationship between cancer and smoking, but may be biased by self-interest on the question of government funding for medical research. As you read your in-depth material, you may discover that one book is frequently mentioned. Read it, and check the *Book Review Index* for summaries of reviews of it.

When you need facts and figures, consult an almanac, yearbook, or atlas. Almanacs and yearbooks provide accurate, up-to-date compilations of information on a wide range of topics. Such materials go beyond simple lists to include short articles and graphics that you can adapt for presentation aids. Atlases are useful when your topic calls for geographical information. They often include data on such things as population density or industrial production and are a good source of materials for presentation aids. Biographical resources can provide information about the qualifications of experts you might cite in a speech. Books of quotations can offer material for the introductions and conclusions of speeches. Most such books are indexed by topic and author, making it easy for you to find what others had to say about your subject. Most of these resources are available on the Internet as well as in the library.

A word of caution: As we noted in Chapter 1, *the articles you find do not provide you with a speech;* rather, they provide ideas, information, opinions, examples, and narratives for use in the speech that you prepare for your particular audience. If you simply summarize an article and present it as though it were your own, you are committing **plagiarism**. Although some guidelines for avoiding plagiarism were presented earlier, they are important enough to bear repeating:

- *Do not summarize a single article for a speech.* Get information and ideas from a variety of sources and blend them into a unique approach to your topic.

- *Introduce the sources of quotations in your speech*—for example, "The late comedian George Jessel once noted, 'The mind is a wonderful organ. It begins working at birth and doesn't quit until you stand up to make a speech.'"

- *Identify your sources of information*—for example, "According to *The 1998 World Almanac* you are almost twice as likely to be disabled by an accident in the home than by a car or work accident."

- *Give credit to the originators of ideas* that you use—for example, "Maria Martinez, director of student counseling services, suggests that there are two techniques test-anxious students can use to get through final exams."

Sources of Current Information. The timeliness of information is important for topics that change rapidly, such as medical research or computer technology. In addition, if you are not aware of current happenings related to your topic, your credibility may suffer. The best source of timely information is the Internet. By logging on to local newspapers and television stations throughout the world, you can keep abreast of what is happening during crisis situations. Ecola Newsstand (http://www.ecola.com/) lists online newspapers in the United States and around the world. One of the best library sources for current information is *Facts on File*, a weekly publication that reports on current events by topics. Additional sources of current information include the most recent issues of newspapers and weekly news magazines.

Sources of Local Applications.   To involve your audience with your subject, you should show them how it relates to them and their community. For example, if you were presenting a speech on problems of hazardous waste, it would be better to talk about that problem in your own area than in some place halfway across the country. Many libraries maintain a vertical file that contains newspaper clippings, pamphlets, and other materials about important local people or issues. These materials may contain the names of people you could interview for additional information or opinions. Your library may also have an index of your local newspaper and subscribe to regional magazines. Your local newspaper may have archives that you can search through the Internet. For a list of searchable newspaper archives, check the Ecola Newsstand at http://www.ecola.com/archive/press/.

Developing a Research Strategy.   The "Research Strategy Worksheet" shown in Figure 5.6 should help you plan your research efficiently. Begin by having your topic and specific purpose clearly in mind. Use the guide at the end of this chapter or the Internet to identify one or more sources of general information to start your search. Read that background material, take notes, and write down the key terms you will use to access in-depth information. Using library indexes and abstracts or an Internet search engine, build a bibliography on your topic. From your bibliography, identify those articles or books that seem most relevant to your specific purpose. If timeliness is important for your topic, find one or two current references. Finally, check for local applications.

Interviewing for Information

Personal interviews can be an excellent source of facts, examples, and testimony for your speeches. Material from interviews adds credibility to your speech. If you can say, "Carolyn Jenkins, the director of research and development at Richardson Electronics, told me . . . ," your audience will sit up and listen. But as with personal experience, there are also problems with interviewing. Finding the right person to interview can be difficult. Or you may feel so grateful to someone for granting you an interview that you simply accept that person's word without further investigation. If you do not know very much about the subject, it may be hard for you to evaluate what you hear.

To minimize these problems, check your library's local clipping service or local newspaper archives to help you identify nearby prospects for interviews. Put out a call for suggestions in one of the Internet's forum discussions. What you discover from these sources can also help you frame questions to ask during the interview. Do as much reading as you can before the interview.

FIGURE 5.6

Research Strategy Work-sheet

TOPIC: _____

SPECIFIC PURPOSE: _____

GENERAL INFORMATION SOURCES: (List sources of general information applicable to your topic) _____

KEY TERMS AND ACCESS TO INFORMATION SOURCES: (List the key terms you will use and 2 sources of access to information you will use to identify specific and/or in-depth references)

Key Terms   1. _____   2. _____

Access   1. _____   2. _____

SPECIFIC AND/OR IN-DEPTH INFORMATION REFERENCES: (List 3 or 4 references to specific and/or in-depth information applicable to your topic of which at least 2 must be from periodicals or books)

1. _____

_____

2. _____

_____

3. _____

_____

4. _____

_____

CURRENT INFORMATION REFERENCES: (List 1 or 2 sources of current information if applicable to your topic)

1. _____

_____

2. _____

_____

LOCAL APPLICATIONS SOURCES: (List 1 or 2 sources for local applications material if applicable to your topic)

1. _____

_____

2. _____

_____

If an interview seems desirable, you must find the right person, determine how to conduct the interview, establish contact, prepare for the interview, conduct the interview, and record what you learn so that it is readily accessible as you prepare your speech.

speaker's notes

Interviewing for Information

1 Locate and contact an expert on your topic.
2 Research your topic before the interview.
3 Plan a series of questions that relate to your specific purpose.
4 Be on time.
5 Be courteous and tactful.
6 Do not ask leading questions.
7 Let your expert do most of the talking.
8 Summarize what you hear so that your expert can verify it.

Find the Right Person to Interview.   Use your library's local resource file or the Internet archives of your local newspaper to identify someone who is qualified as an expert on your subject by education, training, or experience. Don't overlook the most obvious source available to you—your own campus. Every college and university has faculty members with expertise on a wide array of topics, and they are typically willing to take the time to talk to students in their offices.

Determine How to Conduct the Interview.   It is usually preferable to conduct an interview face to face, but sometimes that is not practical. Telephone interviews can be used to verify information, acquire a brief quotation, or discover a person's opinion.[5] You can also interview a person via email on the Internet. When preparing a speech on the effects of a recent NCAA regulation on college athletics, one University of Memphis student phoned the athletic directors at her own school and the Universities of Tennessee, Mississippi, and Arkansas for their opinions. All of these officials were willing to talk with her, and she was able to quote them in her speech. That material definitely enhanced her credibility on the subject.

Establishing Contact.   It is best to initiate contact with a letter that gives your expert an opportunity to prepare for the interview. You might include a list of the questions you wish to discuss. A well-written request can help establish your credibility. Follow up the letter with a phone call to schedule the interview. If time is short, however, you may initiate contact through a telephone call or email either directly to the person you wish to interview or to that person's secretary. Tell her or him why you wish to conduct the interview and what kind of questions you want to ask. Don't be shy. A request for an interview is a compliment because it suggests that you value that person's opinion.

Preparing for the Interview.   Complete most of your library and Internet research before you conduct an interview so that you know what questions to ask and can converse intelligently on the subject. Write out your interview questions so that the responses will be relevant to your specific purpose. Keep your list of questions short—your expert is probably a busy person whose time is valuable.

Plan open questions that invite discussion, not yes or no answers.[6] Never supply the answer you want in your question, as in "Don't you think that air pollution is a crisis that demands our attention?" Design your questions in a sequence so that the answers form a coherent line of thought:

What are the causes of air pollution in Silver City?

What is the impact of air pollution on people's lives?

Is there a serious effort underway to minimize air pollution?

Are polluters cooperating in this campaign? Why or why not?

What can students do to help the effort?

Plan your wording so that your questions do not threaten your expert. Questions such as, "When are you intellectuals going to climb down from the ivory tower and get involved in the campaign for a better environment?" may be seen as argumentative and offensive. Save any controversial questions for late in the interview, after you have established rapport. Ask such questions tactfully: "Some people say that experts like you need to 'dirty their hands more' in the day-by-day effort to improve the environment. How do you respond to such criticism?" If asked with sincerity rather than hostility, this kind of question can produce the most interesting part of your interview.

Should you tape-record your interview? A tape recorder can free you from having to take notes in order to get the exact wording of answers. However, some people dislike being tape-recorded. Never attempt to record an interview without obtaining prior consent. A good time to seek such consent is during your initial contact. If your expert seems reluctant, don't press the point.

Conducting the Interview. Arrive for the interview on time. Dress nicely to show that you take the interview seriously and as a sign of respect for the person you are interviewing. When you meet your expert, take time for a little small talk before you get into your prepared questions. Try to establish common ground.

Let the expert do most of the talking while you do the listening. Allow the person you are interviewing to complete the answer to one question before you ask another. Don't interrupt and jump in with another question every time your expert pauses. Your expert may go from one point to another and may even answer a question before you ask it. You should adapt to the spontaneous flow of conversation.

Be alert for opportunities to follow up on answers by using probes, mirror questions, verifiers, or reinforcers.[7] **Probes** are questions that ask the expert to elaborate on a response: "Could you tell me more about the part played by auto emissions?" **Mirror questions** reflect part of a response to encourage discussion. The sequence might go as follows:

> **"So I told Joan, 'If we want people to change their attitudes, we're going to have to start marching in the front of the movement.'"**
> **"You felt you were moving toward a leadership role?"**

A **verifier** confirms the meaning of something that has been said, such as "If I understand you correctly, you're saying. . . ." Finally, a **reinforcer** provides encouragement for the person to communicate further. Smiles, nods, or comments such as "I see" are reinforcers that can keep the interview moving.

Material from face-to-face interviews can add much to a speech.

If you feel the interview beginning to drift off course, you can often steer it back with a transition. As your expert pauses, you can say, "I believe I understand now the causes of air pollution. But can you tell me more about how this level of pollution affects our lives?"

Do not overstay your welcome. As the interview draws to a close, summarize the main points you have heard and how you think they may be useful in your speech. A summary allows you to verify what you have heard and reassures the expert that you intend to use the information fairly and accurately. Thank your expert for his or her time, then follow up with a telephone call or thank-you note in which you report the successful results of your speech.

Recording What You Learn.   If you plan to take notes during an interview, tell your expert that you want to be sure to quote him or her correctly in your speech. If you are not certain that you wrote down an answer correctly, read it back for confirmation. After you have completed the interview, find a quiet place to go over your notes and write out the answers to important questions while your expert's wording is still fresh in your mind.

Taking Notes on Your Research

The best research in the world will not do you any good unless you take notes to help you prepare your speech. Take notes on anything you read or hear that *might* be usable in your speech. It is better to have too much material to work with than too little. Even if you download your research material, you may find it useful to prepare research cards because they are easy to handle and sort by categories. You will need to prepare both source and information cards for each article or book you might use.

FIGURE 5.7
Information Card

HEADING	Yellowstone Grizzlies in "Fragile" Condition
SOURCE	Chadwick, "Grizzly Country," p. 12.
INFORMATION	"Today, the entire 6-million-acre greater Yellowstone ecosystem is estimated to hold just 200 to 250 grizzlies. Isolated as if on an island, they have become vulnerable to inbreeding as well as catastrophic wildfire, drought or disease epidemics. The word _fragile_ doesn't seem to go with _horribilis_, yet it describes their future in Yellowstone all too well at the moment."

Your **source cards** should contain standard bibliographical information: the author's name, the title of the article or book, the title of the periodical for an article, the place and date of publication for a book, the date of publication for an article, and the page references (see Figure 5.7). You also may wish to include a short summary of the material, information about the author's qualifications, and any of your own comments or reactions to the material. Use **information cards** to record facts and figures, examples, or quotations (see Figure 5.8). Use a different card for each item of information you think you might use. Each card should have a heading that describes the information it contains, the source from which the material was taken, and the information itself.

Testing Information

When you find material that you think might be usable, you must test it carefully. As you research your topic, ask yourself: Does this article contain relevant and useful information? Does it cite experts that I can quote in my speech to support my ideas or position? Are there interesting examples that I can use to make my ideas clearer? Are there stories that will bring my topic to life? Your quest for responsible knowledge should help you find nuggets of information that add value to your message.

Once you have found such material, you must test its reliability, thoroughness, recency, and precision. **Reliability** refers to the trustworthiness of information. Ask yourself:

- Are these sources qualified as experts on this topic?
- Are these sources trustworthy?
- Is there general agreement among the experts on these points?

FIGURE 5.8
Source Card

BIBLIOGRAPHIC INFORMATION	Douglas H. Chadwick, "Grizzly Country," _Nature Conservancy_, 45 (July/August 1995): 11-15.
SUMMARY AND COMMENTS	Draws disturbing picture of the fate in the lower 48 of the grizzly bear, described as "the untamed soul of the Rockies." Explains what is being done to help the dwindling population. The author, a wildlife biologist, wrote _The Fate of the Elephant_. The Nature Conservancy is one of the most effective environmental action groups.

Thoroughness of information is also an important consideration. Don't be satisfied with reading just one or two articles. Read until you stop being surprised by what you discover. **Recency** is essential when knowledge on a subject is changing rapidly. Last year's readings on the state of the economy are today's old news. If someone in your audience points out that more recent data contradict your point, you'll have to pick your credibility up off the floor. **Precision** is important if you are speaking on a topic that varies widely from place to place, such as unemployment rates or the incidence of AIDS. You must be certain that your information applies in the locale where you are speaking. We show you in the next chapter how to apply such tests specifically to the different types of supporting materials.

In Summary

To give a successful speech, you must find a good topic, realize the general function and specific purpose of your speech, frame a clear thesis statement, and expand your knowledge so that you can speak responsibly. A good topic is one that involves and fascinates both you and your audience. It will be limited so that you can research it adequately and develop a speech that will fit within the allotted time.

Finding a Good Topic.   One way to discover promising topic areas is to chart your interests by using prompt questions and by scanning the media. Next, chart audience interests as disclosed in previous speeches and class discussions and match them with your own. To develop topic possibilities, use an analysis based on six questions: who, what, when, where, why, and how. When applied to a topic area, these questions can guide you to specific topics. As you move toward your selection, consider whether a given topic fits the assignment, whether you can speak on it within the time limits, and why you would want to speak on it.

Determining Your Purpose.   The *general function* of your speech might be to inform listeners, to persuade them, or to celebrate some occasion with them. Your *specific purpose* identifies the kind of response you would like from your audience. Your *thesis statement* is the hub of your message, expressed in a single sentence. It is followed by the *preview,* which highlights the main points of your speech.

Acquiring Responsible Knowledge.   *Responsible knowledge* implies that you have a good grasp of the main issues surrounding a topic, what experts say about it, the most recent developments, and how it applies specifically to your listeners. You can acquire responsible knowledge from personal experience, Internet and library research, and interviews. Personal experience can make your speech seem credible and authentic, but you should not rely on it as your only source of information. Internet and library research can add objective, authoritative information to your speech. The knowledge you obtain through interviews can add freshness, vitality, and local relevance to your speech.

Recording Information.   As you conduct research, record what you learn on index cards. Use *information cards,* which pinpoint exact quotations and precise bits of information, and *source cards* for each article, book, or interview. The source card identifies the author, date, and place of publication. It may be used to record background information about the source and to summarize and evaluate the material. As you conduct research for your speech, you should ask four basic questions: Does this material satisfy the tests of *reliability*, *thoroughness*, *recency*, and *precision* so that I can use it responsibly in my speech?

Terms to Know

topic area inventory chart	verifier
general function	reinforcer
specific purpose	source cards
thesis statement	information cards
preview	reliability
responsible knowledge	thoroughness
plagiarism	recency
probes	precision
mirror questions	

Notes

1. Robert J. Kriegel, *If It Ain't Broke . . . Break It!* (New York: Warner, 1991), pp. 167–168.
2. William Norwood Brigance, in his classic public speaking text, *Speech: Its Techniques and Disciplines in a Free Society* (New York: Appleton-Century-Crofts, 1952), entitled his chapter on researching a speech "Earning the Right to Speak."
3. James C. McCroskey, *An Introduction to Rhetorical Communication,* 5th ed. (Englewood Cliffs, N.J.: Prentice-Hall, 1986), p. 72.
4. Study by J. Berger and R. Vartabedian (*Journal of Applied Social Psychology,* vol. 15, no. 2), cited in Jeff Meer, "Political Intimacies: Better Left Unsaid," *Psychology Today*, January 1986, pp. 19–20.
5. Michael Schumacher, "The Interview and Its Uses," in *1992 Writer's Market,* ed. Mark Kissling and Roseann Shaughnessy (Cincinnati: F & W Publications, 1991), p. 9.
6. See the discussion in Jeanne Tessier Barone and Jo Young Switzer, *Interviewing Art and Skill* (Boston: Allyn and Bacon, 1995), pp. 89–99.
7. Lois J. Einhorn, Patricia Hayes Bradley, and John E. Baird, Jr., *Effective Employment Interviewing: Unlocking Human Potential* (Glenview, Ill.: Scott, Foresman, 1982), pp. 135–139.

A Guide to Library and Internet Resources

Library Resources

General Information and Background

General Encyclopedias and Dictionaries

American Heritage Dictionary
Collier's Encyclopedia
Encyclopedia Americana
Enclyclopaedia Brittannica
Oxford English Dictionary

Specialized Encyclopedias and Dictionaries

Black's Law Dictionary
Dictionary of American History
Dictionary of Americanisms
Dictionary of the History of Ideas
Dictionary of Psychology
Dictionary of Science
Dictionary of Word and Phrase Origins
Encyclopedia of Associations
Encyclopedia of Education
Encyclopedia of Philosophy
Encyclopedia of Religion and Ethics
Encyclopedia of Science and Technology
Encyclopedia of World Art
Harper's Bible Dictionary
International Encyclopedia of the Social Sciences
Safire's Political Dictionary
Scientific Encyclopedia
Webster's New World Dictionary of Business Terms

Sources for Access to Information

Periodical Indexes and Abstracts

American Statistics Index: a master guide to government statistical publications
Art Index: covers photography, films, architecture, fine arts, graphic arts, and design
Biography Index: lists current articles and books containing biographical information
Business Index: covers business and industry periodicals
Business Periodicals Index: covers business, economics, computers, advertising, etc.

Congressional Information Service: Index and Abstracts: two volumes covering congressional working papers, hearings, reports, and special publications of congressional committees

Education Index: covers articles relating to children and/or education

Engineering Index: covers international journals and special technical reports

Environment: Index and Abstract: covers articles relating to environmental issues

Federal Index: covers *Congressional Record, Weekly Compilation of Presidential Documents, Federal Register, Code of Federal Regulations, United States Code,* etc.

General Science Index: covers fields such as astronomy, botany, genetics, mathematics, physics, and oceanography

Humanities Index: covers fields such as archaeology, folklore, history, language and literature, performing arts, and philosophy

Index Medicus: covers journal articles, editorials, and biographies related to medicine

MLA International Bibliography: covers modern languages, literatures, and linguistics

Music Index: covers popular music, dance, jazz, and classical music

Psychology Abstracts: covers articles in psychology and related journals

Reader's Guide to Periodical Literature: covers popular periodicals

Social Sciences Index: covers anthropology, psychology, sociology, and related areas

United Nations Document Index (UNDEX): covers publications of the United Nations

Women's Studies Abstracts: covers books, pamphlets, and periodicals on topics relevant to women.

Newspaper Indexes

New York Times Index

Christian Science Monitor Index

Wall Street Journal Index

The Newspaper Index (1972), includes a variety of regional and major market newspapers

Computerized and CD-ROM Indexes

General Periodicals Index: 1,100 general, business, and academic publications since 1987

Reader's Guide to Periodical Literature: going back to 1983

Magazine Index: covers 350 popular magazines going back to the 1940s

Infotrac: covers general periodicals and government documents from 1985 to present

Educational Resources Information Center (ERIC): covers all aspects of education

Business Index: covers business periodicals, books, the *New York Times* financial section, and the *Wall Street Journal*

National Newspaper Index: covers the *New York Times, Christian Science Monitor, Wall Street Journal, Washington Post,* and *Los Angeles Times*

Sources for Specific and/or In-depth Information

Almanacs, Yearbooks, etc.

Annual Register of World Events
Book of Lists
Canadian Almanac and Directory
Economic Almanac
Information Please Almanac
Information Please Environmental Almanac
Old Farmer's Almanac
Statistical Abstract of the United States
World Almanac and Book of Facts
Whitaker's Almanak: Great Britain

Atlases

The Times Atlas of the World
Rand McNally World Atlas
Township Atlas of the United States
Webster's New Geographic Dictionary

Biographical Information

Who's Who: published since 1849; mainly Britons
Who's Who in America: biannually since 1899
Who's Who of American Women: since 1958
International Who's Who: since 1935
Notable American Women
The Dictionary of Canadian Biography
The Dictionary of American Biography: deceased Americans
The Directory of American Scholars
American Men and Women of Science
Current Biography

Quotations

Bartlett's Familiar Quotations
Oxford Dictionary of Quotations
Peter's Quotations: Ideas for Our Time
Simpson's Contemporary Quotations
The Quotable Woman
Beyond Bartlett: Quotations by and About Women

Selected Periodicals

American Demographics: focuses on demographic trends and changing demographics

American Heritage: an interesting history magazine

Americana: contemporary approach to American history focusing on preservation

Business Week: concentrates on business news, patterned after weekly newsmagazines

Changing Times: Kiplinger's monthly report on personal finance

Columbia Journalism Review: critical analysis of media issues

Consumer Reports: a good source of information on consumer goods and services

Discover: popular science magazine

Ebony: articles for and about black readers

Equinox: in-depth profiles of Canadian people, places, and wildlife

Foreign Affairs: establishment quarterly, very influential in government circles

Gray's Sporting Journal: upscale outdoor magazine

Harper's: high-quality general issue magazine

Harvard Business Review: upscale articles on business and management

Harvard Medical School Health Letter: source of reliable, up-to-date medical information written so the lay reader can understand it

Inquiry: libertarian publication (pro free enterprise, anti big government)

Modern Maturity: publication of the American Association of Retired Persons

Money: covers personal finance and consumer issues

Mother Jones: radical left-wing publication, occasionally has good exposés

Nation (The): liberal perspective on contemporary political issues

National Parks: publication of the National Parks and Conservation Association

National Review: conservative perspective on contemporary issues

Natural History: published by the American Museum of Natural History

New Republic (The): liberal perspective on contemporary issues

Newsletter on Intellectual Freedom: published by the American Library Association, contains lists of censored books

Nucleus: quarterly report of the Union of Concerned Scientists

Omni: science for nonscientists

Quarterly Review of Doublespeak: excellent exposé on the uses of language to con the public

Science News: good weekly on what's new in science

Scientific American: good science monthly, difficult reading for lay audience

Sierra: emphasizes conservation and environmental politics

Smithsonian: articles cover popular culture and the fine arts, history, and natural science

Soviet Life: slick Soviet monthly patterned after *Life*

Today's Health: published by the American Medical Association

Village Voice: left-wing, good political exposés

Wilderness: quarterly publication of the Wilderness Society a nonprofit organization devoted to conservation and preservation

Wilson Quarterly: summaries of articles in other magazines plus original articles on many contemporary subjects

Sources for Current Information

Facts on File: A Weekly Digest of World Events with Cumulative Index
Recent issues of periodicals, especially newsweeklies
Recent issues of newspapers

Sources for Local Applications

Vertical File Index
Index to major local or area newspaper
City or state magazines from your area

Internet Resources

Web Browsers and Search Tools

BrowserWatch (up-to-date news on browser downloads): http://www.browserwatch.com/
Netguide Live (search tool and more): http://www.netguide.com
Lexis-Nexis: http://www.lexis-nexis.com
ERIC: http://ericir.syr.edu/
Research It: http://www.itools.com/research-it/research-it.html
One Look: http://www.onelook.com/browse.shtml

Miscellaneous Pages with Relevant Web Site Links

Scoop: http://scoop.evansville.net
Carnegie Mellon English Server: http://english-www.hss.cmu.edu/
University of Iowa Communication Studies: www.uiowa.edu/~commstud/index.html
Libraries Online: http://library.usask.ca/hytelnet/usa/usall.html
Internet Public Library: http://www.ipl.org/
Virtual Library: http://www.w3.org/vl/
Research It: http://www.itolls.com/research-it/research-it.html
New York Times Navigator: http://www.nytimes.com/library/tech/reference/cynavi.html

Multimedia Resources

Multimedia Links: http://www.cdmi.com/Lunch/multimedia.html
Index to Multimedia Information Resources: http://viswiz.gmd.de/MultimediaInfol.
Interactive Multimedia Association: http://www.ima.org/

Health Issues

Prevention: http://www.prevention.com/
Centers for Disease Control and Prevention: http://www.cdc.gov

Medline: http://www.healthgate.com

National Library of Medicine: http://www.nlm.nig.gov/

Merck Manual (guide to diseases): http://www.merck.com/

World Health Organization: http://www.who.ch

Hardin Library for the Health Science: http://www.arcade.uiowa.edu/hardin-www/md.html

Medline: http://www.ncbi.nlm.nih.gov/PubMed/

RxList: The Internet Drug List: http://www.rxlist.com/

Museums and Art Galleries

Guide to Museums and Cultural Resources: http://www.lam.mus.ca.us/webmuseums/

Museum Online Resource Review: http://www.okc.com/morr/

National Museum of the American Indian: http://www.si.edu/nmai

National Civil Rights Museum: http://www.mecca.org/~crights/ncrm.html

American Museum of Natural History: http://www.amnh.org

The Louvre: http://www.paris.org/Musees/Louvre

National Museum of American Art: http://www.nmaa.si.edu:80

Smithsonian: http://www.si.edu/i+d

Environmental Concerns

EnviroLink: http://www.envirolink.org/

Greenpeace: http://www.greenpeace.org/greenpeace.htm

Sierra Club: http://www.sierraclub.org/

Environmental Ethics: http://www.cep.unt.edu/

National Environmental Information Service: http://www.neis.com/neis.html

National Parks and Convervation Association: http://www.npca.org/

National Recycling Coalition: http://www.recycle.net/recycle/Associations/rs000145.html

Women's Resources

The Web for Women (directory of sites for women): http://www.dogpatch.org/women.html

WWWomen: http://www.wwwomen.com/

Women Leaders Online: http://www.wlo.org/

National Organization for Women: http://now.org/now

Books and Literature

Project Gutenberg: http://jg.cso.uiuc.edu/PG/welcome.html

Shakespeare: http://the-tech.mit.edu/Shakespeare/works.html

The Bible (in seven languages): http://www.gospelcom.net/bible

Alex (electronic texts catalog): http://www.lib.ncsu.edu/staff/morgan/alex/alex-index.html

Electronic Books and Text Sites: http://www.awa.com/library/omnimedia/links.html

Online Books Page: http://www.cs.cmu.edu/Web/books.html

Online Literature Library: http://www.literature.org/Works/

News

Vanderbilt University TV News Archive: http://tvnews.vanderbilt.edu/

Newslink: http://www.newslink.org

Ecola Newsstand: http://www.ecola.com/news/

Campus Newspapers on the Internet: http://beacon-asa.utk.edu/resources/papers.html

Pathfinder (Time Warner publications): http://www.pathfinder.com

New York Times: http://www.nytimes.com

USA Today: http://www.usatoday.com

CNN Interactive: http://www.cnn.com

AP Wire Service: http://www.trib.com/NEWS/APwire.html

U.S. News & World Report: http://www.usnews.com

Washington Post: http://www.washingtonpost.com/

Los Angeles Times: http://www.latimes.com/

Times of London: http://www.the-times.co.uk/

Communication—General

American Communication Association: http://www.uark.edu/depts/comminfo/www/ACA.html

Archives of American Public Address: http://douglass.speech.nwu.edu/

Historical Speeches Archive: http://www.webcorp.com/sounds/index.htm

National Communication Association: http://www.natcom.org

Gifts of Speech (speeches by women): http://ripley.wo.sbc.edu/departmental/library/gos/

Science—General

Scientific American: http://www.sciam.com/

Discovery: http://www.discovery.com

Science Frontiers: http://www.knowledge.co.uk/frontiers/

Humanities—General

HNet: http://h-net2.msu.edu/

History Net: http://www.thehistorynet.com/

World Lecture Hall: http://www.utexas.edu/world/lecture/com/

Humanities Hub: http://www.gu.edu.au/gwis/hub/hub.culture.html

Biography Find: http://www.biography.com/find.html

Edsitement: http://edsitement.neh.fed.us

Philanthropies and Charities

Better Business Bureau Philanthropy Advisory Service: http://www.igc.apc.org/cbbb/pas.html

Philanthropy Journal Online (links to charities): http://www.philanthropy~journal.org

Select Nonprofit Organizations on Internet: http://www.fiu.edu/~time4chg/non-profit.html

CHARITIESUSA: http://www.charitiesusa.com

International Service Agencies: http://www.charity.org

United Way: http://www.unitedway.org

Diversity Concerns

American Demographics: http://www.demographics.com

Diversity University: http://www.du.org/places/du/

Diversity Links: http://www.latino.sscnet.ucla.edu/diversity/html#AA

NAACP: http://www.bin.com/assocorg/naacp/naacp.htm

Latino Web: http://www.catalog.com/favision/latnoweb.htm

Native American Information: http://www.freenet.ufl.edu/~native

Asian American Network: http://www.aaa.net rk

Jewish Family & Life: http://www.jewishfamily.com

Anti-Defamation League: http://www.adl.org/

B'nai B'rith: http://bnaibrith.org/ijm/

Media Literacy

Disinform: http://www.disinform.com/disInfo/PROP/media/PROP_media.htm

Center for Media Literacy: http://websites.earthlink.net/~cml

University of Oregon Media Literacy Project: http://interact.uoregon.edu/MediaLit/HomePage

Visual Literacy: http://www.pomona.edu/visual-lit/intro/html

New Mexico Media Literacy Project: http://www.aa.edu

Freedom of Information Center: http://www.missouri.edu/~foiwww

Government and Politics

Great American Web Site (citizen's guide to government sites): http://www.uncle-sam.com

Central Intelligence Agency (World Fact Book): http://www.odci.gov/cia

Department of Justice (includes FBI): http://www.usdoj.gov/

Library of Congress (more than 70 million documents): http://www.loc.gov

United Nations: http://www.un.org

FedWorld Information Network: http://fedworld.gov/

U.S. Historical Documents: http://www.wiretap.spies.com/Gopher/Gov/us-history

U.S. Census Bureau: http://www.census.gov

White House: http://www.whitehouse.gov

U.S. House of Representatives: http://www.house.gov

Political Scientists Guide to the Internet: http://www.trincoll.edu/~pols/guide/home.html

First Amendment Center: http://www.freedomforum.org/first/welcome

Political Commercials Archive: http://www.ou.edu/pcarchiv/

U.S. Senate: http://www.senate.gov

U.S. Department of Education: http://www.ed.gov

C-Span: http://www.c-span.org

Political Education for Everyday Life: http://english-www.cmu.edu/bs/

Business and Commerce

Business Connections: http://www.nytimes.com/library/cyber/reference/buscom.html

Global Interactive Business Directory: http://www.pronett.com

Consumer Information Catalog: http://www.gsa.gov/staff/pa/cic/cic.htm

Netsearch Business Web Pages: http://www.netmail.com/

Business Netiquette International: http://www.wp.com/fredfish/Netiq.html

Business Women's Network: http://www.tpag.com/bwn.html

Minority/Women's Business Connection: http://www.mwbe.com/mwbe/default.htm

Business Week: http://www.businessweek.com

Language

American Slanguage: http://www.slanguage.com

StreetSpeak: http:///www.jayi.com/jayi/Fishnet/StreetSpeak

Quotations: http://www.cc.columbia.edu/aci/bartleby/bartlett

Roget's Thesaurus: http://humanities.uchicago.edu/forms_unrest/ROGET.html

Jack Lynch's Grammar Notes: http://www.english.upenn.edu/~jlynch/grammar.html

ERIC Clearinghouse on Reading, English, and Communication: http://www.indiana.edu/~eric_rec/

Legal Concerns

Findlaw: http://www.findlaw.com

LawInfo: http://www.lawinfo.com/

Internet Legal Resource Guide: http://uts.cc.utexas.edu/~juris/

Law Journal Extra!: http://www.ljx.com/

West's Legal Directory: http://www.wld.com/

Decisions of U.S. Supreme Court: http://www.law.cornell.edu/supct/supct.table.html

Religion

The Bible Browser: http://goon.stg.brown.edu/bible_browser/pbeasy.shtml

Comparative Religion: http://weber.u.washington.edu/~madin

First Church of Cyberspace: http://execpc.com/~chender

The Vatican: http://www.vatican.va

Episcopal Church Home Page: http://www.ai.mit.edu/people/mib/anglican/anglican.html

United Methodist Information: http://www.umc.org

Society of Friends: http://www.misc.org/geeks/bnorum/quaker

Unitarian Universalist Association: http://www.uua.org

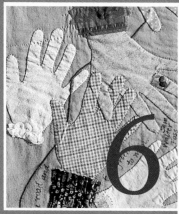

6

Using Supporting Materials in Your Speech

*T*he universe
is made up
of stories, not of
atoms.
—*Muriel Rukeyser*

This chapter will help you

■ understand the nature and forms of supporting materials
■ select the best supporting materials for your speeches
■ learn how to use supporting materials to best advantage

*O*ur home stands atop a ridgeline several hundred feet above the Tennessee River. The terrain slopes at about a 45-degree angle, so that while the front of the home rests upon solid earth, the back of it rises on posts some thirty feet above the ground. You might think that the structure is flimsy, but actually it is quite strong. Our builders selected quality wood, concrete, plastics, and steel, and fashioned and combined these materials into powerful supports.

In the next several chapters we will think of you too as a builder—a builder of ideas. We will think of your speeches as thought structures raised up on solid pillars of supporting materials. Like our builders, you must know your materials and what they can support. You need to know how to select them and how to use them wisely. Just as our home is built to withstand storms and high winds, your speech must withstand doubt and even controversy. When you stand to present it, you must be confident of its structural integrity.

FACTS AND STATISTICS, testimony, examples, and narratives are the major forms of **supporting materials** used in the building of speeches. These materials provide the substance, strength, credibility, and appeal a speech must have before listeners will place their faith in it. Without supporting materials speeches are just empty words blowing in the wind. *Their essential functions are to arouse and sustain interest, to explain the meaning of your ideas, to make your interpretations credible, to underscore their importance to listeners, and to verify controversial or surprising statements you might make.*

Your personal experience, Internet and library research, and interviews with experts, described in Chapter 5, should have provided you with a good stockpile of these materials. We will discuss each type of supporting material, how to identify good and defective forms of it, when it can be most useful, and how to put it to work in your speeches.

Facts and Statistics

Facts and statistics are the most objective forms of supporting material. Unlike other forms, they can stand alone and are independent of any one person's experience of them. Examples, stories, and testimony are more subjective, in that they depend more on the experience of one person or a group. This relatively independent nature of facts and statistics means that you can count on them to add credibility to your ideas. If "the facts are in your favor," this creates a presumption that what you are saying is true. Therefore, facts and statistics are especially important when your topic is unfamiliar or your ideas are controversial.

Facts

Facts are verifiable units of information, which means that independent observers see and report them consistently. Richard Weaver, a prominent communication critic writing in the 1950s, suggested that Americans honor facts and numbers as the highest form of knowledge, much as some other societies respect divine revelation.[1] Although we may believe that we are more sophisticated consumers of communication than the audiences of the 1950s, a recent Gallup survey confirmed that 86 percent of those polled still agree that "references to scientific research in a story increased its credibility."[2] We still worship at the altar of science.

The following statements are factual because they can be shown to be either true or false:

> **Chevrolet Tahoe is an American-made utility vehicle.**
> **Most students at our school earn their degrees in five years.**
> **Television ads often rely on emotional appeals.**

While factual statements can stand by themselves, speakers rarely use them without interpreting them. Interpretations usually add a few words that transform factual statements into claims:

> **Chevrolet Tahoe is a *superior* American-made utility vehicle.**
> **Most *hard-working* students at our school earn their degrees in five years.**
> **Television ads often rely on *unethical* emotional appeals.**

There is nothing wrong with making interpretations or claims. We often must shape factual statements to fit our purpose. The problem comes when speakers and audiences forget that these are no longer simply factual statements that can stand alone without further demonstration. The addition of such words as "superior," "hard-working," or "unethical" means that these speakers have added another burden of proof to their speeches. They now must produce other facts or statistics, examples, testimony, or stories to prove that the claims are justified—that they are more than just opinions.

We usually cannot verify directly the accuracy of such claims. We have no idea how we might proceed on our own to verify that Chevrolet Tahoes actually are "superior." We therefore have to look to independent authorities who are competent to verify such claims and who have no economic axe to grind. So we might say in a speech, "According to the latest issue of *Consumer Reports,* which did extensive tests with many utility vehicles, the Chevrolet Tahoe is superior." If our reading of *Consumer Reports* is correct, we have introduced a factual statement in support of a claim. Because this factual statement comes from an expert source, we have combined fact and expert testimony, which we discuss later in this chapter. Incidentally, note also how we reassure careful listeners: Our source is the "latest," and *CR* was responsible in its work ("did extensive tests").

Sources of information have ethos just as speakers do. For example, *Consumer Reports* enjoys a reputation for responsible, objective testing of products. On social or political issues, the ideological position of the source may be important. For example, if you cited William F. Buckley, Jr.'s *National Review* in support of a claim, skeptical listeners might respond, "Well, that's a conservative magazine. Of course Buckley will support this right-wing claim!" On the other hand, if you also cite *The New Republic,* a more liberal publication, then skeptical listeners might think, "Well, if both left and right agree, then maybe what she's saying is true."[3]

Even seemingly neutral sources present "factual" information that is colored by its cultural environment. Compare the following excerpts from the same encyclopedia in its 1960 and 1990 editions:

> *1960:* Kiowa Indians hunted buffalo on the southwestern plains of the United States. The Kiowa and their allies, the Comanche, raided many Texas ranches. They probably killed more whites than any other Indian tribe. . . . By [a] treaty signed in 1868, the Kiowa agreed to go with the Comanche to a reservation in Indian territory (now Oklahoma). But only the Kiowa chiefs had signed the treaty, and no chiefs could force their young men to make such a sacrifice. Many struggles and arrests occurred before the Kiowa finally went to live on the reservation. When trouble broke out in 1874, Satanta, one of the most daring Kiowa leaders, was arrested and sentenced to prison. There he committed suicide. The Kiowa then "put their hands to the plow." They now live peacefully as farmers. Several have become well-known artists.

> *1990:* Kiowa Indians are a tribe that lives largely in Oklahoma and elsewhere in the Southwestern United States. The tribe has about 8,000 members, most of whom live in rural communities near Anadarko, Carnegie, and Mountain View, Oklahoma. Other tribal members live in urban areas and work in law, medicine, teaching, and other professions. . . . [In] 1970 the Kiowa adopted their own tribal constitution. The tribe is governed by the Kiowa Indian Council, which consists of all members who are at least 18 years old. The Kiowa Business Committee, an elected group, manages tribal programs in such fields as business, education, and health.[4]

Both of these accounts are "factual," but the first dwells upon past conflict, defining the Kiowas as adversaries of the dominant culture, while the second emphasizes their present assimilation. The contrast reminds us that even relatively objective descriptions are selective and incomplete. We should always ask ourselves what any given description leaves out, and whether that omission might be critical. In short, we should try to determine what is information and what is **disinformation**, "misplaced, fragmented, irrelevant, or superficial information . . . that creates the illusion of knowing something but which, in fact, leads one away from knowing."[5]

Statistics

Statistics are numerical facts that can describe the size of something, make predictions, illustrate trends, or show relationships. Americans are almost as much in awe of numbers as they are of science. In the same Gallup study cited earlier in this chapter, 82 percent of those surveyed said that statistics increased a story's credibility.[6] These figures suggest that statistics can be one of the most powerful forms of supporting material.

The following example from a student speech demonstrates how statistical information can appear in speeches:

> **The Environmental Protection Agency is saying that secondhand smoke causes 3,000 lung cancer deaths a year; 35,000 heart disease deaths a year; and contributes to 150,000 to 300,000 respiratory infections in babies, mainly bronchitis and pneumonia, resulting in 7,500 to 15,000 hospitalizations. It triggers 8,000 to 26,000 new cases of asthma in previously unaffected children and exacerbates symptoms in 400,000 to 1 million asthmatic children.**

When presented orally, statistics can be a bit overwhelming. Using a brief explanation, example, or presentation aid (see Chapter 9) can make numerical information more understandable in your speeches. Compare the example cited above with the way a physician used similar figures to help his listeners understand the extent of the medical problems caused by smoking:

> **I ask you to check your watches. Because in this hour, by the time I'm done speaking, 50 Americans will die from smoke-related diseases. By the time you sit down to breakfast in the morning, 600 more will have joined them: 8,400 by the end of the week—every week, every month, every year—until it kills nearly half-a-million Americans, year in, year out. That's more than all the other preventable causes of death combined. Alcohol, illegal drugs, AIDS, suicide, car accidents, fires, guns—all are killers. But tobacco kills more than all of them put together.**
>
> **These are hard, cold realities, defined by hard, cold statistics. But I'd ask you to remember this most important fact. Every statistic is an encoded memorial to what was once a living, breathing—loving and loved—mother, father, sister, brother. Not numbers, real people, and the toll is as terrible as the most horrific war.[7]**

The contrast provided by these two examples is revealing. The first speaker almost drowns the listener with numbers. The second uses fewer numbers, but connects them into a clearer pattern. Moreover, by comparing smoking to other forms of preventable death, he builds its importance in our minds. Finally, he increases the impact by describing the people his numbers represent. We shall discuss these techniques of comparison and description in more detail later in this chapter.

Evaluating Facts and Statistics

For almost any topic you select, your research notes should contain a wide assortment of facts and statistics. Before you decide which of these materials you will actually use in your speeches, use the critical thinking skills we discussed in Chapter 3 to evaluate them. Ask the following questions:

- Is this information relevant?
- Is this information the most recent available?

- Are the sources of this information credible?
- Is this information reliable?

As you review your research notes, you may discover a great deal of interesting information about your topic that does not relate directly to your specific purpose. No matter how fascinating it seems, if the information does not fit, don't use it. A speech that is cluttered with interesting digressions is hard for listeners to follow. You should also be certain that any statistics you cite are relevant to your locale. If you talk about the "crisis of unemployment" in your area, basing your claim on a national average of 7 percent, you could have a problem if someone points out that the local rate is only 4 percent.

You must also consider how current the information is, especially when your topic is one on which information changes rapidly. On certain fast-breaking subjects, yesterday's news is already obsolete. When you speak on such topics, be sure you are up to date. Save yourself the embarrassment of having a listener point out that your claims are invalid because of what happened just this morning!

It is also important that you evaluate the sources of your information. Test even "factual" material for potential bias, distortions, or omissions. Don't be taken in by "scientific sounding" names, especially if the information contradicts common sense. Cynthia Crossen, a reporter and editor with the *Wall Street Journal,* exposes many instances of such deception in her book *Tainted Truth.* For example, she points to a claim made by "the Cooper Institute for Aerobic Research" that "white bread will not make you gain weight." It turns out that the study that produced this amazing conclusion was funded by the makers of Wonder Bread.[8]

To guard against deceptive information, do not rely too heavily on any one source. Compare what different expert sources have to say. The more controversial your topic, the more important it is that your information be sound. In your speech, tell listeners how you have tested vital pieces of information. They will appreciate your efforts to offer them the truth.

As you weigh the use of facts and statistics, be careful not to read into information what you want to find or to exaggerate the results. Be on guard against the tendency to distort facts and statistics by the way you word them. Don't ignore information that contradicts your claims by rejecting it out of hand as atypical or irrelevant.

Be especially careful when using statistics. Keep in mind that statistical predictions are based on probability, not certainty, and that they are subject to misuse and abuse. Peter Francese, founder and president of *American Demographics,* has pointed out that while statistics are supposed to represent reality, they may also be used to create reality:

Politicians and lobbyists carefully select the numbers they use to talk about crime (it's always rampant) or immigration (it's always out of control). The numbers are typically used to prove there is a "big" problem. It's like rounding up vicious dogs to prove that all dogs bite. . . . No number can represent truth perfectly. Every survey has some error or bias. Data from public records, such as crime reports, can be underreported or misclassified. And even perfectly collected data are open to different interpretations.[9]

Chapter 14's discussion of other misuses of facts and statistics as evidence in persuasive speaking will give you additional help in evaluating information and using it ethically.

Using Facts and Statistics

Three techniques for framing facts and statistics into powerful supporting materials are definitions, explanations, and descriptions.

Definitions.   A **definition** helps your audience understand what you are talking about by translating your topic into words your listeners will understand. It helps to ensure that speaker and listeners are talking about the same thing. Audience analysis should help you determine whether you need to provide definitions in your speech. As a general rule, you should provide definitions for any technical terms that are unfamiliar to your audience the first time you use them. In her informative speech at Vanderbilt on genetic testing, Ashlie McMillan first offered a technical definition: "According to 'The Genetic Revolution,' an article in *Scientific Magazine,* genetic testing 'is correlating the inheritance of a distinctive segment of DNA, a marker localizing the mutant gene on a DNA strand which composes our chromosomes.'" Noting the puzzled look on her listeners' faces, Ashlie then said, "I found that a little confusing too, so I tried to put it in my own words: Genetic testing is simply looking at people's DNA to find a pattern of a mutant gene. That's basically what it is."

Definitions can be persuasive as well as informative. A persuasive definition reflects your way of looking at a controversial subject. It presents your perspective in such a way that your listeners will want to share it. A persuasive definition usually puts the subject in an emotional context. In a speech on domestic violence against women Donna Shalala, U.S. Secretary of Health and Human Services, provided the following persuasive definition of domestic violence: "Domestic violence is terrorism. Terrorism in the home. And that is what we should call it."[10]

Explanations.   Longer and more detailed than definitions, **explanations** combine facts and statistics to clarify a topic or demonstrate how it works. The following explanation of "old growth," combined perhaps with an enlarged photograph as a presentation aid, might work well in a speech on forest preservation:

> **From a traditional forester's view, old-growth forests are those in which wood production has reached its peak. . . . Old-growth forests contain many large, live, ancient trees. They are forests that have never been harvested. The Wilderness Society defines "classic" old growth as "containing at least eight big trees per acre exceeding 300 years in age or measuring more than 40 inches in diameter at breast height."[11]**

Again, it is important to offer explanations early in your speech to help your listeners easily grasp your meaning.

Descriptions.   **Descriptions** are "word pictures" that help listeners visualize information. The best descriptions evoke vivid images in the minds of the audience. The great Roman rhetorician Longinus once said of images that

Using Facts and Statistics

speaker's notes

1   Use the most recent, reliable facts and statistics.
2   Don't over-rely on one source; check several sources to verify important information.
3   Use information from unbiased sources who have no vested interest in the results they report.
4   Interpret information accurately. Do not stretch or twist its meaning.
5   When using statistics in speeches, round off numbers whenever you can do so without distorting results.
6   Make statistics understandable by amplifying them with examples or visual aids.
7   Don't overwhelm your audience with a barrage of facts and statistics.

they occur when, "carried away by enthusiasm and passion, you think you see what you describe, and you place it before the eyes of your hearers."[12] Images color information with the speaker's feelings; they establish a mood in addition to increasing understanding. Note how the following description of the monument at Wounded Knee, which commemorates the massacre of hundreds of Sioux men, women, and children (the complete text of this speech is in Appendix B), both paints a picture and establishes a mood:

> **Two red brick columns topped with a wrought iron arch and a small metal cross form the entrance to the grave site. The column to the right is in bad shape: Cinder blocks from the base are missing; the brickwork near the top has deteriorated and tumbled to the ground; graffiti on the columns proclaim an attitude we found repeatedly expressed about the Bureau of Indian Affairs: "The BIA sucks!" Crumbling concrete steps lead you to the mass grave. The top of the grave is covered with gravel, punctuated by unruly patches of chickweed and crabgrass.**

Such descriptions help bring information to life for an audience. But a word of caution is in order. The description above works well because it is *understated*. All too often beginning speakers indulge in emotional overkill. They add too many adjectives, too much emotional coloration. If "grave site" here were "lonely grave site," if "attitude" were "angry attitude," if "mass grave" were "abandoned mass grave," we would begin to think more about the speaker's feelings than about the subject being portrayed. *Let listeners supply the adjectives in their own minds.* That way, they will *participate* in creating the image. They will feel engaged by the speech rather than manipulated by it.

Testimony

You use **testimony** when you cite the words and ideas of others in support of your message. When you repeat the exact words of others, you are using a **direct quotation**. Direct quotations are useful when the material is brief, the exact wording is important, or the language is especially eloquent. When

When Arnold Schwarzenegger speaks on physical fitness his words become a combination of both prestige and expert testimony—powerful forms of support.

points are controversial, direct quotations can also seem especially authoritative and conclusive. You also may **paraphrase** material, or restate in your own words what others have said. When you paraphrase testimony, you must still cite the source: who said it, why we should respect that person, where it was said, and when it was said.

There are three types of testimony that are useful as supporting material. Expert testimony comes from sources who are authorities on the topic. Lay testimony involves citing ordinary citizens who may have firsthand experience with the topic. Prestige testimony comes from someone who is highly regarded but is not necessarily an expert on the topic.

Expert Testimony

Expert testimony comes from people who are qualified by training or experience to serve as authorities on a subject. As you review your research notes, you will probably discover statements by experts offering opinions, information, or simply interesting quotations. When you cite experts in your speeches, you are calling on them as qualified witnesses to support your case. Using expert testimony allows you to borrow their credibility to make your own message more convincing. Expert testimony is especially important when your topic is innovative, unfamiliar, highly technical, or controversial.

When you use expert testimony, remember that competence is area-specific. That means that your experts can speak *as experts* only within their area of expertise. For example, emergency room physicians who can provide expert testimony on the physical effects of gunshot wounds may not qualify as experts on gun control legislation. As you introduce expert testimony in your speeches, be sure to present the credentials of your experts. Emphasize the recency of their statements, and, when appropriate, indicate that their words appeared in a prestigious journal, book, or newspaper.

sia, who come together regularly in the village to discuss nutrition, family planning, and baby care. . . . I have met women in South Africa who helped lead the struggle to end apartheid and are now helping build a new democracy. . . . I have met women in India and Bangladesh who are taking out small loans to buy milk cows, rickshaws, thread and other materials to create a livelihood for themselves and their families. I have met doctors and nurses in Belarus and Ukraine who are trying to keep children alive in the aftermath of Chernobyl. The great challenge of this conference is to give voice to women everywhere whose experiences go unnoticed, whose words go unheard.[21]

Examples also provide emphasis. When you make a statement and follow it with an example, you are pointing out that what you have just said is IMPORTANT. Examples amplify your ideas. They say to the audience, "This bears repeating." Examples are especially helpful when you introduce new, complex, or abstract material. Not only can they make such information clearer, they also allow time for the audience to process what you have said before you move on to your next point.

Types of Examples

Examples take different forms, and these forms have different functions. An example may be brief or extended and may be based either on an actual event or on something that might have happened.

Brief Examples.   A **brief example** mentions a specific instance to demonstrate a more general statement. Brief examples are concise and to the point. To open the speech cited above on effective marketing for people with disabilities, Sue Suter, former president of the World Institute on Disabilities, used the following brief example:

> You do vital work. And much of it deals with marketing. That reminded me of a message found on an old tombstone in Springdale, Ohio. It reads: "Here lies Jane Smith, wife of Thomas Smith, marble cutter. This monument was erected by her husband as a tribute to her memory and a specimen of his work. Monuments of the same style $350."[22]

Extended Examples.   An **extended example** contains more detail and allows you to dwell more fully on a single instance. In her speech on disabilities, Suter used two extended examples, one contained within the other, to allow her audience to focus on her theme. The wider, inclusive example was her tribute to Franklin Delano Roosevelt, who was also disabled by polio. The extended example contained within this tribute was her own experience:

> Back in 1990, I became the first person with a disability to be nominated by a major party to run for a statewide office in Illinois. That was tough. Wondering how people would accept me. Having to crawl into small planes (they were free rides) so that I could make the next engagement. Riding in parades and waving while other candidates

walked and shook hands along the route. And being hoisted onto hay stacks to address crowds. These were accommodations I accepted. Just as Roosevelt had done years before.

We lost a close race. Yet looking back on it all, one impression especially touched me. Most people, I'm convinced, saw the real Sue Suter. A major party candidate fighting in a tough election. Not a cripple to pity. And I'm convinced that is the way people would see FDR today.[23]

Extended examples give us more detailed information. They allow the speaker to convey feeling about a topic that might be lost if the speech relied solely on brief examples.

Factual Examples.   A **factual example** is based on an actual event or a real person. Factual examples provide strong support for your ideas because they actually did happen. University of Memphis student Mark Thompson used the following factual example to define the meaning of generosity:

Generosity? I'll tell you what it means. Last week, tennis champion Arthur Ashe died—one more innocent victim of AIDS. Yesterday, a retired secretary and grandmother who is dying of lung cancer in Brooklyn gave $400,000 to St. Jude Children's Research Hospital to help create the Arthur Ashe Chair for Pediatric AIDS Research. She wanted his name remembered, not hers. We know only that she is a person "of very modest means" who received the money in a malpractice suit when doctors failed to recognize her symptoms of cancer. She wanted to reach out to children who, like her, are fighting terminal illness.

While she remains anonymous, this obscure woman is a champion too—a champion of the human spirit. She has given us a gift far more precious than her money.

Hypothetical Examples.   Examples need not be real to be effective. A **hypothetical example** is a composite of actual people, situations, or events. Although created by the speaker, it claims to represent reality and therefore must be plausible. The following hypothetical example was used by University of New Mexico student Susan Romero to illustrate the meaning of "cabin fever":

Picture the following: you're in a room with five other people—four of them under ten years old, brimming with energy. It's been raining for six days—a cold, heavy rain. No one can go outside. The kids run in circles and fight with one another. The other adult nags at you when awake and snores when asleep. Would you feel the walls closing in on you? Would you have an irresistible impulse to go somewhere, anywhere, to escape? That, my friends, is cabin fever.

You should use hypothetical examples when the factual examples you find don't adequately represent the *truth* of a situation, or when a factual example might embarrass actual, living people. Be especially careful that your hypothetical examples are truly representative, and that they don't distort the truth just to make your point. Always alert your listeners to the hypothetical

Using Examples

speaker's notes

1   Use examples to arouse and sustain attention, clarify abstract or technical ideas, and emphasize major points.

2   Make your examples specific by naming the people and places in them.

3   Use factual examples whenever possible.

4   Use examples that are believable and representative of a situation.

5   Keep examples brief and to the point; do not ramble.

6   Be selective in your use of examples. Save them for points of major importance.

nature of your example; such introductory phrases as "imagine yourself," "picture the following," or "let's pretend that" should caution audiences that they will be hearing a hypothetical example that nevertheless purports to represent the truth. The standards of ethical speech require that you never present a hypothetical example as though it were factual.

Evaluating and Using Examples

Evaluate examples in terms of their relevance, representativeness, and believability. No matter how interesting an example may seem, if it does not advance your specific purpose, leave it out. Examples must also fairly represent situations as they actually exist. Remember, what works well with one audience may seem out of place with another. Examples must meet the tests of taste and propriety. They should fit the mood and spirit of the occasion. Risk offending listeners only when they must be shocked into attention before they can be informed or persuaded.

Examples often make the difference between a speech that is humdrum and one that is successful. Highlight their authenticity by providing concrete details—the names of the people, places, times, and institutions involved in them. It is much easier for a listener to relate to Matt Dunn of the local General Motors plant than to some anonymous worker in an unnamed company. Use transitions to move smoothly from statement to example and from example to statement. Phrases such as "For instance . . ." or "As you can see . . ." work nicely.

Narratives

A **narrative** goes beyond an example by *telling a story* within the speech. Humans have been storytellers from the dawn of time. Most children are brought up on narratives—stories that entertain, fables that warn of dangers, and parables that teach virtues. People organize their experiences and memories in terms of the stories they tell.[24] Moreover, when information seems odd (e.g., a Harvard-educated plumber), people look for the stories that will explain the phenomenon and satisfy their curiosity.[25]

Narratives are especially effective in speeches because they draw listeners into the action. Because listeners can often "see" themselves enacting certain roles within the stories, narratives can encourage those transformations of identity and behavior that ethical public speaking makes possible. Moreover, narratives stimulate the process of constructive listening that we discussed in Chapter 3. Because stories prompt listeners to create meaning from what they hear, the audience becomes involved in the creation of the message. It becomes *their* discovery, *their* truth. Such involvement enhances the impact of the message.

Personal narratives also increase identification between speakers and audiences. They can help bridge the cultural differences that separate people of diverse backgrounds. According to Vice President Gore, storytelling can even help old enemies make peace. On one occasion, when Palestinian, Israeli, Jordanian, and Syrian leaders met to discuss a peace treaty, Gore saw the negotiations coming to a standstill. The situation looked unpromising until, in Gore's words, "The breakthroughs came when they told stories about their families. I have seen time and time again how storytelling brings people together."[26]

Narratives serve many of the same functions as examples. They make a speech livelier and help sustain attention. They clarify abstract or technical ideas. They emphasize a point by telling a story that illustrates it. A narrative functions as a speech within a speech—it begins with an attention-getting introduction, continues with a body in which the story develops, and ends with a conclusion that wraps up the message. Facts and statistics fade with time, but narratives leave the audience with something to remember.

For all these good reasons, the ability to tell stories effectively has become one of the most sought-after skills among candidates for top entry-level positions in American business. More than fifty corporate recruiters surveyed in

Narratives are an important form of supporting material. A well-told story involves the audience in the creation of meaning.

1994–1995 by the Owen Graduate School of Management at Vanderbilt University identified communication skills in general, and storytelling ability in particular, as key to successful interviewing for top positions. Peter Veruki, director of career planning at Owen, concluded:

> **It is becoming increasingly important for candidates to be adept at the art of storytelling. The more the candidate can make his or her experience vivid and memorable for the recruiter, the greater the odds are of advancing to the next stage of the interview process. M.B.A.s should engage the interviewer by adding rich, visual detail to what they relate about their work and personal histories.**[27]

Because they can be so effective at involving the audience, narratives are often used in the introductions of speeches. Narratives that contain a light touch of humor also help make the audience comfortable.[28] Bob Newhart opened his 1997 commencement speech at Catholic University of America with the following story:

> **When I was asked to be the commencement speaker I was reminded of a story about Jascha Heifetz, the famed violinist, who was asked to play in Grange Hall in Minot, North Dakota. He agreed to do it sometime in December. As December came around the weather turned terrible in New York and he called up and said, "I'm sorry, I won't be able to make it." The man who arranged for him to appear there said, "We have 3,000 people in Grange Hall here in Minot, could you try to?" And he said, "I will." So he finally got out of New York and flew to Denver, caught a small plane, and finally got into Minot at about 11 o'clock at night and walked into Grange Hall and there were 12 people waiting.**
>
> **He said, "I'm sorry I can't appear in front of such a small audience. You said there were 3,000 people here." And he said, "Well there were, but they were afraid you wouldn't show up." He said "I've never appeared in front of such a small audience." And the man who had arranged for him to be there said, "Jascha, if you could just sing one or two songs, that would be . . ."**
>
> **So I feel somewhat like that. . . . I'm not sure you have the right man, but I'm very honored.**[29]

Concluding narratives leave the audience with something to remember and extend the impact of a message. They can establish a mood that will last long after the closing words have been spoken. In a speech presented in April 1997 to the Economic Club in Chicago, Newton Minow, former chair of the Federal Communications Commission, concluded his plea for campaign finance reform with the following:

> **I leave you with a story President Kennedy told a week before he was killed. The story was about French Marshal Louis Lyautey, who walked one morning through his garden with his gardener. He stopped at a certain point and asked the gardener to plant a tree there the next morning. The gardener said, "But the tree will not bloom for one hundred years!" The Marshal looked at the gardener and replied, "In that case, you had better plant it this afternoon."**[30]

In a narrative, dialogue is usually preferable to paraphrase. When speakers use dialogue, they reproduce conversation directly. Paraphrasing can save time, but it can also rob a narrative of power and a sense of immediacy. Let people speak for themselves in your narratives. The late Senator Sam Ervin of North Carolina was a master storyteller. Note how he used dialogue in the following narrative, which opened a speech on the Constitution and our judicial system:

> **Jim's administrator was suing the railroad for his wrongful death. The first witness he called to the stand testified as follows: "I saw Jim walking up the track. A fast train passed, going up the track. After it passed, I didn't see Jim. I walked up the track a little way and discovered Jim's severed head lying on one side of the track, and the rest of his body on the other." The witness was asked how he reacted to his gruesome discovery. He responded: "I said to myself, 'Something serious must have happened to Jim.'"**
>
> **Something serious has been happening to constitutional government in America. I want to talk to you about it.[31]**

Had "Mr. Sam" paraphrased this story as "The witness reported that he knew instantly that the victim had had a serious accident," he would have destroyed its effect. Dialogue makes a narrative come alive by bringing listeners close to the action. Paraphrase distances the audience.

Evaluating Narratives

Speakers sometimes "borrow" a narrative from an anthology of stories or jokes and then strain to connect it with their topic. Narratives should never be used simply to amuse listeners. They must also help you make your point. An irrelevant narrative distracts listeners. The audience can also be turned off by stories that foster negative stereotypes or that contain offensive language. Finally, ask yourself whether the narrative will seem fresh and original. If listeners have already heard your story, they may decide you have nothing new to say.

Storytelling is an important folk art. Set off the story from the rest of your speech by pausing as you begin and end the story. Slow down! Tales are to be savored, and the pause is essential to the unfolding drama. Your language should be colorful and active, and you can use voice and dialect changes to signal listeners that a "character" is speaking. Create a sense of anticipation and suspense as you build to the punchline or conclusion. If your story evokes laughter, wait for it to subside before going on. Since storytelling is an intimate form of communication, reduce the distance between yourself and your listeners—either by actually moving toward them or by being less formal. Finally, you should practice telling your story to get the wording and timing just right.

Avoid stories that are funny at the expense of others. If you poke fun at anyone, let it be yourself. Speakers who tell amusing stories about themselves sometimes rise in the esteem of listeners. When this technique is effective, the stories that seem to put the speakers down are actually building them up.[32] Note how former President Jimmy Carter used this type of humor as he acknowledged his introduction as a speaker at commencement exercises at Rice University:

speaker's notes

> I didn't know what Charles [the person who introduced him] was going to say. For those who have been in politics and who are introduced, you never know what to expect. There was a time when I was introduced very simply. "Ladies and gentlemen, the President of the United States," period. But then when I left office I was quite often invited by lowly Democrats who were in charge of a program at an event. Then when I got there with two or three TV cameras, the leaders of the organization—almost invariably Republicans—would take over the introduction of me, and quite often the introduction would be a very negative one derived primarily from President Reagan's campaign notes. I had to do something to heal my relationship with the audience before I could speak so I always would tell them after that, "Ladies and gentlemen, of all the introductions I've ever had in my life, that is the most recent."[33]

A well-told narrative can add much to a speech, but the use of narrative should be reserved for special occasions. Too many narratives can turn a speech into a rambling string of stories without a clear focus. Use narratives to arouse or sustain attention, to create a special mood for your message, or to demonstrate some important truth.

Three Techniques for Using Supporting Materials

The best materials for building homes on hilltops are only as good as the builders who use them. Similarly, the best supporting materials for speeches depend for their effectiveness on the skill of speechmakers. Much of the art of building speeches depends upon the wise use of three major techniques. *Comparison, contrast,* and *analogy* are general techniques for using all the forms of supporting materials—to best advantage.

Comparison

A **comparison** helps an audience grasp a subject by pointing out its similarities to something else. These similarities provide a context or frame in which the subject can be understood. In this way, comparison can make an unfamiliar or controversial idea seem more clear or acceptable by connecting it with something the audience already understands or accepts. Or comparison can help the audience see the significance of supporting materials. Consider how Maurice Johnson used comparison in a classroom speech to point up the meaning of a statistic:

> Let's suppose that you have a job offer here in Memphis that pays $35,000 per year. You're not really sure you want to stay in Memphis, and you know salaries are higher in other cities. But how do these salaries really compare? Will that higher salary in Boston, or New York City, or Chicago actually be higher than what you could earn in Memphis? *Money Magazine's* Web site has a "Salary Comparator" that lets you see how things stack up. For example, in 1998, to equal the Memphis $35,000 salary, you'd have to make $63,000 in Chicago; in Boston, you'd have to make $69,000; and in New York City, you'd have to make a whopping $104,000.

Here the background of similarities really makes the meaning of the hypothetical salary offer stand out in bold relief. Before you decide to use a comparison, ask yourself these questions:

- *Are there enough similarities to justify the comparison?* The similarities among four places that are all large urban cities in the United States might be enough to justify a comparison.

- *Are the similarities significant to the idea you wish to support?* The fact that crime statistics are higher (or lower) in New York City than in the other cities cited would not be especially pertinent to the point of the comparison.

- *Are there important differences that might invalidate the comparison?* Here you must imagine yourself as an unfriendly critic of the comparison. An unfriendly critic might argue that while the dollar has more purchasing power in Memphis, there might well be less for it to purchase. You will have to decide whether the comparison is strong enough to overcome such objections.

Contrast

A **contrast** emphasizes the differences among things. Just as a red cross stands out more vividly against a white background than against an orange one, contrasts make facts and statistics, examples, testimony, and narratives stand out. Newton Minow, in the speech cited previously on campaign finance reform, used contrast in his introduction to heighten the effects of both example and statistics:

> Campaign spending is as old as the republic. When George Washington ran for the Virginia House of Burgesses in 1757, his total campaign expenditures, in the form of "good cheer," came to "28 gallons of rum, 50 gallons of rum punch, 34 gallons of wine, 36 gallons of beer, and 2 gallons of cider royal."
>
> Today, the era of good cheer is gone. For four decades now, campaign expenditures have been driven relentlessly upward by one thing: television. In 1960, in what would be the first presidential cam-

paign to make wide use of television, Democrats and Republicans together spent $14.2 million on radio and television commercials. In 1996, candidates for federal office spent more than 128 times that amount on television and radio commercials, an estimated $1.8 billion.[34]

As you consider whether to use a particular contrast, ask yourself the following:

- *Is the sense of contrast dramatic enough to help my case?* The contrasts between 1757, 1960, and 1996 are quite striking.

- *Is the difference relevant to the point I wish to make?* The point that per capita consumption of alcoholic beverages also differed during these three eras would hardly serve the point of the contrast.

- *Are there other points of difference that might invalidate the point?* Again, take the point of view of an unfriendly critic. Such a person might point out that George Washington had to appeal to a highly elite electorate, all of whom lived in one small area of a state. The costs of federal elections with a national electorate are the price, such a critic might argue, of modern democracy.

Analogy

An **analogy** combines the principles of both comparison and contrast: *It points out the similarities between things or concepts that are essentially dissimilar.* Analogies come in two forms. The first, literal analogies, are much the same as comparisons in that they tie together subjects from the same realm of experience, such as football and soccer, in order to reinforce a point. The second form, **figurative analogy**, combines subjects from different realms of experience. Our opening to this chapter uses a figurative analogy between building homes and building speeches. We will return to this analogy over the next several chapters, because it seems to be a productive way of thinking about what we are describing. Analogies make concepts or ideas that are remote or abstract more immediate and comprehensible. They are especially useful near the beginnings of speeches, where they establish a frame of thinking in which the speech can develop. M. George Allen, senior vice president of research and development for the 3M Company, combined comparison, contrast, and analogy as he established a perspective for his speech, "Succeeding in Japan":

> I think of doing business in Japan as being like a game of football. But first, you need to know which game of football it is you are playing. Is it the American gridiron sport—or what the rest of the world calls football and what we call soccer?
>
> American football is a bruising battle. The players are huge and strong. They have nicknames like "Refrigerator." And the game is played in short bursts of intense energy. In soccer-football, the players are smaller, but faster. Play is continuous. And a soccer fullback weighs less than lunch for a gridiron fullback.
>
> In a nutshell, gridiron football is trench warfare: soccer football is the cavalry. Likewise, when it comes to business, the Japanese play a different game than we do.[35]

In this example, Mr. Allen first draws a *comparison* with football, perhaps to emphasize the aggressive, competitive qualities of international business. He next proceeds to develop a *contrast* between the sports of football and soccer, in order to establish the basis for a *figurative analogy:* Just as similar forms of sport can be quite different, so can styles of business reflect the fundamentally different lifestyles of nations.

As you weigh the use of an analogy, ask yourself the following:

- *Will the analogy help me make some fundamental point about my subject?*

- *Will the analogy distract my listeners?* In the above example, Mr. Allen risked losing some listeners who would prefer to think more about soccer and football than about international business practices.

- *Does the analogy establish a beneficial association for my subject?* Some critics complain that the analogy between sports and politics, so popular among American journalists who describe the "horserace" of political campaigning, both trivializes politics and dehumanizes politicians. The above example could illustrate a similar problem in talking about international business.

Deciding What Supporting Material You Should Use

The following general guidelines may help you make wise choices as you select supporting materials for your speech and ways to combine them:

1. If an idea is *controversial,* rely primarily on facts, statistics, factual examples, or expert testimony from sources that the audience will respect and accept.

2. If your ideas or concepts are *abstract,* use examples and narratives to bring them to life. Use comparisons, contrasts, or analogies so that your listeners grasp your ideas and develop appropriate feelings about them.

3. If an idea is highly *technical,* supplement facts and statistics with expert testimony. Use definitions, explanations, and descriptions to aid understanding. Use examples, comparisons, contrasts, and analogies to help listeners integrate information.

4. If you need to *arouse emotions,* use lay and prestige testimony, examples, or narratives. Excite listeners by using contrast and analogy.

5. If you need to *defuse emotions,* emphasize facts and statistics and expert testimony. Keep the focus on definitions and explanations.

6. If your topic is *distant* from the lives of listeners, draw it closer to them through information, examples, and narratives, activated by descriptions, comparisons, and analogies.

Although the need for particular types of supporting material may vary with different topics and audiences, a good rule of thumb is to *support each main point with the most important and relevant facts and statistics available.* To clarify each point, use testimony, and provide sufficient definitions, explanations, and descriptions. Additionally, *support each main point with at least one interesting example or narrative.* To make your presentation more dramatic or memorable, emphasize examples and narratives, brought to life through striking comparisons, contrasts, or analogies.

In Summary

Facts and statistics, testimony, examples, and narratives are the major forms of *supporting materials.* They provide the substance, strength, credibility, and appeal that a speech must have before listeners will place their faith in it.

Facts and Statistics.   Information in the form of facts and statistics is the most objective form of supporting material, especially useful for unfamiliar or controversial topics. *Facts* are verifiable, which means that independent observers see and report them consistently. *Statistics* are numerical facts that describe the size of something, make predictions, illustrate trends, or show relationships. Be careful not to confuse factual statements with interpretations and claims. Be sure that your information meets the tests of relevance, recency, credibility, and reliability.

Use definitions, explanations, and descriptions to frame facts and statistics into powerful supports. A *definition* states the meaning of an unfamiliar term concisely in words the audience can understand. An *explanation* more fully expands on what something is or how it works. *Descriptions* are word pictures that help the audience visualize what you are talking about.

Testimony.   *Testimony* cites the ideas or words of others in support of your message. When you repeat the exact words of others, you make use of *direct quotation.* When you summarize what others say, you *paraphrase* them. *Expert testimony* comes from recognized authorities who support the validity of your claims. *Lay testimony* represents "the voice of the people" on a topic; sometimes it takes the form of a *testimonial. Prestige testimony* connects your message with the general wisdom of some revered figure.

Be sure that the sources you cite are free from bias. State their credentials as you introduce their testimony, and never quote them out of context.

Examples.   *Examples* serve as verbal illustrations. They help arouse interest, clarify ideas, sustain attention, personalize a topic, emphasize your major points, demonstrate how your ideas can be applied, and make it easier for listeners to remember your message. *Brief examples* mention specific instances. *Extended examples* contain more detail and give the speaker more time to build impressions. *Factual examples* are based on actual events and persons. *Hypothetical examples* are invented by the speaker to represent reality. Use people's names to personalize examples and magnify their power.

Narratives.   A *narrative* tells a story that illustrates some truth about the topic. Good narratives draw listeners into the action and help establish a mood. They should be told in colorful, concrete language, using dialogue and characterization. A lively and informal style of presentation can enhance narration. Avoid narratives that demean others or reinforce negative stereotypes.

Three Techniques for Using Supporting Materials.   Comparison, contrast, and analogy are general techniques used to make the most of supporting materials. *Comparison* points out the similarities of an unfamiliar or controversial topic to something the audience already understands or accepts. *Contrast* emphasizes the differences among things to make some important point. *Analogy* combines the principles of comparison and contrast in order to heighten awareness. *Figurative analogy* especially can help us see a topic in a new way by pointing out previously unexpected relationships.

Terms to Know

supporting materials	testimonial
facts	prestige testimony
disinformation	examples
statistics	brief example
definition	extended example
explanations	factual example
descriptions	hypothetical example
testimony	narrative
direct quotation	comparison
paraphrase	contrast
expert testimony	analogy
lay testimony	figurative analogy

Notes

1. Richard Weaver, "Ultimate Terms in Contemporary Rhetoric," in *The Ethics of Rhetoric* (Chicago: Henry Regnery, 1953), pp. 211–232.
2. Cynthia Crossen, *Tainted Truth: The Manipulation of Fact in America* (New York: Simon & Schuster, 1994), p. 36.
3. For similar commentary on other periodicals, see Howard Kahane, *Logic and Contemporary Rhetoric: The Use of Reason in Everyday Life* (Belmont, Calif.: Wadsworth, 1984), pp. 337–338.
4. Reprinted by permission of *World Book Encyclopedia*. This material was brought to our attention by professor Gray Matthews of the University of Memphis.
5. Neil Postman, "Critical Thinking in the Electronic Era," *Phi Kappa Phi Journal* Winter 1985, p. 7. Reprinted from *National Forum: The Phi Kappa Phi Journal*, Volume 65, Number 1 (Winter 1985). Copyright © by Neil Postman. By permission of the publishers.
6. Crossen, p. 36.
7. Lonnie R. Bristow, "Protecting Youth from the Tobacco Industry," in *Vital Speeches of the Day*, 15 March 1994, pp. 333–334.
8. Crossen, p. 42.
9. Peter Francese, "Editorial: Lies, Damned Lies . . . ," *American Demographics*, November 1994, p. 2.
10. Donna E. Shalala, "Domestic Terrorism: An Unacknowledged Epidemic," in *Vital Speeches of the Day*, 15 May 1994, p. 451.

11. Adapted from *The 1992 Information Please Environmental Almanac* (Boston: Houghton Mifflin, 1992), p. 144.

12. Longinus, *On the Sublime,* trans. W. Rhys Roberts, in *The Great Critics: An Anthology of Literary Criticism,* 3rd ed., ed. James Harry Smith and Edd Winfield Parks (New York: W. W. Norton & Company, 1951), p. 82.

13. She appeared as a panelist on the CNN special report, "Investigating the President: Media Madness?" aired on 28 January 1998.

14. The power of lay testimony is one possible implication of Michael Calvin McGee's "In Search of the People: A Rhetorical Alternative," *Quarterly Journal of Speech* 61 (1975): 235–249.

15. Bill Moyers, "Best of Jobs: To Have and Serve the Public's Trust," keynote address at the PBS annual meeting, 23 June 1996, reprinted in *Current,* 8 July 1996.

16. Colin Powell, "Sharing in the American Dream," in *Vital Speeches of the Day,* 1 June 1997, p. 484. Langston Hughes excerpt from COLLECTED POEMS by Langston Hughes. Copyright © 1994 by the Estate of Langston Hughes. Reprinted by permission of Alfred A. Knopf, Inc.

17. Brock Evans, "A Time of Crisis: The Giveaway of Our Public Lands," in *Vital Speeches of the Day,* 1 September 1995, p. 691.

18. "On the Campaign Trail," *Reader's Digest,* March 1992, p. 116.

19. *Newsweek,* 27 January 1997, p. 86.

20. Sue Suter, "Disability Is No Big Deal: Seeing People as They Really Are," in *Vital Speeches of the Day,* 15 August 1997, pp. 650–651. Reprinted by permission from the author.

21. Hillary Rodham Clinton, "Women's Rights Are Human Rights," in *Vital Speeches of the Day,* 1 October 1995, p. 739.

22. Suter, p. 649.

23. Suter, p. 650.

24. Jerome S. Bruner, *Acts of Meaning* (Cambridge, Mass.: Harvard University Press, 1990) and "The Narrative Construction of Reality," *Critical Inquiry* 18 (1991): 1–21.

25. Z. Kunda, D. T. Miller, and T. Claire, "Combining Social Concepts: The Role of Causal Reasoning," *Cognitive Science* 14 (1990): 551–577.

26. Associated Press, "Gore Promotes Benefits of Good Storytelling," *Memphis Commercial Appeal,* 8 October 1995, p. B2.

27. "M.B.A.s Who Tell Stories Get a Jump on the Job Search," *Spotlight,* 15 September 1995.

28. Roger Ailes, *You Are the Message* (New York: Doubleday, 1988), pp. 70–74.

29. Bob Newhart, "Humor Makes Us Free: Laughter Gives Us Distance," in *Vital Speeches of the Day,* 15 July 1997, p. 607.

30. Newton Minow, "Campaign Finance Reform: We Have Failed to Solve the Problem," in *Vital Speeches of the Day,* 1 July 1997, p. 558.

31. Sam J. Ervin, Jr., "Judicial Verbicide: An Affront to the Constitution," presented at Herbert Law Center, Louisiana State University, Baton Rouge, 22 October 1980, in *Representative American Speeches 1980–1981,* ed. Owen Peterson (New York: H. W. Wilson, 1981), p. 62.

32. Charles R. Gruner, "Advice to the Beginning Speaker on Using Humor—What the Research Tells Us," *Communication Education* 34 (1985): 142–147; and Christie McGuffee Smith and Larry Powell, "The Use of Disparaging Humor by Group Leaders," *Southern Speech Communication Journal* 53 (1988): 279–292.

33. Jimmy Carter, "Excellence Comes from a Repository that Doesn't Change: The True Meaning of Success," in *Vital Speeches of the Day,* 1 July 1993, p. 546.

34. Minow, pp. 555–556.

35. M. George Allen, "Succeeding in Japan: One Company's Perspective," in *Vital Speeches of the Day,* 1 May 1994, p. 430.

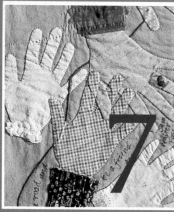

7 Structuring Your Speech

Every discourse ought to be a living creature; having a body of its own and head and feet; there should be a middle, beginning, and end, adapted to one another and to the whole.

—*Plato*

This chapter will help you

■ develop a simple, balanced, and orderly speech design
■ select and arrange your main points
■ plan transitions to make your speech flow smoothly
■ prepare effective introductions for your speeches
■ prepare memorable conclusions for your speeches

Global warming is a gradual warming of the earth caused by human activities that dump carbon dioxide into the atmosphere. August 1998 was the hottest month since weather records have been kept. Fossil fuel use has more than doubled since 1950. One cause of global warming is industrial emissions. The ten hottest years in recorded history have occurred since 1970. Skin cancers could increase as much as 26 percent if the ozone level drops another 10 percent. El Niño seems to be related to global warming. Global warming is a danger to our world.

HOW MUCH OF this randomly scrambled information would you remember if you heard it presented this way? There seems to be important news here, but it gets lost because it is poorly organized. A well-organized presentation makes it easier for listeners to understand and remember your message.[1]

Suppose you must take basic physics next semester and you get the following material from Students for Better Teaching about the instructors who teach the course:

JOHNSON, DENNIS Professor Johnson is very entertaining. He tells a lot of funny stories and puts on demonstrations that seem like a "magic show." But he doesn't explain difficult material in any systematic fashion, so it's hard to take notes. When it's time for departmental examinations, you often don't know how or what to study.

MARTINEZ, MARIA Professor Martinez is very businesslike. She starts each lecture by reviewing the material covered in the last session and asking if anyone has questions. Her lectures are easy to follow. She points out what is most important for students to know and uses clear examples that make difficult ideas easier to understand and apply.

Which would you choose? When a message is important, most of us would choose the well-organized person over the entertainer. In fact, a recent study indicated that students dislike instructors who go off on tangents, jump from one idea to another, ramble, or are generally disorganized.[2]

How well-organized your presentation is affects your ethos.[3] As we noted in Chapter 2, "competence" is an important part of credibility. It is hard for listeners to think of you as competent when your speech is poorly organized. They may conclude either that you lack the capacity to organize or that you did not care enough to prepare carefully.

In this chapter we look at the principles that underlie well-organized messages to explain how to structure the body of your speech. Next, we consider the important role of transitions in making a speech flow smoothly. Finally, we discuss how to prepare effective introductions and conclusions.

Principles of Good Form

The structure of a speech should follow the ways people naturally arrange things in their minds. People rarely store information in individual bits. Instead they "chunk" material for easy recall. For example, people recall telephone numbers as two or three chunks of numbers, such as 219-555-2830, not as individual numbers, such as 2-1-9-5-5-5-7-2-8-3-0.[4] Information is organized according to a few simple principles of **good form**.[5] To develop good form, you should keep your presentation simple, balance the parts of your speech, and arrange your main points so that they flow smoothly. In other words, good form depends on simplicity, balance, and order.

Simplicity

A simple design makes it easy for listeners to follow, understand, and remember your message. Simplicity is important in oral presentations because listeners usually do not have manuscripts to refer to if material is confusing. To achieve **simplicity**, you should limit the number of your main ideas and keep your design direct and to the point.

Number of Main Points.   The fewer the main points in a speech, the better because each main point must be developed.[6] It takes time to present information, examples, narratives, and testimony effectively. Short classroom speeches usually should have no more than four main points. Look at what happens when a speech becomes overburdened with main points:

Thesis statement: Government welfare programs aren't working.

Main points: I. There are too many programs.

II. The programs often duplicate coverage.

III. Some people who need help are left out.

IV. The programs are poorly funded.

V. The programs waste money.

VI. Recipients have no input into what is needed.

VII. The programs create dependence.

VIII. The programs stifle initiative.

IX. The programs rob the poor of self-respect.

Each of these points may be important, but presenting them this way could be confusing. It would be hard for listeners to remember them. They are not organized into a meaningful pattern. Let's see how these ideas might be clustered into a simpler structural pattern:

Thesis statement: Our approach to welfare in America is inadequate, inefficient, and insensitive.

Main point: I. Our approach is inadequate.
Subpoints: A. We don't fund it sufficiently.
            B. Some people who need help get left out.

Main point: II. Our approach is inefficient.
Subpoints: A. There are too many programs.
            B. There is too much duplication.
            C. There is too much waste of money.

Main point: III. Our approach is insensitive.
Subpoints: A. It creates dependence.
            B. It stifles initiative.
            C. It robs people of self-respect.

This simpler structure makes the speech easy to follow. Each main point has subpoints that extend its meaning. Overlapping points have been combined, and unnecessary ideas have been omitted. The result is a design that helps listeners remember.[7]

Phrasing Main Points.   You should state your main points simply. In our example, the new wording of main points is clear and direct. The repeated phrase ("Our approach is . . .") suggests that these are *main* points and helps listeners remember them. It allows the speaker to refer to the "Three I's" of welfare (Inadequate, Inefficient, and Insensitive) in the introduction and conclusion, a strategy that ties the speech together.

Balance

Balance means that each of the major parts of your speech—the introduction, body, and conclusion—receives appropriate development. Instructors typically specify time limits for speeches, so keep these in mind as you plan your message. It can be very upsetting to finish the first point of your speech and find that you have only one minute left and two more points plus your conclusion to present. Time yourself as you practice your speech to be sure it fits within the allotted time limits. The following suggestions will help you plan a balanced presentation:

1. *The body should be the longest part of your speech.* It contains your major ideas. If you spend three minutes on your introduction, a minute and a half on the body, and thirty seconds on the conclusion, your speech will be out of balance.

2. *Consider the development of each main point.* If your main points seem equally important, you might give each point *equal emphasis.* This strategy might be appropriate for the speech on the "three I's" of welfare policy, in which each point merits equal attention. If your main points vary in importance, however, you must take this into account. You might start with the most important point, then present the other points in a *descending order,* spending less time on each. For example, in a problem-solution speech, you may need to convince listeners that

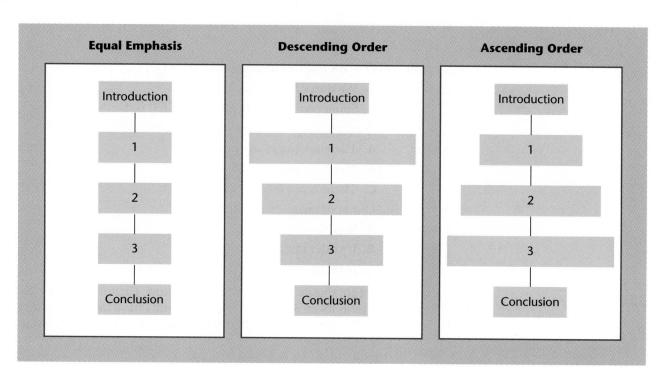

FIGURE 7.1
Balanced Speeches

there actually is a problem. In such a case, you would devote most of your time to meeting the challenge of establishing this first main point. Alternatively, you might wish to develop your main points in an *ascending order.* If listeners agree that there is a problem, but don't know what to do about it, then you should devote most of your time to your solution, the second main point. Figure 7.1 graphically illustrates how these designs can work.

3. *The introduction and conclusion should be about equal in length.* The total amount of time spent on your introduction and conclusion should be less than the amount spent on the body of your speech. As a general rule, in a five-minute presentation, the combined length of the introduction and conclusion should be about a minute. This leaves four minutes to develop the main points of the message.

Order

A speech that meets the requirement of **order** follows a consistent pattern of development from beginning to end. It should start with an introduction, present the main ideas in the body of the speech, then end with a conclusion. You should develop the body of the speech first because it contains the essence of your message. Once you have organized the body of your speech, you can prepare an introduction and conclusion tailored to your message.

Order also applies to the way you arrange your main points. If you propose a solution, you should first present the problem. Why? Because that is how our minds work. We don't normally come up with solutions, then look for problems to fit them. An orderly arrangement is also important when you are presenting the steps in a process. Begin with the first step, then cover the rest in the order they occur. If you jump around, the audience may get lost.

Structuring the Body of Your Speech

In developing the body of your speech, you have three major tasks to accomplish:

1. You must select your main points.
2. You must arrange your main points effectively.
3. You must decide on supporting materials.

Select Your Main Points

Your **main points** are the most important ideas of your message. They are the ideas you should emphasize. As you review your research, you may find some ideas coming up over and over. These are the most important issues connected with your topic. Consider how they relate to your specific purpose, your thesis statement, and the needs and interests of your listeners. They will become the main points of your speech.

Let's look at how you might select the main points for a speech on global warming. Begin with a **research overview** listing your main sources of information and a summary of the major ideas from each. Figure 7.2 presents a research overview based on four sources of information: an encyclopedia entry, an article from *Discover,* reports from Greenpeace, and articles from the Union of Concerned Scientists. Scanning the overview, you might come up with the following themes:

- Increased temperatures are evidence of global warming.
- Human activities cause global warming.
- Global warming will cause climate changes.
- Global warming may cause health, environmental, and economic problems.

Encarta Encyclopedia
1. Increase in Earth's temperature
2. Build-up of greenhouse gases
3. Flooding and climate changes
4. Attributed to human influences

Discover
1. Use less energy
2. Drive efficient vehicles
3. Go with solar or gas energy
4. Geoengineering ideas

Greenpeace
1. CO_2 problems
2. Climate changes
3. What we can do
   A. Learn more about it
   B. Save energy
   C. Drive less

Union of Concerned Scientists
1. Climate changes
2. U.S. largest polluter
3. Energy and global warming
4. Transportation and global warming

FIGURE 7.2
Sample Research Overview

Once you have identified the major themes from the research, you need to determine how these relate to your specific purpose and your audience. In this example, your specific purpose is "to inform my audience about the problem of global warming." You anticipate that your audience's understanding of global warming may be faulty because business and environmental groups often differ on its causes, consequences, and remedies.

In light of these considerations, you realize that you must start by defining global warming to establish a shared base of meaning. When you present any technical topic to a lay audience, you must provide simple, clear, understandable definitions throughout your speech. These definitions should go beyond simple translations. You should use explanations and descriptions (discussed in Chapter 6) to clarify the topic. If your purpose were to persuade listeners, you might stress the predicted consequences of global warming in order to motivate your listeners to support changes in public policy. In your informative speech, however, you decide to mention these consequences in order to arouse interest and to motivate your audience to listen. Once you have their interest, you can proceed to discuss the causes. In this case, from the major themes revealed by your research overview, you might fashion the following main points:

- Global warming is a gradual warming of the earth's surface.

- Global warming may cause climate changes and health problems.

- The major causes of global warming are deforestation, industrial emissions, and personal energy use.

Arranging Your Main Points

Once you have determined your main points, you must decide how to arrange them. You need to come up with a way of ordering them that is appropriate for your audience, fits your material, and serves your specific purpose. For example, in the above case, the first main point will provide needed definitions and heighten interest. The next point will establish the possible negative effects of global warming. The final main point will cover the major causes of global warming.

As we noted earlier in this chapter, people mentally organize information into patterns that are easy to remember. These patterns set up expectations that are used to process further experiences. They function like mental templates into which we fit new information. We see and experience the world through them. The way we arrange our speeches must be in harmony with these expectations. *These templates are based on the principles of similarity, proximity, and closure.* In this section we discuss some basic speech designs that relate to these principles. More detailed examples of speech designs are provided in Chapters 12 and 13, which cover informative and persuasive speaking.

Similarity.   The **principle of similarity** leads people to group together things that seem alike. This tendency underlies the *categorical design* for speeches. Speakers use categories when they discuss "three major causes of global warming" or "the four basic components of a good stereo system." Categories can be based on the actual divisions of a topic, such as the symptoms of a disease. They also may represent customary ways of thinking about a subject, such as the four basic food groups. Such factors go together because they seem alike in some important way.

Proximity.   The **principle of proximity** suggests that things that usually occur together in time or space should be presented in the order in which they naturally occur. For example, a how-to speech should have a *sequential design* that presents the steps in the order in which they should be taken. If you want to discuss the events that led to a present-day problem, you might use the sequential design to present a historical perspective on the situation. Your research may show that the major events occurred in 1955, 1970, and 1987. If you follow this chronological pattern, your speech will be easy to understand. But if you start talking about 1970, then jump back to 1955, then leap ahead to the present before doubling back to 1987, you will probably lose most of your listeners by violating the principle of proximity.

If you were preparing a speech on the wineries in California's Napa Valley, you might best use a *spatial design*. Such a design is based on physical relationships, such as east-west, up-down, or points around a circle. You might begin at Domaine Chandon at the southernmost end of the valley, take listeners next to the wineries along the Silverado Trail, and end up with the cable ride to the top of the hill at the Sterling Winery. This way your audience gets a verbal map to follow as well as a picture of the major wineries in the valley.

Closure.   The **principle of closure** is based on people's natural tendency to seek completion.[8] We like to have patterns carried through so that we feel we have the "whole story." Have you ever started reading a magazine article in a waiting room, only to find that someone had torn out the last page of the story? Do you remember how frustrated you felt? Your need for closure had been violated.

The principle of closure applies to several speech designs. For example, if you omit an important category when developing your topic, listeners may notice its omission. If you leave out a necessary step in a sequence, audiences may sense the flaw. Although all speeches should satisfy this need, there are two speech patterns for which closure is absolutely essential. These are *cause-effect* and *problem-solution designs*. Because we want the world to seem purposeful and controllable, we want all events to have clear causes and all problems to have satisfactory solutions.

A cause-effect speech can go in two directions: It can begin by focusing on some present situation as an effect and then seek its causes, or it can look at the present as a potential cause of future effects. Sometimes these variations can be combined. You might take a current situation such as a budget deficit on campus and develop a speech tracing its origins. If you had enough time, you might continue by predicting the future effects of the deficit, such as tuition increases. Understanding the causes could help your listeners see what needs to be done to reduce the deficit. Predicting future effects might make them want to reduce it.

Determining and Arranging Your Main Points

1   Prepare a research overview to identify repeated ideas.
2   Select main points with regard to your purpose and the needs of your audience.
3   Limit your main points to four or fewer for a short speech.
4   Use the principle of similarity to develop categories.
5   Use the principle of proximity to arrange main points in sequential or spatial patterns.
6   Use the principle of closure to provide completeness in causation and problem-solution designs.

The problem-solution design focuses attention on a problem and then provides a solution for it. Such speeches often must arouse strong feelings in order to motivate listeners. Once you have aroused these emotions, your solutions must show listeners a way out of the problem, or they will feel frustrated.

Use the principles of similarity, proximity, and closure to select the most effective design for your speech.

Adding Supporting Materials

Once you have selected and arranged your main points, you must support them with facts and figures, testimony, examples, or narratives. As you develop your main points, also consider whether you need to divide them into subpoints. The subpoints should contain information or ideas that listeners need in order to understand or accept the main point. For example, assume that you have framed your main point as "The answer to environmental waste on campus is a recycling program." To support this main point, you realize that you must discuss two subpoints: "My recycling plan will work" and "My recycling plan is affordable."

You strengthen both main points and subpoints by providing supporting materials. In the instance just mentioned, you could support your subpoint on workability by citing the example of another college that used a similar plan. You might develop a before-and-after narrative to describe how that college dealt with its waste disposal problem. To convince listeners that your proposal is cost-efficient, you might use statistics and expert testimony. Once you have developed these supporting materials, reasonable listeners should find your main points acceptable.

In Chapter 6 we provided general guidelines for selecting supporting materials. Here we show how to work supporting materials into the structure of your speech. Supporting materials help to fortify a message against the doubts or disagreements of reasonable listeners. They answer the basic questions that listeners often ask:

1. *What is the basis of that idea?* (You answer with facts or statistics.)

2. *How do you know? Who else says so?* (You supply testimony.)

3. *How does it work? Where is it true?* (You offer an example.)

4. *So what? Why should I care?* (You develop a narrative that explains why.)

Although the situation will vary from topic to topic, speaker to speaker, and audience to audience, it is possible to set up an ideal model for the support of any main point or important subpoint. This model includes the point plus the following supporting materials

- The most important relevant facts and statistics
- The most authoritative judgments made by respected sources
- At least one story or example that clarifies the idea or brings it to life

Figure 7.3 provides a format for applying this model to support a point. Assume that you want to demonstrate the main point that suntans are not a sign of good health. Here is one way you could follow this format to support the point:

Statement:	Suntans are not as "good" for you as they look on you.
Transition:	Let's examine some of the evidence.
Facts/statistics:	According to a 1995 report by the American Cancer Society, prolonged exposure without protection is responsible for about 90 percent of all skin cancers.
Transition:	Moreover, exposure without protection also accelerates the aging process.
Expert testimony:	According to Dr. John M. Knox, head of dermatology at the Baylor University College of Medicine, "If you do

FIGURE 7.3

Outline Format for Supporting a Point

Statement: _____

_____

Transition into facts or statistics: _____

    1. Factual information or statistics that support statement: _____

_____

_____

Transition into testimony: _____

    2. Testimony that supports statement: _____

_____

_____

Transition into example or narrative: _____

    3. Example or narrative that supports statement: _____

_____

_____

_____

Transition into restatement: _____

Restatement of original assertion: _____

_____

biopsies on the buttocks of people ages seventy-five and thirty-five, you won't see any differences under the microscope . . . protected skin stays youthful much longer."

Transition:	Let's look at one person who suffered from overexposure.
Example:	Jane was a fair-skinned, blond-haired girl who loved swimming and sunbathing. She often sunburned but didn't think there would be any effects other than the short-term pain. Having a good tan seemed so healthy, she didn't dream it could harm her. Now, at forty-five, she knows better. She couldn't believe it when her doctor told her she had skin cancer. Now she can't go out into the sun, even for a few minutes, without using a sunscreen and wearing a hat, a long-sleeved shirt, and long pants.
Transition:	What does all this mean?
Restatement:	A suntan may make you look healthy, but it is not healthy. Overexposure to the sun causes cancer and premature aging. Are you willing to take that risk just to look good for a brief time?

In this example, three forms of supporting material—statistical information, expert testimony, and example—work together to establish the main point. Each contributes its special strength. If each of your main points is well supported, your message should stand up even if challenged.

Using Transitions

Our example of using supporting materials also illustrates the way **transitions** work in a speech. Transitions show your listeners how your ideas connect with one another. They help your listeners focus on the meaning of what you have already discussed and prepare them for what is still to come. They serve as signposts that help listeners see the overall pattern of your message. Transitions connect your main points and tie the body of a speech to its introduction and conclusion.

Some transitions are simple, short phrases such as "Another point that must be made is. . . ." More often, however, transitions are worded as phrases that link ideas. For example, the sentence "Having looked at why people don't pay compliments more often, let's consider some ways to give them" summarizes what you have just said and directs listeners to your next point.

Certain stock words or phrases can be used to signal changes in a speech. For example, words and phrases like *until now* or *only last week* point out time changes. Transitions such as *in addition* show that you are expanding on what you have already said. The use of the word *similarly* indicates that a comparison will follow. Phrases such as *on the other hand* cue listeners to a contrast. Cause-and-effect relationships can be suggested with words like *as a result* or *consequently*. Introductory phrases like *traveling north* can indicate spatial rela-

FIGURE 7.4

Common Transitions

To Indicate	Use
Time Changes	until, now, since, previously, later, earlier, in the past, in the future, meanwhile, five years ago, just last month, tomorrow, following, before, at present, eventually
Additions	moreover, in addition, furthermore, besides
Comparison	compared with, both are, likewise, in comparison, similarly, of equal importance, another type of, like, alike, just as
Contrast	but, yet, however, on the other hand, conversely, still, otherwise, in contrast, unfortunately, despite, rather than, on the contrary
Cause-Effect	therefore, consequently, thus, accordingly, so, as a result, hence, since, because of, due to, for this reason
Numerical Order	first, second, third, in the first place, to begin with, initially, next, eventually, finally
Spatial Relations	to the north, alongside, to the left, above, moving eastward, in front of, in back of, behind, next to, below, nearby, in the distance
Explanation	to illustrate, for example, for instance, case in point, in other words, to simplify, to clarify
Importance	most importantly, above all, keep this in mind, remember, listen carefully, take note of, indeed
The Speech Is Ending	in short, finally, in conclusion, to summarize

tionships. Phrases or words like *in short, finally,* or *in conclusion* signal that the speech is coming to its end. Figure 7.4 contains a list of some commonly used transitions.

An **internal summary** is a special type of transition that reminds listeners of the points you have covered before you move on to the next part of your message. Internal summaries are especially useful in cause-effect and problem-solution speeches where they signal that you have finished your discussion of the causes or problem and are now going to describe the effects or solution. In addition, an internal summary condenses and repeats your ideas, which can help your listeners remember your message. If your listeners have somehow missed the point, the transition helps get them back on track. Consider the following example:

> **So now we see what the problem is. We know the cost in human suffering. We know the terrible political consequences and the enormous economic burden. The question is, what are we going to do about it? Let me tell you about a plan that experts agree may turn things around.**

Internal summaries should be brief and to the point so that they highlight the major features of your message.

A lack of planned transitions may cause beginning speakers to overuse words and vocalized pauses such as *well, you know, okay,* or *"er."* Plan a variety of transitions to help your speech flow smoothly. If you have trouble developing effective transitions, rethink the structure of your message. Outline your thoughts to be sure that they move in a clear direction and an orderly sequence. We cover outlining in Chapter 8.

Once you have identified and arranged your main points, decided how to develop them with supporting materials, and planned how to connect them with transitions, you can prepare an introduction and conclusion that will begin and end your speech effectively. Introductions and conclusions are very important because listeners tend to be most affected by what they hear at the beginning and end of a message.[9] The introduction allows you to make a good first impression and to set the stage for how your audience will respond. The conclusion gives you a final opportunity to make a lasting impression.

Introducing Your Message

The introduction to your speech is the invitation you give your audience to listen. When you first begin to speak, the audience will have two basic concerns in mind: *Why should I listen to this speech?* and *Why should I listen to this speaker?* These questions relate to two of the three basic functions of an introduction. First, it should capture attention and arouse interest so that your audience wants to listen to your message. Second, it should help establish your ethos as a competent, trustworthy, and likable person with whom the audience can identify. Finally, your introduction should preview your message to make it easier for the audience to follow.

A successful introduction also helps prepare you to present the rest of your speech. When you get off to a good start, you have less performance anxiety. Therefore, you should prepare your introduction carefully. Practice until you are confident and comfortable with your opening words. Establish good eye contact with listeners. *Do not read your introduction!*

Capturing Attention

All too often, speakers open their presentations with something like "Good evening. My speech tonight is on . . ." and then jump right into their message. Needless to say, this is not a good way to begin a speech. It does not make the audience want to listen.

There are several ways to attract, build, and hold the interest of your audience. You may

- Involve the audience
- Ask questions
- Relate a personal experience
- Tell a story
- Use humor
- Develop suspense

The introduction of your speech must immediately engage your audience. If you don't get their attention within the first minute of speaking, they may be lost to you forever.

- Begin with a quotation
- Use a presentation aid
- Startle the audience

Involve the Audience. You involve listeners when you connect them with your message. One of the most frequently used involvement techniques is to offer sincere, well-deserved compliments. Does the group, the location, the occasion, or an audience member merit praise? People like to hear good things about themselves and their community. This technique is often used in formal speeches when custom requires a speaker to make such acknowledgements before moving into the actual presentation. These introductory remarks can be very brief, as illustrated by the opening words of President John F. Kennedy in a speech given at a White House dinner honoring Nobel Prize winners:

> **I think this is the most extraordinary collection of talent, of human knowledge, that has ever been gathered together at the White House, with the possible exception of when Thomas Jefferson dined alone.[10]**

With this elegant tribute, Kennedy was able to honor his guests without embarrassing them or going overboard with praise. His witty reference to the genius of Thomas Jefferson also paid tribute to the past.

Involvement is especially important if your topic seems distant from the audience's immediate concerns or experiences. A student at Kutztown University wanted to give an informative speech on the Black Plague of the Middle Ages. He knew that he had to do something dramatic to involve his audience from the outset in order to make the topic interesting and relevant. Here is how he handled it.[11]

> **As the students entered the classroom, a confederate gave each a card containing the name of a profession, such as clergyman, sailor, farmer, merchant. The number of cards for each profession was proportional to that profession's representation in European society at the time of the plague. When the student's name was called, he entered from the back of the room wearing an oversized black sweatshirt, hood up, cinched around the waist with a length of sash cord. He opened with a rhetorical question, "If the Black Plague were to strike Kutztown today, given the same medical limitations, how many do you think would survive?" He then asked everyone to stand, and after a pause, continued as follows: "Will all of you with a card reading 'physician' please sit down. In tending the sick, you have come in contact with the disease and have become one of its victims." A student took her seat. He followed with "Will all of those identified as 'sailor' or 'merchant' please be seated. You have traveled about the country or the world and so have also come close to other victims and have sealed your fate." Five more students sat down. He then called out the clergy, city dwellers, dock workers, soldiers, and others who would have been exposed to the disease.**
>
> **By the time he finished reading the list of those most susceptible to the disease, only three of his twenty-five classmates were left standing. He then explained that if the plague were to strike Kutztown the way it did many cities during the Middle Ages, those three would have the awesome task of rebuilding society.**

Your introduction need not be this dramatic to involve the audience. If you can demonstrate that what you are talking about matters to the audience, your speech will be more effective.[12] You also can involve your listeners by relating your topic to their motivations or attitudes and by using inclusive pronouns such as *we* and *our.*

Ask Questions.   Speakers will often open a presentation with a question or series of questions. Questions start the audience thinking about a topic and also get them actively involved. Sometimes the questions will call for a direct answer. For example, Holly Carlson, a student at Vanderbilt, opened a speech on censorship by reading a list of banned books. As she read off the title of each book, she asked listeners to raise their hands if they had read it.

Not all questions used in speeches call for direct answers, however. **Rhetorical questions** (such as, "Have you ever thought about what your life would be like if you were a different color?") arouse curiosity and start listeners thinking about the topic. Wendy Liebmann, president of WSL Strategic Retailers, opened a speech to the Non-Prescription Drug Manufacturers Association with the following series of rhetorical questions:

Have you ever wondered of late what's going on with consumers? Why they are so full of contradictions when it comes to spending money? Why they will buy a $500 leather jacket at full price but wait for a $50 sweater to go on sale? Will buy a top-of-the-line sports utility vehicle then go to Costco to buy new tires? Will eagerly pay $3.50 for a cup of coffee but think $1.29 is too expensive for a hamburger? Will spend $2.00 for a strawberry-smelling bath soap but wait for a coupon to buy a 99 cent twin pack of toilet soap?

The economy is booming. Unemployment is at a 25-year low. Real income has increased. Why isn't everyone out spending like they did in the 1980s—shopping everywhere, buying everything? Why are so many companies struggling? What is this paradox? Is there a paradox? Well, that's what we are going to talk about today. This apparent consumer paradox: what it is, what it means, and how to make sense of it.[13]

Relate a Personal Experience.   An old adage suggests that people are interested first in themselves, next in other people, then in things, and finally in ideas. This may explain why relating a topic to personal experience heightens audience interest. When speakers have been personally involved with a topic, they gain credibility. We are more willing to listen to others and take their advice if we know that they have traveled the road themselves. Jason Shafer, a Dean's List student at Vanderbilt University, related the following personal experience as he began his self-introductory speech:

With a lot of hard work, your son will hopefully make it through a trade school. That heart-gripping statement was what my parents heard when I was in third grade. You see, I was a terrible student in grade school. I was the worst. I'm sure most of you just flew through grade school, getting As and Bs. No problem whatsoever. Me, on the other hand, not at all. I got Cs and Ds. And I had to work for them. All of my teachers tried. They didn't know what was wrong. They tried different techniques, but nothing really seemed to work. I guess the point of crisis came in third grade when my teacher realized that I couldn't even read yet. It just about killed my parents. They wanted the best for me. So they had some testing done, and found out I had a learning disability.

Relating your subject to personal experience can be very important if you face an unfriendly audience. Brock Evans, vice president of the Audubon Society, recently addressed the Seattle Rotary Club on the Endangered Species Act. Because this speech was presented amid a controversy concerning logging restrictions in that area, his introduction before this group was especially critical. Evans combined the techniques of involving the audience and relating the topic to personal experience in this introduction:

It is always a distinct honor to be invited to speak before a prestigious group like the Rotary Club of Seattle. I thank you for inviting me to be here today, and not just because of the opportunity to share a few thoughts about this very important subject. Those of you who know me know that my roots here run very deep. It was 30 years ago that I moved here from the Midwest, because I wanted to live in what I thought then—and still do now—was the most beautiful part of the country.

And those of you who know me know that my passion for this special Northwest land, its unique blend of mountain and forest and sea, goes even deeper. . . . It caused me to leave a law practice here, in order to devote my life to fight to help keep our way of life, to keep the Northwest the special place it is. It has now become a life's work that has taken me many places, first all across the Northwest, and finally into "exile" as I now believe—in the nation's capital—that other Washington, where for better or worse, so many of the great issues of our time are finally resolved.[14]

In this example, the love of the area and its beauty unites the speaker and his listeners. The fact that the speaker "adopted" the area lends special credence to his passion for it.

Tell a Story.   We humans began our love affair with stories around the campfires of ancient times. It is through stories that we remember the past and pass on our heritage to future generations. Stories also entertain and educate us—they depict abstract problems in human terms. In introductions, stories help capture audience attention and involve listeners in creating the meaning of the message. Marie D'Aniello opened a speech on the nature of friendship with the following story:

It's nine o'clock at night. I'm curled up in the back seat of a new truck and my friends, Cammy and Joe, are in the front singing along with the radio. As I listen to them sing, and I'm lying there, I start to think about my life and all the changes that have occurred in the past year. A year ago I didn't even know who Cammy and Joe were. And now they're two of my dearest friends. It made me think about friendship and its meaning.

Narratives are also good at establishing a mood for your message. In a self-introductory speech, Ashlie McMillan began with the following sensory narrative:

Imagine you're sitting aboard a dive boat. It's rocking back and forth; you can feel the sun beating down on you. You can feel the wind blowing on you. You smell the ocean, the salt water. You can hear the waves crashing up against the boat. You put on your dive pack with your heavy oxygen tank and you walk unsteadily across the deck of the rocking boat. And all of a sudden you plunge into a completely different environment. All around you is vast blueness and infinite space, a world completely different from the one you left above. But all you have to do is turn on your back and look above you and you see the sunlight streaming in through the top of the water. And you can see the world that you left behind.

An opening narrative may also be based on a historical event. Sandra Baltz, a premed major, opened a speech on setting priorities for organ transplants with the following narrative:

On a cold and stormy night in 1841 the ship *William Brown* struck an iceberg in the North Atlantic. Passengers and crew members frantically scrambled into the lifeboats. To make a bad disaster even worse, one of the lifeboats began to sink because it was overcrowded. Fourteen men were thrown overboard that horrible night. After the survivors were rescued, a crew member was tried for the murders of those thrown overboard.

Fortunately, situations like this have been few in history, but today we face a similar problem in the medical establishment: deciding who will live as we allocate scarce medical resources for transplants. Someday, your fate—or the fate of someone you love—could depend on how we resolve this dilemma.

In the preceding example, the story sets a somber mood for the serious message that follows. Stories can also be used to establish a lighter mood through the use of humor.

Use Humor.   Humor can enliven an introduction and, when used appropriately, can put your audience in a receptive mood for your message. But humor may also be the most misused technique for introducing speeches. Because someone once told them that starting with a joke will assure success, beginning speakers often search through anthologies of humor to find something that will make people laugh. Unless it is carefully adapted, however, such material often sounds canned, inappropriate, or only remotely relevant to the topic or occasion. If you wish to use humor in your introduction, be certain the material is fresh and pertinent.

Be especially careful when using humor to open a speech. It can be grossly inappropriate for some topics and occasions. Also, don't let a humorous introduction "upstage" the rest of your speech. We once heard a student open a speech with a rather risqué quotation from Mae West: "Is that a gun in your pocket, or are you happy to see me?" It drew an initial gasp followed by some hearty laughter. Unfortunately, as the speech continued, one student would chuckle over the remembered joke, then the audience would start laughing all over again even when nothing funny had been said. After the speaker finished, we questioned the audience about their "inappropriate" responses. Their reply? "We kept remembering that Mae West line. We just couldn't help it." And to this day, neither of your authors can remember the topic of the speech, just the opening humor.

Develop Suspense.   You can attract and hold your listeners' attention by arousing their curiosity, then making them wait before you satisfy it. The following introduction creates curiosity and anticipation:

Getting knocked down is no disgrace. Champions are made by getting up just one more time than the opponent! The results are a matter of record about a man who suffered many defeats: Lost his job in 1832, defeated for legislature in 1832, failed in business in 1833, defeated for legislature in 1834, sweetheart died in 1835, had nervous breakdown in 1836, defeated for nomination for Congress in 1843, elected to Congress in 1846, lost renomination in 1848, rejected for land officer in 1849, defeated for Senate in 1854, defeated for nomination for Vice-President in 1856, defeated for Senate in 1858.

> **In 1860 Abraham Lincoln was elected President of the United States. Lincoln proved that a big shot is just a little shot who keeps shooting. The greatest failures in the world are those who fail by not doing anything.[15]**

The list of failures aroused the audience's curiosity. Who was this loser? Many were surprised when they discovered it was Abraham Lincoln. This effective introduction set the stage for the speaker's message that perseverance is the key to success.

Begin with a Quotation. Starting your speech with a striking quotation or paraphrase from a well-known person or respected authority, with the possible exception of one from Mae West, can both arouse interest and give you borrowed ethos. The person you cite should be someone the audience knows, respects, or can identify with. Historical figures are especially apt, particularly in ceremonial speeches, where they evoke a sense of cultural heritage. Elissa Scadron opened her speech celebrating the United States as a sanctuary of human rights by saying: "We are, in the words of Abraham Lincoln, 'the last best hope of earth.'"

Most effective opening quotations are short and to the point. They are used to lead into the message. One student used a very brief quote from folklore as a lead-in to an informative speech on cystic fibrosis:

> **"Woe to the child who when kissed on the forehead tastes salty. He is bewitched and he soon will die." This northern European folk adage is a reference to the genetic disorder cystic fibrosis. Well, we know today that children with cystic fibrosis aren't bewitched. And we have a lot better ways to test for cystic fibrosis than to kiss them on the forehead.**

Most books of quotations (see Chapter 5) are indexed by key words and subjects as well as by authors. Collections of quotations are also available on the Internet. They are an excellent source of statements that you might use to introduce your topic.

Use a Presentation Aid. Sometimes using a presentation aid at the beginning of a speech can help to establish a mood or set a theme that carries on throughout the message. One of our students placed a photograph face down on each seat in the audience. At the beginning of her speech, she had her listeners turn over the photos, then asked them, "Do you think the girl in the photo is at risk?" Her speech on volunteer services for at-risk teenagers presented the stories of the girls pictured in the photos.

The use of presentation aids is not confined to the classroom. Let's look at how Carol Quinn, director of human resources for Argonne National Laboratory, integrated a novel visual aid into a speech presented at a Secretary's Day breakfast in Chicago:

> **Good morning, everyone. I am delighted to be here and am honored that you have selected me as your keynote speaker for Secretary's Day. Most of you have coffee or juice, or perhaps tea. What I have here in this glass is Kool-Aid. But I'm not going to drink it.**

> Why I have this Kool-Aid and why I'm not going to drink it are in a sense what I want to talk about this Secretary's Day. What I would like to share with you today are six suggestions for maximizing your career success by playing to your strengths.
>
> This glass of Kool-Aid represents the worst job I've ever had. Yes, you are looking at a former "Kool-Aid tester" for General Foods. There really is—or at least "was"—such a job. When we weren't testing Kool-Aid, we were expected to taste daiquiri mixes, or nibble potato chips, or smell soap, or otherwise play the role of "average consumer." I came away from that with a long-standing aversion to Kool-Aid, which is why I'm not going to drink this.[16]

Additional references to the Kool-Aid were artfully woven into the speech.

Startle the Audience.   Anything truly unusual draws attention to itself and arouses curiosity. Consider the headlines from the sensationalist tabloids: "BIGFOOT SPOTTED IN NORTHWEST ARKANSAS!" "WOMAN PREDICTS EARTHQUAKES WITH HER TOES!"

One of our students at Vanderbilt opened with the following narrative:

> Imagine a warm, sunny June day. A bride stands at the back of the church. It is beautifully decorated with fresh flowers, and the music of a pipe organ fills the sanctuary. There is not a dry eye as the father gives the bride away. The couple recite their vows, and upon pronouncing the couple married, the minister proclaims, "Katie, you may kiss the bride."
>
> The surprise that many of you just experienced is the reaction gay rights activists have been trying to eliminate since 1969. This fight simply to be accepted as part of everyday life is one that continues today.

The startle technique must always be used with care. You don't want your introduction to arouse more interest than the body of your speech can satisfy. If your opening is too sensational, it will "upstage" the rest of your speech. Similarly, be careful not to go beyond the bounds of propriety. You want to startle your listeners into attention, not offend them.

Capturing Attention

speaker's notes

1 Involve listeners.
2 Call on personal experience.
3 Ask questions.
4 Create suspense and anticipation.
5 Open with a story.
6 Engage listeners with humor.
7 Begin with a quotation.
8 Use a presentation aid.
9 Startle the audience.

Establishing Your Credibility

The second major function of an effective introduction is to establish your-self as a competent, trustworthy, and likable person. People tend to form first impressions of speakers that color their later perceptions.[17] In Chapter 2 we discussed the importance of the impressions you make on listeners in terms of your competence, integrity, likableness, and forcefulness—your ethos. As you make later presentations, you will carry over some of the initial ethos you established with your first presentation and with your interactions in class. You must confirm or strengthen this initial ethos in the introduction of each speech.

Establishing their qualifications to speak on a subject is often difficult for beginning speakers. As we noted in Chapter 2, you can seem competent only if you know what you are talking about. People listen more respectfully to those who speak from both knowledge and personal experience.[18] As we noted in Chapter 5, the perception of competence can be fortified by select-ing topics you already know something about and by doing research to qual-ify yourself as a responsible speaker. In your introduction you can allude to your research to reinforce your credibility:

> **I was amazed to learn in psychology class that research does not sup-port a strong link between exposure to persuasive communications and behavior. This discovery led me to do more reading on the rela-tionship between advertising and consumer activity. What I found was even more surprising, especially when you consider that, accord-ing to *American Demographics,* advertisers routinely paid over $550,000 for a half minute of air time on *ER.***

Here the specific reference to a respected source of information suggests that you have done the research needed to make a responsible speech. It would not be effective, however, to simply announce at the beginning of your speech:

> **The information for my speech comes from my psychology textbook, two articles from the *Journal of Applied Psychology,* and an article in *American Demographics.***

That would seem forced, awkward, and artificial. It would interrupt the nat-ural flow of your introduction.

Your perceived competence will be further strengthened if your speech is well organized, if you use language ably and correctly, and if you have prac-ticed so that your presentation flows smoothly.

To create a perception of integrity, you must seem ethical and honest. Au-diences are more receptive to speakers who are straightforward, sincere, and concerned about the consequences of their words.[19] You can enhance your integrity by showing respect for those who hold different opinions while still maintaining your personal commitment to your topic and position.

You should also present yourself as a likable and forceful speaker. Likable speakers are pleasant and tactful. They treat their listeners as friends, inspiring affection in return.[20] Likable speakers share their feelings and are able to laugh at themselves. To come across as a forceful speaker, you must project self-confidence. Your introduction should show your enthusiasm for your message. A smile and direct eye contact signals listeners that you want to communicate.

When you establish favorable ethos at the outset, you also lay the foundation for one of the most powerful effects of communication: identification between yourself and listeners. **Identification** occurs when people overcome the personal and cultural differences that separate them and share thoughts and feelings as though they were one.[21] When you seem likable, sincere, competent, and forceful, your listeners want to identify with you, and your effectiveness as a communicator is magnified.

Preview Your Message

The final function of an introduction is to preview the body of your speech. The **preview** indicates the main points you will cover and offers your listeners an overview of the speech to come.

Martha Radner offered the following preview for her speech on campus security problems.

> **This campus will be a much safer place if we adopt my plan to improve campus security. First, I want to show you how dangerous our situation has become. Second, I'll explore the reasons why current security measures on our campus are ineffective. And third, I'll present my plan for a safer campus environment.**

By informing her listeners of her intentions and her speech design, Martha helped her audience listen intelligently.

Selecting and Using Introductory Techniques

There are no hard and fast rules for determining exactly how you should open a speech. As you review your research notes, look for material that would make an effective introduction. The following guidelines may help you make a wise selection:

- Consider your audience. Use your introduction to tie your topic to their needs, interests, or well-being.
- Consider the mood you want to establish. Some topics will mandate a light touch, and others may call for more solemnity.
- Consider your time constraints. If you are to speak for seven minutes, you can't get bogged down in a five-minute introduction.
- Consider what you do best. Some people are effective storytellers, and others are better using striking statistics or quotations. Go with your strength!

Developing an Effective Conclusion

Many beginning speakers end their presentations awkwardly. The conclusion of your speech should not be just the point where you just got tired of talking or ran out of time. "That's all, folks!" may be an effective ending for a cartoon, but in a speech such a conclusion violates the audience's need for closure. Saying "That's it, I guess" or "Well, I'm done," accompanied by a sigh of relief, suggests that you have not planned your speech carefully. The final words of your speech should stay with your listeners, remind them of your message, and, when appropriate, move them to action.

Summarizing Your Message

Your conclusion will normally include a summary and final remarks. Most often, you should begin the conclusion with a brief **summary statement** of the main points made in your speech. The more complicated your topic, the more important this becomes. The summary statement then may function as a transition between the body and your final remarks. It signals the audience that you are about to finish.

Concluding Remarks

Although a summary statement can offer listeners a sense of closure, to seal that effect you need to provide some concluding remarks that stay with your listeners. Many of the techniques that create effective introductions can also be used to develop memorable conclusions.

Echo the Introduction.   A conclusion that echoes the introduction provides a nice sense of closure for the audience. Note that we have said "echoes," not "repeats." A conclusion that echoes the introduction may use the same technique. For example, if you began with a story, you might end with a different story that reinforces the meaning. You could also finish a story that you started in the introduction. The speaker who recited the long list of Lincoln's failures might have waited until the end before satisfying audience curiosity as to who this "loser" actually was. Carol Quinn came back to her glass of Kool-Aid for the conclusion of her speech:

> **If I really wanted to end this speech with flair, I would now drink this glass of Kool-Aid. But there being no power on the planet which could force me to drink another glass of Kool-Aid, I will instead wish you health, happiness, a wonderful day, and—you know what?— strawberry Kool-Aid is really the best. Thanks for inviting me.[22]**

Many persuasive speeches end with a call for action.

Involve the Audience.   At the beginning of a speech, you involve the audience by showing them how your message relates directly to their lives. At the conclusion of your speech, you should remind them of what they personally have at stake. In the speech on global warming, the summary statement was followed immediately by remarks that echoed the opening and placed the speech in perspective:

> **Global warming is a monster we are creating. If we don't stop, we and our children face more and more drastic climate changes and serious health problems.**

In persuasive speeches, concluding remarks also often urge listeners to take the first step to confirm their commitment to action and change.

Ask Rhetorical Questions.   When used in an introduction, rhetorical questions help arouse attention and curiosity. When used in a conclusion, such questions give your audience something to think about after you have finished. Annette Berrington opened a speech on the use of seat belts with a rhetorical question, "How many of you buckled up on your way to class this morning?" Her final words were, "Now that you know what a lifesaver seat belts are, how many of you will buckle up on the way home?"

When used at the end of a persuasive speech, concluding questions may be more than rhetorical. They may actually call for a response from the audience. During political campaigns, the Reverend Jesse Jackson often used this technique to register voters. He would end a speech by asking:

> **How many of you are not registered to vote? Raise your hands. No, stand up so we can see you! Is that all of you who aren't registered? Stand up! Let me see you!**

Such questioning and cajoling would be followed by on-site voter registration. Evangelists who issue an invitation to salvation at the end of their sermons often use concluding questions in a similar way. To be effective, this technique must be the climax of a speech that has prepared its audience for action.

End with a Story.   Stories are remembered long after facts and figures are forgotten. A concluding narrative can help your audience *experience* the essence of your message. To conclude a speech on domestic terrorism, which she had opened with a narrative, Donna E. Shalala, then secretary of health and human services, told the following story:

> **Let me conclude by telling you about a child psychologist named Sandra Graham-Berman who took responsibility for doing even more [about the problem of domestic abuse]. Several years ago she became aware of a support group for battered women. But she heard that there was no professional support for their children. On her own time and with her own money she began a support group for the children of these battered women. She began to see the girls and boys act out, talk out, and draw out their fears and their frustrations. She helped them learn they are not alone in their pain. And she taught them that when mommy is in trouble—when she is being hurt by daddy—it's possible to get help by dialing 9-1-1.**

A few years later, a shy 8-year-old girl walked in on a fight. Her father—if you can believe it, a child psychiatrist—was beating her mother on the head with a hammer. Try to imagine that. Try to imagine what you would do. Well, that little girl knew what to do. She remembered the lesson taught to her by a caring adult. And so she went to that phone, picked it up, pressed 9-1-1, and saved her mother's life. The father is in prison now and the family's trying its best to build a new life. If that little girl can have the courage to pick up the telephone, surely we can have the courage to prevent such stories from happening.[23]

Close with a Quotation.   Brief quotations that capture the essence of your message make effective conclusions. For example, if one historic quotation opens a speech, another on the same theme or from the same person can provide an elegant sense of closure. Elissa Scadron closed her ceremonial speech honoring America as a sanctuary of human rights by completing the quotation from Abraham Lincoln she had cited in her opening:

> The best way to complete this speech is to fill in what Lincoln said about our responsibilities a century and a half ago: "Fellow citizens, we cannot escape history. . . . In giving freedom to the slave, we assure freedom to the free. . . . honorable alike in what we give and what we preserve. We shall nobly save, or meanly lose, the last best hope of earth."

End with a Metaphor.   A striking **metaphor** can end your speech effectively.[24] As we will discuss at greater length in Chapter 10, metaphors combine things that are apparently unlike so that we see unexpected relationships. As a conclusion to a speech, an effective metaphor reveals a hidden truth about the speaker's subject in a memorable way. Melodie Lancaster, president of Lancaster Resources, used such a metaphor, combined with a narrative, as she concluded a speech to the Houston Council of the American Business Women's Association:

> We recall the story of the three stonemasons who were asked what they were doing. The first said, "I am laying brick." The second replied, "I am making a foundation." And the third said: "I am building a cathedral." Let's you and I set our sights that high. Let's build cathedrals of success today, tomorrow, and the day after tomorrow.[25]

Consider the many meanings this metaphor might evoke in the minds of listeners. First, the speaker suggests that listeners must work hard. Second, she suggests that they must work with specific goals in mind. Third, she suggests that they must work with a vision that gives significance to what they do. All these meanings are packed into the metaphor, making it memorable for her audience.

Whatever closing technique you select should satisfy your audience that what was promised in the beginning has now been delivered. Plan your summary statement and concluding remarks very carefully, just as you did your introduction. Practice them until you are confident that you will end your speech impressively. After your final words, pause a moment to let them sink in, then take your seat.

In Summary

A carefully structured speech helps the audience understand the message and enhances the speaker's ethos.

Good Form. A well-structured speech has *good form:* It is simple, balanced, and orderly. *Simplicity* occurs when you limit the number of main points and use clear, direct language. A speech has *balance* when the major parts receive proper emphasis and work together. The requirement of *order* means that a speech follows a consistent pattern of development.

Structuring the Body of Your Speech. You should structure the body first, so that you can build an introduction and conclusion that fit your message. To develop the body, determine your *main points,* decide how to arrange them, then select effective supporting materials. To discover your main points, prepare a *research overview* of the information you have collected. This summary can help you spot major themes that can develop into main points.

Arrange your main points so that they follow natural mental patterns based on the principles of similarity, proximity, and closure. The *similarity* of objects or events may suggest a categorical design for structuring main points. *Proximity* suggests that things should be discussed as they happen together in space or time. If they occur in a time sequence, use a sequential design for your speech. If they occur in physical relationship to one another, a spatial design might be appropriate. The structure of the body satisfies the principle of *closure* when it completes the design it begins. Cause-effect and problem-solution designs require closure in order to be effective.

Supporting materials fill out the speech and buttress ideas. In an ideal arrangement, you should support each point with information, testimony, and an example or story that emphasizes its human aspects.

Using Transitions. Effective *transitions* point up the relationships among ideas in your speech and tie the speech together. *Internal summaries* remind listeners of the points you have made in one part of your speech before you move on to another.

Preparing an Effective Introduction. The introduction to a speech should arouse your listeners' interest, establish your credibility, and focus and *preview* your message. Some useful ways to introduce a speech include involving the audience, relating your subject to personal experience, asking *rhetorical questions,* creating suspense, telling a story, using humor, beginning with a quotation, using a presentation aid, or startling the audience. As you build credibility, you also make possible *identification* between yourself and the audience.

Developing an Effective Conclusion. An effective conclusion should review the meaning of your speech in a *summary statement,* provide a sense of closure, leave the audience with *final reflections* on the significance of the speech, and, if appropriate, motivate listeners to act. Techniques that are useful for conclusions include echoing the introduction, involving the audience, asking questions, closing with a quotation, telling a story, and ending with a *metaphor.* Your speech will seem more symmetrical and satisfying if your conclusion ties into your introduction.

Terms to Know

good form	principle of closure
simplicity	transitions
balance	internal summary
order	rhetorical questions
main points	identification
research overview	preview
principle of similarity	summary statement
principle of proximity	metaphor

Notes

1. Patricia R. Palmerton, "Teaching Skills or Teaching Thinking," *Journal of Applied Communication Research* 20 (1992): 335–341; and Robert G. Powell, "Critical Thinking and Speech Communication: Our Teaching Strategies Are Warranted—Not!" *Journal of Applied Communication Research* 20 (1992): 342–347. Most of the research on the effects of structure was conducted in the 1960s and 1970s. Notable among these studies are Arlee Johnson, "A Preliminary Investigation of the Relationship Between Organization and Listener Comprehension," *Central States Speech Journal* 21 (1970): 104–107; Christopher Spicer and Ronald E. Bassett, "The Effect of Organization on Learning from an Informative Message," *Southern Speech Communication Journal* 41 (1976): 290–299; and Ernest Thompson, "Some Effects of Message Structure on Listeners' Comprehension," *Speech Monographs* 34 (1967): 51–57.
2. Patricia Kearney, Timothy G. Plax, Ellis R. Hayes, and Marily J. Ivey, "College Teacher Misbehaviors: What Students Don't Like About What Teachers Say and Do," *Communication Quarterly* 39 (1991): 309–324.
3. J. C. McCroskey and R. S. Mehrley, "The Effects of Disorganization and Nonfluency on Attitude Change and Source Credibility," *Communication Monographs* 36 (1969): 13–21.
4. Saul Kassin, *Psychology* (Boston: Houghton Mifflin, 1995), pp. 208–251.
5. Material in this section is based on the work of the Gestalt psychologists as summarized in Kassin, pp. 78–129.
6. Charles Hulme, Steven Roodenrys, Gordon Brown, and Robin Mercer, "The Role of Long-term Memory Mechanisms in Memory Span," *British Journal of Psychology* 86 (1995): 527–536.
7. Douglas A. Bernstein, Edward J. Roy, Thomas K. Srull, and Christopher D. Wickens, *Psychology,* 2nd ed. (Boston: Houghton Mifflin, 1991), p. 308.
8. Kassin, p. 111.
9. Loren J. Anderson, "A Summary of Research on Order Effects in Communication," in *Concepts in Communication,* ed. Jimmie D. Trent, Judith S. Trent, and Daniel J. O'Neill (Boston: Allyn & Bacon, 1973), pp. 129–130.
10. Cited in Arthur M. Schlesinger, Jr., *A Thousand Days: John F. Kennedy in the White House* (Boston: Houghton Mifflin, 1965), p. 733.
11. Our thanks for this example go to Professor Reno Unger, Kutztown University.
12. James Price Dillard, "Persuasion Past and Present: Attitudes Aren't What They Used to Be," *Communication Monographs* 60 (1993): 91.
13. Wendy Liebmann, "How America Shops: The Consumer Paradox," in *Vital Speeches of the Day,* 15 July 1998, p. 595.
14. Brock Evans, "The Endangered Species Act: Implications for the Future," in *Vital Speeches of the Day,* 15 March 1993, p. 339.

15. Bob Lannom, "Patience, Persistence, and Perspiration," *Parsons (Tenn.) News Leader,* 20 September 1989, p. 9.

16. Carol Quinn, "Playing to Your Strengths," in *Vital Speeches of the Day,* 1 June 1998, p. 508. Reprinted by permission.

17. Sharon S. Brehm and Saul M. Kassin, *Social Psychology,* 2nd ed. (Boston: Houghton Mifflin, 1993), pp. 127–128.

18. R. G. Hass, "Effects of Source Characteristics on the Cognitive Processing of Persuasive Messages and Attitude Change," in *Cognitive Responses in Persuasion,* ed. R. Petty, T. Ostrom, and T. Brock (Hillsdale, N.J.: Erlbaum, 1981), pp. 141–172; M. Heesacker, R. E. Petty, and J. T. Cacioppo, "Field Dependence and Attitude Change: Source Credibility Can Alter Persuasion by Affecting Message-Relevant Thinking," *Journal of Personality* 51 (1983): 653–666; and J. E. Maddux and R. W. Rogers, "Effects of Source Expertness, Physical Attractiveness, and Supporting Arguments on Persuasion: A Case of Brains over Beauty," *Journal of Personality and Social Psychology* 39 (1980): 235–244.

19. A. H. Eagly, W. Wood, and S. Chaiken, "An Attribution Analysis of Persuasion," in *New Directions in Attribution Research,* ed. J. Harvey, W. Ickes, and R. Kidd (Hillsdale, N.J.: Erlbaum, 1981), pp. 37–62.

20. Brehm and Kassin, pp. 220–221.

21. Kenneth Burke, *A Rhetoric of Motives* (Berkeley and Los Angeles: University of California Press, 1969), pp. 20–23.

22. Carol Quinn, "Playing Your Strengths," in *Vital Speeches of the Day,* 1 June 1998, p. 510.

23. Donna E. Shalala, "Domestic Terrorism: An Unacknowledged Epidemic," in *Vital Speeches of the Day,* 15 May 1994, p. 453.

24. John Waite Bowers and Michael Osborn, "Attitudinal Effects of Selected Types of Concluding Metaphors in Persuasive Speeches," *Speech Monographs* 33 (1966): 148–155.

25. Melodie Lancaster, "The Future We Predict Isn't Inevitable: Refraining Our Success in the Modern World," in *Vital Speeches of the Day,* 1 August 1992, p. 638.

8 Outlining Your Speech

*O*ur plans
miscarry be-
cause they have
no aim. When a
man does not
know what har-
bor he is making
for, no wind is
the right wind.

—Seneca

This chapter will help you

- understand why outlining is important
- learn how to develop a working outline
- prepare a formal outline
- condense your formal outline to a key-word outline

For several years our residential neighborhood was caught up in zoning disputes. Once, at a zoning meeting on another matter, we learned that a proposal to construct a helicopter port was on the agenda. With just minutes to prepare, we organized our arguments. Our purpose was clear: We did not want a heliport in the neighborhood! We felt it would destroy the tranquility of our neighborhood. We also believed that the applicant had violated the law by operating without a permit. We jotted down our main arguments on the back of a civil defense bulletin:

I. A heliport would intrude on the tranquility of the neighborhood.

A. It would disturb the peace and quiet of residents.

B. It would bother patients in a nearby nursing home.

II. The applicants had already violated the law.

A. They had not applied for a license before operating.

B. They had ignored FAA operating regulations.

This simple outline helped us structure our presentation. We defeated the heliport proposal! Had we tried to speak before the zoning board without first organizing our thoughts, we would have lost.

 DEVELOPING AN OUTLINE gives you a picture of what you want to say. An effective outline helps you identify your most important points, determine the most effective order in which to arrange them, and select your supporting material. It allows you to plan a speech that is simple, balanced, and orderly. Just as you wouldn't try to build a house without a blueprint, you shouldn't try to prepare a speech without an outline.

Outlining objectifies your thinking: It takes ideas out of your head, where they can get all tangled up, and puts them down on paper, where you can work with them.[1] It is both a creative and a corrective process: As you think about the relationships of ideas, you may come up with new ideas. You can see where you need more research, whether a point is really relevant, and whether the overall structure is well balanced.[2] You may need to add something here, subtract something there. Outlining helps you find and correct problems *before* they become mistakes. Finally, an outline points out where you need transitions and helps you see whether your introduction and conclusion fit your speech.

To outline your speech, all you need is a pencil and paper (plus your research notes). However, outlining is easier with a computer: You can type in material, move it around, and print out different versions of your outline to evaluate. In this chapter we provide you with sample outline formats suitable for the general structure of any speech. In Chapter 12 we offer specific outline formats for informative speech designs: spatial, sequential, categorical, comparative, and causation. In Chapter 13 we provide outline formats for the major persuasive speech designs: problem-solution, motivated sequence, and refutative.

In the process of preparing your speech, your outline should evolve from working outlines to a full-sentence outline to a key-word outline to use as a prompt during presentation. As you prepare your speeches, you will probably develop several working outlines, a formal outline, and a key-word outline for each speech.

Developing a Working Outline

A **working outline** is a *tentative* plan of your speech. It is a work in process in which you display the relationships among ideas and identify potential trouble spots. Why should you start with a working outline? Assume that you plan to present an informative speech on "global warming." You have done some research, but you are not completely sure how your speech should develop. Your working outline is a tool that can help reduce your uncertainty. Figure 8.1 provides you with a format for developing a working outline.

You should not think of this format as a rigid structure. Adapt it so that it works for you. In this early stage of developing your speech, don't worry about the formalities of outlining.[3] Your working outline is a disposable tool to help you arrange your ideas. You will probably prepare and discard several working outlines before you find the right approach. Nonetheless, the working outline should already include your main points and subpoints. Even at this stage you should be thinking about the relative importance of ideas and about their logical relationship to one another.

A good starting point for your working outline is to write out your specific purpose and thesis statement. You need to have these clearly in mind so that you can check how well your main points fit them. Your specific purpose and thesis statement form the foundation for your speech.

Specific purpose:	To inform my audience of the problem of global warming.
Thesis statement:	Today I want to share what I've learned about global warming and its causes.

Developing Your Main Points

The second step in preparing a working outline is to sketch the body of your speech. Following the process discussed in Chapter 7, write out your main points. You may recall that in selecting main points, you work from a research overview. Consider the major themes from this overview in light of

FIGURE 8.1

Format for a Working Outline

Topic: _____
Specific purpose: _____
Thesis statement: _____

INTRODUCTION

Attention material: _____
Credibility material: _____
Thesis statement: _____
Preview: _____

(Transition to body of speech)

BODY

First main point: _____
  Subpoint: _____
    Sub-subpoint: _____
    Sub-subpoint: _____
  Subpoint: _____

(Transition to second main point)

Second main point: _____
  Subpoint: _____
  Subpoint: _____
    Sub-subpoint: _____
    Sub-subpoint: _____

(Transition to third main point)

Third main point: _____
  Subpoint: _____
  Subpoint: _____

(Transition to conclusion)

CONCLUSION

Summary: _____
Concluding remarks: _____

the purpose of your speech, your audience's needs, and the amount of time available for you to speak. In our ongoing example of preparing a speech on global warming, the first working outline contained the following main points:

First main point: Industrial emissions accelerate global warming.

Second main point: Increased energy consumption magnifies global warming.

Third main point: The loss of woodlands adds to global warming.

Once you have your main points written out, ask yourself the following questions:

- Will these points make my message clear to my audience?
- Is this the right order in which to develop them?
- Have I left out anything important?

As you consider these questions, you realize that you have indeed left some-thing out. You remember that all of your sources explained what global warming was before discussing its causes. You note that your original list of main points neither explains global warming nor gives the audience a reason to be interested in it. You also see another potential trouble spot: There is no clear, logical order in your arrangement of main points. But if you put the third point first, the first point second, and the second point third—wood-lands, industrial emissions, and consumption—you would be following an order of increasing importance in the presentation of these points. This would allow your speech to build toward its conclusion. You decide to toss out your first working outline and to revise the main points as follows:

First main point: Global warming is a gradual increase in the temper-ature of the Earth caused by human activities.

Second main point: The loss of woodlands adds to global warming.

Third main point: Industrial emissions accelerate global warming.

Fourth main point: Increased energy consumption magnifies global warming.

Developing Subpoints

Once you have determined and arranged your main points, you can break them down into more specific statements that explain and support them. These more specific statements belong at the **subpoint** level of your outline. Usually each main point will be buttressed by two or more subpoints that substantiate and clarify it. Each subpoint must relate directly to the main point it follows and should make that point more understandable, believable, or compelling.[4]

To identify the subpoints for each of your main points, imagine a critical listener in front of you. When you state the main point, this listener will want to know:

- What do you mean?
- Why should I care?
- How do I know this is true?

The subpoints of each main point should answer these questions. If the main points are columns built upon the foundation of your purpose and thesis statement, the subpoints reinforce these columns so that they will stand up under scrutiny. For example, as you develop your working outline, you might list the following subpoints for your first main point:

First main point: Global warming is a gradual increase in the tempera-ture of the Earth caused by human activities.

Subpoints:
A. It comes from a high concentration of carbon dioxide in the atmosphere.
B. It holds the heat.
C. It is related to a hole in the ozone layer.
D. The hole lets ultraviolet radiation through.

    E. It can cause climate problems.

    F. It can cause health problems.

As you look back over your first main point, you notice that you have listed six subpoints. Recalling the principles of good form learned in Chapter 7, you conclude rightly that you have *too many* subpoints for your speech to remain simple, balanced, and orderly.

At this point, examine how your subpoints relate to one another. Can you combine any of them? Do you need to break out the material to a more detailed level of **sub-subpoints**? Just as subpoints reinforce and clarify main points, sub-subpoints strengthen and specify subpoints. You should also include some supporting materials as you work out the sub-subpoints. For example, you might expand the first main point in this working outline as follows:

First main point:	Global warming is a gradual increase in temperatures caused by human activities.
Subpoint A:	It comes from a high concentration of carbon dioxide (CO_2) in the air.
Sub-subpoints:	1. Five tons of CO_2 per person yearly in U.S.
	2. CO_2 traps heat.
	3. 1998 set temperature records.
Subpoint B:	It is related to the hole in the ozone layer.
Sub-subpoints:	1. In 1998 the size of this hole hit a record high.
	2. More ultraviolet radiation comes through.
Subpoint C:	Global warming can cause serious problems.
Sub-subpoints:	1. It can cause climate problems [*cite possibilities*].
	2. It can cause health problems [*describe potential problems*].

Follow this same procedure as you develop each main point. When you finish, review the working outline of the body of your speech and ask yourself:

- Will a speech based on this outline fulfill what I promise in my thesis statement?
- Will I be able to do all of this in the time available?

Be honest with yourself. It's better to be frustrated now than disappointed later during your presentation. In addition, be sure your ideas are arranged in an orderly manner that is easy to follow. Make certain that each subpoint relates directly to the main point above it and that you have enough supporting material to build a strong, responsible structure of ideas. If you are lacking in any of these areas, now is the time to discover and correct the problem.

Completing Your Working Outline

To complete your working outline (see figure 8.2 on the following pages), prepare an introduction that gains attention, establishes your credibility, and previews your speech, as we discussed in Chapter 7. Next, prepare a conclusion that

FIGURE 8.2

Sample Working Outline

Begin the working outline by writing down your topic, specific purpose, and thesis statement so that you have them clearly in mind as you work.

In the working outline, sketch out your introduction, including short notes on attention and credibility materials. As planning proceeds, revise any of these elements as needed.

Include transitions to remind yourself to tie material together and make it flow smoothly.

Labeling the body of the speech points out its importance. Remember to develop the body of the speech *before* you develop the introduction or conclusion.

Note that the working outline does not follow the numbering and lettering system of a formal outline. The purpose of the working outline is to allow you to organize ideas and see how they fit together.

The working outline serves as your guide and provides a check on the structure of the speech and the adequacy of your preparation.

Topic:	Global warming
Specific purpose:	To inform my audience about the problem of global warming.
Thesis statement:	Today I want to share what I've learned about global warming and its causes.

INTRODUCTION

Attention material:	Twain story on "exaggerated death": Death of global warming also exaggerated. Antarctic icebergs breaking loose.
Credibility material:	Love outdoors and want to see environment safe for future generations. Audience also shares fate.
Thesis statement:	Today I want to share what I've learned about global warming and its causes.
Preview:	We need to be concerned about the loss of woodlands, industrial emissions, and overall increases in energy consumption.

(**Transition** to body of speech:
"Let's begin by understanding more about global warming.")

BODY

First main point:	Global warming is a gradual increase in temperatures on the Earth caused by human activities.
Subpoint A:	It comes from a high concentration of carbon dioxide (CO_2) in the air.
Sub-subpoints:	1. Five tons of CO_2 per person per year in the U.S. 2. CO_2 traps heat. 3. 1998 set temperature records.
Subpoint B:	It is related to the hole in the ozone layer.
Sub-subpoints:	1. In 1998 the size of this hole hit a record high. 2. More ultraviolet radiation comes through.
Subpoint C:	Global warming can cause serious problems.
Sub-subpoints:	1. It can cause climate problems [*cite possibilities*]. 2. It can cause health problems [*describe potential problems*].

(**Transition** to second main point: "So what are the causes?")

Second main point:	The loss of woodlands adds to global warming.
Subpoint A:	Lose woods the size of a football field every second.
Sub-subpoints:	1. Loss from cutting. 2. Loss from burning.
Subpoint B:	Burning adds more CO_2 because of smoke.

(**Transition** to third main point: "An even greater cause is industrial emissions.")

Third main point:	Industrial emissions accelerate global warming.
Subpoint A:	More than 20 percent of all air pollution.
Subpoint B:	CO_2 and nitrogen oxides released when wood, coal, oil, and gas are burned.
Subpoint C:	Recent changes are slowing the growth of industrial emissions.

(continued)

Since this main point covers the largest single cause of global warming, it should be more thoroughly developed than the second and third main points.

(Transition to fourth main point: "Finally, let's consider the most important cause of global warming — ourselves.")

Fourth main point: Personal energy consumption magnifies global warming.
Subpoint A: Energy consumption is single largest cause of global warming.
Sub-subpoints: 1. Fossil Fuel use accounts for 90 percent of America's energy consumption.
2. Transportation-related energy use accounts for half of all air pollution.
Subpoint B: America is on an energy binge.
Sub-subpoints: 1. We are using more fuel in our homes.
2. We are using more fuel for transportation.

(Transition: "In conclusion . . .")

CONCLUSION

Like the introduction, the conclusion is merely sketched in the working outline. Note that this speech ends with a narrative as well as starts with one. These opening and closing stories provide balance and closure.

Summary statement: Global warming threatens our world. It may cause drastic climate changes and serious health problems. Major causes are loss of woodlands, industrial emissions, and increased personal energy consumption.
Concluding remarks: Gore story about the frog in boiling water.

includes a summary and concluding remarks. Finally, add transitions to tie your speech together. Remember that your transitions should connect the introduction to the body, connect each main point to the next main point, and move the speech from the body to the conclusion.

Now, take a final look at your working outline. Figure 8.2 is a sample working outline for a speech on global warming.

Review the outline using the Checklist for a Working Outline. If possible, go over the outline with someone whose judgment you respect. Another

Checklist for a Working Outline

speaker's notes

_____ 1 My topic, specific purpose, and thesis statement are clearly stated.

_____ 2 My introduction contains attention-getting material, establishes my credibility, and focuses and previews my message.

_____ 3 My main points represent the most important ideas on my topic.

_____ 4 I have an appropriate number of main points to cover my material in the time allotted.

_____ 5 Each subpoint breaks its main point into more specific detail.

_____ 6 My conclusion contains a summary statement and concluding remarks that reinforce and reflect upon the meaning of my speech.

_____ 7 I have planned transitions to use between the introduction and body, between each of my main points, and between the body and conclusion of my speech.

person can sometimes see problems that you might miss because you are too close to the material.

As you review your working outline, keep the audience at the center of your thinking. Remember the advice given to beginning journalists: *Never overestimate your audience's information, and never underestimate their intelligence!* Ask yourself the following questions:

- Are my main points arranged so that they are easy to understand and remember?
- Do I have enough supporting material for each main point?
- Do I have different types of supporting materials for each main point?

Remember, speech preparation often proceeds in fits and starts, periods of frustration followed by moments of inspiration and revision. You may find yourself making and revising several working outlines for each of your major presentations.

Developing a Formal Outline

Once you are satisfied with your working outline, you can prepare a formal outline. The **formal outline** is the final step in a process leading from your first rough draft of ideas through a series of working outlines to the finished product. It imposes a helpful discipline upon your preparation to speak, and indicates to your instructor that the research and planning phase of your work is completed. The formal outline for a speech follows many of the established conventions of outlining. Figure 8.3 shows a formal speech outline format illustrating these conventions:

1. Identification of the speech topic, specific purpose, and thesis statement
2. Separation of speech parts: introduction, body, and conclusion
3. Use of numbering and lettering to display coordination and subordination
4. Wording of main points and subpoints as simple declarative sentences
5. A title
6. A list of major sources consulted

Topic, Specific Purpose, and Thesis Statement

Some student speakers recite their topic, specific purpose, and thesis statement at the beginning of each speech as though they had been programmed: "My topic is . . . My specific purpose is . . . My thesis statement is . . ." This is not a good way to begin a speech! Nevertheless, you should write these headings out at the top of your outline. The headings help you focus your message.

FIGURE 8.3

Format for a Formal Outline

TITLE

Topic: _____

Specific purpose: _____

Thesis statement: _____

INTRODUCTION

Attention material: _____

Credibility material: _____

Thesis statement: _____

Preview: _____

(Transition into body of speech)

BODY

I. **First main point:**
   A. Subpoint or supporting material: _____
   B. Subpoint or supporting material: _____
      1. Sub-subpoint or supporting material: _____
      2. Sub-subpoint or supporting material: _____

(Transition into next main point)

II. **Second main point:**
   A. Subpoint or supporting material: _____
      1. Sub-subpoint or supporting material: _____
      2. Sub-subpoint or supporting material: _____
   B. Subpoint or supporting material: _____

(Transition into next main point)

III. **Third main point:**
   A. Subpoint or supporting material: _____
   B. Subpoint or supporting material: _____
      1. Sub-subpoint or supporting material: _____
      2. Sub-subpoint or supporting material: _____
         a. Sub-sub-subpoint or supporting material: _____
         b. Sub-sub-subpoint or supporting material: _____

(Transition into conclusion)

CONCLUSION

Summary statement: _____

Concluding remarks: _____

WORKS CONSULTED

Separation of Speech Parts

The introduction, body, and conclusion of the speech should be separated in the outline. Separating the major parts of your speech helps ensure that you give each section the careful attention it requires. Only when your introduction, body, and conclusion are fully developed and joined by transitions can they work together to achieve your specific purpose.

Note that in Figure 8.3, only the body of the speech follows an outline format.[5] As we suggested in Chapters 2 and 7, it is best to plan your introduction and conclusion carefully to ensure that you get into and out of your speech gracefully and effectively. Although there may be times when you must change your introduction (we discussed this under "Context" in Chapter 4), as a general rule a carefully worded beginning works best. Knowing *exactly* what you want to say and how you want to say it gets you off to a good start and helps build the confidence you need if you are to make your presentation effective. At the end of your speech, the exact wording of your concluding remarks can determine whether you make a lasting impression.

Numbering and Lettering Your Outline

Figure 8.3 shows you how to use letters, numbers, and indentation to set up a formal outline that follows the principles of coordination and subordination. The actual number of main points and levels of subpoints may vary, but the basic format remains the same. Roman numerals (I, II, III) identify the main points of your speech. Capital letters (A, B, C) identify the subpoints under each main point. Arabic numbers (1, 2, 3) identify the sub-subpoints under any subpoint. Lowercase letters (a, b, c) identify any sub-sub-subpoints in your outline.

The principle of **coordination** requires that all statements at a given level (your *I*'s and *II*'s, your *A*'s and *B*'s, your *1*'s and *2*'s, and your *a*'s and *b*'s) be of similar importance. In the sample formal outline (shown later in this chapter), the main points include an explanation of global warming and its three major causes. Because the causes vary in importance, you might arrange them in ascending order of importance. Think how strange it would seem if a fifth main point, "Global warming will decrease our recreational opportunities," were added to this outline. That statement would not be coordinate with the other main points. It would not equal them in importance, nor would it fit within the pattern. Adding such a main point would violate the principle of coordination.

The principle of **subordination** requires that material descend in importance from the general and abstract main points to the concrete and specific subpoints, and sub-subpoints related to them, as shown below:

more important	I. Main point	**more general**
	A. Subpoint	
	1. Sub-subpoint	
less important	a. Sub-sub-subpoint	**more specific**

The more important a statement is, the farther to the left it is positioned. If you rotate an outline so that it rests on its right margin, the "peaks" will represent the main points, the most important ideas in your speech, with the height of the subpoints representing their relative significance.

The easiest way to demonstrate the importance of coordination and subordination is to look at an abbreviated sample outline that violates these principles:

I. Computers can help you develop writing skills.
   A. Using PCs can improve your schoolwork.
   B. PCs can be useful for organizing class notes.
II. Computers can help you keep better financial records.
   A. They can help you plan personal time more effectively.
   B. They can be useful in your personal life.
   C. They can help organize your research notes for class projects.

This collection of ideas may look like an outline, but it isn't. It violates the principles of coordination and subordination. The points at each level are not equal in importance, nor are they logically related to one another. To straighten out this problem, look at points I and II. They are neither the most important nor the most general statements. The main points are actually I-A and II-B: the ideas that PCs can improve your schoolwork and can be useful in your personal life. Once we put the main points where they belong, we can see where the subpoints go:

I. Computers can improve your schoolwork.
   A. PCs can help you develop writing skills.
   B. PCs can be useful for organizing class notes.
   C. PCs can help organize your research notes for class projects.
II. Computers can be useful in your personal life.
   A. PCs can help you keep better financial records.
   B. PCs can help you plan personal time more effectively.

Wording Your Outline

Each main point and subpoint in your outline should be worded as a simple declarative sentence. As the name suggests, such a sentence makes a simple declaration, like "Computers can be useful in your personal life." It is not weighted down with qualifying, dependent clauses, like *"Even though they are expensive,* computers can be useful in your personal life." If the points in your outline start sprouting such clauses, you should simplify the structure of your speech. You may need to break down complex main points into subpoints or complex subpoints into sub-subpoints. For example, the following does not make a good main point sentence: "Bad eating habits endanger health and lower feelings of self-worth, reducing life span and causing personal anguish." The sentence is too complex, and therefore is not entirely clear. It works better if it is simplified in the following way:

I. Bad eating habits are a threat to our well-being.
   A. Such habits endanger health.
      1. They can result in increased heart disease.
      2. They can shorten the life span.
   B. Such habits can damage self-image.
      1. Obese people sometimes dislike themselves.
      2. They can feel that they have nothing to offer others.

Breaking the complex sentence down into outline form helps you to focus what you are going to say. It simplifies and clarifies both the structure and the logic of your speech.

Try to use **parallel construction** when wording the main points of your speech. If you were developing a speech on the need for reforms in political campaign financing, you might word your main points as follows:

I. We need reform at the national level.

II. We need reform at the state level.

III. We need reform at the local level.

IV. But first, we need to reform ourselves.

You could use these words in the introduction of your speech. The parallel construction would give listeners a guide to the structure of your speech. You could also repeat the parallel pattern as you summarize your speech, further imprinting its message upon the minds of your listeners.

Parallel construction has many advantages. Because each sentence has the same basic structure, any variations stand out sharply. Thus parallel construction emphasizes important points. In this example, the parallel structure helps the speech narrow its focus like a zoom lens as it moves from a national to an individual perspective.

Parallel construction for your main points can also be used in internal summaries: "Having looked at reform at the national, state, and local levels, we come to the most important part of the problem—ourselves." Since it involves repetition, it makes your message easy to remember. It satisfies the principles of good form and closure discussed in Chapter 7. Not all material lends itself easily to parallel construction, but look for opportunities to use it when you can.

Supporting Your Main Points

Your formal outline should show how your supporting material fits into your speech. As we noted in Chapter 6, supporting materials strengthen the points you make in your speech. For example, a subpoint that states "Global warming is causing climate changes" might need a factual example and expert testimony to support the claim: "According to climatologist Allen Myerson, writing in the *New York Times*, the summer of 1998 was the hottest on record." In particular, be sure that each main point receives the type and amount of supporting material it needs in order to be effective. In Chapter 6 we offered guidelines for deciding what supporting materials you should use if your ideas are controversial, abstract, technical, or distant from the lives of your listeners. In Chapter 7 we described how to work supporting materials into your speech. You should go back and review this material as you prepare your outline.

Title

For speeches given outside the classroom, a title may serve to attract listeners to a presentation. A good title arouses curiosity. It makes people want to hear the message. You may wish to mention your title in your introduction and then refer to it throughout the speech as a reminder of your thesis statement.

However, you don't want to begin your speech by simply stating your title. Rather, you should find some way to weave your title into your introduction to help you gain attention.

You should wait until you have outlined your speech before you select a title. Your title should not promise too much or deceive the audience. Titles that promise everything from eternal peace of mind to the end of taxation often disappoint listeners. Overblown titles can damage your ethos. The speech on global warming is titled "Warming Our World and Chilling Our Future." What do you think of this title? Can you come up with a better one?

Changing Your Working Outline to a Formal Outline

Let's look at how you can change your working outline to a formal outline. In the working example provided in Figure 8.2, the fourth main point appears as follows:

Fourth main point:	Personal energy consumption magnifies global warming.
Subpoint A:	Energy consumption is the single largest cause of global warming.
Sub-subpoints:	1. Fossil fuels account for 90 percent of America's energy consumption.
	2. Transportation-related energy use accounts for half of all air pollution.
Subpoint B:	America is on an energy binge.
Sub-subpoints:	1. We are using more fuel in our homes.
	2. We are using more fuel for transportation

To change this into a formal outline, you need to use the proper system of numbering and lettering. You also need to write your ideas as complete sentences. In the formal outline, the fourth main point would take the following form:

IV. Personal energy consumption magnifies global warming. (Myerson)
    A. Energy consumption is the single largest cause of global warming.
        1. Fossil fuel use accounts for 90 percent of America's energy consumption.
        2. Transportation-related energy use accounts for half of all air pollution.
    B. America is on an energy binge.
        1. We are using more fuel in our homes.
        2. We are using more fuel for transportation.

Notice that a source of supporting materials is indicated in parentheses at the end of the statement of the main point. This **source citation** is brief, because it refers to the full listing in "Works Consulted" at the end of the formal outline. Placement of the citation at the end of the statement of the main point means that this source supports all claims in the subpoints and sub-subpoints below it. If the citation were placed at the end of a subpoint or sub-subpoint, it would apply only to that statement.

The sample formal outline in Figure 8.4 includes source citations. Putting them in your outline reminds you of the importance of documenting points as you speak. These citations tell your instructor that you have integrated your research into your speech. They help affirm that you have met the challenge of responsible knowledge.

Source citations such as those in Figure 8.4 should be brief cues to the materials in Works Consulted. The Modern Language Association of America suggests the following procedures for citations in a text:

- List the last name of the author plus the page number when more than one page is cited.
- List the author's last name accompanied by an abbreviated title if there is more than one work by the same author in Works Consulted.
- If the "author" is a group, list the name (e.g., Greenpeace); if the author is not provided, list the first word of the title (Thirteen).

Remember, documenting your sources in your outline does not satisfy the need for oral documentation as you present your speech. For example, you must say, "In its recent in-depth investigation, 'The Future Is Here: Earth at the Summit,' *Newsweek* revealed that one acre of tropical forest disappears every second from logging or burning." Your audience will be listening to your speech, not reading the formal outline. Full oral documentation in your presentation allows you to give credit where credit is due, and to enjoy credit for careful research. Moreover, actually citing expert sources enhances your ethos and helps prevent any suspicion of plagiarism.

Listing Your References

A list of your major sources of information should appear at the end of your formal outline as "**Works Consulted.**" Arrange your sources alphabetically by the last name of the author or person interviewed, or by the title of printed materials if the author is not specified. The following guidelines are based on the format suggested by Joseph Gibaldi in *MLA Handbook for Writers of Research Papers* (New York: Modern Language Association of America, 1995). If questions arise concerning these guidelines, consult this book directly. Should your instructor wish you to follow one of the other available formats, such as that developed by the American Psychological Association, he or she will provide additional information.

Books. For a book by one author, list the author's name (last name first), followed by the title, city of publication, publisher, and date:

> **Damasio, Antonio. *Descartes' Error.* New York: Putnam, 1994.**

If the book has two or three authors, list the first author's name (last name first), followed by the names of the second and third authors (first names first), the title, city of publication, publisher, and date:

> **Combs, James E., and Dan Nimmo. *The New Propaganda.* White Plains: Longman, 1993.**

FIGURE 8.4
Sample Formal Outline

Stating your specific purpose and thesis statement helps you keep them in mind as you outline your speech.

Labeling the introduction shows that it is an important part of the speech.

Opening with humor helps gain attention.

Dramatic evidence of global warming rivets audience attention.

A light metaphor personalizes the topic, helps establish credibility, and involves the audience.

The use of transitions helps listeners track the progress of the speech.

The first main point defines global warming and gives the audience good reasons to listen to the speech. Placing a source indicator after the first main point ("Union") indicates that the source supplies material for all subpoints and sub-subpoints below it.

Subpoint A is supported with facts and figures.

Subpoint B discusses how pollutants cause a hole in the ozone layer.

Subpoint C points out possible future problems.

The next transition helps the audience change their focus from the explanation to the causes of global warming.

Title: WARMING OUR WORLD AND CHILLING OUR FUTURE
Topic: Global warming
Specific purpose: To inform my audience about the problem of global warming.
Thesis statement: Today I want to share what I've learned about global warming and its causes.

INTRODUCTION

Attention material: When Mark Twain was in London in 1897, a rumor reached the editor of the *New York Journal,* who immediately wired his London correspondent: "HEAR MARK TWAIN DIED, SEND 1000 WORDS." "REPORT OF MY DEATH GREATLY EXAGGERATED."
Global warming is alive and well and thriving in Antarctica. In winter 1995, an iceberg the size of Rhode Island broke off. In October 1998, an iceberg the size of Delaware broke off.
Credibility material: Now, I'm what you might call a "country mouse." I love the outdoors. You can be a "city mouse," and like clean air, good water, and not having to worry about sun. So all of us have a lot at stake here.
Thesis statement: Today I want to share what I've learned about global warming and its causes.
Preview: We need to consider the loss of woodlands, industrial emissions, and increases in energy consumption.

(**Transition:** "Let's begin by understanding more about global warming.")

BODY

I. Global warming is a gradual warming of the earth from human activities (Union).
   A. It is characterized by a high concentration of carbon dioxide in the atmosphere.
      1. Each year five tons of CO_2 are pumped into the atmosphere.
      2. The carbon dioxide traps heat.
      3. 1998 set temperature records.
   B. Carbon pollutants also eat a hole in the ozone layer (NOAA).
      1. In 1998 this hole set a size record.
      2. This allows more ultraviolet radiation to reach Earth.
   C. If this problem is not corrected, we may see disastrous results (National Issues Forums).
      1. There could be dramatic climate changes.
         a. There could be drought in the middle of continents.
         b. There could be many severe storms.
         c. There could be rising sea levels that would destroy coastal areas.
      2. There could be serious health problems.
         a. There could be an increase in skin cancer.
         b. There could be an increase in cataracts.
         c. There could be damaged immune systems.

(continued)

The speaker develops three causes of global warming, arranged in order of increasing importance.

(Transition: Now that you understand what global warming is and why it is important, let's examine its major causes.)

II. The loss of woodlands adds to global warming (Union).
   A. One football-field-sized area of forest is lost every second.
   B. Some loss occurs through cutting trees.
   C. Burning adds more carbon dioxide from smoke.

This transition announces that the speaker is moving on to another cause.

(Transition: An even greater cause of global warming, . . .)

This third main point is rich in facts and figures, but can be more interesting if examples, vivid language, or presentation aids are used.

III. Industrial emissions accelerate global warming (Union).
   A. These account for more than 20 percent of our air pollution.
   B. Americans are the worst offenders.
      1. We use 26 percent of the world's oil.
      2. We release 26 percent of nitrogen oxides.
      3. We release 22 percent of carbon dioxide.
   C. There is light on the horizon.
      1. The rate of emission is slowing (Dept. of Energy).
      2. Companies are uniting to arrest climate change ("New Initiative").

Again the transition signals a change of focus.

(Transition: "Finally, we come to the biggest cause of global warming—ourselves.")

This final main point is more fully developed than the others. All the subpoints and sub-subpoints contain only factual information. The actual speech will require examples or narratives to bring it to life.

IV. Personal energy consumption magnifies global warming (Union).
   A. Energy consumption is the single largest cause of global warming.
      1. Fossil fuel use accounts for 90 percent of America's energy consumption.
      2. Transportation-related energy accounts for half of all air pollution.
   B. America is on an energy binge (Myerson).
      1. We are using more fuel in our homes.
         a. New homes are much larger.
         b. People have more energy-hungry equipment.
      2. We are using more fuel for transportation.
         a. Commutes are longer.
         b. Vehicle horsepower is increasing.
         c. People are buying gas guzzlers.

CONCLUSION

The phrase "in conclusion," introducing the summary statement, acts as a transition to cue the audience that the end is coming.

Summary statement: In conclusion, if you want to know why we have global warming, listen for the falling trees, watch the industrial smokestacks darkening the sky, and smell the exhaust fumes we are pumping into the air.

The speaker both begins and ends the speech with a striking story, providing a nice sense of closure.

Concluding remarks: Gore story on how global warming can sneak up on us. Addressing the National Academy of Sciences, the vice president said, "If dropped into a pot of boiling water, a frog will quickly jump out. But if the same frog is put into a pot and the water is slowly heated, the frog will stay put until boiled alive. So it is with pollution. . . . If we do not wake up to the slow heating of our environment, we may jump too late." The more we know about global warming, the more likely we are to jump and the less likely we are to be cooked.

(continued)

The references follow the format recommended by the Modern Language Association of America.

WORKS CONSULTED

Energy Information Administration, "U.S. Greenhouse Gas Emissions Growth Slows," *United States Department of Energy,* http://www.eia.doe.gov/neic/press/press111.html. Posted November 3, 1998. Downloaded November 18, 1998.

Lemonick, Michael D. "One Big, Bad Iceberg," *Time,* 20 Mar. 1995: 65.

Myerson, Allen R. "U. S. Splurging on Energy After Falling Off Its Diet," *New York Times Online,* http://www.nytimes.com/library/financial/. Posted October 22, 1998. Downloaded November 20, 1998.

National Issues Forums Institute, *The Environment at Risk: Responding to Growing Dangers.* Dayton: Kettering Foundation, 1989.

National Oceanic and Atmospheric Administration, "Antarctic Ozone Hole Sets New Record," http://www.noaa.gov/public-affairs/pr98/oct98/noaa98-064.html. Posted October 6, 1998. Downloaded November 17, 1998.

National Oceanic and Atmospheric Administration, "New Iceberg Breaks Off Ronne Ice Shelf in Antarctica," http://www.publicaffairs.noaa.gov/stories/sir23.html. Posted October 15, 1998. Downloaded November 17, 1998.

"A New Initiative," *Pew Center on Global Climate Change,* http://www.pewclimate.org/init.html. Undated posting. Downloaded September 30, 1998.

"Thirteen Companies Form Climate Coalition," *MSNBC,* http://www.msnbc.com/news/164240.asp. Posted May 8, 1998. Downloaded September 30, 1998.

Union of Concerned Scientists, "The Causes of Global Warming," http://www.ucsusa.org/warming/gw.causes.html. Undated posting. Downloaded November 18, 1998.

If the book has more than three authors, list the lead author's name (last name first), followed by the abbreviation *et al.,* the title, city of publication, publisher, and date:

> **Belenky, Mary Field, et al. *Women's Ways of Knowing.* New York: Basic Books, 1986.**

If the book has a corporate author, use the name of the corporation in place of the given name of an author:

> **Boston Women's Health Book Collective. *Our Bodies, Ourselve*s. New York: Simon and Schuster, 1973.**

If your material comes from a signed article in a reference book, list the author's name (last name first), the title of the article in quotation marks, the title of the reference book, and the edition date:

> **Tobias, Richard. "Thurber, James." *Encyclopedia Americana.* 1991 ed.**

If your material comes from an unsigned article in a reference book, list the title of the article in quotation marks, the title of the reference book, and the edition number and date:

> **"Twyla Tharp." *Who's Who of American Women.* 17th ed. 1991–92.**

If your material comes from a government document, list the source of the document, the title of the document, the edition (if given), city of publication, publisher, and date:

United States. Cong. House Committee on the Judiciary. *Immigration and Nationality Act with Amendments and Notes on Related Laws.* 7th ed. Washington: GPO, 1980.

Periodicals. The general format is the same for all periodicals. List the author's name (last name first), followed by the title of the article, the name of the periodical, volume number if applicable, date of publication, and page numbers. For example:

Mechling, Elizabeth Walker, and Jay Mechling. "The Atom According to Disney." *Quarterly Journal of Speech* 81 (1995): 436–53.

If the author of the article is not specified, begin with the title of the article. If the magazine is published every month or every two months, give the month or months and year, but omit the volume and issue numbers. For example:

"Ozone Mystery Solved." *National Wildlife* Apr./May 1995: 6.

Materials taken from daily newspapers should include the edition of the paper if applicable, full date of publication, and the section as well as the page numbers. For example:

Perrusquia, Marc. "Farewell to Innocence: School Kids Take Up Arms." *Commercial Appeal* [Memphis] 5 Nov. 1995, final ed.: A:1.

Online Materials and CD-ROMs. Since the use of computer-accessed materials for research is fairly new, the guidelines for citing such sources are still evolving. Both the MLA and the APA have published their current citation guidelines on the World Wide Web. The MLA guidelines may be accessed at http://www.mla.org/main_stl.htm#sources. The APA guidelines may be accessed at http://www.apa.org/journals/webref.html. As a general rule, when citing material from these sources, you should provide the following types of information: author's name (last name first), article title in quotation marks, periodical title, volume and/or date, pages, title of database, publication medium (e.g., CD-ROM, online), name of service, electronic publication date, and date of access. Since these guidelines do change, it would be best to check for updates on the web sites.

If your material comes from a CD-ROM, use the following format:

West, Cornel. "The Dilemma of the Black Intellectual." *Critical Quarterly* 29 (1987): 39–52. *MLA International Bibliography.* CD-ROM. Silver-Platter. Feb. 1995.

If your material comes from an online database, use the following format (note that in this example, the plus sign after the page indicates that the article begins on this page, but is not printed on consecutive pages):

Gray, John. "The Virtues of Toleration." *National Review* 5 Oct. 1992: 28+. *Magazine Database Plus.* Online. CompuServe. Oct. 1995.

If your material comes from a computer network electronic journal, newsletter, or conference, use the following format:

Schreibman, Vigdor. "Closing the 'Values Gap.'" *FINS* 1.5 (8 March 1993): n.pag. Online posting. Internet. 10 April 1995.

Checklist for a Formal Outline

_____ **1** My topic and specific purpose are clearly stated.

_____ **2** My thesis statement is written as a simple, declarative sentence.

_____ **3** My introduction contains material to create attention, establish my credibility, and preview my message.

_____ **4** My main points represent my most important ideas.

_____ **5** My main points are related in kind and importance.

_____ **6** My main points are stated as simple, declarative sentences.

_____ **7** Each main point is supported by facts, statistics, testimony, examples, or narratives.

_____ **8** My subpoints clarify and make specific the main points they follow.

_____ **9** My conclusion contains a summary statement that repeats my message and concluding remarks that reflect on its meaning.

_____ **10** I have provided transitions to make my speech flow smoothly.

_____ **11** I have compiled a list of works used in preparing my speech.

If your material comes from computer network electronic mail, use the following format:

> **Pierson, Michael. "Internet Freedom." 30 April 1995. Online posting: alt.culture. Internet.** *Usenet.* **3 May 1995.**

Miscellaneous References.   You may use other sources of information in your speech, such as radio or television programs, films, interviews, advertisements, lectures, or speeches.

For a radio or television show or film, use the following format:

> **"The Hero's Adventure."** *Moyers: Joseph Campbell and the Power of Myth.* **Prod. Catherine Tatge. PBS. WNET, New York. 23 May 1988.**

For an interview, use the following format:

> **Frentz, C. R. Telephone interview. 25 July 1991.**

For an advertisement, use the following format:

> **Chevrolet. "Send Yourself to Camp." Advertisement.** *National Geographic* **July 1995: 142–143.**

For a speech or lecture, use the following format:

> **Webb, Lynn. "Presidential Address." Southern States Communication Association Convention. Memphis, 28 March 1996.**

After you have completed your formal outline, review it using the Checklist for a Formal Outline.

Developing a Key-Word Outline

Your formal outline is a blueprint of your speech, not the speech itself. *Do not use your formal outline as you present your speech.* If you do, you will be tempted to read it. You will lose eye contact with your listeners and miss feedback from them. Instead, prepare a **key-word outline** that reduces your formal outline to a few essential words that will jog your memory and remind you of the order of your main points.

Your key-word outline should fit on a few sheets of paper or index cards. Number the pages or cards to help keep them in order. If you are preparing your key-word outline by hand, use a dark felt-tip marker and print in letters large enough to read without straining. If you are preparing it on a computer, choose a large font size (14-point or larger). Choose the **BOLD TEXT** command. Your key-word outline will be easier to read if you use capital letters.

Because your key-word outline will be used strictly as a memory jogger, you may want to leave out the introduction, body, and conclusion headings. You should follow the same format for lettering, numbering, and indentation that you used in your formal outline. If you are preparing your outlines by hand, go through a copy of your formal outline and highlight the numbers, letters, and key words. Copy these onto another piece of paper or onto note cards for use as a key-word outline. If you are working on a computer, make a copy of your formal outline. On the copy, select the numbers, letters, and key words, change them to **bold**, delete the rest of the material, and save. With a few final stylistic changes, you will create your key-word outline. Be sure to include your source citations to help you remember them during your presentation. You may also wish to copy brief quotations word for word so that you can present them accurately.

Let's return to the fourth main point of the formal outline for the global warming speech to see how it can be turned into a key-word outline format (see also figure 8.5).

IV. **Personal energy consumption** magnifies global warming **(Myerson)**.

    A. Energy consumption is the **single largest cause** of global warming.

        1. **Fossil fuels** account for **90 percent** of America's energy consumption.

        2. **Transportation**-related energy use accounts for **half** of all air pollution.

    B. America is on an **energy binge.**

        1. We are using more fuel in our **homes.**

        2. We are using more fuel for **transportation.**

In this example we have highlighted the key words for the main point, each subpoint, and each sub-subpoint. These then yield the following key-word outline:

IV. PERSONAL ENERGY CONSUMPTION (MYERSON)

    A. SINGLE LARGEST CAUSE

        1. FOSSIL FUELS = 90 PERCENT

        2. TRANSPORTATION = 1/2 AIR POLLUTION

FIGURE 8.5

Sample Key-Word Outline

The speaker has added prompts for presentation.

This key-word outline follows the same format of indenting used in the formal outline. It makes it easier for the speaker to check at a glance. The outline contains just enough information to keep the speaker focused on the planned sequence of points and subpoints. The single words and short phrases prevent the speaker from being tempted to read the speech.

INTRODUCTION

MARK TWAIN ANECDOTE   (Make eye contact)
GLOBAL WARMING ALIVE AND WELL
COUNTRY MOUSE–CITY MOUSE   (Slower and more expressive)
THREE CAUSES: WOODLAND LOSS, INDUSTRY, ENERGY   (Pause)

BODY

I. GRADUAL WARMING FROM HUMAN ACTIVITIES
  A. HIGH CONCENTRATION OF CARBON DIOXIDE
    1. FIVE TONS PER YEAR
    2. TRAPS HEAT
    3. 1998 RECORD HIGHS
  B. HOLE IN OZONE
    1. 1998 HOLE RECORD SIZE
    2. MORE ULTRAVIOLET RADIATION
  C. FUTURE PROBLEMS
    1. CLIMATE CHANGES
    2. HEALTH PROBLEMS   (Pause and look around room: transition here)

II. CAUSE: LOSS OF WOODLANDS
  A. FOOTBALL FIELD PER SECOND
  B. CUTTING
  C. BURNING   (Pause)

III. CAUSE: INDUSTRIAL EMISSIONS
  A. 20 PERCENT OF AIR POLLUTION
  B. AMERICANS WORST OFFENDERS
  C. LIGHT ON HORIZON   (Pause and be emphatic!)

IV. CAUSE: PERSONAL ENERGY CONSUMPTION
  A. SINGLE LARGEST CAUSE   (Stress these points)
    1. FOSSIL FUELS = 90 PERCENT
  B. ENERGY BINGE
    1. HOMES
    2. TRANSPORTATION   (Longer pause)

CONCLUSION

LISTEN, WATCH, SMELL
GORE STORY ABOUT FROG   (End strong!)

      B. ENERGY BINGE

        1. HOMES

        2. TRANSPORTATION

As you practice your speech, you may be able to reduce your key-word outline even further. *Remember, the more the speech is outlined in your head rather than on paper, the better.* Begin practicing using your formal outline. Go through the speech two or three times, referring to this outline, until you feel comfortable with what you are going to say and how you are going to say it. Then practice from your key-word outline until your speech flows smoothly. As you practice, you may want to write brief presentation notes, such as "pause" or "slow down," on your key-word outline. Make these notes in a different color so that you don't confuse them with the outline during your presentation. Put your outline aside for a while, then rehearse again, using the key-word outline. If the key words still jog your memory, your preparation has been effective. We provide more suggestions for rehearsing your speech in Chapter 11. Figure 8.5 shows a key-word outline for the speech on global warming.

In Summary

An outline gives you an overview of what you want to say and how you want to say it. It can sharpen the logic and improve the structure of your speech. Your *working outline* is a tentative plan of your speech. It helps you work out the relationships of your ideas, showing the relative importance of your points and how they fit together. As working outlines for a speech evolve, they indicate how and where you will use supporting materials. By developing working outlines, you can judge the effectiveness of your research and determine if you need additional material.

The *formal outline* is the final product of the research and planning phase of your speech. It follows a number of conventions, including coordination and subordination. *Coordination* requires that statements that are alike in importance be placed on the same level in the outline. *Subordination* requires that statements descend in importance and that each level logically include the level below it. As you descend through the outline, points become more specific and concrete.

The main points in a formal outline should be worded as declarative sentences. *Parallel construction* helps the audience remember your message. *Source citations* provide documentation. They show how you have integrated your research into your speech. A formal outline includes a list of *works consulted*.

A *key-word outline* can aid you in your presentation of a speech. It reduces the formal outline to a few essential words that remind you of the content and design of your speech, and sources of supporting materials during your presentation. Notes on the key-word outline can also remind you of presentation strategies.

Terms to Know

working outline	subordination
subpoint	parallel construction
sub-subpoints	source citation
formal outline	works consulted
coordination	key-word outline

Notes

1. Robert DiYanni and Pat C. Hoy, II, *The Scribner Handbook for Writers* (Needham Heights, Mass.: Allyn & Bacon, 1995) p. 14.
2. Douglas Hunt, *The Riverside Guide to Writing,* 2nd ed. (Boston: Houghton Mifflin, 1995) pp. 503–504.
3. Hunt, p. 503.
4. Robert T. Oliver, Harold P. Zelko, and Paul D. Holtzman, *Communicative Speaking and Listening* (New York: Holt, Reinhart & Winston, 1968) p. 125.
5. This procedure is consistent with the advice offered by DiYanni and Hoy that the "outline is used primarily to organize the difficult middle portion of an essay" (p. 14).

Annotated Sample Speech

Warming Our World and Chilling Our Future

When Mark Twain was in London in 1897, a rumor reached the editor of the *New York Journal,* who immediately wired his London correspondent: "HEAR MARK TWAIN DIED, SEND 1000 WORDS." The correspondent showed the telegram to Twain, who wired back this message: "REPORT OF MY DEATH GREATLY EXAGGERATED." This response applies to my speech topic today. Despite the efforts of some to write its obituary, and to erase it from the public agenda, global warming is a growing, not a declining problem. The reports of its death have been greatly exaggerated.

Almost thirty years ago, environmentalists urged scientists to look to Antarctica for signs of what they called "global warming"—the gradual warming of the earth because of human activity. During the winter of 1995, *Time* magazine reported that a gigantic iceberg—23 miles wide and 48 miles long, almost as large as the state of Rhode Island—broke off the Larsen Ice Shelf in the Antarctic Peninsula. In October of 1998, according to a National Oceanic and Atmospheric Administration report, another iceberg—this one the size of Delaware—broke off of the Ronne Ice Shelf in Antarctica. These reports simply cannot be ignored. They are ominous signs for our future.

Now, I'm what you might call a "country mouse." I love the outdoors—hiking, camping, and fishing. Therefore, I have a great deal of concern for the environment. But you can be a "city mouse," and still like to breathe clean air and drink good water and not have to worry about the effects of the sun on your skin. So we all have a lot at stake here. Today I want to share what I've learned about global warming and its causes. There are three factors that contribute to global warming: first, the loss of woodlands; second, industrial emissions; and finally—and most important—our own energy consumption.

Let's begin by understanding more about global warming. According to the Union of Concerned Scientists, global warming is characterized by a high concentration of carbon dioxide in the atmosphere. Each year five tons of carbon are pumped into the atmosphere for each man, woman, and child in the United States. You heard me right: <u>that's five tons for each and every one of us!</u> These "greenhouse" gases, of which carbon dioxide is the major component, trap solar heat like a car parked in the sun with the windows closed. The more carbon dioxide there is in the atmosphere, the more heat is trapped and the higher the temperatures. The first nine months of 1998 had record high temperatures. In fact, <u>the ten warmest years in this century have all occurred since 1980!</u> This is carrying "toasty" a bit too far.

A closely related problem is the hole in the ozone layer. According to Anne Douglas, deputy project director at NASA, carbon pollutants are also punching a hole in the ozone layer. This ozone hole reduces the earth's ability to protect us from ultraviolet radiation. During the fall of 1998, the size of the hole in the ozone layer in the Antarctic hit a record high. If this problem is not corrected, mother earth won't seem quite so motherly.

For instance: There could be dramatic climate changes causing widespread drought in the middle of continents. There could be dangerous and costly increases in the frequency and severity of storms—like the hurricanes that raked the Caribbean during the fall of 1998. If present conditions continue, the glaciers in Glacier National Park will be gone in 30 years. There could be floods from rising sea levels that might destroy coastal cities and small islands. If even a tenth of Antarctica's ice melts, sea levels would rise 12 to 30 feet. Think twice before you invest in real estate at the seashore.

Beyond the spectacular effects on the environment, there could be serious health problems as well. These are problems for you, but even more for your children, and more still for your grandchildren. Skin cancers could increase as much as 26 percent if ozone levels drop by 10 percent. There could be a similar dramatic increase in the number of cataracts. Even our immune systems could be damaged, creating a problem that could dwarf even the AIDS epidemic. If we don't change our trajectory, if we don't do something about these causes of global warming, then all these health problems could result from the increased exposure to ultraviolet radiation.

So what are the causes? Let's examine three of the major problems. The first one I want to talk about is the loss of woodlands that convert carbon dioxide into oxygen. Without trees to make this conversion, the carbon escapes into the ozone layer. When we clear out forests, we are putting the heat on Mother Nature to make more room for human activities. One football-field-sized area of forest is lost every second from cutting or burning. And the burning of forests increases the carbon dioxide in the atmosphere because of the smoke from the fires. Forest loss occurs in the rain forests in Central and South America where teak and mahogany are logged for furniture and houses. It also occurs in the national forests in the United States, where timber companies cut down trees for use in construction. Much of this American wood is shipped overseas. Forest loss also comes when land is cleared for development.

An even greater cause of global warming is industrial emissions. The burning of wood, coal, and oil releases large amounts of carbon dioxide into the atmosphere. Industrial refrigeration and air conditioning units add their foul contribution. Nitrogen oxides are spewed out of vehicle exhausts and smokestacks. These industrial contaminants account for more than 20 percent of air pollution. And according to a recent report of the Union of Concerned Scientists, we Americans are the worst offenders. We have only 5 percent of the world's population, but we use 26 percent of the world's oil, release 26 percent of the world's nitrogen oxides, and produce 22 percent of the world's carbon dioxide emissions. It's time we did something about it!

Although this picture is dark, there is some light on the horizon. On the world front, the United Nations Intergovernmental Panel on Climate Change is addressing this problem. In the United States, the U.S. Department of Energy reports that the rate of increases in emission of greenhouse gases is slowing. Also in the United States, under the auspices of the Pew Center on Global Climate Change, thirteen major companies have banded together to convince the business community that businesses can work to arrest climate change without damaging the economy. These changes may move us in the right direction in terms of industrial emissions.

Finally, I want to address the most important cause of global warming: personal energy consumption. It's as though each of us was a smokestack, fouling the air. We consume oxygen and emit carbon dioxide into the atmosphere. The more of us there are, especially in industrialized countries, the more energy we consume.

This direct appeal to listeners' concern for themselves and their offspring would be more effective if it used an example or narrative and cited the sources of the information.

The use of stylistic touches is important here: The phrase "putting the heat on Mother Nature" is apt, and the comparison to a "football field" helps bring the magnitude of the problem into focus. Active verbs like "spew" create ugly mental images. On the other hand, oral documentation is conspicuously lacking in this section. In a longer speech presented before an American audience, the speaker should say more about the logging problem in the United States, even though the problem is clearly global in scope.

The struggle to make this technical subject understandable makes this speech interesting to analyze for its use of style. Note the dramatic image that compares people to smokestacks.

According to the U.S. Department of Energy, 90 percent of America's energy consumption comes from fossil fuels. Fossil fuels, such as gas and oil, and electricity generated from fossil fuels, heat and cool our homes and provide our transportation. In a lengthy business section feature, the *New York Times* on October 22, 1998, reported that the United States is on an energy binge. Since the early 1970s, the size of the average new home has grown from 1600 square feet to 2100 square feet. And even modest homes are stuffed with energy-hungry equipment such as home computers, dishwashers, and central air conditioning. This means more personal energy use.

Not only are we using more energy in our homes, but we are using more for transportation. Transportation-related energy use accounts for approximately half of all air pollution in our country. The average daily commute to work has risen by a third, and the average horsepower of cars is also increasing. Speed limits are going up. More and more people are driving trucks and sport utility vehicles. And all of this means more gas, and more gas means more air pollution. The great American love affair with the car continues, even though this is a "fatal attraction." Environmental damage from air pollution costs us $60 to $100 billion a year. In short, we have to pay through the nose for the problems we create by driving too much.

In conclusion, if you want to know why we have global warming, listen for the falling trees, watch the industrial smokestacks darkening the sky, and smell the exhaust fumes we are pumping into the air. Global warming is a monster we are creating. And if we don't stop, we and our children face more and more drastic climate changes and serious health problems.

Vice President Al Gore used the following story to illustrate how global warming can sneak up on us. In an address to the National Academy of Sciences, he said, "If dropped into a pot of boiling water, a frog will quickly jump out. But if the same frog is put into a pot and the water is slowly heated, the frog will stay put until boiled alive. So it is with pollution. . . . If we do not wake up to the slow heating of our environment, we may jump too late." The more we know about this problem, and the better we understand it, the more likely we are to jump and the less likely we are to be boiled alive.

WORKS CONSULTED

Energy Information Administration, "U.S. Greenhouse Gas Emissions Growth Slows," *United States Department of Energy*, http://www.eia.doe.gov/neic/press/press111.html, Posted November 3, 1998. Downloaded November 18, 1998.

Lemonick, Michael D. "One Big, Bad Iceberg," *Time*, 20 Mar. 1995: 65.

Myerson, Allen R. "U.S. Splurging on Energy After Falling Off Its Diet," *New York Times Online*, http://www.nytimes.com/library/financial/. Posted October 22, 1998. Downloaded November 20, 1998.

National Issues Forums Institute, *The Environment at Risk: Responding to Growing Dangers*. Dayton: Kettering Foundation, 1989.

National Oceanic and Atmospheric Administration, "Antarctic Ozone Hole Sets New Record," http://www.noaa.gov/public-affairs/pr98/oct98/noaa98-064.html. Posted October 6, 1998. Downloaded November 17, 1998.

National Oceanic and Atmospheric Administration, "New Iceberg Breaks Off Ronne Ice Shelf in Antarctica," http://www.publicaffairs.noaa.gov/stories/ sir23.html. Posted October 15, 1998. Downloaded November 17, 1998.

"A New Initiative," *Pew Center on Global Climate Change*, http://www. pewclimate.org/init.html. Undated posting. Downloaded September 30, 1998.

"Thirteen Companies Form Climate Coalition," MSNBC, http://www.msnbc.com/ news/164240.asp. Posted May 8, 1998. Downloaded September 30, 1998.

Union of Concerned Scientists, "The Causes of Global Warming," http://www. ucsusa.org/warming/gw.causes.html. Undated posting. Downloaded November 18, 1998.

PART THREE

Developing Presentation Skills

9

Presentation Aids

10

Using Language Effectively

11

Presenting Your Speech

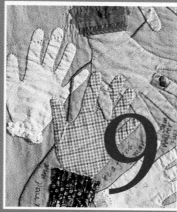

9 Presentation Aids

Seeing . . . , most of all the senses, makes us know and brings to light many differences between things.

—Aristotle

During your summer vacations, you run a small landscaping business. Most of your work has come from neighbors who want you to mow their grass and carry off trash. To attract new business, you posted notices on a community bulletin board. You have just gotten a call from a small company asking you to present a landscaping plan for its property next week. This may be your chance to make enough money to pay your tuition and buy books next fall. You will be competing against other, better established landscaping companies.

If you want to have a shot at that contract, you will need some well-designed presentation aids as you introduce your plan. You could construct a model that shows the building and the landscaping. If that isn't feasible, you could draw sketches that show your landscaping plan. You could have these made into slides or transparencies. If the proper equipment is available, you could make a computer-assisted presentation. You can choose any of these forms, but without presentation aids you won't stand a chance against the competition.

USING PRESENTATION AIDS is not new even to beginning speakers. The first "public speeches" you ever gave probably involved "show and tell." You may have brought an object that you were going to talk about—a new toy, something you made, the family pet. The object helped you explain or describe your subject. The presentation aids discussed in this chapter go far beyond "show and tell" in sophistication, but they still serve many of the same purposes.

In our world of advanced technology, the types and uses of presentation aids are multiplying rapidly. A recent article in *Sales and Marketing Management* suggests that we are at the "beginning of a complete transformation in the way we communicate information on one-to-one and one-to-many basis."[1] In this chapter we describe the kinds of presentation aids that can be used in speeches, identify the ways in which they can be presented, offer suggestions for preparing them, and present guidelines for their use.

Uses and Advantages of Presentation Aids

Presentation aids give your audience sensory contact with your message. They are helpful because words simply *represent* objects and ideas. Words must be translated into mental images, a process that can be difficult and confusing. It requires both words *and* presentation aids to explain some topics. Presentation aids can help speeches in the following ways:

1. *Presentation aids enhance understanding.* Presentation aids often are better than words at conveying meaning. It is easier to give directions when you have a map in front of you.

2. *Presentation aids establish authenticity.* When you show listeners what you are talking about, you demonstrate that it actually exists. This is useful in both informative and persuasive speeches because presentation aids enhance both learning and attitude change.[2]

3. *Presentation aids add variety.* The use of presentation aids in a speech provides variety. This helps sustain audience interest and attention.

4. *Presentation aids can improve your delivery.* Presentation aids often move you out from behind the lectern, making you more visible and encouraging gesture. Such movement can energize a speech. Moreover, purposeful movement such as pointing out the features of a model directs your attention away from your nervousness.

5. *Presentation aids give a speech impact.* Presentation aids are easy to remember because they are concrete. A photograph of a hungry child sticks in the mind and makes people more likely to contribute to a charity.

6. *An attractive presentation aid enhances your credibility.* It tells the audience that you put forth extra effort. Speakers who use presentation aids are judged more professional, better prepared, clearer, more credible, more interesting, and more persuasive than speakers who do not use aids.[3]

Presentation aids are almost mandatory in organizational settings.[4] They are used in public relations presentations, budget meetings, training and development, and employee orientation programs.[5] They can be seen in Congress and in courtrooms.[6] Even when meetings are called on short notice, presentation aids such as handouts or transparencies are frequently used.[7] In business and professional settings, audiences *expect* presentation aids. If you don't have them, you may disappoint listeners.

Kinds of Presentation Aids

The number and kinds of presentation aids are limited only by your imagination. We examine some of the more frequently used types and the situations in which they are most helpful.

People

As a speaker, you are a presentation aid.[8] Your body, grooming, actions, gestures, voice, facial expressions, and demeanor always provide an added dimension to your speech. Use these factors to help convey your message.

What you wear can function as a presentation aid. If you will be talking about camping and wilderness adventures, blue jeans and a flannel shirt might be appropriate attire. What you wear, however, should not be more interesting than what you say. Here, as in all other cases, presentation aids should enhance, not overshadow, your verbal message. We discuss personal appearance in more detail in Chapter 11.

You also can use other people as presentation aids. Neomal Abyskera used two of his classmates to illustrate the lineup positions in the game of rugger as played in his native Sri Lanka. At the appropriate moment, Neomal said, "Peter and Jeffrey will show you how the opposing team members line up." While his classmates demonstrated the arm-locked shoulder grip position, Neomal explained when and why the position was assumed. This demonstration was more understandable than if he had tried to describe the position verbally or drawn it on the chalkboard with stick figures.

If you plan to have other people act as a presentation aid, be sure that they are willing to help you. Rehearse your presentation with them until it goes smoothly. When you give your speech, have them sit in the front row so that they can come forward and then sit down again as quickly as possible when their part is completed.

Objects and Models

Nothing is better than using exactly what you are talking about. However, objects that are extremely large, very small, or quite valuable may not lend themselves to use as presentation aids. In such cases, models may be a better option.

Objects. If you are speaking about something that can be carried easily and that listeners anywhere in the room can see without straining, you may use the object itself as a presentation aid. The object should also be small enough to be kept out of sight until it is time to use it. If you display the object throughout your speech, your listeners may focus on it rather than on your message. We once had a student bring six objects to illustrate a speech on Montessori preschool education. Before she spoke, she lined these objects up in front of the lectern. They were so distracting that a student in the front row actually picked up one of the objects to examine it. Her presentation would have been more effective had she brought the objects out one at a time.

Inanimate objects make better presentation aids than living things. One of our students brought a very young puppy for a speech on caring for animals. As she began, she spread some newspapers on the speaker's table, and placed the puppy on them. You have probably already guessed what happened. The first thing the puppy did was wet the papers (including her note cards). The first thing the audience did was giggle. From there it was all downhill. The puppy squirmed and tried to jump on the speaker while yipping and barking throughout the speech. The speaker was totally upstaged by her presentation aid.

Another problem arises when presentation aids are used to shock the audience into attention. This is especially true if the objects are dangerous, illegal, or possibly offensive, such as guns, drugs, or pornography. One of our students once brandished a realistic "toy" weapon during a speech on gun control. The effect was both dramatic and frightening. Several audience members became too upset to listen effectively to his message. Another student was more successful at shocking the audience into attention with a presentation aid. At the beginning of a speech on regulating the sale of tobacco products to minors, Allison McIntyre held up a gallon jar of cigarette butts that she had collected on the Vanderbilt campus. A Weight Watchers lecturer once shocked the audience by displaying fat cuttings she had gotten from a butcher. She told members who were disappointed with a five-pound weight loss that "This is what that five pounds of fat you lost looks like!" Be careful when using dramatic presentation aids. If you have questions about the appropriateness of an object, check with your instructor.

Objects are frequently used in speeches of demonstration. Just before Halloween, a student gave a speech on jack-o'-lanterns. He demonstrated how to outline the face on a pumpkin and how to make a beveled cut around the stem so that the top wouldn't fall in. As he was showing listeners how to do these things, he also told the story of the origins of jack-o'-lanterns. His presentation aid and his words worked together. The demonstration enlivened his speech, and the stories gave the demonstration depth and meaning. As he came to his conclusion, he reached under the lectern and produced a lighted jack-o'-lantern. The effect was memorable.

Models. When an object is too large to carry; too small to be easily seen; very rare, expensive, or fragile; or simply unavailable, a scale-sized replica of the object can serve as a presentation aid. One advantage of a model is that you can provide a cross section or cutaway of the object to show its interior.

When using a model as a presentation aid, be sure that it is constructed to scale and maintains the proper proportions between parts. The model should also be large enough for all listeners to see from their seats. Any presentation aid that the audience must strain to see will be more of a distraction than a help.

Graphics

Graphics include sketches, maps, graphs, charts, and textual materials. Graphics used in speeches may differ from graphics designed for the print media. Because graphics will be displayed for only a short time as you present a speech, they must be immediately understandable.[9] They must be simpler than graphics designed for print, which readers can study at their leisure. Each graphic should focus on one idea. Because presentation aids will be viewed from a distance, the colors should be intense and should contrast sharply with the background and with each other. The audience should be able to read any print without straining. We will cover such considerations more fully in our section on "Preparing Presentation Aids" later in this chapter.

Sketches. Sketches are simplified representations of what you are talking about. If you don't draw well, check out children's coloring books for line drawings of objects that you can trace. Make the sketch first on paper, then enlarge it or transfer it onto a transparency with a copier. Mark Peterson used a sketch on an overhead transparency to illustrate a speech on buying a bicycle. As he talked about making bar-to-pedal and seat-to-handlebar measurements, he said, "Let me show you how to take some basic measurements." When he finished his demonstration, he turned off the projector so that it would not be a distraction during the rest of his speech.

FIGURE 9.1

Map of Yellowstone Park

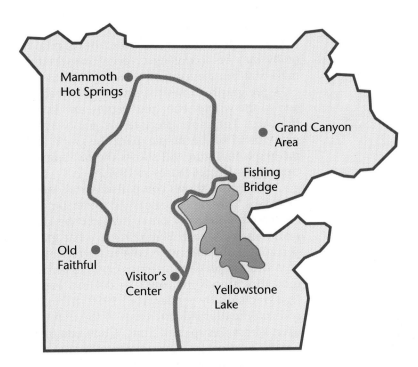

Maps. Commercially prepared maps contain too much irrelevant detail to serve as presentation aids. The best maps are those that you make specifically for your speech so that they are simple, relevant to your purpose, and uncluttered. Maps are particularly useful for speeches based on spatial relationships.

The map in Figure 9.1 was used to indicate the distances and routes between major attractions at Yellowstone National Park. Seeing a map helps the audience put locations and distances into perspective. Stephen Huff used a map to help his listeners see where a series of earthquakes occurred along the New Madrid Fault and to understand how a recurrence of such earthquakes might endanger them (see his speech and presentation aids in Appendix B).

How well a map works as a presentation aid depends on how well you can integrate it into your presentation. Elizabeth Walling used a map of the wilderness canoe area in northern Minnesota to familiarize her Memphis audience with that area. She made a double-sided poster that she was able to keep hidden behind the speaker's table until she was ready for it. On one side she highlighted the wilderness canoe area on an outline map of northern Minnesota, pointing out various places of interest. To illustrate how large the area is, Elizabeth said, "Let me put this in a more familiar context for you." She then turned the poster over, revealing an outline map of western Tennessee on which she had superimposed the wilderness area. At a glance we could see that this area would extend from Memphis to past Jackson, some eighty miles away. By using maps this way, she created a striking visual comparison. The same type of effect could be obtained by overlaying transparencies.

Graphs. Mrs. Robert A. Taft once commented, "I always find that statistics are hard to swallow and impossible to digest. The only one I can ever remember is that if all the people who go to sleep in church were laid end to end, they would be a lot more comfortable."[10] Many people share Mrs. Taft's feelings about statistics. As we noted in Chapter 6, masses of numbers presented orally may be confusing or even overwhelming. A well-designed graph can make statistical information easier for listeners to understand.

A **pie graph** shows the size of a subject's parts in relation to one another and to the whole. The "pie" represents the whole, and the "slices" represent the parts. The most effective pie graphs have five or fewer categories.[11] Too many divisions of the pie make the graph cluttered and difficult to read. The pie graph in Figure 9.2 shows the relationships between murderers and victims in the United States in 1992.[12]

A **bar graph** shows comparisons and contrasts between two or more items or groups. Bar graphs are easy to understand because each item can be readily compared with every other item on the graph. Bar graphs also have a dramatic visual impact. Figure 9.3 is a bar graph illustrating differences in the percentage of adults with college degrees by race and ethnicity.

A **line graph** demonstrates changes across time and is especially useful for indicating trends in growth or decline. Figure 9.4 shows the number of college graduates by gender from 1950 through 1997. The upward-sloping lines confirm the dramatic increases in the numbers of both male and female graduates across this span of time. When you plot more than one line on a graph, use different colors. Never try to plot more than three lines on a graph.

A **mountain graph** is a variation of a line graph that uses different colors to fill in the areas. Mountain graphs are especially effective when there are extreme variations in the data. Figure 9.5 (on page 254) is a mountain graph charting the amount of snowfall in an area from 1980 through 1996.

Charts. Charts provide convenient visual summaries of processes and relationships that are not in themselves visible. However, they are difficult to use in speeches because they must often be oversimplified to keep them from being cluttered and distracting. The more frequently used type of chart is a flow chart.

Flow charts detail the steps in a process. The lines and arrows in a flow chart indicate what steps occur simultaneously and what steps occur sequentially. In Chapter 5 we used a flow chart to illustrate the major steps in the

FIGURE 9.2

Sample Pie Graph

Murder/Victim Relationships

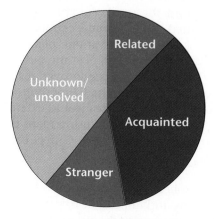

Information Please Almanac, 1995

FIGURE 9.3

Sample Bar Graph

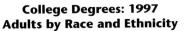

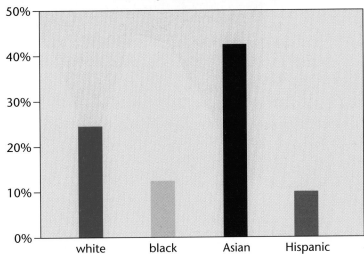

**College Degrees: 1997
Adults by Race and Ethnicity**

1998: U.S. Dept. of Education

preparation of a speech (see Figure 5.1 on page 126). Flow charts are also used to show power and responsibility relationships, such as who reports to whom in an organization.

One major problem that often arises when using charts in oral presentations is that you may be tempted to load them with too much information. If they are too complicated, they may confuse rather than enlighten listeners. One way around this problem is to use **sequence charts**, which are presented in succession. For example, you might choose to illustrate information on the

FIGURE 9.4

Sample Line Graph

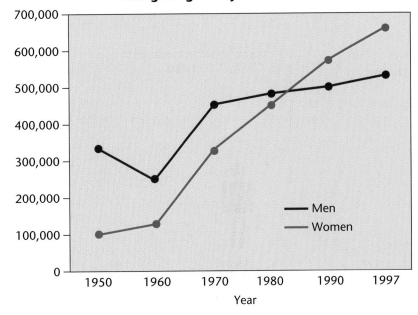

College Degrees by Gender: 1950–1997

1998, U.S. Dept. of Education

FIGURE 9.5
Sample Mountain Chart

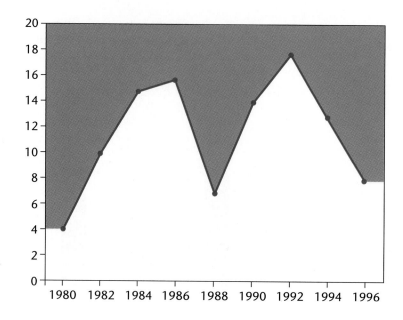

awarding of college degrees by gender in a series of charts. On such charts you might use **pictographs**, or symbolic representations. Figure 9.6 reveals the first and last charts in a series showing the number of degrees by gender across the years. In the first chart, the figure of a man is three times the size of the figure of a woman, representing the 3:1 ratio in earned degrees during 1950. The second chart shows larger pictographs for each gender, indicating the overall increase in the number of college degrees awarded to both men and women in 1997. It also reveals that the number of degrees awarded to women surpassed the number awarded to men. Intermediate charts for decade years could show the more gradual changes in the relative sizes of these figures.

FIGURE 9.6
Sequence Charts

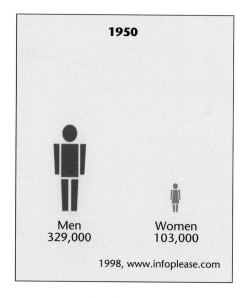

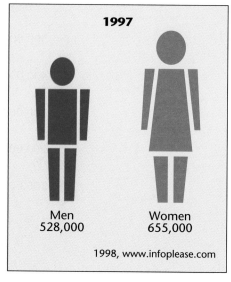

Textual Graphics. **Textual graphics** are lists of phrases, words, or numbers. Unfamiliar material is clearer and easier for listeners to remember when they can both hear and see the message. Presenting the key words in a message visually can help an audience follow complicated ideas more easily. For example, as you describe a process, you might write on a flip chart or chalkboard the number "1" with a key word or phrase, then do the same for "2" and "3" as you discuss those steps. That way you would guide your audience to the main points of your speech. You can present textual graphics using poster board, the chalkboard, transparencies, slides, or handouts.

The most frequently used textual graphics contain **bulleted lists** of information such as that in the computer-generated slide shown in Figure 9.7. When you make a bulleted list, begin with a headline or title, then indent and arrange the material under it. Keep the graphic simple. Use intense colors for contrast. Have no more than six lines of information and no more than six words to a line.[13]

Another frequently used type of textual graphic presents an **acronym** composed of the initial letters of words to implant an idea in your audience's mind and help them remember your message. The acronym can also help you remember the order of ideas as you present your speech. The computer-generated transparency shown in Figure 9.8 (on the following page) used the acronym EMILY in a persuasive speech urging students to begin saving early for retirement. When preparing such a graphic, use the acronym as a title, then list the words under it. Use size and/or color to make the first letters of the words stand out.

Textual graphics may also be used to present numerical information. When you use a textual graphic to present columns of numbers or other information as a poster, transparency, or slide, you should keep it very simple. Have only two or three columns and no more than five rows of data. Textual graphics designed for handouts can contain more information, but not so much that they compete with your words for attention. Figure 9.9 (on the following page) illustrates a complicated textual graphic that would be inappropriate as a poster, transparency, or slide. Figure 9.10 (on page 257) shows the same material adapted for such media.

FIGURE 9.7
Bulleted List

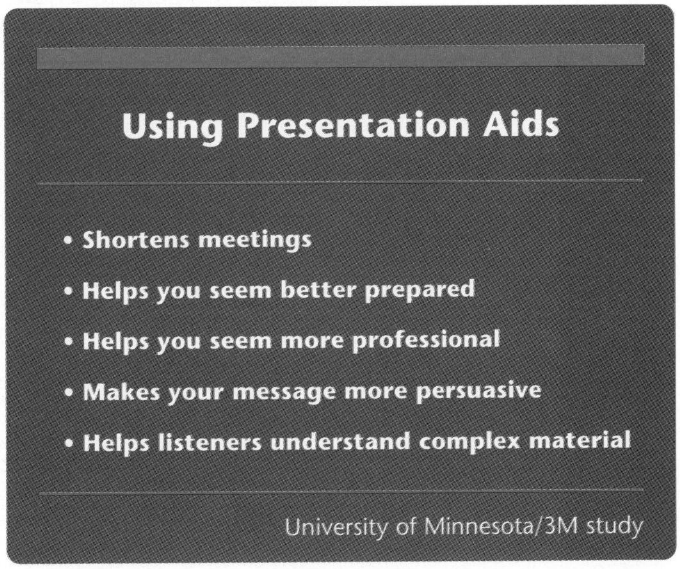

Using Presentation Aids

- Shortens meetings
- Helps you seem better prepared
- Helps you seem more professional
- Makes your message more persuasive
- Helps listeners understand complex material

University of Minnesota/3M study

FIGURE 9.8

Acronym Textual Graphic

EMILY

EARLY
MONEY
IS
LIKE
YEAST

IT MAKES
DOUGH GROW!

Pictures

An old Chinese proverb suggests that a picture is worth a thousand words. While this is true, it is also true that pictures and photographs are difficult to use effectively in speeches. Nonetheless, a good photograph can authenticate

FIGURE 9.9

Overly Complicated Textual Graphic

THE MIRACLE OF COMPOUNDING

Here's what happens to $1,000 in an account earning 8 percent a year, compounded annually.

End of Year	Amount	End of Year	Amount
1	$1,080	11	$2,332
2	$1,166	12	$2,518
3	$1,259	13	$2,720
4	$1,360	14	$2,937
5	$1,469	15	$3,172
6	$1,587	16	$3,426
7	$1,714	17	$3,700
8	$1,851	18	$3,996
9	$1,999	19	$4,316
10	$2,159	20	$4,661

Berger, *Feathering Your Nest,* 1993.

FIGURE 9.10
Simplified Textual Graphic

INVESTMENT GROWTH
$1,000 – 8%

5 years	$1,469
10 years	$2,159
15 years	$3,172
20 years	$4,666

Berger, *Feathering Your Nest*, 1995.

a point in a speech in a way that words alone cannot. It can make a situation seem more vivid and realistic. For instance, the sample speech at the end of Chapter 8 contains the following words, "If present conditions continue, the glaciers in Glacier National Park will be gone in thirty years." Suppose the speaker had expanded this section and used the contrasting photographs in Figure 9.11 (on the following page) to demonstrate the changes that had already taken place. How much do you think seeing these pictures would add to the effectiveness of the words?

On the negative side, photographs and pictures can include irrelevant details. They can also be a disadvantage if speakers rely on them too heavily, forgetting that words are the primary means of communication in a speech. Pictures can also depict incidents that are so disturbing that they are distracting. A student of ours who was a paramedic showed several pictures of child abuse victims that had been taken in a hospital emergency room. Some members of the audience became so upset that they were not able to concentrate on her message.

If you plan to use pictures as presentation aids, you must be sure that they are large enough for everyone to see and you must plan carefully for their use. One of our students tried to illustrate a speech on baseball by showing the audience pictures from a book. He marked the pages that contained pictures he wanted to show with paper clips, so that he could open directly to them. Unfortunately, the order of the pictures in the book did not match the order of the ideas in his speech, so he kept opening to the wrong pages. Also, the pictures in the book were too small to be seen except by people in the front row. This presentation aid made his speech less effective and damaged his ethos. Finally, it is hard to resist the temptation to circulate photographs among the audience as you give your speech. The pictures then compete with your words for attention.

Pictures should be controlled just as you control charts and graphs—revealed only to illustrate a point and then put out of sight. Color copiers can make inexpensive eleven-by-seventeen-inch enlargements from snapshots.

FIGURE 9.11

Photos as Presentation Aids

These two photos illustrate the dramatic reduction in size of the glacier at Glacier National Park between 1910 and 1997.

This is probably the minimum acceptable size for most classroom speeches. Mount pictures on poster board for ease of presentation. Photographs can also be scanned into a computer for use in multimedia presentations.

Museum prints and commercial posters are made to be seen from a distance and are usually large enough to use as presentation aids. In his speech describing an extended camping trip, Michael McDonald used a print of Thomas Moran's painting of the Green River in the American West to convey his feelings about the landscape and to give context to his words. Paintings can invoke a mood, especially when used in combination with eloquent language.

Presentation Media

There are many different types of presentation media. You may choose flip charts, posters, handouts, chalk or marker boards, transparencies, videos, or audiotapes. Most corporate conference rooms, school classrooms, and public meeting places are equipped to handle most of these types of presentation aids. In addition, computerized multimedia presentations that can incorporate slides, videotapes, and sound are increasingly being used in organizational and educational settings.[14]

Flip Charts

A flip chart is a large, unlined tablet. Most flip charts are newsprint pads that measure about two feet wide by three feet high. They are placed on an easel so that the pages can be flipped over the top when you are done with them. Flip charts are convenient, inexpensive, and adaptable to most speech settings. They are helpful when you want to present a series of presentation aids. Business presentations, decision-making groups, and organizational training sessions often use flip charts.

Because flip charts are portable, you can prepare your materials before your speech. Flip charts can also be used spontaneously. This makes them especially useful when subjects come up in a meeting that should be written out so that they can be analyzed and understood.

When preparing presentation aids on a flip chart, keep each page as simple as possible. Because felt-marker ink bleeds through newsprint, you should back each page of prepared material with one or two blank pages stapled at the bottom. Check to be sure that the print from the next page is not visible. Leave the first page of the flip chart blank so that your written materials are hidden from view until you are ready to reveal your message or drawing.

Susan Larson used flip charts effectively to illustrate a speech on nautical navigation. On her first page, she used the acronym POSH (Port Out Starboard Home) as a device for demonstrating how to navigate a boat through river channel markers. Susan kept her writing to a minimum so that the material stood out clearly and emphatically. Had she tried to write out the message "Keep the marker buoys to your left (port) as you leave the marina and to your right (starboard) coming home," the flip-chart page would have looked cluttered.

Susan's second and third flip-chart sheets contained color drawings of Coast Guard navigation markers found in the inland waterways. Her fourth sheet, illustrated in Figure 9.12 (on the following page), was a line drawing of a navigational chart, showing the channel markers. As she spoke, Susan drew the path a boat would take between the markers, adding spontaneity to her presentation. The flip chart was less cumbersome than handling four separate posters.

Poster Board

Not too long ago, large (about two feet by three feet) poster-board visuals were the primary type of presentation aid used in classroom speeches. They were used to display sketches, simplified maps, charts, graphs, or textual graphics. We no longer recommend large poster-board displays as the medium of choice for the following reasons:

1. They are seldom used in presentations outside of a public speaking classroom.

2. They are difficult to transport to the place where you will be speaking. If you roll them up in order to carry them, they may snap back up during your speech, distracting both you and your listeners.

3. They encourage the display of a large amount of material, and thus tend to become cluttered.

4. They are awkward to place on display and difficult to integrate into your speech. It is hard to keep them out of sight before and after you use them.

FIGURE 9.12

Flip Chart Used to Illustrate the Course a Boat Should Follow Returning to Home Port

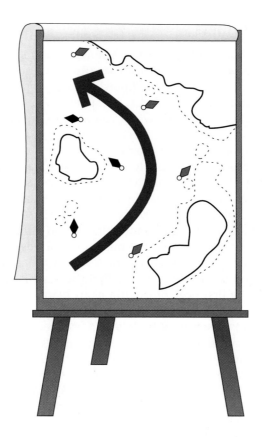

5. They tempt you to talk to your presentation aid rather than to your audience.

6. They often look messy and amateurish, negatively affecting your ethos.

In the typical college classroom or corporate conference room, smaller posters (about fourteen by seventeen inches) work better. Instead of putting a lot of material on one poster, you can use a series of posters as sequence charts, with one idea, point, chart, or graphic on each. You can place them face down on the lectern or table and display them as you refer to them. You can also use the back as a "cheat sheet" that cues you to the next point in your presentation. Just be sure to number the posters on the back so that they don't get out of sequence. Rehearse your speech using the posters so that you integrate them smoothly into your presentation. If you are speaking in a large lecture hall, you should dispense with the smaller posters, and use overhead transparencies, slides, or computerized presentation aids.

Handouts

Handouts are useful when your subject is complex, your message contains a lot of statistical information, or you need to introduce new vocabulary. When the speech is concluded, your listeners have your handout to remind them of your message.

There is one serious drawback to using handouts: They can distract listeners from what you are saying. If you distribute a handout before your speech, it will compete with you for attention. The audience may decide to read the handout instead of listening to you. Therefore, you should distribute handouts before your speech *only* when it is necessary for listeners to refer to them as you speak and you are confident of your ability to command attention. Never distribute handouts during your speech; this is a sure-fire way to divert, confuse, and lose listeners.

Dwight Davidson distributed a handout at the beginning of his speech entitled "Job Trends in the Twenty-first Century." Dwight's audience was able to follow him as he explained the statistical tables in the handout. Without such a visual supplement, his listeners would have been lost. George Stacey distributed a handout listing the steps involved in CPR *after* he ended his presentation. By waiting until he was finished, he avoided distracting listeners during his speech but still helped his audience remember the process. Your decision whether to distribute a handout before or after a speech must be based on the nature of the subject, how confident you are of your ability to control attention, and how you want your handout to function.

Chalk and Marker Boards

A chalkboard or plastic marker board (used with broad-tipped markers) is a presentation medium available in almost every corporate conference room or classroom. These boards work well when you want to emphasize certain words or ideas, or to clear up something the audience doesn't understand by creating a spontaneous presentation aid.

Writing terms or names on the board calls the audience's attention to their importance and helps your listeners remember them. This is especially important if the word or name is spelled differently from the way it is pronounced. For example, if you mentioned the leader of the underground Christianity movement in China, Lin Xiangao, it would be advisable to write the name on the board. As you turn to the board, you might say, "Let me write this name for you." Print the word or words quickly but legibly as you continue speaking, then immediately regain eye contact with your audience.

A chalk or marker board also is a good audience-adaptation tool. Despite your best preparation, there may be moments when you look at your listeners and realize that some of them have not understood what you have just said. You can respond to this feedback by writing a few words on the board or drawing a simple diagram to help reduce their confusion.

Be careful when using chalk or marker boards. When you write on a board, print the words in large letters so that people in the back of the room can read them without straining. Clear the board before you begin and, as a courtesy to later speakers, erase the board when you are finished.

Finally, don't overuse or misuse a chalk or marker board. You should not use these media for anything that will take more than a few seconds to write or draw. When you are writing or drawing, you lose contact with your audience. We have all had teachers who talked more to the chalkboard than to the class. Talk to the audience, not to the chalk or marker board. Stand to the side of your drawing or writing and maintain eye contact with your listeners. Never use chalk or marker boards simply because you do not want to take the time to prepare a polished presentation aid.

Overhead Projections and Slides

Overhead projections and slides allow audiences to see graphics or photographs more easily or to look at an outline of your main points while you are making them. They help listeners remain on track during long or complicated presentations. Business speakers often prefer overhead projections and slides to poster boards or flip charts because of their professional quality and adaptability. Most personal computers now come packaged with graphics software for the preparation and presentation of projections and slides. Projections are most useful for audiences of up to fifty people; for larger audiences, slides presented on large screens are better.[15]

Overhead projections are popular because they are easy to make, inexpensive, and adaptable. Transparency projectors transmit an image from an acetate original. You can draw, print, or type your material on plain paper and convert it to a transparency on a copying machine. Transparencies are also one of the best ways to use computer-generated graphics. You can create transparencies directly through your computer printer. If you have access to a color printer, the transparencies can be quite professional-looking and dramatic. If you have only a black-and-white printer, once you have made your transparency, you can add color with markers.

Overhead projections lend themselves easily to your needs. You don't have to darken the room to use overhead projections, and you can continue to face your audience, maintaining direct contact with them. You can revise a transparency while it is being shown, adding flexibility and spontaneity to your presentation. You can use a pencil as a pointer to direct listeners' attention to features you want to emphasize.

To prepare materials for use as projections, you should follow the general guidelines presented earlier for the use of graphics. You should frame your transparencies to avoid glare from light showing around the outside edges of the projection. Frames can be purchased at most copy shops or made from construction paper or poster board.

With traditional equipment, such as a carousel projector, you will find that slides are more difficult to handle than transparencies. Often the room has to be darkened, and the illuminated screen becomes the center of attention instead of you. When you arrange slides in a carousel, be sure that they are in the proper order and that none of them are upside down. Traditional slides also require specialized equipment to prepare. Today, however, many personal computers are packaged with software that allows you to prepare and present slide presentations. We will discuss this in greater detail as we discuss computer assisted presentations.

The major disadvantage of overhead projections and slides is that often you must speak from where your equipment is located. Unless you have remote-control equipment, you may have to stand behind or in the middle of the audience to run the projector. As a result, you may be talking to someone's back. If you do not have remote-control equipment, your best solution may be to have a classmate change the projections or slides on cue. You will need to practice with this assistant to coordinate the showing of the projections with your words.

If you decide to use overheads or slides, check the equipment ahead of time and become familiar with its operation. You may need a long extension cord in order to position your equipment where you want it. Check the location of electrical outlets in advance, and be sure the cord fits. Practice using the equipment as you rehearse your speech. Be sure you have a spare light bulb for the machine. A burned-out light bulb has ruined many a presentation. Finally, don't use too many slides or transparencies in a short speech. A presentation aid should do just that—*aid* your speech, not compete with or replace it.

Videotapes and Audiotapes

Videotapes and audiotapes can authenticate a speech and add variety to your presentation. Today's audiences, described by Roger Williams, senior writer for *Newsweek Interactive,* as "the first generation that has never watched television without a remote control," may regard such presentation aids as essential to a polished presentation.[16] Videos are especially useful for transporting the audience to distant, dangerous, or otherwise unavailable locations.[17] Although you could verbally describe the scenic wonders of the Grand Canyon, you could reinforce your word-pictures with actual photos of the site or, better still, with living scenes from a videotape. An effective speaker uses video clips for support, but still supplies "the live human touch needed to help move an audience of one, or of hundreds, to the desired conclusion or action."[18]

Using videotapes presents some special problems. Moving images attract more attention than the spoken word, so they can easily upstage you. Moreover, a videotape segment should be edited so that splices blend without annoying static. Editing videotapes takes special skill and equipment. Finally, it can be difficult to work videotapes into a short speech without consuming all of your time. If they are not carefully managed, properly cued, and artistically edited, they can become more of a handicap than an aid.

For certain topics, however, carefully prepared videos can be more effective than any other type of presentation aid. One student at Northwest Mississippi Community College, who was a firefighter by trade, used videotape in an informative speech on fire hazards in the home. By customizing the videotape to fit the precise needs of his speech, he was able to show long shots of a room and then zoom in on the various hazards.[19] He prepared the videotape without sound so that his speech provided the commentary needed to interpret and explain the pictures seen by the audience. Using this technique, he made his subject come to life. When in doubt about the wisdom or practicality of using such aids, consult your instructor.

Audiotapes may also be useful as presentation aids and are not as difficult to handle and integrate into your speech. If you wanted to describe the alarm cries of various animals or the songs of different birds, an audiotape could be essential. Consult your instructor about the availability of equipment if you think your speech would benefit from such a tape.

Computer-Generated Materials and Computer-Assisted Presentations

The world of tomorrow has already pushed the world of today into the past. Your speech classroom may not be equipped now for multimedia presentations, but as you move from college into the business world, you will encounter more and more sophisticated equipment for use in presentations. By the mid 1990s, over 65 percent of all corporations relied on multimedia presentations.[20] Moreover, the present generation is growing up in a multimedia environment. Grade school and middle school students in Louisville and New York City use computers, videos, and digitizers to produce daily news shows.[21] Your audience, and the audience you can expect to address in later business and professional presentations, may be quite attuned to multimedia presentations.

It is one thing to note this trend in the style of presentation aids and quite another to offer useful advice about it. Technology is changing so rapidly that any specific advice we give concerning multimedia presentations will in all likelihood be obsolete by the time you read these words. Because computers are central to such presentations, however, we can offer some helpful general guidelines and directions.

Most personal computers can generate a wide variety of presentation aids. They can be used to develop sketches, maps, graphs, charts, and textual graphics for handouts, slides, and transparencies. Materials produced on computers are usually much neater and more accurate than those done by hand and can be prepared more quickly. Presentation software programs such as PowerPoint, Persuasion, or Harvard Graphics are available for use on most computers.[22] You can also find multimedia shareware on the World Wide Web. The Shareware Shop (http://www.shareware-shop.com/media.htm) provides reviews and links for software available online. These programs are either free or reasonably priced (most of them are under $50). At the time of this writing, the highest-rated shareware programs are IconForge, with a rating of 98 (http://www.davecentral.com/2928.htm), IrFanView, with a rating of 95 (http://stud1.tuwien.ac.at/~9227474/); and SnagIt, with a rating of 95 (http://www.techsmith.com/products/snagit/index.htm). Specialized publications sponsored by computer and software manufacturers, such as *Presentations.Com* (http://www.presentations.com/), are available free or for minimal cost both online and in hard-copy versions.[23] Your campus computer lab may have training programs to help you learn how to access and use these materials.

Computerized slide presentations and flip charts are frequently used as presentation aids in business meetings.

Computer-assisted presentations can bring together text, numbers, pictures, and artwork made into slides, videos, animations, and audio materials. Materials such as graphs and charts that are generated with the computer can be changed at any time, even during a presentation. The programs come with a variety of templates that allow you to concentrate on your message rather than worrying about the design and development of your presentation aids.[24] The templates can be adapted to suit your particular needs. To make a computer-assisted presentation, you need specialized equipment in addition to the computer and software necessary to prepare the aids. You may need a laptop computer, a CD-ROM drive, an audioboard, and a color monitor for use in small-group settings. You will need additional special projection equipment for use with large groups.[25] The standard large-group projection equipment includes LCD (liquid crystal display) projection panels that connect to the output port on a computer and are then sent through an overhead projector to a screen.

As you move into this new technology for developing preparation aids for use in speeches, be careful not to get so caught up with the glitz and glitter that you lose sight of the fact that *it is your message that is most important.*[26] Using sophisticated technology in your presentation does not excuse you from the usual requirements for speaking.[27] In fact, if your presentation aids draw more attention than your ideas, they may be more of a hindrance than a help. Be especially careful not to get caught up with flashy transitions. Remember, it is better to be subtle than sensational. You are giving a speech, not putting on a Disneyland production. Even when you are preparing computer-generated materials or developing computer-assisted presentations, follow the customary guidelines for developing and using presentation aids put forth in this chapter.

Ethical Considerations

Presentation aids can be powerful, but they can also deceive. They can raise challenging ethical questions.[28] For example, the most famous photographer of the Civil War, Matthew Brady, rearranged bodies on the battlefield to enhance the impact of his pictures. Eighty years later, another American war photographer carefully staged the now celebrated photograph of marines planting the flag at Iwo Jima.[29] Fifty years after that, *Time* magazine electronically manipulated a cover photograph of O. J. Simpson to "darken it and achieve a brooding, menacing quality."[30] On the one hand, these famous images may be fabrications: They pretend to be what they are not. On the other hand, they may bring home the reality they represent more forcefully. In other words, the form of the photos is a lie, but the lie may work to reveal a deeper truth. Are these photographs unethical, or are they simply artistic?

Perhaps we can agree that with today's technology, the potential for abuse looms quite large. Video editing easily produces illusions of reality. Consider how moviemakers depicted Forrest Gump shaking hands with Presidents Kennedy, Johnson, and Nixon. Or call to mind the image of the late Fred Astaire dancing with a vacuum cleaner in a recent television commercial. In movies and ads, such distortions can be amusing. When they purportedly convey real-life images, as when television networks and newspapers "stage" crashes and other visuals to make their stories more dramatic without letting us in on the artifice, they can be quite deceptive.[31]

All these practices may relate to the ancient adage, "Seeing is believing." People are taught by tradition to be vulnerable to the "reality" revealed by their eyes. Our position on these ethical issues is the following:

■ As a speaker, whenever you manipulate images so that they reveal your message more forcefully, you should alert your listeners to the illusion.

■ You should be prepared to defend the illusion you create as a "better representation" of some underlying truth.

■ As a listener, you should cultivate a healthy skepticism concerning visual images—for you, seeing should no longer be the same as believing.

■ Whenever important claims are made, and visual images are offered in support of them, you should ask for further confirmation and for additional evidence.

Preparing Presentation Aids

To develop a good presentation aid and use it effectively, you have to go through a process of planning, designing, and preparing it, and practicing its use. As your speech evolves through your working outlines, you should also consider whether a presentation aid might help your message. To create an effective presentation aid, follow basic principles of design and color.

Principles of Design

The best presentation aids are classically simple. When you apply the basic principles of design—visibility, emphasis, and balance—to presentation aids, you have to consider how such aids will function before an audience.

Visibility. Listeners in the back of the room must be able to see your presentation aid without difficulty. Otherwise, the aid will *not* be an aid. When preparing a large poster or flip-chart presentation aid for a speech in a standard classroom, follow these minimum size guidelines: Titles should be about three inches high and other text at least an inch and a half high. On smaller posters, titles should be about two inches high and other text about one inch high.

If you generate slides or transparencies on a computer, use a large font. Computer print is typically sized in terms of points (pt). Such presentation aids should use the following sizes of letters:

	Transparencies	Slides	Handouts
Title	36 pt	24 pt	18 pt
Subtitles	24 pt	18 pt	14 pt
Other text	18 pt	14 pt	12 pt

Use a plain font that is easy to read instead of one that is fancy but harder to read. For example, which of the following do you think would work better?

𝔥𝔬𝔴 𝔈𝔞𝔰𝔶 𝔍𝔰 𝔗𝔥𝔦𝔰 𝔱𝔬 𝔯𝔢𝔞𝔡?

compared with

How Easy Is This to Read?

Emphasis.   Keep presentation aids simple, so that they emphasize only what your speech emphasizes. Each aid should make only one point. Your listeners' eyes should be drawn immediately to what you want to illustrate. The map of Yellowstone Park (Figure 9.1) eliminates all information except what the speaker wishes to stress. Had the speaker added pictures of bears to indicate grizzly habitat and drawings of fish to show trout streams, the presentation aid would have been more distracting than helpful. Avoid irrelevant cuteness! Graphics prepared for handouts may be more detailed than those used for posters, slides, or transparencies, but they should not contain extraneous material. When in doubt, leave the details out. Let your words provide the elaboration.

Balance.   Proper balance, discussed in Chapter 7 as an important requirement for speech structure, is also important for visual materials. Your presentation aid should be balanced so that it is pleasing to the eye. The focal point of the aid can be the actual center of the chart or poster, or it can be deliberately placed off-center for the sake of variety. You should have a margin of about two inches at the top and bottom of a flip chart or large poster board. On computer-generated graphics, you should leave blank space at both the top and the bottom. You should also have equal side margins. For poster boards and flip charts, these margins should be at least one and a half inches wide. On computer-generated graphics, they should be at least an inch wide.

Principles of Color

As many of the illustrations in this chapter show, color adds impact to presentation aids.[32] Clearly, most colored presentation aids can attract and hold attention better than black-and-white aids. Color also is a subtle way to convey or enhance meaning. For example, a speech about crop damage from a drought might use an enlarged outline map showing the least affected areas in green, moderately damaged areas in orange, and severely affected areas in brown. The natural colors would reinforce the message.

Color can also be used to create moods and impressions. For example, blue suggests power, authority, and stability (blue chip, blue ribbon, royal blue). Using blue in your graphics can invest them with these qualities. Red signals excitement and may be used to indicate the presence of crisis (in the red, red ink). Line graphs tracing the rise in cases of AIDS could be portrayed in red to convey a sense of urgency. You should avoid using red when presenting financial data unless you want to focus on debts or losses. In our American culture, green is associated with both money (greenbacks) and environmental concerns (Greenpeace). The use of color in Figure 9.8 resonates with the green of U.S. currency and reinforces the compounded effects of early investments. When selecting colors, you should also be aware of cultural differences. For example, in the United States, white is associated with weddings, baptisms, confirmations, and other happy ritual occasions. In Japan, white has an entirely different connotation. There it is a funeral color, associated with sadness.[33]

Combining colors in particular ways can convey subtle nuances of meaning. An **analogous color scheme** uses colors that are adjacent on the color wheel, such as green, blue-green, and blue. Although this type of color scheme shows the differences among the components represented, it also suggests their connection and compatibility. For example, a pie graph could use analogous colors to represent the students, faculty, and administration of a university. The different colors suggest that these parts are indeed separate, but the analogous color scheme and the inclusion of these parts within a circle imply that they belong together. In this subtle way, the presentation aid itself makes the statement that the components of a university ought to work together.

A **complementary color scheme** uses colors that are opposites on the color wheel, such as red and green. Complementary color schemes suggest tension and opposition among elements in a speech. Because they heighten the sense of drama, they may enliven informative speaking and encourage change in persuasive speaking.

The colors you use for text should always stand out from the background of your presentation aid. With poster board, it is best to use a white or cream-colored board and strong primary colors such as red, blue, and green, for contrast. For slides or projections, a light background can create glare. Therefore, you might want to use a strong primary color for the background and have the text or other graphic elements printed in white. Color contrast is especially important for computer-generated slides and transparencies, because the colors may wash out and appear less distinct when projected than they do when seen on a monitor. Colors like pink, light blue, and pale yellow may not be strong enough for good graphic emphasis in any type of presentation aid.

Making Presentation Aids

To prepare hand-made charts, graphs, or other poster and flip-chart aids, begin with a rough draft that allows you to see how your aid will look when it is finished. If you will be using poster board, prepare your draft on cheaper paper of the same size. With a light pencil, mark off the margins to frame your aid. Divide your planning sheet into four equal sections to help you bal-

speaker's notes

Planning and Preparing Presentation Aids

1   Design a presentation aid that will increase the impact of your speech.
2   Limit the number of presentation aids you will use. Keep the focus on your message.
3   Make a rough draft of your presentation aid to see how well it works.
4   Be sure your presentation aid is simple, balanced in design, and easily visible from the back of the room.
5   Use colors to increase your presentation aid's effectiveness.
6   Prepare a neat presentation aid. A sloppy one will damage your credibility and reduce the effectiveness of your speech.

ance the placement of material. Use a wide-tipped felt-tip marker to sketch in your design and words. Now step back to view your presentation aid from about the same distance as the back row of your audience. Will your most distant listeners be able to read the words without straining? Is everything spelled correctly? Is your eye drawn immediately to the most important elements in the poster? Have you positioned your material so that it will be most effective? Is the poster balanced, or does it look lopsided? Once you are satisfied with your rough draft of the aid, construct the final product using stick-on letters and numbers.

Don't try to crowd too much information into a single presentation aid. Are your margins and borders large enough to provide ample "white space"? Is there anything you can eliminate? If the poster looks cluttered, consider making a series of presentation aids instead of just one.

If you use computer-generated graphics to produce slides, transparencies, or handouts, experiment with several different designs. Don't get so caught up with what the program can do that you try to incorporate everything into a single presentation aid. If you do, you will wind up with something that is so "busy" that it will detract from your message, rather than enhance it. Be consistent in the use of background color and fonts. Simplicity should be your rule of thumb.

Using Presentation Aids

As we discussed each of the specific kinds of presentation aids, we offered suggestions on how to use it in presentations. Here we review these suggestions and extract some basic guidelines:

- Practice using your presentation aid. Be sure to integrate it smoothly into your speech with transitions.
- Go to the room where you will be speaking to decide where you will place your aid both before and during your speech.
- Check out any electronic equipment you will use (slide projector, overhead projector, VCR, etc.) in advance of your presentation. Be certain that you can operate it and that it is working properly.
- Do not display your presentation aid until you are ready to use it. When you have finished with the aid, cover or remove it so that it does not distract your audience.
- Do not stand directly in front of your presentation aid. Stand to the side of it and face the audience as much as possible. Maintain eye contact with listeners. You want them to see both you and your presentation aid.
- When you refer to something on the presentation aid, point to what you are talking about. Don't leave your audience searching for what you are describing.
- Do not distribute materials during your speech. If you have prepared handouts, distribute them before or after you speak.
- Do not use too many presentation aids in one speech. Remember, they should help your verbal message, not replace it.

In Summary

Presentation aids are tools to enhance the effectiveness of speeches. They can increase comprehension, authenticate a point, add variety, increase your credibility, and help your speech have lasting impact.

Kinds of Presentation Aids.   Every speech has at least one presentation aid: the speaker. Your appearance, clothing, and body language must all be in concert with your message and appropriate to the audience and situation. Another form of presentation aid is an object. Unless the object is large enough to be seen, small enough to be portable, and strictly under your control, you may have to use a model or a sketch instead.

Visual representations of information, or *graphics*, provide a number of options for presentation aids. Maps can be useful in speeches based on spatial designs. Draw them specifically for your speech so that they contain only the material you wish to emphasize. Graphs can help make complex numerical data more understandable to an audience. *Pie graphs* illustrate the relationships between parts and a whole. *Bar graphs* highlight comparisons and contrasts. *Line graphs* show changes over time. *Mountain graphs* are variations of line graphs that use different colors to fill in the areas.

Charts are visual representations that give form to abstract relationships. *Flow charts* may be used to outline the steps in a process or to show power and authority relationships within an organization. *Sequence charts* that are presented in succession can be especially effective in speeches to emphasize and illustrate various stages in a process. *Textual graphics* are lists of phrases, words, or numbers. They are often presented as *bulleted lists, acronyms,* or *columnar data.*

Photographs and pictures can add authenticity to a speech if handled correctly. Photographs provide slice-of-life realism but can also include irrelevant detail. Any photograph used in a speech should be enlarged so that everyone in the audience can see it.

Presentation Media.   Speakers may use flip charts, poster boards, handouts, chalk or marker boards, projections, videotapes, and audiotapes as presentation aids. Flip charts provide an easy way to present a sequence of presentation aids. They are adaptable and inexpensive, and can be quite colorful and striking. Posterboard aids should be small and easy to handle. Handouts are effective in explaining complex or unfamiliar material; these should be distributed either before or after a speech. Chalkboards and marker boards should be used sparingly to emphasize points or to clarify questions that may arise during the presentation of a speech.

Overhead projections and slides help audiences see graphics or pictures more clearly. Overhead projections are popular because they are easy to make, inexpensive, and adaptable. Videotapes and audiotapes add variety to a message. They should be used sparingly in presentations because they can easily upstage the speaker.

Most personal computers now have the capacity to generate effective, professional-looking presentation aids such as transparencies, handouts, or slides. With specialized equipment you can make computer-assisted presentations.

Preparing Presentation Aids. As you plan your presentation aids, follow the basic principles of design and color. The presentation aid must be easy for listeners to see. It should emphasize what the speech emphasizes, excluding all extraneous material. It should seem balanced and pleasing to the eye. Plan your layout as you develop the speech itself through the working outlines. Consider using strong colors to add interest and impact.

Using Presentation Aids. Practice using the presentation aid until it seems a natural part of your presentation. Always talk to your audience and not to your presentation aid, and keep the aid out of sight when it is not in use. As you consider the use of presentation aids, be sensitive to their potential ethical impact. Be certain that your presentation aid represents its subject without distortion.

Terms to Know

presentation aids	pictographs
graphics	textual graphics
pie graph	bulleted lists
bar graph	acronym
line graph	computer-assisted presentations
mountain graph	analogous color scheme
flow charts	complementary color scheme
sequence charts	

Notes

1. Robert L. Lindstrom, "The Presentation Power of Multimedia," *Sales and Marketing Management* (September 1994): 51(7), *Magazine Database Plus,* online, CompuServe, November 1995; see also Reid Goldsborough, "Well-Crafted Visual Aids Give Presentations a Zing," *Personal Computing,* 19 February 1998, online, http:www.elibrary.com, downloaded 28 November 1998.
2. Lindstrom; William J. Seiler, "The Effects of Visual Materials on Attitudes, Credibility, and Retention," *Speech Monographs* 38 (1971): 334; and Douglas R. Vogel, Gary W. Dickson, and John A. Lehman, "Persuasion and the Role of Visual Presentation Support: The UM/3M Study," 3M Corporation (1986), pp. 1–20.
3. See studies conducted by Wharton Business School's Applied Research Center and the Management Information Services Department of the University of Arizona, cited by Lindstrom and by Dona A. Meilach, "Even the Odds with Visual Presentations," *Inc.* Annual (1994): 1(6), *Magazine Database Plus,* online, CompuServe, November 1995.
4. "The Low-Down on A-V Use," *Sales and Marketing Management* (August 1991): 25, *Magazine Database Plus,* online, CompuServe, November 1995; and Jan Ozer, "Presentations Come to Life," *Home Office Computing* (December 1994): 74, *Magazine Database Plus,* online, CompuServe, November 1995.
5. David T. Bottoms, "Multimedia Delivers the Message: Interactivity Livens Up Training, Presentations, and the Budget at TRW," *Industry Week,* 4 April 1994, 70(2), *Magazine Database Plus,* online, CompuServe, November 1995; Ken

Jurek, "Portable Computers: Compact Presentations Receive Rave Reviews," *Presentation Products Magazine* (December 1992): 32–38; Thomas R. King, "Visual Aids: Moving into the 21st Century," Southern States Communication Association Convention, New Orleans, April 1995; and James J. McGivney, "Multimedia Educational Systems," *The FBI Law Enforcement Bulletin* (February 1993): 6(4), *Magazine Database Plus,* online, CompuServe, November 1995.

6. Michael Barrier, "How He Helps Jurors Stay Awake by Turning Trials into 'Multimedia Events'," *Nation's Business* (October 1991): 18, *Magazine Database Plus*, online, CompuServe, November 1995.

7. "Low-Down," p. 25.

8. Dona A. Meilach, "Visually Speaking," Special Advertising Section, *Presentation Products Magazine,* June 1993, sec. J-L.

9. Richard Kern, "Making Visual Aids Work for You," *Sales and Marketing Management* (February 1989): 45(4), *Magazine Database Plus*, online, CompuServe, November 1995.

10. Cited in Laurence J. Peter, *Peter's Quotations: Ideas for Our Time* (New York: Bantam, 1979), p. 478.

11. Kern, p. 45(4).

12. Deborah Prothrow-Stith, "Stop Violence Before It Begins," *USA Today,* 24 February 1994, p. 11A.

13. Meilach, "Even the Odds," p. 1(6).

14. "The Art of Business Presentations," *Managing Office Technology* (March 1994): 83, *Magazine Database Plus*, online, CompuServe, November 1995; Robert Burroughs, "New Teaching, New Learning," *Electronic Learning* (January 1990): 52(3), *Magazine Database Plus*, online, CompuServe, November 1995; Isabelle Bruder, "Multimedia: How It Changes the Way We Teach and Learn," *Electronic Learning* (September 1991): 22(5), *Magazine Database Plus*, online, CompuServe, November 1995. Ripley Hatch, "Making the Best Presentations," *Nation's Business* (August 1992): 37(2), *Magazine Database Plus*, online, CompuServe, November 1995; Lindstrom, p. 51(7); and Ozer, p. 74.

15. Meilach, "Visually Speaking," p. B.

16. Todd Oppenheimer, "Exploring the Interactive Future: Newsweek's Voyage Through Cyberspace," *Columbia Journalism Review* (November–December 1993): 34(4), *Magazine Database Plus*, online, CompuServe, November 1995.

17. Lindstrom, p. 51(7).

18. Meilach, "Visually Speaking," p. H.

19. Our thanks for this example go to Professor Mary Katherine McHenry, Northwest Mississippi Community College, Senatobia, Mississippi.

20. Ozer, p. 74.

21. Borroughs, p. 52(3); and Bruder, p. 22(5).

22. Stephen C. Miller, "Presentation Programs Can Give Public Speakers a Leg Up," *New York Times,* online edition, 21 October 1977, http://www.nytimes.com/library/cyber/travel-log/, downloaded 1 December 1988; and Erik Sherman, "Multimedia Presentations Picking Up Speed," *MacWeek*, online, 4 September 1977, http://www.macromedia.com/macromedia/pr/1994, downloaded 3 May 1998. At the time of this writing, we were awaiting a preview copy of Microsoft PowerPoint 2000. See Tad Simons, "Playing Catch-Up with the Software of the Millennium," *Presentations.Com,* http://www.presentations.com/resources/trends/1998/11/22_po_pla.html, undated posting, downloaded 28 November 1998.

23. For information on subscriptions to *Presentation Products Magazine,* write the Circulation Department, *Presentation Products Magazine,* 23410 Civic Center Way, Suite 10, Malibu, CA 91320.

24. Hatch, p. 37.

25. Daniel Grotta and Sally Wiener, "Personal Productivity: When the Presentation Is Everything, Hardware Counts," *HomePC,* 1 May 1997, pp. 139+, online, E-Library, http://www.elibrary.com, downloaded 28 November 1998; and Stephen C. Miller, "Presentation Programs Part II: Hardware Hassles," *New York Times,* online edition, 4 November 1977, http://www.nytimes.com/library/cyber/travel-log/, downloaded 1 December 1998.

26. Tom Bunzel, "Content—Not Technology—Is What Counts," *Computer Pictures* (May–June 1993): 23, *Magazine Database Plus,* online, CompuServe, November 1995.

27. John T. Phillips, Jr. "Professional Presentations," *Records Management Quarterly* (October 1994): 44(3), *Magazine Database Plus,* online, CompuServe, November 1995.

28. Kenneth Brower, "Photography in the Age of Falsification," *Atlantic Monthly,* May 1998, pp. 92–111.

29. Cornelia Brunner, "Teaching Visual Literacy," *Electronic Learning* (November–December 1994): 16(2), *Magazine Database Plus,* online, CompuServe, November 1995.

30. Arthur Goldsmith, "Digitally Altered Photography: The New Image Makers," *Britannica Book of the Year: 1995* (Chicago: Encyclopaedia Britannica, 1995), p. 135.

31. Gloria Borger, "The Story the Pictures Didn't Tell," *U.S. News and World Report,* 22 February 1993, pp. 6–7; and John Leo, "Lapse or TV News Preview?" *The Washington Times*, 3 March 1993, p. G3.

32. John Hanke, "The Psychology of Presentation Visuals," *Presentations.com,* http://www.presentations.com/deliver/audience/1998/95/13_fl_psy_01.html, posted 13 May 1998, downloaded 18 May 1998.

33. Kern, p. 45(4).

10

Using Language Effectively

This chapter will help you

- understand the power of words
- express your thoughts clearly, simply, and correctly
- bring your ideas to life through powerful images
- use symbols to bring listeners together
- choose words that move an audience to action

A legislator was asked how he felt about whiskey. He replied, "If, when you say whiskey, you mean the Devil's brew, the poison scourge, the bloody monster that defiles innocence, dethrones reason, creates misery and poverty—yes, literally takes the bread from the mouths of little children; if you mean the drink that topples Christian man and woman from the pinnacle of righteous, gracious living into the bottomless pit of degradation, despair, shame and helplessness, then certainly I am against it with all my power.

"But if, when you say whiskey, you mean the oil of conversation, the philosophic wine, the ale that is consumed when good fellows get together, that puts a song in their hearts and the warm glow of contentment in their eyes; if you mean Christmas cheer; if you mean the stimulating drink that puts the spring in an old gentleman's step on a frosty morning; if you mean that drink, the sale of which pours into our treasury untold millions of dollars which are used to provide tender care for our crippled children, our blind, our deaf, our dumb, pitiful, aged and infirm, to build highways, hospitals, and schools, then certainly I am in favor of it.

"That is my stand, and I will not compromise."[1]

WE SOMETIMES UNDERESTIMATE the power of words. But as this example shows, language can be both deceptive and richly expressive—at the same time! *When words work ethically and effectively, they bring the reality of a situation home to listeners.* In this chapter we consider how to weave a fabric of words that expresses your message with clarity, power, and beauty so that listeners will understand, remember, and apply what you say. We first describe what effective oral language can do for you. Then we discuss techniques to help you realize this potential. Finally, we identify standards to follow in oral language use.

The Power of the Spoken Word

To understand the power of the spoken word, let us begin with the differences between oral and written language. The first striking difference is that oral language is more spontaneous and less formal than written language. For example, instead of saying, "Eight thousand, three hundred twenty-three cases of measles have been reported in Shelby County," you might say, "More than eight thousand cases of measles have been reported in Shelby County!" It's not really important that listeners remember the exact number of cases. What is important is that they see the magnitude of the problem. Rounding off numbers helps listeners focus on the big picture.

Oral language is also more colorful and intense than written language. Sentence fragments and slang expressions are more acceptable in speeches than in essays. Oral language also is more interactive. It depends on audience involvement for its effectiveness. Consider the following excerpt from a speech:

> **You want to know what we're going to do? I'll tell you what we're *not* going to do. We're *not* going to play along. This is a rule that deserves to be broken. Yes, broken! And we're going to do the breaking.**

This brief example illustrates the spontaneous, informal, intense, fragmentary, and interactive qualities of oral language. The speaker is keenly aware of her audience. Her words reflect the quality of expanded conversation that we discussed in Chapter 1. Moreover, in oral communication, pauses, vocal emphasis, and pitch variations can be used to clarify and reinforce meaning. Such resources are not available in written communication.

In oral communication, time is also important. Jerry Tarver, professor of speech communication at the University of Richmond, emphasizes three significant time differences between spoken and written language.[2] First, he offers "Tarver's Law of Conciseness: *It takes more words per square idea to say something than to write it.*" Because listeners cannot reread a spoken statement, oral language must be simple and speakers must repeat themselves. Examples and illustrations must amplify the speaker's point to ensure that listeners get the message.

Tarver's second time difference concerns the *order in which spoken thoughts develop in a sentence.* His example is excellent:

> **I recently read in a newspaper column a spirited defense of a public figure. The last line of the column was, "For that he should be congratulated, not chastised." Well and good. The reader gobbles up the line in an instant and digests the contrast between congratulations and chastisement. But when we speak the line we feed it to a listener morsel by morsel. And the last two words prove to be rather bland. We need to *hear* "For that he should not be chastised, he should be congratulated." More words; but more important, a different order. . . . In the slower pace of speech, individual words stand out more, and thus *time* accords a special emphasis to the last idea, the climactic idea in the sentence.**
>
> **As a rule, then, the stronger, more impressive idea should be saved for the end. And it will often be the case that the punch comes from a positive rather than a negative thought.[3]**

Tarver's advice to *build up* to your most important point within a sentence repeats a structural principle discussed in Chapter 7—that the main points of a speech often work best when arranged in an order of ascending importance.

Tarver's third effect of time is that "*the beat or flow or rhythm of the syllables is even more important in words written to be heard than in words written to be seen.*" Spoken language often beats on the senses like a drum. The rhythms of oral speech embed the meanings of words in memory. The beat adds emotionality. Rhythm may also be paired with rhyme to make oral language even more memorable. During the O. J. Simpson murder trial, the prosecution asked Simpson to try on a glove that had allegedly been worn by the killer during the crime. It was a high point of the trial, but a low point for the prosecution, when Simpson struggled to put on the glove. Who then can forget how defense attorney Johnny Cochran, in his summary to the jury, impressively intoned: "If it doesn't fit, you must acquit"?

When skillfully used, the spoken word can reach others in ways that the written word cannot. There are four ways in which effective oral language can help you influence the lives of listeners

- By revealing subjects in certain ways
- By arousing intense feelings about subjects
- By bringing your listeners together
- By moving your audience to action[4]

To be an effective and ethical speaker and listener, you must understand how these functions of language can be used or abused.

The Power to Make Listeners See

Speakers and listeners often see subjects in different ways. The artful use of language, however, can close the gap that separates them. Consider, for example, the problem that confronted one of our students, Scott Champlin. For his self-introductory speech, Scott decided to talk about an experience he had had while in the military. His challenge was determining how to share that experience, so that others would understand what it meant to him. One option was to describe the experience matter-of-factly:

While I was parachuting into Panama as part of Operation "Just Cause," I was wounded by a tracer bullet.

Ten Features of Spoken Language

speaker's notes

1   Spoken language is more personal.
2   Spoken language is less formal.
3   Spoken language uses round numbers to focus on the overall meaning.
4   Spoken language is more colorful and intense.
5   Spoken language uses shorter, more simple, even fragmentary sentences.
6   Spoken language is more repetitious.
7   Spoken language uses more examples and narratives.
8   Spoken language emphasizes the rhythm of speech.
9   Spoken language saves important points for the ends of sentences.
10 In framing contrasts, the spoken sentence ends with the positive rather than the negative idea.

The more he thought about that description, the less adequate it seemed. How could he use words to convey to listeners the true sense of that experience? The depiction he developed allowed listeners to share his leap into danger:

> **The darkness of two o'clock in the morning was multiply penetrated by streaks of red marking the paths of tracer rounds as they cut their way through the night. Suddenly, I felt a surge of heat knock me in the right leg with a force that spun me around like a twisted yo-yo at the end of a string.**

Here the use of color contrast—between "darkness" and "streaks of red"— paints a vivid picture. Lively verbs such as "penetrated," "cut," "knock," and "spun" fill the picture with action. A brief comparison—"like a twisted yo-yo at the end of a string"—brings the picture into sharp focus. Through his artful choice of words, Scott found a way to share his meaningful experience.

This power to shape how an audience sees something is especially important when your subject is unfamiliar or unusual. In such cases, the speaker's words become windows that reveal a subject with startling clarity. When listeners don't have a clear perception to compare with the speaker's depiction, they are vulnerable. The Renaissance scholar Francis Bacon suggested over four hundred years ago that such windows can be "enchanted." The perspective they offer may be distorted by the speaker's interests and values. Words can color and alter objects of perception, allowing speakers to disguise or obscure reality. The power to make us see can also become a power that blinds.

The Power to Awaken Feelings

Language also can arouse intense feelings. It can touch our hearts and change our attitudes. This power is ethical when it *supplements* sound reasoning and credible evidence to involve us in the action urged by the speech. It is abused when speakers *substitute* appeals to feelings for evidence or reasoning. To arouse intense feelings in ethical ways, language must overcome the barriers of time, distance, and apathy.

Overcoming Time.   Listeners live in the present. Therefore, it can be difficult to awaken feelings about events that lie in the remote past or distant future. Fortunately, the language of feeling has a time-machine quality. Speakers can use language skills to bring past and future events into the present and make them seem real.

Stories that recapture feelings from the past are often told at company meetings or used in advertisements to counter impressions that a business is too large and impersonal to care about its employees and customers. Such narratives can also establish a sense of corporate heritage and culture. In the following story, the speaker reminds listeners of one of the legends of Federal Express, a pioneer in overnight delivery:

> **You know, we take a lot for granted. It's hard to remember that Federal Express was once just a fly-by-night dream, a crazy idea in which a few people had invested—not just their time and their money, but their lives and futures. I remember one time early on when things weren't going so well. We were really up against it. Couldn't even make the payroll that week. It looked like we were going to crash.**

> Fred [Smith, founder of the company] was in in a deep funk. Never saw him quite like that before or since. "What the hell," he said, and flew off to Las Vegas. The next day he flew back and his face was shining. "We're going to make it," he said. He had won $27,000 at the blackjack table! And we made it. We met the payroll. And then things began to turn around, and Federal Express grew into the giant it is today.[5]

This story enlivens the past by emphasizing the contrast of emotions—the "deep funk" versus the "shining" face. "What the hell" and "We're going to make it" express depression and confidence. Such use of dialogue to express feelings recreates the excitement and brings the scene into the present. In using dialogue, the speaker steps back and lets Fred Smith voice his own feelings. It would have been less effective if the speaker had simply said: "Fred was depressed, but after he got back from Las Vegas he was confident." Offering such a summary would have diluted the emotional strength of the scene.

Language can also make the future seem close at hand. Because language can transport us across the barrier of time, both tradition and a vision of tomorrow can guide us through the present.

Overcoming Distance.   The closer something is to us, the easier it is for us to develop feelings about it. But what if speakers must discuss faraway people and places? Language can telescope such subjects and bring them close. Consider how one student used language to reduce the distance between her urban audience and her rural subject:

> James Johnson has lived in Perry County for eighty-four years. He taught me some important things: why the mist rises on a lake at night, how to make the best wild blackberry jam you've ever put in your mouth, and how to take care of baby rabbits that are abandoned. Today, I want to tell you more about James—and about myself through him.

By focusing on concrete details involving the senses of sight, taste, and touch—the mist, the jam, the rabbits—the speaker conquered distance and aroused feelings about a subject that might otherwise have seemed remote.

Overcoming Apathy.   We live in an age of communication overkill. Modern audiences have become jaded by an endless barrage of mass-mediated information, persuasion, and entertainment. The personal contact of public speaking, even when mediated, allows speakers to reach out and touch listeners with language. Jesse Jackson stirred the audience of the 1988 Democratic National Convention with the following message:

> America's not a blanket woven from one thread, one color, one cloth. When I was a child growing up in Greenville, South Carolina, and grandmother could not afford a blanket, she didn't complain and we did not freeze. Instead, she took pieces of old cloth—patches, wool, silk, gabardine, crockersack on the patches—barely good enough to wipe off your shoes with.
>
> But they didn't stay that way very long. With sturdy hands and a strong cord, she sewed them together into a quilt, a thing of beauty and power and culture.

> Now, Democrats, we must build such a quilt. Farmers, you seek fair prices and you are right, but you cannot stand alone. Your patch is not big enough. Workers, you fight for fair wages. You are right. But your patch, labor, is not big enough. Women, you seek comparable worth and pay equity. You are right. But your patch is not big enough. Women, mothers, who seek Head Start and day care and pre-natal care on the front side of life, rather than jail care and welfare on the back side of life, you're right, but your patch is not big enough.
>
> Students, you seek scholarships. You are right. But your patch is not big enough. Blacks and Hispanics, when we fight for civil rights, we are right, but our patch is not big enough. Gays and lesbians, when you fight against discrimination and [for] a cure for AIDS, you are right, but your patch is not big enough. Conservatives and pro-gressives, when you fight for what you believe, right-wing, left-wing, hawk, dove—you are right, from your point of view, but your point of view is not enough.
>
> But don't despair. Be as wise as my grandmama. Pool the patches and the pieces together, bound by a common thread. When we form a great quilt of unity and common ground we'll have the power to bring about health care and housing and jobs and education and hope to our nation.[6]

Jackson's references to poverty and his grandmother's loving care aroused sympathetic feelings in many viewers. The image of a quilt—suggesting the traditional warmth of home and the ability to create things of lasting value and beauty from humble materials—gave the audience a vision to unite them. When artfully used, language can overcome the barriers of time, distance, and apathy to make us care about a subject.

The Power to Bring Listeners Together

On many issues, individual action is not enough. It may take people acting together to bring about or resist change. The Jesse Jackson example, while it aroused strong feeling, also reminded listeners that they were part of an important larger group. Only if they acted together—as Democrats rather than as individual interest groups—would they have a chance to win the election. The quilt metaphor also invoked this sense of belonging to a larger group.

Just as language can unite people, it can also drive them apart. During a nationally televised debate in the 1996 New Hampshire primary campaign, eight Republican presidential hopefuls attacked and belittled each other. One candidate, Rep. Robert Dornan of California, reminded them that their attacks on each other threatened party unity:

> I wish the spirit of Ronald Reagan would descend on New Hampshire . . . and [remind us of] his eleventh commandment, that no Republi-can should speak ill of another. . . . We have to stop tearing at one another. . . . The target is Clinton [and] the moral crisis in the White House. . . . Gentlemen, we're a family here. Let's unify ourselves and make sure we take the White House on November 5th.[7]

Note that as Dornan pleaded for unity, he invoked a common hero, Ronald Reagan. He used the "family" metaphor to heal the division. And he reminded listeners of a common enemy and a shared goal—President Clinton and their desire to defeat him.

Heroes and enemies, common goals, shared values, and metaphors of inclusion—all can work together to heighten the value of group membership. We discuss these techniques more fully later in this chapter.

The Power to Encourage Action

Even if your listeners share an identity, they still may not be ready to act. What might stand in their way? For one thing, they may not be convinced of the soundness of your proposal. They may not trust you, or they may not think that they can do anything about a problem. Action requires energy, commitment, and risk.

Your words must convince listeners that action is necessary, that your ideas are sound and well motivated, and that success is a realistic hope. Anna Aley, whose speech is printed in Chapter 13, wanted her audience to help improve off-campus housing conditions for students at Kansas State University. In her speech, she painted vivid word-pictures of deplorable and dangerous off-campus housing, supported by both factual materials and personal experience. She also reminded listeners of their group membership— they were all students, responsible for one another's welfare:

> **What can one student do to change the practices of numerous Manhattan landlords? Nothing, if that student is alone. But just think of what we could accomplish if we got all 13,600 off-campus students involved in this issue! Think what we could accomplish if we got even a fraction of those students involved!**

Anna then offered specific proposals that her listeners might support— proposals that did not call for great energy or risk on their part; in short, she made commitment as easy as possible. Finally, she concluded her speech with an appeal to action:

> **Kansas State students have been putting up with substandard living conditions for too long. It's time we finally got together to do something about this problem. Join the Off-Campus Association. Sign my petition. Let's send a message to these slumlords that we're not going to put up with this any more. We don't have to live in slums.**

Anna's words expressed both her indignation and the urgency of the problem. Her references to time—"too long" and "it's time"—called for immediate action. Her final appeals to join the association and sign the petition were expressed in short sentences that packed a lot of punch and encouraged the impulse to action. Her repetition of "slumlords" and "slums" motivated her listeners to transform their indignation into action.

Anna also illustrated another strategy that is important to the language of action. You must be able to depict real-life dramas that reveal what is at stake and challenge listeners to take on certain roles.[8] Such scenarios draw clear lines between right and wrong. In the words of an early union organizing song, the audience may be asked, "Which side are you on?"[9] Be careful, however, not to go overboard with such techniques. Ethical communication requires that you maintain respect for all those involved in any conflict. As both speaker and listener, be wary of melodramas that offer stark contrasts between good and evil. Such depictions usually distort reality.

The power of language is great, ranging from shaping perceptions to inciting action. How can you harness this power in ways that are both ethical and elevating? We have already pointed out some of the ways as we illustrated the power of words. Now we cover these special techniques in more detail.

Using Language Resources

In this section we consider some ways in which you can help listeners share your perceptions and feelings, connect with you and with one another, and take appropriate action.

Resources that Shape Audience Perceptions

You can close the gap between the way you and your listeners see things by making abstract subjects more concrete and complex subjects easier to comprehend.

Abstract Subjects.   Subjects are abstract when we do not have direct access to them through our senses. Abstract subjects include intangible qualities of things, beliefs, and values. People may see subjects like *justice* or *courage* in different ways. We may agree that the object before us is a '59 Mustang convertible—here are its lights, its fenders, its hood ornament. But what are the physical features of *fairness* or *honor*? As we talk about such subjects, we may discover that speakers and listeners assign different meanings to them. In order to share our perceptions, we must fall back on the three *R*'s of language techniques: Relationship, Replacement, and Representation.

One way to handle an abstraction is to show a **relationship** between the subject and some concrete object of comparison. When words such as *like* or *as* are used to connect the abstract and the concrete, or the obscure and the well-known, the comparison is called a **simile**. Remember Scott Champlin's words, "a force that spun me around *like* a twisted yo-yo at the end of a string"? Most of us, we hope will never be hit by a tracer bullet while parachuting, but helped by the simile, we can imagine the scene.

Aristotle once warned that what you select for comparison can either enhance or diminish a subject. An ill-advised simile can make your subject seem trivial or repulsive and make you seem tasteless. Some critics thought President Clinton was ineffective when he suggested that stalling action on health care reform "will make it just like a hangnail or an ingrown toenail. It's just going to get worse."[10] When they work well, however, similes do important work in controversies. Thus one speaker complained that the government's demand that Microsoft add Netscape Navigator to its Windows 98 operating system was "like forcing Coca-Cola to add two cans of Pepsi to each six-pack of Coke."[11] At one point the simile played a major role in Microsoft's case in that controversy.

Martin Luther King, Jr. was famed for his rhetorical style. He made use of many rhetorical techniques such as metaphors and parallel construction in his messages.

Another technique for overcoming abstraction involves the **replacement** of expected words with unexpected words in the form of a **metaphor**. When you use a fresh metaphor, you pull a rabbit out of the language hat. A listener's first reaction is apt to be, "Wait a minute; words are not rabbits, and language is not a hat." But when a metaphor works, the next reaction is, "Ah, I see what she means!" Good metaphors may reveal unexpected similarities in dramatic ways. They substitute concrete words for abstractions and bring a subject into focus.

For these reasons, metaphors are perhaps our most useful and versatile language tool. They help to both inform and persuade, as Jesse Jackson's metaphor of the quilt demonstrated, and they also work well in speeches of celebration. When Martin Luther King, Jr., spoke in Memphis the night before he was assassinated, he talked of the "spiritual journey" that his listeners had traveled. He said that he had climbed the mountain ahead of them—that he had "seen the Promised Land." These metaphors of the journey, the mountain, and the view of the land beyond lifted his listeners and allowed them to share his vision, just as he had earlier invited them to share his "dream" in his famous "I Have a Dream" speech. More than just being a vivid way of communicating, such metaphors reveal the speaker's soul.

Because metaphors can be so powerful, you should select them carefully and use them with restraint. Mixing metaphors, combining images that don't fit well together, can confuse listeners and even create an inappropriate comic effect. The speaker who intoned, "Let us *march forward* into the *seas* of prosperity," got a laugh he didn't want and hadn't intended. Finally, avoid trite similes and metaphors, such as "his idea is as dead as a doornail," "she has the courage of a lion," or "our team is on an emotional roller coaster." Overuse has dimmed these comparisons until people are no longer affected by them. Such clichés can damage your ethos because tired comparisons can suggest a dull mind.

Complex Subjects.   When a subject is complex, you cannot hope to describe it in its entirety. Your words must focus on essential features of the subject, especially those aspects that convey your point of view. One such technique is to focus on part of a subject as a **representation** of it, as in "The *tongue* is mightier than the *sword.*" This seven-word sentence expresses in concrete form the complex idea that the power of speech, represented by the tongue, is greater than the force of arms, represented by the sword. One important representation of our time is the word "movement," often used to characterize campaigns of social change such as the civil and human rights movements or the women's movement. This term focuses on the marching and demonstrating often associated with such campaigns to underscore their activity and strength.

In addition to using representation, speakers sometimes simplify complex issues by offering sharp moral contrasts, such as *good-evil* or *right-wrong.* Be aware, however, that this kind of simplification can invite distortion and create an ethical problem. And when you are a listener, be wary when speakers try to paint the world in black and white.

In summary, the verbal techniques of relationship, replacement, and representation can help you communicate your perceptions of the world.

Resources that Help Arouse Feelings

The *denotative meaning* of a word is its dictionary definition or generally agreed-upon objective usage. For example, the denotative definition of *alcohol* is "a colorless, volatile, flammable liquid, obtained by the fermentation of sugars or starches, which is widely used as a solvent, drug base, explosive, or intoxicating beverage."[12] How different this is from the two connotative definitions in the opening example of this chapter! *Connotative meaning* invests a subject with emotional coloration. Thus, the "intoxicating beverage" is no longer just a chemical substance but either "the poison scourge" or "the oil of conversation." Connotative language intensifies feelings, whereas denotative language encourages detachment.

speaker's notes

How Language Helps Us See: The Three *R*'s and Their Techniques

1 *Relating* abstract subjects to concrete objects to convey an idea and bring the subject into focus ("Her heart was as big as a Montana sky."—*simile*).

2 *Replacing* expected, abstract words with unexpected, concrete words to startle listeners into awareness ("You might think you're bright, but your bulb has burned out."—*metaphor*).

3 *Representing* complex subjects by focusing on selected features or associations that serve the speaker's purpose ("There's blood on her hands."—*representation*).

Many of the techniques of language that help listeners see subjects can also arouse feelings. Simile and metaphor may kindle emotion by the relationships and associations they suggest. Representation can arouse by the focus it gives to a subject. For example, Leslie Eason impressed her Vanderbilt class members with her ability to frame metaphors that stirred deep feeling as well as reflection. She began her speech on the disease of racism by reciting lines of a poem she had written: "What if I go to Heaven, and then to me they tell, White Angels enter here, Black Angels go to hell." In another speech, she used a traditional metaphor to describe the plight of ambitious women: "Glass ceilings still exist." Women, she said, can rise just so far in the workplace before they bump into invisible barriers. But soon she gave the metaphor a novel twist. Other women, she said, never even get a chance to rise. They are stuck in low-pay, low-ability jobs, the victims of "sticky floors."

Such techniques are well suited to stimulate emotions. They produce what Longinus called the **image**, the natural language of the passions. Writing some two thousand years ago, this Roman rhetorician noted that images intensify feelings when "you think you see what you describe, and you place it before the eyes of your hearers."[13] During World War II, when London was bombed every night, the British people needed reassurance that they would prevail. Sir Winston Churchill built images of hope in his radio speeches. One example is the following, developed around a metaphor of fire:

> **What he [Hitler] has done is to kindle a fire in British hearts . . . which will glow long after all traces of the conflagration he has caused in London have been removed. He has lighted a fire which will burn with a steady and consuming flame until the last vestiges of Nazi tyranny have been burnt out of Europe.[14]**

Another useful technique to arouse feeling is **onomatopoeia**, the tendency of the sounds of certain words, such as *buzz* and *hiss,* to imitate the objects of their meaning. Suppose you were trying to describe the scene of refugees fleeing from war and starvation. How could you bring that scene into focus for listeners who are far away? One way would be to describe an old man and his granddaughter as they *trudge* down a road to nowhere. The word "trudge" is an example of onomatopoeia. Its very sound suggests the weary, discouraged walk of the survivors. Onomatopoeia can bring us into a scene by allowing us to hear its noises, smell its odors, taste its flavors, or touch its surfaces. As it overcomes distance, it also arouses feeling.

Hyperbole, or purposeful exaggeration, can also arouse feeling. Speakers often use hyperbole to encourage action or force listeners to confront problems. Note the use of hyperbole in Martin Luther King, Jr.'s final speech:

> **Men for years now have been talking about war and peace, but now no longer can they just talk about it. It is no longer the choice between violence and nonviolence in this world, it's nonviolence or nonexistence. . . . And in the human rights revolution, if something isn't done and done in a hurry to bring the colored peoples of the world out of their long years of poverty, their long years of hurt and neglect, the whole world is doomed.[15]**

Are the choices really that simple, the consequences that inescapable? Perhaps not, but King wanted his listeners to understand what would happen if they neglected their moral responsibility. His use of hyperbole was meant to make his audience think and feel simultaneously. As a speaker, you should be careful when using hyperbole. The line between exaggerating and lying is all too easy to cross. Save hyperbole for those moments when it is vital for listeners to get your message.

A final technique that helps awaken feelings, especially when the subject is abstract, is **personification.** Personification involves treating inanimate subjects, such as ideas or institutions, as though they had human form or feeling. In the late spring of 1989, Chinese students demonstrating for freedom marched in Tiananmen Square carrying a statue they called the "Goddess of Liberty." They were borrowing a personification that has long been used in the Western world: the representation of liberty as a woman.[16] When those students then had to confront tanks, and their oppressors destroyed the symbol of liberty, it was easy for many, living thousands of miles away in another culture, to feel angry and to identify with their cause. Personification makes it easier to arouse feelings about people and values that might otherwise seem distant.

Speakers and listeners must be careful in using and responding to the language of feeling. Such techniques can backfire if listeners believe you are trying to exploit their emotions. We should be equally careful, however, of **euphemisms,** words that numb our feelings by hiding rather than revealing reality. About a half century ago, the British writer George Orwell warned of a developing language of bureaucracy that can deaden rather than awaken feelings. Sadly, this danger has materialized in our time. The Minnesota Board of Education voted to consider requiring all students to do "volunteer work" as a prerequisite to high school graduation.[17] The medical establishment sometimes describes malpractice as a "therapeutic misadventure" and death as a "terminal episode."[18] Government planners may gloss over destructive or costly policy blunders by admitting, "Mistakes were made."[19] In such cases "mistakes" may vastly understate the blunder, and the passive construction, "were made," allows the speaker to avoid taking responsibility or assigning blame. Similarly, "friendly fire" means killing your own troops by mistake, and "collateral damage" means bombs hitting civilian targets such as hospitals and schools. As Orwell noted, such language "falls upon the facts like soft snow, blurring the outlines and covering up all the details."[20] Your ethical goal must be to avoid extremes of language that arouse or block feeling without justification.

Resources that Bring People Together

You can create a sense of togetherness by using inclusive pronouns, applying identity words, or evoking universal images.

Inclusive Pronouns.   Successful speakers rarely refer to *my* feelings, *my* plans, or *my* cause, but rather *our* feelings, *our* plans, *our* cause. Similarly, they do not say that *I* will do something or *you* will do something, but that *we* will do it together. These inclusive pronouns help unite speakers and listeners. Their importance can be shown best by a negative example. When Ross Perot addressed an NAACP convention during the 1992 presidential campaign, he repeatedly referred to his African American audience as "you people." These words highlighted separation and alienated many listeners.

Identity Words. Groups tend to develop a set of words or **culturetypes** that express their values, identity, and goals.[21] The rhetorical critic Richard Weaver called one such set of words "god and devil terms."[22] He suggested that *progress* was the primary "god term" of American culture in the mid-twentieth century. People were willing to do almost anything to achieve the benefits the word suggested. Other terms of the 1950s, such as *science, modern,* and *efficient,* enjoyed similar power because they were rooted in American values. On the other hand, words like *Communist* and *un-American* were "devil terms." Devil terms strengthen group ties by suggesting what we are not. Culturetypes can change over time: By the mid-1970s, words like *natural, peace,* and *communication* were emerging god terms; *liberal* and *pollution* were emerging devil terms.

Other words also seem charged with unusual power, perhaps because they refer to basic needs. The term *security* expresses our desire for safe, stable surroundings. According to political scientist Murray Edelman, expressions like "national security" and "social security" have a kind of built-in resonance that makes the programs they advance hard to resist.[23] "Home security systems" may seem like an especially good investment, even when they are expensive. Communication scholar Michael Calvin McGee has also introduced the idea of **ideographs,** special words that express a country's basic political beliefs.[24] McGee suggests that words like *freedom, liberty,* and *democracy* are important because they are shorthand expressions of political identity. Expressions like "*freedom* fighters" or "*democracy* in action" have unusual power because they use ideographs. But one person's "freedom fighter" can be another person's "terrorist." We need to look behind such glittering words to inspect the agendas they may hide.

In addition to national culturetypes, you should also consider whether there may be special words that express group identity for your audience. In what does your school take pride? Who are its rivals? One student at Indiana University strengthened her appeal for blood donations by arguing: "Purdue students have done it—why can't we?" Presumably, student speakers at Purdue University could use Indiana in the same way.

Culturetypes add strength to a speech when used ethically. They remind us of our heritage and suggest that we must be true to that identity. However, you must prove that they are properly applied to your topic.

Universal Images. Some words draw on experiences that persist across the generations and that cross most cultural boundaries. They express many of the needs discussed in Chapter 4, and can be especially useful for diverse groups. Among them is a set of metaphors that seem especially powerful and popular in speeches. These metaphors connect their particular, timebound subjects with timeless themes: With light and darkness, storms, the sea, disease, war, the impulse to build, the family, and space. They tap into the human experience. A brief look at three of these metaphors demonstrates their potential power in communication.[25]

Light and Darkness. From the beginnings of time, people have made negative associations with darkness. The dark is cold, unfriendly, and dangerous. On the other hand, light brings warmth and safety. It restores one's sense of control. When speakers use the light-darkness metaphor, they usually equate problems or bad times with darkness and solutions or recovery with light.

However, Wuer Kaixi, a leader of the Chinese freedom movement, used the image in a unique way. He expressed his horror over the Tiananmen Square massacre of 1989 by referring to a "black sun that rose on the day in June that should have belonged to a season of fresh flowers."[26] If you can find such creative ways to use this traditional metaphor, your audience should listen with special attention.

Storms and the Sea.   The storm metaphor is often used when describing catastrophes. Quite often the storm occurs at sea—a dangerous place under the best of conditions. The student speaker who argued that "our society is cut adrift—it has lost its moorings, and we don't see the dark cloud on our horizon" used these metaphors in combination to give dramatic expression to his fears of the future.

Disease.   This metaphor reflects our fears of illness and our ongoing search for cures. The plague was the great symbolic disease of the past; more recently, cancer is the metaphoric illness that dominates public discourse.[27] The speaker using such a metaphor usually offers a cure. If the disease has progressed too far, radical surgery may be the answer. On the night before he was assassinated, Dr. King warned that "the nation is sick, trouble is in the land, confusion all around." Only the commitment of his listeners to political, economic, and spiritual reform, he suggested, might cure that illness.

Similarly, metaphors of *war and peace* reflect our fascination with war and our yearning for peace.[28] *The impulse to build*, as when we talk about "constructing" speeches or "laying the foundations" for the future, emphasizes our ancient instinct as tool-makers to create and control the conditions of our lives. *Family* metaphors often express the dream of a close, even loving relationship among people through such images as "the family of humanity."[29] And *spatial* metaphors often reflect striving upward and forward toward goals and the desire to avoid falling or retreating into failure.

Culturetypes and universal images can help bring listeners together and set the stage for group action. *Be careful not to overdo such language.* If you strain to use such words, they will seem artificial. But if you use them appropriately with an abundance of supporting materials, they can make your speech more effective.

Resources that Encourage Action

The work of language is cumulative: That is, to achieve action, we must help listeners see a situation clearly, arouse their feelings about what they see, and bring them together into a group prepared to act. This implies that all the language techniques we have described—from simile to universal images—can contribute to the work of encouraging action. There are, however, certain techniques especially suited to meet this challenge. These resources can help speakers build the kind of ethos that will make them respected advice-givers and leaders in persuasive and ceremonial situations.

In persuasive situations especially, the ethos of the speaker is a central consideration. After all, taking action requires time and trouble and often involves cost and risk. Do we really trust this speaker? Do we respect his judgment? Does she have our good at heart? These questions rise as we hesitate on the threshold of action.

Special techniques that help build the ethos of the speaker and stir listeners to act include alliteration, parallel construction, inversion, and antithesis.

Alliteration.   **Alliteration** is the repetition of initial consonant sounds in closely connected words. One student speaker who was criticizing the lowering of educational standards paused near the conclusion of her speech, then made the following emphatic statement: "We *d*on't need the *d*octrine of *d*umbing *d*own." Her repetition of the "*d*" sound was distinctive, and helped listeners remember her point. It made her and her case seem strong and impressive. Alliteration can be effective in the introductions and conclusions of action-oriented speeches. But be careful not to overdo it—if used too frequently, it can sound contrived. Save it for the moments that really count.

Parallel Construction.   **Parallel construction** is the repetition of the same initial words in a sequence of phrases or sentences. We have already discussed this technique in Chapter 8 as a desirable way to word the main points within the overall structure of a speech. But parallel construction also works in introductions as a way to focus listeners on a vital first thought. Note, for example, how Leslie Eason introduced her classroom tribute to golfer Tiger Woods:

> You're at the Western Open where Tiger Woods could be Elvis resurrected. People clap when he pulls out the club, they clap when he hits the ball, they clap no matter where that ball lands. They clap if he smiles. They clap because he is.

Parallel construction also can work in conclusions, when it puts the final imprint on thoughts developed in the speech. Senator Dan Coats of Indiana, speaking at the Stony Brook School after a discussion of the Holocaust, used the following parallel construction:

> Hate is not dead. It does not even sleep.
> We see it displayed in racism that finds new victims, and reopens old wounds.
> We see it when a synagogue is desecrated.
> We see it when a homosexual is attacked and beaten.
> We saw it when flame touched tinder in Los Angeles and Asian shopkeepers were assaulted in the riot.
> We saw it in Florida when a murder was committed in the name of the pro-life cause.[30]

Parallel construction suggests strength of conviction, a desirable trait of ethos.

Inversion.   **Inversion** changes the expected word order to make statements more memorable and emphatic. One student speaker concluded his criticism of religious intolerance with a paraphrase of the poet John Donne: "Ask not for whom the bell tolls. It tolls for me. And it tolls for thee. For all of us who love the Bill of Rights, it tolls." The "ask not" that begins this statement and the concluding sentence are both inverted from their usual order. The unusual order of the words gains attention and makes the statement distinctive and impressive.

Antithesis.   **Antithesis** is the arrangement of opposing ideas in the same or adjoining sentences to create striking contrasts. Antithesis suggests that you have a clear grasp of options. One student used antithesis as she summarized her speech on educational reform:

> **The lack of funding does not cheat us as much as the lack of leader-ship. The root of our problem is not small budgets, but small people. Shakespeare put it well: "The fault is not in our stars but in ourselves."**

The following quotation from President John F. Kennedy's inaugural address is a famous example that interweaves antithesis, inversion, and parallel construction. See if you can identify these techniques at work together:

> **And so, my fellow Americans: Ask not what your country can do for you—ask what you can do for your country.**
> **My fellow citizens of the world: Ask not what America will do for you, but what together we can do for the freedom of man.**[31]

These language resources can help you use the power of the spoken word to promote good causes. Keep in mind, however, that this power can be abused as well as used. Keep your guard up.

Standards for Using Language Resources

As you use the various resources we have described, there are certain standards you should strive to achieve. We call these the six C's: Clarity, Color, Concreteness, Correctness, Conciseness, and Cultural sensitivity.

Clarity

Clarity comes first on our list for good reason: Unless you are clear, your speech will fail from the outset. This may seem obvious, but it is often ignored! Many speakers lapse into **jargon**, using technical language before an audience that doesn't understand it. Technical vocabularies are necessary for specialized communication in many professions, but when speakers use these vocabularies with listeners who may not understand their meaning, problems are sure to arise. "Positive vorticity advective" may be a perfectly useful expression at a convention of meteorologists, but for general audiences "It's going to rain" would be much better. Speakers who fall into the jargon trap forget how much time and trouble it took for them to acquire a technical vocabulary, so they don't bother to translate the unusual terms into lay language. Therefore they march happily forward into a jungle of unfamiliar ver-

speaker's notes

The Six C's of Effective Language Use

1 Strive for *clarity* by using familiar words in a simple, direct way.
2 Use *colorful,* vivid language to make your message memorable.
3 Develop *concrete* images so that the audience can picture what you're talking about.
4 Check the *correctness* of the words you use.
5 Be *concise.*
6 Be *culturally sensitive*: Avoid stereotyping and racist or sexist language.

biage, leaving their bewildered listeners lost behind them. The cost can be more than confusion. Such language also can increase the receiver apprehension we discussed in Chapter 3, adding tension and even resentment to the speaker/listener interaction.[32]

Closely related to jargon are words that are needlessly overblown. A notorious example occurred at the Barnum museum, when signmakers wanted to tell visitors how they could leave the building. Rather than a simple arrow with "Exit" over it, these wordsmiths came up with "To The Egress." There's no telling how many visitors left the museum by mistake, thinking that they were going to see that rare creature—a living, breathing "Egress."

While misunderstandings may result from such innocent incompetence, at other times jargon can seem purposely befuddling. Some speakers like to satisfy their egos and intimidate others by displaying their technical vocabularies. The parent of a student in Houston received a message from the high school principal regarding a special meeting on a proposed educational program. The message read:

> **Our school's cross-graded, multiethnic, individualized learning program is designed to enhance the concept of an open-ended learning program with emphasis on a continuum of multiethnic, academically enriched learning, using the identified intellectually gifted child as the agent or director of his own learning. Major emphasis is on cross-graded, multiethnic learning with the main objective being to learn respect for the uniqueness of a person.**

The parent responded:

> **Dear Principal: I have a college degree, speak two foreign languages and know four Indian dialects. I've attended a number of county fairs and three goat ropings, but I haven't the faintest idea as to what you are talking about. Do you?[33]**

While some people seem to take a strange joy in *not* communicating, others may try to hide the truth behind a smokescreen of technobabble that is closely related to the problem of euphemism we discussed earlier. Public television commentator Bill Moyers warned an audience at the University of Texas against the dangers of such jargon:

> **If you would . . . serve democracy well, you must first save the language. Save it from the jargon of insiders who talk of the current budget debate in Washington as "megapolicy choices between freeze-feasible base lines." (Sounds more like a baseball game played in the Arctic Circle.) Save it from the smokescreen artists, who speak of "revenue enhancement" and "tax-base erosion control" when they really mean a tax increase. . . . Save it from . . . the official revisionists of reality, who say that the United States did not withdraw our troops from Lebanon, we merely "backloaded our augmentation personnel."[34]**

Fearing what might happen if audiences actually understood their meaning, such speakers attempt to hide behind cloudy technical language. In contrast, ethical speaking is clear and direct.

One way to achieve clarity is through **amplification**, in which you rephrase ideas to emphasize or clarify them. Providing important bits of information and giving examples that compare and contrast are other ways to amplify an idea. In effect, you tell listeners something, then you expand and repeat what you are saying. Observe the techniques of amplification at work in the following speech sample, in which each sentence expands and repeats the meaning of the sentence that precedes it:

> **The roadrunner is not just a cartoon character that makes a fool of Wile E. Coyote. It is a member of the cuckoo family and state bird of New Mexico. Still, the cartoon roadrunner and the real roadrunner have much in common. Both are incredibly fast, real roadrunners having been tracked at ground speeds over 15 miles per hour. Neither takes to the air to chase prey or escape a predator. Both look rather awkward as they run, with strides up to 20 inches long—a real feat for a bird that is only 24 inches long with over half its length in its tail.**

Color

Color refers to the emotional intensity or vividness of language. Colorful words are memorable because they stand out in our minds. Those who use them also are remembered.

During the 1996 presidential primaries, each of the contenders was searching for a way to capture the imagination of voters and to stand out from the pack. In such a contest, those who use language colorfully have an advantage. Patrick Buchanan moved from a long-shot candidate to a leading contender at least partially because of his skill with words. Early in the campaign, Steve Forbes gained a lot of attention through an advertising campaign in which he proposed a flat tax. Senator Phil Gramm, a candidate who later

Vivid imagery and impassioned language can move people to action.

withdrew from the race, criticized Forbes on the grounds that his plan would favor the wealthy by eliminating taxes on dividend and interest income. About the flat tax Gramm said, "I reject the idea that income derived from labor should be taxed and that income derived from capital should not."[35]

A nice use of contrast, but look how Buchanan expressed the same idea: "Under Forbes' plan, lounge lizards in Palm Beach would pay a lower tax rate than steelworkers in Youngstown." Later he added that Forbes' plan had been drawn up by "the boys down at the yacht basin." While Gramm's words are a study in abstraction, Buchanan's language is both colorful and concrete. The use of the animal metaphor, "lounge lizards," is striking. So is the use of contrast, setting the "lounge lizards" and the "boys down at the yacht basin" against the steelworkers, Palm Beach against Youngstown. It's sloth and privilege against character and virtue, and we know which side Buchanan is on. These colorful symbols reflected his commitment.

Colorful language paints striking pictures for listeners. Notice how Leslie Eason made Tiger Woods come alive in the speech of tribute she made in her Vanderbilt class:

> **Mothers with daughters of a certain age (mine included) describe him as the son-in-law they'd like to have. Six foot two, a hundred fifty-five pounds, smart—Stanford, remember. Clean-cut in his creased khakis. Curly hair, gorgeous teeth. Skin the color of what they used to call "suntan" in the Crayola box. And rich. Very rich.**
>
> **He's the very opposite of the gangsta boys in the hood. Boys who wear their pants hanging below their belt as though they were already in the penitentiary. Next to them he's prep school and Pepsodent.**

When you use colorful language, your audience will find *you* to be interesting as well. Your ethos will rise as your listeners assign you high marks for competence and attractiveness. For all these reasons, color is an important standard as you develop your capacity to use language.

Concreteness

It is virtually impossible to discuss anything of significance without using some abstract words. However, if the language in your speech is overly abstract, listeners may lose interest. Moreover, because abstract language is more ambiguous than concrete language, a speech full of abstractions invites misunderstanding. Consider this continuum of terms describing a cat.

Mehitabel is a/an

creature	animal	mammal	cat	Persian cat	gray Persian cat

abstract> - >concrete

A similar continuum can be applied to active verbs. If we wanted to describe how a person moves, we could use any of the following terms:

Jennifer

moves	walks	strides

abstract > - >concrete

The more concrete your language, the more pictorial and precise the information you can convey. Concrete words are also easier for listeners to remember. Your language should be as concrete as the subject permits.

Correctness

Nothing can damage your ethos more quickly than a glaring misuse of language. Mistakes in grammar or word selection can be disastrous because most audiences attribute such errors to incompetence. They are likely to reason that anyone who misuses language can hardly offer good advice. When you select your words, be careful that they say exactly what you mean to say.

Occasionally beginning speakers, wishing to impress people with the size of their vocabularies, get caught up in the "thesaurus syndrome." They will look up a simple word to find a synonym that sounds more impressive or sophisticated. What they may not realize is that the words shown as synonyms often have slightly different meanings. For example, the words "disorganize" and "derange" are sometimes listed as synonyms. But if you refer to a disorganized person as "deranged," you will see what we mean.

People often err by using words that sound similar to the word they want. Such confusions are called **malapropisms**, after Mrs. Malaprop, a character in an eighteenth-century play by Richard Sheridan. She would say, "He is the very *pineapple* of politeness," when she meant *pinnacle*. Thus a major league baseball player trying to explain why he had forgotten a talk show interview, said: "I must have had *ambrosia*" (which probably caused his *amnesia*, which is what he apparently meant). Archie Bunker in *All in the Family* was prone to malapropisms, such as "Don't let your imagination run *rancid*" when he meant *rampant*. William J. Crocker of Armidale College in New South Wales, Australia, collected the following malapropisms from student speeches in his classes:

> A speaker can add interest to his talk with an *antidote*. [anecdote]
> Disagreements can arise from an unintended *conception*. [Indeed they can!]
> The speaker hopes to arouse *apathy* in his audience. [sympathy? empathy?]
> Good language can be reinforced by good *gestation*. [gestures]
> The speaker can use either an inductive or a *seductive* approach.[36] [deductive]

Students, ballplayers, and fictional characters are not the only ones who make such blunders. A reporter once praised an attorney for his ability to *dissemble* a bicycle. As a colleague observed with heavy irony, no doubt the man could "dissemble"—after all, he was a lawyer. But "dissemble" means to conceal and deceive, often by talking around a point. What the unfortunate reporter was praising was the lawyer's ability to "disassemble" the bicycle.[37] Elected officials are also not above an occasional malapropism. One former United States senator declared that he would oppose to his last ounce of energy any effort to build a "nuclear waste *suppository*" [repository] in his state.[38] And the Speaker of the Texas legislature once acknowledged an award by saying, "I am filled with humidity" (perhaps he meant moist hot air as well as humility).

The lesson is clear: To avoid being unintentionally humorous, use a current dictionary to check the meaning and pronunciation of any word you feel uncertain about.

Conciseness

In discussing clarity, we talked about the importance of amplification in speeches. Although it may seem contradictory, you must also be concise, even while you are amplifying your ideas. You must make your points quickly and efficiently. Follow the advice on speaking given by President Franklin Delano Roosevelt to his son James: "Be sincere . . . be brief . . . be seated!"

Long-drawn-out speeches lose audience interest. They kill the impulse toward action in persuasive speeches. A concise speech helps listeners see more clearly and feel more powerfully.

To achieve conciseness, work for simple, direct expression. Thomas Jefferson once said, "The most valuable of all talents is that of never using two words when one will do." Use the active voice rather than the passive in your verbs: "We want action!" is more concise—and more direct, colorful, and clear—than "Action is wanted by us."

You can also be concise by using comparisons that reduce complex issues to the essentials. Sojourner Truth, a nineteenth-century human rights activist, once had to counter the argument that society should not educate African Americans and women because of their alleged "inferiority." She destroyed that then-powerful position with a simple parable: "If my cup won't hold but a pint, and yours holds a quart, wouldn't you be mean not to let me have a little half-measure full?"[39]

The goal of conciseness encourages the use of **maxims**, those wise but compact sayings that summarize the beliefs of a people. During the Chinese freedom demonstrations of 1989, a sign carried by students in Tiananmen Square, "Give Me Democracy or Give Me Death," adapted Patrick Henry's famous maxium, "Give me liberty or give me death." Sadly, the Chinese authorities took them at their word. In Colorado, demonstrators at a nuclear plant carried a sign reading "Hell No, We Won't Glow!"—a variation on a chant often heard in anti–Vietnam war rallies of the 1960s, "Hell no, we won't go!" And, to reinforce his point that we need to actively (and audibly) confront the problems of racism, sexism, and homophobia, Haven Cockerham, vice president of human resources for Detroit Edison, said: "Sometimes silence isn't golden—just yellow."[40]

As these examples suggest, maxims can have special power in attracting mass-media attention. When printed on signs, they satisfy the hunger of the press for visual messages. Their brevity makes them ideally suited to the rigid time constraints of television news. Of even greater importance, maxims evoke cultural memories and invite identification. When the Chinese students adapted Patrick Henry's maxim and displayed the goddess of liberty, they were in effect both declaring that they shared American values and appealing for our assistance in their desperate struggle. When their cause was crushed, many Americans felt the injustice in a personal way, and the resulting tension between the Chinese government and our own lingers to this day.

Maxims serve well within speeches when they focus the message in a compact, memorable statement. However, they cannot substitute for careful, well-supported arguments. Once you have developed a responsible and substantive speech, consider how you might use maxims to reinforce your message.

Cultural Sensitivity

Respect for the power of words reveals how language can lift and unite or wound and hurt the diverse members of your audience. This respect develops into **cultural sensitivity**. If you read the historic writings on human communication, you will find little about cultural sensitivity. The ancient Greeks, for example, worried only about speaking to other male Athenians who were "free men" and citizens. Only in today's world, with its emphasis on empowering a wide spectrum of cultures, lifestyles, and races and its pursuit of gender equity, has cultural sensitivity emerged as an important standard for effective language usage.

As we noted in Chapter 4, there is a high probability that your classroom audience will include people from different cultures. As listeners, they may be sensitive to clumsy efforts by speakers to identify with folkways that aren't their own. Campaigning for the presidential nomination in his native South in 1992, Bill Clinton was comfortable using such folksy expressions as "my opponents are squealing like a pig caught under a gate." Speaking in Georgia in the same campaign, however, Senator Bob Kerrey from Nebraska was less adept. At Atlanta's Spelman College, Kerrey declared that if Clinton got the nomination, Bush would open him up "like a soft peanut." Kerrey's listeners looked at each other with puzzled faces. Someone must have spoken with his speechwriters, because in later speeches in that peanut-producing area Kerrey changed the expression to "boiled peanut."[41] The lesson seems clear: Don't try to be what you're not, or you may look ridiculous.

A lack of cultural sensitivity almost always has negative consequences. At best, audience members may be mildly offended; at worst, they will be irate enough to reject both you and your message. Cultural sensitivity begins with being attuned to the diversity of your audience, appreciative of the differences between cultural groups, and careful about the words you choose when referring to those who may be different from you. Although you must make some generalizations about your audience, avoid getting caught up in stereotypes that suggest that one group is inferior to another in any way. Stay away from racial, ethnic, religious, or gender-based humor, and avoid any expressions that might be interpreted as racist or sexist. (See the Speaker's Notes in Chapter 4, p. 107, guidelines on Avoiding Racist and Sexist Language.)

In Summary

Many of us underestimate the power of our words. The language we select can determine whether we succeed or fail as communicators.

The Power of the Spoken Word.   Oral language is more spontaneous, less formal, and more interactive than written communication. The spoken word is more expansive, alters the structure of sentences, and depends more on the cadence or rhythm of language as it is voiced.

Words can shape our perceptions. They invite us to see and share the world from the speaker's point of view. Words can also distort reality and block certain ways of seeing. Words can arouse intense feeling by overcoming the barriers of time, distance, and audience apathy. The spoken word can bring listeners together in a common identity. Finally, words can prompt us to action.

Language Resources. Speakers utilize certain techniques to activate the power of language. To help audiences see your point of view, *simile* can clarify abstract subjects by showing their *relationship* to things that are more concrete and familiar. *Metaphor* offers new perspectives by following the principle of *replacement*, surprising audiences with unexpected uses of words. *Representation* helps simplify complex subjects by focusing on essential, strategic features or associations.

To arouse feelings, use words that activate connotative meanings. The *image* is the natural language of the emotions. *Onomatopoeia* stimulates our senses to make us feel that we are in the presence of subjects. *Hyperbole* can help overcome audience lethargy and kindle powerful feelings. *Personification* helps us relate emotionally to abstractions or impersonal institutions.

To bring listeners together, use inclusive pronouns such as "our" and "we." *Culturetypes* express and invoke values in a compact way, and universal images based on certain metaphors remind us of our shared heritage as human beings. When properly used, such techniques as *alliteration*, *parallel construction*, *inversion*, and *antithesis* can enhance appeals for action.

Using Language Effectively. As you use the resources of language, strive to meet the standards of *clarity*, *color*, *concreteness*, *correctness*, *conciseness*, and *cultural sensitivity*. Clear language is simple and direct and draws its comparisons from everyday life. Amplification promotes clarity by dwelling on important, difficult points.

Color refers to the emotional intensity and vividness of language and is especially vital to the sharing of feeling. The more concrete a word, the more specific the information it conveys. Correctness is vital to ethos because grammatical errors and improper word choices can lower perceptions of your competence. *Malapropisms,* confusions among words based on similarities of sound, can be quite damaging. Concise speakers strive for brevity, often using comparisons that reduce complex issues to the essentials. *Maxims* are the ultimate in conciseness. *Cultural sensitivity* demands that a speaker be aware of the diversity within an audience and respectful of cultural differences.

Terms to Know

relationship	hyperbole
simile	personification
replacement	euphemisms
metaphor	culturetypes
representation	ideographs
image	alliteration
onomatopoeia	parallel construction

inversion   malapropisms

antithesis   maxims

jargon   cultural sensitivity

amplification

Notes

1. William Raspberry, "Any Candidate Will Drink to That," *Austin American Statesman,* 11 May 1984, p. A–10. The "Whiskey Speech," a legend in Southern politics, was originally presented some years ago by N. S. Sweat, Jr., during a heated campaign to legalize the sale of liquor-by-the-drink in Mississippi. Because about half of his constituents favored the question and the other half were vehemently opposed, Representative "Soggy" Sweat decided to defuse the issue with humor.

2. Jerry Tarver, "Words in Time: Some Reflections on the Language of Speech," *Vital Speeches of the Day,* 15 April 1988, p. 410.

3. Tarver, pp. 410–412.

4. These powers of language were first explored in Michael Osborn, *Orientations to Rhetorical Style* (Chicago: Science Research Associates, Inc., 1976), and are developed further in Michael Osborn, "Rhetorical Depiction," in *Form, Genre, and the Study of Political Discourse,* ed. Herbert W. Simons and Aram A. Aghazarian (Columbia: University of South Carolina Press, 1986), pp. 79–107.

5. Based on the account in Claire Perkins, "The Many Symbolic Faces of Fred Smith: Charismatic Leadership in the Bureaucracy," *The Journal of the Tennessee Speech Communication Association* 11 (1985): 22.

6. Jesse Jackson, "Common Ground and Common Sense," *Vital Speeches of the Day*, 15 August 1988, pp. 649–653.

7. From a transcription of the debate, CNN, 15 February 1996.

8. Listeners whose lives seem dull and unrewarding are especially susceptible to such dramas. See the discussion in Eric Hoffer, *The True Believer: Thoughts on the Nature of Mass Movements* (New York: Harper, 1951).

9. Union organizing song written in 1932 by Florence Reece, wife of a leader of the National Miners Union in Harlan County, Kentucky.

10. "Southern-speak: Clinton Uses It Well," *Norfolk Virginian-Pilot and the Ledger-Star,* 10 April 1994, p. A6.

11. John Markoff, "Metaphors Fly Back and Forth in Microsoft Dispute," *The New York Times on the Web,* 21 May 1998 (http://www.nytimes.com/library/tech/yr/mo/biztech/articles/21 microsoft-rhetoric.html), accessed 21 May 1998.

12. Adapted from *The American Heritage Dictionary,* 2nd ed. (Boston: Houghton Mifflin, 1985), p. 92. Copyright ©1996 by Houghton Mifflin Company. Reproduced by permission from *The American Heritage Dictionary of the English Language,* Third Edition.

13. Longinus, "On the Sublime," trans. W. Rhys Roberts, in *The Great Critics: An Anthology of Literary Criticism,* ed. James Harry Smith and Edd Winfield Parks (New York: Norton, 1951), p. 82.

14. Winston Churchill, *Blood, Sweat, and Tears* (New York: Putnam, 1941), pp. 367–369.

15. Martin Luther King, Jr., from a transcription of "I've Been to the Mountaintop," delivered in Memphis, Tenn., 4 April 1968. For complete text, see *Texts in Context: Critical Dialogues on Significant Episodes in American Political Rhetoric,* ed. Michael C. Leff and Fred J. Kauffeld (Davis, Calif.: Hermagoras Press, 1989), pp. 311–321.

16. Michael Calvin McGee, "The Origins of Liberty: A Feminization of Power," *Communication Monographs* 47 (1980): 27–45.
17. From the *Quarterly Review of Doublespeak,* retrieved 19 June 1998 from the World Wide Web: http://www.netins.net/showcase/clevad/double.htm.
18. "Stamp Out 'Doublespeak'," *Parade*, 10 January 1988, p. 16.
19. "'To Be' in Their Bonnets: A Matter of Semantics," *Atlantic*, February 1992, p. 20.
20. "Politics and the English Language," *Shooting an Elephant and Other Essays* (London: Secker and Warburg, 1950), p. 97.
21. Osborn, *Orientations to Rhetorical Style,* p. 16.
22. Richard Weaver, "Ultimate Terms in Contemporary Rhetoric," in *The Ethics of Rhetoric* (Chicago: Henry Regnery, 1953), pp. 211–232.
23. Murray Edelman, "Language, Myths and Rhetoric," *Transaction: Social Science and Modern Society* 12 (July/August 1975): 14–21.
24. Michael Calvin McGee, "The Ideograph: A Link Between Rhetoric and Ideology," *Quarterly Journal of Speech* 66 (1980): 1–16.
25. For further insights into the function of universal images, see Michael Osborn, "Archetypal Metaphor in Rhetoric: The Light-Dark Family," *Quarterly Journal of Speech* 53 (1967): 115–126, and "The Evolution of the Archetypal Sea in Rhetoric and Poetic," *Quarterly Journal of Speech* 63 (1977): 347–363.
26. *Time,* 10 July 1989, p. 32.
27. For an insightful discussion of the metaphors we use to construct our ideas about our illnesses, see Susan Sontag, *Illness as Metaphor* (New York: Vintage Books, 1979) and *AIDS and Its Metaphors* (New York: Farrar, Straus, and Giroux, 1988).
28. See Robert Ivie, "Images of Savagery in American Justifications for War," *Communication Monographs* 47 (1980): 279–294.
29. See another side of this image in J. Vernon Jensen, "British Voices on the Eve of the American Revolution: Trapped by the Family Metaphor," *Quarterly Journal of Speech* 63 (1977): 43–50.
30. "The Virtue of Tolerance," *Vital Speeches of the Day*, 21 August 1993, p. 646.
31. John F. Kennedy, "Inaugural Address," in *Presidential Rhetoric: The Imperial Age, 1961–1974,* ed. Theodore Windt (Dubuque, Iowa: Kendall Hunt, 1978), p. 11.
32. Joe Ayres, A. Kathleen Wilcox, and Debbie M. Ayres, "Receiver Apprehension: An Explanatory Model and Accompanying Research," *Communication Education* 44 (1995): 223–235.
33. Ann Landers, "Translate Gobbledygook, Please," *The Commercial Appeal* 21 August 1992, p. C3.
34. Bill Moyers, "Commencement Address," presented at the Lyndon B. Johnson School of Public Affairs, University of Texas, Austin. Cited in *Time,* 19 June 1985, p. 68.
35. All quotations are from *USA Today,* 18 January 1996, p. 4A.
36. "Malapropisms Live!" *Spectra,* May 1986, p. 6.
37. Memphis *Commercial Appeal,* 24 July 1991, p. A-13.
38. Richard Lacayo, "Picking Lemons for the Plums?" *Time,* 31 July 1989, p. 17.
39. Sojourner Truth, "Ain't I a Woman?" in *Feminism: The Essential Historical Writings,* ed. Miriam Schneir (New York: Random House, 1972), p. 95.
40. Haven E. Cockerham, "Conquer the Isms that Stand in Our Way," *Vital Speeches of the Day*, 1 February 1998, p. 240.
41. *Time,* 9 March 1992, p. 19.

11

Presenting Your Speech

There is no gesture that does not speak.

—*Montaigne*

This chapter will help you

- make more effective presentations
- respond to audience feedback
- participate in a question-and-answer session
- improve your voice as an instrument of communication
- understand the dynamics of body language
- prepare for video presentations

L ou had worked hard preparing his speech. He had selected a topic that he cared about, and he had researched and developed it carefully. Despite all this work, Lou's speech fell flat. Within the first minute of his presentation he had lost much of his audience.

The trouble began when Lou opened his mouth. His voice did not project energy or enthusiasm. He never varied his pitch or loudness. He looked down at his notes or up at the ceiling, seldom making eye contact with his listeners. His soft voice almost lulled his listeners to sleep. Lou's presentation suggested that he was not really interested in his topic or in trying to communicate. Little wonder that his listeners found their daydreams more interesting and that a potentially worthy speech never had a chance that day.

IN THIS CHAPTER we focus on the **presentation** of a speech. We consider the major ways to present speeches and the factors that make presentations effective or ineffective. We offer advice on responding to audience feedback, handling questions and answers, developing an effective speaking voice, using your body to communicate, and practicing effectively. At the end of the chapter, we indicate how to adapt many of these skills for video presentations.

Developing your ability to present speeches should help you in other settings, such as job interviews, meetings, and even social occasions. Learning how to present yourself as well as your ideas tends to stay with you over the years, providing what Francis Bacon once called "continual letters of recommendation."

What Makes a Presentation Effective?

The word *communication* stems from the Latin word for *common*. An effective presentation allows a speaker and audience to hold ideas and feelings in common, even when they come from different cultural backgrounds. Such a presentation makes use of a verbal and nonverbal system of symbols that should work together to create meaning.

At the end of Chapter 12, we reprint the text of a speech first presented at Vanderbilt University by Marie D'Aniello. In her speech Marie traced how friendship evolves from childhood to young adulthood. As she presented this

301

speech, her manner was warm and open, and her face was responsive to audience reactions. *In short, Marie herself seemed the perfect model of a friend!* Her presentation illustrated the harmonious interplay of verbal and nonverbal symbols.

On the other hand, we also remember a student who described her childhood in these terms: "I was always getting into trouble." But as she said these words, she seemed listless; she slouched at the podium, chewed gum, and avoided eye contact. Her passive manner did not reinforce her portrait of herself as a boisterous child. Instead, *there was an incongruity between what she claimed and what she showed.* Whenever verbal and nonverbal symbols seem out of sync, listeners give more credit to the nonverbal message. Yet scholars often give priority to written language. Clearly, as these positive and negative examples indicate, written language alone cannot invoke the immediacy, the rich totality of human communication.[1]

An effective presentation begins with your attitude. You must be committed to your topic and want to share this commitment. The way you speak should bring your ideas to life. In brief, *you should want to communicate.* This may seem obvious, but we remember another student in whom this desire to communicate seemed oddly missing. She had done well in high school speaking contests, and in her first speech she told her listeners that she thought of herself as a good speaker. And in a technical sense, she was correct. Her voice was pleasant and expressive, her manner direct and competent. But there was a false note, an overtone of artificiality. In consequence, her listeners gave her a rather chilly reception. It was clear that for her, speaking was an exhibition. She was more important than her ideas. Her listeners sensed that she had her priorities wrong.

Beyond the right attitude, any good presentation has certain requirements. Your presentation must be loud enough to be heard easily in the back of the room where you are speaking. It should not call attention to itself or distract from your message. Consequently, you should avoid pompous pronunciations, artificial vocal patterns, and overly dramatic gestures. An effective presentation sounds natural and conversational—as though you were talking *with* listeners, not *at* them. This helps reduce the psychological distance between you and your audience.

Immediacy is the term used to describe the closeness between speaker and listeners in successful communication.[2] Communication scholar James McCroskey has written:

> **Immediacy increases the audience's attentiveness; it reduces tension and anxiety for both speaker and audience; it creates greater liking between speaker and audience; and it increases the probability that the speaker's purpose will be accomplished.**[3]

Immediacy relates to the likableness dimension of ethos, which we discussed in Chapter 2. It encourages listeners to open their minds to you and to be influenced by what you say.[4] How, then, can you encourage immediacy? You can start by reducing the actual distance between yourself and your listeners. Step out from behind the lectern and move closer to them. Smile at them when appropriate, maintain eye contact, use gestures to clarify and reinforce ideas, and let your voice express your feelings. Even if your heart is pumping, your hands are a little sweaty, and your knees feel a bit wobbly, the self you show to listeners should be a person in control of the situation. Listeners admire and identify with speakers who maintain what Ernest Hemingway once called "grace under pressure."

Your goal should be a speech characterized by an **expanded conversational style**, which we discussed in detail in Chapter 1. An expanded conversational style is direct, spontaneous, colorful, and tuned to the responses of listeners. Such a style, however, is a bit more careful and formal than everyday conversation.

To summarize, *an effective presentation makes your ideas come alive while you are speaking*. It blends nonverbal with verbal symbols, so that reason and emotion, heart and head, work together to advance your message. The remainder of this chapter will help you move closer to this goal of effective presentation.

Methods of Presentation

In this section we consider the four major methods of speech presentation: impromptu speaking, memorized text presentation, reading from a manuscript, and extemporaneous speaking. We also include suggestions for responding to audience feedback and handling questions and answers.

Impromptu Speaking

Impromptu speaking is sometimes called "speaking off the cuff," a phrase that suggests that you could put all your notes on the cuff of your shirt. Impromptu speaking is useful when you have little or no time for preparation or practice. The incident we described in Chapter 8, in which we learned during a zoning hearing that developers were proposing a helicopter port in our neighborhood, called for an impromptu speech. At work you might find yourself being asked to make a presentation "in fifteen minutes." In meetings you may want to "say a few words" about something. You can also use impromptu speaking skills in other classes—to answer a question or comment on a point made by your professor.

When you have just a few minutes to prepare, first determine your purpose. What do you want the audience to know? Why is this important? Next, decide on your main points. Don't try to cover too much. Limit yourself to no more than three main points. If you have access to any type of writing material—a note pad, a scrap of paper—jot down a memory-jogging word for each idea, either in order of importance or as the ideas seem to flow naturally. The skeletal outline on the following page will keep you from rambling or forgetting something that is important. Stick to the main points, enumerating them as you go: "My first point is. . . . Second, it is important to. . . . Finally, it is clear that. . . ." Use the **PREP formula**: State a *p*oint, give a *r*eason or *e*xample, then restate the *p*oint. Keep your presentation short and end with a summary of your remarks.

Speakers in public meetings must adapt to the situations that confront them.

Point:	The proposal to allow John Clark to operate a helicopter port in the neighborhood is not sound.
Reason(s)/ Example(s):	The noise generated by helicopters taking off and landing would destroy the tranquility of this quiet residential neighborhood. It would be especially disturbing to the residents of the nursing home one block from the proposed facility.
Restatement of *Point:*	Therefore, we ask you to vote against this proposal.

An impromptu speech often is one of several such speeches as people express their ideas in meetings. The earlier speeches create the context for your presentation. If others stood at the front of the room to speak, you should do so as well. If earlier speakers remained seated, you may wish to do the same. However, you should consider whether earlier speakers have been successful. If these speakers offended listeners while making standing presentations, you may wish to remain seated to differentiate yourself from them. If seated speakers have made trivial presentations, you may wish to stand to signal that what you are going to say is important.

Fortunately, most impromptu speaking situations are relatively casual. No one expects a polished presentation on a moment's notice. However, the ability to organize your ideas quickly and effectively and to present them confidently puts you at a great advantage. The principles of preparing speeches that you learn in this course can help you become a more effective impromptu speaker.

Memorized Text Presentation

Memorized text presentations, are written out, committed to memory, and delivered word for word. In general, you should avoid trying to memorize entire speeches because this method of presentation poses many problems. However, because the introduction and conclusion of a speech are important, the introduction for gaining audience attention and the conclusion for leaving a lasting impression, their wording should be carefully planned, and you may want to memorize them. You might also want to memorize short congratulatory remarks, a toast, or a brief award acceptance speech.

Beginning speakers who try to memorize their speeches usually get so caught up with *remembering* that they forget about *communicating*. The result often sounds stilted or "sing-songy." Speaking from memory also inhibits adapting to feedback. It can keep you from clarifying points that the audience doesn't understand or from following up on ideas that seem especially effective.

Another problem with memorized speeches is that they must be written out in advance. Most people do not write in an effective oral style. The major differences between oral and written language, covered in Chapter 10, bear repeating. Good oral style uses short, direct, conversational patterns. Even sentence fragments can be acceptable. Repetition, rephrasing, and amplification are more necessary in speaking than in writing. The sense of rhythm and saving the most forceful idea for the end of the sentence are more important in oral style. Imagery can be especially useful to help the audience visualize what you are talking about.

If you must memorize a speech, commit the speech so thoroughly to memory that you can concentrate on communicating with your audience. If you experience a "mental block," keep talking. Restate or rephrase your last point to get your mind back on track. If this doesn't work, you may find yourself forced into an extemporaneous style and discover that you can actually express your ideas better without the constraints of exact wording!

Reading from a Manuscript

When you make a **manuscript presentation**, you read to an audience from either a text or a teleprompter. Manuscript presentations have many of the same problems as memorized presentations. Because speakers must look at a script, they lose eye contact with listeners. This in turn causes a loss of immediacy and inhibits adapting to feedback. Moreover, as with memorized presentations, you may have trouble writing in an oral style.

Some problems are exclusive to manuscript presentations. Most people do not read aloud well. Their presentations lack variety. Also, when people plan to read a speech, they often do not practice enough. Unless speakers are comfortable with the material, they end up glued to their manuscripts rather than communicating with listeners. Other problems may arise if your manuscript pages get out of order, or if you pick up the wrong paper or teleprompter material on your way to a presentation.

Although this last predicament may sound improbable, it can happen, as President Clinton can confirm. In September of 1993 Clinton presented a speech on health care to a joint session of Congress. He had been working on the speech for some time and finished revising it on the ride to the Capitol. The final changes were entered onto computer disks immediately before he was to speak. Here is a report of what happened:

> **No one realized that a White House communications aide had already accidentally merged the new speech with an old file of the February 17 speech to Congress. . . . When Clinton took the podium minutes later, he was understandably alarmed to see a seven-month-old speech on the teleprompter's display screens. Clinton told the news to Gore. . . . Gore summoned Stephanopoulos, who scrambled to fix the mistake, eventually downloading the correct version. . . . But for seven minutes, Clinton vamped with just notes.[5]**

During the first seven minutes of his presentation, the president was forced into an extemporaneous style—the method of presentation most communication instructors recommend. The speech was received with high acclaim:

> **For a man reading the wrong speech off his teleprompter, Bill Clinton spoke with persuasive passion as he addressed Congress and the nation about health care last week. Gone was the Slick Willie. . . . Suddenly Clinton looked the leader millions of Americans hoped they were voting for: decisive, forceful, even visionary.[6]**

Manuscript presentations are most useful when the speaker seeks accuracy or eloquence, or when time constraints are severe, as in legal announcements, formal political speeches, or media presentations that must be timed within seconds. Extemporaneous presentations may also include quotations or technical information that must be read if they are to achieve their effect. Because you will need to read material from time to time, we offer the following suggestions:

- Use large print to prepare your manuscript so that you can see it without straining.
- Use light pastel rather than white paper, to cut down on glare from lights.
- Double- or triple-space the manuscript.
- Mark pauses with slashes.
- Highlight material you want to emphasize.
- Practice speaking from your manuscript so that you can maintain as much eye contact as possible with your audience.

Figure 11.1 shows a sample manuscript prepared for presentation. Note that two or three slashes together indicate longer pauses. The speaker highlights emphasized material by underlining it.

As you make final preparations, ask a friend to videotape your rehearsal. Review the tape and ask yourself: Do I sound as though I'm *talking with* someone or reading a text? Do I maintain eye contact with my imaginary audience? Do I pause effectively to emphasize the most important points? Does the presentation flow smoothly? Revise and continue practicing until you are satisfied.

FIGURE 11.1
Sample Speech Script

WE AMERICANS ARE BIG ON MONUMENTS. / WE BUILD MONUMENTS

IN MEMORY OF OUR HEROES. // WASHINGTON, JEFFERSON, AND LIN-

COLN LIVE ON IN OUR NATION'S CAPITAL. // WE ERECT MONUMENTS

TO HONOR OUR MARTYRS. / THE MINUTE MAN STILL STANDS GUARD

AT CONCORD. / THE FLAG IS EVER RAISED OVER IWO JIMA. / SOME-

TIMES WE EVEN CONSTRUCT MONUMENTS TO COMMEMORATE VIC-

TIMS. // IN ASHBURN PARK DOWNTOWN THERE IS A MONUMENT TO

THOSE WHO DIED IN THE YELLOW FEVER EPIDEMICS. /// HOWEVER,

<u>THERE ARE SOME THINGS IN OUR HISTORY THAT WE DON'T MEMORI-</u>

<u>ALIZE</u> // PERHAPS WE WOULD JUST AS SOON FORGET WHAT HAP-

PENED. /// LAST SUMMER I VISITED SUCH A PLACE — // <u>THE</u>

<u>MASSACRE SITE AT WOUNDED KNEE</u>.

Extemporaneous Speaking

Extemporaneous speaking is prepared and practiced but not written out or memorized. It offers a spontaneous and natural-sounding presentation, and makes it easier to establish immediacy with an audience. The speaker is not the prisoner of a text, and each presentation will vary according to the audience, occasion, and inspiration of the moment. Another large advantage is that it encourages interaction with an audience. A Vanderbilt speaker who distributed photographs and then instructed listeners on how to view them, and another student who asked listeners to close their eyes and imagine themselves living as dwarfs, were playing up these advantages. Such interaction encourages the audience to participate in constructing the message of the speech. It becomes their creation as well, which is especially important when persuading listeners.

Extemporaneous speaking involves preparation and practice, and is therefore more polished than impromptu speaking. But it also allows you to respond to feedback and to adapt accordingly, giving it a strong advantage over manuscript and memorized presentations. Because extemporaneous speaking combines the best characteristics of these various modes of presentation, many instructors require that you use it for most classroom speeches.

Responding to Feedback from Your Audience.   As we saw in Chapter 1, **feedback** is the message listeners send back to you as you speak. Facial expressions, gestures, or sounds of agreement or disagreement let you know how you are coming across. Since most feedback is nonverbal, you should maintain eye contact with your audience so that you can respond to these signals. Use feedback to monitor whether listeners understand you, are interested, and agree with what you are saying. Negative feedback in particular can alert you to the need to make on-the-spot adjustments.

Feedback that Signals Misunderstanding.   Listeners' puzzled expressions can signal that they don't understand what you are saying. You may need to define an unfamiliar word or rephrase an idea to make it simpler. You could add an example or story to make an abstract concept more concrete. It might help to compare or contrast an unfamiliar idea with something the audience already knows and understands. When you detect signs of misunderstanding, you can say, "Let me put it another way." Then provide a clearer explanation.

Feedback that Signals Loss of Interest.   Bored listeners wiggle in their seats, drum their fingers, or develop a glazed look. Remind them of the importance of your topic. Provide an example or story that makes your message come to life. Involve your listeners by asking a question that calls for a show of hands. Startle them with a bold statement. Keep in mind that enthusiasm is incendiary: Your interest can ignite theirs. Move from behind the lectern and come closer to them. Whatever happens, do not become disheartened or lose faith in your speech. In all likelihood, some people—probably more than you think—will have found the speech interesting.

Feedback that Signals Disagreement.   A number of techniques can help you deal with disagreement. If you anticipate resistance, work hard to establish your ethos in the introduction of your speech. Listeners should see you as a competent, trustworthy, and likable person who has their best interests at heart.

To be perceived as competent, you must *be* competent. Arm yourself with a surplus of information, examples, and testimony from sources your audience will respect. Practice your presentation until it is polished. Set an example of tolerance by respecting positions different from your own.

You may find that although you differ with listeners on methods, you agree with them on goals. In such cases, stress the values that you share. Appeal to the listeners' sense of fair play and their respect for your right to speak. You should be the model of civility in the situation. Avoid angry reactions and the use of inflammatory language. Think of these listeners as offering an opportunity for your ideas to have impact.

In Figure 11.2 we summarize the uses, advantages, and disadvantages of these major methods of presentation.

Handling Questions and Answers

If you are successful in arousing interest and stimulating thinking, your listeners may want to ask questions at the end of your speech. The following suggestions should make handling questions easier for you.[7]

METHOD	USE	ADVANTAGES	DISADVANTAGES
Impromptu	When you have no time for preparation or practice.	Spontaneity, ability to meet demands of the situation, open to feedback.	Less-polished, less use of supporting material, less well-researched, less well-organized.
Memorized	When you will be making brief remarks such as a toast or award acceptance; when the wording of your introduction or conclusion is important.	Eloquent wording can be planned, can sound well-polished.	Focusing on remembering can make you forget to communicate, speech must be written out in advance, style can become sing-songy.
Manuscript	When exact wording is important, time constraints are strict, or your speech will be telecast.	Precise wording can be planned in advance, timing can be down to seconds.	Most people don't read well, inhibits responding to feedback and adapting speech accordingly, may not practice enough.
Extemporaneous	For most public speaking occasions.	Spontaneity, ability to respond to audience feedback, encourages focusing on the essence of your message.	Requires considerable time for preparation and practice, excellence comes through experience.

FIGURE 11.2
Methods of Presentation

First, *prepare for questions.* Try to anticipate what you might be asked, think about how you will answer these questions, and do the research required to answer them effectively. Practice your speech before friends and urge them to ask you tough questions.

Second, *repeat or paraphrase the question.* This is especially important if the question was long or complicated and your audience is large. Paraphrasing ensures that everyone in the audience hears the question. It gives you time to think of your answer, and it helps you be sure you understood the question. Paraphrasing also enables you to steer the question to the type of answer you are prepared to give.

Third, *maintain eye contact with the audience as you answer.* Note that we say "with the audience," not just "with the questioner." Look first at the questioner, then make eye contact with other audience members, returning your gaze to the questioner as you finish your answer. The purpose of a question-and-answer period should be to extend the understanding of the entire audience, not to carry on a private conversation with one person.

Fourth, *defuse hostile questions.* Reword emotional questions in more objective language. For example, if you are asked, "Why do you want to throw away our money on people who are too lazy to work?" you might respond with something like, "I understand your frustration and think what you really want to know is 'Why aren't our current programs helping people break out of the chains of unemployment?'"

Simply saying "I don't know" can also help defuse a hostile questioner. Roger Ailes, a political media adviser for three U.S. presidents, described how former New York City Mayor Ed Koch once used this technique. Koch had spent three hundred thousand dollars putting bike lanes in Manhattan. Cars were driving in the bike lanes. Cyclists were running over pedestrians. The money seemed wasted. Soon thereafter, when Koch was running for reelection, he appeared on a "meet-the-press" type of show. This is how the questioning went:

> **One reporter led off with "Mayor Koch, in light of the financial difficulties in New York City, how could you possibly justify wasting three hundred thousand dollars on bike lanes? . . ." Koch smiled and he said, "You're right. It was a terrible idea." He went on. "I thought it would work. It didn't. It was one of the worst mistakes I ever made." And he stopped. Now nobody knew what to do. They had another twenty-six minutes of the program left. They all had prepared questions about the bike lanes, and so the next person feebly asked, "But, Mayor Koch, how could you do this?" And Mayor Koch said, "I already told you, it was stupid. I did a dumb thing. It didn't work." And he stopped again. Now there were twenty-five minutes left and nothing to ask him. It was brilliant.[8]**

Fifth, *keep your answers short and direct.* Don't give another speech.

Sixth, *handle nonquestions politely.* If someone starts to give a speech rather than ask a question, wait until he or she pauses for breath and then cut in with something like, "Thank you for your comment" or "I appreciate your remarks. Your question, then, is . . ." or "That's an interesting perspective. Can we have another question?" Don't get caught up in a shouting match. Stay in command of the situation.

Finally, *bring the question-and-answer session to a close.* Call for a final question and, as you complete the answer, summarize your message again to refocus listeners on your central points.

speaker's notes

Handling Questions and Answers

1 Practice answering tough questions on your topic before an audience of friends.

2 Repeat or paraphrase the question you are asked.

3 Maintain eye contact with the audience as you answer. Don't look at just the person who asks the question.

4 Defuse hostile questions by rewording them in unemotional language.

5 Don't be afraid to say, "I don't know."

6 Keep answers short and to the point.

7 Handle nonquestions politely.

8 Bring the question-and-answer session to a close by reemphasizing your message.

Using Your Voice Effectively

Your voice plays a major role in the effectiveness of your oral communication. Consider the following simple sentences:

I don't believe it.

You did that.

Give me a break.

How many different meanings can you create as you speak these words, just by changing the rhythm, pace, emphasis, pitch, or inflection of your voice?

Your ethos as well as your message can be affected by the quality of your voice. A good speaking voice enhances your image in the ears of listeners. But if you sound tentative, people may think you are not very competent. If you mumble, they may think you are trying to hide something. If you are overly loud or strident, they may find you not very likable.

How you talk is also part of your identity. Someone who talks in a soft, breathy voice may be labeled "sexy"; someone who speaks in a more forceful manner, may be considered "authoritative." For some speakers, a dialect is part of their ethnicity, a valued part of their personality.[9]

While you may not wish to make radical changes in your speaking voice, minor improvements can yield big dividends. As one voice specialist put it, "Though speech is a human endowment, how well we speak is an individual achievement."[10] With a little effort and practice, most of us can make positive changes. We caution, however, that simple vocal exercises will not fix serious impairments. If you have such a problem, contact the nearest speech pathology clinic for professional help.

The first step in learning to use your voice more effectively is to evaluate how you usually talk. Tape-record yourself while speaking and reading aloud. When you hear yourself, you may say, "Is that really me?" Most tape recorders will slightly distort the way you sound because they do not exactly replicate the spectrum of sounds made by the human voice. Nevertheless, a tape recording gives you an idea of how you may sound to others. As you listen, ask yourself:

1. Does my voice convey the meaning I intend?
2. Would I want to listen to me if I were in the audience?
3. Does my voice present me at my best?

If your answers are negative, you may need to work on pitch, rate, loudness, variety, articulation, enunciation, pronunciation, or dialect. Save your original tape so that you can hear yourself improve as you practice.

Pitch

Pitch is the placement of your voice on the musical scale. Vocal pitches can range from low and deep to high and squeaky. For effective speaking, find a pitch level that is comfortable and that allows maximum flexibility and variety. Each of us has a **habitual pitch**, the level at which we speak most frequently. Additionally, we have an **optimum pitch**, the level that allows us to produce our strongest voice with minimal effort and that allows variation up and down the scale. You can use the following exercise to help determine your optimum pitch:

> Sing the sound *la* down to the lowest pitch you can produce without feeling strain or having your voice break or become rough. Now count each note as you sing up the scale to the highest tone you can comfortably produce. Most people have a range of approximately sixteen notes. Your optimum pitch will be about one-fourth of the way up your range. For example, if your range extends twelve notes, your optimum pitch would be at the third note up the scale. Again, sing down to your lowest comfortable pitch, and then sing up to your optimum pitch level.[11]

Tape-record this exercise, and compare your optimum pitch to the habitual pitch revealed during your first recording. If your optimum pitch is within one or two notes of your habitual pitch, then you should not experience vocal problems related to pitch level. If your habitual pitch is much higher or lower than your optimum pitch, you may not have sufficient flexibility to raise or lower the pitch of your voice to communicate changes in meaning and emphasis. You can change your habitual pitch by practicing speaking and reading at your optimum pitch.

The lyrical, melodic writing of Kiowa author N. Scott Momaday offers an opportunity to practice reading for vocal improvement. See if you can make your voice convey the meaning of the passage through variations in pitch and rate.

Read the following paragraphs from N. Scott Momaday's *The Way to Rainy Mountain* at your optimum pitch level, using pitch changes to provide meaning and feeling. To make the most of your practice, tape-record yourself so that you can observe both problems and progress.

> **A single knoll rises out of the plain in Oklahoma, north and west of the Wichita Range. For my people, the Kiowas, it is an old landmark, and they gave it the name Rainy Mountain. The hardest weather in the world is there. Winter brings blizzards, hot tornadic winds arise in the spring, and in the summer the prairie is an anvil's edge. The grass turns brittle and brown, and it cracks beneath your feet. There are green belts along the rivers and creeks, linear groves of hickory and pecan, willow, and witch hazel. At a distance in July or August the steaming foliage seems almost to writhe in fire. . . . Loneliness is an aspect of the land. All things in the plain are isolate: there is no confusion of objects in the eye, but one hill or one tree or one man. To look upon that landscape in the early morning, with the sun at your back, is to lose the sense of proportion. Your imagination comes to life, and this, you think, is where Creation was begun.**[12]

The purpose of this exercise is to explore the full range of variation around your optimum pitch and to make you conscious of the relationship between pitch and effective communication. Tape yourself reading the passage a second time, this time exaggerating the pitch variations as you read it. Play back both of the taped readings. If you have a problem with a narrow pitch range, you may discover that exaggerating makes you sound more effective.

When you speak before a group, don't be surprised if your pitch seems higher than usual. Your pitch is sensitive to your emotions and will usually go up when you are under pressure. If pitch is a serious problem for you, hum your optimum pitch softly to yourself before you begin to speak so that you start out on the right note.

Rate

Your **rate**, or the speed at which you speak, helps set the mood of your speech. Serious material calls for a slow, deliberate rate; lighter topics need a faster pace. For a speech to be effective, there should be rate variations that reflect changes in the material being presented. These variations may include the duration of syllables, the use of pauses, and the overall speed of presentation. The rate patterns within a speech produce its **rhythm**. Rhythm is an essential component of all communication.[13] With rhythmic variations you point out what is important and make it easier for listeners to comprehend your message.

Beginning speakers who feel intimidated typically speed up their presentations and run their words together. What this rapid-fire delivery communicates is the speaker's desire to get it over with and sit down! At the other extreme, some speakers become so deliberate that they almost put themselves and their audiences to sleep. Neither extreme lends itself to effective communication.

As we noted in Chapter 3, the typical rate for extemporaneous speaking is about 125 words per minute. You can check your speed by timing your reading of the excerpt from *Rainy Mountain*. If you were reading at the average rate, you would have taken about sixty seconds to complete that material. If you allowed time for pauses between phrases, appropriate for such formal material, your reading may have run slightly longer. If you took less than fifty seconds, you were probably speaking too rapidly or not using pauses effectively.

Pausing before or after a word or phrase highlights its importance. Pauses also give your listeners time to contemplate what you have said. They can help build suspense and maintain interest as listeners anticipate what you will say next. Moreover, pauses can clarify the relationships among ideas, phrases, and sentences. They are oral punctuation marks, taking the place of the commas and periods, underlinings and exclamation marks, that occur in written communication. For all these good reasons, experienced speakers learn how to use pauses to maximum advantage. Humorist William Price Fox once wrote of Eugene Talmadge, a colorful Georgia governor and fabled stump speaker, "That rascal knew how to wait. He had the longest pause in the state."[14]

Read the following passage aloud again, using pauses (where indicated by the slash marks) and rate changes (a faster pace is indicated by italic type and a slower pace by capital letters) to enhance its meaning and demonstrate mood changes. This exercise will give you an idea of how pausing and changing rate can emphasize and clarify the flow of ideas:

> **A single knoll rises out of the plain in Oklahoma / north and west of the Wichita Range // For my people / the Kiowas / it is an old landmark / and they gave it the name Rainy Mountain /// The hardest weather in the world is there //** *Winter brings blizzards / hot tornadic winds arise in the spring / and in the summer the prairie is an anvil's edge // The grass turns brittle and brown / and it cracks beneath your feet //* **There are green belts along the rivers and creeks / linear groves of hickory and pecan, willow, and witch hazel // At a distance / in July or August / the steaming foliage seems almost to writhe in fire /// LONELINESS IS AN ASPECT OF THE LAND // ALL THINGS IN THE PLANE ARE ISOLATE /// THERE IS NO CONFUSION OF OBJECTS IN THE EYE // BUT ONE HILL // OR ONE TREE // OR ONE MAN /// To look upon that landscape in the early morning / with the sun at your back / is to lose the sense of proportion // Your imagination comes to life // AND THIS / YOU THINK / IS WHERE CREATION WAS BEGUN.**

Just as pausing can work for you, the wrong use of a pause can be a liability. Some speakers habitually use "ers" and "ums," "wells" and "okays," or "you knows" in the place of pauses without being aware of it. These **vocal distractions** may fill in the silence while the speaker thinks about what to say next, or they may be signs of nervousness. To determine if you have such a habit, tape-record yourself speaking extemporaneously about one of the main points for your next speech. Often simply becoming aware of such vocal distractions is enough to help you control them. Also, don't use "okay," "well," or "you know" as transitions in your speech. Plan more effective transitions (see Chapter 7). Practice your presentation until the ideas flow smoothly. Finally, don't be afraid of the brief strategic silence that comes when you pause. Make silence work for you.

If your natural tendency is to speak too slowly, you can practice developing a faster rate in practice sessions by reading light material aloud. Read the following poem by Charlotte Perkins Gilman in a lively, expressive manner:

There was once an Anthropoidal Ape,
   Far smarter than the rest,
And everything that they could do
   He always did the best;
So they naturally disliked him,
   And they gave him shoulders cool,
And when they had to mention him
   They said he was a fool.

Cried this pretentious Ape one day,
   "I'm going to be a Man!
And stand upright, and hunt, and fight
   And conquer all I can!
I'm going to cut down forest trees,
   To make my houses higher!
I'm going to kill the Mastodon!
   I'm going to make a fire!"

Loud screamed the Anthropoidal Apes
   With laughter wild and gay;
They tried to catch that boastful one,
   But he always got away.
So they yelled at him in chorus,
   Which he minded not a whit;
And they pelted him with cocoanuts,
   Which didn't seem to hit.
And then they gave him reasons
   Which they thought of much avail,
To prove how his preposterous
   Attempt was sure to fail.
Said the sages, "In the first place
   The thing cannot be done!
And, second, if it could be,
   It would not be any fun!
And, third, and most conclusive,
   And admitting no reply,
You would have to change your nature!
   We should like to see you try!"
They chuckled then triumphantly,
   These lean and hairy shapes,
For these things passed as arguments
   With the Anthropoidal Apes.[15]

If you enjoy this exercise, try reading stories by Dr. Seuss to children. Such tales as *The Cat in the Hat* and *Green Eggs and Ham* should bring out the ham in you! Children normally provide an appreciative audience that encourages lively, colorful, dramatic uses of the voice.

Different cultures have different speech rhythms. In the United States, for example, northerners often speak more rapidly than southerners. These variations in the patterns of speech can create misunderstandings. Californians, who use longer pauses than New Yorkers, may perceive the latter as rude and aggressive, while New Yorkers may see Californians as too laid back or as not having much to say.

Such problems can even go beyond simple misunderstanding. Sociologist Ron Scollon reports that Native American Alaskans show deference to authority by slowing their speech and pausing before responding to questions. Unfortunately, non-Native law enforcement officials often interpret these speech customs as signs of antagonism or hostility, and the Native Americans typically receive longer jail sentences than non-Natives.[16] Guard against stereotyping individuals on the basis of what may be culturally based speech rate variations.

Loudness

No presentation can be effective if the audience can't hear you. Nor will your presentation be successful if you overwhelm your listeners with a voice that is too loud. When you speak before a group, you usually need to speak louder than you do in general conversation. The size of the room, the presence or absence of a microphone, and background noise may also call for adjustments. Take your cues from audience feedback. If you are not loud enough, you may see listeners leaning forward, straining to hear. If you speak too loudly, they may unconsciously lean back, pulling away from the noise.

You should also be aware that different cultures have different norms and expectations concerning appropriate loudness. For example, in some Mediterranean cultures, a loud voice signifies strength and sincerity, whereas in some Asian and American Indian cultures, a soft voice is associated with good manners and education.[17] When members of your audience come from a variety of cultural and ethnic groups, be especially attentive to feedback on this point.

To speak at the proper loudness, you must have good breath control. If you are breathing improperly, you will not have enough force to project your voice so that you can be heard at the back of a room. Improper breathing can also cause you to run out of breath before you finish a phrase or come to an appropriate pause. To check whether you are breathing properly for speaking, do the following:

> **Stand with your feet approximately eight inches apart. Place your hands on your lower rib cage, thumbs to the front, fingers to the back. Take a deep breath—in through your nose and out through slightly parted lips. If you are breathing correctly, you should feel your ribs moving up and out as you inhale.**

Improper breathing affects more than just the loudness of your speech. If you breathe by raising your shoulders, the muscles in your neck and throat will become tense. This can result in a harsh, strained vocal quality. Moreover, you probably will not take in enough air to sustain your phrasing, and the release of air will become difficult to control. The air and sound will all come out with a rush when you drop your shoulders, leading to unfortunate oral punctuation marks when you don't want or need them. To see if you have a problem, try this exercise:

> **Take a normal breath and see how long you can count while exhaling. If you cannot reach fifteen without losing volume or feeling the need to breathe, you need to work on extending your breath control. Begin by counting in one breath to a number comfortable for you, then**

gradually increase the count over successive tries. Do not try to compensate by breathing too deeply. Deep breathing takes too much time and attracts too much attention while you are speaking. Use the longer pauses in your speech to breathe, and make note of your breathing pattern as you practice your speech.

You should vary the loudness of words and phrases in your speech, just as you vary your pitch and your rate of speaking. Changes in loudness are often used to express emotion. The more excited or angry we are, the louder we tend to become. But don't let yourself get caught in the trap of having only two options: loud and louder. Decreasing your volume, slowing your rate, pausing, or dropping your pitch can also express emotion quite effectively. Vanderbilt student speaker Leslie Eason illustrated this dramatically as she introduced her speech on racism. As she read the concluding lines of her poem ("What if I go to heaven, and then to me they tell, White angels enter here, Black angels go to hell"), Leslie reduced her loudness, lowered her pitch, and slowed her rate. These vocal contrasts had a dramatic impact on listeners.

To acquire more variety in loudness, practice the following exercise recommended by Hillman and Jewell: "First, count to five at a soft volume, as if you were speaking to one person. Then, count to five at medium volume, as if speaking to ten or fifteen people. Finally, count to five, as if speaking to thirty or more people."[18] If you tape-record this exercise, you should be able to hear the clear progression in loudness.

Variety

The importance of vocal variety shows up most in speeches that lack it. Speakers who drone on in a monotone, never varying their pitch, rate, or loudness, send a clear message: They tell us that they have little interest in their topic or in their listeners, or that they fear the situation they are in. Variety can make speeches come to life by adding color and interest. One of the best ways to develop variety is to read aloud materials that demand variety to express meaning and feeling. As you read the following selection from *the lives and times of archy and mehitabel*, strive for maximum variation of pitch, rate, and loudness. Incidentally, archy is a cockroach who aspires to be a writer. He leaves typewritten messages for his newspaper-editor mentor, but, because he is a cockroach, he can't type capital letters and never uses punctuation marks. His friend mehitabel, whom he quotes in this message, is an alley cat with grandiose dreams and a dubious reputation.

archy what in hell have i done
to deserve all these kittens
life seems to be just one damn litter after another
after all archy i am an artist
this constant parade of kittens
interferes with my career
its not that i am shy on mother love archy
why my heart would bleed if anything happened to them
and i found it out
a tender heart is the cross i bear
but archy the eternal struggle between life and art
is simply wearing me out[19]

Tape-record yourself while reading this and other favorite poems or dramatic scenes aloud. Compare these practice tapes with your initial self-evaluation tape to see if you have improved in the use of variety in your presentations.

Patterns of Speaking

People often make judgments about others based on their speech patterns. If you slur your words, mispronounce familiar words, or speak with a dialect that sounds unfamiliar to your audience, you may be seen as uneducated or socially inept. When you sound "odd" to your listeners, their attention will be distracted from what you are saying to the way you are saying it. In this section we cover articulation, enunciation, pronunciation, and dialect as they contribute to or detract from speaking effectiveness.

Articulation.   **Articulation** refers to the way you produce individual speech sounds. Some people have trouble making certain sounds. For example, they may substitute a *d* for a *th*, saying "dem" instead of "them." Other sounds that are often misarticulated include *s, l,* and *r.* Severe articulation problems can interfere with effective communication, especially if the audience cannot understand the speaker or if the variations suggest low social or educational status. Such problems are best treated by a speech pathologist, who retrains the individual to produce the sound in a more acceptable manner.

Enunciation.   **Enunciation** refers to the way you pronounce words in context. In casual conversation it is not unusual for people to slur their words— for example, saying "gimme" for "give me." However, careless enunciation causes credibility problems for public speakers. Do you say "Swatuh thought" for "That's what I thought"; "Harya?" for "How are you?"; or "Howjado?" for "How did you do?" These lazy enunciation patterns are not acceptable in public speaking. Check your enunciation patterns on the tape recordings you have made to determine whether you have such a problem. If you do, concentrate on careful enunciation as you practice your speech. Be careful, however, to avoid the opposite problem, inflated, pompous, and pretentious enunciation. Very few speakers can make this work without sounding phony. You should strive to be neither sloppy nor overly precise.

Pronunciation.   **Pronunciation** involves saying words correctly. It includes both using the correct sounds and placing the proper accent on syllables. Because written English does not always indicate the correct pronunciation, we may not be sure how to pronounce words that we first encounter in print. For instance, does the word *chiropodist* begin with an *sh*, a *ch*, or a *k* sound?

If you are not certain how to pronounce a word, consult a dictionary. An especially useful reference is the *NBC Handbook of Pronunciation,* which contains 21,000 words and proper names that sometimes cause problems.[20] When international stories and new foreign leaders first appear in the news, newspapers frequently indicate the correct pronunciation of their names. Check front-page stories in the *New York Times* for guidance with such words.

In addition to having problems pronouncing unfamiliar words, you may find that there are certain words you habitually mispronounce. For example, how do you pronounce the following words?

government	library
February	picture
ask	secretary
nuclear	just
athlete	get

Unless you are careful, you may find yourself slipping into these common mispronunciations:

goverment	liberry
Febuary	pitchur
aks	sekaterry
nuculer	jist
athalete	git

Mispronunciation of such common words can damage your ethos. Most of us know what words we chronically mispronounce and are able to pronounce them correctly when we think about it. The time to think about it is when you are practicing your speech.

Dialect.   A **dialect** is a speech pattern typical of a geographic region or ethnic group. Your dialect usually reflects the area of the country where you were raised or lived for any length of time, or your cultural and ethnic identity.[21] In the United States there are three commonly recognized dialects: eastern, southern, and midwestern. Additionally, there are local variations within the broader dialects. For example, in South Carolina, one finds the Gullah dialect from the islands off the coast, the Lowcountry or Charlestonian accent, the Piedmont variation, and the Appalachian twang.[22] And then there's always "*Bah-stahn*" where you buy a "*lodge budded pup con*" at the movies!

There is no such thing in nature as a superior or inferior dialect. However, there can be occasions when a distinctive dialect is a definite disadvantage or advantage. Listeners prefer speech patterns that are familiar to their ears. Audiences may also have stereotyped preconceptions about people who speak with certain dialects. For example, those raised in the South often associate a northeastern dialect with brusqueness and abrasiveness, and midwesterners may associate a southern dialect with slowness of action and mind. Comedian Jeff Foxworthy has noted:

> **A lot of people think everyone in the South is a redneck. . . . I went to Georgia Tech. I was an engineer at IBM. I just sound stupid. I can't help this, because where I grew up everybody else talked this way. People hear the accent and they want to deduct 100 IQ points.[23]**

You may have to work to overcome such a prejudice against your dialect.

Your dialect should reflect the standard for educated people from your geographic area or ethnic group. You should be concerned about tempering your dialect only if it creates barriers to understanding and identification between you and your audience. Then you may want to work toward softening your dialect so that you lower these barriers for the sake of your message.

Using Your Body to Communicate

Communication with your audience begins before you ever open your mouth. Your facial expression, personal appearance, and air of confidence all convey a message. How do you walk to the front of the room to give your speech? Do you move with confidence and purpose, or do you stumble and shuffle? As you begin your speech, do you look your listeners directly in the eye, or do you stare at the ceiling as though seeking divine inspiration? This **body language** is a nonverbal message that accompanies your speech. It affects how your audience responds to what you say.[24] For public speaking to be effective, your body language must reinforce your verbal language. If your face is expressionless as you urge your listeners to action, you are sending inconsistent messages. Be sure that your body and words both "say" the same thing. Although we discuss separate types of body language in this section, in practice they all work together and are interpreted as a totality by listeners.[25]

Facial Expression and Eye Contact

I knew she was lying the minute she said it. There was guilt written all over her face!

He sure is shifty! Did you see how his eyes darted back and forth? He never did look us straight in the eye!

Most of us believe we can judge people's character, determine their true feelings, and tell whether they are honest from their facial expressions. If there is a conflict between what we see and what we hear, we will usually believe our eyes rather than our ears.

The eyes are the most important element of facial expressiveness. In our culture, frequent and sustained eye contact suggests honesty, openness, and respect. We may think of a person's eyes as windows into the self. If you avoid looking at your audience while you are talking, you are drawing the shades on these windows of communication. A lack of eye contact suggests that you do not care about your listeners, that you are putting something over on them, or that you are afraid of them. Other cultures view eye contact quite differently. For example, in Japan, downcast eyes may signal attentiveness and agreement, while Chinese, Indonesians, and rural Mexicans may lower their eyes as a sign of deference, and some Native Americans may find direct eye contact offensive or aggressive.[26]

When you reach the podium or lectern, turn, pause, and look at your audience. This signals that you want to communicate and prepares people to listen. During your speech, try to make eye contact with all sectors of your audience. Don't just stare at one or two people. You will make them uncomfortable, and other members of the audience will feel left out. First look at people at the front of the room, then shift your focus to the middle, and finally look at those in the rear. You may find that those sitting in the rear of the room are the most difficult to reach. They may have taken a back seat because they don't want to listen or be involved. You may have to work harder to gain and hold their attention. Eye contact is one way you can reach them.

Start your speech with a smile unless this is inappropriate to your message. A smile signals your goodwill toward listeners and your ease in the speaking situation—qualities that should help your ethos.[27] We noticed that several of our Vanderbilt students combined a smile, a pause, and a nod to certain of their listeners to acknowledge a connection between the point they were making and previous speeches by those listeners. This smile-pause-nod combination illustrates an implied *intertextual signifier*. Such signifiers connect and bridge the various speeches heard by a group. They demonstrate that speakers are aware of the overall communication context in which they are speaking, and help listeners make connections as well.

After the initial moment of speaking, your face should reflect and reinforce the meanings of your words. An expressionless face suggests that the speaker is afraid or indifferent. The frozen face may be a mask behind which the speaker hides. The solution lies in selecting a topic that excites you, concentrating on sharing your message, and having the confidence that comes from being well prepared.

You can also try the following exercise:

Utter these statements, using a dull monotone and keeping your face as expressionless as possible:

I am absolutely delighted by your gift.

I don't know when I've ever been this excited.

We don't need to beg for change—we need to demand change.

All this puts me in a very bad mood.

Now repeat them with *exaggerated* vocal variety and facial expression. You may find that your hands and body also want to get involved. Encourage such impulses so that you develop an integrated system of body language.

Movement and Gestures

Most actors learn—often the hard way—that if you want to steal a scene from someone, all you have to do is move around, develop a twitch, or swing a leg. Before long, all eyes will be focused on that movement. This theatrical trick shows that physical movement sometimes can attract more attention than words. All the more reason that your words and gestures should work in harmony and not at cross-purposes. This also means that you should avoid random movements, such as pacing back and forth, twirling your hair, rubbing your eyes, or jingling change in your pockets. Once you are aware of such mannerisms, it is easy to control them.

Your gestures and movement should grow out of your response to your material.[28] They should always appear natural and spontaneous, prompted by your ideas and feelings. They should never look contrived or artificial. For example, you should avoid making a gesture to fit each word or sequence of words you utter. Perhaps every speech instructor has encountered speakers like the one who stood with arms circled above him as he said, "We need to get *around* this problem." That's not a good way to gesture!

Effective gestures involve three phases: *readiness, execution,* and *return.* In the readiness phase, you must be prepared for movement. Your hands and body should be in a position that does not inhibit free action. For example, you cannot gesture if your hands are locked behind your back or jammed into your pockets, or if you are grasping the lectern as though it were a life preserver. Instead, let your hands rest in a relaxed position either at your sides, on the lectern, or in front of you, where they can easily obey the impulse to gesture in support of a point you are making. As you execute a gesture, let yourself move naturally and fully. Don't raise your hand halfway, then stop with your arm frozen awkwardly in space. When you have completed a gesture, let your hands return to the relaxed readiness position, where they will be free to move again when the next impulse to gesture arises.

Do not assume that there is a universal language of gesture. A study of Rwandan culture reveals that Rwandans learn an elaborate code of gestures that is a direct extension of their spoken language.[29] In contrast, our "gesture language" is far less complex and sophisticated. Even more, assuming a universal language of gesture could get you in big trouble with a culturally diverse audience. For example, the American sign for A-OK (thumb and index finger joined in a circle) has an obscene meaning in some cultures, and nodding the head up and down may mean "no" instead of "yes."[30] Management consultant Marc Hequet provides additional insight:

> **The "Hook 'em, Horns!" hand signal beloved of fans who follow the fortunes of the University of Texas Longhorns college football team once started a brawl in a crowded Italian nightclub when Texans at separate tables merrily flashed each other the sign—hand raised, middle fingers held down by thumb, index and pinky extended. The innocents didn't know it but in Italy the gesture is referred to as cuckold horns. It means, "Your wife is being unfaithful."[31]**

From **proxemics**, the study of how humans use space during communication, we can derive two additional principles that help explain the effective use of movement during speeches. The first of these principles suggests that *the physical distance between speakers and listeners affects their sense of closeness or immediacy.* Bill Clinton made effective use of this principle during the second of the televised debates of the 1992 presidential campaign. In the town meeting setting of that debate, Clinton actually rose from his seat after one question and approached the audience as he answered it. His movement towards his listeners suggested that he felt a special closeness for that problem and for them. Clinton's body language also enhanced his identification with the live audience and with the larger viewing audience they represented. In contrast, his opponents, President Bush and Ross Perot, were made to seem distant from these audiences.

It follows also that the greater the physical distance between speaker and audience, the harder it is to achieve identification. This problem gets worse when a lectern acts as a physical barrier. Short speakers can almost disappear behind it! If this is a problem, try speaking from either beside or in front of the lectern so that your body language can work for you. A different problem arises if you move so close to listeners that you make them feel uncomfortable. If they pull back involuntarily in their chairs, you know you have violated their sense of personal space. You should seek the ideal physical distance between yourself and listeners to increase effectiveness.

The second principle of proxemics suggests that *elevation will also affect the sense of closeness between speakers and listeners.* When you speak, you often stand above your seated listeners in a "power position." Because we tend to associate *above* us with power over us, speakers may find that this arrangement discourages identification. Often they will sit on the edge of the desk in

Reducing the physical distance between the speaker and audience can help increase identification.

front of the lectern in a more relaxed and less elevated stance. If your message is informal and requires close identification, or if you are especially tall, you might try this approach.

Personal Appearance

Your clothing and grooming affect how you are perceived. These factors also influence how you see yourself and how you behave. A police officer out of uniform may not act as authoritatively as when dressed in blue. A doctor without a white jacket may behave like just another person. You may have a certain type of clothing that makes you feel comfortable and relaxed. You may even have a special "good luck" outfit that raises your confidence.

When you are scheduled to speak, you should dress in a way that puts you at ease and makes you feel good about yourself. Since your speech is a special occasion, you should treat it as such. By dressing a little more formally than you usually do, you emphasize both to yourself and to the audience that your message is important. As we noted in Chapter 9, your appearance can serve as a presentation aid that complements your message. Like any other aid, it should never compete with your words for attention or be distracting. Always dress in good taste for the situation you anticipate.

The Importance of Practice

It takes a lot of practice to sound natural. Although this statement may seem contradictory, it should not be surprising. Speaking before a group is not your typical way of communicating. Even though most people seem spontaneous and relaxed when talking with a small group of friends, something happens when they walk to the front of a room and face a larger audience of less familiar faces. They often freeze or become stilted and awkward. This blocks the natural flow of communication.

The key to overcoming this problem is to practice until you can respond fully to your ideas as you present them. Your voice, face, and body should express your feelings as well as your thoughts. On the day of your speech, you become a model for your listeners, showing them how they should respond in turn.

To develop an effective extemporaneous style, practice until you feel that the speech is part of you. During practice you can actually hear what you have been preparing and try out the words and techniques you have been considering. What looked like a good idea in your outline may not seem to work as well when it comes to life in spoken words. It is better to discover this fact in rehearsal than before an actual audience.

You will probably want privacy the first two or three times you practice. Even then you should try to simulate the conditions under which the speech will be given. Stand up while you practice. Imagine your listeners in front of you. Picture them responding positively to what you have to say. Address your ideas to them, and visualize your ideas having impact.

If possible, go to your classroom to practice. If this is not possible, find another empty room where the speaking arrangements are similar. Such on-site rehearsal helps you get a better feel for the situation you will face, reducing its strangeness when you make your actual presentation. Begin practicing from your formal outline. Once you feel comfortable, switch to your key-word outline, then practice until the outline transfers from the paper to your head.

Keep material to be read to a minimum. Type or print quotations in large letters so that you can see them easily. Put each quotation on a separate index card or sheet of paper. If you will be using a lectern, position this material so that you can maintain frequent eye contact while reading. If you will speak from beside or in front of the lectern, hold your cards in your hand and raise them when it is time to read. Practice reading your quotations until you can present them naturally while only glancing at your notes. If your speech includes presentation aids, practice handling them until they are smoothly integrated into your presentation. They should seem a natural extension of your verbal message.

speaker's notes

Practicing for Presentation

1 Practice standing up and speaking aloud, if possible in the room where you will be making your presentation.

2 Practice first from your formal outline, then switch to your key-word outline when you feel you have mastered your material.

3 Work on maintaining eye contact with an imaginary audience.

4 Practice integrating your presentation aids into your message.

5 Check the timing of your speech. Add or cut if necessary.

6 Continue practicing until you feel comfortable and confident.

7 Present your speech in a "dress rehearsal" before friends. Make final changes in light of their suggestions.

During practice, you can serve as your own audience by recording your speech and playing it back. If videotaping equipment is available, arrange to record your speech so that you can see as well as hear yourself. Always try to be the toughest critic you will ever have, but also be a constructive critic. Never put yourself down or give up on yourself. Work on specific points of improvement.

In addition to evaluating yourself, you may find it helpful to ask a friend or friends to listen to your presentation. This outside opinion may be more objective than your self-evaluation, and you will get a feel for speaking to real people rather than to an imagined audience. Seek constructive feedback from your friends by asking them specific questions. Was it easy for them to follow you? Do you have any mannerisms (such as twisting your hair or saying "you know" after every other sentence) that distracted them? Were you speaking loudly and slowly enough? Did your ideas seem clear and soundly supported?

On the day that you are assigned to speak, get to class early enough to look over your outline one last time so that it is fresh in your mind. If you have devoted sufficient time and energy to your preparation and practice, you should feel confident about communicating with your audience.

In Summary

An effective *presentation* integrates the nonverbal aspects of voice and body language with the words of your speech. It is characterized by enthusiasm and naturalness. Your voice and bearing should project your sincere commitment but should not call attention to themselves. You should sound and look spontaneous and natural, not contrived or artificial.

Methods of Presentation.   The four major methods of speech presentation are impromptu speaking, memorized presentation, reading from a manuscript, and extemporaneous speaking. In *impromptu speaking* you talk with minimal or no preparation and practice. To present an effective impromptu speech, follow the *PREP formula:* State your *p*oint, give a *r*eason or *e*xample, then restate your *p*oint.

Both *memorized* and *manuscript presentations* require that your speech be written out word for word. Be sure that your speech is written in good oral style. An *extemporaneous presentation* requires careful planning, but the wording is spontaneous. Instructors usually require that you present speeches extemporaneously. Extemporaneous speaking allows you to adapt to *feedback* from your audience. Be especially alert for signs that your audience doesn't understand, has lost interest, or disagrees with you, then make adjustments to your message to overcome these problems.

Following any presentation you may need to answer questions about your material and ideas. While your responses will be impromptu, you should prepare for questions in advance and plan appropriate responses.

Using Your Voice Effectively.   A good speaking voice conveys your meaning fully and clearly. Vocal expressiveness depends on your ability to control your *pitch,* rate, loudness, and variety. Your *habitual pitch* is the level at which you usually speak. Your *optimum pitch* is the level at which you can produce a clear, strong voice with minimal effort. Speaking at your optimum pitch gives your voice flexibility. The *rate* at which you speak can affect the impression you make on listeners. You can control rate to your advantage by using pauses and by changing your pace to match the moods of your material. To speak loudly enough, you need proper breath control. Vary loudness for the sake of emphasis. Vocal variety adds color and interest to a speech, makes a speaker more likable, and encourages identification between speaker and audience.

Articulation, enunciation, pronunciation, and dialect refer to the unique way you give voice to words. *Articulation* concerns the manner in which you produce individual sounds. *Enunciation* refers to the way you utter words in context. Proper *pronunciation* means that you say words correctly. Your *dialect* may identify the area of the country in which you learned language or your cultural or ethnic background. Occasionally, dialect can create identification and comprehension problems between speaker and audience.

Using Your Body Effectively.   You communicate with *body language* as well as with your voice. Eye contact signals listeners that you want to communicate. Your facial expressions should project the meanings of your words. Movement attracts attention; therefore, your movements and gestures must complement your speech, not compete with it. *Proxemics* is the study of how humans use space during communication. Two proxemic principles, distance and elevation, can affect your identification with an audience as you speak. Be sure your grooming and dress are appropriate to the speech occasion and do not detract from your ability to communicate.

The Importance of Practice.   You should practice your speech until you have the sequence of main points and supporting materials well established in your mind. It is best to practice your presentation in conditions similar to those in which you will give your speech. Keep citations or other materials that you must read to a minimum. Tape recording or videotaping can be useful for self-evaluation during rehearsal.

Terms to Know

presentation	optimum pitch
immediacy	rate
expanded conversational style	rhythm
impromptu speaking	vocal distractions
PREP formula	articulation
memorized text presentations	enunciation
manuscript presentation	pronunciation
extemporaneous speaking	dialect
feedback	body language
pitch	proxemics
habitual pitch	

Application

Making Video Presentations

It is quite likely that at some time in your life you will make a video presentation. You may find yourself speaking live on closed-circuit television, videotaping instructions or training materials at work, using community access cable channels to promote a cause, or even appearing on commercial television. Many of these video presentations will be made using a manuscript printed on a teleprompter. At other times you may need to speak impromptu or extemporaneously. With some minor adaptations, the training you receive in this class should serve you well in such situations.[32]

We live in a culture in which the mass media have changed audience expectations. Television especially seems to bring speakers into our homes, giving mass communication more the feeling of personal communication and encouraging a more intimate style of presentation.[33] Because television brings you close to viewers, it magnifies every aspect of your appearance. Therefore, you should dress conservatively, avoiding shiny fabrics, glittery or dangling jewelry, and flashy prints that might "swim" on the screen and distract viewers. You also should not wear white or light pastels because they reflect glare. Ask in advance about the color of the studio backdrop. If you have light hair or if the backdrop will be light, wear dark clothing for contrast. If you have a dark skin tone, request a light or neutral background and consider wearing light-colored clothes.

Both men and women need makeup to achieve a natural look on television. Have powder available to reduce skin shine or hide a five o'clock shadow. Women should use makeup conservatively because the camera will intensify it. Avoid glasses with tinted lenses: They will appear even darker on the screen. Even untinted lenses may cause problems, as they reflect glare from the studio lights. Wear contact lenses if you have them. If you can see well enough to read the monitor without glasses, leave them off.

Television requires a conversational mode of presentation. Your audience may be single individuals or small groups assembled in their homes. Imagine yourself talking with another person in an informal setting. While intimate, however, television is also remote. Since you will have no immediate feedback to help you, your meaning must be instantly clear. Use language that is colorful and concrete so that your audience will remember your material. Use previews and internal summaries to keep viewers on track. You may use visual aids to enhance comprehension, but be sure to confer in advance with studio personnel to be certain your materials will work well in that setting. For example, large poster boards displayed on an easel are more difficult to handle in video presentations than smaller materials. (See related considerations in Chapter 9.)

Vocal variety and facial expressions will be your most important forms of body language. Remember that television will magnify all your movements and vocal changes. Slight head movements and underplayed facial expressions should be enough to reinforce your ideas. Avoid abrupt changes in loudness as a means of vocal emphasis. Rely instead on subtle changes in tempo, pitch, and inflection, and on pauses, to drive your point home.

For most televised presentations, timing is crucial. Five minutes of air time means five minutes, not five minutes and ten seconds. If you run over the time, you may be cut off in midsentence. For this reason, television favors manuscript presentations read from a teleprompter. The teleprompter controls timing and preserves a sense of direct eye contact between speakers and listeners. Ask studio personnel how to use the equipment.

Try to rehearse your presentation in the studio with the production personnel. Develop a positive relationship with the studio technicians. Your success depends in large part on how well they do their jobs. Provide them with a manuscript marked to show when you will move around or use a visual aid. Practice speaking from the teleprompter if you will be using one. Use the microphone correctly. Don't blow into it to see if it's working. Remember that the microphone will pick up *all* sounds, including shuffling papers or tapping on a lectern. If you use a stand or hand-held microphone, position it about 10 inches below your mouth. The closer the microphone is to your mouth, the more it will pick up unwanted noises like whistled "*s*" sounds or tongue clicks. Remember that microphones with cords will restrict your movement. If you plan to move about during your presentation, know where the cord is so that you don't trip over it.

Don't be put off by distractions as you practice and present your speech. Studio technicians may need to confer with one another while you are speaking. This is a necessary part of their business. They are not being rude. Even though they are in the room with you, they are not your audience. Keep your mind on your ideas and your eyes on the camera. The camera may seem strange at first, but think of it as a friendly face waiting to hear what you have to say. Your eye contact with the camera becomes your eye contact with your audience. Be prepared for lighting and voice checks before the actual taping begins. Use this time to run through your introduction. Before you begin your speech and after you finish, always assume that any microphone or camera near you is "live." Don't say or do anything you wouldn't want your audience to hear or see.

Even though the situation is strange, try to relax. If you are standing, stand at ease. If you are sitting, lean slightly forward as if you were talking to someone in the chair next to you. The floor director will give you a countdown before the camera starts to roll. Clear your throat and be ready to start on cue. Begin with a smile, if appropriate, as you make eye contact with the camera. If several cameras are used, a red light on top will tell you which camera is on. During your presentation, the studio personnel may communicate with you using special sign language. The director will tell you what cues they will use.[34]

If you are using a teleprompter script, it will appear directly below or on the lens of the camera. Practice your speech ahead of time until you *almost* have it memorized so that you can glance at the script as a whole. If you have to read it word for word, your eyes may be continually shifting (which will make you look suspicious). If you make a mistake, keep going. Sometimes "mistakes" are improvements. Do not stop unless the director says "cut." If appropriate, smile when you finish and continue looking at the camera to allow time for a fade-out.

Notes

1. Janet Beavin Bavelas, "Redefining Language: Nonverbal Linguistic Acts in Face-to-Face Dialogue," 1992 Aubrey Fisher Memorial Lecture, presented at the University of Utah, October 1992.
2. James C. McCroskey, *An Introduction to Rhetorical Communication*, 3rd ed. (Englewood Cliffs, N.J.: Prentice-Hall, 1993), pp. 263–264.
3. McCroskey, p. 264.
4. Virginia P. Richmond, James C. McCroskey, and S. K. Payne, *Nonverbal Behavior in Interpersonal Relations*, 2nd ed. (Englewood Cliffs, N.J.: Prentice-Hall, 1991), pp. 208–228.
5. Michael Duffy, "Picture of Health," *Time*, 4 October 1993, pp. 28+, *Time Almanac Reference Ed*, CD-ROM, Compact, 1994.
6. "A Letter to Our Readers," *Newsweek*, 4 October 1993, p. 29.
7. These guidelines for handling questions and answers are a compendium of ideas from the following sources: Stephen D. Body, "Nine Steps to a Successful Question-and-Answer Session," *Management Solutions*, May 1988, pp. 16–17; Teresa Brady, "Fielding Abrasive Questions During Presentations," *Supervisory Management*, February 1993, p. 6; J. Donald Ragsdale and Alan L. Mikels, "Effects of Question Periods on a Speaker's Credibility with a Television Audience," *Southern States Communication Journal* 40 (1975): 302–312; Dorothy Sarnoff, *Never Be Nervous Again* (New York: Ballantine, 1987); Laurie Schloff and Marcia Yudkin, *Smart Speaking: Sixty-Second Strategies* (New York: Holt, 1991); and Alan Zaremba, "Q and A: The Other Part of Your Presentation," *Management World*, January–February 1989, pp. 8–10.
8. Roger Ailes, *You Are the Message: Getting What You Want by Being Who You Are* (New York: Doubleday, 1988), p. 170.
9. Howard Giles and Arlene Franklyn-Stokes, "Communicator Characteristics," in *Handbook of International and Intercultural Communication*, ed. Molefi Kete Asante and William B. Gudykunst (Newbury Park, Calif.: Sage, 1989), pp. 117–144.
10. Jon Eisenson, *Voice and Diction: A Program for Improvement* (New York: Macmillan, 1974), p. vii.
11. Adapted from Stewart W. Hyde, *Television and Radio Announcing*, 6th ed. (Boston: Houghton Mifflin, 1991), pp. 80–85.
12. N. Scott Momaday, *The Way to Rainy Mountain* (Albuquerque: University of New Mexico Press, 1969), p. 5.
13. Carole Douglis, "The Beat Goes On: Social Rhythms Underlie All Our Speech and Actions," *Psychology Today*, November 1987, p. 36(6), *Magazine Database Plus*, online, CompuServe, November 1995.
14. William Price Fox, "Eugene Talmadge and Sears Roebuck Co.," *Southern Fried Plus Six* (New York: Ballantine Books, 1968), p. 36.
15. Poem, "Similar Cases," by Charlotte Perkins Gilman, from *In This Our World* (reprinted in Wayland Maxfield Parrish, *Reading Aloud: A Technique in the Interpretation of Literature* (New York: The Ronald Press Company, 1941), pp. 144–145).
16. Cited in Douglis, p. 36(6).

17. Michael L. Hecht, Peter A. Andersen, and Sidney A. Ribeau, "The Cultural Dimensions of Nonverbal Communication," in *Handbook of International and Intercultural Communication*, pp. 163–185; and Larry A. Samovar and Richard E. Porter, *Communication Between Cultures* (Belmont, Calif.: Wadsworth, 1991), pp. 205–206.

18. Ralph Hillman and Delorah Lee Jewell, *Work for Your Voice* (Murfreesboro, TN: Copymatte, 1986), p. 63.

19. Don Marquis, adapted from "mehitabel and her kittens," in *the lives and times of archy and mehitabel.* Copyright ©1927 by Doubleday and Company, Inc. Reprinted by permission of the publisher.

20. *NBC Handbook of Pronunciation*, 4th ed. (New York: Harper, 1991).

21. William B. Gudykunst et al., "Language and Intergroup Communication," in *Handbook of International and Intercultural Communication*, pp. 145–162.

22. Carolanne Griffith-Roberts, "Let's Talk Southern," *Southern Living*, February 1995, p. 82. For a detailed explication of regional dialect variances, see Charles K. Thomas, *An Introduction to the Phonetics of American English*, 2nd ed. (New York: Ronald, 1958), pp. 191–260.

23. "Jeff Foxworthy: From Hootenanny to Hoosier," *Satellite TV Week*, 28 July–3 August 1996, p. l.

24. Samovar and Porter, p. 177.

25. Peter A. Andersen, "Nonverbal Immediacy in Interpersonal Communication," in *Multichannel Integrations of Nonverbal Behavior*, ed. A. W. Siegman and S. Feldstein (Mahwah, N.J.: Erlbaum, 1985).

26. S. Ishii, "Characteristics of Japanese Nonverbal Communication Behavior," *Communication,* Summer 1973, pp. 163–180; Samovar and Porter, pp. 198–200; "Understanding Culture: Don't Stare at a Navajo," *Psychology Today,* June 1974, p. 107.

27. Research psychologist Carolyn Copper has found that newscasters influence voters when they smile while speaking of candidates, further evidence of the power of facial expression ("A Certain Smile," *Psychology Today*, January–February 1992, p. 20).

28. Charlotte I. Lee and Timothy Gura, *Oral Interpretation*, 8th ed. (Boston: Houghton Mifflin, 1992), pp. 118–119.

29. Edouard Gasarabwe-Laroche, "Meaningful Gestures: Nonverbal Communication in Rwandan Culture," *UNESCO Courier,* September 1993, pp. 31–33.

30. Mary Munter, "Cross Cultural Communication for Managers," *Business Horizons*, May–June 1993, p. 69(10). For additional insights into cultural differences in nonverbal communication, see Roger Axtell, *Gestures: The Do's and Taboos of Body Language Around the World* (New York: Wiley, 1991); E. Hall, *Understanding Cultural Differences* (Yarmouth, Me.: Intercultural Press, 1990); J. Mole, *When in Rome . . . A Business Guide to Cultures and Customs in Twelve European Nations* (New York: AMACOM, 1991); D. Ricks, *Big Business Blunders* (Homewood, Ill.: Dow Jones-Irwin, 1983); and C. Storti, *The Art of Crossing Cultures* (Yarmouth, Me.: Intercultural Press, 1990).

31. Marc Hequet, "The Fine Art of Multicultural Meetings," *Training,* July 1993, p. 29(5).

32. The authors are indebted to Professor Roxanne Gee of the television and film area in the Department of Communication at the University of Memphis for her assistance and suggestions in putting together this advice.

33. Ailes, pp. 15–19.

34. Illustrations of major video hand signals may be found in Hyde, pp. 80–85.

PART FOUR

Types of Public Speaking

12 Informative Speaking

*T*he improvement of understanding is for two ends: first, our own increase of knowledge; secondly, to enable us to deliver that knowledge to others.

—John Locke

This chapter will help you

- understand the functions of informative speaking
- apply principles of motivation and attention to help listeners learn
- learn the types of informative speeches and how to design them
- prepare and present informative speeches

*I*n ancient Greek mythology Prometheus was punished by the other gods for showing humans how to make fire. These jealous gods knew that people would now be able to warm themselves, cook food, take advantage of the extended light, and share knowledge as they huddled around their campfires. They would build a civilization and challenge the gods themselves through the power of their learning. These mythical gods had every right to be angry with Prometheus. He had given the first significant speech of demonstration.

THIS TALE OF Prometheus reminds us that information is power. Because we cannot personally experience everything that may be important or interesting to us, we must rely on the knowledge of others to expand our understanding and competence. *Sharing knowledge is the essence of informative speaking.*

Shared information can be important to survival. Early detection and warning systems alert us to impending natural disasters, and news of medical breakthroughs tells us how to increase our life span. Beyond simply enabling us to live, information helps us to live better. Information can help us control the world around us and even manage people. It follows that people who can deliver information are highly valued. In this chapter we look at the functions of informative communication, suggest ways to help your listeners learn, discuss the major types of informative speeches, and explain some basic speech designs that are appropriate to these types of speeches. Our objective is to help you bring fire to your listeners.

The Functions of Informative Speaking

Informative speaking is defined by its function. In the same speech, you might introduce yourself, provide information, urge action, and celebrate values. *But if your main purpose is to share knowledge, then we call the speech informative.*

Sharing knowledge can be vital in four ways. First, informative speaking can empower listeners by giving them new ideas and increasing their competence. Second, informative speaking can shape listener perceptions. Third, informative speaking can help set the agenda of public concerns. Finally, informative speaking can clarify options for action.

333

Sharing Information and Ideas

An informative speech *gives to* listeners rather than *asks of* them. The demands on the audience are relatively low. As an informative speaker, you want enthusiastic attention from your listeners. You want them to understand and use what you tell them, but you do not try to make them change values or enact reforms. For example, one student speaker gave an informative speech in which she revealed the dangers of prolonged exposure to ultraviolet radiation, but she did not urge her audience to boycott tanning salons. Although informative speaking makes modest demands on the listener, the demands on the speaker are high. Good informative speakers must have a thorough understanding of their subject. It is one thing to know something well enough to satisfy yourself. It is quite another to know it well enough to assume the responsibilities of communication.

By sharing information, an informative speech reduces ignorance. An informative speech does not simply repeat something the audience already knows. Rather, *the **informative value** of a speech is measured by how much new and important information or understanding it provides the audience.* As you prepare your informative speech, ask yourself the following questions:

> Is my topic significant enough to merit an informative speech?
>
> What do my listeners already know about my topic?
>
> What more do they need to know?
>
> Do I have sufficient understanding of my topic to help others understand it better?

The answers to these questions should help you plan a speech with high informative value.

In informative speaking, the speaker functions basically as a teacher. To teach people effectively, you must arouse and sustain their attention by adapting your message to their interests and needs. You must make listeners aware of how important the new information is. When you have finished, they should feel enriched by the communication transaction.

Shaping Audience Perceptions

When speakers share information with audiences, they also share their points of view. It is virtually impossible to cover everything there is to know about any important subject in a short message. Therefore, speakers are always selective with regard to what information they communicate, highlighting the ideas and material that they believe best represent the subject. When we see the subject through their eyes, we really see their interpretations of it. The images they provide are often colored by their feelings. This selective exposure can influence the way we respond to later communications on the subject, especially when this is our first exposure to it.

This power of informative speaking to influence our perceptions can serve a **prepersuasive function**, preparing us for later persuasive speaking. Suppose, for example, you heard *one* of two speeches on teaching as a career choice. One was presented by an enthusiastic teacher who described the personal rewards he obtained from teaching and stressed the joys of helping children learn. The other was presented by a teacher suffering from "burnout" who focused on classroom discipline problems and administrative red tape. Neither speaker suggested that you should or should not become a teacher. Each provided what he or she believed was an accurate picture of teaching as a profession. But each created a different predisposition. If you heard only the first speaker, you might be more inclined to consider a message urging you to become a teacher than if you heard only the second speaker.

If you have strong feelings about your subject, you must work hard *not* to present a distorted perspective. If listeners feel you are blurring the truth or displaying a bias, they will dismiss your message as unreliable and lower their estimation of your character and competence.

Setting the Agenda

The amount of information reaching people today is almost overwhelming. This flood of information from the mass media serves an **agenda-setting function.**[1] As the media present the "news," they also tell us what we *should* be thinking about. By the amount of coverage allotted to a topic, the media establish the importance of that topic in the public mind.

Informative speaking also performs an agenda-setting role. As it directs our attention to certain subjects, it influences what we feel is important. The informative speech "The 'Monument' at Wounded Knee," which appears in Appendix B, demonstrates this agenda-setting function as it shapes perceptions about our country's policy toward Native Americans. Hearing such a message could predispose listeners both to believe that the issue is important and to favor better treatment for this group. As you prepare an informative speech, remember the power you have to establish the importance of your topic in the minds of your listeners. Consider the ethical consequences of your words.

Clarifying Options

An informative speech also can reveal and clarify options for action. Information expands our awareness, opens new horizons, and suggests fresh possibilities. Information can also help us discard unworkable options. The better we understand a subject, the more intelligent the choices we can make on issues that surround it. For example, what should we know about obesity? Informative speeches may tell us about the consequences of doing something or nothing to correct this condition. They may teach us about the medical soundness of different diets. They may also inform us about the roles of exercise and counseling in weight control. Such information would expand our options for dealing with obesity.

Informative speakers carry a large ethical burden: They must communicate responsible knowledge of their topics. A responsible informative speech should cover all major positions on a topic and present all vital information. Although speakers may have strong feelings on a subject, it is unethical to deliberately omit or distort information that is necessary for audience understanding. Similarly, speakers who are unaware of options or information because they have not done the research that will *make* them aware also are irresponsible. As you conduct your research, seek out material from sources that present different perspectives. The two speeches on the teaching profession mentioned earlier demonstrate potential abuses of the option-clarifying

FIGURE 12.1

The Functions of Informative Speaking

Function	Important When
1. Sharing information and ideas	You wish to introduce new ideas and knowledge of a subject.
2. Shaping audience perceptions	You want to prepare listeners for future persuasive messages by revealing a situation they have not been aware of.
3. Setting the agenda	You wish to make listeners realize that a topic is important and merits their serious consideration.
4. Clarifying options for action	You want to provide information that makes listeners aware of the positive and negative aspects of options for action so that they can make informed, intelligent decisions.

function of informative speaking. If the speeches are presented as *representative* of teaching as a career, then both speakers are guilty of overgeneralizing from limited personal experience.

Helping Your Audience Learn

The success of an informative speech can be measured by the answer to one simple question: "Does the listener learn from the speech?" As an informative speaker, you need to apply basic principles of learning to make your speeches effective. To help your listeners learn and remember your message, you must motivate them by establishing the relevance of your message for their lives, hold their attention throughout your message, and structure your speech so that it is clear and readily understood.

Motivation

To motivate listeners, you must tell them why your message is important to them. In Chapter 4 we discussed motivation as a factor in audience analysis. Now we consider motivation in terms of giving listeners a reason to learn. Go back to the list of seven motives summarized in Figure 4.1 (page 94) and determine which of these might be most relevant to your topic and your audience. Then tie your message to these motives, either through direct statements or through interesting examples or narratives. For example, you might relate a speech on how to interview for a job to the motives of control and independence. You could begin by talking about the problem of finding a good job in today's marketplace and provide an example that illustrates how a successful interview can make the difference between who gets hired and who does not. As you preview the body of your speech, you might say, "Today, I'm going to describe four factors that can determine whether you get the job of your dreams. First. . . ." In this case you have given your audience a reason for wanting to listen to the rest of your speech. You have begun the learning process by motivating your listeners.

Attention

Once you have established the importance of your message, you must sustain your listeners' attention throughout your speech. In this section we examine six basic factors that affect attention: *intensity, repetition, novelty, activity, contrast,* and *relevance.* We also explain how to use these factors to maintain interest and promote learning.

Intensity.   Our eyes are drawn automatically to bright lights, and we turn to investigate loud noises. In public communication, intense language and vivid images can be used to attract and hold attention. You can emphasize a point by supplying examples that magnify its importance. You can also achieve intensity through the use of presentation aids and vocal variety. Note how Stephen Huff holds attention through the intensity of his descriptions of the New Madrid earthquakes that struck the south-central area of the United States in the early nineteenth century:

> **The Indians tell of the night that lasted for a week and the way the "Father of Waters"—the Mississippi River—ran backwards. Waterfalls were formed on the river. Islands disappeared. Land that was once in Arkansas—on the west bank of the river—ended up in Tennessee—on the east bank of the river. Church bells chimed as far away as New Orleans and Boston. Cracks up to ten feet wide opened and closed in the earth. Geysers squirted sand fifteen feet into the air. Whole forests sank into the earth as the land turned to quicksand. . . . Reelfoot Lake—over ten miles long—was formed when the Mississippi River changed its course.**

Repetition.   Sounds, words, or phrases that are repeated attract our attention and embed themselves in our consciousness. Skillful speakers frequently repeat key words or phrases to stress the importance of points, to help listeners focus on the sequence of ideas, to unify the message, and to help people remember what they have heard.

Repetition is the strategy that underlies alliteration and parallel construction. As we saw in Chapter 10, alliteration can lend vividness to the main ideas of informative speeches: "Today, I will discuss how the *Mississippi* River *m*eanders from *M*innesota to the sea." The repetition of the *m* sound catches our attention and emphasizes the statement. In like manner, parallel construction can establish a pattern that sticks in your listeners' minds (see Chapters 7, 8, and 10). For example, repeated questions and answers such as "What is our goal? It is to . . ." sustain attention through parallel construction.

Novelty.   We are attracted to anything new or unusual. A novel phrase can fascinate listeners and hold their attention. In the speech reprinted at the end of Chapter 14, James Cardoza found a novel way to describe the magnitude of pollution in this country. After documenting that nineteen million tons of garbage are picked up each year along the beaches of the United States, Jim concluded: "And that's just the tip of the wasteberg." His invented word, "wasteberg," was effective because it reminded listeners of "iceberg," and that in turn connoted for them the vastness of the problem. Some famous novel expressions in American history that have aroused attention for political programs and philosophies are "New Deal," "the New Frontier," "the Great Society," "Star Wars" (Strategic Defense Initiative), and "Contract with America."

Activity. Our eyes are attracted to moving objects. Gestures, physical movement, and presentation aids can all add activity to your speech. You can also create a sense of activity in a speech by using concrete words, vocal variety, and a narrative structure that moves your speech along. Note the sense of action and urgency, as well as the invitation to act, in the conclusion of this student's speech:

> **I don't know what you're going to do, but I know what I'm going to do. I'm going to march right down tomorrow and register to vote. There's too much at stake not to. Why don't you join me?**

A lively example or an exciting story can also bring a speech to life and engage your listeners.

Contrast. Opposites attract attention. If you work in a noisy environment and it suddenly becomes quiet, the stillness can seem deafening. Similarly, abrupt changes in vocal pitch or rate of speaking will draw attention. Presenting the pros and cons of a situation creates a sense of conflict and drama that listeners often find arresting. You can also highlight contrasts by speaking of such opposites as life and death, light and dark, or the highs and lows of a situation.

In a speech dramatizing the need to learn more about AIDS, a speaker introduced two or three specific examples with the statement "Let me introduce you to *Death*." Then, as the speech moved to the promise of medical research, she said, "Now let me introduce you to *Life*." This usage combined repetition and contrast to create a dramatic effect.

Surprise is necessary for contrast to be effective. Once people become accustomed to an established pattern, they no longer think about it. They notice any abrupt, dramatic change from the pattern.

Relevance. Things that are related to our personal needs or interests attract our attention. Research has indicated that sleepers respond with changes in brain-wave patterns when their names are mentioned. Parents have been known to sleep through severe thunderstorms, yet be wakened by the faint sounds of their infant crying. Relevance is essential to public speaking as well.

Allison McEntire created relevance for her agenda-setting speech on smoking advertisements by placing a large jar of cigarette butts on the table by the lectern.

> **So you think the cigarette advertisers are losing their fight to recruit smokers at American colleges and universities? Here's what I collected myself in about 45 minutes at noon yesterday, right around the outside of this building. These are our butts. Vanderbilt student butts. Think of all the damaged lungs these represent, right here in this building.**

The striking relevance of the presentation aid she used made it hard to ignore her point.

Retention

Even the best information is useless unless your listeners remember and use it. Repetition, relevance, and structural factors can all be used to help your audience remember your message. The more frequently we hear or see anything, the more likely we are to retain it. This is why advertisers bombard us with slogans to keep their product names in our consciousness. These slogans may be repeated in all of their advertisements, regardless of the visuals or narratives presented. The repetition of key words or phrases in a speech also helps the audience remember. In his famous civil rights speech in Washington, D.C., Martin Luther King's repetition of the phrase "I have a dream . . ." became the hallmark of the speech and is now used as its title.

Relevance is also important to retention. Our minds filter new information as we receive it, associating it with things we already know and unconsciously evaluating it for its potential usefulness or importance. Our advice seems simple, but is profoundly important. *If you want listeners to remember your message, tell them why and how it relates to their lives.*

As we saw in Chapter 7, structural factors also affect how readily a message can be understood and retained. Previews, summaries, and clear transitions can help your audience remember your message. The way you organize your material also has an effect on retention. Suppose you were given the following list of words to memorize:

> **north, man, hat, daffodil, green, tulip, coat, boy, south, red, east, shoes, gardenia, woman, purple, marigold, gloves, girl, yellow, west**

It looks rather difficult, but see what happens when we rearrange the words:

> **north, south, east, west**
> **man, boy, woman, girl**
> **daffodil, tulip, gardenia, marigold**
> **green, red, purple, yellow**
> **hat, coat, shoes, gloves**

In the first example, you have what looks like a random list of words. In the second, the words have been organized by categories: Now you have five groups of four related words to remember. Material that is presented in a consistent and orderly fashion is much easier for your audience to understand

Helping Listeners Learn

1 Approach your topic in a fresh and interesting way.
2 Show listeners how they can benefit from your information.
3 Sustain attention with vivid examples and exciting stories.
4 Organize your material clearly to make it easy to understand.
5 Use strategic repetition to help listeners remember.
6 Provide previews and summaries to aid retention.

speaker's notes

and retain. In the remainder of this chapter, we look at the major types of informative speeches and the design formats that are most often used to structure informative messages.

Types of Informative Speeches

As we mentioned earlier, the major purpose of an informative speech is to share knowledge in order to expand your listeners' understanding or competence. To meet this challenge, an informative speech will typically describe, demonstrate, or explain its subject. These different procedures divide informative speaking into types. As we discuss them, we will also consider briefings as an important subtype of informative speaking.

Speeches of Description

Often the specific purpose of a speech is to describe a particular activity, object, person, or place. A **speech of description** should give the audience a clear picture of your subject, such as the one Stephen Huff painted of the New Madrid earthquakes of 1811. An effective speech of description relies

Speeches of description often provide background information to aid understanding.

heavily on the artful use of language. The words must be clear, concrete, and colorful to carry both the substance and the feeling of the message. The speech "The 'Monument' at Wounded Knee" in Appendix B provides vivid word-pictures. Thus, the landscape is not simply desolate; it is characterized by "flat, sun-baked fields and an occasional eroded gully." The speaker goes on to describe the monument:

> **The monument itself rests on a concrete slab to the right of the grave. It's a typical, large, old-fashioned granite cemetery marker, a pillar about six feet high topped with an urn—the kind of gravestone you might see in any cemetery with graves from the turn of the century. The inscription tells us that it was erected by the families of those who were killed at Wounded Knee. Weeds grow through the cracks in the concrete at its base.**

The topic, purpose, and materials selected for a descriptive speech should suggest the appropriate design. The "Monument" speech follows a spatial pattern. Other designs that may be used for speeches of description include the sequential, categorical, and comparative designs, which are discussed later in this chapter.

Speeches of Demonstration

The **speech of demonstration** shows the audience how to do something important or pleasurable. Dance instructors teach us how to do the Texas two-step. Others may tell us how to access the Internet, or how to prepare for the Law School Admission Test, or even how to build a fire. The tip-off to the speech of demonstration is the phrase *how to*. What these examples have in common is that they demonstrate a process.

Successful speeches of demonstration empower listeners so that they can perform the process themselves. Jeffrey O'Connor gave his New Mexico audience some vital how-to information as he demonstrated the process of reading a textbook efficiently. He took them through a five-step tour of the process, with each step constituting a main point of his speech. His presentation is outlined later in this chapter as an example of sequential design, often appropriate for speeches of this nature.

Another form of speech of demonstration is illustrated by a speech first presented by Suzanne Jones at the University of Memphis. Suzanne took her listeners on a verbal tour of Yellowstone Park, showing them how to access major attractions there. Her speech is outlined later as an example of spatial design.

One final consideration: Most speeches of demonstration are helped by the use of presentation aids. The aids can range from yourself as a model performing the activity, to objects used in the process you are demonstrating, to an overhead projection or poster listing the steps in order. Stephen Huff distributed a handout that listed the steps to follow in case of an earthquake (he circulated this *after* his speech so that it would not compete for his listeners' attention). If you are preparing a speech of demonstration, review the materials on presentation aids in Chapter 9 to determine what you could use to help your audience better understand your message. When you are demonstrating a process, "show and tell" is usually much more effective than just telling.

Speeches of Explanation

The **speech of explanation** offers information about subjects that typically are more abstract than the subjects of descriptive or demonstrative speeches. Abstract subjects are sometimes harder to understand. Katherine Rowan, a communication scholar at Purdue University, suggests that speakers should:

1. Define the subject in terms of its critical features.
2. Compare an example with a nonexample. (Show an instance that *could* be considered an example, but is not.)
3. Provide more examples to reinforce what listeners have learned.[2]

Note how Stephen Lee uses this technique in his speech of explanation "The Trouble with Numbers." (The complete text of this speech may be found in Appendix B.) Stephen observes that when military personnel were added to the employment pool used to compute unemployment figures, the rate of unemployment went down. But did the actual number of the unemployed? Here is how Stephen handled this technique:

> There is a more important question that needs to be answered. Look at what happened to the number. It changed. Look at what happened to the way the number was computed. It changed, too. But what happened to the very real problem of civilian unemployment, which we all assumed this number to represent? It had not changed at all. It all goes back to what Lester T. Thurow said in his basic theory of economics, "A difference is only a difference if it truly makes a difference." Many times a difference in a number does not represent a difference in the real world. This also was the case in the late 1970s when housing was taken out of the consumer price index.[3]

Speeches of explanation face an even greater challenge when the information they offer runs counter to generally accepted beliefs or lay theories of technical phenomena. For example, at one time it was difficult for the Western world to accept that the earth was not the center of the universe. That idea ran counter to religious doctrine and got many scientists in serious trouble. Less than four hundred years ago, Galileo was persecuted and imprisoned for advancing such a view. Rowan describes a more contemporary case:

> Perhaps there is no better example of the problems created by lay theories than in research on seat belt safety campaigns. . . . A particularly resilient obstacle to belt use is the erroneous but prevalent belief that hitting one's head on a windshield while traveling at 30 miles per hour is an experience much like doing so when a car is stationary. . . . If people understood that the experience would be much more similar to falling from a three-story building and hitting the pavement face first, one obstacle to the wearing of seat belts would be easier to overcome.[4]

As her example indicates, dramatic analogies—such as comparing an auto accident at thirty miles per hour to falling out of a building—can help break through our resistance to new ideas that defy folk wisdom. Rowan also recommends that speakers

1. State the prevalent view.
2. Acknowledge its apparent legitimacy.
3. Demonstrate its inadequacy.
4. Show the greater adequacy of the more expert view.

Such a strategy of comparisons and contrasts can help listeners accept the new information and use it in their lives. Speeches of explanation may also use other designs described later in this chapter.

Briefings

A **briefing** is a short informative presentation in an organizational setting. Briefings often take place during meetings, as when you are called upon to give a status report or update on a project for which you have responsibility. Briefings also take place in one-on-one situations, as when you report to your supervisor at work.

Most "how-to" books on communicating in organizations stress the importance of brevity, clarity, and directness.[5] When executives in eighteen organizations were asked, "What makes a poor presentation?" they responded with the following list of factors

- Confusing organization
- Poor delivery
- Too much technical jargon
- Too long
- No examples or comparisons[6]

These observations suggest some clear guidelines to follow as you prepare to make a briefing.

Informative presentations are basic to many employee training programs.

speaker's notes

Preparing for a Briefing

1 Always be prepared to report in a meeting.
2 Keep your remarks short and to the point.
3 Start with a preview and end with a summary.
4 Have no more than three main points.
5 Use facts and statistics, expert testimony, brief examples, and comparison and contrast for emphasis.
6 Avoid technical jargon.
7 Present your report with assurance.
8 Be prepared to answer tough questions.

First, a briefing should be what its name suggests: brief. This means that you must cut out any material that is not related directly to your main points. Keep your introduction and conclusions short. Begin with a preview and end with a summary.

Second, organize your ideas before you open your mouth. How can you possibly be organized when you are suddenly called upon in a meeting to "tell us about your project"? The answer is simple: Prepare in advance. (Also, see our guidelines for making an impromptu presentation in Chapter 11.) *Never go into any meeting in which there is even the slightest possibility that you might be asked to report without a skeleton outline of a presentation.* Select a simple design and make a key-word outline of the points you would cover and the order in which you would cover them. Put this outline on a note card and carry it in your pocket. Your supervisors and colleagues will be impressed by your foresight.

Third, rely heavily on carefully verified facts and figures, expert testimony, and short examples for supporting materials. Don't drift off into long stories. Use comparison and contrast to make your points clearly and directly.

Fourth, adapt your language to your audience. If you are an engineer reporting on a project to a group of nonengineer managers, use the language of management, not the language of engineering. Tell them what they need to know in language they can understand.

Fifth, present your message with confidence. Be sure everyone can see and hear you. Stand up, if necessary. Look listeners in the eye. Speak firmly with an air of assurance. After all, the project is yours, and you are the expert on it.

Finally, be prepared to deal with questions, especially tough ones. Answer questions forthrightly and honestly. No one likes bad news, but worse news will come if you don't deliver the bad news to those who need to know it *when they need to know it.* Review our suggestions for handling question-and-answer sessions in Chapter 11.

Speech Designs

There are five major design formats that are appropriate for most informative speeches: spatial, sequential, categorical, comparative, and causation. These designs may also be used in persuasive and ceremonial speeches.

Spatial Design

A **spatial design** is appropriate for speeches that locate subjects within some actual, physical context. Because the order of discussion is based upon the nearness of things to one another, the pattern follows the principle of proximity, discussed in Chapter 7. Suppose someone asked you to name the time zones in the United States. If you live in Washington, D.C., you would probably reply, "Eastern, Central, Mountain, and Pacific." If you live in Washington state, you might answer, "Pacific, Mountain, Central, and Eastern."[7] Either answer would follow a spatial pattern, taking yourself as the point of reference.

Most people are familiar with maps and can readily visualize directions. A speech using a spatial design provides listeners with a verbal map. Spatial designs are especially useful for speeches of description, so that listeners can visualize clearly the relationships of objects to one another, or for speeches of demonstration, which show listeners how to actually go through the pattern.

To develop a spatial design, first select a starting point and then take your audience on an *orderly*, systematic journey to some destination. Once you begin a pattern of movement, you should stay with it to the end of the speech. If you change directions in the middle, the audience may get lost. Be sure to complete the pattern so that you satisfy listeners' desire for closure.

The body of a speech of demonstration using a spatial design might have the following general format:

> *Preview:* When you visit Yellowstone, stop first at the South Entrance Visitor's Center, then drive northwest to Old Faithful, north to Mammoth Hot Springs, and southeast to the Grand Canyon of the Yellowstone.

I. Your first stop should be at the South Entrance Visitor's Center.
   A. Talk with a park ranger to help plan your trip.
   B. Attend a lecture or film to orient yourself.
   C. Pick up materials and maps to make your tour more meaningful.
II. Drive northwest through the Geyser Valley to Old Faithful.
   A. Hike the boardwalks in the Upper-Geyser Basin.
   B. Join the crowds waiting for Old Faithful to erupt on schedule.
   C. Have lunch at Old Faithful Inn.
III. Continue north to Mammoth Hot Springs.
   A. Plan to spend the night at the lodge or in one of the cabins.
   B. Attend the evening lectures or films on the history of the park.
IV. Drive southeast to the Grand Canyon of the Yellowstone.
   A. Take in the view from Inspiration Point.
   B. Hike down the trail for a better view of the waterfalls.

Sequential Design

While the spatial design moves listeners through space, a **sequential design** moves them through time. Speeches built upon sequential design may present the steps in a process, appropriate to a speech of demonstration, or provide a historical perspective in a speech of explanation.

A sequential design is effective for a speech of demonstration because it allows you to take the audience step by step through a process as you talk with them about it. You begin by determining the necessary steps in the process and then decide the order in which they must take place. These steps become the main points of your speech. In a short presentation, you should have no more than five steps as main points. If you have more, try to cluster some of them into subpoints. It is also helpful to enumerate the steps as you make your presentation.

The following abbreviated outline, developed by Jeffrey O'Connor, illustrates a sequential design for a speech of demonstration:

> *Preview:* The five steps toward efficient textbook reading include skimming, reading, rereading, reciting, and reviewing.
>
> I. First, *skim* through the chapter to get the overall picture.
>
>   A. Identify from large-print section headings the major ideas that will be covered.
>
>   B. Find and read any summary statements.
>
>   C. Find and read any boxed materials.
>
>   D. Begin a key-word skeleton outline of major topics that will be covered.
>
> II. Second, *read* the chapter a section at a time.
>
>   A. Make notes to yourself in the margins.
>
>   1. Write questions about material you do not understand.
>
>   2. Write a brief summary of ideas you do understand.
>
>   3. Make numbered lists of any materials presented in series.
>
>   B. Look up the definitions of unfamiliar words in the book's glossary or a dictionary.
>
>   C. Go back and highlight the section you have just read.
>
>   1. Highlight only the major ideas.
>
>   2. Highlight no more than 10 percent of the text.
>
> III. Third, *reread* the chapter.
>
>   A. Fill in your skeleton outline with more detail.
>
>   B. Try to answer the questions you wrote in the margin.
>
>   C. Write out questions to ask your instructor on anything that is still not clear.
>
> IV. Fourth, *recite* what you have read.
>
>   A. Use your skeleton outline to make an oral presentation to yourself on the chapter.
>
>   B. Talk about what you have read with someone else.
>
>   1. Ask your roommate, a classmate, or a friend to listen.
>
>   2. See if you can explain the material so that your listener understands it.
>
> V. Finally, *review* the material within twenty-four hours.
>
>   A. Review your skeleton outline.

B. Reread the highlighted material.

C. See if you can answer any more of your questions now that you have had time to digest the material.

Presenting the steps in this orderly manner helped Jeffrey "walk and talk" his listeners through the process. After his speech, they understood how to begin and what to do in the proper order.

The historical variation of a sequential design places the subject in a specific time frame. Often you "tell the story" of the subject, emphasizing the narrative form of supporting material. You may start with the beginning of an idea or issue and trace it up to the present through its defining moments. Or, you may start with the present and trace an issue or situation back to its origins. Because of your own time limitations, you must be careful to narrow your topic to manageable proportions. You must be selective, choosing landmark events that are relevant to your purpose and representative of the process you are describing. These landmark events become the main points in your message. Arrange them in their natural order, going either forward or backward in time. A speech on the evolution of the T-shirt using a sequential design might be structured as follows:

Preview: The T-shirt began its life as an undergarment, developed into a bearer of messages, and has emerged as high-fashion apparel.

I. The T-shirt originated as an undergarment at the beginning of the twentieth century.
   A. The first undershirts with sleeves were designed for sailors so that sensitive people were spared the sight of hairy underarms.
   B. Sleeved undershirts were first sold commercially by Sears and Hanes in the late 1930s.
   C. During World War II, T-shirts were standard military issue and were used as outerwear in the tropics.

II. After World War II, civilians began using T-shirts as outerwear.
   A. Veterans liked them because they were comfortable and absorbent.
   B. They were popularized in movies like *A Streetcar Named Desire* and *Rebel Without a Cause*.
   C. Parents liked them for children because T-shirts were easy to care for.

III. T-shirts soon became embellished with pictures and messages.
   A. Children's T-shirts had pictures of cartoon characters like Mickey Mouse.
   B. Adult T-shirt designs were usually related to sports team logos.
   C. T-shirts soon were used for "political" statements.
      1. The first "political" T-shirt was made in 1948 and read "Dew-It with Dewey."
      2. Peace symbols were popular during the 1960s.
      3. Ideological slogans such as "A Woman's Place Is in the House (and in the Senate)" appeared during the 1970s.
   D. During the 1990s, T-shirts became walking billboards, especially for sports equipment.

IV. Today you have a choice of unique designs for T-shirts.
   A. T-shirt print shops will customize a message for you.
   B. Craft fairs often offer air-brushed T-shirts.
   C. Your local copy shop will put your picture on a T-shirt.
   D. You can buy dressy T-shirts with rhinestone and pearl decorations.
   E. You can even spend over $800 for a Gianni Versace abstract print of mercerized cotton that feels like silk.

Categorical Design

The **categorical design** is based on the principle of similarity, discussed in Chapter 7, and is useful for subjects that have natural or customary divisions. Natural divisions may exist within the subject itself, such as, for wines, red, white, and blended. Customary divisions represent typical ways of thinking about a subject, such as the four food groups that are essential to a healthy diet. Therefore, categories are the mind's way of ordering the world by either seeking the patterns within it or supplying patterns useful to arrange it. They help us sort out incoming information so that we can make sense of it.

Each category in the design becomes a main point for development. For a short presentation, you should limit the number of categories to four or at most five. Any subject that breaks out into six or more categories will be too complex for most classroom speeches. If you have too many categories, try to cluster some of them as a single main point. If you cannot condense your categories into a manageable number, you should consider another way to design the speech or rethink your specific purpose to narrow your focus.

In her informative speech on child abuse presented at Vanderbilt University, Amanda Watkins first established its relevance to her audience, which included prospective teachers. She then defined the problem, described its magnitude, and discussed the four major types (categories) of child abuse. Following is an abbreviated outline of the body of her speech:

Preview: There are four types of child abuse: physical abuse, neglect, sexual abuse, and mental abuse.

I. Physical abuse involves inflicting bodily harm on a child by such means as beating, kicking, biting, or burning.
   A. This may result from overdiscipline by the caregiver.
   B. There may be no intent to harm the child; the abuser may even apologize afterwards.
   C. Symptoms of physical abuse may include:
      1. Repeated instances of bruises on the body.
      2. Fright in the presence of the abuser.
      3. Protest over having to go home.
      4. Sudden change in performance at school.
II. Abusive neglect means failure to provide for the child's basic needs.
   A. Physical needs, such as adequate health care, may be neglected.
   B. Educational neglect occurs when the child is allowed to stay out of school excessively.

    C. Emotional neglect occurs when the child is ignored, often because of drug or alcohol abuse.

    D. Symptoms of neglect may include:

       1. Frequent absences from school.

       2. Child is often dirty or smells bad.

       3. Child reports no caregiver at home.

III. Sexual abuse can involve fondling of the genitals, incest, sodomy, or sexual exploitation of any form.

    A. Sexual abuse may be committed by a person responsible for the well-being of the child.

    B. Sexual abuse is typically underreported because of the child's shame or a conspiracy of silence.

    C. Symptoms of sexual abuse may include:

       1. Child has difficulty walking or sitting.

       2. Child shies away from any physical contact.

       3. Child attempts to run away.

IV. Mental abuse involves emotional, verbal, and psychological abuse.

    A. This can have serious behavioral or cognitive impact.

    B. Sometimes involves unusual forms of torment.

    C. Symptoms of mental abuse may include:

       1. Child exhibits behavioral withdrawal.

       2. Child exhibits unusual behavioral traits or immaturity.

       3. Child is abusive of other children.

Comparative Design

A **comparative design** is useful when your topic is new to your audience, abstract, highly technical, or simply difficult to understand. It can also help you describe dramatic changes in a subject. Comparative designs aid comprehension by relating the topic to something the audience already knows and understands. They are especially useful in speeches of description, speeches of explanation, and briefings because they help bring out the meanings more clearly. In speeches of demonstration, comparative design can also show the right and wrong ways of doing something.

    There are three basic variations of the comparative design. In a **literal analogy**, the subjects compared are drawn from the same field of experience. For example, a student in one of our classes related the game of rugger as played in his native Sri Lanka to the American game of football. Since both rugger and football are contact sports, the comparison between them is literal.

    In a **figurative analogy**, the subjects compared are drawn from different fields of experience: for example, a speaker might relate the body's struggle against infection to a military campaign. In such a design, the speaker might identify the nature of the armies, the ways they fight, and the consequences of defeat and victory. Figurative analogies are basically extended metaphors, which we discussed in Chapter 10. As such, figurative analogies transform a technique of language into a technique of structure. The strength of such a design is that it can be insightful and imaginative, helping listeners to see the significance of subjects in often surprising and impressive ways. When well selected, it can strengthen the competence dimension of a speaker's ethos. But an analogy can damage the speaker's ethos and the speech if the comparison seems far-fetched. The advice we gave for metaphor also holds for figurative analogy designs: Avoid stretching the comparison too far, or the design will collapse under the strain.

A **comparison and contrast** design points out the similarities and/or differences between subjects or ideas. In this design, each similarity or difference becomes a main point. In the interest of simplicity, you should limit yourself to five or fewer points of similarity and difference in a short presentation. The following example places the emphasis on contrast as it designs the body of a speech:

> *Preview:* Over two decades—from the late 1960s to the late 1980s—the women we saw in advertisements began to change.

I. The products that women were used to advertise changed.
   A. In the late 1960s, 75 percent of the women shown were in ads for kitchen or bath products.
   B. By the late 1980s, only 45 percent of the women were in such ads.
   C. By the late 1980s, women were in more ads for alcohol, phone services, automobiles, and other high-ticket products.

II. Women began to appear in different roles.
   A. The percentage of women shown in domestic (wife/mother) roles changed.
      1. In the late 1960s, two-thirds of women were in domestic roles.
      2. By the late 1980s, less than half of the women were in such roles.
   B. The occupational roles of women in advertisements also changed.
      1. In the late 1960s, only 9 percent of the females had an identifiable occupation.
      2. By the late 1980s, this number had doubled.
      3. In the late 1960s, working women were restricted to low-paying, traditionally female occupations.
      4. By the late 1980s, the majority were shown in nontraditional careers.

III. The apparent ages of women also changed.
   A. In the late 1960s, 80 percent appeared to be under thirty.
   B. By the late 1980s, this number had dropped to about 50 percent.

IV. The overall attitude toward women in ads has changed.
   A. In the late 1960s, most women were portrayed in demeaning ways, as dumb and dependent sex objects.
   B. By the late 1980s, more women appeared as intelligent, achieving, and independent individuals.

FIGURE 12.2

Selecting Informative Designs

Design	Use When
Spatial	Your topic can be discussed in terms of how it is positioned in a physical setting or natural environment. This design allows you to take your audience on an orderly "oral tour" of your topic as you move from place to place.
Sequential	Your topic can be arranged by time. This design is useful for describing a process as a series of steps or explaining a subject as a series of developments.
Categorical	Your topic has natural or customary divisions. Each category becomes a main point for development. This design is useful when you need to organize large amounts of material.
Comparative	Your topic is new to your audience, abstract, technical, or simply difficult to comprehend. This design helps make material more meaningful by comparing or contrasting it with something the audience already knows and understands.
Causation	Your topic involves a situation, condition, or event that is best understood in terms of its underlying causes. This design may also be used to predict the future from existing conditions.

Causation Design

A **causation design**, often used in speeches of explanation, interprets a situation, condition, or event in terms of the causes that led up to it. The speaker usually begins with a description of an existing condition, then probes for its causes. The description often becomes the first main point, with the causes following as subsequent main points. A causation design may also be used to predict events or conditions in the future. In that case, the present condition is usually the first main point and the predictions become the subsequent main points. The causes or predictions may be grouped into categories that can be arranged in order of their importance. They may also be presented sequentially.

Speeches of causation are subject to one serious limitation: The tendency to oversimplify. Any complex situation will generally have many underlying causes. And any given set of conditions may lead to many different future effects. Be wary of overly simple explanations and overly confident predictions. Such explanations and predictions are one form of faulty reasoning (fallacy) discussed further in Chapter 14.

The speech on global warming that appears at the end of Chapter 8 used a causation design. Its first main point defined global warming, while the second, third, and fourth main points discussed major causes in order of ascending importance.

> *Preview*: We need to be concerned, first, about the loss of woodlands; second, about industrial emissions; and third, about overall increases in energy consumption.

> I. Global warming is the artificial warming of the earth as a result of human activities.
>
>   A. It is characterized by a high concentration of carbon dioxide in the atmosphere.

    B. Carbon pollutants are eating a hole in the ozone layer.

    C. If this problem is not corrected, we may see disastrous results.

        1. There could be dramatic climate changes.

        2. There could be serious health problems.

II. One cause of global warming is the loss of woodlands that convert carbon dioxide into oxygen.

    A. One football-field-sized area of forest is lost every second to cutting or burning.

    B. Burning forests add more carbon dioxide.

III. Industrial emissions also add to global warming.

    A. Industrial contaminants produce more than 20 percent of air pollution.

    B. Carbon dioxide is released in large quantities when fossil fuels are burned.

    C. Chlorofluorocarbons come from refrigeration and air conditioners.

    D. Nitrogen oxides are spewed out of vehicle exhausts and smokestacks.

IV. Increased energy consumption magnifies global warming.

    A. Both population growth and prosperity fuel the problem.

        1. More people means more energy consumption.

        2. Improved living standards add to the problem.

    B. Energy consumption is the largest cause of global warming.

        1. Fossil fuel use has more than doubled since 1950.

        2. Fossil fuels account for 90 percent of America's energy consumption.

        3. Transportation-related use accounts for half of all air pollution.

Combined Speech Designs

Although we have presented these designs as simple patterns for speeches, effective speeches sometimes combine two or more of them. This is especially the case when you wish both to demonstrate or describe a subject and to provide an explanation for it in the same speech. In such speeches, spatial or sequential designs are often linked with categorical or causation designs. Obviously, the time restrictions for most classroom speeches prevent you from developing elaborate combined designs for most subjects. But occasionally such combinations are both practical and desirable. If you believe that a combined design will work best for your material, first be sure you have time to develop it, then plan it carefully so that you do not confuse listeners as you move from one pattern to another.

    Karen Lovelace wanted her Vanderbilt classmates to understand that those who suffer from muscular dystrophy are victims not just of a disease but of insensitivity on the part of their fellow citizens. She used a combined sequential and categorical design to convey her prepersuasive message. In the first part of her speech, she described a day in the life of her friend Donald Morgan, as she had experienced it with him. Her day with Donald began in his apartment, which is retrofitted so that he can live comfortably. As soon as she and Donald left the apartment, troubles began. At the grocery store, some unthinking soul had parked illegally in the handicapped space, and there was no ramp. At the taco shop where they went to eat, every facility—from the self-serve drink dispenser to the door to the bathroom—was ill-suited to Donald's needs. At the movie they attended, there were no empty spaces for his wheelchair. They returned to his apartment exhausted and humiliated after the inconveniences of the day. At this point in the speech, Karen made a transition into her categorical design: "What are the forms of inconvenience and inhumanity that we impose upon disabled people?" She then identified these forms, drawing upon the earlier part of her speech for examples. By the end of her speech, her classmates better understood what it means to experience a disability in our society. They were prepared for her later persuasive speech in which she would propose specific reforms to the Americans with Disabilities Act.

In Summary

Sharing knowledge is the essence of informative speaking. It helps us to live better and work smarter. In short, information is power.

Functions of the Informative Speech.   Informative speaking serves four basic functions. First, informative speaking empowers listeners by sharing information and ideas. Second, informative speaking shapes listener perceptions for later persuasive speeches. Third, informative speaking sets an agenda of public concerns by suggesting what is important. Finally, informative speaking clarifies options for decision making. In short, informative speaking teaches people what they need to know.

Helping Your Audience Learn.   To make it easier for listeners to learn, motivate them by showing how your subject relates to their basic needs. To grasp and hold attention, design your message in light of the principles of intensity, repetition, novelty, activity, contrast, and relevance. Help your audience remember your message by organizing your material and providing previews and summaries.

Types of Informative Speeches.   Informative speeches include speeches of description, demonstration, and explanation. *Speeches of description* create word-pictures that help the audience visualize a subject. *Speeches of demonstration* show the audience how something is done. They may give listeners an understanding of a process or teach them how to perform it. Speeches of demonstration are often more effective when presentation aids are used. *Speeches of explanation* inform the audience about abstract and complex subjects, such as concepts or programs. Such speeches normally present a more difficult challenge, especially when the information presented contradicts common knowledge or threatens cherished beliefs. Briefings, an important subtype of informative speaking, are presented mainly in organizational settings. Briefings are usually status reports or updates on projects for which you have responsibility.

Speech Designs.   The patterns most frequently employed in informative speeches are spatial, sequential, categorical, comparative, and causation designs. A *spatial design* orders the main points according to the arrangement of a subject in space. Spatial designs are especially appropriate for describing objects or places. Most speeches of demonstration use a *sequential design,* which follows a time pattern to present steps in a process as they occur or a series of historical events. *Categorical designs* may represent natural divisions of your subject or traditional ways of thinking. In a short speech, you should limit your number of categories to no more than five. *Comparative designs* are especially effective when your topic is new to the audience, when it has undergone dramatic changes, or when you wish to establish right and wrong procedures. These designs are often based on *literal* or *figurative analogies,* depending on whether the compared subjects are drawn from the same or different fields of experience. A *causation design* explains how one condition generates or is generated by another. The causation design is subject to the problem of oversimplification. Sometimes you may decide to incorporate two or more designs into a speech. In that case, be certain to provide transitions so that listeners are not confused by the changing patterns.

Terms to Know

informative value

prepersuasive function

agenda-setting function

speech of description

speech of demonstration

speech of explanation

briefing

spatial design

sequential design

categorical design

comparative design

literal analogy

figurative analogy

comparison and contrast

causation design

Notes

1. D. L. Shaw and M. E. McCombs, *The Emergence of American Political Issues: The Agenda-Setting Function of the Press* (St. Paul, Minn.: West, 1977).
2. Katherine E. Rowan, "Goals, Obstacles, and Strategies in Risk Communication: A Problem-Solving Approach to Improving Communication About Risks," *Journal of Applied Communication Research* 19 (1991): 314.
3. Stephen Lee presented this informative speech of explanation in his public speaking class at the University of Texas, Austin. The speech won the Southern division of the 1991 Houghton Mifflin Public Speaking Contest.
4. Rowan, p. 314.
5. Notable among such books are Jeff Scott Cook, *The Elements of Speech Writing and Public Speaking* (New York: Macmillan, 1989); Joan Detz, *Can You Say a Few Words? How to Prepare and Deliver* (New York: St. Martin's Press, 1991); Milo O. Frank, *How to Get Your Point Across in 30 Seconds or Less* (New York: Simon & Schuster, Inc., 1986); Sunja Hamlin, *How to Talk So People Listen* (New York: Harper & Row, 1988); Burton Kaplan, *The Manager's Complete*

Guide to Speech Writing (New York: Free Press, 1988); Dorothy Leeds, *Power-Speak* (New York: Berkeley Books, 1991); William Parkhurst, *The Eloquent Executive: How to Sound Your Best: High-Impact Speaking in Meetings Large & Small* (New York: Avon, 1988); Laurie Schloff and Marcia Yudkin, *Smart Speaking: Sixty-Second Strategies* (New York: Holt, 1991); and Lilly Walters, *Secrets of Successful Speakers: How You Can Motivate, Captivate and Persuade* (New York: McGraw-Hill, 1993).

6. J. E. Hollingsworth, "Oral Briefings," *Management Review,* August 1968, pp. 2–10.

7. Adapted from material supplied by Randy Scott, Department of Communication, Weber State University, Ogden, Utah.

Sample Informative Speech

What Friends Are All About
Marie D'Aniello

It's nine o'clock at night. I'm curled up in the back seat of a new truck and my friends, Cammy and Joe, are in the front singing along with the radio. As I listen to them sing, and I'm lying there, I start to think about my life and all the changes that have occurred in the past year. A year ago I didn't even know who Cammy and Joe were. And now they're two of my dearest friends. It made me wonder about friendship and its meaning.

According to Webster's dictionary, to be a friend means that you're someone who someone else feels comfortable with and is fond of. But friendship is so much more than that. According to Plato, true friendship rises out of basic human needs and desires, such as striving for goodness, reaching out to others, and seeking self-understanding. And loving and being loved. Friendship should benefit all who are involved in it and should occur between people who value each other's good qualities. As human beings we need friends in order to survive and grow.

Through our friends we learn who we are, and what we like and don't like. We learn about strengths we never knew we had, weaknesses that maybe we can overcome. Think about your friendships. I'll bet you've learned a great deal and grown a great deal because of them.

If you're like me you probably have one or two really close friends and a lot of great acquaintances. But that's good because that's what you need. According to Dr. John Litwac of the University of Massachusetts medical center, people in modern society require a variety of friends to meet their needs. And the variety of friends we need varies over time. What Dr. Litwac says in a book, *Adult Friendships,* is that the friendships we enjoy when we are young differ a lot from those we experience as we grow older. As we develop, so does the complexity and intimacy of our relationships.

In this speech I'm going to take you through the development of friendship, beginning in childhood, going up through adolescence all the way to young adulthood. I'm going to talk about how we define our friends, the roles that friends play in our lives, and the effect conflicts have on friendship during each stage.

The saga of friendship begins in our lives when we are quite young. And, the concepts we have of friendship change dramatically over the first decade of life. Psychologists classify childhood as the stage occurring between the ages of 4 and 10. During childhood a child's friends are the people they have the most contact with, the people whom they play with. In childhood that's what friendship is all about. According to Dr. William Rawlings, friendships exist while children are playing together. For example, when I was in kindergarten, I was friends with Michelle when we were playing tag. But the next day I would go and play with someone else and make friends with them. The friendship vanished until the next time we played together. Because the friendship was based on an activity. It existed for the sake of fun, and had little to do with who Michelle really was. She was simply there and I could play with her.

But when we play as children, we're not only having fun, we're also learning how to assimilate into society and how to develop more lasting friendships. We learn to inhibit our actions, to deal with other people's emotions, and to follow rules. Because we're just starting out and just trying to figure out how everything works, we may run into a lot of conflicts with our friendships during childhood. We may get into silly fights about whose toy is this and whose toy is that, but the fights don't usually last very long and can be resolved fairly easily. Behavior is based on the moment, and the moment is based on what things appear to be.

During childhood friendship often depends on looks. Maybe that's why some children are so popular and others are ignored. In fact, a study conducted by Dr. William Lipit concluded that children between the ages of 4 to 9 base their descriptions of their friends completely on their looks. That may be sad, but it's just the way it is. Think of this as a phase in the process of growing up.

At the end of childhood, friends become more than just playmates. They're people who share our interests—they're the ones we share our feelings with. Play becomes less, talk becomes more important. Friendship evolves steadily to a new level, called adolescence.

I'm sure you remember adolescence. It usually occurs between the ages of 11 and 17. As we live through it, friendship involves revealing and discussing one's personal thoughts and feelings. Just talking can be more important than anything, especially for girls. Boys, male friendships, still involve a lot of activity, like sports, but the activities involve more verbal communication than before. The critical task of adolescence is to develop one's identity and friends are crucial in that respect. According to Dr. Graham Allen in his book, *Friendship*, people in adolescence, more than at any other time in their lives, need to share strong, often confusing emotions. Did you have a best friend in junior high school? A friend you would sit and talk on the phone with for hours on end? Well if you did, that's good, that's normal. According to Dr. Allen, that's what you needed.

Think back. Think back to friendship pins, and side pony tails and matching outfits, and sleep-over parties. Think of your first best friend. That person probably knew more about you than anyone in the whole world. They were probably your age, in your class, lived pretty close by and pretty much had the same social status you did. In adolescence we seek out people who are like us because they make us feel more normal. Because the level of intimacy is so much greater in adolescence, the potential for conflict and jealousy also increases. There's so much emotion at stake that an argument in adolescence can easily ruin a friendship. The way we deal with such problems in adolescence prepares us for young adulthood.

Now young adulthood is classified as the stage between 18 and 24, the stage we're all in now. Here at Vanderbilt and I suppose elsewhere, friendship has a lot of potential. Friends can be playmates, confidants, lovers, listeners. They can be anything. According to Rosemary Adams, also writing in *Adult Friendship*, during the college years friends may provide a crucial input regarding self-conceptions, career options, and recreational activities. Patterns of friendship vary a lot and we have many different types of friends. We have party friends. We have classroom friends. And then we have our good, good friends. But you need all of those kinds of friends as you grow older because you are becoming a more complex individual.

Marie relied strongly on examples as supporting materials. In her first main point, she discussed her personal experiences. In the second point, she asked listeners to supply examples from their own experiences. She used rhetorical questions to highlight the points and stimulate reflection. She also used the contrast between play and talk to underscore the difference between the childhood and adolescent phases of friendship.

In her final main point, Marie continued to engage listeners with rhetorical questions and invited them to reflect upon their own friendships.

Why do you like your good friends? Do you like them because they have the best toys? Or do you like them because you can relate to them and share a bond with them? Our friends prevent us from being lonely. In fact 40 percent of college freshmen who reported they felt homesick also reported not having made new friends in college.

Why do some people make friends easily while others struggle to? Researchers speculate that how open and honest you are with people and how much you are willing to give of yourself can affect your forming friendships. Talking and sharing is very important because it creates a sense of intimacy. Friendship also depends a great deal on attraction. Whatever attracts you to people is why you like them. Maybe you like people who smile a lot, or maybe you like those who are serious. Maybe you like people who are the complete opposite of you and who possess qualities you wish you had. Or maybe you like people who are just like you, who you feel you know inside and out.

When we're younger, friendships are based on what people appear to be. As we get older, friendships are based more on what people really are. If you got in a fight with your best friend, would you tell him to hit the road? Chances are you'd probably try to work it out. As we get older, it's easier for us to accept differences in other people. Serious betrayals could end friendships. But the researchers I read concluded that the older you get and the older the friendship is, the harder you're going to work to try to preserve it.

▨ *At this point, Marie reflects on the general meaning of her subject, signalling that she is moving into her conclusion. By beginning with Plato and ending with Yeats, she dignified her subject and emphasized its importance in her listeners' lives.*

Friendship is hard to define and I think that's probably because it involves your heart and your soul. But out of all the research I've done and all the people I've talked to, no one said that they thought friendship was a bad thing. Of course there are downsides like peer pressure and conflict and sometimes stress, but 91 percent of the college freshmen that Dr. Adams studied claim that the benefits of friendships outweigh the hardships. All I know is that from the day we're born until the day we die, people affect our lives. If we're lucky, maybe we'll come to know some of them as friends.

The dynamics of friendship change rapidly throughout our lives. During childhood friendship is based on play. In adolescence, more on emotion. In young adulthood, I think friendship is based on a combination of acceptance, respect, and trust. I'd like to leave you with some words by William Butler Yeats, who said, "Think where man's glory most begins and ends. And say my glory was to have such friends."

WORKS CONSULTED

Blieszner, Rosemary and Rebecca G. Adams. *Adult Friendship*. Newbury Park: Sage Publications, 1992.

Brenton, Myron. *Friendship*. New York: Stein and Pay, 1974.

Cates, Diana Fritz. *Choosing to Feel: Virtue, Friendship and Compassion for Friends*. Notre Dame: University of Notre Dame Press, 1997.

Gilligan, Carol, Nona P. Lyons, and Trudy J. Hammer. *Making Connections: The Relational Worlds of Adolescent Girls at the Emma Willard School*. Cambridge: Harvard Press, 1990.

Gottman, John M., and Jeffrey G. Parker. *Conversation of Friends: Speculations and Affective Development*. Cambridge: Cambridge University Press, 1986.

Griffiths, Vivienne. *Adolescent Girls and their Friends*. Aldershot: Avebury, 1995.

Meyer, Luanna H., et al. *Making Friends*. Baltimore: Paul H. Brookes Publishing Co., 1998.

Rawlins, William K. *Friendship Matters*. New York: Aldine de Gruyter, 1992.

Web Sources:

The Friendship Page, http://www.geocities.com/Athens/Acropolis/9761/quofrend.html

http://www.ozemail.com

13

Persuasive Speaking

Because there has been implanted in us the power to persuade each other . . . , not only have we escaped the life of the wild beasts but we have come together and founded cities and made laws and invented arts.

— Isocrates

This chapter will help you

- understand the persuasive process
- meet the major challenges of persuasion
- learn the functions of persuasive messages
- select a design for your persuasive speech

You awaken to a world that is trying to persuade you. On the radio, a DJ sells tickets to a rock concert. The weather forecaster advises you to carry an umbrella. Students urge you to join their organizations. Stores advertise for your business. Politicians plead for your vote. Billboards tout everything from animal rights to zoo attendance. Novels, movies, and television shows promote social or political causes.

You, in turn, are constantly trying to persuade others. You may want your roommate to go out for pizza with you. To convince him, you describe the pizza in mouth-watering ways. You think some questions on a chemistry test were unfair. But if you want your grade changed, you'll have to make the case. You've just met someone you want to date. How can you excite his or her interest? Your friends are traveling to Florida for spring break. Can you convince your parents that you deserve to go on the trip? To get the job you want, you'll first have to impress an interviewer. Once you get the job, you'll have to sell yourself and your ideas.

Whatever path you take, you can't avoid persuading and being persuaded.

WHAT DOES IT mean to say that we live in a world of persuasion? It means that we live among competing interests. Your roommate's need to study for an exam may take priority over pizza. Your instructor may have good reasons *not* to change your grade. And the object of your romantic interest may, alas, have other options.

In such a world, **persuasion** *is the art of getting others to give fair and favorable consideration to our point of view.* When we persuade, we want to influence how others believe and behave. We may not always prevail—other points of view may be more persuasive, depending on the listener, the situation, and the merits of the case. But when we practice the art of persuasion, we try to ensure that our position receives the attention it deserves.

Some people, however, object to the very idea of persuasion. They may regard it as an unwelcome intrusion into their lives or as manipulation or domination.[1] In contrast, we believe that persuasion is inevitable—to live is to persuade. Persuasion can be ethical or unethical, selfless or selfish, inspiring or degrading. Persuaders may enlighten our minds or prey on our vulnerability. Ethical persuasion, however, calls on sound reasoning and is sensitive to the feelings and needs of listeners. Such persuasion can help us apply the wisdom of the past to the decisions we now must make. Therefore, an essential part of education is learning to resist the one kind of persuasion and to encourage and practice the other.

Beyond its personal importance to us, persuasion is essential to society. The right to persuade and be persuaded is the bedrock of the American political system, guaranteed by the First Amendment to the Constitution. According to the late Supreme Court Justice Louis D. Brandeis, "Those who won our independence believed that the final end of the State was to make men [and women] free to develop their faculties; and that in its government the deliberative forces should prevail over the arbitrary."[2] Open discussion and persuasion are required for these "deliberative forces" to operate.

Deliberation involves the consideration of all sides of an issue before a decision is made. When decisions are arbitrarily imposed, force is often required to back them up. During the debate in the House of Representatives over the impeachment of President Clinton, Rep. Richard Gephardt was asked in the course of a television interview whether the many speeches delivered on the floor of the House had any real purpose. Gephardt responded that persuasion is society's alternative to violence. We strongly agree. Our political system is based on the premise that persuasion is more ethical and more practical than force. We should make commitments because we are persuaded, not because we are coerced.

Although you may find the expression of some views to be objectionable, if not downright obnoxious, the freedom to voice unpopular opinions is the very soul of liberty. The English philosopher John Stuart Mill put the matter eloquently (although in the sexist language of his time):

> **If all mankind, minus one, were of the one opinion, and only one person were of the contrary opinion, mankind would be no more justified in silencing that one person, than he, if he had the power, would be justified in silencing mankind.**
>
> **. . . We can never be sure that the opinion we are endeavoring to stifle is a false opinion; and if we were sure, stifling it would be an evil still.[3]**

There are also practical reasons for tolerating opposing opinions. Exposure to different perspectives can produce better decisions.[4] For example, even though Nick may never agree with Hailey's view that we should register guns, her arguments may prompt him to reexamine his thoughts, to understand his convictions better, or perhaps even to modify his position.

Although speaking out on public issues is important, many people shy away from it. They may feel: "What difference can one person make? My words don't carry much weight." Perhaps not, but words make ripples, and ripples can come together to make waves. Just ask Anna Aley, a student at Kansas State University who gave a persuasive speech on substandard student housing. Her classroom speech was later presented in a public forum on campus. The text of her speech was reprinted in the local newspaper, which followed it up with investigative reports and a supportive editorial. Brought to the attention of the mayor and city commission, Anna's speech helped promote reforms in the city's rental housing policies. Her words are still reverberating in Manhattan, Kansas.

Perhaps your classroom speech will not have that much impact, but you never know who or what may be changed by it. In this chapter we consider the characteristics of persuasive speaking, the process of persuasion, some of the challenges facing persuasive speakers, the functions of persuasive speeches, and the designs that are appropriate for the structure of these speeches.

Seven Characteristics of Persuasive Speaking

Seven characteristics define persuasive speaking. They are best understood when contrasted with characteristics of informative speaking:

Informative speeches reveal options; persuasive speeches urge a choice from among options. Informative speakers expand our awareness. For example, an informative speaker might say, "There are three different ways we can deal with the budget deficit. Let me explain these." In contrast, a persuasive speaker would weigh these options and urge support of one of them: "Of the three different ways to deal with the budget deficit, we should take this course of action because it is best."

Implied in this contrast is the assumption that persuasion comes into play with questions that are not yet resolved, and with listeners many of whom may not share your point of view. Just as you can't inform listeners who already know everything you will tell them, you can't persuade listeners who already accept your position and are already committed to the action you propose.

Informative speakers function as teachers: Persuaders are advocates. The difference is one of passion and engagement: While informative speakers typically discuss a situation in relatively calm and dispassionate tones, persuaders are more often vitally engaged, committed to a cause. This does not necessarily mean that persuaders are loud; the most passionate and intense moments of a speech can be very quiet.

Informative speeches provide supporting material to enlighten listeners; persuasive speeches provide such material to justify advice. While both informative and persuasive speeches must be based on responsible knowledge, persuasive speeches apply that knowledge to how we should feel, believe, and act. An ethical persuasive speech justifies recommendations with **good reasons** that are based on responsible knowledge and sensitivity to the best interests of listeners.

Persuasive speeches can help raise support for worthy causes. Here Sharon Stone speaks out on behalf of Race for the Cure.

Persuasive speeches ask for more audience commitment than informative speeches. Although there is risk in being exposed to new ideas, more is at stake when listening to a persuasive message. You risk little when you listen to an informative speaker describe off-campus living conditions. A persuasive speaker wants you *to do something* about these conditions. What if that speaker isn't honest? What if the actions backfire? *Doing* always involves a greater risk than *knowing.* Your commitment could cost you. Because of the risks involved, audiences for persuasive speeches must practice critical listening skills.

Leadership is more important in persuasive than in informative speeches. Because persuasive speeches involve risk, listeners will weigh the character and competence of the speakers more closely. Do they really know what they are talking about? Do they have their listeners' interests at heart? Are they willing to place themselves on the line? As you speak out against slumlords, your ethos will be on public display and will be scrutinized carefully.

Appeals to feelings are more appropriate in persuasive than in informative speeches. Because of the risk involved, listeners may balk at accepting recommendations, even when they are backed up by good reasons. To overcome such inertia, persuaders must often appeal to feelings.[5] This is why persuasive speakers often use appeals to emotions to open their speeches. For example, the statement "A 10 percent rise in tuition will reduce the student population by about 5 percent next term" may work well in an informative speech but would not be sufficient in a persuasive speech. Look at another way of putting the matter:

> **The people who are pushing for the tuition increase don't think a couple hundred dollars more will have much effect. They think we can handle it. They say that the one in twenty who won't be back doesn't make much difference!**
>
> **Well, let me tell you about my friend Tricia. Both her parents lost their jobs when the plastics plant closed down. Tricia's on the Dean's List in chemistry. She'll get a great job when she graduates—if she graduates! But if this increase goes through, Tricia won't be back next term. Her dreams of success will be delayed, perhaps denied! What do the legislators care about that? What do they care about Tricia's dreams?**
>
> **Perhaps you're in the same boat as Tricia—paddling like mad to keep going. But even if you're not, she is one of us, and she needs our help *now.***

Emotional language is often needed to help people see the human dimension of problems and move them to action.

The ethical obligation for persuasive speeches is greater than that for informative speeches. As Isocrates indicated in the quotation that opens this chapter, persuasion can be a great blessing to humankind. At their best, persuasive speakers confront us with our obligation to believe and act in socially responsible ways. By describing how they themselves became persuaded, they model how we should deliberate the options open to us in difficult choice situations. By making intelligence and morality effective in public affairs, they help the world evolve in more enlightened ways, and help humans to control their destiny.

FIGURE 13.1

Informative versus
Persuasive

Informative Speaking	Persuasive Speaking
1. Reveals options	1. Urges a choice among options
2. Speaker acts as teacher	2. Speaker acts as advocate
3. Uses supporting material to enlighten listeners	3. Uses supporting material to justify advice
4. Asks for little commitment	4. Asks for strong commitment
5. Speaker's leadership less important	5. Speaker's leadership more important
6. Fewer appeals to feelings	6. More appeals to feelings
7. High ethical obligation	7. Higher ethical obligation

This blessing can also be a great curse. In the final analysis, you must be able to accept the consequences of your persuasion. Will your plan for improving off-campus housing result in safer living, or will it merely raise rents? Are your reasons free from logical flaws? Are they built on responsible knowledge? Is your plan worth the cost and risk?

To summarize, persuasion asks us to make a choice that will affect how we believe or act. To justify this choice, persuaders must present good reasons based on sound knowledge and sensitivity to the audience's values and interests. Persuaders ask listeners to assume risks, which raises the issue of credibility. Can we depend on these speakers? Are they trustworthy? To overcome inertia, persuaders often must arouse feelings to make us act. Finally, the possible personal and social impact of persuasion creates an ethical obligation. Persuasion should not be undertaken lightly. The major differences between informative and persuasive speaking are shown in Figure 13.1.

The Process of Persuasion

To understand both how to persuade and how to resist persuasion when we should, we must look at how persuasion works. William J. McGuire, professor of psychology at Yale University, suggests that effective persuasion is a complicated process involving up to twelve phases.[6] For our purposes, these phases may be grouped into five stages: awareness, understanding, agreement, enactment, and integration (see Figure 13.2 on the following page). Familiarity with these stages helps us see that persuasion is not an all-or-nothing affair. A persuasive message may be successful if it moves people through the process toward a goal.

The first stage in the persuasive process is awareness. Awareness includes knowing about a problem, paying attention to it, and understanding how it affects our lives. This phase is often called **consciousness-raising**. As we noted in Chapter 12, informative speaking can build such awareness and help prepare us for persuasion.[7] Creating awareness is especially important when people do not believe that there actually is a problem. For example, before feminists could change the way females were depicted in children's

FIGURE 13.2

McGuire's Model of the Persuasive Process

books, they had to make people understand that always showing boys in active roles and girls in passive roles was a serious problem. They had to demonstrate that this could thwart the development of self-esteem or ambition in young girls.[8] Similarly, Anna Aley had to draw people's attention to substandard student housing, and Bonnie Marshall had to start listeners thinking about who would make life-and-death decisions for them if they did not prepare living wills (see her speech in Appendix B).

Beyond acquainting listeners with a problem, persuasive messages aimed at building awareness must demonstrate that the problem is important and show listeners how it affects them directly. Persuasive speakers must raise awareness before moving on to the next stage in the process.

The second phase of the persuasive process is understanding. Listeners must understand what you are telling them. They must be moved by your ideas and know how to carry out your proposals. To provide understanding, Anna Aley used an "inside-outside" approach. She took listeners *inside* the housing problem in Manhattan by vividly describing her basement apartment. Then she took listeners *outside* the problem by showing them the total picture of substandard student housing: the number of students involved and the causes of the problem. Helping listeners understand is important when listeners admit that there is a problem but don't know what to do about it. Ethical persuasion expands our knowledge of arguments, demonstrates how some arguments are stronger than others, and provides evidence to support a position.[9]

Effective persuasive messages strike sparks in the minds of listeners. For instance, an example may remind listeners of a similar situation they encountered. An argument may generate additional supporting arguments or counterarguments. This interplay engages the audience in *both* critical and constructive listening (described in Chapter 3). It invites listeners to participate in the communication process. Finally, the audience must understand *how* to put the speaker's proposals into effect. Bonnie Marshall clearly spells out the steps she wants her listeners to take, enumerating these as she presents them.

The third stage in the persuasive process is agreement. Agreement means that listeners accept recommendations and remember their reasons for accepting them. Agreement can range from small concessions to total acceptance. Lesser degrees of agreement could represent success, especially when listeners have to change their attitudes or risk a great deal by accepting your ideas. During the Vietnam War, classroom speeches attacking or defending our involvement in that conflict were often heard. Feelings about the war ran so high that just to have a speech heard without interruption could be an accomplishment. If a reluctant listener were to nod agreement, or concede, "I guess you have a point," then one could truly claim victory.

Often you achieve agreement by presenting indisputable facts and well-reasoned interpretations that make your conclusions seem beyond question. You can help listeners remember their agreement by providing vivid images or telling interesting stories that embody your message. While reasoning is important to secure agreement, stories and images will stay with your audience after they have forgotten the details of your argument.

The fourth stage in the persuasive process is enactment. It is one thing to get listeners to accept what you say. It is quite another to ask them to act on it. If you invite listeners to sign a petition, raise their hands, or voice agreement, you give them a way to enact agreement. *By enacting their agreement, listeners make a commitment.* The student speaker who mobilized his audience against a proposed tuition increase

- Brought a petition to be signed
- Distributed the addresses of local legislators to contact
- Urged listeners to write letters to campus and local newspapers

He channeled their agreement into constructive action.

Changing agreement to action often requires the use of emotional appeals. Stirring stories and examples, vivid images, and colorful language can arouse sympathy. As she told the story of Harry Smith, who died an agonizing death because he had not signed a living will, Bonnie Marshall moved her listeners to act on behalf of themselves and their loved ones. Anna Aley's concluding story of her neighbor's accident helped motivate her audience to take action against substandard student housing.

The final stage in the persuasive process is *the integration of new attitudes and commitments with the listeners' beliefs and values.* For a persuasive speech to have lasting effect, listeners must see the connection between the attitudes and actions you propose and their important values. Your ideas must fit comfortably within their belief system. As she presented her case for living wills, Bonnie Marshall anchored her appeals in the right to control one's destiny. Anna Aley tied her attack on housing conditions to the values of fair treatment and safe living conditions.

All of us seek some consistency among our values and behaviors. For example, it would be inconsistent for us to march against substandard housing on Monday and contribute to a landlord's defense fund on Tuesday. This is why people sometimes seem to agree with a persuasive message, then change their minds. It dawns on them that this new commitment means that they must rearrange other cherished beliefs and attitudes.

You are asking a great deal when you invite dramatic changes. You must offer listeners compelling reasons to change—even appealing to their humanity. To provide such reasons, point out how the new position is consistent with their cherished values. Show listeners how the change will benefit them and their loved ones. Finally, plan responses to objections. Help listeners see a situation in a new way. On some issues this may require an almost biblical conversion—listeners must be "born again." Obviously, this degree of integration is rarely achieved through a single message. Such dramatic changes may require a campaign of persuasion in which any single speech plays a small but vital role.

Applying McGuire's Model to Persuasive Speeches

1 Arouse attention with your introduction.
2 Relate your message to your listeners' interests and needs.
3 Define complex terms, use concrete examples, and organize your material clearly.
4 Base your persuasion on solid supporting material.
5 Include a clear plan of action.
6 Use vivid language to make your message memorable.
7 Ask listeners to make a public commitment.
8 Relate your proposal to your audience's values.

To conclude, persuasion is a complicated process. Any persuasive message must focus on the stage where it can make its most effective contribution: raising awareness, building understanding, seeking agreement, encouraging action, or promoting the integration of beliefs, attitudes, and values. To determine where to focus your persuasive efforts, carefully analyze your audience and adapt your message to the specific challenge of the persuasive situation you anticipate.

The Challenges of Persuasion

The challenges that persuaders face range from confronting a reluctant audience to framing messages that meet the most demanding ethical tests. As you plan a persuasive speech, you need to consider the audience's position on the topic, how listeners might react to you as an advocate, and the situation in which the speech will be presented. At this point, the information and techniques concerning audience analysis that we introduced in Chapter 4 become crucial to success.

Begin preparing your persuasive speech by determining where your listeners stand on the issue. Do they hold varying attitudes about the topic, or are they united? If listeners are divided, you might hope to unify them around your position. If listeners are already united—but in opposition—you might try to divide them and attract some toward your position. Also consider how your listeners might regard you as a speaker on the subject. If you do not have their respect, trust, and goodwill, use testimony from highly regarded sources to enhance your ethos and improve your chances for success.

Evaluating the relationships among the audience, the topic, and you as speaker will help you determine how far you can go in a particular speech. These relationships also may suggest what strategies you should use and the kind of supporting materials you will need.

Enticing a Reluctant Audience to Listen

When attitudes and beliefs are important to your listeners, they are especially hard to change. If you face an audience that opposes your position, success may be represented by small achievements, such as simply getting thoughtful

Persuasive speakers must often entice a reluctant audience to action, remove barriers to commitment, and move listeners to participate.

attention. One way to handle a reluctant audience is to adopt a **co-active approach**, which seeks to bridge the differences between you and your listeners.[10] The major steps in this approach include:

1. *Establish identification and goodwill early in the speech.* Emphasize experiences, background, beliefs, and values that you share with listeners.

2. *Start with areas of agreement before you tackle areas of disagreement.* Starting out by reminding listeners of areas of disagreement may make them want to think up refutations rather than listen.

3. *Emphasize explanation more than argument.* Create an atmosphere in which your message has a fair chance of being heard. Explaining the reasons for your position gives listeners a chance to consider the merits of your position without risking their own.

4. *Cite authorities that the audience will respect and accept.* If you can find statements by such authorities that are favorable to your position, you can gain "borrowed ethos."

5. *Set modest goals for change.* Don't try to push your audience too far too fast. If reluctant listeners have listened to you—if you have raised their awareness and built a basis for understanding—you have accomplished a good deal.

6. *Make a multisided presentation that compares your position with others in order to demonstrate its superiority.* In taking such an approach, you indicate respect for other positions, but show how they are deficient.

Let's look at how you might apply these steps in a speech against capital punishment. You could *build identification* by pointing out the common beliefs, attitudes, and values you share with the audience, such as "We all respect human life. We all believe in fairness." At the same time, you would be *starting with areas of agreement and working toward the acceptance of common values.* It might also help to take an indirect approach in which you present your evidence and reasoning before you announce your purpose.

What if I were to tell you that we are condoning unfairness, that we are condemning people to death simply because they are poor and cannot afford a good lawyer? What if I were to show you that we are sanctioning a model of violent behavior in our society that invites more violence and more victims in return?

As you present evidence, cite authorities that *your audience will respect and accept.* "FBI statistics tell us that if you are poor and black, you are three times more likely to be executed for the crime of murder."

Keep your goals modest. Ask only for a fair hearing. If you propose too much change, you may create a **boomerang effect**, in which the audience reacts by opposing your position even more strongly.[11] To hope for a major change on the basis of any single persuasive effort is what McGuire calls the **great expectation fallacy**.[12] Be patient. Try to move your audience a step at a time in the direction you would like them to go. Give listeners information that may *eventually* change their minds.

I know that many of you may not like to hear what I'm saying, but think about it. If capital punishment does not deter violent crimes, if indeed it may encourage *more* violent crimes, isn't it time we put capital punishment itself on trial?

Finally, *make a* **multisided** presentation. Acknowledge the arguments in favor of capital punishment, showing that you respect and understand that position, even though you do not accept it.

I know that the desire for revenge can be strong. If someone I love had been murdered, I would want the killer's life in return. I wouldn't care if capital punishment wasn't fair. I wouldn't care that it condones brutality. I would just want an eye for an eye. But that doesn't mean you should give it to me. It doesn't mean that society should base its policy on my anger and hatred.

A multisided approach helps make those you do persuade resistant to later counterattacks, because you show them how to answer such arguments. This is often called the **inoculation effect**, because you "inoculate" your listeners against later exposure to differing messages.[13] When you acknowledge and then refute arguments, you also help your credibility in two ways. First, you enhance your *trustworthiness* by showing respect for your opposition. You suggest that their position deserves consideration, even though you have a better option. Second, you enhance your *competence* by showing your knowledge of the opposing position, both of the reasons why people may find it attractive and of how it is defective.

After your speech, you should continue to show respect for the audience. Even if some listeners want to argue or heckle, keep your composure. Others may be impressed by your self-control and may be encouraged to rethink their positions in light of your example.

There may be times when you and your audience are so far apart that you decide simply to acknowledge your disagreement. You might say that although you do not agree with your listeners, you respect their right to their position and hope that they will respect yours. Such openness may help establish the beginnings of trust. Even if audience members do not see you as an ally, they may at least start to see you as an honest, committed opponent and give you a hearing. If you emphasize that you will *not* be asking them to change their minds, but simply asking them to hear you out and to listen to the reasons why you believe as you do, you may be able to have your day in court.

We once heard a student speak against abortion to a class that was sharply divided on that issue. She began with a personal narrative, the story of how her mother had been given thalidomide (a drug that was later found to induce birth defects) and was faced with a decision on terminating the pregnancy. The student concluded by saying that if her mother had chosen the abortion route, she would not be there speaking to them that day. She paused, smiled, and said, "Although I know some of you may disagree with my views on abortion, I must say I am glad that you are here to listen and that I am here to speak. Think about it." If your reasons are compelling and your evidence is strong, you may soften the opposition and move waverers toward your position.

Do not worry if the change you want does not show up immediately. There often is a delayed reaction to persuasion, a **sleeper effect,** in which change shows up only after listeners have had time to integrate the message into their belief systems.[14] Even if no change is apparent, your message may serve a consciousness-raising function, sensitizing your listeners to the issue and making them more receptive to future persuasion.[15] Even when a cause is truly deserving, moving people through all the steps in the persuasive process may still require a series of messages.

Facing a reluctant audience is never easy. But you can't predict what new thoughts your speech might stimulate among listeners or what delayed positive reactions to it there might be. Even if it only keeps alive the American tradition of dissent, it will have served a valuable function.

Removing Barriers to Commitment

Listeners may be reluctant to commit to a position because they need more information, because they do not see a connection between their values and interests and your position, or because they may not feel certain that they can trust your judgment. To deal with these challenges, you should provide needed information, show listeners how your proposal relates to their values or interests, or strengthen your credibility.

Provide Needed Information.   Often a missing fact or unanswered question stands in the way of commitment. "I know that many of you agree with me but are asking, 'How much will this cost?'" Anticipating reservations and supplying the necessary information can help move listeners toward your position.

Affirm and Apply Values.   Persuasive speeches that threaten audience values are not likely to be effective. You must show listeners that your proposal agrees with what they believe. For example, if your listeners resist an educational program for the disadvantaged because they think that people ought to take care of themselves, you may have to show them that your program represents "a *hand up,* not a *handout.*" Show them that your proposal will lead to other favorable outcomes, such as reductions in crime or unemployment.

As we noted in Chapter 4, values are resistant to change. If you can reason from the perspective of your listeners' values, using them as the basis for your arguments, you will create identification and remove a barrier to commitment.

Encouraging Uncommitted Listeners

speaker's notes

1 Provide all necessary information.
2 Show how your proposal meets listeners' needs and strengthens their values.
3 Borrow ethos by citing authorities the audience respects.
4 Do not overstate your case or rely too heavily on emotional appeals.

Strengthen Your Credibility. When audiences hesitate because they question your credibility, you can "borrow ethos" by citing expert testimony. Call on sources that your listeners trust and respect. Uncommitted audiences will scrutinize both you and your arguments carefully. Reason with such listeners, leading them gradually and carefully to the conclusion you would like them to reach. Provide supporting material each step of the way. Adopt a multisided approach, in which you consider all options fairly, to confirm your ethos as a trustworthy and competent speaker.

When addressing uncommitted listeners, don't overstate your case. Let your personal commitment be evident through your sincerity and conviction, but be careful about using overly strong appeals to guilt or fear. These might backfire, causing listeners to resent and reject both you and your message.[16] It is also important not to push uncommitted listeners too hard. Help them move in the desired direction, but let them take the final step themselves.

Moving from Attitude to Action

Just as opponents may be reluctant to listen, sympathetic audiences may be reluctant to act. It is one thing to agree with a speaker and quite another to accept the inconvenience and risk that action may require. Listeners may believe that the problem does not affect them personally. They may not know what they should do or how they should do it. Or, they may feel that the situation is hopeless.[17] To move people to action, you must give them a reason to act. You may have to remind them of their beliefs, demonstrate the need for involvement, present a clear plan of action, and make it easy for them to comply.

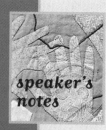

Moving People to Action

speaker's notes

1 Remind listeners of what is at stake.
2 Provide a clear plan of action.
3 Use examples and stories that provide models for action.
4 Visualize the consequences of acting and not acting.
5 Demonstrate that you practice what you preach.
6 Ask for public commitment.
7 Make it easy for listeners to act.

Revitalize Shared Beliefs.   When speakers and audiences celebrate shared beliefs, the result is often a renewed sense of commitment. Such occasions may involve telling stories that resurrect heroes, giving shared beliefs new meaning.[18] At political conventions, Jefferson, Lincoln, Roosevelt, Kennedy, and Reagan are often invoked in speeches. These symbolic heroes can help bridge audience diversity by bringing differing factions together.

Demonstrate the Need for Involvement.   Show your listeners how the quality of *their* lives depends on action. Demonstrate that the results will be satisfying. It often helps if you can associate the change with a vision of the future. In his final speech, Martin Luther King, Jr., said, "I may not get there with you, but I can see the Promised Land." King's vision of the Promised Land helped justify the sacrifice called for in his plan of action.

Present a Clear Plan of Action.   Listeners may exaggerate the difficulty of a proposal or insist that it is impossible. To overcome such resistance, show them how others have been successful. Use examples or narratives that depict listeners undertaking successful action. Stress that "we *can* do it, and this is *how* we can do it." Give listeners a clear plan. A speaker urging classmates to work to defeat a proposed tuition raise said:

> **How many of you are ready to help defeat this plan to raise tuition? Good! I see your heads nodding. Now, if you're willing to sign this petition, hold up your hands. Hold them higher! I want to see you! Good! Now, I'm going to pass around this petition, and I want each of you to sign it. If we act together, we can make a difference.**

Be specific in your instructions. Your plan must show listeners what to do and how to do it. It may take strong feelings to move people to action. Declare your own commitment and ask listeners to join you. Once people have voiced their commitment, they are more likely to follow through on it.[19]

Make It Easy for Your Audience to Comply.   Instead of simply urging listeners to write their congressional representatives, provide them with addresses and telephone numbers, a petition to sign, or preprinted addressed postcards to return.

The Challenge of Ethical Persuasion

Ours is a skeptical and cynical age, perhaps because of large-scale abuses of communication ethics. Ads promise that products will make us sexier or richer. Persuasive messages disguised as information appear in "infomercials" seen on television. Public officials may present suspicious statistics, make dubious denials, or dance around questions they don't want to answer directly. Television networks have staged visuals to dramatize their stories. Talk show hosts may play fast and loose with facts and use inflammatory language. Our government has more than once subjected us to "disinformation" campaigns that deceive the public. Little wonder that people have lost trust in their major institutions.

As a consumer of persuasive messages, you can at least partially protect yourself by applying the critical thinking skills we discussed in Chapter 3. As a producer of persuasive messages, you can help counter this trend toward

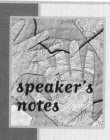

Guidelines for Ethical Persuasion

speaker's notes

1   Avoid name-calling: Attack problems, proposals, and ideas—not people.
2   Be open about your personal interest.
3   Don't adapt to the point of compromising your convictions.
4   Argue from responsible knowledge.
5   Don't try to pass off opinions as facts.
6   Don't use inflammatory language to hide a lack of evidence.
7   Be sure your proposal is in the best interest of your audience.
8   Remember that words can hurt.

unethical communication. While ethical questions in communication are often complex, depending upon the interaction of topic, situation, audience, and technique, you can start by keeping three simple questions in mind as you prepare your persuasive speech:[20]

- What is my ethical responsibility to my audience?
- Could I publicly defend the ethics of my message?
- What does this message say about my character?

Your responses to these questions should light your way through the complexities of ethical persuasion.

As we noted in Chapter 1, an ethical speech is based fundamentally on respect for the audience, responsible knowledge of the topic, and concern for the consequences of your words. The guidelines in the Speaker's Notes above should help you apply these precepts to persuasive messages.

Major Persuasive Functions

The three major functions that persuasive speeches perform are (1) addressing attitudes and values, (2) urging action, and (3) contending with opposition. A persuasive speech may perform all these functions, but it will usually emphasize just one of them.

Addressing Attitudes and Values

The basic goal of a persuasive speech **addressing attitudes and values** is to form, change, or reinforce listeners' feelings and beliefs about something. To do this, a speaker might wish to raise doubt or discontent. For example, in addressing "Are We Harassing the Harassers?" Jennifer DeSantis described specific situations in which sexual harassment had been or might be alleged to occur. She then posed questions about these situations, complicating her listeners' reactions to them and raising doubt as to what is and what is not sexual harassment. In a later speech, Jennifer built on this doubt by proposing a new policy for controlling sexual harassment in the workplace. Thus, speeches addressing attitudes and values often pave the way for speeches urging action.

When they are most ambitious, speeches addressing attitudes aim for a total change of conviction. A speech on "Putting Football in Its Place"—urging us to de-emphasize intercollegiate sports—might attempt such far-reaching influence. Obviously, the greater the change of attitude advocated, the more difficult it will be to achieve your goal. As we noted in Chapter 4, beliefs, attitudes, and values are an integral part of our personality. Deep changes in any of these can have a real impact on how we live, so audiences are usually resistant to extreme proposals. Such persuasive efforts might even cause listeners to reject the speaker and cling more stubbornly to their previous beliefs.

To be effective, speeches addressing attitudes must begin on common ground. Betty Nichols's classroom speech on responsible drinking and driving began by assuming that she and her listeners shared the belief that drunk driving is a serious problem. She reinforced that shared belief and then proposed a change in attitude as part of a solution for the problem. To encourage such change, offer audience members good reasons for modifying their convictions.[21]

Urging Action

Speeches **urging action** go beyond attitude change and encourage listeners to take action, either as individuals or as members of a group. Bonnie Marshall asked audience members to take individual action to assure their right to die with dignity: to write their state representatives in support of appropriate legislation, draw up a living will, assign durable power of attorney to a trusted friend or family member, and let their personal physicians know their wishes. When a persuasive speech urges individual action, listeners must see the necessity for action in personal terms.

When a speech advocates group action, the audience must see itself as having a common identity and purpose. As we noted in Chapter 10, the speaker can reinforce group identity by using inclusive pronouns (*we, our, us*), telling stories that emphasize group achievements, and referring to common heroes, opponents, or martyrs. Anna Aley used an effective appeal to group identity as she proposed specific actions:

> **What can one student do to change the practices of numerous Manhattan landlords? Nothing, if that student is alone. But just think of what we could accomplish if we got all 13,600 off-campus students involved in this issue! Think what we could accomplish if we got even a fraction of those students involved!**

By identifying and uniting them as victims of unscrupulous landlords, Anna encouraged her student listeners to act as members of a group.

Speeches advocating action usually involve risk. Therefore, you must present good reasons to overcome your audience's natural caution. The consequences of acting and not acting must be clearly spelled out. Your plan must be practical and reasonable, and your listeners should be able to see themselves enacting it successfully.

Contending with Opposition

When **contending with opposition**, you directly refute opposing arguments to clear the way for what you are proposing. "There are those who say that we cannot afford to land explorers on Mars in the next century," said Marvin

Andrews to his public speaking class. "I say we can't afford not to." Marvin then went on to describe the benefits that might come from such exploration. "But we really have no idea of all the benefits, any more than Queen Isabella could have foreseen the benefits of the voyage of Columbus. Fortunately, she did not listen to advisers who said his trip would cost too much."

On highly controversial topics such as abortion or gun control, you often can't avoid speeches of contention. If some audience members hold opposing views, your criticism of their position may offend them, make them defensive, or even make them more difficult to persuade. Why, then, would you risk giving such a speech? When immediate action is needed, other approaches may take too long to be effective. To secure immediate action, you may have to address opposing beliefs directly and discredit the arguments that support them with indisputable facts and figures or expert testimony.

Speeches that contend with opposition may also be the best strategy when your audience is divided in their attitudes toward the topic. In such cases, your primary audience will be uncommitted listeners and reasonable opponents. By presenting tactful, carefully documented counterarguments, you may reach some of them. A refutational approach may also help strengthen the resolve of supporters who need assurance that an opposing position can be effectively countered.

Finally, in some situations that are extremely important to you personally, you may want to give a speech of contention as a last-ditch tactic. You may feel that listeners are so strongly entrenched in their opposition that your only hope is to shock them with a direct, frontal attack that shows them why they are wrong. You hope for a positive delayed effect after their first negative reaction. Or you may even decide that your chances for persuasion are small, but your position deserves to be heard with all the power, reason, and conviction you can muster. You can have your say and feel better for it.

Designs for Persuasive Speaking

As you determine the function of your persuasive speech, you must also decide how to structure your speech (see Figure 13.3). Many of the designs used for informative speeches are also appropriate for persuasive speeches. The categorical design can be used to develop a persuasive argument, such as asserting that a plan is *needed*, that it will *work*, and that it offers *benefits*. The sequential design can outline the steps in a plan of action. The comparative design works well for speeches of contention in which you contrast the weaknesses of an opposing argument with the strengths of your own.

In the remainder of this chapter, we look at three designs that are especially suited to persuasive speeches. We shall examine the problem-solution design, the motivated sequence design, and the refutative design.

Problem-Solution Design

The **problem-solution design** first convinces listeners that there is a problem, then shows them how to deal with it. The solution can involve changing an attitude or taking an action. It is sometimes hard to convince listeners that a problem exists or that it is serious. People have an unfortunate ten-

FIGURE 13.3

Selecting Persuasive
Designs

Design	Use When
Categorical	Your topic invites thinking in familiar patterns, such as proving a plan will be *safe, inexpensive,* and *effective.* Can be used to change attitudes or to urge action.
Comparison/ Contrast	You want to demonstrate why your proposal is superior to another. Especially good for speeches in which you contend with opposing views.
Sequential	Your speech contains a plan of action that must be carried out in a specific order.
Problem-Solution	Your topic presents a problem that needs to be solved and a solution that will solve it. Good for speeches involving attitudes and urging action.
Motivated Sequence	Your topic calls for action as the final phase of a five-step process that involves, in order, arousing attention demonstrating need, satisfying need, picturing the results, and calling for action.
Refutative	You must answer strong opposition on a topic before you can establish your position. The opposing claims become main points for development. Attack weakest points first and avoid personal attacks.

dency to ignore problems until they reach a critical stage. You can counteract this tendency by vividly depicting the crisis that will surely emerge unless your audience makes a change.

When you prepare a problem-solution speech, do not overwhelm your listeners with details. Cover the most important aspects of the problem, then show the audience how your solution will work. A problem-solution speech opposing a tuition increase might build on the following general design:

Thesis statement: We must defeat the tuition increase proposal.

I. *Problem:* The proposal to raise tuition is a disaster!
   A. The increase will create hardships for many students.
      1. Many current students will have to drop out.
      2. New students will be discouraged from enrolling.
   B. The increase will create additional problems for the university and the community.
      1. Decreased attendance means decreased revenue.
      2. Decreased revenue will reduce the university's community services.
      3. Reduced service will mean reduced support from contributors.
II. *Solution:* Defeat the proposal to raise tuition!
   A. Sign our petition against the tuition increase.
   B. Write letters to your state legislators.
   C. Write a letter to your local newspaper.
   D. Attend our campus rally next Wednesday.

When the problem can be identified clearly and the solution is concrete and simple, the problem-solution design works well in persuasive speeches.

The **stock issues design** is a variation of the problem-solution design. In this design, the speaker first establishes a need for change, then develops a plan for change, and finally demonstrates that the plan fits the need. The stock issues design attempts to answer the major questions that a reasonable, careful person would ask before agreeing to a change in policies or procedures.[22] Such questions include:

   I. *Is there some significant problem?*
     A. How did the problem originate?
     B. What caused the problem?
     C. How widespread is the problem?
     D. How long has the problem persisted?
     E. What harms are associated with the problem?
     F. Will these harms continue and grow unless there is change?
   II. *What is the solution to this problem?*
     A. Will the solution actually solve the problem?
     B. Is the solution practical?
     C. Would the cost of the solution be reasonable?
     D. Might there be other consequences to the solution?
  III. *Who will put the solution into effect?*
     A. Are these people responsible and competent?
     B. What role might listeners play?[23]

Motivated Sequence Design

The **motivated sequence design** is also related to the problem-solution design, but it is distinctive enough that we can discuss it separately.[24] This design has five steps, beginning with arousing attention and ending with a call for action. Therefore, it is especially suited for speeches that have action as their goal. The steps in the motivated sequence are as follows:

1. *Arouse attention.* As in any speech, you begin by stimulating interest in your subject. In Chapter 12 we discussed six factors that affect attention: Intensity, Repetition, Novelty, Activity, Contrast, and Relevance. These same techniques may be used to gain attention in persuasive speeches.

2. *Demonstrate a need.* Show your listeners that the situation you wish to change is urgent. Help them see what they can win or lose if they accept or reject your plan for change. To create such understanding, tie your proposal to the basic needs discussed in Chapter 4.

3. *Satisfy the need.* Present a way to satisfy the need you have demonstrated. Set out a plan of action and explain how it would work. Offer examples that show how your plan has worked successfully in other places.

4. *Visualize the results.* Paint verbal pictures that illustrate the positive results listeners can expect. You could show your listeners how their lives will be better when they have enacted your plan. Such a picture of

the future can help overcome resistance to action. You could also paint a dire picture of what life could be like if they do not go along with your suggestions. You might even put these positive and negative verbal pictures side by side to strengthen their impact through contrast.

5. *Call for action.* Your call for action may be a challenge, an appeal, or a statement of personal commitment. The call for action should be short and to the point. Give your listeners something specific that they can do right away to start the change. If you can get them to take the first step, the next will come more easily.

Let's look at how this model might work in a persuasive speech that appeals to audience motivations for recognition, friendship, and nurturance, using language that activates feelings of sympathy and identification:

1. *Arouse attention*	Have you ever dreamed about being a hero or heroine? Have you ever wished you could do something that would really make a difference in our world? Well, I'm here to tell you how you can if you invest only three hours a week.
2. *Demonstrate a need*	Our community needs volunteers to help children who are lonely and neglected. Big Sisters and Big Brothers of Omaha have a program for these children, but it takes people to make the program work. Last year they had forty-eight student volunteers. This year only thirty have signed up to help. They need at least thirty more. They need you.
3. *Satisfy the need*	Volunteering to be a big brother or a big sister will help keep this vital program going. It will also make you a hero or heroine in the eyes of a child.
4. *Visualize the results*	Maybe you can have an experience that will be as rewarding as mine has been. Last year I worked with ten-year-old Kevin two afternoons a week. He needed help with his homework because his grades were just barely passing. But more than school help, he needed someone who cared about him. The first six weeks his grades went from D–'s to C–'s, and I took him to a basketball game one weekend. The next six weeks his grades went up to C's and C+'s, and I took him to a movie. This year Kevin is doing well in school. He's making C's and B's in all his courses, but we still meet and work together because I couldn't bear not to see him. I guess this is a small contribution to humankind, but not to Kevin. When I look in his eyes, I see a large reflection of myself.
5. *Call for action*	Won't you make the commitment to become one of the heroines or heroes of our community? Just one or two afternoons a week can make a difference in the life of a child and in

our future. The pay is not good—nothing!—but the rewards are enormous. I've got the applications with me. Let me sign you up now!

If you plan to use the motivated sequence design, first determine where your listeners stand on the issue, then focus on the steps that will carry persuasion forward. For example, if you are speaking to an audience that is already convinced of the need for a change but lacks a plan to make it work, you could focus on step 3, "satisfy the need." However, if you are facing an audience that contests the need, your emphasis should be on step 2, "demonstrate a need."

Refutative Design

In the **refutative design**, the speaker tries to raise doubt about a competing position by revealing its inconsistencies and weaknesses. To bring off an effective refutation, you must understand the opposition's motivations, arguments, and evidence. It is often wise to take on your opponent's weakest point first. Your refutation then raises doubt about other opposing arguments. The point of attack may be illogical reasoning or flimsy, insufficient evidence, as we shall discuss further in Chapter 14, or even the self-interest of an opposing speaker. However, be sure to keep the dispute constructive. Avoid personal attacks unless credibility issues are central and inescapable. Above all, be fair!

There are five steps in developing an effective refutation. These five steps should be followed in sequence for each point you plan to refute.

1. State the point you are going to refute and explain why it is important.
2. Tell the audience how you are going to refute this point.
3. Present your evidence, using facts and figures, examples, and testimony. Cite sources and authorities that the audience will accept as competent and credible.
4. Spell out the conclusion for the audience. Do not assume that listeners will figure out what the evidence means. Tell them directly.
5. Explain the significance of your refutation—show how it discredits or damages the position of the opposition.

For example, you might refute an argument against sex education in public high schools in the following manner:

State the point you will refute and explain its importance.
Tell how you will refute this point.

Present your evidence, using credible sources.

Our well-intentioned friends would have you believe, and this is their biggest concern, that birth-control information increases teenage sexual activity.

I want to share with you some statistical evidence that contradicts this contention—a contention that is simply not supported by the facts.

The latest study on this issue by the Department of Health, Education, and Welfare compared sexual activity rates in sixty high schools across the United States—thirty with sex education programs and thirty without. Their findings show that there are no significant differences in sexual activity rates between these two groups of schools.

■ *State your conclusion.*

Therefore, the argument that access to birth-control information through sex education programs increases sexual activity simply does not hold water.

■ *Explain the significance of your refutation.*

That's typical of the attack on sex education in the schools—to borrow a line from Shakespeare, it's a lot of "sound and fury, signifying nothing."

You can strengthen this design if you follow your refutation by proving a similar point of your own, thus balancing the negative refutation with a positive demonstration. The result supplies the audience with an alternative belief to substitute for the one you have refuted. Use the same five-step sequence to support your position. For example, you might follow the preceding refutation with the following demonstration:

■ *State the point you will support and explain its importance.*

I'm not going to try to tell you that birth-control information reduces sexual activity. But I want to tell you what it does reduce. It reduces teenage pregnancy.

■ *Tell how you will support this point.*

There is reliable evidence that fewer girls become pregnant in high schools with sex education programs.

■ *Present your evidence, using credible sources.*

The same study conducted by Health, Education, and Welfare demonstrated that in high schools with sex education programs, the pregnancy rate dropped from one out of every sixty female students to one out of ninety within two years of the program's going into effect.

■ *State your conclusion.*

Therefore, sex education is a good program. It attacks a devastating social problem—the epidemic of children having children.

■ *State the significance of your demonstration.*

Any program that reduces unwanted teenage pregnancy is valuable—valuable to the young women involved, valuable to society. We all pay in so many ways for this personal and social tragedy—we should all support a program that works to reduce it. And we should reject the irrational voices that reject the program.

As should now be clear, the study of persuasive speaking is a study of the arts of effective living. Learning how to use persuasion ethically and effectively, and how to avoid being abused by unethical persuaders, provides skills that are central to successful lives. In the next chapter, we shall learn more about persuasion by studying patterns of evidence, proof, and argument that drive the persuasive process.

In Summary

Persuasion is the art of getting others to consider our point of view fairly and favorably. Persuasion is vital to our political system, which is based on the principle of rule by *deliberation* and choice rather than by force. The right to express opinions—no matter how unpopular—also serves practical goals. Groups that have been exposed to different positions usually make better decisions because they are stimulated to examine a situation and to think about their options.

Characteristics of Persuasive Speaking. In contrast with informative speaking, persuasive speaking urges a choice among options and asks for a commitment. Rather than speaking as a teacher, the speaker assumes the role of advocate. Ethical persuasive speaking centers on *good reasons* based upon responsible knowledge and a sensitive consideration of audience interests. Persuasive speeches rely more on emotional involvement than do informative speeches, and they carry a heavier ethical burden.

The Process of Persuasion.   When persuasion is successful, people listen, learn, agree, and change as a result of what they hear. These behaviors parallel McGuire's categories of awareness, understanding, agreement, enactment, and integration of persuasive material. Awareness suggests that we know of a problem, that it commands our serious attention. Understanding implies that we can see the connection between the problem and our lives, and that we know how to carry out the speaker's proposals. Agreement implies our acceptance of a speaker's interpretations and recommendations. Enactment suggests our commitment and readiness to carry out the speaker's ideas. Integration involves consolidating the new attitudes and commitments into our overall belief and value system.

The Challenges of Persuasion.   Persuading others can pose many challenges. You may have to entice a reluctant audience to listen, remove barriers that block commitment, move listeners from agreement to action, and be scrupulously ethical. To encourage reluctant listeners, use a *co-active approach* that seeks to bridge differences and to build identification. Avoid a *boomerang effect* by not pushing listeners too hard in one speech. Remove barriers to commitment by providing vital information, pointing out the relevance to listeners' lives, and building credibility. To move partisan listeners from agreement to action, use vivid language and examples to bring abstract principles to life, prove the need for their involvement, present a clear plan, declare your own commitment as a model, and make it easy for listeners to take the first step into involvement. To be an ethical persuader, be sure that your messages are based on respect for the audience, responsible knowledge of the topic, and concern for the consequences of your words.

Functions of Persuasive Speeches.   Persuasive speeches address attitudes and values, urge action and the support of policies, and contend with opposition. While *addressing attitudes and values*, remember that the more change you ask for, the more difficult your challenge will be. Avoid the *great expectation fallacy*, which asks for more change than one could reasonably expect after one speech. When *urging action*, you ask listeners to take action, either as individuals or as members of groups. While *contending with opposition*, you confront opponents by systematically refuting their claims. Speeches that emphasize contention usually do not seek to convert opponents, but rather seek to win over the uncommitted and to influence opinion leaders.

Designs for Persuasive Speaking.   While many of the designs discussed for informative speaking can also serve the purposes of persuasion, three designs in particular serve the needs of persuasive speaking. In a *problem-solution design*, you must first convince the audience that a problem exists, and then advance a solution that corrects it. The *motivated sequence design* has five steps: arousing attention, demonstrating a need, satisfying the need, visualizing results, and calling for action. To use the *refutative design*, state the point you intend to refute, tell how you will refute it, present your evidence, draw a conclusion, and explain the significance of the refutation. Refutation is often followed by demonstration, in which you prove a point to replace the one you have just disproved.

Terms to Know

persuasion

deliberation

good reasons

consciousness-raising

co-active approach

boomerang effect

great expectation fallacy

multisided presentation

inoculation effect

sleeper effect

addressing attitudes and values

urging action

contending with opposition

problem-solution design

stock issues design

motivated sequence design

refutative design

Notes

1. Sonja K. Foss and Cindy L. Griffin, "Beyond Persuasion: A Proposal for an Invitational Rhetoric," *Communication Monographs* 62 (1995): 2–18.
2. *Whitney* v. *California*, 274 U.S. 357, 375 (1927).
3. *On Liberty* (Chicago: Henry Regnery, 1955 [originally published 1859]), p. 24.
4. Charlan Jeanne Nemeth, "Differential Contributions of Majority and Minority Influence," *Psychological Review* 93 (1986): 23–32.
5. Mark A. Hamilton and John E. Hunter, "The Effect of Language Intensity on Receiver Attitudes Toward Message, Source, and Topic," in *Persuasion: Advances Through Meta-Analysis,* ed. M. Allen and R. W. Preiss (Beverly Hills, Calif.: Sage, 1998).
6. William J. McGuire, "Attitudes and Attitude Change," in *The Handbook of Social Psychology,* ed. Gardner Lindzey and Elliot Aronson (New York: Random House, 1985), I: 258–261.
7. Roger Brown, *Social Psychology* (New York: Free Press, 1965), pp. 709–763.
8. Gloria Steinem, *Revolution from Within: A Book of Self-Esteem* (New York: Little, Brown, 1992), p. 120.
9. John C. Reinard, "The Empirical Study of the Persuasive Effects of Evidence: The Status After Fifty Years of Research," *Human Communication Research* 15 (1988): 3–59.
10. Adapted from Herbert W. Simons, *Persuasion: Understanding, Practice, and Analysis*, 2nd ed. (New York: Random House, 1986), p. 138.
11. N. H. Anderson, "Integration Theory and Attitude Change," *Psychological Review* 78 (1971): 171–206.
12. McGuire, p. 260.
13. Mike Allen, "Meta-Analysis Comparing the Persuasiveness of One-sided and Two-sided Messages," *Western Journal of Speech Communication* 55 (1991): 390–404; M. Allen et al., "Testing a Model of Message Sidedness: Three Replications," *Communication Monographs* 56 (1990): 275–291; Jerold L. Hale, Paul A. Mongeau, and Randi M. Thomas, "Cognitive Processing of One- and Two-sided Persuasive Messages," *Western Journal of Speech Communication* 55 (1991): 380–389; Carl I. Hovland, Arthur A. Lumsdaine, and Fred D.

Sheffield, "The Effects of Presenting 'One Side' Versus 'Both Sides' in Changing Opinions on a Controversial Subject," in *Experiments on Mass Communication* (Princeton, N.J.: Princeton University Press, 1949), pp. 201–227; and William J. McGuire, "Inducing Resistance to Persuasion," in *Advances in Experimental Social Psychology,* ed. L. Berkowitz (New York: Academic Press, 1964), pp. 191–229.

14. Mike Allen and James B. Stiff, "Testing Three Models for the Sleeper Effect," *Western Journal of Speech Communication* 53 (1989): 411–426; and T. D. Cook et al., "History of the Sleeper Effect: Some Logical Pitfalls in Accepting the Null Hypothesis," *Psychological Bulletin* 86 (1979): 662–679.

15. M. E. McCombs, "The Agenda-setting Approach," in *Handbook of Political Communication,* ed. D. D. Nimmo and K. R. Sanders (Beverly Hills, Calif.: Sage, 1981), pp. 121–140.

16. Franklin J. Boster and Paul Mongeau, "Fear-arousing Persuasive Messages," in *Communication Yearbook 8,* ed. R. Bostrom (Beverly Hills, Calif.: Sage, 1984), pp. 330–377, and Richard E. Petty and Duane T. Wegener, "Attitude Change: Multiple Roles for Persuasion Variables," in *The Handbook of Social Psychology,* 4th ed., Daniel T. Gilbert, Susan T. Fiske, and Gardner Lindzey (Boston: McGraw-Hill, 1998), pp. 353–354.

17. Katherine E. Rowan, "Goals, Obstacles, and Strategies in Risk Communication: A Problem-solving Approach to Improving Communication About Risks," *Journal of Applied Communication Research* 19 (1991): 322.

18. Michael Osborn, "Rhetorical Depiction," in *Form, Genre, and the Study of Political Discourse,* ed. Herbert W. Simons and Aram A. Aghazarian (Columbia: University of South Carolina Press, 1986), pp. 79–107.

19. R. A. Wicklund and J. W. Brehm, *Perspectives on Cognitive Dissonance* (Hillsdale, N.J.: Erlbaum, 1976).

20. Adapted from Richard L. Johannensen, *Ethics in Communication,* 3rd ed. (Prospect Heights, Ill.: Waveland, 1990), pp. 17–20.

21. See Walter R. Fisher, "Toward a Logic of Good Reasons," *Quarterly Journal of Speech* 64 (1978): 376–384; and Karl R. Wallace, "The Substance of Rhetoric: Good Reasons," *Quarterly Journal of Speech* 49 (1963): 239–249.

22. J. W. Patterson and David Zarefsky, *Contemporary Debate* (Boston: Houghton Mifflin, 1983).

23. The structure of the stock issues design has been adapted from Charles U. Larson, *Persuasion: Reception and Responsibility,* 8th ed. (Belmont, Calif.: Wadsworth, 1998), pp. 293–295; and Charles S. Mudd and Malcolm O. Sillars, *Public Speaking: Content and Communication* (Prospect Heights, Ill.: Waveland, 1991), pp. 100–102.

24. This design was introduced in Alan Monroe's *Principles and Types of Speech* (New York: Scott, Foresman, 1935) and has been refined in later editions.

Sample Persuasive Speech

We Don't Have to Live in Slums
Anna Aley

Slumlords—you'd expect them in New York or Chicago, but in Manhattan, Kansas? You'd better believe there are slumlords in Manhattan, and they pose a direct threat to you if you ever plan to rent an off-campus apartment.

I know about slumlords; I rented a basement apartment from one last semester. I guess I first suspected something was wrong when I discovered dead roaches in the refrigerator. I definitely knew something was wrong when I discovered the leaks: the one in the bathroom that kept the bathroom carpet constantly soggy and molding and the one in the kitchen that allowed water from the upstairs neighbor's bathroom to seep into the kitchen cabinets and collect in my dishes.

Then there were the serious problems. The hot water heater and furnace were connected improperly and posed a fire hazard. They were situated next to the only exit. There was no smoke detector or fire extinguisher and no emergency way out—the windows were too small for escape. I was living in an accident waiting to happen—and paying for it.

The worst thing about my ordeal was that I was not an isolated instance; many Kansas State students are living in unsafe housing and paying for it, not only with their money, but their happiness, their grades, their health, and their safety.

We can't be sure how many students are living in substandard housing, housing that does not meet the code specifications required of rental property. We can be sure, however, that a large number of Kansas State students are at risk of being caught in the same situation I was. According to the registrar, approximately 17,800 students are attending Kansas State this semester. Housing claims that 4,200 live in the dorms. This means that approximately 13,600 students live off-campus. Some live in fraternities or sororities, some live at home, but most live in off-campus apartments, as I do.

Many of these 13,600 students share traits that make them likely to settle for substandard housing. For example, many students want to live close to campus. If you've ever driven through the surrounding neighborhoods, you know that much of the available housing is in older houses, houses that were never meant to be divided into separate rental units. Students are also often limited in the amount they can pay for rent; some landlords, such as mine, will use low rent as an excuse not to fix anything and to let the apartment deteriorate. Most importantly, many students are young and, consequently, naive when it comes to selecting an apartment. They don't know the housing codes; but even if they did, they don't know how to check to make sure the apartment is in compliance. Let's face it—how many of us know how to check a hot water heater to make sure it's connected properly?

Adding to the problem of the number of students willing to settle for substandard housing is the number of landlords willing to supply it. Currently, the Consumer Relations Board here at Kansas State has on file student

Here the problem-solution design becomes apparent. Having established the reality of the problem, Anna turns to the causes, which she must identify before she can propose a solution.

complaints against approximately one hundred landlords. There are surely complaints against many more that have never been formally reported.

There are two main causes of the substandard student housing problem. The first—and most significant—is the simple fact that it is possible for a landlord to lease an apartment that does not meet housing code requirements. The Manhattan Housing Code Inspector will evaluate an apartment, but only after the tenant has given the landlord a written complaint and the landlord has had fourteen days to remedy the situation. In other words, the way things are now, the only way the Housing Code Inspector can evaluate an apartment to see if it's safe to be lived in is if someone has been living in it for at least two weeks!

A second cause of the problem is the fact that campus services designed to help students avoid substandard housing are not well known. The Consumer Relations Board here at Kansas State can help students inspect apartments for safety before they sign a lease, it can provide students with vital information on their rights as tenants, and it can mediate in landlord-tenant disputes. The problem is, many people don't know these services exist. The Consumer Relations Board is not listed in the university catalogue; it is not mentioned in any of the admissions literature. The only places it is mentioned are in alphabetically organized references such as the phone book, but you have to already know it exists to look it up! The Consumer Relations Board does receive money for advertising from the student senate, but it is only enough to run a little two-by-three-inch ad once every month. That is not large enough or frequent enough to be noticed by many who could use these services.

Anna appeals to her audience as a group and assures them that there is power in numbers. She spells out what they need to do. Her petition provides for immediate action. She could have strengthened her appeal to "join the Off-Campus Association" by having membership forms and a roster for her listeners to sign.

It's clear that we have a problem, but what may not seem so clear is what we can do about it. After all, what can one student do to change the practices of numerous Manhattan landlords? Nothing, if that student is alone. But just think of what we could accomplish if we got all 13,600 off-campus students involved in this issue! Think what we could accomplish if we got even a fraction of those students involved! This is what Wade Whitmer, director of the Consumer Relations Board, is attempting to do. He is reorganizing the Off-Campus Association in an effort to pass a city ordinance requiring landlords to have their apartments inspected for safety before those apartments can be rented out. The Manhattan code inspector has already tried to get just such an ordinance passed, but the only people who showed up at the public forums were known slumlords, who obviously weren't in favor of the proposed ordinance. No one showed up to argue in favor of the ordinance, so the city commissioners figured that no one wanted it and voted it down. If we can get the Off-Campus Association organized and involved, however, the commissioners will see that someone does want the ordinance, and they will be more likely to pass it the next time it is proposed. You can do a great service to your fellow students—and to yourself—by joining the Off-Campus Association.

A second thing you can do to help ensure that no more Kansas State students have to go through what I did is sign my petition asking the student senate to increase the Consumer Relations Board's advertising budget. Let's face it—a service cannot do anybody any good if no one knows about it. The Consumer Relations Board's services are simply too valuable to let go to waste.

Anna concludes with a true-life narrative to ensure that listeners will retain her message and integrate it into their belief systems. Her speech ends with a forceful appeal to action.

An important thing to remember about substandard housing is that it is not only distasteful, it is dangerous. In the end, I was lucky. I got out of my apartment with little more than bad memories. My upstairs neighbor was not so lucky. The main problem with his apartment was that the electrical wiring was done improperly; there were too many outlets for too few circuits, so the fuses were always blowing. One day last November, Jack was at home when a fuse blew—as usual. And, as usual, he went to the fuse box to flip the switch back on. When he touched the switch, it delivered such a shock that it literally threw this guy the size of a football player backwards and down a flight of stairs. He lay there at the bottom, unable to move, for a full hour before his roommate came home and called an ambulance.

Jack was lucky. His back was not broken. But he did rip many of the muscles in his back. Now he has to go to physical therapy, and he is not expected to fully recover.

Kansas State students have been putting up with substandard living conditions for too long. It's time we finally got together to do something about this problem. Join the Off-Campus Association. Sign my petition. Let's send a message to these slumlords that we're not going to put up with this any more. We don't have to live in slums.

WORKS CONSULTED

Kansas State University. *K-State! Campus Living*.

Registrar's Office. Kansas State University. Personal interview. 10 March 1989.

Residential Landlord and Tenant Act. State of Kansas. 1975.

Whitmer, Wade. Director, Consumer Relations Board. Personal interview. 10 March 1989.

14 Evidence, Proof, and Argument

*S*peech is power: Speech is to persuade, to convert, to compel.

—*Ralph Waldo Emerson*

This chapter will help you

- transform supporting materials into evidence
- develop evidence into proofs
- arrange proofs into arguments
- avoid defects of evidence, proofs, and arguments

A *s he completed the "problem" phase of the design for his persuasive speech, Jim Cardoza could see from his listeners' faces that he had expanded their awareness of the environmental problem. They seemed concerned as they pondered his* evidence. *They nodded as he* proved *his points to their satisfaction. They appeared ready to agree with his* argument *that environmental recovery should be a high priority. They were now prepared to give serious consideration to his solution (see his entire speech at the end of this chapter).*

WHAT DO THE terms—evidence, proof, and argument—mean? They form the tapestry of reasoning that we see displayed in successful persuasive speeches. They provide the "good reasons" we talked about in the last chapter. They explain why we sometimes listen to speakers with whom we disagree, why we may take seriously facts and testimony that contradict our established attitudes, and why we occasionally integrate new convictions into our belief systems. In this chapter we discuss these elements, show how they may be woven together, explain how to use them ethically and effectively, and demonstrate how to avoid mistakes that can rob persuasion of its power.

Using Evidence Effectively

In Chapter 13 we explained that the good reasons that justify persuasion are based on responsible knowledge of a subject. In persuasive speaking, responsible knowledge means having an adequate base of supporting material from which one can draw conclusions. When supporting materials are used in persuasion, they function as **evidence**.

Consider the following situation: A speaker says, "We should all sign up as organ donors." A listener asks, "Why?" The speaker replies, "Well, I think we should. That's my opinion." Now consider a different approach. Paul B. Fowler, a student at Alderson-Broaddus College, presented a speech urging his classmates to become organ donors. Instead of just voicing his personal opinion, Paul said:

According to the *United Network for Organ Sharing*, nearly 200,000 kidney transplants have been performed since 1963. Pittsburgh surgeons

> alone transplant hundreds of kidneys per year. However, only 25 percent of kidney patients can receive a kidney from a living family member. Many must wait for years for an organ from a donor, and many will die waiting. In the Pittsburgh area alone, nealy one thousand patients are waiting right now for a phone call telling them a kidney has become available. Nationwide, more than 30,000 people are waiting.

The contrast is clear. The person listening to our hypothetical speaker might respond, "You have a right to your opinion, but I have a right to ignore it." Paul's listeners *had* to take his message seriously, even if they did not agree with all his recommendations. The combination of facts and expert testimony lifted his message above personal opinion. His evidence added strength, authority, and objectivity to his speech.

To better understand the power of evidence, let us look briefly at each of the forms of supporting material identified in Chapter 6 and contrast the work they do in informative and persuasive speeches.

Facts and Statistics

In informative speaking, facts and statistics enrich our understanding; in persuasive speaking, they alert us to a situation that should be changed. Therefore, facts and figures are especially important during the awareness phase of the persuasive process to prepare listeners for what will follow. Juli Pardell, arguing for more effective safety regulations in air travel, showed how the judicious use of facts, interlaced with testimony and examples, can create strong evidence:

> The Los Angeles airport deserves special attention. The *Christian Science Monitor* of October 29th of this year contends that it "exemplifies the growing congestion that decreases safety margins." Thirty other airports lie within a ninety-mile radius of Los Angeles airport, creating a hubbub of planes in the sky. Within a forty-five-mile radius, 197 planes vie for space in the skies at any given moment. Overcongestion only increases the chance for planes to crash, such as they did last October.

By the time Juli had finished presenting her carefully documented facts, the audience felt that she had strong evidence for her case.

Examples

In informative speeches, examples illustrate ideas and create interest. In persuasive speeches, examples can also move listeners by arousing emotions such as sympathy, fear, or anger. Factual examples are especially useful. When you can say, "This really happened," you strengthen your position. LaDell Patterson demonstrated the value of factual examples in a speech opposing discrimination against women in news organizations. In her speech she cited the experiences of Laura Stepp, a reporter for the *Washington Post*:

> Ms. Stepp recalled . . . that while a *Washington Post* lawyer was reading one of her stories, she commented that she hoped it would land on the front page because of its importance. His reply to her was, "All

Exhibits can become powerful persuasive evidence in speeches.

you have to do is shake your little fanny and they'll put it on the front page." When she objected, he said he had no idea that the remark was offensive.

This example, one of many in LaDell's speech, helped move her listeners in favor of the reforms she recommended.

In circumstances in which no one factual example adequately conveys the meaning you want to communicate, a hypothetical example may work better. At the beginning of this book, when we wanted to persuade you of the usefulness of the public speaking course, we invented the hypothetical example of "Mary," a composite person who represented all the successful students we have taught. To be ethical, you must let your listeners know when an example has been fabricated to fit the purposes of your persuasive speech.

Narratives

In informative speeches, narratives illustrate the meaning of ideas. In persuasive speeches, narratives create a sense of reality that must be changed or preserved. They can carry listeners to the scene of a problem and engage them in a living drama. They can build identification among listeners, speaker, and the theme of the speech. Kirsten Lientz illustrated these functions when she opened a speech with the following narrative:

It's a cold, icy December afternoon. You hear a distant crash, then screams, and finally the unending moan of a car horn fills the silence. You rush the short distance to the scene of the crash, where you find a Ford Bronco overturned with a young woman and two small boys inside. The woman and one of the boys climb from the wreckage

> unhurt; the other boy, however, is pinned between the dashboard and the roof of the car, unconscious and not breathing. Would you know what to do? Or would you stand there wishing you did? These events are real. Bob Flath saved this child with the skills he acquired at his company's first aid workshop.

After this dramatic narrative introduction, Kirsten's listeners were prepared to listen to her speech urging them to take the first aid course offered at her university.

Testimony

Testimony is critical in persuasive speaking. When you use testimony in a persuasive speech, you call upon experts to support your position. Introduce these witnesses carefully, describing their credentials. To support her call for air safety improvements, Juli Pardell cited eight authoritative sources of information. In his plea for organ donors, Paul Fowler cited four reputable books. It was not just Juli or Paul speaking—it was all these sources of testimony together.

Witnesses who testify against their self-interest are called **reluctant witnesses.** They provide some of the most powerful evidence available for persuasion. For example, if student reform leaders admit that the latest campus demonstrations have gone too far or if government officials confirm that they have made mistakes, their statements provide strong evidence for speakers to use.

In ethical persuasive speaking, you should rely mainly on expert testimony, using prestige and lay testimony as secondary sources of evidence. You can use prestige testimony to stress values that you want listeners to embrace. You can use lay testimony to relate your subject to the lives of listeners and increase identification. Keep in mind that when you quote others, you are associating yourself with them—for better or for worse. Be careful with whom you associate!

As a matter of fact, select all your evidence carefully. Consider different points of view on a problem, so that you don't simply present one perspec-

speaker's notes

Guidelines for the Ethical Use of Evidence

1 Does my evidence come from credible sources?

2 Have I adequately identified these sources in my speech?

3 Would my evidence be verified by other experts?

4 Have I acknowledged disagreements among experts?

5 Is my evidence relevant?

6 Is my evidence complete? Has anything important been withheld?

7 Is my evidence the most recent available?

8 Have I used testimony properly—i.e., expert testimony to establish facts, prestige testimony to enhance credibility, lay testimony to create identification?

9 Have I quoted or paraphrased testimony accurately?

10 Are my examples and narratives truly representative and not exceptions to the rule?

tive without being aware of others. Gather more research materials than you think you will need so that you have a wide range from which to choose. Be sure you have facts, figures, or expert testimony for each of your main points. Use multiple sources and types of evidence to strengthen your case.

Proving Your Points

To prove a point is to present evidence that requires your listeners to take your conclusions seriously. *Therefore, a* **proof** *weaves evidence into a justification for the advice offered in a persuasive speech.*

The nature of proof has been studied since the Golden Age of Greece. In his *Rhetoric,* Aristotle suggested that there are three fundamental types of proof, based on the susceptibilities of audiences. The first, **logos,** recognizes that we are thinking animals who respond to well-reasoned demonstrations. The second, **pathos,** affirms that we are creatures of emotion who can be touched by appeals to such emotions as fear, pity, and anger. The third, **ethos,** recognizes that we respond to the leadership qualities of speakers, especially our perceptions of their competence, character, likableness, and forcefulness. In our time, the work of many scholars has confirmed the presence of a fourth dimension of proof, **mythos,** that recognizes that we also respond to appeals to the traditions and values of our culture.[1] The dimensions of proof are actually the many dimensions of ourselves.

A persuasive speech rarely relies on a single kind of proof. Each type of proof brings its own coloration and strength to the fabric of persuasion (see Figure 14.1). In the sections that follow, we identify the strengths and qualities of these types of proof, so that you may weave them effectively into your own persuasive speech.

Logos

Logos is both practically and ethically important to persuasion. Logos demonstrates that a situation is *real*—that it is not a figment of the speaker's imagination. Therefore, it relies on facts, statistics, and expert testimony to ground a problem in reality. Logos also shows the audience what the facts

FIGURE 14.1

Weaving the Fabric of Proof

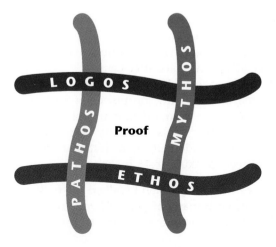

mean. This happens when a speaker interprets facts and reasons from them to a conclusion.

How does logos contribute to proof? The process follows a simple basic pattern:

1. An *assertion* is made that must be proved.
2. *Evidence* is provided to support the claim.
3. A *conclusion* is drawn that ties together the assertion and the evidence.

In a classroom speech on drinking and driving responsibly, Betty Nichols wanted to demonstrate that the sense of security people may feel in a car can be dangerous. To prove this assertion, Betty presented these facts:

> **Drunk driving causes 24,000 deaths per year and 65,000 serious injuries.**

Although this evidence is strong, Betty recognized that the facts alone might not be compelling enough to fully support the idea. She needed to interpret them for listeners. Therefore, she added a dramatic contrast to make these figures come to life:

> **Let's compare these numbers with the risk of being a homicide victim. We have a 1 in 150 chance of being murdered, but we have a 1 in 33 chance of being killed or crippled in an alcohol-related accident.**

Notice that as she draws this contrast, Betty weaves into her logos a strand of pathos: Listeners begin to see the personal threat involved. This appeal to fear, based upon the statistics, becomes even more evident in the following striking conclusion:

> **Therefore our car—which makes us feel so safe, so secure, so powerful—can become our assassin, our coffin.**

Betty's example demonstrates how logos can work as proof in a speech. An appeal to logos demonstrates the speaker's faith in the audience's intelligence. It implies that if people are offered facts and shown how to interpret them, they will come to the proper conclusion. When interwoven with pathos, *the proof gives listeners a vivid sense of the reality of the message.*[2]

Pathos

Appeals to pathos recognize that we act on feelings as well as on information. People usually respond strongly when they feel angry, afraid, guilty, excited, or compassionate toward others. When used ethically, pathos can help change attitudes or advance causes.

When speakers tell personal stories, pathos can be especially effective. Personal narratives blend the power of pathos with the authenticity of ethos. During a congressional debate on handgun control legislation, James Brady, the presidential press secretary who was shot during the assassination attempt on President Reagan, testified before the U.S. Senate Judiciary Subcommittee. Speaking from his wheelchair, he said:

> **There was a day when I walked the halls of this Senate and worked closely with many of you and your staffs. There was a wonderful day when I was fortunate enough to serve the President of the United**

States in a capacity I had dreamed of all my life. And for a time, I felt that people looked up to me. Today, I can tell you how hard it is to have people speaking down to me. But nothing has been harder than losing the independence and control we all so value in life. I need help getting out of bed, help taking a shower, and help getting dressed.

There are some who oppose a simple seven-day waiting period for handgun purchases because it would inconvenience gun buyers. Well, I guess I am paying for their convenience. And I am one of the lucky ones. I survived being shot through the head. Other shooting victims are not as fortunate.[3]

Often, threads of pathos woven into a proof are the only way to convince people of the human dimensions of a problem or the need for immediate action. Still, as powerful as emotional appeals may be, they should be used with caution. If the appeal to feeling is too obvious, audiences may suspect you of trying to manipulate them. Appeals to negative emotions such as fear or guilt are especially tricky, since they can boomerang, discrediting both the speaker and the speech. When you use pathos, be sure to back up what you say with facts and figures. *Always support pathos with logos.* In your presentation, let your voice and body language understate rather than overstate an emotional appeal. Don't engage in theatrics!

Ethos

The use of ethos recognizes that listeners are persuaded by the credibility of message sources. As a speaker, you are one such source. The sources of information you cite in your speech are another.

In Chapter 2 we discussed ways to establish your personal ethos. Here we are concerned with the ethos of your sources of evidence. Listeners will also evaluate these sources in terms of their competence, character, goodwill, and power. If this evaluation of your sources is positive, your audience will be more inclined to accept your proof. Let's look at how Heide Nord used the ethos of her sources to help persuade her listeners to change their attitudes about suntanning. To support the claim "We should avoid prolonged exposure to the sun," Heide emphasized expert testimony supplemented with lay testimony:

The most recent *Consumer Report* of the Food and Drug Administration tells us that "Prolonged exposure to sunlight without protection is responsible for about 90 percent of skin cancer." It describes the case of Wendell Scarberry, a skin cancer patient with over a hundred surgeries behind him. Wendell talks about the seriousness of the disease and urges that we be careful about sun exposure. "You can't cure skin cancer," he says, "by just having the doc whack it off." Finally, the American Cancer Society in its pamphlet *Fry Now Pay Later* says that skin cancer most often occurs among people who spend a lot of time in the sun, especially if they have been exposed in their teens or twenties. Well, that's where most of us are right now.

This combination of expert and lay testimony helped Heide urge listeners to protect themselves from prolonged exposure to the sun.

Clearly, proof based on the testimony of reliable, competent, and trust-worthy sources is extremely important in persuasive speaking. *Identify your sources and point out why they are qualified to speak on the subject.* It is also help-ful if you can say that the testimony is recent. For maximum effect, quote experts directly rather than paraphrasing them.

Mythos

Mythos has emerged as an important element of proof in today's society. *Mythos* appeals to the values, faith, and feelings that make up our social char-acter. It is most often expressed through traditional stories, sayings, and sym-bols. Proof that emphasizes mythos assumes that people value their member-ship in a culture and share its heritage. Communication scholar Martha Solomon Watson has noted, "Rhetoric which incorporates mythical elements taps into rich cultural reservoirs."[4]

Appeals to mythos call on patriotism, pride, and heroes or enemies for evi-dence. In the United States we are raised on political narratives, such as those that stress the hardships of Washington's winter at Valley Forge or the triumphs of the suffragists who won women the right to vote. Such stories impress on us the meaning and value of political freedom. We may think of our country as "a frontier" or "the land of opportunity."[5] Appeals to mythos also may be based on economic legends, such as the American stories of success through hard work and thrift made popular by the Horatio Alger books of the late nineteenth cen-tury. The Horatio Alger myth celebrates the rise to power from humble begin-nings. It justifies economic power in our society, while assuring the powerless that they can make it, if only they have "the right stuff." Appeals to mythos may also draw on religious narratives. Religious documents such as the Bible or the Koran provide a rich storehouse of parables that are often used as proof—not just in religious sermons but also in political discourse.[6]

To create mythos, stories need not be retold in their entirety each time they are invoked. Because they are so familiar, allusions to them may be suffi-cient. The culturetypes discussed in Chapter 10 are often called into service because they compress myths into a few choice words that are easily recog-nized throughout the culture. In his speech accepting the Democratic presi-dential nomination in 1960, John F. Kennedy called on the myth of the American frontier to move Americans to action:

> **The New Frontier of which I speak is not a set of promises—it is a set of challenges. It sums up not what I intend to offer the American peo-ple, but what I intend to ask of them.**[7]

This appeal to mythos emerged as a central theme of Kennedy's presidency. He didn't need to refer directly to the legends of Daniel Boone and Davy Crockett or to the tales of wagons pushing west to meet the dangers and chal-lenges that lay ahead—he was able to conjure up those thoughts in listeners with the phrase "the New Frontier."

How can you use appeals to mythos in a classroom speech? Let us look at how Robert Owens used mythos to urge stronger action against drug traffic in urban slums. Robert wanted to establish that "We must win the battle against drugs on the streets of America." He supported this statement by creating a sense of outrage in listeners over the betrayal of the American dream in urban America:

The Western frontier is a major source of mythos in American speeches. "American Progress," a painting by American artist John Gast, portrays many icons and ideographs. Which ones can you identify?

Read the latest issue of *Time* magazine, and you'll meet an America you never sang about in the songs we learned in school. It's an America in which hope, faith, and dreams are nothing but a bitter memory. They call America a land of hope, but it's hard to hope when your mother is a cocaine addict on Susquehanna Avenue in North Philadelphia. They call America a land of faith, but what faith can you cling to when even God seems to have abandoned the street corners to the junkies and the dealers? They call America a land of dreams, but what kind of dreams can you have when all you hear at night as you lie in bed are the curses and screams of buyers and dealers?

We might be able to redeem the hope, the faith, and the dream Americans like to talk about. But we're going to have to move in a hurry. Our president has said that we've got to declare war on drugs, but we need to do more than declare war. We've got to *go* to war, and we've got to win! If we don't, the crack in the Liberty Bell may soon symbolize—not freedom—but a deadly drug that is destroying the American spirit all over this land.

These appeals to a betrayed mythos justified Robert's concluding plea for a broad-based, aggressive campaign to rid America of its drug culture. *The unique function of mythos is to help listeners understand how the speaker's recommendations fit into the total belief and value patterns of their group.* This gives such proof a special role in the persuasive process we discussed in the last chapter. It can help integrate new attitudes and actions into the group's culture.

Like appeals to pathos, appeals to mythos can be a great good or a considerable evil. At its best, mythos heightens our appreciation of our social identity and promotes consistency between community values and public policy. However, when misused, appeals to mythos can make it seem that there is only one *legitimate* culture. It can make us forget that the freedom we honor must also affirm the right to practice different lifestyles. American culture is richly diverse. Mythos can be misused to justify action against people who do not conform to dominant-group values. Speakers may do grave damage by careless, ill-considered appeals to mythos.

Weaving the Fabric of Proof

Much of the art of persuasion lies in the way speakers blend the various strands of proof into a convincing demonstration. To fashion such a demonstration, you must (1) determine the type of proof that is most appropriate to your message, and (2) understand how different types of proof can work together.

When audience awareness or understanding of a problem is uncertain, persuasion should emphasize logos. If a problem calls for human understanding, proof by pathos with moving examples may be needed. If a situation is uncertain or confusing, proof by ethos, based on expert testimony or the speaker's personal witnessing, rises in importance. If traditions and values are relevant to a situation, mythos becomes vital. Mythos can help overcome the differences among people and create a group spirit that is receptive to a message.

Consider again the speech that begins and ends this chapter. Jim Cardoza believed that his audience accepted the problem phase of his speech: Pollution of the environment is a serious problem. The proof he offered was therefore meant simply to strengthen their conviction before he moved on to the solution phase of his speech. So he provided striking facts to validate his statement that the environment is in crisis. He added personal ethos to the

speaker's notes

When and How to Use Proof

1   When you must increase awareness and understanding, use logos (facts and statistics).

2   When you need to communicate the human dimensions of a problem, stir listeners with pathos (examples and narratives).

3   When situations are complex and much is at stake, emphasize ethos (personal witness and expert testimony, carefully documented).

4   When group traditions and values are relevant, stress mythos (group symbols and legends).

proof design by talking about his own interest in the subject, and borrowed ethos by citing experts. By reminding listeners that the problem involves the water they drink and the air they breathe, he added pathos. Finally, by his descriptions of nature that definitely are *not* "America the Beautiful" and by calling listener responsibility "environmental stewardship," Jim added mythos to the fabric of proof. By combining these various appeals and forms of evidence, he developed a compelling argument to support the conclusion that a serious problem exists.

Forming Arguments

An **argument** *is the overall case that a speaker develops in order to answer questions that are vital to the fate of persuasion.* These questions are inherent in the persuasive designs we considered in Chapter 13. In a problem-solution design, there are two vital questions:

1. Is there a serious problem?
2. Would the proposed solution solve the problem ethically and effectively?

In the refutative and comparative designs, there are also two vital questions:

1. Is the attack on the position justified?
2. Would an alternative plan be better?

In the categorical design, the speaker builds arguments that apply to particular patterns of thinking. For example, when the categorical concerns are whether a plan would be *safe*, *inexpensive*, and *effective*, the speaker must build arguments that address each of these concerns.

An argument represents the speaker's best effort to weave a pattern of evidence and proofs in response to such questions. The speaker wants his or her arguments to be judged sound and persuasive by judicious, critical, and constructive listeners. Arguments assume such listeners, and are therefore inherently ethical. They respect the right of listeners to inspect the patterns of evidence and proof and draw their own conclusions from them.

Arguments are based on basic forms of human reasoning that imply three fundamental tests:

■ Is the case based on acceptable principles or rules of conduct?
■ Are the interpretations drawn from a careful inspection of reality?
■ Can we learn something by considering related situations?

The major patterns of argument—deductive, inductive, and analogical—relate respectively to these tests.

Deductive Argument

As we absorb the faiths and beliefs of our culture, we acquire a set of principles and rules of conduct that guide the way we live. These principles and rules are not necessarily scientifically correct—for example, for a long time, people believed that the earth was flat and the sun was the center of the universe. Rules of conduct are a part of the working faith of a people: "Freedom of speech," for example, is written into the Constitution of the United States as a principle of government.

These principles and rules are basic to persuasion because we *deduce* from them specific lessons to apply in everyday life—hence the name **deductive argument**. Such argument starts with a generally accepted rule or principle:

"We all believe in freedom of speech."

It then relates a specific issue to that principle:

Obnoxious Melvin would like to speak.

Finally, it reaches a conclusion:

Even though he is obnoxious, we should let Melvin speak.

Because it is based on widely shared principles or values, deductive argument is especially useful for establishing common ground with reluctant audiences. Deductive argument can also point out inconsistencies between beliefs and behaviors—between what we preach and what we practice. For example, if you can show that the censorship of song lyrics is inconsistent with freedom of speech, then you will have presented a good reason for people to condemn the censorship. We are more likely to change a practice that is inconsistent with cherished principles or values than we are to change the principles or values. Because people like to be consistent and maintain the integrity of their values, deductive argument is a powerful way to change specific attitudes and behaviors. It includes a major premise, a minor premise, and a conclusion.

The **major premise** is the generally accepted belief on which the argument is based. In our chapter-opening example, the unstated major premise might be reconstructed as follows: "We have a responsibility to protect the environment in which we live from serious pollution." Similarly, the unstated major premise in Cesar Chavez's "Pesticides Speech," reprinted in Appendix B, might be reconstructed as: "We should not poison food to grow more of it."

One of the major tasks in understanding arguments is to recognize and evaluate the major premises that support the reasoning. We must realize that some people may not agree with the items of faith that we accept without question. For example, some researchers discovered that if you read the Bill of Rights to people without telling them that it was part of the U.S. Constitution, an alarming percentage would describe it as "radical" or "communistic." Therefore, when you are devising deductive arguments, you cannot always take your major premises for granted. You may have to defend them and explain them to reinforce your listeners' belief in them.

Another problem with deductive reasoning is that people may give lip service to a principle, but not be committed to its meaning. As a speaker, you may have to reawaken their faith in the principle. In other situations, basic principles may come into conflict, making disputes difficult to resolve. Arguments over environmental policy, for example, often invoke what appear to be contradictory principles concerning rights to employment versus rights to clean air and water. Advocates must either prove the priority of their principle in the particular case or show that the supposed contradiction does not really exist. An advocate might have to prove, for example, that people don't really have to choose between conserving the environment and expanding the economy.

The **minor premise**—which is actually *not* minor in terms of its importance in argument—affirms the reality of some specific relevant situation. For example, Jim Cardoza's evidence affirmed that pollution of our environment has risen to a serious level. Similarly, Cesar Chavez affirmed that California growers were poisoning food—and agricultural workers and consumers—in order to grow more. As you will quickly discover, the minor premise is often the major point of controversy in a dispute. People may not argue passionately about the *principle* of environmental protection, but allegations about specific instances of pollution are subject to a great deal of dispute. The proof you weave around your minor premise must support it without question.

Once the audience accepts the major premise and agrees that the minor premise describes reality, then the **conclusion** logically follows: "Yes, we'd better assume personal responsibility for improving our environment." "Yes, we'd better boycott grapes." If we accept the major and minor premises, the argument *compels* us to accept its conclusion. To be consistent, we must believe or do what it tells us to.

Yet, as Aristotle implied in his *Rhetoric*, logic and life may be two very different things. When we reason in the real world, we have to account for uncertainty. Jim's proposal that his listeners assume personal responsibility for pollution might not help the situation very much. Chavez may have exaggerated the situation to dramatize his plea for action. Because of this uncertainty, a British logician, Stephen Toulmin, recommends that we add a *qualifier* or acknowledge a possible *rebuttal* as we draw conclusions in real-life arguments.[8]

Qualifiers are words like "probably" or "most likely" or "in most cases." They suggest the degree of confidence we have in the conclusion. We use qualifiers to offset possible **rebuttals** that point out conditions under which the conclusion might not hold. Examples of qualifiers might be "*unless* conditions change rapidly during the next six months, we should adopt the Cardoza plan" or "*unless* growers can prove they have changed the way they do business, we should join the grape boycott." If you carefully qualify your conclusions, recognizing rebuttals when appropriate, you should come across as a careful persuasive speaker who is not trying to force listeners into an unreasoned commitment. Rather than being a sign of weakness, qualifiers can strengthen your ethos before critical listeners.

As you develop a deductive pattern of reasoning for your speech, keep these cautions in mind:

1. *Be certain that your audience will accept your major premise.* If you have any suspicion that listeners may not agree with your major premise, you should support that premise carefully. Remind listeners *why* they believe as they do. Cite prestige sources who testify to the importance of the premise. Use the pathos of moving examples and the mythos of exciting narratives that stir patriotic feelings about the principle. Weave in threads of logos to show the practical importance of the premise.

2. *Once your major premise is established, concentrate on supporting the minor premise.* This, as we shall see in the next section, is where inductive reasoning joins with deductive reasoning to build a compelling argument.

3. *Demonstrate the relationship between your major and minor premises.* Don't expect your listeners to get the connection automatically. Will listeners see the relationship between environmental conditions and their moral responsibility to maintain the natural beauty of their country? Will they be willing to grant that pesticide poisoning of foods is the result of grower practices? Even if what you say is true, you must establish the connection between your premises. Critical listeners and opponents will demand that you meet this responsibility.

4. *Be certain your reasoning is free from logical errors and fallacies.* We discuss such flaws of argument in the final section of this chapter.

5. *Be sure your conclusion offers a clear direction for listeners.* Don't leave them floundering without a clear idea as to what you want them to do.

Inductive Argument

As we develop critical listening and thinking abilities, we require persuaders to base their conclusions on conditions that actually exist. While we are learning to be critical listeners, we may be gullible—we may buy into arguments without checking to see whether their claims coincide with reality. We may be deceived by people who use appeals based solely on tradition and authority. These deceivers invite us to live in a deductive world in which major premises predetermine our experiences. For example, we may be taught that "African Americans are _____" or "White people are _____" (you fill in the blanks). It becomes a matter of faith to honor these beliefs, regardless of what violence they do to fairness or reality. We then live imprisoned in our minds, confined by the rules we have learned.

These reflections suggest the ethical importance of an inductive orientation. An inductive orientation means that we open ourselves to life as it actually is and that we are willing to change our conduct and our beliefs based on our experiences. An inductive orientation also means that we should ask whether conclusions are drawn from a careful observation of reality. It elevates the importance of a second pattern of reasoning, **inductive argument**. While deductive argument is driven by faith in general principles and values, inductive reasoning emphasizes observation and concrete experiences.

Although these two forms of argument may seem to be opposites, they actually work together. Persuasion based on inductive reasoning helps verify major premises so that they are no longer simply items of faith. Arguments based on premises that have been justified by inductive investigation lead to more reliable conclusions. For example, if we can demonstrate that "Freedom of discussion results in better public deliberation," then we bring reality and practicality to the support of morality, and defend our faith in freedom of speech.

Beyond demonstrating major premises, *the artful joining of deductive and inductive reasoning in a speech is essential to persuasive success*. In deductive reasoning, there is a point at which facts become critical. That point is the assertion that some situation related to the major premise actually exists. Proving this assertion is sometimes easy, at other times more difficult. Jim Cardoza's task, to prove that "pollution has reached a critical stage in our country," was not that hard. An earlier classroom speech had presented evidence that supported much of what Jim claimed, and discussion following that speech suggested that listeners were convinced. Jim's task was to reawaken and strengthen that acceptance. Therefore, the major emphasis of his speech was

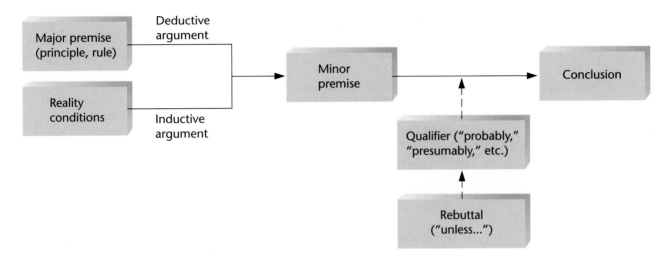

FIGURE 14.2
Deductive and Inductive Reasoning in Public Argument

on his attempt to sell his plan. On the other hand, Cesar Chavez faced a different challenge. In his audience, many listeners questioned whether growers actually were using pesticides irresponsibly. Chavez had to prove that they were.

As these examples indicate, deductive and inductive patterns of reasoning converge at the minor premise. Figure 14.2 shows how this process works.

This model suggests that speakers can lead audiences to accept their conclusions *if* they present a major premise that is accepted by listeners, and *if* they verify the conditions claimed in the minor premise. The major premise grounds the argument in a powerful deductive principle, such as "We should protect our environment." The minor premise presents an inductive claim about the present state of affairs, such as "We are trashing our environment." This interaction of principle and reality—the interweaving of deductive and inductive arguments—justifies the conclusion, "We need an aggressive policy to restore the environment." The strength of this conclusion may be qualified by words such as "probably" or "presumably," in light of possible rebuttal conditions such as "unless conditions change dramatically."

It seems clear that inductive argument is logos-centered. Cesar Chavez, for example, used statistics to dramatize and authenticate the severity of conditions in the fields of California.

> **The World Resources Institute reported that over three hundred thousand farm workers are poisoned every year by pesticides. Over half of all reported pesticide-related illnesses involve the cultivation or harvesting of table grapes. They receive *more* restricted-use application permits, which allow growers to spray pesticides known to threaten humans, than *any* other fresh food crop. The General Accounting Office, which does research for the U.S. Congress, determined that *34* of the *76* types of pesticides used *legally* on grapes pose potential human health hazards and could *not be detected* by current multi-residue methods. (The script of the speech supplies the italicized words. They indicate points that Chavez particularly wished to emphasize in oral presentations.)[9]**

Chavez could bring powerful personal testimony to bear, but, sensing that some might suspect him of bias, he also used an abundance of expert testimony, including "reluctant" testimony from sources that might be expected to speak against him.

> **Even the growers' own magazine, *The California Farmer*, admitted that growers were *illegally* using a very dangerous growth stimulator, called *Fix*, which is quite similar to *Agent Orange*, on the grapes.**

Therefore, he wove into the fabric of his argument the authority of both personal and borrowed ethos. As he pointed out examples of the victims of pesticide poisoning—especially among children—he added the coloration of pathos:

> **This is a very technical problem, with very *human* victims. One young body, Felipe Franco, was born without arms or legs in the agricultural town of McFarland. His mother worked for the first three months of her pregnancy picking grapes in fields that were sprayed repeatedly with pesticides believed to cause birth defects. . . . *And the children are dying.* They are dying *slow, painful, cruel* deaths in towns called *cancer clusters*. In cancer clusters like McFarland, where the childhood cancer rate is *800 percent* above normal. . . . There are at least *four* other children suffering from cancer and similar diseases, which the experts believe were caused by pesticides in the little town of Earlimart, a rate *1200 percent* above normal. In Earlimart, little Jimmy Caudillo died recently from leukemia at the age of three.**
>
> **The grape vineyards of California have become America's Killing Fields.**

Interestingly, Chavez underplayed mythos, perhaps because he sensed that he and his farm workers did not share the cultural background of many of his listeners. Perhaps his willingness to appeal to "the court of last resort: the American people" affirms his faith in the essential mythic goodness of American character. What makes this argument inductive is its effort to convince listeners that it pictures reality. By proving his minor premise inductively, Chavez added a powerful sense of this reality to his speech.

In addition to its special usefulness in problem-solution designs, where it is used to validate the seriousness of the problem, inductive argument also serves refutative designs in speeches that directly confront the opposition. Refutative speeches closely examine contending positions and criticize specific weaknesses in their evidence or proof. They often argue that opponents have not presented an accurate picture of reality.

The conclusion seems inescapable that inductive argument is the foundation of reason in constructive discussions of public issues. Before they do anything, listeners must be convinced that they are dealing with reality, not phantoms of the speaker's imagination. As you plan the inductive reasoning in your persuasive speech, keep in mind the healthy skepticism of potential listeners, and ask yourself these questions:

- If you are relying on the observations of experts, can you trust the adequacy, fairness, and objectivity of their reports?
- Are these reports the most recent available?
- Do they appear in publications that will be respected by your listeners?

- Can you find at least three experts, representing different interests and institutions, who agree on the reality of your inductive argument?
- If you are the source of observations, can listeners trust your reports?
- Are your interpretations justified by your observations?
- Are these observations representative of the situation, reflecting the typical rather than the atypical?
- If you are surveying the views of others, have you talked to enough people, and are these people representative of the population specified in your inductive reasoning?

Analogical Argument

Analogical argument assumes that we can learn about a problem, and how to respond to it, by considering a highly similar situation. The related situation becomes a model from which we can learn.

Analogical reasoning is useful for framing an unfamiliar, abstract, or difficult subject in terms of something that is familiar, concrete, and easily understood. Such argument can associate the subject with another that has strong positive or negative feelings associated with it, and thus predispose listener reactions. If we argue that a proposed policy has already been tried—in Stalinist Russia, we are in effect indicting the proposed policy. Needless to say, this can create "guilt by association," and be unethical. The argument may "beg the question," assuming in advance what it should be proving with evidence. In either of these cases, the argument would be a fallacy; fallacies are discussed in greater detail later in this chapter.

On the positive side, an analogical argument can demonstrate that a proposed plan of action will or will not work. For example, some of Chavez's opponents might have argued that the grape boycott would be ineffective. Chavez anticipated such arguments by emphasizing that previous boycotts had worked. He presented an analogical argument for the grape boycott by comparing it with the Montgomery bus boycott of the Civil Rights movement:

> **I have seen many boycotts succeed. The Reverend Martin Luther King Junior, who so generously supported our first fast, led the way with the bus boycott. And with our first boycott, we were able to get DDT, Aldrin, and Dieldrin banned, in our first contracts with grape growers. Now, even more urgently, we are trying to get deadly pesticides banned.**

In some cases analogical argument can be central to the success or failure of persuasion. For example, in the ongoing debate over our nation's drug policy, those who favor legalizing "recreational" drugs frequently base their arguments on an analogy to Prohibition.[10] They contend that the Prohibition amendment caused more problems than it solved because it led to the rise of a criminal empire. They further suggest that our efforts to outlaw recreational drugs have had the same result. In developing this analogical argument, those who favor legalization claim that it is impossible to ban a human desire, and that trying to do so simply encourages contempt for the law. Moreover, they assert that legalizing drugs would help put the international drug dealers out of business, just as the repeal of Prohibition helped bring about the downfall of the gangsters of the 1930s. Finally, they argue, if drug

speaker's notes

Developing Powerful Arguments

1 Base deductive arguments on an accepted principle, assumption, or rule of conduct.

2 Remind listeners why the major premise is important.

3 Convince listeners of the reality of the minor premise with inductive reasoning.

4 Reason inductively from representative observations drawn from an adequate sample.

5 In analogical argument, relate a novel problem to a similar familiar situation.

6 Remember that argument by analogy is only as reliable as the similarities you point out. It is subject to criticism based on dissimilarities.

7 Provide adequate definitions of basic terms to achieve clarity and force.

sales were legal, it would be easier to control the quality of drugs, thus reducing the danger to users (parallel to the health problems associated with bootleg whiskey during Prohibition).

As this example shows, analogical argument emphasizes strategic points of comparison between similar situations. People on both sides of an issue will focus on these points, using evidence and proofs to defend or attack them. Those opposed to legalizing drugs claim that there are many important differences between drugs and alcohol.[11] They say that alcohol is not as addictive for casual users as heroin or cocaine. They contend that legalization would multiply the drug problem, not reduce it. They further suggest that since many drug abusers are prone to violence, the cost to society would be increased. Moreover, they argue that the campaign against drugs can point to some success, whereas enforcement of the Prohibition laws was a disaster from the beginning. Thus, the public debate rages on over these crucial points of comparison.

What makes an analogical argument work? Analogy is similar to induction in that it seeks insight through careful observation. It differs from induction in that *observations are concentrated on one similar situation* rather than ranging across many. This means that although an analogical argument may seem more concrete and interesting than an inductive argument, it can also be less reliable. Before you decide to use an analogical argument, be certain that the important similarities between the situations outweigh the dissimilarities. If you must strain to make an analogy fit, use the other forms of argument.

The Importance of Defining Terms

All forms of argument depend on clear definitions of terms. Have you ever had a heated discussion with someone, only to discover later that the two of you were not talking about the same things? Socrates suggested that all persuasive messages should start with definitions of terms, so that speakers and listeners can share understanding from the outset. Opening definitions clarify what you mean, reveal your intentions, and show listeners how you see a subject. When the speaker and audience come from different backgrounds, careful definitions are even more important.

Many problems of definition are based more on disagreements than on misunderstanding. Should alcohol be defined as a drug? Should the fetus be defined as a human being? Such questions lead speakers to *ethical* definitions. In the 1968 Memphis sanitation strike that led to the assassination of Dr. Martin Luther King, Jr., the workers marched carrying signs that read, "I Am a Man." This simple-looking statement was actually the tip of an underlying moral argument. The strikers, all of whom were African American, were claiming that they were *not* treated like men, either in social or in economic terms. As you develop your arguments, keep in mind that definitions can be the *fundamental issues at the heart of controversies*. Define key terms clearly, and support all controversial definitions with evidence and proof.

Avoiding Defective Persuasion

It takes hard work to prepare a persuasive speech—analyzing your audience, researching your topic, planning your strategy, and designing arguments to make your message effective. Do not ruin all this work by committing **fallacies**, or errors of reasoning. Fallacies may crop up in the evidence you use, the proof you develop, or the pattern of your arguments. There are also fallacies that are specific to some of the speech designs discussed in the previous chapter. In this section we identify some of these major errors so that you can guard against them, both as speaker and as listener.

Defective Evidence

Evidence is defective if the speaker misuses facts, statistics, or testimony.

Misuse of Facts. A major misuse of facts is the **slippery slope fallacy**, which assumes that once something happens, it will establish an irreversible trend leading to disaster. The slippery slope fallacy often involves oversimplification and outlandish hyperbole. For example, a prominent religious leader once suggested that feminism was "a socialist, anti-family political movement that encourages women to leave their husbands, kill their children, practice witchcraft, destroy capitalism, and become lesbians."[12] In an advertisement, the R. J. Reynolds Tobacco Company presented lay testimony by a Florida state employee:

> **The Government is considering a substantial increase in excise taxes as a deterrent to smoking. . . . And restricting smoking in your own home is also under review. . . . I don't think they'll be content with regulating tobacco. There isn't any reason they can't use a similar argument about other products such as meat, cheese, or anything they say we shouldn't consume. When they start regulating they rarely know when to stop.**

In the slippery slope fallacy, it is not logic, but rather our darkest fears, that drives the prediction of events.

A second misuse of evidence involves *the confusion of fact and opinion*. A factual statement is objective and verifiable, such as "Most Republican governors support the lowering of taxes." An opinion is a personal interpretation of information: A statement of belief, feeling, attitude, or value. Normally, factual statements and opinions stay in their proper places. The problem comes when speakers make impassioned claims based on opinions, such as: "The Republicans have done it now! They're violating our Constitution. They're tossing children out into the cold. They're depriving retired people of their right to a secure old age. These are the *facts* of what they're doing." Opinions can be useful in persuasive speeches when they represent careful interpretations that are supported by evidence. However, treating an opinion as a fact, or a fact as an opinion, is the source of many problems. It can make you seem to claim too much or too little and can raise real questions about your competence and ethics.

At one time hunters used to distract their dogs from a trail by dragging a smoked herring across it. In our time, the **red herring fallacy** occurs when persuaders try to draw attention away from the real issues in a dispute, perhaps because they feel vulnerable on those issues or because they see a chance to vilify the opposition. The "red herring" they use is quite pungent—formed by sensational facts dragged across the trail of the discussion. In the current abortion controversy, some "pro-choice" advocates attempt to discredit the entire opposition by depicting their opponents as terrorists, assassins, and bombers. In return, some "pro-life" advocates try to smear their opponents by arguing that many abortion clinics are underwritten by "mafia money." Such charges from both sides divert attention from the central issues of the controversy.

Statistical Fallacies.   Audiences are often intimidated by numbers. We've all been taught that "figures don't lie" without being advised that "liars sometimes figure." Speakers can exploit this weakness by creating statistical deceptions. For example, consider the **myth of the mean**, or the "illusion of the average." If you've ever vacationed in the mountains, you are well aware that a stream may have an "average depth" of six inches, yet a person could drown in one of its deep pools. A speaker might tell you not to worry about poverty in Plattsville because the average income is well above the poverty level. Yet this average could be skewed by the fact that a few families are very wealthy, creating an illusion of well-being that does not reflect reality for many people. Averages are useful to summarize statistical information, but be sure they do not hide the reality of a situation.

Another statistical fallacy occurs when we offer *conclusions drawn from statistical comparisons that start from unequal bases.* Many years ago, during a college debate, we heard an opponent make a dark prediction: "The gross national product of the United States is growing at an annual rate of only 6 percent, while that of the Soviet Union is growing at a rate of 14 percent. Therefore, the Soviets are rapidly overtaking us." The problem was that the bases of this comparison were radically unequal: A 6 percent rise in the American GNP at that time represented more actual economic growth than a 14 percent rise in the Soviet GNP—6 percent of $500 billion is greater than 14 percent of $150 billion. It was not the Americans who were losing ground! Figure 14.3 illustrates these defective uses of facts and figures.

Defective Testimony.   Testimony can be misused in many different ways. Speakers may omit when a statement was made to hide the fact that the testimony is outdated. They may deceive us by leaving out important facts about their experts, instead intimidating us with titles: "*Dr.* Michael Jones reported

FIGURE 14.3

Examples of Defective
Evidence

1. Slippery Slope:
"an event will become
 a trend"

2. Red Herring:
"diversion of attention"

3. Myth of the Mean:
"averages can create
 illusions"

**4. Incomparable
 Percentages:**
"unequal bases make for
 defective comparisons"

that smoking does not harm health." What the speaker *didn't* reveal was that Dr. Jones was a marketing professor who was writing public relations material for the Tobacco Growers Association. Speakers also abuse testimony when they cite words out of context that are not representative of a person's position. As we noted in Chapter 6, prestige and lay testimony can be misused if they replace expert opinion when facts must be established. Finally, the "voice of the people" can be easily misrepresented, depending on *which* people you choose to quote.

Inappropriate Evidence.   Other abuses occur when speakers deliberately use one form of evidence when they should be using another. For example, you might use facts and figures when examples would bring us closer to the human truth of a situation. Welfare statistics are sometimes misused in this way. It is as though the speaker preferred to talk about poverty in the abstract, distancing listeners from its concrete reality. On the other hand, speakers may use examples to arouse emotions when what is needed is a dispassionate picture supported with facts and figures. Testimony is abused when it is used to compensate for inadequate facts. Narratives that create mythos may also be used inappropriately. Calling someone a "Robin Hood who steals from the rich to give to the poor" has been used to justify more than one crime.

Defective Proof

Any element of proof can be defective. We have already pointed out the danger of overreliance on proof by pathos when appeals to feelings overwhelm good judgment and cloud the perception of issues. Speakers may also misuse proof by mythos to promote intolerance, such as "When are Native Americans going to start being *good* Americans?"

In a similar manner, speakers may misuse proof by ethos by attacking the person rather than the argument. This is called an **ad hominem fallacy**. Such persuaders try to avoid issues by calling the opposition derogatory names. Therefore, this fallacy is related to the "red herring" fallacy mentioned earlier. For example, during a recent environmental dispute, one side charged that its opponents were "little old ladies in tennis shoes" and "outside agitators." Not to be outdone, the other side labeled its antagonists "rapists of public parkland."[13] Senator Jennings Randolph, speaking before the U.S. Senate in the not-so-distant past, dismissed arguments in favor of the Equal Rights Amendment for women on grounds they were offered by a "small band of bra-less bubbleheads."[14] Speakers also misuse proof by ethos when they overemphasize it. An example of this fallacy occurs when speakers try to intimidate listeners by citing an overwhelming number of authorities while neglecting to present information or good reasons for accepting their claims.

Finally, speakers neglect their responsibility to prove their points when they merely assert what they have not proved, thereby committing the fallacy, mentioned earlier in this chapter, of **begging the question.** Those who "beg the question" usually rely on colorful language to disguise the inadequacy of their proofs, so that the words themselves *seem* to establish the conclusion. Some anti-abortion advocates may be guilty of this practice when they refer to the fetus as the "unborn *child*" without bothering to address first the difficult moral question of when human life actually begins. A similar abuse may occur when the speaker taps into the mythos of the audience without adequate justification or preparation. A conclusion such as "Be *patriotic!* Support the *American way of life!* Speak out against gun control!" tacked onto a speech without further explanation begs the question because the speaker has not proved that being against gun control is a legitimate form of patriotism.

Defective Arguments

Major fallacies may infest all forms of argument. It is unethical to commit them purposely, and irresponsible to commit them accidentally. In your role as critical listener, be on guard against them at all times.

Errors of Deduction.   Because deductive reasoning builds on the major premise, an argument can be only as good as the major premise is sound. *If your major premise is faulty, the entire argument will crumble.* We once heard a student begin a line of argument with the premise "College athletes are not really here to learn." She was instantly in trouble. When her speech was over, the class assailed her with questions: How did she define *athletes*? Was she talking about intercollegiate or intramural athletes? How about the tennis team? How did she define learning? Was she aware of the negative stereotype at the center of her premise? Wasn't she being unfair, not to mention arrogant? It's safe to say that the speaker did not persuade many people that day. To avoid such a fiasco, be sure that you can defend each word in your major premise and that you are on sound footing as you begin.

Confusing probability and certainty is another fallacy common to deductive argument. Aristotle reminded us that the logic of everyday life is rarely absolutely certain. Suppose a friend from the Tau Beta fraternity calls you to set up a blind date. If the premise "Tau Betas are handsome" holds about 90 percent of the time, in your experience, and if you are about 90 percent certain that your blind date is a Tau Beta, then your conclusion that your date will be attractive is at best an assumption qualified by two factors of uncertainty. There is a 10 percent chance that your date is not a Tau Beta, and even if he is, there is another 10 percent chance that he is not one of the handsome ones. If you assert probabilities as though they were certainties, you are guilty of a reasoning error. It is better to use qualifiers that point out the uncertainty: "There is a *good chance* that my date will be handsome." If you point out the uncertainty factor in advance as you deal with important matters, you may not lose the audience's trust if a prediction does not come true.

Another error common in deductive argument is *reasoning that if something happens after an event, it was therefore caused by the event.* This fallacy, called the **post hoc fallacy** after its abbreviated Latin name, confuses association with causation. It is the basis of many superstitious beliefs. The same people who wear their lucky boots and shirts to ball games may also argue that we should have a tax cut because the last time we had one we avoided war, increased employment, or reduced crime. One of our students fell into the post hoc trap when she argued that low readership of certain books in areas that ban these books in the public schools proves that the bans are effective. There are many reasons why people don't read books, and banning certain books in public school libraries may or may not be among these reasons. It is just as likely that the book bans themselves are merely symptoms of deeper cultural conditions, and that the only real effect of such bans is to increase curiosity concerning the books they proscribe. A speaker always must demonstrate that events are causally connected, not just make the assumption based on association.

Finally, a **non sequitur fallacy** occurs when the minor premise is not related to the major premise, when the conclusion does not necessarily follow from the relationship between premises, or when the evidence presented is irrelevant. Former Speaker of the House Newt Gingrich, lecturing students on why men are more suited than women to traditional military combat roles, provided a remarkable example that appears to fit all the conditions of non sequitur reasoning: "If combat means living in a ditch, females have biological problems staying in a ditch for 30 days because they get infections . . . [moreover] males are biologically driven to go out and hunt for giraffes."

Former Rep. Pat Schroeder responded to this wisdom as follows: "I have been working in a male culture for a very long time, and I haven't met the first one who wants to go out and hunt a giraffe."[15] And then there is the cockeyed logic of Marge Schott, owner of the Cincinnati Reds baseball team. Schott told a Denver radio audience that she would rather see children smoke than take drugs. Her reason? "We smoked a peace pipe with the Indians, right?"[16]

Errors of Induction.   A common error in inductive reasoning is a **hasty generalization** that is based on insufficient or nonrepresentative observations. Suppose a student reasoned: "My big sister in Alpha Chi got a D from Professor Osborn. The guy who sits next to me in history got an F from her. I'm struggling to make a C in her class. Therefore, Professor Osborn is a tough grader." To avoid hasty generalization, you would need to know what Professor Osborn's grade distribution looks like over an extended period of time and across courses, plus how her grades compare with those given by other professors teaching the same courses.

Defective Analogy.   A **faulty analogy** occurs when the things compared are dissimilar in some important way. If the points of dissimilarity outweigh the similarities, an analogy is in trouble. For example, assume that you have transferred from a college with 1,500 students to a university with 15,000 students. You present a speech proposing new campus security measures, arguing that because they worked well at the college, they should also work well at the university. Would such an analogical argument be valid? That would depend on the similarities and dissimilarities between the two schools. Is the size difference important? Are the crime problems similar? Are the schools located in similar settings? Are the students from roughly the same social and economic backgrounds? Dissimilarity on any of these points could raise doubts about the analogy. You would have to overcome these doubts for the analogy to be convincing.

Fallacies Related to Particular Designs

In addition to fallacies of evidence, proof, and argument, there are at least two major fallacies related to particular persuasive designs. **Either–or thinking,** sometimes called *false dilemma,* makes listeners think that they have only two choices—one desirable, the other not. This fallacy is attractive because it is dramatic: It satisfies our yen for conflict and simplicity. It occurs in political behavior when we think we must choose between two political parties. It shows up in policy debates: "Pass our 'Contract with America,'" say the Republicans, "or accept a doomed America." "If you pass the Republican 'Contract *on* America,'" answer the Democrats, "you will sacrifice our basic values." Either–or thinking blinds listeners to other options, such as compromise or creative alternatives that have not yet been considered. Such thinking often infests problem-solution speeches when speakers oversimplify the choices to encourage commitment to their cause. We should be wary of being boxed into either–or decisions by impassioned speakers.

People who have gardens sometimes make up a "straw man" to scare off crows. As the name suggests, the straw is formed into the "likeness" of a man. (Presumably, a "straw woman" would work as well, as far as the crows are concerned!) Whatever the gender, the "straw man" is obviously much less than what it represents. From this name comes the **straw man fallacy,** making up a "likeness" of an opponent's view that makes it seem trivial, ridiculous, or easy to refute. As you might suspect, the straw man fallacy appears most often in speeches that contend with opposition. It understates and distorts the position of opponents, and is unethical. Dismissing Steve Forbes's "flat tax" proposal as simply an effort to reduce his own taxes was a "straw man" of the 1996 Republican primaries, as the candidates trashed each other with negative ads. As an ethical persuasive speaker, you have an obligation to represent an opposing position fairly and fully, even as you refute it. Only then will critical listeners respect you and your arguments. The straw man fallacy is an implicit admission of weakness or desperation and can damage what may well be a legitimate case.

Persuasion is constantly threatened by flaws and deception. In a world of competing views, we often see human nature revealed in its petty as well as its finer aspects. As you plan and present your arguments or listen to the arguments of others, be on guard against fallacies.

In Summary

Evidence, proof, and argument form the substance of reasoning that we see at work in any successful persuasive speech.

Using Evidence Effectively.   When supporting materials serve persuasion, they become *evidence*. Facts and statistics alert us to a situation that we must change. Examples move listeners, creating a favorable emotional atmosphere for the speaker's recommendations. Narratives bring a sense of reality, and help listeners identify with the issue. Testimony calls upon witnesses to support a position. When you use evidence, strive for recent facts and figures, emphasize factual examples, engage listeners through stories that make your point, and rely primarily on expert testimony.

Proving Your Points.   A *proof* is an arrangement of evidence that provides listeners with good reasons for accepting your advice. The elements of proof, based upon deep human qualities, are logos, pathos, ethos, and mythos. *Logos* recognizes that we are thinking animals who respond to well-reasoned demonstrations. *Pathos* affirms that we are creatures of emotion as well. *Ethos* recognizes that we respond to leadership qualities in speakers and their sources of evidence. *Mythos* relates to our nature as social beings who respond to group traditions and values. Powerful proofs weave a fabric of evidence that appeals to these various dimensions of ourselves. To develop sound proof, you must determine what to emphasize in your particular message, and you must be able to combine the strengths of these different elements.

Forming an Argument.   An *argument* is the overall case a speaker develops to answer questions that are vital within the particular persuasive design. An argument combines evidence and proof to satisfy the scrutiny of critical and constructive listeners. Arguments are based on underlying forms of reasoning, and can be identified as deductive, inductive, or analogical. *Deductive argument* develops around a major premise, minor premise, and conclusion. The *major premise*, often unstated but understood by listeners, is a generally accepted principle, assumption, or rule on which the argument rests. The *minor premise* focuses on some specific issue relevant to the major premise. The *conclusion*, drawn from the relationship between the major and minor premises, tells us what to believe or do. *Inductive argument* satisfies listeners that the speaker has an adequate grasp of reality, especially as reflected in the minor premise. Deductive and inductive patterns of reasoning combine in successful persuasion to build a powerful case. *Analogical argument* compares a proposed plan to closely related programs already in existence. All three forms of argument depend on clear, persuasive definitions for their effectiveness.

Avoiding Defective Persuasion.   *Fallacies* are errors in reasoning that can damage a persuasive speech. Evidence can be defective when the speaker misuses facts, statistics, and testimony. Common errors include the *slippery slope fallacy,* which assumes that a single instance will establish a trend, the confusion of fact with opinion, and the *red herring fallacy,* using irrelevant material to divert attention from the issue. Statistical fallacies include the *myth of the mean,* in which averages create illusions that hide reality, and faulty conclusions based upon flawed statistical comparisons. Evidence can also be used inappropriately, featuring facts and figures when the situation calls for examples, examples when the audience needs facts and figures, testimony to hide the weakness of information, or narratives to justify unethical behavior.

Various defects can reduce the value of proof. Speakers misuse proof by ethos when they commit an *ad hominem* fallacy, attacking the person rather than the argument. When speakers merely assert and assume in their conclusion what they have not proved, they commit the fallacy of *begging the question.*

Fallacies are also common in the patterns of argument. If your major premise is faulty, the entire argument will crumble. Other frequent errors occur when probability is passed off as certainty, and when the speaker confuses association with causation, reasoning that if something happened after an event, it therefore was caused by the event. This is called the *post hoc* fallacy. A *non sequitur* fallacy occurs when irrelevant conclusions or evidence are introduced into argument. Inductive reasoning can suffer from a *hasty generalization* drawn from insufficient or nonrepresentative observations. Argument by analogy is defective when important dissimilarities outweigh similarities.

Either–or thinking can be a special problem in speeches calling for action. This fallacy reduces audience options to only two, one advocated by the speaker, the other undesirable. When speeches that contend with opposition understate, distort, or misrepresent an opposing position for the sake of easy refutation, they commit the *straw man* fallacy.

Terms to Know

evidence	argument
reluctant witnesses	deductive argument
proof	major premise
logos	minor premise
pathos	conclusion
ethos	qualifiers
mythos	rebuttals

inductive argument

analogical argument

fallacies

slippery slope fallacy

red herring fallacy

myth of the mean

ad hominem fallacy

begging the question

post hoc fallacy

non sequitur fallacy

hasty generalization

faulty analogy

either–or thinking

straw man fallacy

Notes

1. Representative of this scholarship are Ernest G. Bormann, "Fantasy and Rhetorical Vision: The Rhetorical Criticism of Social Reality," *Quarterly Journal of Speech* 58 (1972): 396–407; Walter F. Fisher, "Narration as a Human Communication Paradigm: The Case of Public Moral Argument," *Communication Monographs* 51 (1984): 1–22; Michael C. McGee, "In Search of 'The People': A Rhetorical Alternative," *Quarterly Journal of Speech* 61 (1975): 235–249; Michael Osborn, "Rhetorical Depiction," in *Form, Genre and the Study of Political Discourse*, ed. Herbert W. Simons and Aram A. Aghazarian (Columbia: University of South Carolina Press, 1986), pp. 79–107; and Janice Hocker Rushing, "The Rhetoric of the American Western Myth," *Communication Monographs* 50 (1983): 14–32.
2. Antonio R. Damasio, *Descartes' Error: Emotion, Reason, and the Human Brain* (New York: Putnam, 1994).
3. From a brochure distributed by Handgun Control, Inc., 1225 Eye Street NW, Washington, DC 20005, 1990.
4. Martha Solomon, "The 'Positive Woman's' Journey: A Mythic Analysis of the Rhetoric of STOP ERA," *Quarterly Journal of Speech* 65 (1979): 262–274.
5. Rushing, pp. 14–32.
6. Roderick P. Hart, *The Political Pulpit* (West Lafayette, Ind.: Purdue University Press, 1977).
7. John Fitzgerald Kennedy, "Acceptance Address, 1960," *The Great Society: A Sourcebook of Speeches,* ed. Glenn R. Capp (Belmont, Calif.: Dickenson, 1969), p. 14.
8. See his discussion in *The Uses of Argument* (London: Cambridge University Press, 1958) and in Stephen Toulmin, Richard Rieke, and Allan Janik, *An Introduction to Reasoning*, 2nd ed. (New York: Macmillan, 1984).
9. Cesar Chavez, "Pesticides Speech," *Contemporary American Speeches: A Sourcebook of Speech Forms and Principles*, 7th ed., ed. Richard L. Johannesen, R. R. Allen, and Wil A. Linkugel, (Dubuque, Iowa: Kendall/Hunt, 1992), pp. 210–213. Reprinted by permission of the Cesar Chavez Foundation.
10. Lisa M. Ross, "Buckley Says Drug Attack Won't Work," *Memphis (Tenn.) Commercial Appeal,* 14 September 1989, p. B2.
11. Mortimer B. Zuckerman, "The Enemy Within," *U.S. News & World Report*, 11 September 1989, p. 91.
12. Gilbert Cranberg, "Even Sensible Iowa Bows to the Religious Right," *Los Angeles Times*, 17 August 1992, p. B5.
13. Michael M. Osborn, "The Abuses of Argument," *Southern Speech Communication Journal* 49 (1983): 1–11.
14. Howard Kahane, *Logic and Contemporary Rhetoric: The Use of Reason in Everyday Life,* 5th ed. (Belmont, Calif.: Wadsworth, 1998), p. 38.
15. *Newsweek*, 30 January 1995, p. 17.
16. *Memphis (Tenn.) Commercial Appeal*, 6 September 1996, p. C1.

Sample Speech

Reduce, Refuse, Reuse
James Cardoza

Jim's clever opening gains attention and creates identification by referring to a shared cultural experience. He invites listeners to confirm from their own experience the urgency of environmental problems. His unstated major premise is, "We have a responsibility to protect the environment from serious pollution."

"It isn't easy being green." Recognize this line? Kermit the frog, right? Those of us raised on *Sesame Street* know that Kermit's song was all about what it's like to be different—what it's like to be green in a world that isn't. But I want to apply this line in a different context. I want to tell you how "it isn't easy being green" in an environmental sense.

The environment is very important to me. I like camping and hiking and fishing. To me, being outside and enjoying nature is the ultimate high. But sometimes, being outside has its downside. Have you ever walked through the woods, thinking you'd gotten away from it all, and then tripped over a beer can? Have you ever found the beauty of a river spoiled by an old used tire at the edge of the stream? Have you ever gone to the beach and not been able to swim because the water was polluted? Have you ever had trouble seeing the mountains because of the smog? Or, even worse, had trouble breathing the air? Well, I have. And it's things like this that have turned me into a budding environmentalist.

Jim presents himself as an example of how people can change their habits for the better. He presents his thesis statement and previews his speech, using a formula that should be easy to remember.

At first, it wasn't "easy being green." I had to break some bad habits to stop being part of the problem myself. But then it began to get easier to do the right things, and now it's almost second nature. Today I want to convince you that you too should become involved, and tell you what you need to do. I want to introduce you to what I call "the three R's of environmental stewardship: REDUCE . . . REFUSE . . . REUSE. REDUCE the amount of energy you use. REFUSE to buy products that are environmentally unsound or shop at stores that aren't environmentally friendly. And REUSE by finding new uses for things you might otherwise throw away and by recycling all you can.

I don't think many of us would deny that pollution is a problem. We've already heard a speech that pointed out the dangers of global warming. Let me add some fuel to the fire.

Jim uses inductive reasoning to confirm his minor premise, "Pollution has reached a serious level." He reminds listeners of evidence from a previous speech, and adds other facts, statistics, and testimony. Vivid images help dramatize the problem.

According to *U.S. News and World Report*, in 1991 alone 667 pounds of garbage was collected for every mile of beach in the United States. There are more than 28,000 miles of beach in the United States, so that's almost nineteen million pounds of garbage. Just from beaches alone! And that's just the tip of the wasteberg. Figures released by the Environmental Protection Agency as reported in the *Environmental Almanac* show that the average U.S. citizen produces more than one-half ton of solid waste each year. With a population of almost 260 million people, that's over 130 million tons of waste per year. Can you picture how much trash that is? The writing paper alone that we throw out each year is enough to build a twelve-foot-high wall from Los Angeles to New York.

The situation with water isn't much better. According to the *Information Please Almanac*, nearly half of our rivers are too polluted to support their intended uses for drinking water, recreation, or fisheries. And how about the air we breathe? The almanac tells us that this too is getting worse, with cars accounting for over half of all air pollution in the country. Furthermore,

Time magazine warns us that air pollution can reduce life spans as much as two years, even in areas that meet current federal air quality standards.

"Enough already," I hear you thinking. "So we have a problem. What can we do?" Let's look at these "three R's" one at a time. The first stands for REDUCE, and I'm not talking about your weight. I'm talking about the amount of energy you use by driving too much and by using too much gas and electricity in your home.

Need something from a store four blocks away? What do you do? You drive. Drive to campus. Drive to work. Drive on dates. Drive home. Drive just for the fun of it. Drive, drive, drive! It's our national passion. What are the options? Take the bus to school and you won't have to worry about parking. Carpool with other students or coworkers and make some new friends. Ride a bike. Walk anyplace that's closer than a mile or two. The exercise will be good for you. Reduce the amount of energy you use by keeping your car in good shape. And, when you're lucky enough to get a new car, buy one that's energy-efficient.

"Well, all right," you may be thinking, "I know I can drive less, but what about electricity and home heating? I don't want to be uncomfortable." You don't have to be. Here are some easy things to do to save energy and save money. Set your thermostat no higher than 68° in the winter and no lower than 78° in the summer, then dress for comfort. When you go to bed or leave your apartment for any length of time—even just for the day—adjust your thermostat. Your apartment will heat back up or cool back down quickly when you return.

Buy a fan. Ceiling fans are good because they move the warm air down in the winter and keep you cooler in the summer. You can buy one for less than $30 and install it yourself. Some other things you can do. Turn down the thermostat on your water heater to 130°. Water heaters are the second largest energy user in the home. Use your microwave for more than just reheating coffee. It's more energy-efficient than your stove. Buy energy-efficient light bulbs and turn off the lights when you leave a room. These may sound like little things, but little things can add up to big savings—both for yourself and for the environment. The eighteenth-century British statesman Edmund Burke once said, "Nobody made a greater mistake than he who did nothing because he could only do a little."

Now, let's move on to the second "R": REFUSE. Do you remember back in grade school being told, "Just say no!" Well, just say no to products that are environmentally unsound! Just say no to merchants that don't demonstrate an environmental consciousness! Just say no! Money talks.

For starters, learn to recognize the recycling logo [shows small poster with logo] and buy products that carry this symbol. Buy paper products made from recycled paper. They're not much more expensive. For example, this notebook [shows notebook] made of recycled paper costs just ten cents more than one not made with recycled paper. Think of that dime as your gift to the environment. Learn what companies support environmental causes and choose their products. For example, did you know that Kellogg's has packaged its corn flakes in boxes made from recycled paper since 1906? Buy paper products that are unbleached or bleached without chlorine. Buy products with the least amount of packaging. Don't buy six-packs of drinks with plastic rings.

As he discusses the first part of his plan, Jim develops a lively oral style that anticipates reactions and uses rhetorical questions. Missing from his speech at this point is analogical argument that might show how similar programs have reduced energy consumption. As he concludes the first part of his proposal, he makes good use of prestige testimony.

As he moves to his second point, Jim continues to anticipate the reactions of listeners with his interactive style. He uses examples to illustrate how to buy products with the recycling logo. He identifies stores that are friendly to the environment. Still missing is an analogical argument showing how his reforms might meet the need.

Be selective about where you shop. Find stores that encourage recycling. Anderton's Supermarket will give you three cents for every used grocery bag you return and reuse. That'll make up for that dime you lost on the notebook! Some stores have recycling facilities. Others offer information on consumer and environmental concerns. For example, the Safeway supermarkets in northern California polled customers about the importance of environmentally friendly products and packaging, and whether they'd like more information about steps they could take at home. The result? More people wanted information on recycling than wanted free recipes.

So much for groceries, now on to fast foods places. Watch out for Styrofoam; it isn't biodegradable. Go where they use paper instead of plastic. And let manufacturers and merchants know your feelings. Hit them where it hurts—hit them in the pocketbook.

Now, the third "R" of environmental stewardship — REUSE. Buy products that are reusable or recyclable. Did you know that the average college student goes through 500 disposable cups every year? Carry a mug in your backpack and you can cut that number down to nothing. Other students do it. The University of North Carolina, the University of Vermont, Furman, UCLA, James Madison, and the University of Illinois all have successful "use your own mug" programs. Maintain and repair what you already have rather than replacing it. Rinse out plastic bags and reuse them.

Jim seems most successful as he presents the "reuse" part of his program. He relates the problem closely to his audience as he discusses the use of disposable cups by "the average college student." Listing colleges that have successful "use your own mug" programs lays the groundwork for the kind of analogical argument needed for this speech to be most effective. However, Jim needed to provide more detail on the success of these programs. He does use inductive argument effectively to suggest the possible significance of his proposal. Perhaps his most striking demonstration comes when he paints the magnitude of improperly disposed of oil.

Find innovative ways to reuse. Cut up scrap paper for scratch paper. Use both sides of computer paper for rough drafts of homework assignments. Then save what is left for recycling. Every ton of recycled paper saves 380 gallons of gas. Read the newspaper at the library. Swap magazines with friends. Donate anything usable that you no longer need to a thrift shop. If you want more ideas on ways to use things, you can find over thirty pages of them on the Rainforest Web site. The URL is on the list of environmental Web sites I'll distribute after my speech.

Finally, recycle. According to the *Washington Times*, more than 40 percent of landfill material comes from paper, so recycling paper is the single most effective thing we can do to reduce waste. Each ton of recycled paper saves 3.3 cubic yards of space at the local dump. Recycling paper also saves trees. Wastepaper represents the largest untapped forest in the world. You also know that recycled bottles and cans are redeemable for cash, but did you know that recycled plastics show up in cars, carpets, and even clothes? Used tires can be recycled into asphalt for highway construction or mixed with soil for athletic fields.

Last, but not least, when you get an oil change, be sure that the old oil is disposed of properly. Do you remember how horrified we were when the *Exxon Valdez* spilled over 11 million gallons of crude oil in Prince William Sound in Alaska, gravely damaging one of the world's most fragile ecosystems? Well, just listen to this. Each year the amount of improperly disposed of oil in this country is equal to 35 *Exxon Valdez* oil spills! You heard me correctly. And each quart of improperly disposed of motor oil can contaminate two million gallons of drinking water.

Jim develops an elegant conclusion that repeats the "3 R's" and ties the ending of his speech to its beginning. The poetic conclusion of the

In closing, let me urge you to do your part in the battle against pollution. REDUCE, REFUSE, AND REUSE. It isn't always easy being green. It may be a little inconvenient, but the earth will appreciate it, and so will future generations. Let me close by sharing with you a poem written by Ed Stein of the *Rocky Mountain News* (with apologies to William Shakespeare):

speech—Stein's parody of the witches' speech from Macbeth—is quite effective.

Double, double toil and trouble, fire burn and cauldron bubble.
Toxic waste and PCBs, bring on suffering and disease.
Acid rain and nuclear spills, infect all with assorted ills.
Leach into the lake and river, poison both the lung and liver.
Spread this waste upon the land, into the flesh of child and man.
By the damage man has done, something wicked this way comes.
(Source: Ed Stein reprinted by permission of Newspaper Enterprise Association, Inc.)

WORKS CONSULTED

Browning-Ferris Industries and Earthwatch 3. "One Hundred Things You Can Do for Our Planet." Undated brochure.

"Database." *U.S. News and World Report* 15 June 1992: 10.

Information Please Almanac. Boston: Houghton Mifflin, 1996.

Innerst, Carol. "Students Try Cupfuls of Concern." *Washington Times* 12 Aug. 1991: A5.

Parfit, Michael. "Troubled Waters Run Deep." *National Geographic* Nov. 1993: 78–88.

Pisik, Betsy. "Concern for the Environment a Top-Shelf Item for Grocers." *Washington Times* 23 Mar. 1993: C3.

Rainforest. "Reuse Your Trash." Posted 11 April 1998, accessed 6 May 1998; http://www.geocities.com/Rainforest/5002/index.html.

Wetzstein, Cheryl. "'Waste Not, Want Not' Is Good Advice, Might Soon Be Law." *Washington Times* 8 Feb. 1991: C3.

World Resources Institute. *The 1992 Information Please Environmental Almanac.* Boston: Houghton Mifflin, 1992.

15 Ceremonial Speaking

[P]eople] who celebrate . . . are fused with each other and fused with all things in nature.

—*Ernst Cassirer*

This chapter will help you

- appreciate the importance of ceremonial speaking
- present speeches of tribute and inspiration
- develop speeches introducing speakers and accepting awards
- prepare a toast or an after-dinner speech
- act as a master of ceremonies

Your college has just concluded an ambitious fund-raising campaign to create scholarships and attract outstanding teachers, artists, and scholars. As the leader of student volunteers who spent many hours soliciting contributions, you have been invited to be master of ceremonies at a banquet celebrating the campaign. At the banquet, you may both present and listen to many kinds of speeches: speeches offering tribute, conferring and accepting awards, introducing other speakers, evoking laughter, and inspiring listeners. They are all part of what we call ceremonial speaking.

THERE ARE OTHER occasions when you may be called on to make a ceremonial speech. You may be asked to "say a few words" about a coworker or former teacher who is retiring, to toast a friend's wedding or anniversary, to welcome newcomers to an organization or community, or to present a eulogy for a dear friend or family member. Although your remarks at such times may be brief, ceremonial speaking is an important part of our lives.

It is very easy to underestimate the importance of ceremonial speaking. Informative speaking shares knowledge, and persuasive speaking influences attitudes and actions. In comparison, ceremonial speaking, with its occasional moments of humor or inspiration, may not seem that significant. However, it can serve an important purpose. **Ceremonial speaking** stresses the sharing of identities and values that unite people into communities.[1] The philosopher John Dewey observed that people "live in a community in virtue of the things which they have in common; and communication is the way in which they come to possess things in common. What they must have in common . . . are aims, beliefs, aspirations, knowledge—a common understanding."[2] It is ceremonial speaking that celebrates and reinforces our common aims, beliefs, and aspirations.

Rituals and ceremonies are important to all groups because they draw people together.[3] They provide larger-than-life pictures of our identities and ideals.[4] Ceremonial speaking addresses four basic questions: "Who are we?" "Why are we?" "What have we accomplished?" and "What can we become together?" As it answers these questions, ceremonial speaking provides people with a sense of purpose and helps create an "ordered, meaningful cultural world."[5]

Ceremonial speaking also serves a very practical purpose. As our opening example indicates, ceremonies put the spotlight on the speaker. As you conduct the college's celebration of its fund-raising campaign as master of ceremonies, others will be looking at you and thinking, "Wouldn't he make a good student body president?" or "Wouldn't she be a fine candidate for city council?" From the time of Aristotle, scholars have recognized that ceremonial speaking puts leadership on display.[6]

Ceremonial speeches also establish practical standards for action, advancing the major premises that justify arguments and influence behavior.[7] The two student speeches that conclude this chapter illustrate this function. As Leslie Eason paid tribute to Tiger Woods for refusing to accept an identity based on race, she was in effect saying that *we ought not to base our perceptions of ourselves and others on racial criteria*. As Ashlie McMillan told the inspiring story of her cousin who is a dwarf, she was at the same time urging her listeners *not to accept limitations that block their own accomplishments*. Both generalizations could work as premises justifying arguments and influencing behavior.

In this chapter, we discuss the techniques and major forms of ceremonial speaking.

Techniques of Ceremonial Speaking

Two techniques, identification and magnification, are especially vital to the effectiveness of ceremonial speaking.

Identification

Earlier in this book, we defined **identification** as the creation of close feelings for the topic and purpose of the speech, the audience, and the speaker. Kenneth Burke, perhaps the most important communication theorist of our time, suggested that identification was a key element of persuasive speaking.[8] Because ritual and ceremony draw people together, identification is also the heart of ceremonial speaking. Speakers promote identification through the use of narrative, the recognition of heroes and heroines, and the renewal of group commitment.

The Use of Narrative. Ceremonial speaking is the time for reliving shared golden moments. For example, if you were preparing a speech for the fund-raising celebration, you could recall certain things that happened during those long evenings when student volunteers were making their calls. You might remember moments of discouragement, followed by other moments of triumph when the contributions were especially large or meaningful. Your story would draw listeners closer together as they remembered emotions they had shared. Stories that evoke humor are especially effective identifiers, because laughter itself is a shared group experience when it is effective:

> **I don't think that any of us will forget the night that John tripped over a phone cord while carrying a tray of coffee and shorted out the computer network for the phone bank. Although many contributors got "cut off" by the accident, the returned calls netted the highest contributions of any night of the campaign.**

Just be certain your humorous stories don't belittle the people involved.

Ashlie McMillan showed how narrative can advance identification in her tribute to her cousin. In the opening of her speech, she asked listeners to close their eyes and imagine themselves shrinking to the size of a diastrophic dwarf. As they imagined miniature versions of themselves, prompted by her skillful use of language, her listeners could identify more closely with Tina and the enormous problems she had to confront on a daily basis.

The Recognition of Heroes and Heroines. As you speak of the trials and triumphs of fund-raising, you may want to recognize people who made singular contributions. These heroes and heroines can function as role models that inspire future action. As we try to be like them and act like them, the effect again is to draw people together. You must be careful in using this technique, however. You may leave out someone who deserves recognition, and create division rather than identification. Therefore, *recognize specific individuals only when they have made truly unusual contributions or when they are representative.* You might say, for instance,

> **Let me tell you about Mary Tyrer. She is just one of the many who for the last two months have spent night after night on these phones— talking, coaxing, winning friends for our school, and raising thousands of dollars in contributions. Mary, and all the others like you, we salute you, and pledge that we will continue your dedication in the months to come!**

Renewal of Group Commitment. Ceremonial speaking is a time both for celebrating what has been accomplished and for renewing commitments. Share with your listeners a vision of what the future can be like if their commitment continues. Plead with them not to be satisfied with present accomplishments. Renew their identity as a group moving toward even greater goals.

In his first inaugural address, delivered on the eve of the Civil War, Abraham Lincoln used the technique of identification in an effort to reunite the nation:

> **I am loath to close. We are not enemies, but friends. We must not be enemies. Though passion may have strained, it must not break our bonds of affection. The mystic chords of memory, stretching from every battle-field, and patriot grave, to every living heart and hearthstone, all over this broad land, will yet swell the chorus of the Union, when again touched, as surely they will be, by the better angels of our nature.[9]**

Magnification

In his *Rhetoric,* Aristotle noted that when you select certain features of a person or event and then dwell upon these qualities in your speech of tribute, the effect is to magnify these features until they fill the minds of listeners.[10] These magnified features then characterize the subject in terms of the values they represent. They focus listener attention on what is relevant, honorable, and praiseworthy. We may accordingly identify this vital inspirational technique as **magnification.** For example, imagine that you are preparing a speech honoring Jesse Owens's incredible track and field accomplishments in the 1936 Olympic Games. In your research, you come up with a variety of facts, such as:

- He had a headache the day he won the medal in the long jump.
- He had suffered from racism in America.
- He did not like the food served at the Olympic training camp.
- He won his four gold medals in front of Adolf Hitler, who was preaching the racial superiority of Germans.
- Some of his friends did not want him to run for the United States.
- After his victories, he returned to further discrimination in America.

If you used all this information, your speech might seem aimless. Which of these items should you focus on, and how should you proceed? To make your selection, you need to know what themes are best to develop when you are magnifying the actions of a person. These themes include:

1. Overcoming obstacles
2. Unusual accomplishment
3. Superior performance
4. Pure, unselfish motives
5. Benefit to society

As you consider these themes, it becomes clear which items about Jesse Owens you should magnify and how you should go about it. To begin, you would stress that Owens *had to overcome obstacles* such as racism in America to make the Olympic team. Then you would point out that his *accomplishment was unusual,* that no one else had ever won four gold medals in Olympic track and field competition. Moreover, *the performance was superior,* resulting in world records that lasted for many years. Because Owens received no material gain from his victories, *his motives were pure*; his performance was driven solely by personal qualities such as courage, competitiveness, and determination. Finally, you would demonstrate that because his victories repudiated Hitler's racist ideology, causing the Nazi leader public humiliation, *Owens's accomplishments benefited our society.* The overall effect would be to magnify the meaning of Jesse Owens's great performances both for himself and for his nation.

In addition to a focus on these basic themes, magnification relies on the effective use of language to create dramatic word-pictures. *Metaphor* and *simile* can magnify a subject through creative associations, such as, "He struck like a lightning bolt that day." *Parallel structure,* the repetition of key words and phrases, can also help magnify a subject and embed it in our minds. For example, if you were to say of Mother Teresa, "Whenever there was hurt, she was there. Whenever there was hunger, she was there. Whenever there was desperation, she was there," you would be magnifying her dedication and selflessness. This technique should make those qualities seem to resonate in the minds of listeners.

Magnification also favors certain speech designs over others. Comparison and contrast designs promote magnification by making selected features stand out. For example, you might contrast the purity of Owens's motives with the crassness of those of today's well-paid athletes. Historical designs enhance magnification by dramatizing certain events as stories unfold over time. As Ashlie McMillan sketched incidents in the childhood and adulthood of her cousin, she magnified Tina's developing character. The causation design serves magnification when a person's accomplishments are emphasized as the causes of important effects: Jesse Owens's victories, a speaker might say, refuted Nazi propaganda for many people. Whatever designs ceremonial speeches use, it is important that *they build to a conclusion.* Speakers should save their best stories, their most telling points, until the end of the speech. Ceremonial speeches must never dwindle to a conclusion.

Types of Ceremonial Speeches

Ceremonial speeches include the speech of tribute (including award presentations, eulogies, and toasts), the acceptance speech, the speech of introduction, the speech of inspiration, and the after-dinner speech (see Figure 15.1).

The Speech of Tribute

Had you developed a speech honoring Jesse Owens's Olympic victories, you would have prepared a **speech of tribute.** The speech of tribute, which may center on a person or on an event, recognizes and celebrates accomplishments. For example, you might be called on to honor a former teacher at a retirement ceremony, present an award to someone for an outstanding accomplishment, eulogize a person who has died, or propose a toast to a friend who is getting married.

Speeches of tribute can serve several important purposes. If you have presented a series of speeches on related topics in your class, the speech of tribute gives you a chance to extend your efforts to inform and persuade listeners. For example, Holly Carlson chose the banning of books in the public schools as the topic area for all her speeches. In her informative speech, she demonstrated that books are banned in schools all over the country, and

FIGURE 15.1

Types of Ceremonial Speeches

Type	Use When
Tributes	You wish to honor a person, group, occasion, or event. Subtypes include award presentations, eulogies, and toasts.
Acceptance	You need to acknowledge an award or honor.
Introductions	You must introduce a featured speaker in a program.
Inspiration	You want to motivate listeners to appreciate and commit to a goal, purpose, or set of values; this may be religious, commercial, political, or social in nature.
After-Dinner	You want to entertain the audience while leaving a message that can guide future behavior. Here, as elsewhere, brevity is golden.
Master of Ceremonies	You must coordinate a program and see that everything runs smoothly. The master of ceremonies sets the mood for the occasion.

listed the books and authors most often targeted. In her persuasive speech, she offered a stirring plea for intellectual freedom, urging her listeners to support students' right to read and think for themselves. Then for her ceremonial speech, she offered a tribute to one of the most victimized authors, J. D. Salinger. Her tribute to Salinger both made her listeners want to read his works themselves and dramatized for them how hurtful the censorship of Salinger could be. Thus all her speeches were of one fabric, which gave focus and cohesion to her semester's work.

A blend of the speech of tribute and the inspirational speech is perhaps the most popular form of classroom ceremonial speech. As Leslie Eason praised Tiger Woods, she also inspired listeners to apply his principle of *combination* to their own lives. Ashlie McMillan's tribute to her cousin offered listeners an inspiring model of determination to overcome obstacles to their own achievements.

Praiseworthy accomplishments are usually celebrated for two reasons. First, they are important in themselves: The influence of a teacher may have contributed to the success of many of her former students. Second, they are important as symbols. The planting of the American flag at Iwo Jima during some of the most intense fighting of World War II came to symbolize the fortitude of the entire American war effort; it represented commitment and was more important as a symbol than as an actual event. Sometimes the same event may be celebrated for both actual and symbolic reasons. A student speech honoring the raising of $60 million for famine relief celebrated this achievement both as a symbol of global generosity and for the actual help it brought to many starving people. When you plan a speech of tribute, you should consider both the actual and the symbolic values that are represented.

Developing Speeches of Tribute. As you prepare a speech of tribute, there are several guidelines that you should keep in mind. First, *do not exaggerate the tribute*. If you are too lavish with your praise or use too many superlatives, you may embarrass the recipient and make the praise unbelievable. Second, *focus on the person being honored*, not on yourself. Even if you know how much effort the accomplishment required because you have done something similar, don't mention that at this time. It will just seem as though you are tooting your own horn when the focus should be on the honoree. Third, *create vivid, concrete images of accomplishments*. Speeches of tribute are occasions for illustrating what someone has accomplished, the values underlying those accomplishments, and their consequences. Tell stories that make those accomplishments come to life. Finally, *be sincere*. Speeches of tribute are a time for warmth, pride, and appreciation. Your manner should reflect these qualities as you present the tribute.

Award Presentations. When you present an award, you often accompany it with a speech of tribute. An **award presentation** recognizes the achievements or contributions of those on whom the award is bestowed. Most award presentations have two main points: They explain (1) the nature of the award and (2) what the recipient did to qualify for it.

Unless the award is quite well known, such as an Oscar or Nobel Prize, you should always begin an award presentation by talking about the nature of the award. At the very least, you should name the award and tell why it is given. For example, you might say:

Mary Beth Peterson was a graduate assistant in this department who exemplified the best qualities of a teacher: enthusiasm for her subject, the ability to impart it to others, and a real sense of caring for those whom she taught. After her untimely death, her parents and friends endowed the Mary Beth Peterson award, offered each year to the graduate assistant in our department who best exemplifies the qualities Mary Beth brought so generously to the classroom.

The second and most important part of an award presentation involves explaining why the honoree was chosen to receive the award. In talking about the recipient, you should emphasize the uniqueness, superiority, and benefits of his or her achievements. Provide specific examples that illustrate these accomplishments. Finally, you should name the recipient of the award and offer your sincere congratulations and wishes for continued success. The complete text of an award presentation to Olympic track gold medalist Wilma Rudolph may be found in Appendix B.

Eulogies. Earlier we asked you to imagine yourself preparing a speech to honor Jesse Owens. Following his death in 1980, many such speeches were actually presented. A speech of tribute presented upon the death of a person is called a **eulogy**. The following comments by Congressman Thomas P. O'Neill, Jr., then Speaker of the House, illustrate how some of the major techniques we have discussed can work in a eulogy:

O'Neill's opening highlights the themes of unusual and superior accomplishment. He begins with the actual value of Owens's victories, and then describes their symbolic value.

I rise on the occasion of his passing to join my colleagues in tribute to the greatest American sports hero of this century, Jesse Owens. . . . His performances at the Berlin Olympics earned Jesse Owens the title of America's first superstar. . . .

No other athlete symbolized the spirit and motto of the Olympics better than Jesse Owens. "Swifter, higher, stronger" was the credo by which Jesse Owens performed as an athlete and lived as an American. Of his performances in Hitler's Berlin in 1936, Jesse said: "I wasn't running against Hitler, I was running against the world." Owens's view of the Olympics was just that: He was competing against the best athletes in the world without regard to nationality, race, or political view. . . .

Jesse Owens proved by his performances that he was the best among the finest the world had to offer, and in setting the world record in the 100-yard dash, he became the "fastest human" even before that epithet was fashionable. . . .

These comments magnify the values represented by Owens's life and develop the theme of benefit to the community.

In life as well as on the athletic field Jesse Owens was first an American, and second, an internationalist. He loved his country; he loved the opportunity his country gave him to reach the pinnacle of athletic prowess. In his own quiet, unassuming, and modest way—by example, by inspiration, and by performance—he helped other young people to aim for the stars, to develop their God-given potential. . . .

That Owens remained a patriotic American in the face of racism and indifference magnifies his character.

As the world's first superstar Jesse Owens was not initially overwhelmed by commercial interests and offered the opportunity to become a millionaire overnight. There was no White House reception waiting for him on his return from Berlin, and as Jesse Owens once observed: "I still had to ride in the back of the bus in my hometown in Alabama."

> *O'Neill's conclusion emphasizes the symbolic, spiritual values of Owens's life.*

Can one individual make a difference? Clearly in the case of Jesse Owens the answer is a resounding affirmative, for his whole life was dedicated to the elimination of poverty, totalitarianism, and racial bigotry; and he did it in his own special and modest way, a spokesman for freedom, an American ambassador of goodwill to the athletes of the world, and an inspiration to young Americans. . . . Jesse Owens was a champion all the way in a life of dedication to the principles of the American and Olympic spirit.[11]

When presented at memorial services, eulogies should also express the pain of loss and offer comfort.[12] At the funeral of young Ryan White, a hemophiliac who had contracted AIDS from a blood transfusion, the Rev. Raymond Probasco comforted mourners with this reflection:

Ryan and his family always believed there would be a miracle. But that didn't happen. I believe God gave us that miracle in Ryan. He healed a wounded spirit in the world and made it whole. . . . He helped us to care and to believe that with God's help, nothing is impossible, even for a kid. . . . With God's help, and each of yours, we'll make AIDS a disease and not a dirty word.[13]

Eulogies presented by family members are usually brief and focus on the personal characteristics of the deceased. At the funeral of the assassinated Israeli prime minister Yitzhak Rabin, his teenage granddaughter, Noa Ben-Artzi, presented the following eulogy:

> *The speaker indicates in her introduction that she will focus on the personal characteristics of the deceased. Note also the use of the universal images of fire and light and darkness, the biblical allusion, and the connection to the Holocaust, all of which relate Rabin to the mythos of the Jewish people.*

> *This section reveals the speaker's personal struggle to understand what has happened and to somehow place it meaningfully in her life.*

You will forgive me, but I do not want to talk about peace today. I want to talk about my grandfather.

Grandfather, you were the pillar of fire before the camp, and now we are just a camp left alone in the dark, and we're so cold. Very few people knew you truly. They can talk about you, but I feel they know nothing about the depth of the pain, the disaster and, yes, this holocaust, for—at least for us, the family and the friends, who are left only as the camp, without you, our pillar of fire.

People greater than I have already eulogized you, but no one knows the caress that you placed on my shoulder and the warm hug that you saved only for us and your half-smile that always told me so much—the same smile that is no more.

I harbor no feelings of revenge because the pain is too great. The ground was taken from under our feet, and we're trying somehow to make something of this void and have not yet succeeded. Grandpa, you were our hero. I want you to know that everything I did, I always saw you before me.

Your appreciation and your love escorted us through every way and road. You never abandoned us, and here you are, my eternal hero, cold and alone, and there's nothing I can do to save you. We love you, Grandfather, forever.[14]

The importance of sustaining a sense of community is especially critical after the loss of a valued member of the group. While the eulogy primarily mourns and honors the person who has died, it also celebrates the values of those who remain and helps them rededicate to what that person stood for.

Toasts.   A **toast** is a ceremonial speech in miniature, offered as a tribute to people and what they have done, as a blessing for their future, or simply as light-hearted enjoyment of the present moment. You might be asked to toast a coworker who has been promoted or a couple at a wedding reception, or simply to celebrate the beginning of a new year. The occasion may be formal or informal, but the message should always be eloquent. It simply won't do to mutter, "Here's to Tony, he's a great guy!" or "Cheers!" Such a feeble toast is "a gratuitous betrayal—of the occasion, its honoree, and the desire [of the audience] to clink glasses and murmur, 'Hear, hear' in appreciation of a compliment well fashioned."[15]

Whenever you think you might be called upon to offer a toast, plan your remarks in advance.[16] Keep your toast brief. Select one characteristic or event that epitomizes your message, illustrate it with a short example, then conclude. You might toast the "coach of the year" in the following way:

> I always knew that Larry was destined for greatness from the time he led our junior high basketball team to the city championship. In one game in that tournament, Larry scored twenty-eight points, scrambled for eight rebounds, and dished off thirteen assists. And he was only five feet two inches tall! Here's to Larry, coach of the year!

Because a toast is a speech of celebration, you should refrain from making negative remarks. For example, it would be inappropriate at a wedding reception to say, "Here's to John and Mary. I hope they don't end up in divorce court in a year the way I did!" Although most speeches are best presented extemporaneously, a toast should be memorized. Practice presenting your toast with glass in hand until it flows easily. If you have difficulty memorizing your toast, it is probably too long. Figure 15.2 presents samples of toasts for different occasions.

FIGURE 15.2
Sample Short Toasts

May you have warm words on a cold evening, a full moon on a dark night, and a road downhill all the way to your door. (Irish Blessing)
When the roaring flames of your love have burned down to embers, may you find that you've married your best friend. (Wedding toast offered by Jeff Brooks, Newton, Mass.)
As you slide down the bannister of life, may the splinters never point the wrong way.
May the Good Lord take a liking to you, . . . but not too soon!
As you ramble through life, whatever be your goal; keep your eye upon the doughnut, and not upon the hole. (Offered by Sid Pettigrew)
May the road rise to meet you. May the wind be always at your back. May the sun shine warm upon your face. And rains fall soft upon your fields. And until we meet again, May God hold you in the hollow of His hand. (Irish blessing)

Source: These examples were compiled by "Tom's Toasts: Irish Toasts and Blessings," *http://zinnia.umfacad.maine.edu/~donaghue/toasts01.html.* Updated March 1998; downloaded 16 December, 1998.

The elegant use of language is important in ceremonial speaking. Here Toni Morrison accepts the Nobel Prize for Literature.

Acceptance Speeches

If you are receiving an award or honor, you may be expected to respond with a **speech of acceptance**. A speech of acceptance should express gratitude for the honor and acknowledge those who made the accomplishment possible. In addition, a speech of acceptance should focus on the values the award represents and be presented in language that matches the dignity of the occasion.

Consider a situation in which you are being awarded a scholarship by your hometown historical society. The award is being presented at a banquet, and you must make a public acceptance. You would not go amiss if you began with, "Thank you. I appreciate the honor of this award." Let others praise; you should remain modest. When Elie Wiesel was awarded the 1986 Nobel Peace Prize, he began his acceptance speech with these remarks: "It is with a profound sense of humility that I accept the honor you have chosen to bestow upon me."[17] (The complete text of his acceptance speech may be found in Appendix B). Follow his lead and accept an award with grace and modesty.

In an acceptance speech, you should also give credit where credit is due. If your hometown historical society is awarding you a scholarship, it would be appropriate for you to mention some teachers who prepared you for this moment. You might say something like, "This award belongs as much to Mr. Del Rio as it does to me. He opened my eyes to the importance and relevance of history in our world." When Martin Luther King, Jr., accepted his Nobel Peace Prize in 1964, he did so in these words:

Making an Acceptance Speech

speaker's notes

1 Be modest.
2 Express your appreciation for the honor.
3 Acknowledge those who made your accomplishment possible.
4 Highlight the values that the award represents.
5 Be sure your language fits the formality of the occasion.

> **I accept this prize on behalf of all men who love peace and brotherhood. . . . Most of these people will never make the headlines and their names will not appear in *Who's Who.* Yet when years have rolled past . . . men and women will know and children will be taught that we have a finer land, a better people, a more noble civilization— because these humble children of God were willing to suffer for righteousness' sake.[18]**

As you accept an award, express your awareness of its deeper meaning. In their acceptance speeches, both Mr. Wiesel and Dr. King stressed the value of freedom and the importance of involvement—of overcoming hatred with loving concern. Finally, be sure the eloquence of your language fits the dignity of the situation. Dr. King relied heavily on an extended movement metaphor in his acceptance speech. He spoke of the "tortuous road" from Montgomery, Alabama, to Oslo, Norway, a road on which, in his words, "millions of Negroes are traveling to find a new sense of dignity." In a similar manner, Mr. Wiesel told the story of a "young Jewish boy discovering the kingdom of night" during the Holocaust. This personal, metaphorical narrative was introduced early in the speech and repeated in the conclusion when Mr. Wiesel remarked, "No one is as capable of gratitude as one who has emerged from the kingdom of night." Although your rhetorical style may not be as eloquent as that of these Nobel Prize winners, you should make a presentation that befits the dignity of the occasion.

If an award is presented as part of a ceremony involving awards to several people, such as the Academy Awards or a sports banquet, shorter acceptance speeches may be called for. Wilma Rudolph's brief words of acceptance on the National Sports Awards show were appropriate for that situation.

The Speech of Introduction

One of the more common types of ceremonial speeches is the **speech of introduction,** in which you introduce a featured speaker to the audience. The importance of this speech can vary, depending on how well the speaker and the listeners know each other. When both the person being introduced and the introducer are very well known, a formal introduction may seem superfluous and a light touch may be called for. For example, when the singer Madonna introduced Muhammad Ali at a recent gathering of New York sports personalities, she simply said:

> **We are alike in many ways. We have espoused unpopular causes, we are arrogant, we like to have our picture taken, and we are the greatest.[19]**

speaker's notes

Introducing Featured Speakers

1 Be sure you know how to pronounce the speaker's name.

2 Find out what the speaker would like you to emphasize.

3 Focus on those parts of the speaker's background that are relevant to the topic, the audience, or the occasion.

4 Announce the title of the speech and tune the audience for it.

5 Make the speaker feel welcome. Be warm and gracious.

6 Be brief!

A good introduction will usually achieve three goals: It will (1) make the speaker feel welcome, (2) establish or strengthen the ethos of the speaker, and (3) prepare the audience for the speech that will follow. You make a speaker feel welcome by both what you say and how you say it. Deliver your words of welcome with warmth and sincerity.

As soon as you know you will be introducing a speaker, find out as much as you can about the person. Some guidelines that will help build ethos and lay the groundwork for speaker-audience identification are the following:

- Create respect by magnifying the speaker's main accomplishments.

- Don't be too lavish with your praise. An overblown introduction can be embarrassing and distracting. One featured speaker was so overcome by an excessive introduction that he responded, "If you do not go to heaven for charity, you will certainly go somewhere else for exaggeration or downright prevarication."[20]

- Mention achievements that are relevant to the speaker's message, the occasion on which the speech is being presented, or the audience that has assembled.

- Be selective! If you try to present too many details and accomplishments, you may take up the speaker's time and make listeners weary. Introducers who drone on too long can create real problems for the speakers who follow.

The final function of an effective introduction is to tune the audience. In Chapter 4 we discussed how preliminary tuning can establish a receptive mood. You tune the audience when you arouse anticipation for the message that will follow. However, this does not mean that you should attempt to preview the speech. Leave that job to the speaker!

The Speech of Inspiration

The **speech of inspiration** arouses an audience to appreciate, commit to, and pursue a goal, purpose, or set of values or beliefs. Speeches of inspiration help listeners see subjects in a new light. Inspirational speeches may be religious, commercial, political, or social. When a sales manager introduces a new product to marketing representatives, pointing up its competitive advantages and its glowing market potential, the speech is both inspirational and persuasive. The marketing reps should feel inspired to push that product with great zeal and enthusiasm. Speeches at political conventions that praise the principles of the party, such as keynote addresses, are inspirational in tone and intent. Major addresses at conferences, such as that presented by Hillary Rodham Clinton to the United Nations Fourth World Conference on Women at Beijing, China, are inspirational as well. So also are commencement addresses, such as that presented by Elizabeth Dole at Radcliffe when she was president of the American Red Cross. (The texts of the speeches by Ms. Clinton and Ms. Dole are given in Appendix B.) As different as these speech occasions may seem, they have important points in common.

First, speeches of inspiration are enthusiastic. Inspirational speakers accomplish their goals through their personal commitment and energy. Both the speaker and the speech must be active and forceful. Speakers must set an example for their audiences through their behavior both on and off the speaking platform. They must practice what they preach. Their ethos must be consistent with their advice.

Second, speeches of inspiration draw upon past successes and frustrations to encourage future accomplishment. At the 1995 Catalyst Awards Dinner, Sheila W. Welling, the president of Catalyst, evoked vivid memories of what the past was like for women as she urged continued progress toward equality in the workplace in the new millennium:

> **One hundred years ago, at the dawn of the last millennium, our bustled Victorian great-grandmothers could not run for a bus, let alone for Congress. If the race—as the Victorian poet claimed—went to the swift, women lost. Girdled, corseted, enveloped in yards of gingham and lace, women were balanced precariously on their pedestals.**
>
> **. . . Women couldn't vote when my mother was born. Every time I think about it, it startles me, even as Edith Wharton wrote her novels, as Helen Keller graduated from Radcliffe with honors, even as women manufactured the arms that led to victory in WWI and the nation's move to global primacy, women still could not vote.**[21]

In the later years of his life, when his athletic prowess had faded, Jesse Owens became known as a great inspirational speaker. According to his obituary in the *New York Times*, "The Jesse Owens best remembered by many Americans was a public speaker with the ringing, inspirational delivery of an evangelist. . . . [His speeches] praised the virtues of patriotism, clean living and fair play."[22]

Third, speeches of inspiration revitalize our appreciation for values or beliefs. In the Owens speech that follows, the ideals of brotherhood, tolerance, and fair competition are stressed. Such speeches can strengthen our sense of mythos, the distinctive code of values underlying our society.

Speeches of Inspiration: An Illustration.   In his inspirational speeches to budding athletes, Jesse Owens frequently talked of his Olympic achievements. The following excerpts, taken from a statement protesting America's withdrawal from the 1980 Summer Olympic Games, illustrate his inspirational style. Jesse Owens was unable to deliver this message orally. It was prepared shortly before his death from cancer.

■ *Owens's introduction suggests the larger meaning of his victories and sets the stage for identification.*

■ *Note the use of graphic detail to recapture the immediacy of the moment.*

■ *Owens's use of dialogue helps listeners feel that they are sharing the experience.*

■ *This narrative leaves open the meaning of Owens's "inside" victory: Perhaps it was over self-doubt or over his own stereotype of Germans. Perhaps it was over both.*

■ *This scene presents an inspirational model of international competition.*

■ *Owens shows how individuals can rise above ideologies, as Long's final message invites identification.*

■ *Owens ends with a metaphor of the "road to the Olympics."*

What the Berlin games proved . . . was that Hitler's "supermen" could be beaten. Ironically, it was one of his blond, blue-eyed, Aryan athletes who helped do the beating.

I held the world record in the broad jump. Even more than the sprints, it was "my" event. Yet I was one jump from not even making the finals. I fouled on my first try, and playing it safe the second time, I had not jumped far enough.

The broad jump preliminaries came before the finals of my other three events and everything, it seemed then, depended on this jump. Fear swept over me and then panic. I walked off alone, trying to gather myself. I dropped to one knee, closed my eyes, and prayed. I felt a hand on my shoulder. I opened my eyes and there stood my arch enemy, Luz Long, the prize athlete Hitler had kept under wraps while he trained for one purpose only: to beat me. Long had broken the Olympic mark in his very first try in the preliminaries.

"I know about you," he said. "You are like me. You must do it all the way, or you cannot do it. The same that has happened to you today happened to me last year in Cologne. I will tell you what I did then." Luz told me to measure my steps, place my towel 6 inches on back of the takeoff board and jump from there. That way I could give it all I had and be certain not to foul.

As soon as I had qualified, Luz, smiling broadly, came to me and said, "Now we can make each other do our best in the finals."

And that's what we did in the finals. Luz jumped, and broke his Olympic record. Then I jumped just a bit further and broke Luz's new record. We each had three leaps in all. On his final jump, Luz went almost 26 feet, 5 inches, a mark that seemed impossible to beat. I went just a bit over that, and set an Olympic record that was to last for almost a quarter of a century.

I won that day, but I'm being straight when I say that even before I made that last jump, I knew I had won a victory of a far greater kind—over something inside myself, thanks to Luz.

The instant my record-breaking win was announced, Luz was there, throwing his arms around me and raising my arm to the sky. "Jazze Owenz!" he yelled as loud as he could. More than 100,000 Germans in the stadium joined in. "Jazze Owenz, Jazze Owenz, Jazze Owenz!"

Hitler was there, too, but he was not chanting. He had lost that day. Luz Long was killed in World War II and, although I don't cry often, I wept when I received his last letter—I knew it was his last. In it he asked me to someday find his son, Karl, and to tell him "of how we fought well together, and of the good times, and that any two men can become brothers."

That is what the Olympics are all about. The road to the Olympics does not lead to Moscow. It leads to no city, no country. It goes far beyond Lake Placid or Moscow, Ancient Greece or Nazi Germany. The road to the Olympics leads, in the end, to the best within us.[23]

The After-Dinner Speech

Occasions that celebrate special events or that mark the beginning or end of a process often call for an **after-dinner speech.** Political rallies, award banquets, the kickoff for a fund-raising campaign, or the end of the school year may provide the setting for such a speech.

The after-dinner speech is one of the great rituals of American public speaking and public life. In keeping with the nature of the occasion, after-dinner speeches should not be too difficult to digest. Speakers making these presentations usually do not introduce radical ideas that require listeners to rethink their values or that ask for dramatic changes in belief or behavior. Nor are such occasions the time for anger or negativity. They are a time for people to savor who they are, what they have done, or what they wish to do. A good after-dinner speech, however, leaves a message that can act as a vision to guide and inspire future efforts.

The Role of Humor.   Humor is an essential ingredient in most after-dinner speeches. In the introduction, humor can place both the speaker and the audience at ease.[24] It can also relieve tension. Enjoying lighter moments can remind us that there is a human element in all situations and that we should not take ourselves too seriously. At least one study has discovered that the use of humorous illustrations helps audiences remember the message of the speech.[25] In addition, humorous stories can create identification by building an "insider's" relationship between speaker and audience that draws them closer together. In sharing humor, the audience becomes a community of listeners.[26]

As we noted in Chapters 6 and 7, however, humor should not be forced on a speech. If you decide to begin your speech with a joke simply because you think a speech should start that way, the humor may seem contrived and flat. Rather, humor must be functional, useful to make a point.

The humor in a speech is best developed out of the immediate situation. Dick Jackman, the director of corporate communications at Sun Company, opened an after-dinner speech at a National Football Foundation awards dinner by warning those in the expensive seats under the big chandelier that it "had been installed by the low bidder some time ago." His speech also contained lighthearted references to well-known members of the audience, including some who were there to receive an award. In her keynote address at the Democratic National Convention in 1988, Texas state treasurer Ann Richards used pointed humor as she took her party to task for not involving women more directly:

> **Twelve years ago Barbara Jordan, another Texas woman, . . . made the keynote address to the convention, and two women in 160 years is about par for the course.**
> **But if you give us a chance, we can perform. After all, Ginger Rogers did everything that Fred Astaire did. She just did it backwards and in high heels.[27]**

Humor requires thought, planning, and caution to be effective in a speech. If it is not handled well, it can be a disaster. For example, religious humor is usually dangerous, and racist or sexist humor is absolutely forbidden. The first runs the risk of offending some members of the audience and

Humor can help relax listeners. Speakers who tell amusing stories about themselves build bonds of identification with an audience.

can make the speaker seem intolerant. The second reveals a devastating truth about the speaker's character and can create such negative reactions from the audience that the rest of the speech doesn't stand a chance. In general, avoid any anecdotes that are funny at the expense of others.

Often the best kind of humor centers on speakers themselves. Speakers who tell amusing stories about themselves sometimes rise in the esteem of listeners.[28] When this technique is successful, the stories that seem to put speakers down are actually building them up. A rural politician once told the following story at a dinner on an urban college campus:

> You know, I didn't have good schooling like all of you have. I had to educate myself for public office. Along the way I just tried not to embarrass myself like another fellow from around here once did. This man wanted to run for Congress. So he came up here to your college to present himself to all the students and faculty. He worked real hard on a speech to show them all that he was a man of vision and high intellect.
>
> As he came to the end of his speech, he intoned very solemnly, "If you elect me to the United States Congress, I'll be like that great American bird, the eagle. I'll soar high and see far! I won't be like that

other bird that buries its head in the sand, the oyster!" There was a wonderful reaction from the audience to that. So he said it again—said he wasn't going to be no oyster.

Well, I've tried hard not to be an oyster as I represent you, even though I know there's some folks who'd say, "Well, you sure ain't no eagle, either!"[29]

This story, which led into a review of the politician's accomplishments, was warmly appreciated for both its humor and its modesty. It suggests that humor takes time to develop and must be rich in graphic detail to set up its punch line. The story would not have been nearly as effective had the speaker begun with, "Did you hear the one about the politician who didn't know an ostrich from an oyster?"

Developing an After-Dinner Speech. After-dinner speeches are more difficult to develop than their lightness and short length might suggest. Like any other speech, they must be carefully planned and practiced. They must have an effective introduction that commands attention right away, especially since some audience members may be more interested in talking to table companions than in listening to the speaker. After-dinner speeches should be more than strings of anecdotes to amuse listeners. The stories told must either establish a mood, convey a message, or carry a theme forward. Such speeches should build to a satisfying conclusion that conveys the essence of the message.

Above all, perhaps, after-dinner speeches should be mercifully brief. Long-winded after-dinner speakers can leave the audience fiddling with coffee cups and drawing pictures on napkins. After being subjected to such a speech, Albert Einstein once murmured: "I have just got a new theory of eternity."[30]

Master of Ceremonies

Quite often ceremonial speeches are part of a program of events that must be coordinated with skill and grace if things are to run smoothly. Being the master of ceremonies is no easy task. A speaker who served in such a capacity for a community program once noted:

Being an MC was sort of like having to stand up and juggle a dozen oranges in front of an audience. I just kept standing there, fumbling everything and waiting for the whole thing to be over with.[31]

It takes at least as much careful planning, preparation, and practice to function effectively as a master of ceremonies as it does to make a major presentation. As the **master of ceremonies**, you will be expected to keep the program moving along, introduce participants, and possibly present awards. You will also set the tone or mood for the program.

If at all possible, you should be involved in planning the program from the beginning. Then you will have a better grasp of what is expected of you, what events have been scheduled, what the timetable is, who the featured speakers are, and what special logistics (such as meal service) you might have to deal with. The following guidelines should help you function effectively as a master of ceremonies:[32]

- *Know what is expected of you.* Why were you chosen to emcee the program? Remember, as emcee, you are not the "star" of the program, you are the person who brings it all together and makes it work.

- *Plan a good opener for the program.* Your opening remarks as an emcee are as important as the introduction to a major presentation. You should gain the attention of the audience and prepare them for the program. Be sure that the mood you set with your opener is consistent with the nature of the occasion.

- *Be prepared to introduce the participants.* Be sure that you know who they are and that you can pronounce their names correctly. If you prepare the introductions for them, review the relevant material in this chapter. Find out all you can about them: Check *Who's Who* and local newspaper clipping files, and talk to them directly as well as to the organizers of the event to see what they want you to emphasize. If the introductions will be prepared for you, be sure you get them far enough in advance so that you can convert them to your own oral style and practice presenting them (see the guidelines for oral style and manuscript presentations in Chapter 11).

- *Be sure you know the schedule and timetable so that you can keep the program on track.* Also be sure that the participants get this information. They need to know how much time has been allotted for them to speak. Double-check this with them before the program and work out some way to cue them in case they should run overtime. If time restrictions are severe (as in a televised program), be ready to edit and adapt your own planned comments.

- *Make certain that any prizes or awards are kept near the podium.* You shouldn't be fumbling around looking for a plaque or trophy at presentation time.

- *Plan your comments ahead of time.* Develop a key-word outline for each presentation on a running script of the program. Print the name of the person or award in large letters at the top of each outline so that you can keep your place in the program.

- *Practice your presentation.* Although you are not the featured speaker, your words are important (especially to the person whom you will introduce or who will receive the award you will present). Practice your comments the same way you would practice a speech.

- *Make advance arrangements for mealtime logistics.* Speak with the maitre d' before the program to be sure the waiters know the importance of "silent service." If you will be speaking while people are still eating, adapt your message to cope with this distraction by using the attention-gaining techniques discussed in Chapters 7 and 12.

- *Be ready for the inevitable glitches.* Despite your best efforts, Murphy's Law (if anything can go wrong, it will) will surely prevail. Be ready for problems like microphones that don't work or that squeal, trays of dishes being dropped, and people wandering in and out during the course of the program. As you respond to these events, keep your cool and good humor.

- *End the program strongly.* Just as a speech should not dwindle into nothingness, neither should a program. Review the suggestions for speech conclusions provided in Chapter 7. When ending your presentation thank those who made the program possible, then leave the audience with something to remember.

The tribute to Wilma Rudolph (the complete text is in Appendix B) illustrates how one master of ceremonies, Tom Brokaw, performed that role. The text also provides examples of speeches of tribute and acceptance.

As you end this book, we offer our own speech of tribute: this one to you. Public speaking may not have been easy for you. However, it is our hope that you have grown as a person as you have grown as a speaker. Our special wish, expressed in terms of the three basic metaphors that form the vision of this book, is that:

- You have learned how to climb the barriers that sometimes separate people and defeat communication.
- You have learned how to build speeches that are both powerful and ethical.
- You now know how to weave words into eloquent thoughts and evidence into persuasive ideas.

We propose a toast: May you use your new speaking skills to improve the lives and lift the spirits of all who may listen to you.

In Summary

Ceremonial speeches serve important social functions. They reinforce the values that hold people together in a community and give listeners a sense of order and purpose in their lives. They build the major premises for later arguments and put the spotlight on leadership.

Major Techniques of Ceremonial Speaking.   Two major techniques of ceremonial speaking are *identification* and *magnification*. The first creates a close feeling, and the second selects and emphasizes those features of a subject that will convey the speaker's message. Speakers build identification by the use of narratives that remind listeners of shared experiences. Recognizing heroes and heroines also provides ideal models of conduct to draw listeners and speakers closer together. Finally, appeals to group commitment can remind listeners of the values and goals they share. Themes worthy of magnification include overcoming obstacles, achieving unusual goals, performing in a superior manner, having pure motives, and benefiting the community. Eloquent uses of language can also magnify the subjects of ceremonial speeches.

Types of Ceremonial Speeches.   *Speeches of tribute* recognize achievements or commemorate special events. Such speeches should help us appreciate the values these achievements represent. As they describe ideal models of conduct, speeches of tribute also perform an inspirational function. Achievements and events may be significant in themselves or in what they symbolize. *Award presentations* should explain the nature of the award and what the recipient has done to merit it. *Eulogies* are speeches of tribute presented on the death of a person or persons. *Toasts* are ceremonial speeches in miniature that pay tribute, offer blessings, or celebrate the moment.

Speeches of acceptance should begin with an expression of gratitude and an acknowledgment of others who deserve recognition. They should focus on the values that the honor represents. Acceptance speeches often call for more formal language than other speeches and for eloquence that suits the occasion.

Speeches of introduction should welcome the speaker, establish his or her ethos, and tune the audience for the message to follow. Introductions should focus on information about the speaker that is relevant to the speech topic or the occasion or that has special meaning for the audience.

Speeches of inspiration help listeners appreciate values and make them want to pursue worthy goals. Such speeches often call on stories of past successes. *After-dinner speeches* should be lighthearted, serving up humor and insight at the same time. Humor should be functional in such speeches, illustrating a point or serving some larger purpose.

The *master of ceremonies* coordinates a program and sees that things run smoothly. He or she sets the mood of the program, introduces the participants, provides transitions, and sometimes presents awards.

Terms to Know

ceremonial speaking	toast
identification	speech of acceptance
magnification	speech of introduction
speech of tribute	speech of inspiration
award presentation	after-dinner speech
eulogy	master of ceremonies

Notes

1. Celeste Michelle Condit, "The Functions of Epideictic: The Boston Massacre Orations as Exemplar," *Communication Quarterly* 33 (1985): 284–299; Gray Matthews, "Epideictic Rhetoric and Baseball: Nurturing Community Through Controversy," *Southern Communication Journal* 60 (1995): 275–291; Randall Parrish Osborn, "Jimmy Carter's Rhetorical Campaign for the Presidency: An Epideictic of American Renewal," Southern States Communication Association Convention, Memphis, March 1996; Ch. Perelman and L. Olbrechts-Tyteca, *The New Rhetoric: A Treatise on Argumentation* (South Bend, Ind.: University of Notre Dame Press, 1971), pp. 47–54; and Richard M. Weaver, *The Ethics of Rhetoric* (Chicago: Henry Regnery, 1953), pp. 164–185.
2. John Dewey, *Democracy and Education* (New York: Macmillan, 1916), p. 4.
3. Bronislaw Malinowski, "The Problem of Meaning in Primitive Languages," in C. K. Ogden and I. A. Richards, *The Meaning of Meaning: A Study of the Influence of Language upon Thought and of the Science of Symbolism,* 8th ed. (New York: Harcourt, Brace & World, 1946), p. 315.
4. Michael Osborn, *Orientations to Rhetorical Style* (Chicago: Science Research Associates, 1976), p. 32.
5. James W. Carey, "A Cultural Approach to Communication," *Communication* 2 (1975): 6.
6. Walter H. Beale, "Rhetorical Performance Discourse: A New Theory of Epideictic," *Philosophy and Rhetoric* 11 (1978): 221–246; and Bernard K. Duffy, "The Platonic Functions of Epideictic Rhetoric," *Philosophy and Rhetoric* 16 (1983): 79–93.

7. Christine Oravec, "Observation in Aristotle's Theory of Epideictic," *Philosophy and Rhetoric* 9 (1976): 162–174; and Perelman and Olbrechts-Tyteca.

8. See his discussion in "The Range of Rhetoric," in *A Rhetoric of Motives* (Berkeley: University of California Press, 1969), pp. 3–43.

9. From *American Speeches,* ed. Wayland Maxfield Parrish and Marie Hochmuth (New York: Longmans, Green, 1954), p. 43.

10. See the discussion in *The Rhetoric of Aristotle,* trans. Lane Cooper (New York: Appleton-Century-Crofts, Inc., 1932), I.7, I.9, I.14 (pp. 34–44, 46–55, 78–79).

11. *Congressional Record,* 1 April 1980, pp. 7459–7460.

12. For a more detailed account of the functions of eulogies, see Karen A. Foss, "John Lennon and the Advisory Function of Eulogies," *Central States Speech Journal* 34 (1983): 187–194.

13. "Friends Put Ryan White to Rest, but Spirit Lives in AIDS Message," *Washington Times,* 12 April 1990, p. A5.

14. "'The Pillar of Fire': Excerpts from the Eulogies at the Funeral Yesterday of Yitzhak Rabin," *Boston Globe,* 7 November 1995, p. A3.

15. Owen Edwards, "What Every Man Should Know: How to Make a Toast," *Esquire,* January 1984, p. 37.

16. The advice that follows is adapted from Jacob M. Braude, *Complete Speaker's and Toastmaster's Library: Definitions and Toasts* (Englewood Cliffs, N.J.: Prentice-Hall, 1965), pp. 88–123; and Wendy Lin, "Let's Lift a Glass, Say a Few Words, and Toast 1996," *Memphis Commercial Appeal,* 28 December 1995, p. C3.

17. Elie Wiesel, "Nobel Peace Prize Acceptance Speech," 10 December 1986, reprinted in *New York Times,* 11 December 1986, p. A8.

18. Martin Luther King, Jr., "Nobel Peace Prize Acceptance Statement," reprinted in *The Cry for Freedom: The Struggle for Equality in America,* ed. Frank W. Hale, Jr. (New York: Barnes, 1969), pp. 374–377.

19. *Memphis Commercial Appeal,* 23 October 1995, p. D2.

20. Cited in Morris K. Udall, *Too Funny to Be President* (New York: Holt, 1988), p. 156.

21. Sheila W. Welling, "Working Women: A Century of Change," presented at the 1995 Catalyst Awards Dinner, New York, 22 March 1995, in *Vital Speeches of the Day,* 15 June 1995, pp. 516–517.

22. *Congressional Record,* 1 April 1980, p. 7249.

23. *Congressional Record,* 1 April 1980, p. 7249.

24. Roger Ailes, *You Are the Message* (New York: Doubleday, 1988), pp. 71–74.

25. Robert M. Kaplan and Gregory C. Pascoe, "Humorous Lectures and Humorous Examples: Some Effects upon Comprehension and Retention," *Journal of Educational Psychology* 69 (1977): 61–65.

26. For more on the social function of laughter, see Henri Bergson, *Laughter: An Essay on the Meaning of the Comic,* trans. Cloudsley Brereton and Fred Rothwell (London: Macmillan, 1911).

27. Ann Richards, "Keynote Address," delivered at the Democratic National Convention, Atlanta, Ga., 18 July 1988, in *Vital Speeches of the Day,* 15 August 1988, pp. 647–649.

28. Charles R. Gruner, "Advice to the Beginning Speaker on Using Humor—What the Research Tells Us," *Communication Education* 34 (1985): 142–147; and Christie McGuffee Smith and Larry Powell, "The Use of Disparaging Humor by Group Leaders," *Southern Speech Communication Journal* 53 (1988): 279–292.

29. Thanks for this story go to Professor Joseph Riggs, Slippery Rock University.

30. *Washington Post,* 12 December 1978.

31. Cited in Joan Detz, *Can You Say a Few Words?* (New York: St. Martin's, 1991), p. 77.

32. Adapted from Detz, pp. 77–78.

Sample Ceremonial Speeches

A Man for the New Age: Tribute to Tiger Woods
Leslie Eason

You're at the Western Open, where Tiger Woods could be Elvis reincarnated. People clap when he pulls out a club, they clap when he hits the ball, they clap no matter where that ball lands. They clap if he smiles. They clap—because he is.

Not long ago, when not much else was going on and we were tired of O.J. and very much needed a hero, a young man in a red polo shirt materialized out of nowhere doing magical things with a stick in a sport we usually ignored. He was not just good or even outstanding. He was a miracle. His game all but laughed at records set by men twice his age. Nike threw forty million at him. Rolex threw fifty million at him. American Express lined up to give him millions more.

We started having to pay attention to things like the Masters, and opens, and invitationals, and other such things that applied to golf. Other people were playing, but he was all we could see, this young god in a red shirt. Suddenly we had to learn a new language—"fore," "eagle," "birdie," "par," and "bogie"—just to keep up with the latest news about him.

Some people watched him play and bragged that black people could do just about anything. Then we heard that he was only one-fourth black, and that he did not describe himself as black. Now, in a society that honors the rule that one drop of blood is all it takes to be black, this didn't mean much. We ignored his Thai mother, disregarded the Native American and Chinese and Caucasian he said he had in him, and all we saw was his black father, who was always there in the gallery cheering him on.

To us he continued to look a lot like other young black men we knew. Mothers with daughters of a certain age (including my own) said that they wished he was their son-in-law or future son-in-law. Six foot two, a hundred fifty-five pounds, smart—Stanford, remember—clean-cut in his creased khakis, curly hair, gorgeous teeth—gorgeous teeth. Skin the color of what they used to call "suntan" in the Crayola box. And rich—very, very rich.

He's the very opposite of the gangsta boys in the hood—boys who wear their pants hanging below their belt like some people in the penitentiary. Next to them he's prep school and Pepsodent. Some said he put a pretty face on blackness. Others said he couldn't possibly be black.

From the moment the world finally met him at the Nike press conference, people wondered *what*, not *who*, he was. He with the almond eyes, the great-colored skin, the photo-op smile. "What are you?" a reporter asked. He didn't seem quite ready for the question, suggesting he wasn't any one thing, but a lot of everything all rolled up into one. Started going into fractions—one-eighth of this, one-fifth of that, a fourth of something else. Told Oprah he didn't feel comfortable being called black. To describe his ethnicity, he came up with the name Cablinasian, combining his Caucasian, Black, Indian, and Asian ethnicities. It seemed both a naive plea for a color-blind, colorless America and a throwback to the quadroon days of old Louisiana when people measured their bloodlines by the teaspoon.

But in actuality, Tiger Woods was something the world needed very much. He transcended the color barrier. Not because he was the first black to do this or do that in golf, but because he refused to be defined by the color of his skin. In the midst of all his fame, fortune, contracts, money, and marriage offers, he had taken the step to destroy the old racist rule, *one drop is all it takes*. He offered instead a new principle, *combination*: He was a combination of all he came from—Caucasian, black, Indian, and Asian—but that was not *who* he was.

How does all this help Tiger? Well, to some he's considered the best golfer in the world. Not the best black player, but the best player, period. A perfect example of together and the same, instead of separate but equal. How does this help the rest of us? It shows us that race is just a small part of our identity. Our own personal racial equation does not determine who we are or where we're going. Or even what we can do.

You're back at the Western Open. The fan galleries finally look like America—Asian, white, black, Latino, fathers with sons, mothers pushing baby carriages, people who have been playing golf for years, people who didn't know what golf was before Tiger Woods and now want to try it. Everything revolves around Tiger. Even babies go silent when Tiger's about to swing. Once the ball is hit, people resume their conversation and stampede to the next hole to watch him, leaving the next player to struggle by himself.

So what are we to make of him? His father, Earl Woods, has said that his son would change the course of humanity. You can mark that up to a proud father's hyperbole, but perhaps Tiger has already pointed us in a new direction by his refusal to accept an identity imposed by racist custom. Hopefully one day we will see him as a young man who was simply ahead of his time, instead of viewing him as a naive child trying to escape his heritage.

It's not clear yet who he is, but it's quite clear what he is not. His boundaries are not defined and confined by his complex racial background. Instead, he is what he told us, a combination—not of race, but of heart, talent, dedication, attractiveness of person and personality, and grace under the pressure of constant media attention and tournament competition. The most important ingredient in that combination is his stubborn refusal to accept the world's ways of limiting identity, and his polite insistence upon leaving himself open to change and growth. He did not inherit a prearranged identity imposed by race; rather, he is responsible for creating who he is and who he will become. Who he is will emerge over time, a product of his character and accomplishments.

As we watch him grow and become himself, we can only celebrate what he means for a nation and world that must become more comfortable with its incredible diversity of race and culture. Tiger Woods, you are a man for the New Age, and we salute you!

In this section Leslie shifts the focus to Tiger's social significance. She dwells on the importance of creating our own identity rather than accepting a prearranged identity based on race. In the process she expands the principle so that it applies more to character and accomplishment.

In her brief conclusion, Leslie sketches Tiger against the background of a New Age in which the world must come to accept and appreciate its cultural and racial diversity.

WORKS CONSULTED

Garrity, John. "You the Kid." *Sports Illustrated,* http://www.cnnsi.com/features/1996/sportsman/archive/920309.html. Posted March 9, 1992; downloaded April 12, 1998.

Lewis, Andrea. "A Public Course Win—Tiger's Victory Marks a New Stage in Cultural History." *JINN*, http://www.pacificnews.org/jinn/stories/3.08/970416-tiger.html. Posted April 16, 1997; downloaded April 11, 1998.

Montville, Leigh. "On the Job Training." *Sports Illustrated*, http://www.cnnsi.com/features/1996/sportsman/archive/960909.html. Posted September 9, 1996; downloaded April 12, 1998.

Reilly, Rick. "Godness Gracious, He's a Great Ball of Fire." *Sports Illustrated*, http://www.cnnsi.com/features/1996/sportsman/archive/950327.html. Posted March 27, 1995; downloaded April 12, 1998.

Sirak, Ron. "Golf Owes Charlie Sifford a Great Deal." Golfweb Library, http://services.golfweb.com/library/sirak/charlie980224.html. Posted February 24, 1998; downloaded April 11, 1998.

Van Sickle, Gary. "Jackpot!" *Sports Illustrated*, http://www.cnnsi.com/features/1996/sportsman/archive/961014.html. Posted October 14, 1996; downloaded April 10, 1998.

Reach for the Stars!
Ashlie McMillan

In her speech of tribute to her cousin, Ashlie McMillan uses both identification and magnification. Her opening asks listeners to imagine themselves as dwarfs. By picturing her cousin in simple, everyday situations, she invites identification with her.

Please close your eyes. Imagine now that you are shrinking. Can you feel your hands and feet getting smaller, your arms being pulled in closer to your shoulders? Can you picture your legs now dangling off the edge of your seat as your legs shrink up closer to your hips? Now you are only three feet tall. But don't open your eyes yet. This is your first day of being a diastrophic dwarf.

You wake up and get out of bed, which is quite a drop because the bed is almost as tall as you are. You go to the bathroom to wash your face and brush your teeth, but you must stand on a trash can because the faucet is out of your reach. Now you go back to your dorm room, and you're ready to put on your clothes. But again you can't reach the clothes hanging in your closet because you're too short. You have to struggle to get dressed.

Now you have errands that you must run. But how are you going to do them? If you walk, it will take you a long time because you must take many short steps. And you can't drive a car because you can't reach the pedals, much less see over the steering wheel. Finally you get to the bank. But it takes you about five minutes to get the teller's attention because she can't see you below the counter. Next you go to the grocery store. This takes forever because you can't push a cart. You're forced to use a carry basket and to find people who will reach high items for you. Frustrated yet? Okay, open your eyes.

In 1968 my cousin, Tina McMillan, was born. Today she's in her twenty-ninth year as a diastrophic dwarf. What does that mean? It means that she'll never be taller than three feet. It means that her hands will never be able to bend this way [gestures] because she will never have joints in her fingers or toes. She'll always have club feet, and she had to have a rod put in her spine because all diastrophic dwarfs are plagued with scoliosis.

So what does her dwarfism mean to my cousin? Nothing. When you first meet Tina, you might be a little shocked at how tiny she is. But after a while you forget her physical size because her personality is so large and her spirit is so bright. Today I want to tell you the story of how this small person is

After introducing her cousin and defining dwarfism, Ashlie begins magnification by revealing incidents that reveal Tina as a spirited, determined fighter who refuses to accept the role of a disabled person. Ashlie's entire speech is built upon an inspiring irony: that someone so small in physique should be so large in spirit.

reaching for the stars. Her life is a miracle that should teach us never to let obstacles stand in the way of our goals and dreams.

When my aunt and uncle were told that they were going to have a baby who was a diastrophic dwarf, they prepared themselves. They were ready to tell their child that she would never be able to have a Great Dane dog because it would be three times the size that she was. That she would never be able to ride a horse. That she would never be able to drive a car. And that she might not be able to attend college because the dormitories and other facilities were not built for people three feet tall.

What my aunt and uncle were *not* prepared for was a child with a physical disability who refused to see herself as disabled. I can tell you that growing up with Tina was quite an experience. She was always the ham of the cousins, always the center of attention. I remember going over to her house and playing with her *three* Great Dane dogs in the backyard. I remember every Sunday when my grandpa would take us out to the farm and we would fight over who got to ride the horses. And Tina would even fight my grandfather so she could get up on the horse all by herself. And I remember the day, some time after her sixteenth birthday, that she slid behind the wheel of a car. She had teamed up with some engineers down in Texas to have the pedals extended as well as hand gears made on the steering wheel so that she could drive herself. But perhaps my proudest and fondest memory was watching my cousin walk across the graduation stage at Texas Christian University in 1991. She not only got her degree in English, but she went on to get a master's degree in anthropology from TCU. After she graduated, the university invited her to come back to teach in the English Department. But by this time Tina had a new challenge: She declined the teaching job so that she could enter politics as campaign manager for the mayor of Dallas.

Tina has never stopped challenging the perception that she is disabled. Next April she will be marrying a person of normal stature, and once again she will defy society's assumption that something must be wrong about such a marriage. And then in the fall she plans on attending the University of Texas law school. Want to bet against her there?

As she nears the conclusion, Ashlie begins to draw lessons from her cousin's life to inspire listeners. The closing sentence suggests an analogy with a point made earlier in the speech: People must stand on dreams as well as boxes to reach distant goals.

Somehow, against the odds, my cousin has led a normal life. To many people, what she has accomplished might not seem that exceptional. To me, however, she is an inspiration. Whenever I think I've got problems that are too much for me, I think of her and of what she has done, this large and vital person stuffed into such a small body. I think of how she refuses to use her disability as a scapegoat or excuse. And I remember how she does not even consider quitting if something stands in her way. She simply views the obstacle, decides the best way to get around it, and moves on. And although she will lose the ability to walk, probably by the age of forty, I believe that she will still find the way to keep moving toward her goals.

The next time a large obstacle stands in your way, remember Tina, my small cousin who has achieved such noteworthy things. You too may seem too short to grasp your stars, but you never know how far you might reach if you stand upon a dream.

WORKS CONSULTED

Department of Orthopedics, Alfred I. Dupont Institute. http://gait.aidi.udel.edu .res695/homepage/pd_ortho/educat. Undated posting; downloaded April 18, 1998.

Diastrophic Dwarfism. http://chorus.rad.mcw.edu/dpc/01027.html. Undated posting; downloaded April 18, 1998.

Diastrophic Dysplasia. http://gasbone.herston.uq.edu.au/~ortho/regsum/genorth 108. Undated posting; downloaded April 18, 1998.

NORD Research Group. http://www.stepsn.com/nord/rdb_sum/482.htm. Undated posting; downloaded April 18, 1998.

Texgene Genetics Network. "Methods of Inheritance." http://www.tdh.texas .gov/texgene/inherit.htm. Posted March 4, 1998; downloaded April 18, 1998.

APPENDIX A

Communicating in Small Groups

Many important communication interactions are conducted in small group settings. In class, you may be assigned to a project team to study some problem. At work, you may serve on a committee planning the company's future. In your community, a group of neighbors may meet to resolve some issue. In social organizations, you may find yourself planning organizational activities with a few others.

In order to understand how such communication functions, we need to consider the nature of a group. For a collection of people to be considered "a group,"

- More than three people must interact face to face over a period of time in order to reach a goal.
- Those who interact must be part of some larger population that they represent.
- Oral communication must be central to their interaction.

Here we discuss how groups function and how your public communication skills can make you a better participant or leader.

The Advantages and Disadvantages of Group Problem Solving

When we listen to someone present information or make recommendations, we usually hear only one side of a situation. The presentation may be biased or based on self-interest, or it may simply be wrong. When important issues are involved, we need to minimize the risk of such errors. One way to minimize this risk is to empower a small group of people to investigate, analyze, share information and perspectives, and make recommendations about a problem.

Group problem solving has many advantages. When people from different cultures share their various ways of seeing a problem, they enrich our understanding.[1] We begin to see the world through the eyes of others, and this may help us see misconceptions and biases in our own thinking. Listening to others' points of view also can stimulate creative thinking about problems.

In well-run problem-solving groups, people on all sides of an issue have a chance to discuss the similarities and differences of their perspectives. Through discussion, they may discover some areas of agreement that can form a basis for resolving differences. Additionally, in small, face-to-face groups, people are often more willing to examine their differences and may feel free to explore compromises or new options for action. Because of these advantages, organizations often use groups to work on important organizational problems. In fact, it is estimated that approximately twenty million meetings take place each day in the United States.[2]

Although working in groups has many advantages, there are also some problems that can make groups ineffective. **Cultural gridlock**, the inability to communicate because of profound cultural differences, can stand in the way of effective group deliberations. For example, an organization's marketing people and its research and development scientists may see the world quite differently. Culturally diverse participants may bring different perspectives, assumptions, expectations, priorities, agendas, procedures, ways of communicating, and standards of protocol to meetings. The scientists might fancy blue jeans and beards, an anathema to the marketing folks. In any organization, unwritten rules may dictate that some people speak first, while others defer or even remain silent. These differences may sidetrack constructive discussions.

Dealing with cultural gridlock is never easy. To minimize its impact, you should:

- Allow time for people to get acquainted before getting down to business.

- Provide a comfortable environment. Be sure you have enough room so that people don't feel crowded.

- Distribute an agenda so that people know what to expect.

- Minimize technical communication problems. Summarize discussions. Post key points. Discourage the use of jargon that some participants may not understand.

- Be sensitive to cultural differences in protocol and nonverbal communication.[3]

Another problem that groups may encounter is **groupthink**, the uncritical acceptance of decisions.[4] Groupthink is most likely to occur when groups value interpersonal relationships more than they value the ability to perform effectively.[5] Other factors that contribute to groupthink include a leader's strong preference for a certain decision and the lack of a clear set of procedures for approaching problems. Groupthink is dangerous because outsiders may assume that a group has deliberated carefully and responsibly when it has not.

To avoid groupthink, groups need to be aware of its major symptoms. These include

- Putting pressure on people who argue against what most of the group believe

- Censoring thoughts that differ from group beliefs

- Maintaining an illusion of infallibility (the group can do no wrong)

- Reinforcing an unquestioned belief in the group's moral rightness

- Attempting to rationalize group decisions

The problems in decision-making that accompany groupthink include (1) incomplete consideration of objectives, (2) poor information retrieval and analysis, and (3) incomplete consideration of alternative solutions.[6]

Once a group becomes aware that there is a potential groupthink problem, members can initiate actions to minimize its effects. First, they should set standards for "vigilant search and appraisal that counter collective uncritical thinking and premature consensus."[7] This suggests that they must have a systematic way to approach the problem. Leadership behaviors that help reduce groupthink include

- Reminding participants to critically evaluate the group's recommendations

- Reserving one's own opinions until others have expressed their views

- Assigning the role of "devil's advocate" so that someone asks critical questions about ideas
- Bringing in outsiders to discuss the issues under consideration
- Encouraging creative conflict in which members attack and defend points of view rather than uncritically accepting them

Group Problem-Solving Techniques

Group deliberations that are orderly, systematic, and thorough help people reach high-quality decisions. Problem-solving groups can use a variety of methods to achieve their goals.[8]

Reflective Thinking and Problem Solving

The approach we recommend for most problem-solving groups is a modification of the reflective-thinking technique first proposed by John Dewey in 1910.[9] This systematic approach has five steps: (1) defining the problem, (2) generating potential solutions, (3) evaluating solution options, (4) developing a plan of action, and (5) evaluating the results.

Step 1: Defining the Problem.   Sometimes the problem assigned to a group is only a symptom of the actual problem. All problem-solving groups should take time to define the problem carefully before looking for a solution. The following guidelines can help in defining the problem:

- Describe the problem as specifically as possible.
- Explore the causes of the problem.
- Consider the history of the problem.
- Determine who is affected by the problem.
- Decide whether you have the information needed to understand the problem. If you do not, obtain this information.

Step 2: Generating Potential Solutions.   Once a group has defined the problem, members can work on generating solutions. Brainstorming encourages members to identify a variety of possible solutions so that the group is aware of its options.[10] The procedure works best in groups with twelve or fewer members.[11]

While brainstorming, members should adhere to the following rules:

- Feel free to present any ideas they have, no matter how outrageous these may seem. Even an outlandish notion may provide the basis for an eventual solution.
- The more ideas generated, the better.
- Criticism is out of place during the brainstorming process. Nothing should inhibit creativity.
- Consider whether any ideas might be combined to produce additional options.

Brainstorming usually involves a five-step process:

1. The leader asks each member in turn to contribute an idea. If a member does not have an idea, he or she should pass.
2. A recorder writes down all ideas on a flip chart or markerboard so that everyone can see them.
3. Brainstorming continues until all members have passed.
4. The suggestions are reviewed for clarification, and options may be added or combined.
5. The leader designates someone to receive additional ideas that may occur to members after this formal process has concluded. These ideas may be added to the list for consideration during the next phase of the problem-solving process.

There are many variations of brainstorming.[12] When time is short or when member status differences may stifle the expression of ideas, **electronic brainstorming**, in which participants generate ideas in computer chat groups or by email before meeting face to face, may enhance the process.[13]

Step 3: Evaluating Solution Options.   Ideally, a group should take a break between generating solutions and evaluating them. During that time, members can gather information on the feasibility of each option and determine if it has been used elsewhere. When the group reconvenes, it should discuss the options using the following guidelines:

1. Costs of the option
2. Probability of success
3. Difficulty of enactment
4. Time constraints
5. Additional benefits to be expected
6. Additional problems that might be encountered

Groups should summarize these considerations for each option on a flip chart, then post the summaries so that members can refer to them as they compare options. As options are evaluated, some of them will seem weak and will be dropped: others may be strengthened and refined.

The group also may combine options to generate new alternatives. For example, if the group is caught between Option A, which promises improved efficiency, and Option B, which promises lower cost, it may be possible to combine the best features of each into Option C. This approach is similar to the SIL (Successive Integration of Problem Elements) Method developed at the Battelle Memorial Institute, a nonprofit research and development think tank. The SIL Method is useful for groups of six or fewer participants. The process includes the following steps:

1. Members independently generate solution options.
2. Two of the members each read one of his or her ideas to the group.
3. The group discusses ways to combine the two ideas into one solution.
4. A third member reads an idea, and the group attempts to integrate it with the solution from step 3.

5. The "add-an-idea" process continues until all of the participants' ideas have been read aloud and the group has tried to integrate them.

6. The process is complete when the group reaches a consensus on a solution.[14]

After each alternative has been considered, members rank the solutions in terms of their acceptability. The option receiving the highest overall rank is the proposed solution.

It is not unusual for group members to become personally caught up with their own solutions. During evaluation, the leader must keep the group focused on ideas and not on participants. Accept differences of opinion and conflict as a natural and necessary part of problem solving. Discussing the strengths of an option before talking about its weaknesses can take some of the heat out of the process.

Step 4: Developing a Plan of Action.   Once the group has selected a solution, it must determine how this solution can be implemented. For example, to improve company morale, a group might recommend a three-step plan: (1) better in-house training programs to increase upward mobility, (2) a pay structure that rewards success in training programs, and (3) increased employee participation in decision-making. As the group refines this plan, it should consider what might help or hinder it, the resources needed to enact it, and a timetable for completion.

If the group cannot develop a plan of action for the solution, or if insurmountable obstacles appear, the group should return to step 3 and consider other options.

Step 5: Evaluating Results.   Not only must a problem-solving group plan how to implement a solution, it must also determine how to evaluate results once the plan is enacted. The group should establish evaluation criteria that define what will constitute success, when the group can expect results, and contingency plans to use if the original plan doesn't work. To monitor the ongoing success of a solution, such as the three-part plan to improve morale, the group would have to determine reasonable expectations for each stage in the process. That way, the company could detect and correct problems as they occur, before they damaged the plan as a whole. Having a scheduled sequence of expectations also provides a way to determine results while the plan is being enacted, rather than having to wait for the entire project to be completed.

Other Approaches to Group Problem Solving

While the systematic process described above works well in many situations, there are times when a different approach may be needed. When a group consists of people from different areas of the public and private sectors, **collaborative problem solving** may work best.[15] For example, in many urban areas, coalitions of business executives and educators have worked together on plans to train people for jobs in the community. In such situations, the problems are usually important and the resources typically are limited. Because there is no clear-cut authority structure and because the factions may have different expectations or goals, the members of such groups often have difficulty working together. To be effective, they need to spend considerable time defining the problem and exploring one another's perspectives. This should help them to recognize their interdependence and encourage them to work together. In such groups, participants must come to see themselves not as members of group A (the executives) or group B (the educators), but as members of group C, the coalition. Leadership in such groups may pose a special challenge.

One approach that may facilitate collaborative problem solving is **dialogue groups**. According to William Isaacs, director of the Dialogue Project at the Massachusetts Institute of Technology's Center for Organizational Learning, "Dialogue is a discipline of collective thinking and inquiry, a process for transforming the quality of conversation, and, in particular, the thinking that lies beneath it."[16] Such groups focus on understanding the different interpretations of the problem that participants bring to the interaction. Their purpose is to establish a conversation among the participants from which common ground and mutual trust can emerge.[17]

The role of the facilitator is critical in dialogue groups. According to Edgar Schein of the MIT Center, the facilitator must

- Organize the physical space in a circle to create a sense of equality
- Introduce the problem
- Ask people to share an experience in which dialogue led to "good communication"
- Ask members to consider what it was that led to good communication in that situation
- Ask participants to talk about their reactions
- Let the conversation flow naturally
- Intervene only to clarify problems of communication
- Conclude by asking all members to comment however they choose[18]

The dialogue method is not a substitute for other problem-solving techniques, such as the rational-thinking process presented earlier. Instead, it may be used as a precursor because deliberation works only when members understand each other well enough to be "talking the same language."[19] A similar approach may be found in the Kettering Foundation's National Issues Forums.[20]

Participating in Small Groups

To be an effective group member, you must understand your responsibilities. First, you should come to meetings prepared to contribute. You should have read background materials and performed any tasks assigned to you. Second, you should be willing to learn from others and avoid dominating the discussion. Don't be afraid to admit when you are wrong, and don't become defensive when you are challenged. Willingness to change your views is not a sign of weakness, nor is obstinacy a strength. Third, you should listen constructively and not interrupt others. However, do object if you feel consensus is forming too rapidly. You might save the meeting from groupthink.

Analyzing your group communication skills can help you become a more effective communicator. Use the self-analysis form (Figure A.1 on page 454) to steer you toward more constructive behaviors.

FIGURE A.1

Group Communication Skills Self-Analysis Form

		Need to Do Less	Doing Fine	Need to Do More
1.	I make my points concisely.	_____	_____	_____
2.	I speak with confidence.	_____	_____	_____
3.	I provide specific examples and details.	_____	_____	_____
4.	I try to integrate ideas that are expressed.	_____	_____	_____
5.	I let others know when I do not understand them.	_____	_____	_____
6.	I let others know when I agree with them.	_____	_____	_____
7.	I let others know tactfully when I disagree with them.	_____	_____	_____
8.	I express my opinions.	_____	_____	_____
9.	I suggest solutions to problems.	_____	_____	_____
10.	I listen to understand.	_____	_____	_____
11.	I try to understand before agreeing or disagreeing.	_____	_____	_____
12.	I ask questions to get more information.	_____	_____	_____
13.	I ask others for their opinions.	_____	_____	_____
14.	I check for group agreement.	_____	_____	_____
15.	I try to minimize tension.	_____	_____	_____
16.	I accept help from others.	_____	_____	_____
17.	I offer help to others.	_____	_____	_____
18.	I let others have their say.	_____	_____	_____
19.	I stand up for myself.	_____	_____	_____
20.	I urge others to speak up.	_____	_____	_____

As you participate in groups, you should also keep in mind the following questions:

1. What is happening now in the group?
2. What should be happening in the group?
3. What can I do to make this come about?[21]

If you notice a difference between what the group is doing and what it *should be* doing to reach its goals, you have the opportunity to assume group leadership.

Leadership in Small Groups

Interest in leadership is driven by one quite practical consideration: Leaders help get jobs done. For over thirty-five years, social scientists have been studying leadership by analyzing group communication patterns.[22] This research suggests that two basic types of leadership behaviors emerge in most groups. The first is **task leadership behavior,** which directs the activity of the group toward a specified goal. The second is **social leadership behavior,** which helps to build and maintain positive relationships among group members.

Task leaders initiate goal-related communication, including both giving and seeking information, opinions, and suggestions. A task leader might say, "We need more information on just how widespread sexual harassment is on campus. Let me tell you what Dean Johnson told me last Friday. . . ." Or the task leader might ask, "Gwen, tell us what you found out from the Affirmative Action Office."

Social leaders express agreement, help the group release tension, and behave in a supportive manner. A social leader looks for chances to give compliments: "I think Gwen has made a very important point. You really helped us by finding that out." Sincere compliments help keep members from becoming defensive and help maintain a constructive communication atmosphere. In a healthy communication climate, the two kinds of leadership behavior support each other and keep the group moving toward its goal. When one person combines both styles of leadership, that person is likely to be highly effective.

Leadership has also been discussed in terms of how the leader functions. An **autocratic leader** makes decisions without consultation, issues orders or gives direction, and controls the members of the group through the use of rewards or punishments. A **participative leader** functions in a more democratic fashion, seeking input from group members and giving them an active role in decision-making. A **free-rein leader** leaves members free to decide what, how, and when to act, offering no guidance. In effect, such "leadership" abdicates leadership. If you were working in an organization, you might well say that you "worked *for*" an autocratic leader, "worked *with*" a participative leader, and "worked *in spite of*" a free-rein leader.

As we move into the twenty-first century, another way of looking at leadership is emerging. It suggests that leadership styles are either transactional or transformational. **Transactional leadership** takes place in an environment based on power relationships and relies on reward and punishment to accomplish its ends. **Transformational leadership** appeals to "people's higher levels of motivation to contribute to a cause and add to the quality of life on the planet."[23] Transformational leadership carries overtones of stewardship instead of management. Transformational leaders have the following qualities:

- They have a vision of what needs to be done.
- They are empathetic.
- They are trusted.
- They give credit to others.
- They help others develop.
- They share power.
- They are willing to experiment and learn.

In short, transformational leaders lead with both their hearts and their heads. According to John Schuster, a management consultant who specializes in transformational leadership training, "The heart is more difficult to develop. It's easier to get smarter than to become more caring."[24]

To understand your leadership potential, you need to consider the major components of **ethos**: competence, trustworthiness, likability, and forcefulness. An effective leader is competent. This means that the leader understands the problem and knows how to steer a group through the problem-solving process. An effective leader is both trustworthy and trusted. This means that the leader *is* honest, concerned about the good of the group, and willing to place group success above personal concerns. Just as important, the leader is *perceived* to have these qualities by group participants. An effective leader is likable. This means that he or she is friendly and interacts easily with others. Finally, an effective leader is forceful. Forcefulness suggests enthusiasm, energy, and optimism, and implies the ability to get others to act.

Don't be intimidated by this idealized portrait of a leader. Most of us have these qualities in varying degrees and can use them when the need for leadership arises. To be an effective leader, remember this simple overriding goal: *Help others be effective and get the job done.* Cultivate an open leadership style that encourages all sides to air their views.

Planning Meetings

Meetings can sometimes be a waste of time, perhaps because the people who conduct them do not know when to call them or how to prepare for them.[25] Meetings should be called when members need to

- Discuss the meaning of information face to face
- Decide on a common course of action
- Establish a plan of action
- Report on the progress of a plan, evaluate its effectiveness, and revise it if needed

In other words, there should be some specific justification for holding a meeting. If your goal is simply to increase interaction, plan a social event instead.

You also need to know how to plan meetings. The following guidelines should prove useful:

1. Keep the group small. You get more participation and interaction in a small group. In a larger group, people may be reluctant to ask questions or contribute ideas.

2. Assemble a group that invites open discussion. In business settings, the presence of someone's supervisor may inhibit interaction. You will get better participation if group members come from the same or nearly the same working level in the organization.

3. Plan the site of the meeting. Arrange for privacy and freedom from interruptions. A circular arrangement contributes to participation because there is no power position. A rectangular table or a lectern and classroom arrangement may inhibit interaction.

4. Prepare an agenda and distribute it to participants before the meeting. Having an agenda gives members time to prepare and assemble information they might need. Solicit agenda items from participants.

5. Make last-minute preparations. Have extra copies of the agenda on hand. Gather necessary supplies, such as chalk, a flip chart, markers, note pads, and pencils. Check out audiovisual equipment to be sure it is working.

6. Keep the meeting short. After about an hour, groups grow weary and the law of diminishing returns sets in. Don't try to do too much in a single meeting.

Conducting an Effective Meeting

The following checklist should be helpful in guiding your behavior as a group leader:

- Begin and end the meeting on time.
- Present background information concisely and objectively.
- Don't run the meeting, lead it.
- Be enthusiastic.
- Get conflict out in the open so that it can be dealt with directly.
- Urge all members to participate.
- Keep discussion centered on the issue.
- At the close of a meeting, summarize what the group has accomplished.

As a group leader, you may be asked to report to others on the group's work. Depending upon the time allotted, you may summarize how the group deliberated, including the information gathered that was most compelling, the major arguments that developed, and the final recommendations adopted and the reasons for offering them. You should also mention any reservations concerning these recommendations that may have surfaced. As you describe the group's work and defend the wisdom of its proposals, you will combine the functions of both informative and persuasive speaking.

Guidelines for Formal Meetings

The larger a group is, the more it may need a formal procedure to conduct a meeting. Also, if a meeting involves a controversial subject, it is often wise to have a set of rules for conducting business. Having clear-cut guidelines helps keep meetings from becoming chaotic and helps assure fair treatment for all participants. In such situations, many groups choose to operate by **parliamentary procedure.**[26]

Parliamentary procedure establishes an order of business for a meeting and lays out the way the group initiates discussions and reaches decisions (see Figure A.2). Under parliamentary procedure, a formal meeting proceeds as follows:

1. The chair calls the meeting to order.
2. The secretary reads the minutes of the previous meeting, which are corrected, if necessary, and approved.
3. Reports from officers and committees are presented.
4. Unfinished business is considered.
5. New business is introduced.

FIGURE A.2

Guide to the Parliamentary Procedure

Action	Requires Second	Can Be Debated	Can Be Amended	Vote Required	Function
Main Motion	Yes	Yes	Yes	Majority	Commits group to a specific action or position.
Second	No	No	No	None	Assures that more than one group member wishes to see idea considered.
Move to Amend	Yes	Yes	Yes	Majority	Allows group to modify and improve an existing motion.
Call the Question	Yes	No	No	Two-thirds	Brings discussion to an end and moves to a vote on the motion in question.
Move to Table the Motion	Yes	No	No	Majority	Stops immediate consideration of the motion until a later unspecified time.
Move to Postpone Consideration	Yes	Yes	Yes	Majority	Stops immediate discussion and allows time for the group to obtain more information on the problem.
Move to Adjourn	Yes	No	No	Majority	Formally ends meeting.

6. Announcements are made.

7. The meeting is adjourned.

Business in formal meetings goes forward by motions, or proposals set before the group. Consider the following scenario. The chair asks: "Is there any new business?" A member responds: "I move that we allot $100 to build a Homecoming float." The member has offered a main **motion**, which proposes an action. Before the group can discuss the motion, it must be seconded. The purpose of a **second** is to assure that more than one person wants to see the motion considered. If no one volunteers a second, the chair may ask, "Is there a second?" Typically, another member will respond, "I second the motion." Once a motion has been made and seconded, it is open for discussion. It must be passed by majority vote, defeated, or otherwise resolved before the group can move on to other business. With the exception of a few technical motions (such as "I move we take a fifteen-minute recess" or "Point of personal privilege—can we do anything about the heat in this room?"), the main motion remains at the center of group attention until it is resolved.

Let us assume that as the group discusses the main motion in our example, some members believe that the amount of money proposed is insufficient. At this point, another member may say: "I move to amend the motion to provide $150 for the float." The motion to amend gives the group a chance to modify a main motion. It must be seconded and, after discussion, must be resolved by majority vote before discussion goes forward. If the motion to amend passes, then the amended main motion must be considered further.

How does a group make a decision on a motion? There usually comes a time when discussion begins to lag. At this point the chair might say, "Do I hear a call for the question?" A motion to call the question ends discus-sion, and requires a two-thirds vote for approval. Once the group votes to end discussion, it must then vote to accept or reject the motion. No further discussion can take place until the original or amended original motion is voted upon.

Sometimes the discussion of a motion may reveal that the group is confused or sharply divided about an issue. At this point, a member may move to table the motion. This is a way to dispose of a troublesome motion without further divisive or confused discussion. At other times, the discussion of a motion may reveal that the group lacks certain information that is needed to make an intelligent decision. At that point, we might hear from a member: "In light of the uncertainty over costs, I move we postpone further consideration until next week's meeting." The motion to postpone consideration gives the chair a chance to appoint a committee to gather the needed information.

These are just some of the important procedures that can help assure that formal group communication remains fair and constructive. For more information on formal group communication procedures, consult the authoritative *Robert's Rules of Order.*

Notes

1. Marc Hequet, "The Fine Art of Multicultural Meetings," *Training,* July 1993, 29(5), *Business Database Plus,* online, CompuServe, January 1996; William N. Issacs, "Taking Flight: Dialogue, Collective Thinking, and Organizational Learning," *Organizational Dynamics,* Autumn 1993, 24(16), *Business Database*

Plus, online, CompuServe, January 1996; and Edgar H. Schein, "On Dialogue, Culture, and Organizational Learning," *Organizational Dynamics,* Autumn 1993, 40(12), *Business Database Plus,* online, CompuServe, January 1996.

2. Scot Ober, *Contemporary Business Communication* (Boston: Houghton Mifflin, 1995), p. 498.

3. Adapted from Hequet.

4. Paul R. Bernthal and Chester A. Insko, "Cohesiveness Without Groupthink: The Interactive Effects of Social and Task Cohesion," *Group and Organization Management,* March 1993, 66(22), *Business Database Plus,* online, CompuServe, January 1996; and Christopher P. Neck and Charles C. Manz, "From Groupthink to Teamthink: Toward the Creation of Constructive Thought Patterns in Self-Management Work Teams," *Human Relations,* August 1994, 929(24), *Business Database Plus,* online, CompuServe, January 1996.

5. Bernthal and Insko.

6. Neck and Manz.

7. I. L. Janis, *Groupthink: Psychological Studies of Policy Decisions and Fiascoes* (Boston: Houghton Mifflin, 1982), pp. 245–246.

8. For an overview of other methods, see Patricia Hayes Andrews and Richard T. Herschel, *Organizational Communication: Empowerment in a Technological Society* (Boston: Houghton Mifflin, 1996), pp. 213–218.

9. The problem-solving process described here is adapted from William C. Morris and Marshall Sashkin, "Phases of Integrated Problem Solving (PIPS)," *The 1978 Annual Handbook for Group Facilitators,* ed. J. William Pfeiffer and John E. Jones (La Jolla, Calif.: University Associates, 1978), pp. 109–116.

10. Floyd Hurt, "Better Brainstorming," *Training and Development,* November 1994, 57(3), *Business Database Plus,* online, CompuServe, January 1996.

11. Ron Zemke, "In Search of Good Ideas," *Training,* January 1993, 46(6), *Business Database Plus,* online, CompuServe, January 1996.

12. Hurt; Sivasailam Thiagarajan, "Take Five for Better Brainstorming," *Training and Development Journal,* February 1992, 37(6), *Business Database Plus,* online, CompuServe, January 1996; and Zemke.

13. Milam Aiken, Mahesh Vanjami, and James Krosp, "Group Decision Support Systems," *Review of Business,* Spring 1995, 38(5), *Business Database Plus,* online, CompuServe, January 1996; Gail Kay, "Effective Meetings Through Electronic Brainstorming," *Management Quarterly,* Winter 1994, 15(12), *Business Database Plus,* online, CompuServe, January 1996; Michael C. Kettelhut, "How to Avoid Misusing Electronic Meeting Support," *Planning Review,* July–August 1994, 34(5), *Business Database Plus,* online, CompuServe, January 1996; and Srikumar S. Rao, "Meetings Go Better Electronically: Do Hard-Nosed Bosses Stifle Discussion? Try Conferencing Software," *Financial World,* 14 March 1995, 72(2), *Business Database Plus,* online, CompuServe, January 1996.

14. Zemke.

15. Jacqueline N. Hood, Jeanne M. Logsdon, and Judith Kenner Thompson, "Collaboration for Social Problem Solving: A Process Model," *Business and Society,* Spring 1993, 1(17), *Business Database Plus,* online, CompuServe, January 1996.

16. Isaacs.

17. Schein.

18. Schein.

19. Schein.

20. Michael Osborn and Suzanne Osborn, *Alliance for a Better Public Voice: The Communication Discipline and the National Issues Forums* (Dayton, Ohio: National Issues Forms Institute, 1991).

21. Adapted from David G. Smith, "D-I-D: A Three-Dimensional Model for Understanding Group Communication," *The 1977 Annual Handbook for Group Facilitators,* ed. John E. Jones and J. William Pfeiffer (La Jolla, Calif.: University Associates, 1977), p. 106.

22. Robert F. Bales, *Interaction Process Analysis: A Method for the Study of Small Groups* (Cambridge, Mass.: Addison-Wesley, 1950); *Personality and Interpersonal Behavior* (New York: Holt, 1970).

23. John P. Schuster, "Transforming Your Leadership Style," *Association Management,* January 1994, 39(5), *Business Database Plus,* online, CompuServe, January 1996.

24. Schuster.

25. Much of the material in this section is adapted from Becky Jones, Midge Wilker, and Judy Stoner, "A Meeting Primer," *Management Review,* January 1995, 30(3), *Business Database Plus,* online, CompuServe, January 1996; and Robert D. Ramsey, "Making Meetings Work for You," *Supervision,* February 1994, 14(3), *Business Database Plus,* online, CompuServe, January 1996.

26. Darwin Patnode, *Robert's Rules of Order: Modern Edition* (Nashville, Tenn.: Thomas Nelson, 1989).

APPENDIX B

Speeches for Analysis

Self-Introductory

Sandra Baltz, "My Three Cultures"
Rodney Nishikawa, "Free at Last"

Informative

Stephen Huff, "The New Madrid Earthquake Area"
Cecile Larson, "The 'Monument' at Wounded Knee"
Stephen Lee, "The Trouble with Numbers"

Persuasive

Bonnie Marshall, "Living Wills: Ensuring Your Right to Choose"
Gina Norman, "Secondhand Smoke"
Cesar Chavez, "Pesticides Speech"

Ceremonial

Elie Wiesel, "Nobel Peace Prize Acceptance Speech"
Award Ceremony Honoring Wilma Rudolph with presentations by Tom
    Brokaw, Bill Cosby, Gail Devers, Ed Temple, and Wilma Rudolph.
Hillary Rodham Clinton, "Address to the United Nations Fourth World Con-
    ference on Women"
Elizabeth Dole, "Women in Public Life Commencement Address"
John Scipio, "Martin Luther King at the Mountaintop"

My Three Cultures
Sandra Baltz

Sandra Baltz first presented this self-introductory speech many years ago at the University of Memphis. She addressed the themes of cross-culturalism and family values long before these became fashionable. Sandra's deft use of comparison and contrast, and her example of foods illustrating how three cultures can combine harmoniously, are instructive. As her speech developed, she built her ethos as a competent, warm person, highly qualified to give later informative and persuasive speeches on issues involving medical care. Presented at a time when tensions in the Middle East were running high, Sandra's speech served as a gentle reminder that people of goodwill can always find ways to enjoy their differences, and to reaffirm their common membership in the human family.

Several years ago I read a newspaper article in the *Commercial Appeal* in which an American journalist described some of his experiences in the Middle East. He was there a couple of months and had been the guest of several different Arab families. He reported having been very well treated and very well received by everyone that he met there. But it was only later, when he returned home, that he became aware of the intense resentment his hosts held for Americans and our unwelcome involvement in their Middle Eastern affairs. The journalist wrote of feeling somewhat bewildered, if not deceived, by the large discrepancy between his treatment while in the Middle East and the hostile attitude that he learned about later. He labeled this behavior hypocritical. When I reached the end of the article, I was reminded of a phrase spoken often by my mother. "Sandra," she says to me, *"respeta tu casa y a todos los que entran en ella, trata a tus enemigos asi como a tus amigos."*

This is an Arabic proverb, spoken in Spanish, and roughly it translates into "Respect your home and all who enter it, treating even an enemy as a friend." This is a philosophy that I have heard often in my home. With this in mind, it seemed to me that the treatment the American journalist received while in the Middle East was not hypocritical behavior on the part of his hosts. Rather, it was an act of respect for their guest, for themselves, and for their home—indeed, a behavior very typical of the Arabic culture.

Since having read that article several years ago, I have become much more aware of how my life is different because of having a mother who is of Palestinian origin but was born and raised in the Central American country of El Salvador.

One of the most obvious differences is that I was raised bilingually—speaking both Spanish and English. In fact, my first words were in Spanish. Growing up speaking two languages has been both an advantage and a disadvantage for me. One clear advantage is that I received straight A's in my Spanish class at Immaculate Conception High School. Certainly, traveling has been made much easier. During visits to Spain, Mexico, and some of the Central American countries, it has been my experience that people are much more open and much more receptive if you can speak their language. In addition, the subtleties of a culture are easier to grasp and much easier to appreciate.

I hope that knowing a second language will continue to be an asset for me in the future. I am currently pursuing a career in medicine. Perhaps by knowing Spanish I can broaden the area in which I can work and increase the number of people that I might reach.

Now one of the disadvantages of growing up bilingually is that I picked up my mother's accent as well as her language. I must have been about four years old before I realized that our feathered friends in the trees are called "birds" not "beers" and that, in fact, we had a "birdbath" in our backyard, not a "beerbath."

Family reunions also tend to be confusing around my home. Most of my relatives speak either Spanish, English, or Arabic, but rarely any combination of the three. So, as a result, deep and involved conversations are almost impossible. But with a little nodding and smiling, I have found that there really is no language barrier among family and friends.

In all, I must say that being exposed to three very different cultures—Latin, Arabic, and American—has been rewarding for me and has made a difference even in the music I enjoy and the food I eat. It is not unusual in my house to sit down to a meal made up of stuffed grape leaves and refried beans and all topped off with apple pie for dessert.

I am fortunate in having had the opportunity to view more closely what makes Arabic and Latin cultures unique. By understanding and appreciating them I have been able to better understand and appreciate my own American culture. In closing, just let me add some words you often hear spoken in my home—*adios* and *allak konn ma'eck*—goodbye, and may God go with you.

Free at Last
Rodney Nishikawa

Rod Nishikawa presented this sensitive and moving self-introductory speech in his public speaking class at the University of California–Davis. Although most of his classmates were aware of prejudice, Rod's personal narrative—about his first encounter with prejudice as a child—introduced many of them to the Japanese American culture and helped them relate to the problem more closely. Rod's willingness to speak from the heart helped transform his class into a creative, caring community.

Three years ago I presented the valedictory speech at my high school graduation. As I concluded, I borrowed a line from Dr. Martin Luther King's "I Have a Dream" oration: "Free at last, free at last, thank God almighty we're free at last!" The words had only a joyful, humorous place in that speech, but for me personally they were a lie. I was not yet free, and would not be free until I had conquered an ancient enemy, both outside me and within me—that enemy was racial prejudice.

The event in my life that had the greatest effect on me happened over twelve years ago when I was eight years old. I was a shy, naive little boy. I knew I was Japanese, but I didn't consider myself different from my friends, nor did I realize anyone else noticed or even cared. But at least one person did. The "bully" in our class made it a point to remind me by calling me a "Jap." He told me I didn't belong in America, and that I should go back to Japan.

It was hard for me to understand what he meant, because like my parents I was born here in this country. This was my home. I didn't know what to do when I was taunted. All I can remember is going home after school and crying as though my heart were broken. I told my mom that I wished I wasn't Japanese, but that if I did have to be Japanese, why did I have to be born in this country?

Of course my mother knew exactly how I felt. She was about the age I was then when the Japanese attacked Pearl Harbor. She told me how she too had experienced prejudice at school, but that the prejudice she encountered was over a hundred times worse. When my father came home from work, my mom and I told him what had happened. Although my father was understanding, he said that I would never know the meaning of true prejudice because I did not grow up on the West Coast during World War II.

My encounter with the school bully was the beginning of my personal education about prejudice. What I have learned is that prejudice is not a disease that infects only the least educated among us. Rather, it is a bad part of human nature that lies buried deep within all of us. Some people, however, seem to enjoy their prejudice. These people like to feel good by putting others down. But I have also learned how to deal with such problems when they arise. It was the advice from my mother that helped me the most.

My mother explained to me the meaning of the Japanese word *gaman*. *Gaman* means to "bear within" or "bear the burden." It is similar to the American phrase "turn the other cheek," but it means more to "endure" than to "ignore." She told me that when I go back to school, I should practice *gaman*—that even if I am hurt, I should not react with anger or fear, that I should bear the burden within. She said that if I showed anger or fear it would only make things worse, but if I practiced *gaman* things would get better for me. She was right. When I went back to school, I remembered what she had said. I used *gaman*. I bore the burden within. It wasn't easy for an eight-year-old, but I did not show any anger. I did not show any fear to the bully, and eventually he stopped picking on me.

Prejudice has been a bitter teacher in my life, but *gaman* has been an even greater blessing. By learning how to practice it, I feel I have acquired a great deal of inner strength. Whereas Gary [another student in the class] said he is a "competitor," I believe I am a "survivor." I look around my environment, recognize my situation, and cope with it. Because *gaman* has been part of my daily life since I was eight years old, I rarely experience feelings of anger or fear—those negative emotions that can keep a person from really being "free."

Being freed from such negative feelings has also helped me to better understand and accept myself. When I first encountered prejudice, I was ashamed of who I was. I didn't like being different, being a Japanese American. But as I've grown to maturity, I have realized that I'm really proud to be Japanese American: Japanese by blood—with the rich culture and heritage of my ancestors behind me—and American by birth—which makes me equal to anyone in this room because we were all born in this country and we all share the same rights and obligations.

Practicing *gaman* has helped me conquer prejudice. Although my Japanese ancestors might not have spoken as boldly as I have today, I am basically an American, which makes me a little outspoken. Therefore, I can talk to you about racial prejudice and of what it has meant to my life. And because I can talk about it, and share it with you, I am finally, truly, "free at last."

The New Madrid Earthquake Area
Stephen Huff

Stephen Huff's informative speech skillfully related his subject to his immediate audience at the outset. He makes excellent use of comparison and contrast, of presentation aids, and of vivid description to make his subject come alive. Based on the facts he presents, he builds an imaginary disaster narrative to help his audience understand the magnitude of the problem being discussed. Thus he motivates listeners to take seriously his suggestions for earthquake preparation. A more adequate summary at the end of the speech might have made it even more effective.

How many of you can remember what you were doing around seven o'clock on the evening of October 17th? If you're a sports fan like me, you had probably set out the munchies, popped a cold one, and settled back to watch San Francisco and Oakland battle it out in the World Series. Since the show came on at seven o'clock here in Memphis for its pregame hype, you may not have been paying close attention to the TV—until—until—until both the sound and picture went out because of the Bay Area earthquake.

If you're like me, you probably sat glued to the TV set for the rest of the evening watching the live coverage of that catastrophe. If you're like me, you probably started thinking that Memphis, Tennessee, is in the middle of the New Madrid earthquake area and wondering how likely it would be for a large earthquake to hit here. And if you're like me, you probably asked yourself, "What would I do if a major earthquake hit Memphis?"

As I asked myself these questions, I was surprised to admit that I didn't know very much about the New Madrid earthquake area or the probability of a major quake in Memphis. And I was really upset to discover that I didn't have the foggiest idea of what to do if a quake did hit. So I visited the Center for Earthquake Research and Information here on campus; talked with Dr. Arch Johnston, the director; and read the materials he helped me find. Today, I'd like to share with you what I learned about the New Madrid earthquake area, how likely it is that Memphis may be hit by a major quake in the near future, what the effects of such a quake might be, and—most important—what you can do to be prepared.

Let's start with a little history about the New Madrid earthquake area. During the winter of 1811 to 1812, three of the largest earthquakes ever to hit the continental United States occurred in this area. Their estimated magnitudes were 8.6, 8.4, and 8.8 on the Richter scale. [He reveals magnitude chart. (shown on the following page)] I have drawn this chart to give you some idea of how much energy this involves. To simplify things, I have shown the New Madrid quakes as 8.5. Since a one-point increase in the Richter scale equals a thirtyfold increase in energy release, the energy level of these quakes was over nine hundred times more powerful than the Hiroshima atomic

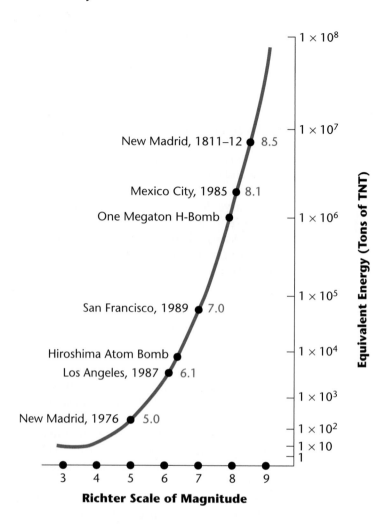

bomb and more than thirty times more powerful than the 7.0 quake that hit San Francisco last October. [He conceals magnitude chart.]

Most of the reports of these early earthquakes come from journals or Indian legends. The Indians tell of the night that lasted for a week and the way the "Father of Waters" —the Mississippi River—ran backwards. Waterfalls were formed on the river. Islands disappeared. Land that was once in Arkansas—on the west bank of the river—ended up in Tennessee—on the east bank of the river. Church bells chimed as far away as New Orleans and Boston. Cracks up to ten feet wide opened and closed in the earth. Geysers squirted sand fifteen feet into the air. Whole forests sank into the earth as the land turned to quicksand. Lakes disappeared and new lakes were formed. Reelfoot Lake—over ten miles long—was formed when the Mississippi River changed its course. No one is certain how many people died from the quakes because the area was sparsely settled with trappers and Indian villages. Memphis was just an outpost village with a few hundred settlers.

[He shows map of epicenters.] As you can see on this map, Memphis itself is not directly on the New Madrid Fault line. The fault extends from around Marked Tree, Arkansas, northeast to near Cairo, Illinois. This continues to be a volatile area of earthquake activity. According to Robert L. Ketter, director

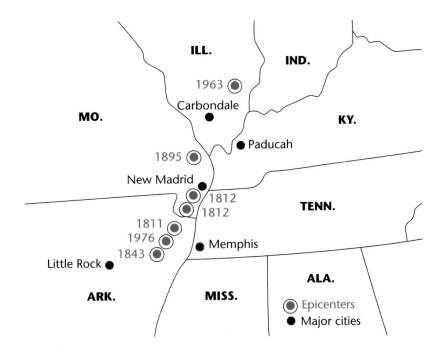

of the National Center for Earthquake Engineering Research, between 1974 and 1983 over two thousand quakes were recorded in the area. About 150 earthquakes per year occur in the area, but only about eight of them are large enough for people to notice. The others are picked up on the seismographs at tracking stations. The strongest quake in recent years occurred here in 1976. [He points to location on map.] This measured 5.0 on the Richter scale.

The New Madrid earthquake area is much different from the San Andreas Fault in California. Because of the way the land is formed, the alluvial soil transmits energy more efficiently here than in California. Although the quakes were about the same size, the New Madrid earthquakes affected an area fifteen times larger than the "great quake" that destroyed San Francisco in 1906.

Although scientists cannot predict exactly when another major quake may hit the area, they do know that the *repeat time* for a magnitude-6 New Madrid earthquake is seventy years, plus or minus fifteen years. The last earthquake of this size to hit the area occurred in 1895 north of New Madrid, Missouri. [He points to epicenter on map.] According to Johnston and Nava of the Memphis Earthquake Center, the probability that one with a magnitude of 6.3 will occur somewhere in the fault area by the year 2000 is 40 to 63 percent. By the year 2035 this probability increases to 86 to 97 percent. The probabilities for larger quakes are lower. They estimate the probability of a 7.6 quake within the next fifty years to be from 19 to 29 percent. [He conceals map of epicenters.]

What would happen if an earthquake of 7.6 hit Memphis? Allan and Hoshall, a prominent local engineering firm, prepared a study on this for the Federal Emergency Management Agency. The expected death toll would top 2,400. There would be at least 10,000 casualties. Two hundred thousand residents would be homeless. The city would be without electricity, gas, water or sewer treatment facilities for weeks. Gas lines would rupture, and fires would sweep through the city. Transportation would be almost impossible, bridges and roads would be destroyed, and emergency supplies would have to be brought in by helicopter. The river bluff, midtown, and land along the Wolfe River would turn to quicksand because of liquification. Buildings there would sink like they did in the Marina area during this past year's San Francisco quake. If the quake hit during daytime hours, at least 600 children would be killed and another 2,400 injured as schools collapsed on them. None of our schools have been built to seismic code specifications.

In fact, very few buildings in Memphis have been built to be earthquake resistant, so it would be difficult to find places to shelter and care for the homeless. The major exceptions are the new hospitals in the suburbs, the Omni Hotel east of the expressway, the Holiday Inn Convention Center, and two or three new office complexes. The only municipal structure built to code is the Criminal Justice Center. The new Memphis Pyramid, being built by the city and county, which will seat over twenty thousand people for the University of Memphis basketball games, is not being built to code. I'd hate to be in it if a major quake hit. The prospects are not pretty.

What can we do to prepare ourselves for this possible catastrophe? We can start out by learning what to do if a quake does hit. When I asked myself what I would do, my first reaction was to "get outside." I've since learned that this is not right. The "Earthquake Safety Checklist" published by the Federal Emergency Management Agency and the Red Cross makes a number of suggestions. I've written them out and will distribute them after my speech.

First, when an earthquake hits, if you are inside, stay there. Get in a safe spot: Stand in a doorway, stand next to an inside wall, or get under a large piece of furniture. Stay away from windows, hanging objects, fireplaces, and tall, unsecured furniture until the shaking stops. Do not try to use elevators. If you are outside, get away from buildings, trees, walls, or power lines. If you are in a car, stay in it; pull over and park. Stay away from overpasses and power lines. Do not drive over bridges or overpasses until they have been inspected. If you are in a crowded public place, do not rush for the exit. You may be crushed in the stampede of people.

When the shaking stops, check for gas, water, or electrical damage. Turn off the electricity, gas, and water to your home. Do not use electrical switches—unseen sparks could set off a gas fire. Do not use the telephone unless you must report a severe injury. Check to see that the sewer works before using the toilet. Plug drains to prevent a sewer backup.

There are also some things you can do in advance to be prepared. Accumulate emergency supplies: At home you should have a flashlight, a transistor radio with fresh batteries, a first-aid kit, fire extinguishers, and enough canned or dried food and beverages to last your family for 72 hours. Identify hazards and safe spots in your home—secure tall, heavy furniture; don't hang heavy pictures over your bed; keep flammable liquids in a garage or outside storage area—look around each room and plan where you would go if an earthquake hit. Conduct earthquake drills with your family.

There's one more suggestion that I would like to add. One that is specific to Memphis. Let our local officials know that you are concerned about the lack of preparedness. Urge them to support a building code—at least for public structures—that meets seismic resistance standards.

In preparing this speech, I learned a lot about the potential for earthquakes in Memphis. I hope you have learned something too. I now feel like I know what I should do if an earthquake hits. But I'm not really sure how I would react. Even the experts don't always react "appropriately." In 1971 an earthquake hit the Los Angeles area at about six o'clock in the morning. Charles Richter, the seismologist who developed the Richter scale to measure earthquakes, was in bed at the time. According to his wife, "He jumped up screaming and scared the cat."

Earthquake Preparedness Suggestions

1. If you are inside, stay there. Get in a safe spot: Stand in a doorway, stand next to an inside wall, or get under a large piece of furniture. Stay away from windows, hanging objects, fireplaces, and tall, unsecured furniture until the shaking stops. Do not try to use elevators.

2. If you are outside, get away from buildings, trees, walls, or power lines. If you are in a car, stay in it; pull over and park. Stay away from overpasses and power lines. Do not drive over bridges or overpasses until they have been inspected.

3. If you are in a crowded public place, do not rush for the exit. You may be crushed in the stampede of people.

4. When the shaking stops, check for gas, water, or electrical damage. Turn off the electricity, gas, and water to your home. Do not use electrical switches—unseen sparks could set off a gas fire. Do not use the telephone unless you must report a severe injury. Check to see that the sewer works before using the toilet. Plug drains to prevent sewer backup.

There are also some things you can do in advance to be prepared:

1. Accumulate emergency supplies: At home you should have a flashlight, a transistor radio with fresh batteries, a first-aid kit, fire extinguishers, and enough canned or dried food and beverages to last for 72 hours.

2. Identify hazards and safe spots in your home—secure tall, heavy furniture; don't hang heavy pictures over your bed; keep flammable liquids in a garage or outside storage area—look around each room and plan where you would go if an earthquake hit; conduct earthquake drills with your family.

The "Monument" at Wounded Knee
Cecile Larson

Cecile Larson's classroom speech serves two informative functions. First, it shapes the perceptions of the audience because of the way it describes the "monument" and the perspective it takes on the situation—most of her classmates had had little or no contact with Native Americans, and this might have been their first exposure to this type of information. Second, the speech serves the agenda-setting function in that it creates an awareness of a problem and thus increases the importance of that problem in the minds of the audience. The speech follows a spatial design. Cecile's vivid use of imagery and the skillful contrasts she draws between this "monument" and our "official" monuments create mental pictures that should stay with her listeners long after the words of her speech have been forgotten.

We Americans are big on monuments. We build monuments in memory of our heroes. Washington, Jefferson, and Lincoln live on in our nation's capital. We erect monuments to honor our martyrs. The Minute Man still stands guard at Concord. The flag is ever raised over Iwo Jima. Sometimes we even construct monuments to commemorate victims. In Ashburn Park downtown there is a monument to those who died in the yellow fever epidemics. However, there are some things in our history that we don't memorialize. Perhaps we would just as soon forget what happened. Last summer I visited such a place—the massacre site at Wounded Knee.

In case you have forgotten what happened at Wounded Knee, let me refresh your memory. On December 29, 1890, shortly after Sitting Bull had been murdered by the authorities, about 400 half-frozen, starving, and frightened Indians who had fled the nearby reservation were attacked by the Seventh Cavalry. When the fighting ended, between 200 and 300 Sioux had died—two-thirds of them women and children. Their remains are buried in a common grave at the site of the massacre.

Wounded Knee is located in the Pine Ridge Reservation in southwestern South Dakota—about a three-hour drive from where Presidents Washington, Jefferson, Theodore Roosevelt, and Lincoln are enshrined in the granite face of Mount Rushmore. The reservation is directly south of the Badlands National Park, a magnificently desolate area of wind-eroded buttes and multicolored spires.

We entered the reservation driving south from the Badlands Visitor's Center. The landscape of the Pine Ridge Reservation retains much of the desolation of the Badlands but lacks its magnificence. Flat, sun-baked fields and an occasional eroded gully stretch as far as the eye can see. There are no signs or highway markers to lead the curious tourist to Wounded Knee. Even the *Rand-McNally Atlas* doesn't help you find your way. We got lost three times and had to stop and ask directions.

When we finally arrived at Wounded Knee, there was no official historic marker to tell us what had happened there. Instead there was a large, handmade wooden sign—crudely lettered in white on black. The sign first directed our attention to our left—to the gully where the massacre took place. The mass grave site was to our right—across the road and up a small hill.

Two red-brick columns topped with a wrought-iron arch and a small metal cross form the entrance to the grave site. The column to the right is in bad shape: Cinder blocks from the base are missing; the brickwork near the top has deteriorated and tumbled to the ground; graffiti on the columns proclaim an attitude we found repeatedly expressed about the Bureau of Indian Affairs—"The BIA sucks!"

Crumbling concrete steps lead you to the mass grave. The top of the grave is covered with gravel, punctuated by unruly patches of chickweed and crabgrass. These same weeds also grow along the base of the broken chain-link fence that surrounds the grave, the "monument," and a small cemetery.

The "monument" itself rests on a concrete slab to the right of the grave. It's a typical, large, old-fashioned granite cemetery marker, a pillar about six feet high topped with an urn—the kind of gravestone you might see in any cemetery with graves from the turn of the century. The inscription tells us that it was erected by the families of those who were killed at Wounded Knee. Weeds grow through the cracks in the concrete at its base.

There are no granite headstones in the adjacent cemetery, only simple white wooden crosses that tell a story of people who died young. There is no neatly manicured grass. There are no flowers. Only the unrelenting and unforgiving weeds.

Yes, Americans are big on monuments. We build them to memorialize our heroes, to honor our martyrs, and sometimes, even to commemorate victims. But only when it makes us feel good.

The Trouble with Numbers
Stephen Lee

Stephen Lee first presented this informative speech of explanation to his public speaking class at the University of Texas–Austin. Later, Stephen's speech won the Southern division of the 1991 Houghton Mifflin speaking contest. The speech is noteworthy for its use of testimony and its illustrative examples. It first gains and holds attention by the novelty of its introduction, as Stephen describes a mythical "average American." The speech is somewhat loosely structured around a categorical design, as Stephen reflects upon the "misuse, abuse, and general overuse" of statistics in various dimensions of modern life. Stephen's presentation skills—his timing, wry sense of humor, eye contact, vocal variety, and gesture—helped bring his speech to life. All in all, he offers a sprightly commentary that critiques our society's overreliance on one of the basic forms of supporting materials, statistical knowledge.

Name, Bill Smith. Address, 103 Main Street, Smalltown, USA. Height, 5'11", weight, 185 pounds. Who is this person? Why, he's the average American. Bill makes a comfortable $32,000 each year. His car gets 18.9 miles to the gallon. He reads 4.2 novels every year, each with 482.73 pages. He receives 9.7 gifts every Christmas, and he brushes his teeth 1.9 times every day. The average American.

Today it seems we hear a lot of this person. Someone who is supposedly like all of us and yet not like any of us. After all, how many men do you know with 2.7 children? No, Bill is by no means real. His composition is not one of flesh and blood. Instead Bill is the product of cold and heartless data. Born of a national almanac, Bill is nothing more than a statistic.

But the characteristics of Bill Smith and the way we interpret them are highly reflective of our society's misuse, abuse, and general overuse of statistics. As Darrell Huff tells us in his essay, *How to Lie with Statistics*, "Americans use statistics like drunks use lamp posts, for support instead of illumination." He was referring to the unfailing dependence that we Americans put on statistics. He continues: "We prefer to record and measure ourselves with numbers and what we can't measure we assume not to exist at all." But what are these mystic symbols and figures? And more importantly, how do they affect us? Humorist Artemus Ward once said, "It ain't so much what we know that gets us in trouble. It's the things we know that ain't so."

Now such was the case in the government. Our government is faulted for many problems. Statistical misuse is perhaps one of the greatest. This was clearly demonstrated in March of 1983 when the computation of the unemployment rate was changed to encompass military personnel. Now this had a significant impact, as the number changed from 10.6% to 10.1%. Some people said this was a political ploy of President Reagan, trying to make himself look good in the public spectrum, while others claimed this was a highly justified move since, after all, military personnel were employed. But I think there is a more important question that needs to be answered. Look at what happened to the number. It changed. Look at what happened to the way the number was computed. It changed, too. But what happened to the very real problem of civilian unemployment, which we all assumed this number to represent? It had not changed at all. It all goes back to what Lester T. Thurow said in his basic theory of economics: "A difference is only a difference if it truly makes a difference." Many times a difference in a number does not represent a difference in the real world. This was the case in the late 1970s when housing was taken out of the consumer price index. Now as contradictory as it might sound, while inflation continued to skyrocket, the inflation rate actually stagnated.

In our society we even misuse something as simple as a baseball statistic, denoting one player is good, batting .350, while another one bad, batting .150. But what do these figures tell us about his moral character, his interaction with other players, his leadership abilities—any of which any coach will tell you is necessary for the well-rounded player? While numbers may be convincing, so much of what they imply, as Ward said, simply "ain't so." Perhaps we can all relate to standardized tests, where the quality of one's education is measured by the quantity of correct circles on a piece of paper. You may not be aware of how misleading statistics are on the university level, but look closer when a university advertises that 95% of its needy students receive financial aid. It sounds good, but the truth behind this claim is the fact that the university is the one who determines who is needy, and thereby allocates aid accordingly.

Perhaps the greatest inadequacy surrounding statistics lies not in what is wrong with these numbers, but instead with the way we use them. Numbers are only numbers. Many times we forget this. We forget that there are very real humans and very real human conditions behind these statistics. And yes, we are all affected by them. The only solution to our statistical dilemma is to better understand what a statistic is and what a statistic is not. We need to more adequately comprehend what a statistic can do, but what a number cannot do.

So when you go home today, read your paper. Eat your meal, watch TV. You don't have to go looking for statistics. They're all around us. But this time be aware of them. Train yourself not to passively sit by as seemingly innocent numbers are flashed before your eyes. Learn to question what hides behind those numbers. I think it's interesting, and indeed fascinating, that statistics have come to dominate our decision making in America today. But don't get me wrong. I am not saying that statistics are bad, but that statistics can be misleading. And without careful management they can do more harm than good. Carl Tucker summed it up best in his book, *The Data Game*. He wrote: "Statistics and lists are obviously useful tools. They, in their own way, can tell us what happened, but never why that mattered." And in the end that is the only question worth answering. So as you leave, remember: three-fourths of the people always comprise 75% of the population.

Living Wills: Ensuring Your Right to Choose
Bonnie Marshall

Bonnie Marshall was a student at Heidelberg College in Ohio when she made the following persuasive presentation. Her speech is noteworthy for its use of an opening narrative to heighten interest in the problem Bonnie was presenting. The speech is also strong in its use of personal and expert forms of testimony. Clearly, Bonnie had responsible knowledge of her subject. In her conclusion, she makes excellent use of anaphora to underscore her message of personal responsibility. She presented the speech with great conviction, and its overall impact led to its selection as a finalist in the Midwest division of the 1991 Houghton Mifflin Public Speaking contest.

Harry Smith was a cranky, obstinate, old farmer. He loved bowling, Glenn Miller music, and Monday night football. He was also dying from cancer of the esophagus, which had metastasized to his lungs. He didn't like doctors, and he liked hospitals and modern medicine even less. Harry used to say that he remembered when three square meals, mom's mustard plaster, and an occasional house call from Doc Jones was all anyone ever needed to stay healthy. Harry didn't want to live in pain, and he hated being dependent on anyone else; yet like so many others, Harry never expressed his wishes to his family. When Harry's cancer became so debilitating that he could no longer speak for himself, his family stepped in to make decisions about his medical care. Since Harry never told them how he felt, his children, out of a sense of guilt over the things they had done and the love they hadn't expressed, refused to let Harry die. He was subjected to ventilators, artificial feedings, and all the wizardry that modern medicine can offer. Harry did die eventually, but only after months of agony with no hope of recovery.

Harry's doctor, my husband, agonized too, over the decisions regarding Harry's care. He knew that the children were acting out of grief and guilt, not for Harry's benefit. Yet because Harry had not documented his wishes, his doctor had no choice but to subject Harry to the senseless torture that he didn't want.

We all know of a similar case that gained national attention. On December 26, 1990, Nancy Cruzan died. The tragic young woman who became the focal point for the right-to-die movement was finally allowed to die after eight long years and a legal battle that reached the hallowed halls of the Supreme Court. Nancy's battle is now over, yet the issue has not been resolved and the need for action is more urgent than ever. Since the Supreme Court ruling on June 25, 1990, public interest in this issue has skyrocketed.

From July 1990 to November 1990, the last month statistics were available, the Society for the Right To Die answered 908,000 requests for information. By comparison, in November of 1989, the first month that the Society kept monthly statistics, they answered only 21,000 requests.

Today I would like to explore this problem and propose some solutions that we all can implement.

The *Cruzan* v. *Missouri* decision was significant because it was the first time that the Supreme Court had rendered an opinion on the right-to-die issue. However, the message from the Court is anything but clear and complete. As Justice Sandra Day O'Connor wrote in her concurring opinion, "Today we decide only that one state's practice does not violate the Constitution. . . . The more challenging task of crafting appropriate procedures for safeguarding incompetents' liberty interests is entrusted to the 'laboratory' of the states." So while the Court has for the first time recognized a "constitutionally protected liberty interest in refusing unwanted medical treatment," it has also given the power over this issue back to the states. According to the July 9, 1990, issue of *U.S. News and World Report,* nine states, including Ohio, have no legislation recognizing the legality of living wills. Of the states that do have living will legislation, about one-half do not allow for the withdrawal of nutrition and hydration, even if the will says the patient does not want such treatment, according to Lisa Belken in the June 25th issue of the *New York Times.* Also according to the *Times,* only 33 states have health care proxy laws. Perhaps as a result of all this indecision and inconsistency, desperate patients with terminal illnesses will continue to seek out the "Dr. Deaths" of the medical community, those who, like Dr. Kevorkian of Michigan, are willing to surpass simply allowing the terminally ill to die, to actively bringing about death.

The right-to-die issue may seem far removed from you today, yet the American Medical Association estimates that 80 to 90% of us will die a "managed death." Even today, according to an editorial by Anthony Lewis in the June 29, 1990, *New York Times,* "The problem is far more acute and far-reaching than most of us realize. Almost two million people die in the United States every year, and more than half of those deaths occur when some life-sustaining treatment is ended." The decision to provide, refuse, or withdraw medical treatment should be made individually, personally, with the counsel of family, friends, doctors, and clergy, but certainly not by the state.

More and more, however, these personal decisions are being taken away from patients and their families and instead are being argued and decided in courts of law. Perhaps it began with Karen Ann Quinlan. It certainly continued with Nancy Cruzan, and these decisions could be taken away from you, if we do not act now to ensure that our right to refuse medical treatment is protected. And our right to refuse medical treatment includes the right to refuse artificial nutrition and hydration, just as it includes the right to refuse antibiotics, chemotherapy, surgery, or artificial respiration. According to John Collins Harvey, M.D., Ph.D from the Kennedy Institute of Ethics at Georgetown University, "The administration of food and fluid artificially is a medical technological treatment. . . . Utilizing such medical treatment requires the same kind of medical technological expertise of physicians, nurses, and dietitians as is required in utilizing a respirator for treatment of respiratory failure or employing a renal dialysis machine for the treatment of kidney failure. This medical treatment, however, is ineffective, for it cannot cause dead brain cells to regenerate; it will merely sustain biological life and prolong the patient's dying. Such treatment is considered by many physicians and medical ethicists to be extraordinary." Additionally, the Center for Health Care Ethics of St. Louis University, a Jesuit institution, prepared a brief for the Cruzan case which states that "within the Christian foundation, the withholding and withdrawing of medical treatment, including artificial nutrition and hydration, is acceptable."

So what can we do to protect ourselves and assure that our wishes are carried out? My plan is fourfold. First, we in Ohio must urge our legislators to pass living will legislation. Representative Marc Guthrie, from Newark, Ohio, has drafted a living will bill, House Bill 70. We must urge our legislators to pass this bill, since it is more comprehensive than the Senate version and will better protect our rights on this crucial issue.

Second, we must draw up our own living wills stating our philosophy on terminal care. I propose the use of the Medical Directive, a document created by Drs. Linda and Ezekiel Emanuel. This document details twelve specific treatments that could be offered. You can choose different treatment options based on four possible scenarios. You can indicate either that you desire the treatment, do not want it, are undecided, or want to try the treatment, but discontinue it if there is no improvement. This directive, which also includes space for a personal statement, eliminates much of the ambiguity of generic living wills and provides clearer guidelines to your physician and family.

Third, designate a person to make health care decisions for you should you become incompetent. This person should be familiar with your personal philosophy and feelings about terminal care and be likely to make the same decisions that you yourself would make. You should name this person in a Durable Power of Attorney for Health Care, a legal document that is now recognized in the State of Ohio.

Fourth, have a heart-to-heart talk with your doctor and be sure that he or she understands and supports your wishes on terminal care. Have a copy of your living will and Durable Power of Attorney for Health Care placed in your medical file. Finally, for more information on living wills, you can contact: The Society for the Right To Die, 250 West 57th St., New York, NY 10107, or send $1.00 to the Harvard Medical School Health Letter, 164 Longwood Ave., Fourth Floor, Boston, MA 02115 for a copy of the Emanuels' Medical Directive form.

I am interested in this issue because, through my husband, I have seen patients suffer the effects of not having an advance directive. You need to ask yourself how you feel about terminal care, but regardless of your personal response, we all must choose to protect our rights on this issue. WE must choose to pressure our legislators to adopt living will legislation. WE must choose to draw up our own living wills and health care proxies. And most importantly, WE must choose to discuss this most personal and sensitive issue with our families and loved ones, so that in the absence of a legal document, or even with one, they may confidently make the decisions concerning our life and death that we ourselves would make. Not all patients end up like Nancy Cruzan or Harry Smith. Many people are allowed to quietly slip away from the pain and suffering of life. But that can only happen after the careful, painful deliberation of a grieving family, who can at least take comfort in the fact that they are carrying out their loved one's wishes.

Secondhand Smoke
Gina Norman

Gina Norman was a student at the University of Memphis, where she presented this persuasive speech in her public speaking class. The strengths of this speech include her effective introduction and conclusion and the use of a wealth of evidence in the body of the speech. Note how her introductory remarks involve the audience directly and how her conclusion sums up her message in a striking analogy that will be easy for listeners to remember. Note also how Gina integrates her evidence into the speech and works in references to the sources of her information.

Have you ever breathed smoke from someone else's cigarette? Have you ever sat beside someone or behind someone, they light up a cigarette, they take one puff, and then they're either holding it out to the side or they sit it in an ashtray? In my case I feel that I usually end up smoking more of that cigarette than the actual smoker does. As an involuntary smoker, a nonsmoker breathing smoke from others, you are at an increased risk for several diseases. According to former U.S. Surgeon General C. Everett Koop, it is now clear that disease risk due to the inhalation of tobacco smoke is not limited to the individual smoking. According to the American Cancer Society and our own *Fitness and Wellness* book here at Memphis State, undiluted sidestream smoke has higher concentrations of the toxic and carcinogenic compounds than found in mainstream smoke.

For the reason of smokers not being able to control the excess smoke from their cigarettes, cigars, and pipes, I believe smoking should be banned in public places. I'd like to share with you today the reasons for my statement, which include personal experiences and some statistics that I've obtained. My first personal experience was when I was little. I suffered from chronic upper respiratory infections, inner ear infections, and colds. I was in and out of the doctor's office all the time. My father smoked two packs of cigarettes a day. When I moved out, when I got older, I didn't have this problem, although I didn't connect it to cigarette smoking at that time. My other personal experience is where I work. As of last year, our office became nonsmoking. The two years previous that I worked there it was a smoking office. Every month it seemed I was going to the doctor for upper respiratory or inner ear infections. Finally they referred me to an allergist. And the allergist, Dr. Philip Lieberman here in Memphis, said I was allergic to smoke. I told him that our office is huge and I sat on the far, far end in the nonsmoking section. He said that didn't matter. In an enclosed area, the air you're breathing is just recirculated. It's the same air that everybody breathes. The air conditioner heating ducts take the air in and then another duct pulls the air back out. So even though you may not be smelling the smoke, you're still breathing the compounds from it.

Our office, as I said, went nonsmoking January of '92. I think I've been maybe twice to the doctor for upper respiratory infections, so it's dropped significantly since our office became nonsmoking. These are just my personal experiences of how smoking aggravates my upper respiratory system, my inner ear, and my sinuses.

Now I'd like to share with you some statistics that I've obtained. According to the American Heart Association, environmental tobacco smoke, ETS, causes an estimated 53,000 deaths annually in the United States—two-thirds from heart diseases and 4,000 from lung disease. The *Journal of the American Medical Association* concluded this January that heart disease is an important consequence of the exposure to environmental tobacco smoke. According again to the *Fitness and Wellness* book here at Memphis State, passive smoke aggravates and may precipitate angina. That's chest pain that is a result of diminished supply of blood to the heart. And it also states that secondhand smoke induces small airway dysfunctions in adults. According to the *American Journal of Public Health,* infants born to women who smoke during pregnancy are more likely to die from sudden infant death syndrome. The American Academy of Pediatrics estimates that nine million American children under the age of five may be exposed to environmental tobacco smoke. The American Cancer Society states that children exposed to secondhand smoke have increased risk of respiratory illnesses and infections, impaired development of lung function, and middle ear infections—which is exactly what I had when I was growing up. This is from *Cancer Facts and Figures* 1992. The Environmental Science Advisory Board, in reviewing evidence that environmental tobacco smoke causes excess lung cancer in adults and respiratory illnesses in children, has recommended that environmental tobacco smoke be classified as a Class A, which is a known human carcinogen.

Now this is taken from *Newsweek* 1992 [she refers to chart]. *Newsweek* got this from the Environmental Protection Agency. It's a draft they put out about the dangers of secondhand smoke. The Environmental Protection Agency is saying that secondhand smoke causes 3,000 lung cancer deaths a year; 35,000 heart disease deaths a year; contributes to 150,000 to 300,000 respiratory infections in babies, mainly bronchitis and pneumonia, resulting in 7,500 to 15,000 hospitalizations. It triggers 8,000 to 26,000 new cases of asthma in previously unaffected children and exacerbates symptoms in 400,000 to 1 million asthmatic children. In a study done by the *Journal of the American Medical Association* earlier this year, out of 663 nonsmokers who either lived with smokers or worked in a smoking environment, 91 percent had metabolic byproducts of nicotine in their urine, including 162 who reported no exposure to environmental tobacco smoke for four days.

Now I know that this sounds like I have no empathy for the smoker, but I do. Someone I am very close to smokes, my husband. He's tried to quit for me, but he's had a lot of problems. He has a lot of physical withdrawal with quitting smoking. The bottom line, too, is he likes it. He likes to smoke. It helps him to concentrate when he's working, it helps him relax, and it's social. A lot of his friends smoke, and when they get together for a game, they like to smoke. I respect his choice for smoking. I respect anybody who smokes; I respect their choice; they have that choice to smoke. However, it's not my choice. And when a smoker smokes in an enclosed area, that smoker takes away the choice for a nonsmoker. I feel that banning smoking in all public places is necessary to protect the health of people who do not smoke.

In closing I'd like to quote Julia Carol—she's with the Americans for Nonsmokers' Rights—when she was quoted in *Newsweek,* June 1992, that separate seating was a nice thought. But sitting in the nonsmoking section of a building is like swimming in the nonchlorinated section of a pool. The difference, of course, is that a little chlorine won't kill you. Other people's smoke may.

Pesticides Speech
Cesar Chavez

Cesar Chavez was the founder and president of the United Farm Workers union, which organized and led national boycotts of table grapes and iceberg lettuce to protest the use of pesticides. The following "generic" speech (dated 1990) was presented to a variety of audiences as Chavez went around the nation speaking to various groups. He would insert names and expand the concluding paragraph depending on the audience. Note the use of statistics in the speech to dramatize the severity of the problem. Consider also how Chavez weaves information and testimony into his message, carefully citing the sources of his information. His citing of "reluctant" testimony from the "growers' own magazine" helps to strengthen his case. Consider also Chavez's use of narratives and analogy to arouse emotion in this speech.

Thank you very much. I am truly honored to be able to speak with you. I would like to thank the many people who made this possible for their kindness and their hospitality (insert names).

Decades ago, the chemical industry promised the growers that pesticides would create vast new wealth and bountiful harvests. Just recently, the experts learned what farm workers, and the truly organic farmers, have known for years. The prestigious National Academy of Sciences recently concluded an exhaustive five-year study, which showed that by using simple, effective organic farming techniques, *instead of pesticides,* the growers could make *more money,* produce *more crops,* and *protect the environment.*

Unfortunately, the growers are not listening. They continue to spray and inject hundreds of millions of pounds of herbicides, fungicides, and insecticides onto our foods.

Most of you know that the United Farm Workers have focused our struggle against pesticides on table grapes. Many people ask me "Why grapes?" The World Resources Institute reported that over three hundred thousand farm workers are poisoned every year by pesticides. Over half of all reported pesticide-related illnesses involve the cultivation or harvesting of table grapes. They receive *more* restricted-use application permits, which allow growers to spray pesticides known to threaten humans, than *any* other fresh food crop. The General Accounting Office, which does research for the U.S. Congress, determined that *34* of the *76* types of pesticides used *legally* on grapes pose potential human health hazards and could *not be detected* by current multi-residue methods.

My friends, grapes are the most dangerous fruit in America. The pesticides sprayed on table grapes are *killing America's children.* These pesticides *soak* the fields, *drift* with the wind, *pollute* the water, and are *eaten* by unwitting consumers. These poisons are designed to kill life, and pose a very real threat to consumers and farm workers alike.

The fields are sprayed with pesticides like captan, a fungicide believed to cause cancer, DNA mutation, and horrible birth defects. Other poisons take a similar toll. Parathion and phosdrin are *"nerve gas"* types of insecticides, which are believed to be responsible for the majority of farm worker poisonings in California. The growers spray sulphites, which can trigger asthmatic attacks, on the grapes. And even the growers' own magazine, *The California Farmer,* admitted that growers were *illegally* using a very dangerous growth stimulator, called *Fix,* which is quite similar to *Agent Orange,* on the grapes.

This is a very technical problem, with very *human* victims. One young boy, Felipe Franco, was born without arms or legs in the agricultural town of McFarland. His mother worked for the first three months of her pregnancy picking grapes in fields that were sprayed repeatedly with pesticides believed to cause birth defects.

My friends, the central valley of California is one of the wealthiest agricultural regions in the world. In its midst are clusters of children dying from cancer. The children who live in towns like McFarland are surrounded by the grape fields that employ their parents. The children contact the poisons when they play outside, when they drink the water, and when they hug their parents returning from the fields. *And the children are dying.* They are dying *slow, painful, cruel* deaths in towns called *cancer clusters.* In cancer clusters like McFarland, where the childhood cancer rate is *800 percent* above normal.

A few months ago, the parents of a brave little girl in the agricultural community of Earlimart came to the United Farm Workers to ask for our help. Their four-year-old daughter, Natalie Ramirez, has lost one kidney to cancer and is threatened with the loss of another. The Ramirez family knew about our protests in nearby McFarland and thought there might be a similar problem in their home town. Our union members went door to door in Earlimart and found that the Ramirez family's worst fears were true. There are at least *four* other children suffering from cancer and similar diseases, which the experts believe were caused by pesticides in the little town of Earlimart, a rate *1200 percent* above normal. In Earlimart, little Jimmy Caudillo died recently from leukemia at the age of three.

The grape vineyards of California have become America's Killing Fields. These *same* pesticides can be found on the grapes you buy in the store. Study after study, by the California Department of Food and Agriculture, by the Food and Drug Administration, and by objective newspapers, concluded that up to *54 percent* of the sampled grapes contained pesticide residues. Which pesticide did they find the most? *Captan,* the same carcinogenic fungicide that causes birth defects.

My friends, *the suffering must end. So many* children are dying, *so many* babies are born without limbs and vital organs, *so many* workers are dying in the fields.

The growers, the supermarket owners, say that the government can *handle* the problem, can *protect* the workers, can *save* the children. It *should,* but it *won't.* You see, agribusiness is *big business.* It is a *sixteen billion* dollar industry in California alone. Agribusiness contributed very heavily to the successful campaign of Republican governor George Deukmajian. He has rewarded the growers by turning the Agricultural Labor Relations Board into a tool for the growers, run by the growers. The governor even vetoed a bill that would have required growers to warn workers that they were entering recently sprayed fields! And only *one percent* of those growers who *are caught* violating pesticide laws were even fined in California.

President Bush is a long-time friend of agribusiness. During the last presidential campaign, George Bush ate grapes in a field just *75 miles* from the cemetery where little Jimmy Caudillo and other pesticide victims are buried, in order to show his support for the table grape industry. He recently gave a speech to the Farm Bureau, saying that it was up to the *growers* to restrain the use of dangerous pesticides.

That's like putting *Idi Amin,* or *Adolph Hitler,* in charge of promoting *peace* and *human rights.*

To show you what happens to pesticides supposedly under government control, I'd like to tell you more about captan. Testing to determine the acceptable tolerance levels of captan was done by Bio-Tech Laboratories, later found *guilty* of falsifying the data to the EPA. The tolerance level set was *ten times* the amount allowed in Canada. Later, government agencies tried to ban captan, but were mysteriously stopped several times. Finally, the government banned captan on 42 crops, but *not on grapes.* Even the General Accounting Office found that the government's pesticide testing is wholly inadequate. The government is *not* the answer, it is part of the problem.

The growers and their allies have tried to stop us with *lies,* with *police,* with *intimidation,* with *public relations agencies,* and with *violence.* But *we cannot be stopped.* In our *life and death struggle* for justice, we have turned to the court of last resort: the American people.

At last we are winning. Many supermarket chains have stopped selling or advertising grapes. Millions of consumers are refusing to buy America's most dangerous fruit. Many courageous people have volunteered to help our cause or joined human chains of people who fast, who go without food for days, to support our struggle. As a result, *grape sales keep falling.* We have witnessed truckloads of grapes being dumped because no one would stoop low enough to buy them. As demand drops, so do prices and profits. This sort of economic pressure is the only language the growers understand.

We are winning, but there is still much work to be done. If we are going to beat the greed and power of the growers, we must work *together. Together,* we can end the suffering. *Together,* we can save the children. *Together,* we can bring justice to the killing fields. I hope that you will join our struggle, for it is *your* struggle too. The simple act of boycotting table grapes laced with pesticides is a powerful statement the growers understand. *Please, boycott table grapes.* For your safety, for the workers, *we must act,* and *act together.* (insert additional pitches)

Good night, and God bless you.

Nobel Peace Prize Acceptance Speech
Elie Wiesel

Elie Wiesel delivered the following speech in Oslo, Norway, on December 10, 1986, as he accepted the Nobel Peace Prize. The award recognized his lifelong work for human rights, especially his role as "spiritual archivist of the Holocaust." Wiesel's poetic, intensely personal style as a writer carries over into this ceremonial speech of acceptance. He uses narrative very effectively as he flashes back to what he calls the "kingdom of night" and then flashes forward again into the present. The speech's purpose is to spell out and share the values and concerns of a life committed to the rights of oppressed peoples, in which, as he put it so memorably, "every moment is a moment of grace, every hour an offering."

It is with a profound sense of humility that I accept the honor you have chosen to bestow upon me. I know: your choice transcends me. This both frightens and pleases me.

It frightens me because I wonder: do I have the right to represent the multitudes who have perished? Do I have the right to accept this great honor on their behalf? I do not. That would be presumptuous. No one may speak for the dead, no one may interpret their mutilated dreams and visions.

It pleases me because I may say that this honor belongs to all the survivors and their children, and through us, to the Jewish people with whose destiny I have always been identified.

I remember: it happened yesterday or eternities ago. A young Jewish boy discovering the kingdom of night. I remember his bewilderment, I remember his anguish. It all happened so fast. The ghetto. The deportation. The sealed cattle car. The fiery altar upon which the history of our people and the future of mankind were meant to be sacrificed.

I remember: he asked his father: "Can this be true? This is the 20th century, not the Middle Ages. Who would allow such crimes to be committed? How could the world remain silent?"

And now the boy is turning to me: "Tell me," he asks. "What have you done with your life?"

And I tell him that I have tried. That I have tried to keep memory alive, that I have tried to fight those who would forget. Because if we forget, we are guilty, we are accomplices.

And then I explained to him how naive we were, that the world did know and remain silent. And that is why I swore never to be silent whenever and wherever human beings endure suffering and humiliation. We must always take sides. Neutrality helps the oppressor, never the victim. Silence encourages the tormentor, never the tormented.

Sometimes we must interfere. When human lives are endangered, when human dignity is in jeopardy, national borders and sensitivities become irrelevant. Wherever men or women are persecuted because of their race, religion or political views, that place must—at that moment—become the center of our universe.

Of course, since I am a Jew profoundly rooted in my people's memory and tradition, my first response is to Jewish fears, Jewish needs, Jewish crises. For I belong to a traumatized generation, one that experienced the abandonment and solitude of our people. It would be unnatural for me not to make Jewish priorities my own: Israel, Soviet Jewry, Jews in Arab lands.

But there are others as important to me. Apartheid is, in my view as abhorrent as anti-Semitism. To me, Andrei Sakharov's isolation is as much a disgrace as Iosif Begun's imprisonment. As is the denial of Solidarity and its leader Lech Walesa's right to dissent. And Nelson Mandela's interminable imprisonment.

There is so much injustice and suffering crying out for our attention: victims of hunger, or racism and political persecution, writers and poets, prisoners is so many lands governed by the left and by the right. Human rights are being violated on every continent. More people are oppressed than free.

And then, too, there are the Palestinians to whose plight I am sensitive but whose methods I deplore. Violence and terrorism are not the answer. Something must be done about their suffering, and soon. I trust Israel, for I have faith in the Jewish people. Let Israel be given a chance, let hatred and danger be removed from her horizons, and there will be peace in and around the Holy Land.

Yes, I have the faith. Faith in God and even in His creation. Without it no action would be possible. And action is the only remedy to indifference: the most insidious danger of all. Isn't this the meaning of Alfred Nobel's legacy? Wasn't his fear of war a shield against war?

There is much to be done, there is much that can be done. One person—a Raoul Wallenberg, an Albert Schweitzer, one person of integrity, can make a difference, a difference of life and death. As long as one dissident is in prison, our freedom will not be true. As long as one child is hungry, our lives will be filled with anguish and shame.

What all these victims need above all is to know that they are not alone: that we are not forgetting them, that when their voices are stifled we shall lend them ours, that while their freedom depends on ours, the quality of our freedom depends on theirs.

This is what I say to the young Jewish boy wondering what I have done with his years. It is in his name that I speak to you and that I express to you my deepest gratitude. No one is as capable of gratitude as one who has emerged from the kingdom of night.

We know that every moment is a moment of grace, every hour an offering; not to share them would mean to betray them. Our lives no longer belong to us alone; they belong to all those who need us desperately.

Thank you Chairman Aarvik. Thank you members of the Nobel Committee. Thank you people of Norway, for declaring on this singular occasion that our survival has meaning for mankind.

A Tribute to Wilma Rudolph

The following material was presented as part of the *National Sports Awards* program telecast on NBC, June 23, 1993. The script, transcribed from the telecast of the show and provided by NBC, includes the beginning of the program. Tom Brokaw, *NBC Nightly News* anchor, was the master of ceremonies. Speeches of tribute were presented by Bill Cosby, entertainer and former college track star; Gail Devers, 1992 Olympic Gold Medal winner in the 100-meter dash; and Ed Temple, Ms. Rudolph's mentor and track coach at Tennessee State University.

*T*om Brokaw (Master of Ceremonies): Good evening and welcome. This is such a fitting national celebration because, after all, what would life be without the games that we play? The greatest athletes—the most memorable—are those who give us a sense of exhilaration off the field as well as on. Heywood Hale Broun once said, "Sports don't build character; they reveal it." What you'll share here tonight is the essence of character as revealed by the lives of these great athletes.

Sports are such an important part of our national culture, our language, our fantasies. Well, tonight the National Sports Awards honors those who played their games at the highest level—and lived their lives at the same heights. They lifted us all by their achievements and by their conduct. Four of them are here in Washington with us tonight; one of them, Ted Williams, has been asked by his doctor not to travel, so he's watching from his home. They were all nominated by a panel of leading sports journalists.

The first that we honor tonight is a woman. When she was born, one of twenty-two children in a Tennessee family, no one could have guessed at that time that her story would echo over the decades, or that it would make even a big impression on the 1962 Middle Atlantic Conference High Jump Champion.

Bill Cosby: She was five foot eleven, she was slender, and she had the manner of a duchess, and you know what they called her in Europe? La Gazelle—La Perle Noire—La Chattanooga Choo-Choo. Wouldn't it be nice to be called "La Chattanooga Choo-Choo?"

I had dreams of being a track star, so I have a particularly vivid memory of this woman who broke barriers, broke records, and brought glory to her country at the 1960 Rome Olympics. Very few Olympians have climbed a bigger mountain than the girl from Clarksville, Tennessee—and her story is one of the most powerful and poignant of the modern Olympics. Madame Choo-Choo, I join the nation in saluting you.

When she was four years old, she contracted polio. Watching other children at play was the cruelest hurt of all. She said, "Only my mother gave me the faith to believe I'd ever walk again." She was the twentieth of twenty-two children. The family scrimped to pay for her therapy at the clinic nearly 90 miles away. But in the end it was her own therapy that did it. She threw away the brace, gritted her teeth, and taught herself to walk . . . to run, to throw herself completely into the Burt High School basketball team. Then a visiting coach who saw her play suggested she try something else.

She was naturally blessed with burning speed—and the passion to push it. Long-legged—and glamorous, there had never been a woman runner who looked like *this* and ran like *that.*

The Tennessee Tigerbelles made their international debut at the '56 Olympics. She was sixteen and green, and while the team had won a bronze, she missed her golden moment in the 200. It would be four years before the next Olympics. The girls track team was at the bottom of the budget, so Coach Ed Temple picked up the tab. Going into the Rome Olympics she was among the world's fastest but she remembered her failure in '56 —the narrow margin between gold and bronze.

Coach Temple's home movies—occasionally in focus—show the athletes settling in. Here's Wilma, and her new hat . . . and her new friends. Then it got serious. "From the moment I walked into the stadium," she said, "I blocked out everything. Everything." Her first event was the 100 meters. Eleven seconds flat. She was the fastest woman in the world. Then came the 200—the excruciating demand of speed and stamina. She simply ran away from the rest of the world. Twenty-four flat. An Olympic record. She wasn't done yet. On the last day she ran the anchor leg of the 400-meter relay, and another record fell. It was her third Olympic gold. No American woman had done that in track before.

From out of these Olympic games, Wilma Rudolph entered the company of American heroines. She was honored at every turn. But the greatest reward was in the eyes of her parents. Her hometown set aside old differences. Everyone came out to greet her. That night, for the first time, black and white sat together at the same table. Thirty years ago she gave women a reason to run. She still encourages. She still inspires. It is the simplest, purest athletic endeavor—to run. And oh my—how Wilma could run.

Tom Brokaw: At last summer's Olympic games in Barcelona, we were reminded once again of the power of the human spirit by another American sprinter, gold metal winner Gail Devers.

Gail Devers: I was diagnosed with Graves Disease in 1990, and until I received the proper medication, I had come within two days of having my feet amputated. Long before any of this ever happened, I had heard of a woman named Wilma Rudolph. I read about her in books and I'd watched the Wilma Rudolph stories several times on television and just like Wilma, during my ordeal my first goal was just to walk again. And once I was back on the track running, I thought about her determination.

I knew that she had overcome a very serious illness and still went on to pursue her dream. I felt that if Wilma could do it, I could do it too. Her strong will and her never-give-up attitude had inspired so many of us to keep going despite any obstacles that we may be faced with. And I want to take this opportunity to tell you, Wilma, thank you from the very bottom of my heart. Not just for the example that you've given, not just to me, but to all women in track and field. We love you.

Tom Brokaw: And the man with the movie camera. He has come from Tennessee to present Wilma Rudolph with her award. Her coach and mentor, who retires this fall after forty-two years as coach of the Tennessee State Tigerbelles, Ed Temple, ladies and gentlemen.

Ed Temple: Wilma, you've worked long and hard to achieve these kinds of honors. I've always talked about the adversity that you've had. I tell people that you were able to meet it, to greet it, and defeat it. Wilma, you were an individual who opened up the doors for women's track and field in the United States, and that will always be your greatest legacy. It is an honor for me to be here tonight with you.

Tom Brokaw: And on this occasion the great ones do a great walk, so Wilma Rudolph, will you please come forward so that Gail Devers and Ed Temple can present you the first National Sports Award. Ladies and gentlemen, the object of our attention and affection, Wilma Rudolph.

Wilma Rudolph: I'm excited. I'll get my breath. I receive this honor, and I dedicate it to the youth of America so they will know that their dreams too can come true. And also to my mother who is eighty-four years old, Blanche Rudolph. Thank you so much for this honor.

On June 23, 1993, *The Great Ones: The National Sports Awards* was broadcast on NBC. The program was conceived and produced by George Stevens, Jr., Don Mischer, and Michael Stevens, and written by George Stevens, Jr. and Brian Brown.

Address to the United Nations Fourth World Conference on Women
Hillary Rodham Clinton

Hillary Rodham Clinton received her undergraduate degree from Wellesley College and a law degree from Yale University. She has been active in such causes as child welfare, health care reform, and women's rights. The following speech of inspiration was presented at the United Nations Fourth World Conference on Women, September 5, 1995. In this speech, Hillary Rodham Clinton speaks for the unseen and unheard women of the world as she shares the problems that beset them. Her use of parallel structure adds strength to her message. As the First Lady of the United States, her presence lends the imprimatur of the U.S. government to her remarks. The speech is strongly embedded in values as it lobbies for human rights for women and protests the violation of such rights.

MRS. CLINTON: Mrs. Mongella, Under Secretary Kittani, distinguished delegates and guests: I would like to thank the Secretary General of the United Nations for inviting me to be part of the United Nations Fourth World Conference on Women. This is truly a celebration—a celebration of the contributions women make in every aspect of life: in the home, on the job, in their communities, as mothers, wives, sisters, daughters, learners, workers, citizens and leaders.

It is also a coming together, much the way women come together every day in every country.

We come together in fields and in factories. In village markets and supermarkets. In living rooms and boardrooms.

Whether it is while playing with our children in the park, or washing clothes in a river, or taking a break at the office water cooler, we come together and talk about our aspirations and concerns. And time and again, our talk turns to our children and our families. However different we may be, there is far more that unites us than divides us. We share a common future. And we are here to find common ground so that we may help bring new dignity and respect to women and girls all over the world—and in so doing, bring new strength and stability to families as well.

By gathering in Beijing, we are focusing world attention on issues that matter most in the lives of women and their families: access to education, health care, jobs and credit, the chance to enjoy basic legal and human rights and participate fully in the political life of their countries.

There are some who question the reason for this conference.

Let them listen to the voices of women in their homes, neighborhoods, and workplaces.

There are some who wonder whether the lives of women and girls matter to economic and political progress around the globe.

Let them look at the women gathered here and at Huairou—the homemakers, nurses, teachers, lawyers, policymakers, and women who run their own businesses.

It is conferences like this that compel governments and people everywhere to listen, look and face the world's most pressing problems.

Wasn't it after the women's conference in Nairobi ten years ago that the world focused for the first time on the crisis of domestic violence?

Earlier today, I participated in a World Health Organization forum, where government officials, NGOs, and individual citizens are working on ways to address the health problems of women and girls.

Tomorrow, I will attend a gathering of the United Nations Development Fund for Women. There, the discussion will focus on local—and highly successful—programs that give hard-working women access to credit so they can improve their own lives and the lives of their families.

What we are learning around the world is that if women are healthy and educated, their families will flourish. If women are free from violence, their families will flourish. If women have a chance to work and earn as full and equal partners in society, their families will flourish.

And when families flourish, communities and nations will flourish.

That is why every woman, every man, every child, every family, and every nation on our planet has a stake in the discussion that takes place here.

Over the past 25 years, I have worked persistently on issues relating to women, children and families. Over the past two-and-a-half years, I have had the opportunity to learn more about the challenges facing women in my own country and around the world.

I have met new mothers in Jojakarta, Indonesia, who come together regularly in their village to discuss nutrition, family planning, and baby care.

I have met working parents in Denmark who talk about the comfort they feel in knowing that their children can be cared for in creative, safe, and nurturing after-school centers.

I have met women in South Africa who helped lead the struggle to end apartheid and are now helping build a new democracy.

I have met with the leading women of the Western Hemisphere who are working every day to promote literacy and better health care for the children of their countries.

I have met women in India and Bangladesh who are taking out small loans to buy milk cows, rickshaws, thread and other materials to create a livelihood for themselves and their families.

I have met doctors and nurses in Belarus and Ukraine who are trying to keep children alive in the aftermath of Chernobyl.

The great challenge of this Conference is to give voice to women everywhere whose experiences go unnoticed, whose words go unheard.

Women comprise more than half the world's population. Women are 70 percent of the world's poor, and two-thirds of those who are not taught to read and write.

Women are the primary caretakers for most of the world's children and elderly. Yet much of the work we do is not valued—not by economists, not by historians, not by popular culture, not by government leaders.

At this very moment, as we sit here, women around the world are giving birth, raising children, cooking meals, washing clothes, cleaning houses, planting crops, working on assembly lines, running companies, and running countries.

Women also are dying from diseases that should have been prevented or treated; they are watching their children succumb to malnutrition caused by poverty and economic deprivation; they are being denied the right to go to school by their own fathers and brothers; they are being forced into prostitution, and they are being barred from the bank lending office and banned from the ballot box.

Those of us who have the opportunity to be here have the responsibility to speak for those who could not.

As an American, I want to speak up for women in my own country—women who are raising children on the minimum wage, women who can't afford health care or child care, women whose lives are threatened by violence, including violence in their own homes.

I want to speak up for mothers who are fighting for good schools, safe neighborhoods, clean air and clean airwaves; for older women, some of them widows, who have raised their families and now find that their skills and life experiences are not valued in the workplace; for women who are working all night as nurses, hotel clerks, and fast food cooks so that they can be at home during the day with their kids; and for women everywhere who simply don't have time to do everything they are called upon to do each day.

Speaking to you today, I speak for them, just as each of us speaks for women around the world who are denied the chance to go to school, or see a doctor, or own property, or have a say about the direction of their lives, simply because they are women. The truth is that most women around the world work both inside and outside the home, usually by necessity.

We need to understand that there is no formula for how women should lead their lives.

That is why we must respect the choices that each woman makes for herself and her family. Every woman deserves the chance to realize her God-given potential.

We also must recognize that women will never gain full dignity until their human rights are respected and protected.

Our goals for this Conference, to strengthen families and societies by empowering women to take greater control over their own destinies, cannot be fully achieved unless all governments—here and around the world—accept their responsibility to protect and promote internationally recognized human rights.

The international community has long acknowledged—and recently affirmed at Vienna—that both women and men are entitled to a range of protections and personal freedoms, from the right of personal security to the right to determine freely the number and spacing of the children they bear.

No one should be forced to remain silent for fear of religious or political persecution, arrest, abuse or torture.

Tragically, women are most often the ones whose human rights are violated.

Even in the late 20th century, the rape of women continues to be used as an instrument of armed conflict. Women and children make up a large majority of the world's refugees. When women are excluded from the political process, they become even more vulnerable to abuse.

I believe that, on the eve of a new millennium, it is time to break our silence. It is time for us to say here in Beijing, and the world to hear, that it is no longer acceptable to discuss women's rights as separate from human rights.

These abuses have continued because, for too long, the history of women has been a history of silence. Even today, there are those who are trying to silence our words.

The voices of this conference and of the women at Huairou must be heard loud and clear:

It is a violation of human rights when babies are denied food, or drowned, or suffocated, or their spines broken, simply because they are born girls.

It is a violation of human rights when women and girls are sold into the slavery of prostitution.

It is a violation of human rights when women are doused with gasoline, set on fire and burned to death because their marriage dowries are deemed too small.

It is a violation of human rights when individual women are raped in their own communities and when thousands of women are subjected to rape as a tactic or prize of war.

It is a violation of human rights when a leading cause of death worldwide among women ages 14 to 44 is the violence they are subjected to in their own homes.

It is a violation of human rights when young girls are brutalized by the painful and degrading practice of genital mutilation.

It is a violation of human rights when woman are denied the right to plan their own families, and that includes being forced to have abortions or being sterilized against their will.

If there is one message that echoes forth from this conference, it is that human rights are women's rights—and women's rights are human rights. Let us not forget that among those rights are the right to speak freely—and the right to be heard.

Women must enjoy the right to participate fully in the social and political lives of their countries if we want freedom and democracy to thrive and endure.

It is indefensible that many women in nongovernmental organizations who wished to participate in this conference have not been able to attend—or have been prohibited from fully taking part.

Let me be clear. Freedom means the right of people to assemble, organize, and debate openly. It means respecting the views of those who may disagree with the views of their governments. It means not taking citizens away from their loved ones and jailing them, mistreating them, or denying them their freedom or dignity because of the peaceful expression of their ideas and opinions.

In my country, we recently celebrated the 75th anniversary of women's suffrage. It took 150 years after the signing of our Declaration of Independence for women to win the right to vote.

It took 72 years of organized struggle on the part of many courageous women and men. It was one of America's most divisive philosophical wars. But it was also a bloodless war. Suffrage was achieved without a shot being fired.

We have also been reminded, in V-J Day observances last weekend, of the good that comes when men and women join together to combat the forces of tyranny and build a better world.

We have seen peace prevail in most places for a half century. We have avoided another world war.

But we have not solved older, deeply-rooted problems that continue to diminish the potential of half the world's population.

Now it is time to act on behalf of women everywhere.

If we take bold steps to better the lives of women, we will be taking bold steps to better the lives of children and families too.

Families rely on mothers and wives for emotional support and care; families rely on women for labor in the home; and increasingly, families rely on women for income needed to raise healthy children and care for other relatives.

As long as discrimination and inequities remain so commonplace around the world—as long as girls and women are valued less, fed less, fed last, over-worked, underpaid, not schooled and subjected to violence in and out of their homes—the potential of the human family to create a peaceful, prosperous world will not be realized.

Let this Conference be our—and the world's—call to action.

And let us heed the call so that we can create a world in which every woman is treated with respect and dignity, every boy and girl is loved and cared for equally, and every family has the hope of a strong and stable future.

Thank you very much.

God's blessing on you, your work and all who will benefit from it.

Women in Public Life Commencement Address, Radcliffe College, June 11, 1993
Elizabeth Dole

Elizabeth Hanford Dole received an undergraduate degree from Duke University, a master's degree and law degree from Harvard. Ms. Dole served as the secretary of transportation and the secretary of labor during the Reagan and Bush administrations. More recently she has been president of the American Red Cross. As secretary of transportation, she instituted campaigns against drunken driving and for automobile safety. As secretary of labor she worked on programs of job training for at-risk youth, job safety regulations, stricter enforcement of child-labor laws, and ways to shatter the glass ceiling that often prevents women from advancing in organizations. Ms. Dole's commencement address is a speech of inspiration aimed at getting the female graduates to realize their own potential and value as women. She suggests public service as a viable alternative to the private sector for women. She uses personal examples and narratives to give authenticity to her advice to the young graduates.

I have been asked to share some thoughts this afternoon on women in public policy—an interesting topic, because while there are more women in public leadership roles than in private, there are still relatively few. While there are greater opportunities for women in public leadership than in private, there are still relatively few. While there are greater opportunities for women in government, there obviously remain impediments.

There are many ways to pursue the goal of involving women in shaping public policy. And there are many reasons to pursue this goal. In the first place, it's right. Too many of our number have felt the sting of discrimination. Secondly, women, I believe, have something very special to offer. And, thirdly, our work force is changing. America must be able to welcome women and minorities into its leadership roles if we are to accommodate that change. Sixty-four percent of the new entrants to the work force over the next 10 years will be women. If the public sector is to attract the best and the brightest, it must be able to attract and reward women.

When I was in law school at Harvard, only 24 of the 550 students were women. There were only a few women, at the time, who had made partner in major law firms. The private sector simply was not a strong option. Public policy beckoned as a rewarding alternative—a call to service, a chance to make a positive difference in people's lives.

There are some observations I could offer [women today] which might smooth the way a little. I could summarize them this way: that our greatest obstacle—that we women are women in a world of men—is really an enormous opportunity.

Remember the question Henry Higgins asked in the film *My Fair Lady*, "Why can't a woman be more like a man?" Because I think it's important to learn the correct lesson from our successes, I believe that further gains do not depend on better answers to the question, "Why can't a woman be more like a man?" The question we should be asking now is "Why can't a woman be more like a woman?"

I'd like to quote for you from a recent article in *Life* magazine: "Women," the article asserts, "are more committed than men to cushioning the hard corners of the country, to making it a safer place. Women want stricter law enforcement against drunk driving and illegal firearms and drug dealing. . . . It's not that men don't care about these issues. It's simply that women care more."

I don't know whether that's true. But perhaps our approach is different. Perhaps our involvement in public policy debates provides a leavening influence. Perhaps more women in public service would result in greater focus on cushioning corners for vulnerable Americans. If that's so, then it is doubly important that we women add our voices to the national debates, that we take our places at the tables of power, that we rise to the challenge of leadership when we believe that to be our calling.

So then, why can't a woman be more like a woman? In other words, progress for women in public policy and private life may indeed hinge on our ability to acknowledge and develop our skills and values as women. It may just be that those are the skills and values our country needs most at this moment.

I have been privileged during my years in public service to work with a number of successful women in public policy and I would like to pass along some of their observations, and some of my own, about drawing on our professional female advantages.

The first is to take full advantage of our trumpeted trait of flexibility—in fact to plan for the unexpected, and relish our ability to think on our feet. Rigid guidelines, set agendas, and line reporting responsibilities all help create the illusion of control in the current management environment. But perhaps a knack for flexibility is more important.

Another observation I have is that to succeed in the public arena, women must learn to trust their instincts. It's not just female intuition—it's a cognitive skill that we are perhaps more open to. Estimation skills are now being taught to children as they come up through elementary and secondary schools, and instinct is oftentimes another word for it. It's an ability to take in a great deal of information and quickly reduce it to a rough but generally accurate picture. It's the soft route to hard data.

Yet too often we women allow ourselves to be intimidated into denying our instincts—whether it's a judgment of people, situations, or the heart of the policy question. The women in the audience have probably all had the experience of sitting across the table from someone—a man, let's say, with whom you disagree. Ask yourselves how many times, in this situation, has your reaction been to question your own judgment rather than his—only to find out later that you were right on the money?

Over the ages, we women have perfected to a high art form this trait of second-guessing ourselves. Perhaps it stems from our early constant exposure to society's message that female traits and talents are inferior; but we have to get over it. It takes confidence to trust ourselves, and if we don't have confidence, our voices will be lost if ever they're heard.

The third common denominator I've seen among successful women leaders is a commitment to those who follow. About twenty years ago, a group of us formed an organization called "Executive Women in Government," which still flourishes today. Its purpose is twofold: to help younger women who want to follow into public service by giving them information and advice, and to make it easier for women in policy-making positions to relate to one another across government. Networking—women reaching out to other women—is a way of using our special opportunities to overcome obstacles. I have been helped many times in the stages of my career by women who were ahead of me. As a result, my door is always open to young women who are in need of a mentor, and I would encourage other women to do the same.

The final challenge for women is not to let others define success for us. Our lives are complicated, balancing personal and professional goals, loving our families while searching for individual fulfillment. And every woman must find her own answers—answers that are right for her. Women must allow ourselves, and each other, the freedom to choose. Women across America are discovering that feeling in as many ways as there are women—some through public service, some in the world of business or as lawyers and doctors, and some as wives, mothers, and volunteers. No one can or should tell us where we will find that feeling, or how we will come to define our own success. These are decisions we alone can make for ourselves.

In the fairy tales we were read as children, once having been rescued by the prince, the "female lead" lives happily ever after. That was the theme in Cinderella, Snow White, and Sleeping Beauty. But now perhaps we need to read our daughters a new bedtime story—with a heroine who isn't a princess, but a woman who sees that there are things that need to be changed to make life better for herself and others. A woman who is not a victim, and who doesn't need a rescuer. We need a tale about a woman whose talents and abilities are valued and admired, a woman who uses those talents to succeed. A woman who is committed, who feels passionately about her life's decisions. Such a story would not be a fairy tale—there are thousands of examples. And if each of us continues to ask the right question, "Why can't a woman be more like a woman?" there will be hundreds of thousands more tomorrow.

Martin Luther King at the Mountaintop
John Scipio

This speech of tribute honoring Dr. Martin Luther King, Jr., was presented by John Scipio in his public speaking class at the University of Memphis. In this speech John uses the technique of magnification by demonstrating that Dr. King had to overcome great obstacles, that his performance was unusual and superior, and that he sacrificed himself for the cause of humanity. Note the colorful use of language in this speech. His graphic descriptions of the stormy April night and of the plight of the sanitation workers in Memphis are good examples. Note that to obtain some of the background information for the speech, John conducted a telephone interview with Dr. Ralph Abernathy of the Southern Christian Leadership Conference. The inclusion of this information increased both the authenticity of the message and the speaker's ethos.

On the stormy night of April 3, 1968, three thousand onlookers came to Mason Temple here in Memphis, Tennessee, to hear what many have considered to be one of the greatest speeches in Martin Luther King, Jr.'s, history. The title: "I've Been to the Mountaintop." Richard Lynch, in his monograph, "Sixty-five Days in Memphis," describes it as being one of the finest speeches of his career, matching the eloquence of his "I Have a Dream" peroration at the 1963 march on Washington. In it, King seemed to foretell his own death.

Now, King may have used this speech as a medium to predict his forthcoming assassination. But no one really knows. Whether or not he was a prophet, no one can really tell. But in his speech, King constantly refers to death. He often talks about "the Promised Land" and how beautiful it is over there. He also refers, at the ending of his speech, that he may not get to the Promised Land with them, but they as a people will get to the Promised Land.

In order to understand the message that Dr. King was trying to convey in his address to the masses that night, we must look beyond the speech to the conditions and events that were taking place during that time. Dr. King had become the leader of the movement for many years. And many of those that were involved in the actions of the day viewed him as their champion. When injustice raised its ugly head, he would come to the rescue like a mighty warrior. When freedom was being denied, he was there. He was there in Selma, in Montgomery, in Birmingham, and, finally, in Memphis.

But what was it that brought Dr. King to Memphis? The answer—thirteen hundred sanitation workers and their families who thought they had been treated unfairly by the city of Memphis in general and by Mayor Loeb in particular. These workers were angered by the fact that the city refused to recognize their union, the American Federation of State, County, and Municipal Employees, Local 1733. Their frustrations reached a boiling point, and they decided to take action and go on strike. Dr. King came to Memphis to give his support to the workers and to urge others to do the same.

Now, many problems had arisen during the course of the civil rights movement that did nothing insofar as to help the cause, but to cripple it. The violence that erupted during the first march led by Dr. King in Memphis caused many to doubt the effectiveness of his nonviolent movement. Many were tired and weary from this long struggle that they had endured. They were almost to the point of surrender.

Through the speech, Dr. King had to give them some type of motivation—a reason to go on and continue the struggle. With all of the problems that were being put upon him, Dr. King was reluctant to speak that particular night. So, in his stead, he sent his closest friend, Ralph Abernathy. Upon

Mr. Abernathy's arrival at Mason Temple and seeing the throngs of people who had come out to hear Dr. King, he immediately phoned him and said, "They're your crowd." They needed a speech that only Dr. King could give.

When asked in a telephone interview what he thought the attraction to Dr. King was, Abernathy stated, "He possessed a power, never before seen in a man of color." What was this power that Abernathy spoke of? It was the power to persuade audiences and change opinions with his words. It was the power of speech. This particular speech is the most evident example of that power. King is a master at using metaphors to dramatize his subject. An example of this is when he states that the nation is sick, there is trouble in the land. He does this to bring life to the suffering that was going on during this time. In his speech, Dr. King had to give these people hope and motivate them to go on. He did this by speaking of the Promised Land and how beautiful it was.

He also makes use of metaphors when he makes reference to the verses of Scripture, which say, "Let justice roll down like waters and righteousness like a mighty stream." King was a master. King's rhetorical style is very effective in conveying his message as well. He uses key phrases time and time again to pound out their meaning. An example of this is when he speaks of a letter, written to him by a little white girl from White Plains. He says that in this letter, she says, "As it should not matter, I am white. I am only writing to say that I read the article in the *New York Times* that stated the blade was so close to your aorta that if you had sneezed, you would have been dead. And I'm just writing to say I'm so happy that you didn't sneeze." Dr. King uses the phrase "if I had sneezed" to backtrack the movement and give us its history.

Another phrase that stands out in this speech is "but I wouldn't stop there." This is a phrase used in the beginning of Dr. King's speech, to give us—take us through—a mental flight of history, up until the present day.

Dr. King's oratorical brilliance is personified in this, his last and greatest speech. Many can be referred to as "speaker," but only a select few have earned the title of "orator." Dr. King was truly an orator.

Glossary

acronym A word composed of the initial letters or parts of a series of words. (9)

addressing attitudes and values A function of persuasive speech that attempts to form, reform, or reinforce audience attitudes. (13)

***ad hominem* fallacy** An attempt to discredit a position by attacking the people who favor it. (14)

after-dinner speech A brief, often humorous, ceremonial speech, presented after a meal, that offers a message without asking for radical changes in attitude or action. (15)

agenda-setting function Employing information to create a sense of what is important. (12)

alliteration The repetition of initial consonant sounds in closely connected words. (10)

amplification The art of developing ideas by strategic repetition in a speech. (10)

analogical argument Creating a strategic perspective on a subject by relating it to something about which the audience has strong positive or negative feelings. (14)

analogous color scheme Colors adjacent on the color wheel; used in a presentation aid to suggest both differences and close relationships among the components represented. (9)

analogy A connection established between two otherwise dissimilar ideas or things. (6, 12)

antithesis A language technique that combines opposing elements in the same sentence or adjoining sentences. (10)

appreciative phase Phase of listening in which we enjoy the beauty of messages, responding to such factors as the simplicity, balance, and proportion of speeches and the eloquence of their language. (3)

argument A combination of evidence and proofs designed to produce a strong case for one side of an issue. (14)

articulation The manner in which individual speech sounds are produced. (11)

assimilation The tendency of listeners to interpret the positions of a speaker with whom they agree as closer to their own views than they actually are. (3)

attitudes Pre-existing complexes of feelings, beliefs, and inclinations that we have toward people, places, events, or ideas. (4)

audience demographics Observable characteristics of listeners, including age, gender, educational level, group affiliations, and sociocultural backgrounds, that the speaker considers when adapting to an audience. (4)

audience dynamics The motivations, attitudes, beliefs, and values that influence the behavior of listeners. (4)

autocratic leader A leader who makes decisions without consultation, issues orders or gives direction, and controls the members of the group through the use of rewards or punishments. (Appendix A)

award presentation A speech of tribute that recognizes achievements of the award recipient, explains the nature of the award, and describes why the recipient qualifies for the award. (15)

balance Achieving a balance among the major parts of a presentation. (7)

bar graph A kind of graph that shows comparisons and contrasts between two or more items or groups. (9)

begging the question Assuming that an argument has been proved without actually presenting the evidence. (14)

beliefs Things accepted as true about a subject. (4)

body The middle part of a speech, used to develop the main ideas. (2)

body language Communication achieved using facial expressions, eye contact, movements, and gestures. (11)

boomerang effect An audience's hostile reaction to a speech advocating too much or too radical change. (13)

brief example A specific instance illustrating a more general idea. (6)

briefing A short, informative presentation given in an organizational setting. (12)

bulleted list A presentation aid that highlights themes by presenting them in a list of brief statements. (9)

call the question A motion that proposes to end the discussion on a motion and to bring it to a vote. (Appendix A)

categorical design The use of natural or traditional divisions within a subject as a way of structuring an informative speech. (12)

causation design A pattern for an informative speech that shows how one condition generates, or is generated by, another. (12)

ceremonial speaking (ceremonial speech) Speaking that celebrates special occasions. Common forms are speeches of tribute, inspiration, eulogies, toasts, introduction, making and accepting awards, and the after-dinner speech. Their deeper function is to share identities and reinforce values that unite people into communities. (3, 15)

co-active approach A way of approaching reluctant audiences in which the speaker attempts to establish goodwill, emphasizes shared values, and sets modest goals for persuasion. (13)

cognitive restructuring The process of replacing negative thoughts with positive, constructive ones. (2)

collaborative problem solving In group communication, an approach that gathers participants from separate areas of the public or private sectors for their input on a problem. (Appendix A)

communication apprehension Anxiety or fear experienced before and during public speaking. (2)

communication environment The setting in which communication occurs, including both physical and psychological factors. (1)

comparative design   A pattern for an informative speech that relates an unfamiliar subject to something the audience already knows or understands. (12)

comparison   Using supporting material to point out the similarities of an unfamiliar or controversial issue to something the audience already knows or accepts. (6)

comparison and contrast   An informative speech design that points out similarities and differences between subjects or ideas. (12)

competence   The speaker's appearance of being informed, intelligent, and well prepared. (2)

complementary color scheme   Colors opposite one another on the color wheel; used in a presentation aid to suggest tension and opposition among various elements. (9)

comprehensive phase   Phase of listening in which we focus on, understand, and interpret spoken messages. (3)

computer-assisted presentation   The use of commercial presentation software to join audio, visual, text, graphic, and animated components. (9)

conclusion   The last part of a speech, which should include a summary statement and concluding remarks (2); the proposition that follows the major and minor premises of a syllogism and directs the audience toward the speaker's point of view. (2, 14)

consciousness-raising   Making an audience more sensitive to an issue and more receptive to future persuasion. (13)

constructive listening   The role of the listener in the creation of meaning. Involves discovering the speaker's intention, tracing out the implications and consequences of the message, and applying the message to one's life. (3)

contending with opposition   A function of persuasive speech that confronts the opposition by systematically refuting its claims. (13)

contrast   Using supporting materials to emphasize difference between two things. (6)

contrast effect   A tendency by listeners to distort the positions of a speaker with whom they disagree and to interpret those positions as even more distant from their own opinions than they actually are. (3)

coordination   The requirement that statements equal in importance be placed on the same level in an outline. (8)

critical listening   The careful analysis and evaluation of message content. (3)

critique   An evaluation of a speech. (3)

cultural gridlock   Occurs when the cultural differences in a group are so profound that the varying agendas, priorities, customs, and procedures create tensions that block constructive discussion. (Appendix A)

cultural sensitivity   The respectful, appreciative awareness of the diversity within an audience. (10)

culturetypes   Terms that express the values and goals of a group's culture. (10)

decoding   The process by which the listener determines the meaning of the speaker's message and decides the speaker's intent. (1)

deductive argument   A kind of proof that begins with a generally accepted truth, connects an issue with that truth, and draws a conclusion based on the connection. (14)

definition   A translation of a word an audience may not be familiar with into understandable terms. (6)

deliberation   Allowing all sides to express their opinions before a decision is made. (13)

demagogues   Political speakers who try to inflame feelings without regard to the accuracy or adequacy of their claims in order to promote their own agendas. (3)

descriptions   Word pictures that help listeners visualize information by evoking vivid, concrete images in their minds. (6)

dialect   A speech pattern associated with an area of the country or with a cultural or ethnic background. (11)

dialogue group   A group assembled to explore the underlying assumptions of a problem but not necessarily to solve it. (Appendix A)

direct quotation   Repeating the exact words of another to support a point. (6)

discriminative phase   Phase of listening in which we detect the vital sounds of spoken communication. (3)

disinformation   Communication that offers what appears to be information, but that actually deceives listeners and impedes their understanding. (6)

egocentrism   Holding the view that one's own experiences and thoughts are the norm. (1)

either-or thinking   A fallacy that occurs when the speaker informs listeners that they have only two options, only one of which is desirable. (14)

electronic brainstorming   A group technique in which participants generate ideas in computer chat groups or by email. (Appendix A)

empathic phase   Phase of listening in which we suspend judgment, allow speakers to be heard, and try to see things from their points of view. (3)

encoding   The process by which the speaker combines words, tones, and gestures to convey thought and feelings to the audience. (1)

enunciation   The manner in which individual words are articulated and pronounced in context. (11)

ethics   The moral dimension of human conduct, governing how we treat others and wish to be treated in return. (1)

ethnocentrism   The tendency of any nation, race, religion, or organized group to believe that its way of looking at and doing things is right and that other perspectives have less value. (1, 4)

ethos   Those characteristics that make a speaker appear honest, credible, and appealing (1, Appendix A); a kind of proof created by a speaker's own favorable impression and by association with credible testimony. (14)

eulogy   A speech of tribute presented upon a person's death. (15)

euphemisms   The use of words to disguise unpleasant subjects, as when we say of someone who has failed a course, "His performance was less than successful." (10)

evidence   Supporting materials used in persuasive speeches, including facts and figures, examples, narratives, and testimony. (14)

examples   Verbal illustrations of the speaker's points. (2, 6)

expanded conversational style   A speaker's style that, while more formal than everyday conversation, preserves its directness and spontaneity. (11)

expert testimony   Information derived from authorities within a field. (6)

explanations   A combination of facts and statistics to clarify a topic or process mentioned in a speech. (6)

extemporaneous presentation (extemporaneous speaking)   A form of presentation in which a speech, although carefully prepared and practiced, is not written out or memorized. (3, 11)

extended example A detailed illustration that allows a speaker to build impressions. (6)

facts and statistics Items of information that can be used to illustrate and prove points made by the speaker. When expressed numerically, such information appears in statistics. (2, 6,)

factual example An illustration based on something that actually happened or that really exists. (6)

fallacies Errors in persuasion. (14)

faulty analogy A comparison drawn between things that are dissimilar in some important way. (14)

feedback The audience's immediate response to a speaker. (1, 11)

figurative analogy A comparison made between things that belong to different fields. (6, 12)

filtering Listening to only part of a message, the part the listener wants to hear. (3)

flow chart A visual method of representing power and responsibility relationships. (9)

forcefulness A favorable impression created by a speaker's competence, integrity, decisiveness, and confidence. (2)

formal outline The final outline in a process leading from the first rough ideas for a speech to the finished product. (8)

free-rein leader A leader who leaves members free to decide what, how, and when to act, offering no guidance. (Appendix A)

gender stereotyping Generalizations based on oversimplified or outmoded assumptions about gender and gender roles. (4)

general purpose (general function) The speaker's overall intention to inform or persuade listeners, or to celebrate some person or occasion. (3, 5)

good form A primary principle of structure, based on simplicity, symmetry, and orderliness. (7)

good reasons The persuasive speaker's justification of a recommendation, based on responsible knowledge and consideration of the listeners' best interests. (13)

graphics Visual representations of information. (9)

great expectation fallacy The mistaken idea that major change can be accomplished by a single persuasive effort. (13)

groupthink Occurs when a single, uncritical frame of mind dominates group thinking and prevents the full, objective analysis of specific problems. (Appendix A)

habitual pitch The level at which people speak most frequently. (11)

hasty generalization An error of inductive reasoning in which a claim is based on insufficient or nonrepresentative information. (14)

hyperbole A technique of language that employs exaggeration to make points and arouse feeling. (10)

hypothetical example A representation of reality, usually a synthesis of actual people, situations, or events. (6)

identification The close involvement of subject, speaker, and listener. (2, 3, 7, 15)

ideographs Words that convey a group's basic political faith or system of beliefs. (10)

image A mental picutre created by the use of vivid examples. (10)

immediacy A quality of successful communication achieved when the speaker and audience experience a sense of closeness. (11)

impromptu speaking A talk delivered with minimal or no preparation. (11)

inductive argument The use of specific instances to build general conclusions. (14)

information cards Records of facts and ideas obtained from an article or book used in research. (5)

informative speech Speech aimed at extending understanding. (3)

informative value A measure of how much new and important information or understanding a speech conveys to an audience. (12)

inoculation effect Preparing an audience for an opposing argument by answering it before listeners have been exposed to it. (13)

integrity The quality of being ethical, honest, and dependable. (2)

interference Any physical noise or psychological distraction that impedes the hearing of a speech. (1)

internal summary Reminding listeners of major points already presented in a speech before new ideas are introduced. (7)

introduction The first part of a speech, intended to gain the audience's attention and prepare it for the rest of the presentation. (2)

inversion Changing the normal word order to make statements memorable and emphatic. (10)

jargon Technical language related to a specific field, but often used before an audience that may not understand it. (10)

key-word outline An abbreviated version of a formal outline, used in presenting a speech. (2, 8)

lay testimony Information that is derived from the first-hand experience of ordinary citizens. (6)

likableness The quality of radiating goodness and goodwill and inspiring audience affection in return. (2)

line graph A visual representation of changes across time; especially useful for indicating trends of growth or decline. (9)

listener A person who interprets the message offered by the speaker to construct its meaning. (1)

literal analogy A comparison made between subjects within the same field. (12)

logos A form of proof that makes rational appeals based on facts and figures and expert testimony. (14)

magnification A speaker's selecting and emphasizing certain qualities about a subject in order to stress the values that they represent. (15)

main motion A proposal that would commit a group to some specific action or declaration. (Appendix A)

main points The most prominent ideas of the speaker's message, and a speech's principal points of focus. (7)

major premise A generally accepted belief upon which an argument is based. (14)

malapropisms   Language errors that occur when a word is confused with another word that sounds like it. (10)

manuscript presentation   A speech read from a manuscript. (11)

marking   Adding a gender reference when none is needed—e.g., "a woman doctor." (4)

master of ceremonies   A person who coordinates an event or program, sets its mood, introduces participants, provides transitions, and may also present awards. (15)

maxims   Brief and particularly apt sayings. (10)

memorized text presentations   Speeches that are committed to memory and delivered word for word. (11)

message   The fabric or words, illustrations, voice, and body language that conveys the idea of the speech. (1)

metaphor   A figure of speech in which anticipated words are replaced by new, surprising language in order to create a new perspective. (7, 10)

minor premise   The claim made in an argument that an important idea is related to a generally accepted truth (or major premise). (14)

mirror questions   Questions that include part of a previous response to encourage further discussion. (5)

motion   Formal proposal for group consideration. (Appendix A)

motivated sequence design   A persuasive speech design that proceeds by arousing attention, demonstrating a need, satisfying the need, visualizing results, and calling for action. (13)

motivation   Internal forces that impel action and direct human behavior toward specific goals. (4)

mountain graph   A variation of a line graph in which different colors are used to fill in the areas above and below the line(s). (9)

move to amend   A parliamentary move that offers the opportunity to modify a motion presently under discussion. (Appendix A)

multisided presentation   A speech in which the speaker's position is compared favorably to other positions. (13)

myth of the mean   The deceptive use of statistical averages in speeches. (14)

mythos   A form of proof that connects a subject to the culture and tradition of a group through the use of narratives. (14)

narrative   A story used to illustrate some important truth about a speaker's topic. (6)

non sequitur fallacy   A deductive error occurring when conclusions are drawn improperly from the premises that preceded them. (14)

onomatopoeia   The use of words that sound like the objects they signify. (10)

optimum pitch   The level at which people can produce their strongest voice with minimal effort and that allows variation up and down the musical scale. (11)

order   A consistent pattern used to develop a speech. (7)

parallel construction   Wording an outline's main points in the same way in order to emphasize their importance and to help the audience remember them. (8, 10)

paraphrase   A summary of something said or written. (6)

parliamentary procedure   A set of formal rules that establishes an order of business for meetings and encourages the orderly, fair, and full consideration of proposals during group deliberation. (Appendix A)

participative leader   A leader who seeks input from group members and gives them an active role in decision-making. (Appendix A)

pathos   Proof relying on appeals to personal motives and emotions. (14)

personification   A figure of speech in which nonhuman or abstract subjects are given human qualities. (10)

persuasion   The art of convincing others to give favorable attention to our point of view. (13)

persuasive speech   Speech intended to influence the attitudes or actions of listeners. (3)

pictographs   On a chart, a visual image symbolizing the information it represents. (9)

pie graph   A circle graph that shows the size of a subject's parts in relation to each other and to the whole. (9)

pitch   The position of a human voice on the musical scale. (11)

plagiarism   Presenting the ideas and words of others without crediting them as sources. (1, 5)

***post hoc* fallacy**   A deductive error in which one event is assumed to be the cause of another simply because the first preceded the second. (14)

postpone consideration (move to postpone consideration)   A motion that defers discussion until some specified time when necessary information will be available. (Appendix A)

precision   Using information that is closely and carefully related to the specific purpose; particularly important when a topic varies widely from place to place. (5)

preliminary tuning effect   The effect of previous speeches or other situational factors in predisposing an audience to respond positively or negatively to a speech. (4)

prepersuasive function   The way in which informative speaking shapes listeners' perceptions, preparing them for later persuasive speeches on a topic. (12)

PREP formula   An outlining technique for an impromptu speech: state a **p**oint, give a **r**eason or **e**xample, and restate the **p**oint. (11)

presentation   Utterance of a speech to an audience, integrating the skills of nonverbal communication, especially body language, with the speech content. (11)

presentation aids   Supplemental materials used to enhance the effectiveness and clarity of a presentation. (9)

prestige testimony   Information coming from a person who is highly regarded but not necessarily an expert on a topic. (6)

preview   The part of the introduction that identifies the main points in the body of the speech and presents an overview of the speech to follow. May follow the thematic statement or be part of the thematic statement itself. (5, 7)

principle of closure   The need for a satisfactory end or conclusion to a speech. (7)

principle of proximity   The idea that things occurring together in time or space should be presented in the order in which they normally happen. (7)

principle of similarity   The principle that like things should be grouped together. (7)

probes   Questions that ask an expert to elaborate on a response. (5)

problem-solution design   A persuasive speech pattern in which listeners are first persuaded that they have a problem and then are shown how to solve it. (13)

pronunciation The use of correct sounds and of proper stress or accent on syllables in saying words. (11)

proof An interpretation of evidence that provides reasons for listeners to change their attitudes or behaviors. (14)

proxemics The study of how human beings use space during communication. (11)

qualifiers Words that suggest the degree of confidence a speaker has in the conclusion of his or her argument. (14)

quoting out of context An unethical use of a quotation that changes or distorts the original speaker's meaning or intent by not including parts of the quote. (1)

rate The speed at which words are uttered. (11)

rebuttals Pointing out conditions under which the conclusion of an argument might not hold. (14)

receiver apprehension Fear of misinterpreting, inadequately processing and/or not being able to adjust psychologically to messages sent by others. (3)

recency Ensuring that the information in a speech is the latest that can be provided. (5)

red herring fallacy The use of irrelevant material to divert attention. (14)

refutative design A persuasive speech design in which the speaker tries to raise doubts about, damage, or destroy an opposing position. (13)

reinforcer A comment or action that encourages further communication from someone being interviewed. (5)

relationship The use of words to identify or characterize a subject by pointing out what it is similar to. The most common form of this technique, the *simile,* typically uses "like" or "as" to make this linkage. (10)

reliability The trustworthiness of information critical to the credibility of a speech. (5)

reluctant witness A person cited as evidence whose testimony is against his or her self-interest. (14)

replacement The use of words in unexpected or surprising applications to characterize subjects in dramatic ways. The most common form of this technique occurs in the metaphor, such as when we speak of the "dawn" of an idea or a "battle" of words. (10)

representation The strategic use of words to focus on certain aspects of complex subjects, as in such expressions as "The tongue is mightier than the sword." The effect is to direct listeners' attention to some features of these subjects and to de-emphasize others. (10)

research overview A listing of the main sources of information used in a speech and of the major ideas from each source. (7)

responsible knowledge An understanding of the major features, issues, experts, latest developments, and local applications relevant to a topic. (1, 5)

rhetorical questions Questions that have a self-evident answer, or that provoke curiosity that the speech then proceeds to satisfy. (7)

rhythm Rate patterns within a speech. (11)

Robert's Rules of Order The authoritative, traditional "bible" of parliamentary procedure. (Appendix A)

second A motion must receive a "second" before group discussion can proceed. Assures that more than one member wishes to have the motion considered. (Appendix A)

self-awareness inventory A series of questions that a speaker can ask to develop an approach to a speech of introduction. (2)

sequence chart Visual illustrations of the different stages of a process. (9)

sequential design A pattern for an informative speech that presents the steps involved in the process being demonstrated. (12)

sexism Allowing gender stereotypes to control interactions with members of the opposite sex. (4)

sexist language The use of masculine nouns and pronouns when the intended reference is to both sexes, or the use of derogatory emotional trigger words when referring to women. (4)

simile A language tool that clarifies something abstract by comparing it with something concrete; usually introduced by *as* or *like.* (10)

simplicity A desirable quality of speech structure. Suggests that a speech have a limited number of main points and that they be short and direct. (7)

skills training Developing abilities and attitudes that help speakers control and transform communication apprehension into a positive factor. (2)

sleeper effect A delayed reaction to persuasion. (13)

slippery slope fallacy The assumption that once something happens, an inevitable trend is established that will lead to disastrous results. (14)

social leadership behavior Occurs when leaders focus upon building and maintaining positive, productive relationships among group members. (Appendix A)

source cards Records kept of the author, title, place and date of publication, and page references for each research source. (5)

source citation Parenthetical reference in a speech outline to sources listed in full under *Works Consulted.* (8)

spatial design A pattern for an informative speech that orders the main points as they occur in physical space. (12)

specific purpose The speaker's particular goal or the response that the speaker wishes to evoke. (5)

speech of acceptance A ceremonial speech expressing gratitude for an honor and acknowledging those who made the accomplishment possible. (15)

speech of demonstration An informative speech aimed at showing the audience how to do something or how something works. (12)

speech of description An informative speech that creates word pictures to help the audience understand a subject. (12)

speech of explanation A speech that is intended to inform the audience about abstract and complex subjects, such as concepts or programs. (12)

speech of inspiration A ceremonial speech directed at awakening or reawakening an audience to a goal, purpose, or set of values. (15)

speech of introduction A ceremonial speech in which a featured speaker is introduced to the audience. (15)

speech of tribute A ceremonial speech that recognizes the achievements of individuals or groups or commemorates special events. (15)

stereotypes Generalized pictures of a race, gender, or group that supposedly represent its essential characteristics. (1, 4)

stock issues design A persuasive speech pattern that attempts to answer the major general questions a reasonable person would ask before agreeing to a change in policies or procedures. (13)

stories Accounts of actions or incidents that demonstrate points the speaker is making. See also **narrative.** (2)

straw man fallacy Understating, distorting, or otherwise misrepresenting the position of opponents for the sake of refutation. (14)

subordination The requirement that material in an outline descend in importance from main points to subpoints to sub-subpoints to sub-sub-subpoints. (8)

subpoint The major division within a speech's main points. (8)

substance A quality possessed by a speech when it has an important message, a careful plan of development, and adequate facts, examples, and testimony. (3)

sub-subpoints Divisions of subpoints within a speech. (8)

summary statement The speaker's reinterpretation of the speech's main idea at the end of a presentation. (7)

supporting materials The facts and figures, testimony, examples, and narratives that constitute the building blocks of successful speeches. (6)

symbolic racism An indirect form of racism that employs code words and subtle, unspoken contrast to suggest that one race is superior to another. (4)

table the motion (move to table the motion) Suspends indefinitely the discussion of a motion. (Appendix A)

task leadership behavior A leadership emphasis that directs the attention and activity of a group towards a specified goal. (Appendix A)

testimonial Lay testimony used to endorse a person, practice, or institution. (6)

testimony The employment of the observations, opinions, or conclusions of other people or institutions to enhance the credibility of a presentation. (2, 6)

textual graphics Visual presentation of key words in a speech using a chalkboard, poster board, flip chart, transparency, slide, or handout. (9)

thesis statement The speech's central idea. (2, 5)

thoroughness Providing complete and accurate information about a topic. (5)

toast A short speech of tribute, usually offered at celebration dinners or meetings. (15)

topic area inventory chart A means of determining possible speech topics by listing topics you find of interest

and subjects your audience finds of interest, and matching them. (5)

transactional leadership A leadership style based on power relationships that relies on reward and punishment to achieve its ends. (Appendix A)

transformation The dynamic effect of successful communication on the identities of the speaker and listener and on public knowledge. (1)

transformational leadership A leadership style based on mutual respect and stewardship rather than on control. (Appendix A)

transitions Connecting elements used in speeches. (2, 7)

trigger words Words that arouse such powerful feelings that they interfere with the ability to listen critically and constructively. (3)

universal human values Eight values identified by the Institute for Global Ethics that transcend cultural differences: love, truthfulness, fairness, freedom, unity, tolerance, responsibility, and respect for life. (4)

urging action A function of persuasive speech that urges the audience to take action, either as individuals or as a group. (13)

values Standards of desirable or ideal behavior. (4)

verbatim Using the exact words of a source. (6)

verifier A statement by an interviewer confirming the meaning of what has just been said by the person being interviewed. (5)

visualization The process of systematically picturing oneself succeeding as a speaker and practicing a speech with that image in mind. (2)

vocal distractions Filler words, such as *er, um,* and *you know,* used in the place of a pause. (11)

working outline A tentative plan showing the pattern of a speech's major parts, their relative importance, and the way they fit together. (8)

works consulted A bibliography included on the formal outline, listing the major sources for a speech. (8)

Photo Credits

Chapter 1:   p. 2 (Opener), Michael Hayman/Stock Boston; p. 7, Bob Daemmrich/The Image Works; p. 13, Dick Blume/The Image Works.

Chapter 2:   p. 28 (Opener), Michelle Bridwell/PhotoEdit; p. 31, Bob Daemmrich/Stock Boston; p. 36, John Eastcott & Yva Momatiuk/The Image Works; p. 42, M. Granitsas/The Image Works.

Chapter 3:   p. 58 (Opener), Seth Resnick/Stock Boston; p. 63, Loren Santow/Impact Visuals; p. 72, Bob Daemmrich/The Image Works; p. 76, Bob Daemmrich/The Image Works.

Chapter 4:   p. 88 (Opener), Bob Daemmrich/The Image Works; p. 97, ©Richard B. Levine; p. 109, Paula Lerner.

Chapter 5:   p. 124 (Opener), Rob Crandall/Stock Boston; p. 129, C. Takagi/Impact Visuals; p. 140, Kenneth Gabrielsen/Liaison Agency; p. 148, James Marshall/The Image Works.

Chapter 6:   p. 162 (Opener), Zillioux/Liaison Agency; p. 170, David Young-Wolff/PhotoEdit; p. 178, Bob Rowan/Progressive Image/Corbis.

Chapter 7:   p. 188 (Opener), Richard Pasley/Stock Boston; p. 201, Asahi Shimbun; p. 210, David Young-Wolff/PhotoEdit.

Chapter 8: p. 216 (Opener), Jennifer Waddell.

Chapter 9: p. 246 (Opener), AP/Wide World Photos; p. 258, (top) Kiser/Glacier National Park Archives, (bottom) Dan Fagre/U.S. Geological Survey; p. 264, Dan Bosler/Tony Stone Images.

Chapter 10:   p. 274 (Opener), Billy E. Barnes/Stock Boston; p. 283, AP/Wide World Photos; p. 292, L. Dematteis/The Image Works.

Chapter 11:   p. 300 (Opener), ©Richard B. Levine; p. 304, AP/Wide World Photos; p. 312, Chris Mooney/BWP Studios; p. 323, ©Richard B. Levine.

Chapter 12:   p. 332 (Opener), Bob Daemmrich/Stock Boston; p. 340, Michael Newman/PhotoEdit; p. 343, Paul S. Howell/Liaison Agency.

Chapter 13:   p. 360 (Opener), Bob Daemmrich/The Image Works; p. 363, Patsy Lynch/Corbis; p. 369, Jonathan Nourok/PhotoEdit.

Chapter 14:   p. 388 (Opener), James Lemass/Liaison Agency; p. 391, ©Frances M. Roberts; p. 397, "American Progress," by John Gast, 1872, oil on canvas, Autry Museum of American Heritage, Los Angeles.

Chapter 15:   p. 420 (Opener), ©Richard B. Levine; p. 430, Pressens Bild AB/Liaison Agency; p. 436, Bob Daemmrich/The Image Works.

Index

505